RESERVE **DATE DUE** 2 HOURS

LIBRARY USE ONLY

SE - 9 '10	MR - 1 '17	
OC 10 '11	2·27	
'13	MR - 8	
FE 28	1127	
1:12		
SE - 9 '13		
6008		
FE 2		
JA 12 '15		
MR 24 '15		
7:00		

DEMCO 38-296

oper's

Writing

Fifth Edition

Axelrod & Cooper's Concise Guide to Writing

Rise B. Axelrod

University of California, Riverside

Charles R. Cooper

University of California, San Diego

Bedford/St. Martin's

Boston ◆ New York

For Bedford/St. Martin's

Senior Developmental Editor: Alexis Walker
Production Editor: Jessica Skrocki
Senior Production Supervisor: Dennis J. Conroy
Market Development Manager: Karita dos Santos
Art Director: Lucy Krikorian
Text Design: Linda M. Robertson
Copy Editor: Virginia Rubens
Indexer: Kirsten Kite
Photo Research: Helane Prottas
Cover Design: Donna Dennison
Cover Art: Detail from the central part of the design for the Paul McCartney New World Tour Stage
        Set, 1992 (acrylic, gouache, and collage on card), by Brian Clarke. Image provided by The
        Bridgeman Art Library.
Composition: Aptara
Printing and Binding: RR Donnelley and Sons

President: Joan E. Feinberg
Editorial Director: Denise B. Wydra
Editor in Chief: Karen S. Henry
Director of Development: Erica T. Appel
Director of Marketing: Karen R. Soeltz
Director of Editing, Design, and Production: Marcia Cohen
Assistant Director of Editing, Design, and Production: Elise S. Kaiser
Managing Editor: Shuli Traub

Library of Congress Control Number: 2009930494

Manufactured in the United States of America.

3 2 1 0 9
e d c b

For information, write: Bedford/St. Martin's, 75 Arlington Street,
Boston, MA 02116   (617-399-4000)

ISBN-10: 0-312-60607-9
ISBN-13: 978-0-312-60607-7

Acknowledgments

Acknowledgments and copyrights are continued at the back of the book on page A-1, which constitutes an exten-
    sion of the copyright page.

Preface
for Instructors

In 1993, we published the first edition of *Axelrod & Cooper's Concise Guide to Writing* in response to requests from instructors who appreciated the pedagogy of *The St. Martin's Guide to Writing* but wanted a briefer text. Our goals in crafting the *Concise Guide* were the same as those for *The Guide*: to take the best of current composition research and practice and turn it into a writing guide that would be useful for both instructors and students. In this fifth edition of the *Concise Guide*, we have enhanced coverage of working with sources, working online, and considering document design and other visual aspects of writing.

An Overview of the Book

The *Concise Guide* is divided into two parts:

Part One, Writing Activities, presents six different essay assignments, all reflecting actual writing situations that students may encounter both in and out of college: narrating a remembered event, profiling a person or a place, explaining a concept, arguing a position, proposing a solution to a problem, and justifying an evaluation.

You may choose among these chapters and teach them in any order you wish, though they are sequenced here from writing based on personal experience and reflection, to writing based on firsthand observation, to writing centered on library or Internet research, and then to writing about ongoing debates over controversial issues and problems.

Each chapter in Part One follows the same organizational plan:

- Three brief illustrated **scenarios** based on the genre covered in the chapter and suggesting the range of occasions when such writing is done — in college courses, in the community, and in the workplace

- A brief **introduction** to the genre suggesting why it is a valuable kind of writing for students to study

- A **collaborative activity** that gives students confidence that they can work with the genre

- A **student essay**, annotated to point out specific strategies or features of the genre

- Two professional **readings** accompanied by activities designed to help students explore connections to their culture and experience and analyze writing strategies used in the genre
- A summary of the **purpose and audience** and the **basic features** of the genre
- A flexible **guide to writing**, tailored to the particular genre, that aids students as they research and compose their essays and includes a **critical reading guide** for peer review of drafts
- Genre-specific advice on **working with sources**
- **Editing and proofreading guidelines,** based on our nationwide study of error in first-year college students' writing, to help students check for one or two sentence-level problems likely to occur in a genre
- A section exploring how writers think about **document design**, expanding on one of the scenarios presented at the beginning of the chapter
- A **reflective activity** designed to help students reflect on and consolidate what they learned about writing in the chapter

Part Two, Strategies for Critical Thinking, Writing, and Research, offers eight chapters covering the following:

- Heuristics for invention and for reading (Chapters 8 and 9)
- Strategies of cueing the reader and of arguing (Chapters 10 and 11)
- Field as well as library and Internet research, including thorough, up-to-date guidelines for using and documenting sources in MLA and APA, and an annotated sample student research paper (Chapters 12, 13, and 14)
- Advice on designing written and online documents (Chapter 15)

Proven Features

Since the first edition, two central features have made the *Concise Guide* such an effective textbook: the practical guides to writing different genres and the systematic integration of reading and writing.

Practical Guides to Writing.   We do not merely talk about composing; rather, we offer practical, flexible guides that help students with different parts of writing, such as invention or revision, as they write. Commonsensical and easy to follow, these writing guides teach students to assess a rhetorical situation, identify the kinds of information they will need, ask probing questions and find answers, and organize an essay to achieve a particular purpose for chosen readers.

Systematic Integration of Reading and Writing.   Because we see a close relationship between the ability to read critically and the ability to write thoughtfully, the *Concise Guide* combines reading instruction with writing instruction. Each reading in

Part One is accompanied by carefully focused apparatus to guide purposeful, productive rereading. First is a response activity, Making Connections to Personal and Social Issues, that relates a central theme of the reading to students' own lives and cultural knowledge. The two sections following, Analyzing Writing Strategies and a brief Commentary, examine how each writer makes use of some of the basic features and strategies typical of the genre. Finally, in Considering Topics for Your Own Essay, students approach the most important decision they have to make with a genre-centered assignment: choosing a workable topic.

Continuing Attention to Changes in Composition

With each new edition, we have tried to turn current theory and research into practical classroom activities—with a minimum of jargon. As a result, recent editions of the *Concise Guide* have incorporated a number of features.

Correlation to the Council of Writing Program Administrators' Outcomes Statement. The WPA statement emphasizes the importance of rhetorical knowledge; critical thinking, reading, and writing; writing processes; and knowledge of conventions. For a table that correlates WPA outcomes to features of the *Concise Guide*, see pp. xii–xv. For a more detailed correlation, see the Instructor's Resource Manual or visit bedfordstmartins.com/conciseguide.

Collaborative Activities. The *Concise Guide* offers multiple opportunities for group work throughout each chapter in Part One. At the start of each chapter is a collaborative activity that invites students to try out some of the thinking and planning they will be engaged in as they complete the chapter's assignment. The Making Connections to Personal and Social Issues section that follows each reading is designed to provoke thoughtful small-group discussions about the social and cultural dimensions of the reading. The Guide to Writing offers a collaborative activity that invites students to discuss their work in progress with two or three other students. A Critical Reading Guide focuses a student's comments on another student's essay draft.

Reflective Activities. Each chapter in Part One concludes with a metacognitive activity to help students become aware of what they have learned about the process of writing. These activities are based on research showing that students who reflect on what they have learned increase their understanding and recall.

Attention to Document Design. We offer one full chapter on document design in Part Two, as well as a separate section on document design in each writing activity chapter in Part One.

Attention to New Modes of Writing and Research. In its previous edition, the *Concise Guide* was thoroughly revised to reflect the fact that both students and instructors now rely on computers, chat rooms, online collaboration and peer review, and other aspects of the increasingly electronic classroom. Sidebars in the assignment chapters in Part One provide concise information and advice about technological topics such as grammar- and spell-checkers and software-based commenting tools, and the Invention section in each Guide to Writing includes an activity that suggests ways students can use the Web selectively and productively.

Changes in the Fifth Edition

In this edition, in response to instructors' concerns to better prepare students to write academic discourse, we have added advice to support students' work with sources in every assignment chapter. We also address the use of visual elements in writing, updating and expanding the parts of the book dealing with visuals and document design. As always, we have inserted new readings on engaging topics.

Additional Advice on Working with Sources.   The Revision section of every Guide to Writing now includes a boxed feature that gives special attention to using sources for the chapter's assignment, with examples drawn from the chapter's readings. Topics include using speaker tags, or signal phrases, to introduce information from sources, citing a variety of sources rather than just one or two, and citing statistics to establish a problem's existence and seriousness.

A New Overall Design with Marginal Annotations of Student Essays.   Perhaps the most noticeable feature of the new design is that the first reading in each chapter in Part One is now a student essay with color-screened marginal annotations instead of the apparatus that accompanies the other readings. Each annotation refers to a specific strategy or feature of the essay, modeling the kind of close reading students must do in order to learn to recognize and use a genre's characteristic features and strategies.

Updated and Expanded Coverage of Visuals and Document Design.   New Thinking about Document Design sections in each chapter in Part One discuss the use of visual elements in writing. In addition, a new Chapter 15, "Designing Documents," offers many examples of designing documents in different genres and more discussion of such issues as the use of color.

New Readings.   Half of the readings (nine out of eighteen) are new to this edition. Selected from a wide variety of contemporary sources, the new readings will engage students with topics such as the usefulness of online professor-evaluation sites and the desirability of same-sex schooling. In addition, a new annotated student research paper has been added to Chapter 14, "Using Sources."

Note on MLA Documentation

As you may know, the Modern Language Association publishes two versions of its guidelines for documenting sources. The *MLA Style Manual and Guide to Scholarly*

Publishing is for scholars and graduate students. The *MLA Handbook for Writers of Research Papers* is for undergraduate and high school students. In May 2008, the guide for scholars was updated with new guidelines for documenting sources. The Modern Language Association strongly discouraged publishers from updating texts intended for undergraduates to reflect the changes in the scholars' guide. Accordingly, the coverage of MLA documentation in the *Concise Guide* reflects the guidelines for undergraduates as put forth in the current edition of the *MLA Handbook for Writers of Research Papers*. When the Modern Language Association publishes the new edition of this guide (anticipated in the spring of 2009), the *Concise Guide* will be revised to reflect these new guidelines.

Additional Resources

Book Companion Site (bedfordstmartins.com/conciseguide). The *Concise Guide*'s companion Web site makes the *Concise Guide* an even more effective teaching resource for improving students' writing. The free site offers many resources for both instructors and students, including a PDF version of the Instructor's Resource Manual, prompts for journaling and discussion, electronic versions of the Critical Reading Guides and collaborative activities, tutorials for the sentence strategies in the Part One chapters, a variety of resources for research and documentation, and the *Exercise Central* database of grammar, punctuation, and word choice exercises (which includes customized feedback for students and a reporting feature that lets instructors monitor student progress).

***The Instructor's Resource Manual*, by Rise B. Axelrod, Charles R. Cooper, Lawrence Barkley of Mt. San Jacinto College–Menifee Valley, and Alison M. Warriner of California State University, East Bay (ISBN-10: 0-312-47808-9 / ISBN-13: 978-0-312-47808-7).** This guide includes a catalog of helpful advice for new instructors, guidelines on common teaching practices such as assigning journals and setting up group activities, guidelines on responding to and evaluating student writing, course plans, detailed chapter plans, an annotated bibliography in composition and rhetoric, and a selection of current background readings from the burgeoning literature of composition studies.

Course management content (ISBN-10: 0-312-55922-4 / ISBN-13: 978-0-312-55922-9). Our content cartridge for course management systems like WebCT, Blackboard, and Angel makes it simple for instructors using this online learning architecture to build a course around the *Concise Guide*. The content is drawn from the Web site and includes activities, models, reference materials, and the new *Exercise Central* 3.0 gradebook.

Premium Resources

The items below can be packaged with the textbook at a small additional cost to your students. Visit **bedfordstmartins.com/conciseguide/catalog** to see these and other packaging options.

CompClass (bedfordstmartins.com/compclass) is the first online course space shaped by the needs of composition students and instructors. In *CompClass*, students can read assignments, do their work, and see their grades all in one place, and instructors can easily monitor student progress and give feedback right away. *CompClass* comes preloaded with the innovative digital content that Bedford/ St. Martin's is known for. Please use ISBN-10: 0-312-55924-0 / ISBN-13: 978-0-312-55924-3 when ordering this package.

Re:Writing Plus (bedfordstmartins.com/rewritingplus) neatly gathers our collections of premium digital content into one online library for composition. Available as a premium resource accessible from the book companion Web site, *Re:Writing Plus* features *Marriage 101 and Other Student Essays,* a new online collection of thirty-two student essays organized according to the chapter structure of Part One. *Marriage 101* also highlights the revision process with three annotated draft-and-revision pairs. Also featured in *Re:Writing Plus* is Peer Factor, an online role-playing game introducing students to the best practices for giving and receiving peer comments. Please use ISBN-10: 0-312-55927-5 / ISBN-13: 978-0-312-55927-4 when ordering this package.

Sticks and Stones and Other Student Essays, Sixth Edition, edited by Ruthe Thompson of Southwest Minnesota State University, Rise B. Axelrod, and Charles R. Cooper, is a collection of thirty-seven essays written by students across the nation using the Guides to Writing in *The St. Martin's Guide.* Each essay is accompanied by a headnote that spotlights some of the ways the writer uses the genre successfully, invites students to notice other achievements, and supplies context where necessary. Please use ISBN-10: 0-312-55926-7 / ISBN-13: 978-0-312-55926-7 when ordering this package.

Who Are We? Readings in Identity and Community and Work and Career, prepared by Rise B. Axelrod and Charles R. Cooper, contains selections that expand on themes foregrounded in *The St. Martin's Guide.* Full of ideas for classroom discussion and writing, the readings offer students additional perspectives and thought-provoking analysis. Please use ISBN-10: 0-312-55925-9 / ISBN-13: 978-0-312-55925-0 when ordering this package.

Acknowledgments

We owe an enormous debt to all the rhetoricians and composition specialists whose theory, research, and pedagogy have informed the *Concise Guide*. We must also acknowledge immeasurable lessons learned from all the writers, professional and student alike, whose work we analyzed and whose writing we used in this and earlier editions.

Many instructors have helped us improve the book. For providing valuable feedback on the fourth edition and our plans for the fifth, we thank Valerie Barbaro, Rasmussen College; Erin Breaux, Louisiana State University; Cassandra D. Chaney, Louisiana State University; Patricia Colella, Bunker Hill Community College; Nissa Dalager, Rasmussen College; Jim Dervin, Winston-Salem State University; Brooks Doherty, Rasmussen College; William Fine, Penn State; Cheryl Finley, Yosemite Community College; Emily Griesinger, Azusa Pacific University; Martha Hayes, Gateway Community College; Andrea Ivanov-Craig, Azusa Pacific University; Jane Laux, Aakers College; Sabine Meyer, Rasmussen College; Katherine Morley, Castleton State College; Keith Otto, University at Buffalo; William Poston, Lander University; Steven Price, Monmouth College; Dorie Goldman Rivera, Central Arizona College; Jane Schreck, Bismarck State College; Ann Smith, Yosemite Community College; Martha Viehmann, Northern Kentucky University; Kristi Walker, Tacoma Community College; Michael Weiser, Thomas Nelson Community College; James Wilson, Victor Valley College; and Mari H. York, Northern Kentucky University.

We want to thank many people at Bedford/St. Martin's, especially Alexis Walker, who helped us make the *Concise Guide* even more concise; John Elliott, whose guidance has been invaluable; and our production team of Jessica Skrocki, Shuli Traub, and Dennis Conroy. Cecilia Seiter capably assisted with reviews and managed updates to the Instructor's Resource Manual and the book companion Web site.

Thanks also to the immensely talented design team—Linda Robertson, who adapted the design created for the eighth edition of *The St. Martin's Guide* by Wanda Kossak and Claire Seng-Niemoeller, as well as Bedford/St. Martin's art directors Anna Palchik and Lucy Krikorian — for making the fifth edition so attractive and usable. Our gratitude also goes to Sandy Schechter and Sue Brekka for their hard work clearing permissions, and Helane Prottas for her imaginative photo research.

We want to thank Erica Appel, who lends her considerable experience as our new director of development. Thanks as well to Joan Feinberg and Denise Wydra for their adroit leadership of Bedford/St. Martin's, and to director of marketing Karen Melton Soeltz, market development manager Karita dos Santos, and the extraordinarily talented and hardworking sales staff for their tireless efforts on behalf of the *Concise Guide*.

Charles dedicates this edition to his three children: Vince, the guitarist and composer; Laura, the artist and garden designer; and Susanna, the writer and political consultant. Rise wishes to thank her husband, Steven, and their son, Jeremiah, for their abiding love, patience, and support. Rise dedicates this book to her friend and colleague, composition instructor *par excellence*, Kathryn O'Rourke.

Features of the *Concise Guide*, Fifth Edition, Correlated to the WPA Outcomes Statement

Desired Student Outcomes	Relevant Features of the *Concise Guide*
Rhetorical Knowledge	
Focus on a purpose	Each Writing Assignment chapter in Part One offers extensive discussion of the purpose(s) for the genre of writing covered in that chapter.
Respond to the needs of different audiences	Each chapter in Part One discusses the need to consider one's audience for the particular genre covered in that chapter. In Chapters 5, 6, and 7, which cover argument, there is also extensive discussion of the need to anticipate opposing positions and readers' objections and alternatives to and their questions about the writer's thesis.
Respond appropriately to different kinds of rhetorical situations	Each chapter in Part One gives detailed advice on responding to a particular rhetorical situation, from remembering an event (Chapter 1) to justifying an evaluation (Chapter 7).
Use conventions of format and structure appropriate to the rhetorical situation	Each chapter in Part One points out features of effectively structured writing, and the Guides to Writing help students systematically develop their own effective structures. Document design is covered in two sections in each of these chapters, as well as in a dedicated Chapter 15, "Designing Documents."
Adopt appropriate voice, tone, and level of formality	Many of the Sentence Strategies sections in each chapter in Part One deal with these issues. Also, see purpose and audience coverage mentioned previously.
Understand how genres shape reading and writing	Each chapter in Part One offers student and professional readings accompanied by annotations, questions, and commentary that draw students' attention to the key features of the genre and stimulate ideas for writing. Each chapter's Guide to Writing offers detailed, step-by-step advice for writing in the genre and for offering constructive peer criticism. In addition, In College Courses, In the Community, and In the Workplace sections that open each Part One chapter show how the various genres are used outside the composition course.
Write in several genres	The Guides to Writing in each of the six chapters in Part One offer specific advice on writing to remember an event; to profile a person or place; to explain a concept; to argue a position; to propose a solution; and to justify an evaluation. In addition, Chapters 12–14 cover research strategies that many students will use while writing in the genres covered in Part One.

Desired Student Outcomes	Relevant Features of the *Concise Guide*
Critical Thinking, Reading, and Writing	
Use writing and reading for inquiry, learning, and communicating	Each Writing Assignment chapter in Part One emphasizes the connection between reading and writing in a particular genre: each chapter begins with a group of readings whose apparatus introduces students to the features of the genre; then a Guide to Writing leads them to apply these features in an essay of their own. Chapter 8, "A Catalog of Invention Strategies," and Chapter 9, "A Catalog of Reading Strategies," prompt students to engage actively in invention and reading. Other Part Two chapters include coverage of specific invention, reading, and writing strategies useful in a variety of genres.
Understand a writing assignment as a series of tasks, including finding, evaluating, analyzing, and synthesizing appropriate primary and secondary sources	The Guides to Writing in each chapter in Part One stage the work of writing projects so that students may more confidently engage in invention and research to find, evaluate, and synthesize information and ideas. Working with Sources sections teach specific strategies of evaluating and integrating source material. Chapter 9, "A Catalog of Reading Strategies," covers various strategies useful in working with sources, including annotating, summarizing, and synthesizing. Chapter 14, "Using Sources," offers detailed coverage of finding, evaluating, using, and acknowledging primary and secondary sources.
Integrate their own ideas with those of others	Chapter 14, "Using Sources," offers detailed advice on how to integrate and introduce quotations, paraphrases, and summaries and how to avoid plagiarism.
Understand the relationships among language, knowledge, and power	Making Connections to Personal and Social Issues, a recurring section in the apparatus following the professional readings in Part One chapters, encourages students to put what they've read in the context of the world they live in. These preliminary reflections come into play in the Guides to Writing, where students are asked to draw on their experiences in college, community, and career in order to begin writing.
Processes	
Be aware that it usually takes multiple drafts to create and complete a successful text	The need for a critical reading of a draft and for revision is emphasized in Chapter 1 as well as in the Guides to Writing in each chapter of Part One.

Desired Student Outcomes	Relevant Features of the *Concise Guide*
Develop flexible strategies for generating ideas, revising, editing, and proofreading	The Guides to Writing in each Part One chapter offer genre-specific activities for invention and research, getting a critical reading of a draft, revising, editing, and proofreading. Chapter 8, "A Catalog of Invention Strategies," offers numerous helpful activities.
Understand writing as an open process that permits writers to use later invention and rethinking to revise their work	The Guides to Writing in each Part One chapter offer extensive, genre-specific advice on revising.
Understand the collaborative and social aspects of writing processes	Each chapter in Part One includes several collaborative activities: Practice at the beginning of the chapter, Making Connections to Personal and Social Issues after the readings, Testing Your Choice, and the Critical Reading Guide.
Learn to critique their own and others' works	See the Critical Reading Guide and Revising sections in the Guides to Writing in each Part One chapter.
Learn to balance the advantages of relying on others with the responsibility of doing their part	This goal is implicit in several collaborative activities: Practice at the beginning of the chapter, Making Connections to Personal and Social Issues after the readings, Testing Your Choice, and the Critical Reading Guide.
Use a variety of technologies to address a range of audiences	Each Guide to Writing in Part One chapters includes a boxed online research activity, as well as "sidebars" providing information and advice about grammar- and spell-checkers and software-based commenting tools. See also Chapter 13, "Library and Internet Research," for extensive coverage of finding, evaluating, and using print and electronic resources and of responsibly using the Internet, e-mail, and online communities for research, and Chapter 15, "Designing Documents," which offers advice on creating visuals on a computer or downloading them from the Web. Finally, the *Concise Guide*'s electronic ancillaries include a companion Web site, with access to a host of useful resources for writers.
Knowledge of Conventions	
Learn common formats for different kinds of texts	Document design is covered in a dedicated Chapter 15 as well as in two sections in each of the Writing Assignment chapters in Part One. Examples of specific formats for a range of texts appear on pp. 438–45 (research paper); p. 462 (memo); p. 464 (business letter); p. 465 (e-mail); p. 467 (résumé); p. 468 (job application letter); pp. 470–71 (lab report); p. 460 (Web page); and pp. 453–58 (table, diagrams, graphs, charts, map, and other figures).

Desired Student Outcomes	Relevant Features of the *Concise Guide*
Develop knowledge of genre conventions ranging from structure and paragraphing to tone and mechanics	Each chapter in Part One presents several basic conventions of a specific genre. These conventions are introduced in the Analyzing Writing Strategies and Commentary apparatus for readings at the beginning of the chapter, summarized in a Basic Features section, and then applied in the Guide to Writing. Genre-specific issues of structure, paragraphing, tone, and mechanics are also addressed in the Sentence Strategies and Editing and Proofreading sections of each Guide to Writing.
Practice appropriate means of documenting their work	Chapter 14, "Using Sources," offers detailed advice on how to integrate and introduce quotations, how to cite paraphrases and summaries so as to distinguish them from the writer's own ideas, and how to avoid plagiarism. This chapter also offers coverage of MLA and APA documentation in addition to an annotated sample student research paper. In addition, Working with Sources sections in each Guide to Writing help students with the details of using and appropriately documenting sources by providing genre-specific examples of what (and what not) to do.
Control such surface features as syntax, grammar, punctuation, and spelling	Genre-specific editing and proofreading advice is given in two sections in each Guide to Writing: A Sentence Strategy and Editing and Proofreading.

Preface for Students: How to Use the *Concise Guide*

We have written this book with you, the student reading and using it, always in the forefront of our minds. Although it is a comprehensive book that covers many different topics, at its heart is a simple message. The best way to become a good writer is to study examples of good writing, then to apply what you have learned from those examples to your own work, and finally to learn even more by reflecting on the challenges that the particular writing task posed for you. Here we explain how the various parts of the book work together to achieve this goal.

■ The Organization of the Book

Following Chapter 1 — an introduction to writing that gives general advice about how to approach different parts of a writing assignment — the *Concise Guide* is divided into two major parts:

Part One: Writing Activities (Chapters 2–7)

Part Two: Strategies for Critical Thinking, Writing, and Research (Chapters 8–15)

The Part One Chapters

For now, to understand how to use the book effectively to improve your writing, you first need to know that the most important part — the part that all of the rest depends on — is Part One, Chapters 2 through 7. Each of the Part One chapters is organized to teach you about one important specific *genre*, or type of writing:

- Autobiography
- Profile
- Concept explanation
- Position paper
- Proposal
- Evaluation

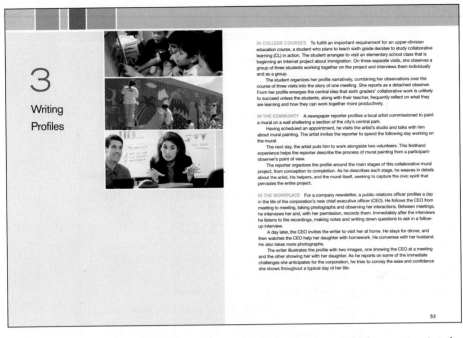

Each Part One chapter follows the same structure, beginning with three scenarios that provide examples of how that kind of writing could be used in a college course, in a workplace, and in a community setting such as a volunteer program or civic organization. Then, after a brief introduction, there are three readings that will help you become familiar with the basic features of the genre. The first reading in each chapter is always one written by a first-year college student. It includes color-coded marginal annotations that point out ways the student writer incorporated the basic features of the genre into his or her essay and also call attention to particular writing strategies—such as quoting, using humor, providing definitions, and comparing and contrasting—that the writer used.

The other two readings in the chapter are by professional writers. Each of these additional essays is accompanied by the following groups of questions, activities, and commentary to help you learn how essays in that genre work:

Making Connections to Personal and Social Issues invites you to explore with other students an issue raised by the reading that is related to your own experience and often to broader social or cultural issues.

Analyzing Writing Strategies helps you examine closely some specific strategies the writer used.

Commentary points out and discusses the ways one or more of the basic features are represented in the essay.

Considering Topics for Your Own Essay suggests subjects related to the reading that you might write about in your own essay.

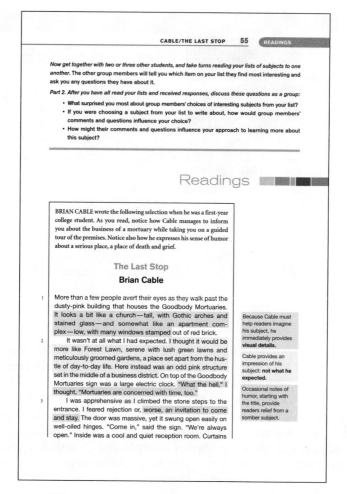

Following the readings, each assignment chapter also includes the following parts:

- A discussion of possible purposes and audiences for the genre
- A summary of the genre's basic features, with examples from the chapter's readings
- A Guide to Writing that will help you write an effective essay in the genre for your particular audience and purpose. The Guides to Writing, the most important parts of the entire book, will be explained fully in the next section
- A Thinking About Document Design section, illustrating possible ways to use visuals in the genre and based on one of the scenarios at the beginning of the chapter
- A concluding section titled Reflecting on Your Writing, which invites you to reflect on your experience with the genre

The Guides to Writing

Just as the Part One assignment chapters are the heart of the book, the heart of each assignment chapter is the Guide to Writing, whose pages are tinted blue so that you can find them easily. Writing an essay does not usually proceed in a smooth, predictable sequence—often, for example, a writer working on a draft will go back to what is usually an earlier step, such as invention and research, or jump ahead to what is usually a later one, such as editing and proofreading. But to make our help with the process more understandable and manageable, we have divided each Guide to Writing into the same six sections that appear in the same order: the Writing Assignment, Invention and Research, Planning and Drafting, a Critical Reading Guide, Revising, and Editing and Proofreading.

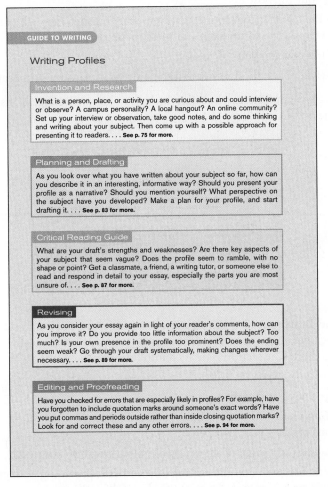

GUIDE TO WRITING

Writing Profiles

Invention and Research

What is a person, place, or activity you are curious about and could interview or observe? A campus personality? A local hangout? An online community? Set up your interview or observation, take good notes, and do some thinking and writing about your subject. Then come up with a possible approach for presenting it to readers. . . . **See p. 75 for more.**

Planning and Drafting

As you look over what you have written about your subject so far, how can you describe it in an interesting, informative way? Should you present your profile as a narrative? Should you mention yourself? What perspective on the subject have you developed? Make a plan for your profile, and start drafting it. . . . **See p. 83 for more.**

Critical Reading Guide

What are your draft's strengths and weaknesses? Are there key aspects of your subject that seem vague? Does the profile seem to ramble, with no shape or point? Get a classmate, a friend, a writing tutor, or someone else to read and respond in detail to your essay, especially the parts you are most unsure of. . . . **See p. 87 for more.**

Revising

As you consider your essay again in light of your reader's comments, how can you improve it? Do you provide too little information about the subject? Too much? Is your own presence in the profile too prominent? Does the ending seem weak? Go through your draft systematically, making changes wherever necessary. . . . **See p. 89 for more.**

Editing and Proofreading

Have you checked for errors that are especially likely in profiles? For example, have you forgotten to include quotation marks around someone's exact words? Have you put commas and periods outside rather than inside closing quotation marks? Look for and correct these and any other errors. . . . **See p. 94 for more.**

To understand how the Guide to Writing works, look closely at the types of activities included in each section:

The Writing Assignment. Each Guide to Writing begins with an assignment that defines the general purpose and basic features of the genre you have been studying in the chapter. The assignment does not tell you what subject to write about or who your readers will be. You will have to make these decisions, guided by the invention and research activities in the next section.

Invention and Research. Every Guide to Writing includes invention activities designed to help you

- find a topic
- discover what you already know about the topic
- consider your purpose and audience
- research the topic further in the library, on the Internet, through observation and interviews, or some combination of these methods
- explore and develop your ideas, and
- compose a tentative thesis statement to guide your planning and drafting.

Each Invention and Research section includes a box with suggestions for researching your topic on the Web.

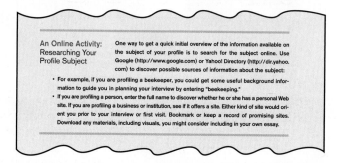

An Online Activity:
Researching Your
Profile Subject

One way to get a quick initial overview of the information available on the subject of your profile is to search for the subject online. Use Google (http://www.google.com) or Yahoo! Directory (http://dir.yahoo.com) to discover possible sources of information about the subject:

- For example, if you are profiling a beekeeper, you could get some useful background information to guide you in planning your interview by entering "beekeeping."
- If you are profiling a person, enter the full name to discover whether he or she has a personal Web site. If you are profiling a business or institution, see if it offers a site. Either kind of site would orient you prior to your interview or first visit. Bookmark or keep a record of promising sites. Download any materials, including visuals, you might consider including in your own essay.

Planning and Drafting. To get you started writing a draft of your essay, each Guide to Writing includes suggestions for planning—setting goals that you try to implement as you write a draft. The section is divided into four parts:

- *Seeing What You Have* involves reviewing what you have discovered about your subject, purpose, and audience.
- *Setting Goals* helps you think about your overall purpose as well as your goals for the various parts of your essay.
- *Outlining* suggests some of the ways you might organize your essay.
- *Drafting* launches you on the writing of your draft, providing both general advice and specific strategies that you might find useful for the genre.

Critical Reading Guide

Now is the time to get a close reading of your draft. Writers usually find it helpful to have someone else read and comment on their drafts, and all writers know how much they learn about writing when they read other writers' drafts. Your instructor may schedule readings of drafts as part of your coursework—in class or online. If not, you can ask a classmate to read your draft. You could also seek comments from a tutor at your campus writing center. The guidelines in this section can be used by anyone reviewing a profile. (If you are unable to have someone else read your draft, turn ahead to the Carrying Out Revisions section on p. 92, where you will find guidelines for analyzing and evaluating your own draft.)

▶ **If You Are the Writer.** To provide comments that are focused and helpful, your reader must know your essay's intended audience, your purpose, and a problem in the draft that you need help solving. Briefly write out this information at the top of your draft.

- *Audience:* Identify the intended audience of your essay.
- *Purpose:* What do you hope your audience will learn about your subject?
- *Problem:* Describe the most important problem you see with your draft.

▶ **If You Are the Draft Reader.** The following guidelines can be useful for approaching a draft with a well-focused, questioning eye.

Making Comments Electronically

Most word processing software offers features that allow you to insert comments directly into the text of someone else's document. Many readers prefer to make their comments in this way because it tends to be faster than writing on a hard copy and space is virtually unlimited; it also eliminates the problem of deciphering handwritten comments. Where such features are not available, simply typing comments directly into a document in a contrasting color can provide the same advantages.

Critical Reading Guide. Once you have finished a draft, you will want to make an effort to have someone else read the draft and comment on how to improve it. Each Guide to Writing includes a Critical Reading Guide, tinted in beige for easy reference, that will help you assess your own and others' drafts.

Ask whether your critical reader would prefer an electronic version of your draft or a hard copy. Even a reader who is going to comment on the draft electronically may prefer to read a hard copy.

Revising. Each Guide to Writing includes a Revising section to help you get an overview of your draft, consider readers' comments, chart a plan for revision, and carry out revisions. The Revising section also includes a boxed feature called Working with Sources, which offers advice on incorporating materials from research sources into your essay.

Editing and Proofreading. Each Guide to Writing ends with a section intended to help you recognize and fix specific kinds of errors in grammar, punctuation, sentence structure, and so on that are common in that genre of writing. In some chapters, the errors include ones particular to students whose first language is not English.

Figure 15.13 Excerpt from sample student paper with figure

Chapters in Part Two

Part Two provides more help and practice with specific kinds of strategies for reading critically as well as for different aspects of writing and research. Also included are up-to-date guidelines for choosing, using, and documenting different kinds of sources (library sources, the Internet, and your own field research) and advice on designing documents.

Finding What You Need

To help you find your way around, besides the color-coded sections that have already been mentioned, you can use the running heads at the tops of the pages and, in the Part One chapters, the color-coded tabs used to mark the four main sections of those chapters. (See the illustration below.) To locate information or additional material on particular topics, besides using the Contents in the front of the book and the Index in the back, you can benefit from the cross-references that appear in the margins throughout the book. Other marginal notes refer you to the companion Web site, where related material or electronic versions of material in the book are available. Still other notes provide useful information and advice about computer-related topics such as editing-tracking, collaborating and reviewing others' work online, and software-based commenting tools.

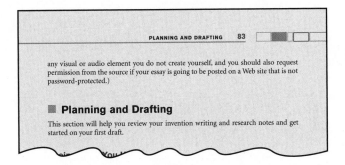

Contents

PART TWO STRATEGIES FOR CRITICAL THINKING, WRITING, AND RESEARCH

8   A Catalog of Invention Strategies   294

9   A Catalog of Reading Strategies   307

10   Cueing the Reader   331

Axelrod & Cooper's
Concise Guide to Writing

Introduction 1

"Why should learning to write well be important to me? What is the connection between writing and thinking? How will reading help me learn to write better? How can I learn to write more inventively, effectively, efficiently?" These are some of the questions you may be asking as you begin this writing course. Read on — for *Axelrod & Cooper's Concise Guide to Writing* offers some answers to these and other questions.

■ Why Writing Is Important

Writing influences and changes the way you learn, enhances your chances of success, contributes to your personal development, and strengthens your relationships with other people.

Writing Contributes to Learning

When you take notes in class, writing helps you identify and remember what is important. Writing in the margins as you read encourages you to question the reading's ideas and information. Writing consolidates your understanding of and response to what you are learning.

Writing essays of various kinds helps you organize and present what you have learned and, in the process, clarify and extend your own ideas. Different kinds of writing contribute to learning in different ways. Arguing a position teaches you not only to support your reasons but also to refute objections to your argument. Researching a profile, you learn to make precise observations and arrange them to create a particular impression. Composing an evaluation requires you to learn about your subject and the values or standards typically used to judge it.

> Writing has been for a long time my major tool for self-instruction and self-development.
> — Toni Cade Bambara

1

Writing Fosters Personal Development

In addition to influencing the ways you think and learn, writing can help you grow as an individual. Writing leads you to reflect on your experience, for example, when you write to understand the significance of a particular event in your life. Writing about a controversial issue can make you examine some of your most basic beliefs. Writing an evaluation requires that you think about what you value and how your values compare to those of others. Perhaps most important, becoming an author confers authority on you; it gives you confidence to assert your own ideas and feelings.

> In a very real sense, the writer writes in order to teach himself, to understand himself, to satisfy himself . . . .   — ALFRED KAZIN

> Some of the things that happen to us in life seem to have no meaning, but when you write them down, you find the meanings for them . . . .
>   — MAXINE HONG KINGSTON

Writing Connects You to Others

It is easier now than ever before to connect with others via e-mail and the Internet. You may use writing to keep in touch with friends and family, take part in academic discussions, and participate in civic debate and decision making. By writing about your experiences, ideas, and observations, you reach out to readers, offering them your own point of view and inviting them to share theirs in return. Writing your own argument, for example, you clarify your different perspectives, reexamine your own reasoning, and may ultimately influence other people's opinions as they influence yours. Similarly, writing a proposal invites you to work collaboratively with others to invent new ways of solving complex problems.

> Writing is the act of saying I, of imposing oneself upon other people, of saying listen to me, see it my way, change your mind.   — JOAN DIDION

> It's the sense of being in contact with people who are part of a particular audience that really makes a difference to me in writing.   — SHERLEY ANNE WILLIAMS

Writing Promotes Success in College and at Work

As a student, you are probably most aware of the many ways writing can contribute to your success in school. Students who learn to write for different readers and purposes do well in courses throughout the curriculum. Eventually, you will need to use writing to advance your career by writing persuasive application letters for jobs or graduate school admission. At work, you will be expected to write effective e-mail messages, letters, and reports that present clear explanations, well-reasoned arguments, convincing evaluations, or constructive proposals.

People think it's sort of funny that I went to graduate school as a biologist and then became a writer. . . . What I learned [in science] is how to formulate or identify a new question that hasn't been asked before and then to set about solving it, to do original research to find the way to an answer. And that's what I do when I write a book.   — BARBARA KINGSOLVER

EXERCISE 1.1

Think of an occasion when writing helped you accomplish something important. For example, you may recall a time when writing helped you better understand a difficult subject, when you used writing to influence someone else, or when you worked through a problem by writing.

Write a page or two describing how you came to write and what you wrote about. Then explain what your writing accomplished. For example, did you use it to help you learn something, express yourself, or connect to others?

◼ How Writing Is Learned

There are many myths about writing and writers. For example, some people assume that people who are good at writing do not have to spend a lot of time learning to write — that they just naturally know how. Others assume that "real" writers write perfectly the first time, every time, dashing off an essay with minimal effort. Writers' testimonies, however, together with extensive research on how people write and learn to write, show that writing can — indeed, must — be learned. All writers work at their writing. Some writers may be more successful and influential than others. Some may find writing easier and more satisfying. But no one is born knowing how to write.

However great a [person's] natural talent may be, the art of writing cannot be learned all at once.   — JEAN-JACQUES ROUSSEAU

Learning to write well takes time and much effort, but it can be done.
— MARGARET MEAD

The *Concise Guide to Writing* has helped many students become more thoughtful, effective, confident writers. From reading and analyzing an array of different kinds of essays, you will learn how other writers make their texts work. From writing for different purposes, you will learn to compose texts that readers want to read. To help you take full advantage of what you are learning, the *Concise Guide* will also help you reflect on your learning so that you will be able to remember, apply, and build on what you have learned.

Reading

Most professional writers are avid readers who read not only for enjoyment and information but also to learn how other writers write. Your reading will help you learn about the types of writing you will do for personal, academic, and career reasons. This section shows how the *Concise Guide* supports your learning about writing from reading.

How Written Texts Work. The expectations of readers are aroused when they recognize a text as a particular *genre* or type of writing. For example, a story about a past event in the writer's life is immediately recognizable as a form of autobiography, which leads readers to expect a story that changes, challenges, or complicates the writer's sense of self or connection with others. If the event seems trivial or the story lacks interest, then readers' expectations will be disappointed and the text will not succeed. Similarly, if the text takes a position on a controversial issue, readers will recognize it as an opinion piece and expect it to not only assert and support that position, but also refute possible objections. If the argument lacks credible support or ignores objections that thoughtful readers may have raised, readers are likely to decide that the essay is not convincing.

Although individual texts within the same genre vary a great deal—no two proposals, even those arguing for the same solution, will be identical—they nonetheless follow a general pattern that provides a certain amount of predictability. But these language patterns, also called *conventions*, should not be thought of as rigid formulas. Genre conventions are broad frameworks within which writers are free to be creative. Most writers, in fact, find that working within a framework allows them to be more creative, not less so.

> You would learn very little in this world if you were not allowed to imitate. And to repeat your imitations until some solid grounding . . . was achieved and the slight but wonderful difference—that made you and no one else— could assert itself. — MARY OLIVER

How Reading Helps You Write Texts That Work. To learn the conventions of a particular genre, you need to read examples of that genre so that you begin to recognize its predictable patterns as well as the possibilities for innovation. At the same time, you should also practice writing in the genre.

> Read, read, read. . . . Just like a carpenter who works as an apprentice and studies the master. Read! — WILLIAM FAULKNER

The *Concise Guide* provides an array of sample essays in the genres you are learning to write and helps you analyze patterns in these essays. It also helps you practice using these patterns in your own writing to achieve your own purposes. Seeing, for example, how writers define key terms and integrate quotations from their sources in an essay explaining a concept introduces you to strategies you may use when you write in this genre.

> I practiced writing in every possible way that I could. I wrote a pastiche of other people. . . . Just as a pianist runs his scales for ten years before he gives his concert: because when he gives that concert, he can't be thinking of his fingering or of his hands, he has to be thinking of his interpretation. He's thinking of what he's trying to communicate. — KATHERINE ANNE PORTER

How Reading Helps You Design Texts That Work.   Writers have long recognized that no matter how well organized, well reasoned, or compelling a piece of writing may be, the way it looks on the page influences to some extent how well it works for readers. Today, writers have more options for designing their documents than ever before. Digital photography, scanning, and integrated word processing and graphics programs make it relatively easy for writers to heighten the visual impact of the page. For example, they can change type fonts and add colors, charts, diagrams, and photographs to written documents. To construct multimedia Web pages or DVDs, writers can add sound, moving images, and hyperlinks.

These multiple possibilities, however, do not guarantee a more effective document. In order to design effective texts, writers need to study documents that capture readers' attention and enhance understanding. As someone who has grown up watching television shows and videos, playing computer games, and looking at the photos, advertisements, cartoons, tables, and graphs in magazines, newspapers, and other sources, you are already a sophisticated visual consumer who has unconsciously learned many of the conventions of document design for different genres and writing situations. This book will help you become aware of what you already know and help you make new discoveries about document design that you may be able to use in your own writing.

> Design is a funny word. Some people think design means how it looks. But of course, if you dig deeper, it's really how it works. — STEVE JOBS

EXERCISE 1.2

Make two lists—one of the genres you have *read* recently, such as explanations of how to do something, stories, news reports, opinion pieces, and movie reviews, and the other of the genres you have *written* recently, both for courses and for other purposes. Then write a few sentences speculating about how your reading influences your writing and the design of your texts.

Writing

This section shows how your writing can become more thoughtful and productive. It also suggests how the *Concise Guide* helps you develop a richer and more flexible repertoire of writing strategies to meet the demands of different writing situations.

How Writing Helps You Think.   We all know what it is like to stare at a blank computer screen or stark white page of paper waiting for inspiration. However, "genius," as the great inventor Thomas Alva Edison famously said, "is one percent inspiration and ninety-nine percent perspiration." This quotation (which incidentally has also been attributed to Albert Einstein, Pablo Picasso, and even Yogi Berra) simply states what is common knowledge to anyone who has tried to write: Writing is work.

> Inspiration usually comes during work, rather than before it.
> — MADELEINE L'ENGLE

Sitting around waiting for inspiration is for amateurs.   — TOM ROBBINS

Like people who write for a living, students need to develop a repertoire of reliable strategies they can use not only to get writing done but also to make writing a way of learning. The *Concise Guide* offers many strategies to help you learn to write productively in a range of genres about different topics. You will have to try the strategies to discover which ones work especially well for you.

How to Think through Writing.   Few writers begin writing with a complete understanding of a subject. Most use writing as a way to learn about the subject—trying out ideas and information they have collected, exploring connections and implications, and reviewing what they have written in order to expand and develop their ideas.

> When I start a project, the first thing I do is write down, in longhand, everything I know about the subject, every thought I've ever had on it. This may be twelve or fourteen pages. Then I read it through, for quite a few days . . . then I try to find out what are the salient points that I must make. And then it begins to take shape.   — MAYA ANGELOU

Using writing for discovery in this way means that you do not think and then write, but that the writing helps you think. Writers often reflect on this so-called generative aspect of writing, echoing E. M. Forster's much repeated adage: "How do I know what I think until I see what I say?" Here are some other versions of the same insight:

> Every book that I have written has been an education, a process of discovery.   — AMITAV GHOSH

> I don't see writing as a communication of something already discovered, as "truths" already known. Rather, I see writing as a job of experiment. It's like any discovery job; you don't know what's going to happen until you try it.   — WILLIAM STAFFORD

> Don't tear up the page and start over again when you write a bad line—try to write your way out of it. Make mistakes and plunge on . . . . Writing is a means of discovery, always.   — GARRISON KEILLOR

Writers obviously do not give birth to a text as a whole, but must work cumulatively, focusing first on one aspect, then on another. Writing therefore may seem to progress in a linear, step-by-step fashion. But in fact it almost always proceeds *recursively*, which means that writers return periodically to earlier stages of their work to reconsider and build upon what they are discovering. In this way, the experience of writing is less like marching in a straight line from first sentence to last and more like climbing a steep trail with frequent switchbacks. It may appear that you are retracing old ground, but you are really rising to new levels.

> It's a matter of piling a little piece here and a little piece there, fitting them together, going on to the next part, then going back and gradually shaping the whole piece into something.   — DAVE BARRY

Discovery does not stop when you finish a draft. Most writers plan and revise their plans, draft and revise their drafts, write and read what they have written, and then write some more. The continual shifting of attention—from discovering new ideas to choosing words, from setting goals to planning, from rereading to reorganizing, from anticipating questions to adding details—characterizes writing as a dynamic, recursive process.

How to Make Your Writing Inventive, Yet Efficient.   Writers, then, need strategies that make writing more systematic but do not stifle inventiveness. Most writers begin drafting with some type of plan—a list, a scratch outline, or a detailed storyboard like that used by filmmakers. Outlines can be very helpful, but they must be tentative and flexible if writers are to benefit from writing's natural recursiveness.

> I began [*Invisible Man*] with a chart of the three-part division. It was a conceptual frame with most of the ideas and some of the incidents indicated.
> — RALPH ELLISON

> You are always going back and forth between the outline and the writing, bringing them closer together, or just throwing out the outline and making a new one.   — ANNIE DILLARD

While composing a draft, writers can benefit from frequent pauses to reread what they have written. Rereading often leads to further discovery—adding an example, choosing different words that unpack or separate ideas, filling in a gap in the logic of an argument. In addition, rereading frequently leads to substantial rethinking and revising: cutting, reorganizing, rewriting whole sections to make the writing more effective. Consequently, drafting always involves both invention and revision.

> You have to work problems out for yourself on paper. Put the stuff down and read it—to see if it works.   — JOYCE CARY

> As a writer, I would find out most clearly what I thought, and what I only thought I thought, when I saw it written down.   — ANNA QUINDLEN

Rereading your own writing in order to improve it can be difficult, though, because it is hard to see what the draft actually says, as opposed to what you were trying to say. For this reason, most writers also give their drafts to others to read. Students generally seek advice from their teachers and other students in the class because they understand the assignment. Published writers also share their work in progress with others. Poets, novelists, historians, scientists, newspaper reporters, magazine essayists, and even textbook writers actively seek constructive critical comments by joining writers' workshops or getting help from editors.

I was lucky because I was always going to groups where the writers were at the same level or a little better than me. That really helped.   — MANIL SURI

[Ezra Pound] was a marvelous critic because he didn't try to turn you into an imitation of himself. He tried to see what you were trying to do.

— T. S. ELIOT

How to Use the Guides to Writing.   As you have seen, students learning to write need to be flexible and yet systematic. The Guides to Writing in Part One of this book are designed to meet this need. The first few times you write in a new genre, you can rely on these guides. They provide scaffolding to support your work until you become more familiar with the demands and possibilities of each genre. The Guides will help you develop a repertoire of strategies for creatively solving problems in your writing, such as deciding how to interest readers, how to refute opposing arguments, what to quote from a source, and how to integrate quotations into your writing.

When people engage in any new and complex activity—driving, playing an instrument, skiing, or writing—they may divide it into a series of manageable tasks. In learning to play tennis, for example, you can isolate lobbing from volleying or work on your backhand or serve. Similarly, in writing an argument on a controversial issue, you can separate tasks such as defining the issue, developing your reasons, and antici-pating readers' objections. What is important is focusing on one aspect at a time. Dividing your writing in this way enables you to tackle a complex subject without oversimplifying it.

Here is a writer's quotation that has been especially helpful for us as we have writ-ten and revised the *Concise Guide.*

You know when you think about writing a book, you think it is overwhelming. But, actually, you break it down into tiny little tasks any moron could do.

— ANNIE DILLARD

EXERCISE 1.3

Write a page or two describing how you went about writing the last time you wrote an essay (or something else) that took time and effort. Use the following questions to help you recall what you did, but feel free to write about any other aspects of your writing that you remember.

- Whom were you writing for, and what was the purpose of your writing?
- What kinds of thinking and planning did you do, if any, before you began writing the first draft?
- If you discussed your ideas and plans with someone, how did discussing them help you? If you had someone read your draft, how did getting a response help?
- If you rewrote, moved, added, or cut anything in your first draft, describe what you changed.

Creating the Best Conditions for Reading and Writing

People can read and write under the most surprising or arduous conditions. Reading and writing are most productive, however, if you can find a time and place ideally suited for sustained and thoughtful work. Many professional writers have a place where they can concentrate for a few hours without repeated interruptions. Try to find such a place for yourself.

Disconnecting is hard to do, but eliminating or at least greatly reducing distractions for sustained periods of time is likely to help you concentrate on intellectually demanding college reading and writing. If at all possible, turn off your cell phone. If you are used to listening to music while reading or writing, you might experiment with turning it off, too, just to see if your attention is better focused with or without it. Or if you find complete silence stressful—or a certain amount of background noise impossible to escape—music might help. Whatever the conditions that prove best for you, make a real effort to create them.

Thinking Critically

To think critically about your learning, you reflect on what you have learned from reading texts in the genre you are writing. Much of human language and genre-learning comes from modeling. As young children, for example, we learn from hearing our parents, teachers, and peers tell stories and from watching stories portrayed on television and in film. We learn ways of beginning and ending, strategies for building suspense, techniques for making time sequences clear, how to use dialogue to develop character, and so on. As adults, we can reinforce and increase our repertoire of storytelling patterns by analyzing these stories and by consciously trying these strategies in our own writing.

The *Concise Guide* helps you talk and write about the hows of reading and writing different genres by providing a shared vocabulary of words and phrases that you can easily learn and add to others which you already know. Words like *significance, narrating,* and *thesis,* for example, will help you identify the features and strategies of essays you are reading in different genres. Words and phrases like *invention, setting goals,* and *revising* will help you describe what you are doing as you write your own essays in these genres.

Each writing assignment chapter in Part One of the *Concise Guide* includes many opportunities for you to think critically about your understanding of the genre you are writing and to reflect on your learning. A section entitled Reflecting on Your Writing concludes each chapter, giving you an opportunity to look back and reflect on how you used the writing process creatively.

> I went back to the good nature books that I had read. And I analyzed them. I wrote outlines of whole books—outlines of chapters—so that I could see their structure. And I copied down their transitional sentences or their main sentences or their closing sentences or their lead sentences.
>
> — ANNIE DILLARD

EXERCISE 1.4

Read the following quotes to see how writers use similes ("Writing is like") and metaphors ("Writing is") to describe the processes and products of writing.

> Writing is like exploring . . . as an explorer makes maps of the country he has explored, so a writer's works are maps of the country he has explored.
> — Lawrence Osgood

> The writer must soak up the subject completely, as a plant soaks up water, until the ideas are ready to sprout.   — Marguerite Yourcenar

> Writing is manual labor of the mind: a job, like laying pipe.
> — John Gregory Dunne

> If we had to say what writing is, we would define it essentially as an act of courage.
> — Cynthia Ozick

Write two or three similes or metaphors of your own that express aspects of your experience as a writer. Then write a page or so explaining and expanding on the ideas and feelings expressed in your similes and metaphors.

Part One

Writing
Activities

2

Remembering
an Event

IN COLLEGE COURSES For a linguistics course, a student is required to select a subject, report research on that subject, and connect findings or conclusions by the researchers to a specific instance of language use in her own experience. The student decides to focus on Deborah Tannen's finding that in problem-solving discussions women expect to spend a lot of time talking about the problem itself, especially their feelings about it. Men, in contrast, typically want to cut short the analysis of the problem and the talk about feelings; they would rather discuss solutions.

Applying Tannen's findings to her own experience, the student recalls a recent conversation with her brother about their father's drinking. She reconstructs the conversation much as it occurred. Next she explains which parts constitute feelings talk and which indicate problem-solving talk. She concludes that her conversation with her brother well illustrates Tannen's findings.

IN THE COMMUNITY As part of a local history project in a small western ranching community, a college student volunteers to help an elderly rancher write about a time in the winter of 1938 when a snowstorm isolated the rancher's family for nearly a month. The student tape-records the rancher talking about how he and his wife made preparations to survive and ensure the health of their infant sons and how he snowshoed eight miles to a logging train track, stopped the train, and gave the engineer a message to deliver to relatives. On a subsequent visit, the student and the rancher listen to the tape recording and afterward talk about further details that might make the event more complete and dramatic for readers.

After the rancher writes a draft, the student helps him revise and edit it, and together they choose two photographs for publication in the local newspaper. (For more information on how the student and rancher chose visuals and selected quotations from the story to accompany the visuals, turn to Thinking About Document Design, p. 50.)

IN THE WORKPLACE To keynote a statewide meeting of highway department regional managers, a respected manager writes a speech describing an incident when he was confronted in his office by an unhappy employee who complained loudly about an overtime assignment and threatened to harm the manager and his family if the manager did not give him the weekend off. When asked to leave, he initially refused and remained, cursing, for several minutes. The manager reflects on his fear and on his frustration about not knowing what to do because the department's procedures seemed not to apply, and he also acknowledges his reluctance to report the incident because he did not want to appear to be ineffective. He concludes by offering guidelines on how to handle an employee's cursing, threats, and refusal to leave the office, based on research he did after the incident.

When you write about remembered events in your life, you rely on a genre of writing known as autobiography. It is a popular genre because reading as well as writing it leads people to reflect deeply on their own lives. Reflecting on the meaning of your experience, you examine the forces within yourself and within society that have shaped you into the person you have become.

When you write about a remembered event, your purpose is to present yourself to readers by telling a story that discloses something significant about you. Autobiographical writers do not just pour out their memories and feelings, however. Instead, they shape those memories into a compelling story that conveys the meaning and importance of an experience.

A Collaborative Activity: Practice Remembering an Event

Part 1. Consider several events, and choose one you feel comfortable telling about in this situation. Then, for two or three minutes, make notes about how you will tell your story.

Now, get together with two or three other students, and take turns telling your stories. Be brief: Each story should take only a few minutes.

Part 2. Take ten minutes to discuss what happened when you told about a remembered event:

- Tell each other how you chose your particular story. How did your purpose and audience—what you wanted your classmates to know and think about you—influence your choice?
- Review what each of you decided to include in your story. Did you plunge right into telling what happened, or did you first provide some background information? Did you describe any of the people, including yourself, or mention any specific dialogue? Did you tell your listeners how you felt at the time the event occurred, or did you say how you feel now looking back on it?
- What was the easiest part of telling a story about a remembered event in your life? What was the most difficult part?

Readings

> JEAN BRANDT wrote this essay as a first-year college student. In it, she tells about a memorable event that occurred when she was thirteen. Reflecting on how she felt at the time, Brandt writes, "I was afraid, embarrassed, worried, mad." As you read, look for places where these tumultuous and contradictory remembered feelings are expressed.

Calling Home
Jean Brandt

1   As we all piled into the car, I knew it was going to be a fabulous day. My grandmother was visiting for the holidays; and she and I, along with my older brother and sister, Louis and Susan, were setting off for a day of last-minute Christmas shopping. On the way to the mall, we sang Christmas carols, chattered, and laughed. With Christmas only two days away, we were caught up with holiday spirit. I felt light-headed and full of joy. I loved shopping—especially at Christmas.

2   The shopping center was swarming with frantic last-minute shoppers like ourselves. We went first to the General Store, my favorite. It carried mostly knickknacks and other useless items which nobody needs but buys anyway. I was thirteen years old at the time, and things like buttons and calendars and posters would catch my fancy. This day was no different. The object of my desire was a 75-cent Snoopy button. Snoopy was the latest. If you owned anything with the Peanuts on it, you were "in." But since I was supposed to be shopping for gifts for other people and not myself, I couldn't decide what to do. I went in search of my sister for her opinion. I pushed my way through throngs of people to the back of the store where I found Susan. I asked her if she thought I should buy the button. She said it was cute and if I wanted it to go ahead and buy it.

3   When I got back to the Snoopy section, I took one look at the lines at the cashiers and knew I didn't want to wait thirty minutes to buy an item worth less than one dollar. I walked back to the basket where I found the button and was about to drop it when suddenly, instead, I took a quick glance around, assured myself no one could see, and slipped the button into the pocket of my sweatshirt. I hesitated for a moment, but once the item was in my pocket, there was no turning back. I had never before stolen anything; but what was done was done. A few seconds later, my sister appeared and asked, "So, did you decide to buy the button?"

4   "No, I guess not." I hoped my voice didn't quaver. As we headed for the entrance, my heart began to race. I just had to get out of that store. Only a few more yards to go and I'd be safe. As we crossed the threshold, I heaved a sigh of relief. I was home free. I thought about how sly I had been and I felt proud of my accomplishment.

The action in this remembered event begins with the first sentence. Verbs move the action along.

Actors other than the narrator are introduced and two of them are named.

A remembered conversation is summarized.

Specific narrative action slows the narrative and focuses readers on a fateful moment.

A remembered conversation is reconstructed as dialogue.

Remembered feelings help to create suspense.

This startling, dramatic moment is simply narrated without any dialogue. The restraint at this point in the narrative heightens the effect of the dramatic interactions later in the essay.

An unexpected tap on my shoulder startled me. I whirled around to find a middle-aged man, dressed in street clothes, flashing some type of badge and politely asking me to empty my pockets. Where did this man come from? How did he know? I was so sure that no one had seen me! On the verge of panicking, I told myself that all I had to do was give this man his button back, say I was sorry, and go on my way. After all, it was only a 75-cent item.

5

Next thing I knew, he was talking about calling the police and having me arrested and thrown in jail, as if he had just nabbed a professional thief instead of a terrified kid. I couldn't believe what he was saying.

6

"Jean, what's going on?"

7

Beginning here, the story of the narrator's arrest is narrated mostly through remembered conversations.

The sound of my sister's voice eased the pressure a bit. She always managed to get me out of trouble. She would come through this time too.

8

"Excuse me. Are you a relative of this young girl?"

9

"Yes, I'm her sister. What's the problem?"

10

"Well, I just caught her shoplifting and I'm afraid I'll have to call the police."

11

"What did she take?"

12

"This button."

13

"A button? You are having a thirteen-year-old arrested for stealing a button?"

14

"I'm sorry, but she broke the law."

15

The man led us through the store and into an office, where we waited for the police officers to arrive. Susan had found my grandmother and brother, who, still shocked, didn't say a word. The thought of going to jail terrified me, not because of jail itself, but because of the encounter with my parents afterward. Not more than ten minutes later, two officers arrived and placed me under arrest. They said that I was to be taken to the station alone. Then, they handcuffed me and led me out of the store. I felt alone and scared. I had counted on my sister being with me, but now I had to muster up the courage to face this ordeal all by myself.

16

More remembered feelings heighten the suspense.

As the officers led me through the mall, I sensed a hundred pairs of eyes staring at me. My face flushed and I broke out in a sweat. Now everyone knew I was a criminal. In their eyes I was a juvenile delinquent, and thank God the cops were getting me off the streets. The worst part was thinking my grandmother might be having the same thoughts. The humiliation at that moment was overwhelming. I felt like Hester Prynne being put on public display for everyone to ridicule.

17

Through a simile, the narrator compares her situation to that of the main character in Nathaniel Hawthorne's novel *The Scarlet Letter*.

18   That short walk through the mall seemed to take hours.
But once we reached the squad car, time raced by. I was read
my rights and questioned. We were at the police station within
minutes. Everything happened so fast I didn't have a chance to
feel remorse for my crime. Instead, I viewed what was happening to me as if it were a movie. Being searched, although
embarrassing, somehow seemed to be exciting. All the movies
and television programs I had seen were actually coming to
life. This is what it was really like. But why were criminals
always portrayed as frightened and regretful? I was having fun.
I thought I had nothing to fear—until I was allowed my one
phone call. I was trembling as I dialed home. I didn't know
what I was going to say to my parents, especially my mother.

19   "Hi, Dad, this is Jean."

20   "We've been waiting for you to call."

21   "Did Susie tell you what happened?"

22   "Yeah, but we haven't told your mother. I think you should
tell her what you did and where you are."

23   "You mean she doesn't even know where I am?"

24   "No, I want you to explain it to her."

25   There was a pause as he called my mother to the phone.
For the first time that night, I was close to tears. I wished I had
never stolen that stupid pin. I wanted to give the phone to one
of the officers because I was too ashamed to tell my mother
the truth, but I had no choice.

26   "Jean, where are you?"

27   "I'm, umm, in jail."

28   "Why? What for?"

29   "Shoplifting."

30   "Oh no, Jean. Why? Why did you do it?"

31   "I don't know. No reason. I just did it."

32   "I don't understand. What did you take? Why did you do
it? You had plenty of money with you."

33   "I know but I just did it. I can't explain why. Mom, I'm sorry."

34   "I'm afraid sorry isn't enough. I'm horribly disappointed in
you."

35   Long after we got off the phone, while I sat in an empty jail
cell, waiting for my parents to pick me up, I could still distinctly
hear the disappointment and hurt in my mother's voice. I cried.
The tears weren't for me but for her and the pain I had put her
through. I felt like a terrible human being. I would rather have
stayed in jail than confront my mom right then. I dreaded each
passing minute that brought our encounter closer. When the
officer came to release me, I hesitated, actually not wanting to

Remembered feelings provide a surprise for readers.

The climax and resolution of the narrative begins here, revealed through a combination of reconstructed conversation and remembered feelings.

leave. We went to the front desk, where I had to sign a form to retrieve my belongings. I saw my parents a few yards away and my heart raced. A large knot formed in my stomach. I fought back the tears.

Not a word was spoken as we walked to the car. Slowly, I sank into the back seat anticipating the scolding. Expecting harsh tones, I was relieved to hear almost the opposite from my father. 36

"I'm not going to punish you and I'll tell you why. Although I think what you did was wrong, I think what the police did was more wrong. There's no excuse for locking a thirteen-year-old behind bars. That doesn't mean I condone what you did, but I think you've been punished enough already." 37

As I looked from my father's eyes to my mother's, I knew this ordeal was over. Although it would never be forgotten, the incident was not mentioned again. 38

ANNIE DILLARD, professor emeritus at Wesleyan College, won the Pulitzer Prize for nonfiction writing with her first book, *Pilgrim at Tinker Creek* (1974). Since then, she has written eleven other books in a variety of genres. They include *Teaching a Stone to Talk* (1988), *The Writing Life* (1990), *The Living* (1993), *Mornings Like This* (1996), and *The Maytrees* (2007). Dillard also wrote an autobiography of her early years, *An American Childhood* (1987), from which the following reading comes.

This reading relates an event that occurred one winter morning when the seven-year-old Dillard and a friend were chased by an adult stranger. Dillard admits that she was terrified at the time, and yet she asserts that she has "seldom been happier since." As you read, think about how this paradox helps you grasp the autobiographical significance of this experience for Dillard.

An American Childhood
Annie Dillard

Some boys taught me to play football. This was fine sport. You thought up a new strategy for every play and whispered it to the others. You went out for a pass, fooling everyone. Best, you got to throw yourself mightily at someone's running legs. Either you brought him down or you hit the ground flat out on your chin, with your arms empty before you. It was all or nothing. If you hesitated in fear, you would miss and get hurt: you would take a hard fall while the kid got away, or you would get kicked in the face while the kid got away. But if you flung yourself wholeheartedly at the back of his knees—if you gathered and joined body and soul and pointed them 1 diving fearlessly—then you likely wouldn't get hurt, and you'd stop the ball. Your fate, and your team's score, depended on your concentration and courage. Nothing girls did could compare with it.

Boys welcomed me at baseball, too, for I had, through enthusiastic practice, what was weirdly known as a boy's arm. In winter, in the snow, there was neither baseball nor football, so the boys and I threw snowballs at passing cars. I got in trouble throwing snowballs, and have seldom been happier since.

On one weekday morning after Christmas, six inches of new snow had just fallen. We were standing up to our boot tops in snow on a front yard on trafficked Reynolds Street, waiting for cars. The cars traveled Reynolds Street slowly and evenly; they were targets all but wrapped in red ribbons, cream puffs. We couldn't miss.

I was seven; the boys were eight, nine, and ten. The oldest two Fahey boys were there—Mikey and Peter—polite blond boys who lived near me on Lloyd Street, and who already had four brothers and sisters. My parents approved of Mikey and Peter Fahey. Chickie McBride was there, a tough kid, and Billy Paul and Mackie Kean too, from across Reynolds, where the boys grew up dark and furious, grew up skinny, knowing, and skilled. We had all drifted from our houses that morning looking for action, and had found it here on Reynolds Street.

It was cloudy but cold. The cars' tires laid behind them on the snowy street a complex trail of beige chunks like crenellated castle walls. I had stepped on some earlier; they squeaked. We could not have wished for more traffic. When a car came, we all popped it one. In the intervals between cars we reverted to the natural solitude of children.

I started making an iceball—a perfect iceball, from perfectly white snow, perfectly spherical, and squeezed perfectly translucent so no snow remained all the way through. (The Fahey boys and I considered it unfair actually to throw an iceball at somebody, but it had been known to happen.)

I had just embarked on the iceball project when we heard tire chains come clanking from afar. A black Buick was moving toward us down the street. We all spread out, banged together some regular snowballs, took aim, and, when the Buick drew nigh, fired.

A soft snowball hit the driver's windshield right before the driver's face. It made a smashed star with a hump in the middle.

Often, of course, we hit our target, but this time, the only time in all of life, the car pulled over and stopped. Its wide black door opened; a man got out of it, running. He didn't even close the car door.

He ran after us, and we ran away from him, up the snowy Reynolds sidewalk. At the corner, I looked back; incredibly, he was still after us. He was in city clothes: a suit and tie, street shoes. Any normal adult would have quit, having sprung us into flight and made his point. This man was gaining on us. He was a thin man, all action. All of a sudden, we were running for our lives.

Wordless, we split up. We were on our turf; we could lose ourselves in the neighborhood backyards, everyone for himself. I paused and considered. Everyone had vanished except Mikey Fahey, who was just rounding the corner of a yellow brick house. Poor Mikey, I trailed him. The driver of the Buick sensibly picked the two of us to follow. The man apparently had all day.

He chased Mikey and me around the yellow house and up a backyard path we knew by heart: under a low tree, up a bank, through a hedge, down some snowy steps, and across the grocery store's delivery driveway. We smashed through a gap in another hedge, entered a scruffy backyard and ran around its back porch and tight between houses to Edgerton Avenue; we ran across Edgerton to an alley and up our own sliding woodpile to the Halls' front yard; he kept coming. We ran up Lloyd Street and wound through mazy backyards toward the steep hilltop at Willard and Lang. 12

He chased us silently, block after block. He chased us silently over picket fences, through thorny hedges, between houses, around garbage cans, and across streets. Every time I glanced back, choking for breath, I expected he would have quit. He must have been as breathless as we were. His jacket strained over his body. It was an immense discovery, pounding into my hot head with every sliding, joyous step, that this ordinary adult evidently knew what I thought only children who trained at football knew: that you have to fling yourself at what you're doing, you have to point yourself, forget yourself, aim, dive. 13

Mikey and I had nowhere to go, in our own neighborhood or out of it, but away from this man who was chasing us. He impelled us forward; we compelled him to follow our route. The air was cold; every breath tore my throat. We kept running, block after block; we kept improvising, backyard after backyard, running a frantic course and choosing it simultaneously, failing always to find small places or hard places to slow him down, and discovering always, exhilarated, dismayed, that only bare speed could save us — for he would never give up, this man — and we were losing speed. 14

He chased us through the backyard labyrinths of ten blocks before he caught us by our jackets. He caught us and we all stopped. 15

We three stood staggering, half blinded, coughing, in an obscure hilltop backyard: a man in his twenties, a boy, a girl. He had released our jackets, our pursuer, our captor, our hero: he knew we weren't going anywhere. We all played by the rules. Mikey and I unzipped our jackets. I pulled off my sopping mittens. Our tracks multiplied in the backyard's new snow. We had been breaking new snow all morning. We didn't look at each other. I was cherishing my excitement. The man's lower pants legs were wet; his cuffs were full of snow, and there was a prow of snow beneath them on his shoes and socks. Some trees bordered the little flat backyard, some messy winter trees. There was no one around: a clearing in a grove, and we the only players. 16

It was a long time before he could speak. I had some difficulty at first recalling why we were there. My lips felt swollen; I couldn't see out of the sides of my eyes; I kept coughing. 17

"You stupid kids," he began perfunctorily. 18

We listened perfunctorily indeed, if we listened at all, for the chewing out was redundant, a mere formality, and beside the point. The point was that he had chased us passionately without giving up, and so he had caught us. Now he came down to earth. I wanted the glory to last forever. 19

But how could the glory have lasted forever? We could have run through every backyard in North America until we got to Panama. But when he trapped us at the lip of the Panama Canal, what precisely could he have done to prolong the drama of the chase and cap its glory? I brooded about this for the next few years. He could only have fried Mikey Fahey and me in boiling oil, say, or dismembered us piecemeal, or staked us to anthills. None of which I really wanted, and none of which any adult was likely to do, even in the spirit of fun. He could only chew us out there in the Panamanian jungle, after months or years of exalting pursuit. He could only begin, "You stupid kids," and continue in his ordinary Pittsburgh accent with his normal righteous anger and the usual common sense.

If in that snowy backyard the driver of the black Buick had cut off our heads, Mikey's and mine, I would have died happy, for nothing has required so much of me since as being chased all over Pittsburgh in the middle of winter—running terrified, exhausted—by this sainted, skinny, furious redheaded man who wished to have a word with us. I don't know how he found his way back to his car.

Making Connections to Personal and Social Issues: Behaving Fearlessly

"The point," Dillard tells us near the end, "was that he had chased us passionately without giving up" (par. 19). What seems to fascinate her is not that the man chased the kids to bawl them out, but that an adult could still do what she thought only children knew how to do—what she had been taught by the neighborhood boys: the joy of flinging yourself wholeheartedly, fearlessly, into play or, indeed, into anything you do in life.

With other students in your class, discuss what you have learned about acting in the way Dillard describes. Begin by telling one another about a particular team or group you belonged to where you had to coordinate your activities to achieve a common goal, activities that posed some risk or challenge or required special effort, such as a swimming team, a newspaper staff, a science project, or a group helping after a natural disaster.

Then, together, discuss what you learned about being challenged, taking risks, or exerting yourself in unexpected ways. Into what other activities, if any, were you able to carry forward this "[flinging] yourself wholeheartedly" and "fearlessly"? If it has not happened again, what special conditions made it possible that one time? How might the expectations of your family, friends, and community have encouraged or thwarted your behaving fearlessly?

Analyzing Writing Strategies

1. By referring to cars early in the essay and ending with the man returning to his car, Dillard uses **framing**, a narrative device that echoes something from the beginning in the ending. In addition to giving the story a sense of closure, framing can help

readers understand an event's significance. *Write a few sentences about the way Dillard uses framing in her story.* What ideas does the frame suggest to you about the man, what he might represent, and the significance to Dillard of their confrontation? Consider that today, a Mercedes or Lexus would be the equivalent of the Buick sedan of the 1950s. How does this social class marker—together with the fact that the man wore a business suit and tie—affect your understanding of the event's significance?

2. **Visual description**—naming objects and detailing their colors, shapes, sizes, textures, and other qualities—is an important writing strategy in remembered-event essays. To see how writers use **naming** and **detailing** to create description, look closely at Dillard's description of an iceball: "I started making an iceball—a perfect iceball, from perfectly white snow, perfectly spherical, and squeezed perfectly translucent so no snow remained all the way through" (par. 6). Notice that she names two things: *iceball* and *snow*. She adds to these names descriptive details—*white* (color), *spherical* (shape), and *translucent* (appearance)—that help readers imagine more precisely what an iceball looks like. She also repeats the words *perfect* and *perfectly* to emphasize the color, shape, and appearance of this particular iceball.

To analyze Dillard's use of naming and detailing to present scenes and people, reread paragraphs 10–13, where she describes the man and the neighborhood through which he chases her and Mikey. Underline the names of objects and people (nearly always nouns), and put brackets around all of the words and phrases that modify the nouns they name. Here are two examples from paragraph 10 to get you started: "[snowy] Reynolds sidewalk" and "[city] clothes."

Notice how frequently naming and detailing occur in these paragraphs and how many different kinds of objects and people are named. Then, in a few sentences, consider these questions: Does naming sometimes occur without any accompanying detailing? How do you think the naming helps you visualize the scene and people? What do you think the detailing contributes?

Commentary: Organizing a Well-Told Story

"An American Childhood" is a **well-told story.** It provides a dramatic structure that arouses readers' curiosity, builds suspense, and concludes the action in a rather surprising way.

Writers of remembered-event essays usually begin at the beginning or even before the beginning. That is how Annie Dillard organizes "An American Childhood"—opening with two introductory paragraphs that give readers a context for the event and prepare them to appreciate its significance. Readers can see at a glance, by the space that separates the second paragraph from the rest of the essay, that the first two paragraphs are meant to stand apart as an introduction. They also do not refer to any particular incident.

In contrast, paragraph 3 begins by grounding readers in specifics. It is not any "weekday morning" but "one" in particular, "after Christmas" and after a substantial snowfall. Dillard goes on to locate herself in a particular place "on a front yard on trafficked Reynolds Street," engaged in a particular set of actions with a particular group of individuals. She has not yet begun to tell what happened but gives us the cast of characters (the "polite blond" Fahey boys, "tough" Chickie McBride) and sets the scene ("cloudy but cold"). In paragraph 9, when the driver of the Buick "got out of it, running," Dillard's narrative itself suddenly springs into action, moving at breakneck speed for the next six paragraphs until the man catches up with the kids in paragraph 15.

We can see this simple narrative organization in the following paragraph-by-paragraph scratch outline:

1. explains what she learned from playing football
2. identifies other sports she learned from boys in the neighborhood
3. sets the scene by describing the time and place of the event
4. describes the boys who were playing with her
5. describes what typically happened: a car would come down the street, they would throw snowballs, and then they would wait for another car
6. describes the iceball-making project she had begun while waiting
7. describes the Buick's approach and how they followed the routine
8. describes the impact of the snowball on the Buick's windshield
9. describes the man's surprising reaction: getting out of the car and running after them
10. narrates the chase and describes the man
11. explains how the kids split up and the man followed her and Mikey
12. narrates the chase and describes how the neighborhood looked as they ran through it
13. continues the narration, describing the way the man threw himself into the chase
14. continues the narration, commenting on her thoughts and feelings
15. narrates the climax of the chase, when the man caught the kids
16. describes the runners trying to catch their breath
17. describes her own physical state
18. relates the man's words
19. explains her reactions to his words and actions
20. explains her later thoughts and feelings
21. explains her present perspective on this remembered event

For more on scratch outlining, see Chapter 9.

Dillard's focus on a single incident that occurred in a relatively short span of time is the hallmark of the remembered-event essay. Although a chase is by nature dramatic because it is suspenseful, Dillard heightens the drama in a couple of ways.

One strategy she uses is identification: She lets us into her point of view, helping us to see what she saw and feel what she felt. In addition, she uses surprise. In fact, Dillard surprises us from beginning to end. The first surprise is that the man gets out of the car. But the fact that he chases the kids and that he continues to chase them beyond the point that any reasonable person would do so ratchets up the suspense. We simply cannot know what such a man is capable of doing. Finally, the story reaches its climax when the man catches Mikey and Dillard. Even then, Dillard surprises readers by what the man says and doesn't say or do. He does not shove them or hit them. Instead, he gives them only a "chewing out." Moreover, Dillard tells us, he says it "perfunctorily," as if it is something he is supposed to say as an adult "in his ordinary Pittsburgh accent with his normal righteous anger and the usual common sense" (par. 20). Dillard's language here is ironic because it is obvious that she feels that the man's behavior was anything but *ordinary, normal,* or *usual*—which is, of course, precisely what she wants us to appreciate.

Considering Topics for Your Own Essay

Like Dillard, you could write about a time when an adult did something entirely unexpected during your childhood, an action that seemed dangerous or threatening to you, or humorous, kind, or generous. List two or three of these occasions. Consider unpredictable actions of adults in your immediate or extended family, adults you had come to know outside your family, and strangers.

RICK BRAGG, a journalist who has taught writing at the University of South Florida, Boston University, and Harvard, won the Pulitzer Prize for feature writing in 1996 and the American Society of Newspaper Editors' Distinguished Writing Award twice. He has also written two autobiographical books: *All Over but the Shoutin'* (1997), about his small-town Alabama childhood, and *Ava's Man* (2001), about the grandfather he never met.

The following selection from *All Over but the Shoutin'* tells what happened the summer before Bragg was a senior in high school. As you read, pay attention to Bragg's vivid descriptions. For example, notice how he helps readers imagine the car and appreciate his feelings for it right down to its orange houndstooth-pattern upholstery and the eight-track *Eagles' Greatest Hits* tape.

100 Miles per Hour, Upside Down and Sideways
Rick Bragg

Since I was a boy I have searched for ways to slingshot myself into the distance, faster and faster. When you turn the key on a car built for speed, when you hear that car rumble like an approaching storm and feel the steering wheel tremble in your hands from all that power barely under control, you feel like you can run away

1

from anything, like you can turn your whole life into an insignificant speck in the rearview mirror.

In the summer of 1976, the summer before my senior year at Jacksonville High School, I had the mother of all slingshots. She was a 1969 General Motors convertible muscle car with a 350 V-8 and a Holley four-barreled carburetor as long as my arm. She got about six miles to the gallon, downhill, and when you started her up she sounded like Judgment Day. She was long and low and vicious, a mad dog cyclone with orange houndstooth interior and an eight-track tape player, and looked fast just sitting in the yard under a pine tree. I owned just one tape, that I remember, *The Eagles' Greatest Hits*.

I worked two summers in the hell and heat at minimum wage to earn enough money to buy her and still had to borrow money from my uncle Ed, who got her for just nineteen hundred dollars mainly because he paid in hundred-dollar bills. "You better be careful, boy," he told me. "That'un will kill you." I assured him that, Yes, Sir, I would creep around in it like an old woman.

I tell myself I loved that car because she was so pretty and so fast and because I loved to rumble between the rows of pines with the blond hair of some girl who had yet to discover she was better than me whipping in the breeze. But the truth is I loved her because she was my equalizer. She raised me up, at least in my own eyes, closer to where I wanted and needed to be. In high school, I was neither extremely popular nor one of the great number of want-to-bes. I was invited to parties with the popular kids, I had dates with pretty girls. But there was always a distance there, of my own making, usually.

That car, in a purely superficial way, closed it. People crowded around her at the Hardee's. I let only one person drive her, Patrice Curry, the prettiest girl in school, for exactly one mile.

That first weekend, I raced her across the long, wide parking lot of the TG&Y, an insane thing to do, seeing as how a police car could have cruised by at any minute. It was a test of nerves as well as speed, because you actually had to be slowing down, not speeding up, as you neared the finish line, because you just ran out of parking lot. I beat Lyn Johnson's Plymouth and had to slam on my brakes and swing her hard around, to keep from jumping the curb, the road and plowing into the parking lot of the Sonic Drive-In.

It would have lasted longer, this upraised standing, if I had pampered her. I guess I should have spent more time looking at her than racing her, but I had too much of the Bragg side of the family in me for that. I would roll her out on some lonely country road late at night, the top down, and blister down the blacktop until I knew the tires were about to lift off the ground. But they never did. She held the road, somehow, until I ran out of road or just lost my nerve. It was as if there was no limit to her, at how fast we could go, together.

It lasted two weeks from the day I bought her.

On Saturday night, late, I pulled up to the last red light in town on my way home. Kyle Smith pulled up beside me in a loud-running Chevrolet, and raced his engine.

I did not squall out when the light changed—she was not that kind of car—but let her rpm's build, build and build, like winding up a top.

I was passing a hundred miles per hour as I neared a long sweeping turn on Highway 21 when I saw, coming toward me, the blue lights of the town's police. I cannot really remember what happened next. I just remember mashing the gas pedal down hard, halfway through that sweeping turn, and the sickening feeling as the car just seemed to lift and twist in the air, until I was doing a hundred miles per hour still, but upside down and sideways. 10

She landed across a ditch, on her top. If she had not hit the ditch in just the right way, the police later said, it would have cut my head off. I did not have on my seat belt. We never did, then. Instead of flinging me out, though, the centrifugal force—I had taken science in ninth grade—somehow held me in. 11

Instead of lying broken and bleeding on the ground beside my car, or headless, I just sat there, upside down. I always pulled the adjustable steering wheel down low, an inch or less above my thighs, and that held me in place, my head covered with mud and broken glass. The radio was still blaring—it was the Eagles' "The Long Run," I believe—and I tried to find the knob in the dark to turn it off. Funny. There I was in an upside-down car, smelling the gas as it ran out of the tank, listening to the tick, tick, tick of the hot engine, thinking: "I sure do hope that gas don't get nowhere near that hot manifold," but all I did about it was try to turn down the radio. 12

I knew the police had arrived because I could hear them talking. Finally, I felt a hand on my collar. A state trooper dragged me out and dragged me up the side of the ditch and into the collective glare of the most headlights I had ever seen. There were police cars and ambulances and traffic backed up, it seemed, all the way to Piedmont. 13

"The Lord was riding with you, son," the trooper said. "You should be dead." 14

My momma stood off to one side, stunned. Finally the police let her through to look me over, up and down. But except for the glass in my hair and a sore neck, I was fine. Thankfully, I was too old for her to go cut a hickory and stripe my legs with it, but I am sure it crossed her mind. 15

The trooper and the Jacksonville police had a private talk off to one side, trying to decide whether or not to put me in prison for the rest of my life. Finally, they informed my momma that I had suffered enough, to take me home. As we drove away, I looked back over my shoulder as the wrecker dragged my car out of the ditch and, with the help of several strong men, flipped it back over, right-side up. It looked like a white sheet of paper someone had crumpled up and tossed in the ditch from a passing car. 16

"The Lord was riding with that boy," Carliss Slaughts, the wrecker operator, told my uncle Ed. With so many people saying that, I thought the front page of the *Anniston Star* the next day would read: LORD RIDES WITH BOY, WRECKS ANYWAY- 17

I was famous for a while. No one, no one, flips a convertible at a hundred miles per hour, without a seat belt on, and walks away, undamaged. People said I had a charmed life. My momma, like the trooper and Mr. Slaughts, just figured God was my copilot. 18

The craftsmen at Slaughts' Body Shop put her back together, over four months. | 19
My uncle Ed loaned me the money to fix her, and took it out of my check. The body
and fender man made her pretty again, but she was never the same. She was fast but
not real fast, as if some little part of her was still broken deep inside. Finally, someone
backed into her in the parking lot of the Piggly Wiggly, and I was so disgusted I sold
her for fourteen hundred dollars to a preacher's son, who drove the speed limit.

Making Connections to Personal and Social Issues: Social Status

Bragg worked hard and saved his money for two years to buy the convertible.
Probably he had several motives for doing so; but after he started driving the car,
he came to think of it as "my equalizer," which "closed" the distance between the
most popular students and himself and gave him immediate "upraised standing"
(par. 4, 5, 7).

With other students, discuss this concern with standing or status in high
school. Was it a concern of yours personally? If not, speculate about the reasons. If
so, what did you try to do, if anything, to raise (or maintain) your status? Why do
you think you made this effort?

Analyzing Writing Strategies

1. One important strategy used for describing people, places, and objects in
   autobiographical writing is **comparing**. Similes use *like* or *as* to make explicit
   comparisons: "you hear that car rumble like an approaching storm" (par. 1).
   Metaphors are implied comparisons: "Since I was a boy I have searched for
   ways to slingshot myself into the distance, faster and faster" (1). Here Bragg
   implies a comparison between himself and a stone launched from a slingshot;
   the stone speeds into space as Bragg hopes to speed into the future, or simply
   to get away.

   There are several comparisons in paragraph 1 and one each in paragraphs 3,
   7, 9, 13, and 16. Locate and underline them. Choose one that you think works especially well, and explain in a few sentences why you think it does. Then consider
   the comparisons as a group. What impression do they give you of the young Bragg
   and the event he is writing about?

2. In the central incident (par. 9–16), Bragg **narrates** a compelling story. To understand more fully how Bragg organizes the incident, make a paragraph scratch
   outline of it. Does the order of events make sense? Are there further details you
   need to know to follow easily what happens? What does Bragg do to arouse your
   curiosity and build **suspense**?

For an example of a paragraph scratch outline, turn to the Commentary following Annie
Dillard's essay on p. 22. For more information on scratch outlining, see Chapter 9, p. 315.

Commentary: Autobiographical Significance

Bragg's essay illustrates the two main ways writers convey the **autobiographical significance** of a remembered event: showing and telling. Bragg shows the event's significance through details and action. For example, he shows us how the car raised his status by describing its power and imposing appearance and the girls he took for rides in it. He shows the importance of the car by recounting how terribly hard he worked to buy it and then to have it repaired after the wreck. Bragg also tells readers what he believes the autobiographical significance might be, and he does so in two ways: by telling his remembered thoughts and feelings from the time of the event as well as by giving his present perspective on the event.

Bragg's **remembered thoughts and feelings** frame his essay. In the first paragraph, he remembers thinking that owning a powerful car makes "you feel like you can run away from anything, like you can turn your whole life into an insignificant speck in the rearview mirror." In the final paragraphs, he remembers his temporary fame for surviving the accident and his disgust when someone damaged his car in a parking lot. These remembered thoughts and feelings reveal perhaps a change of values, from materialism to some yet-to-be-defined values.

Bragg also offers **present perspectives** on this remembered event. Writing in his mid-thirties, Bragg reflects, "I tell myself I loved that car because she was so pretty and so fast. . . . But the truth is I loved her because she was my equalizer" (par. 4). He acknowledges that as a high school student he wanted the car because it made him popular. But he also admits that he loved the feeling the car gave him that he could "run away from anything" (1). By inserting these comments, Bragg reflects on desires that are contradictory but all too familiar: the wish to be accepted socially and, at the same time, the need to feel free and powerful. From his adult perspective, he knows that racing was "an insane thing to do" (6). But instead of moralizing about the recklessness of his wild ride, he tries to give readers a sense of the joy he felt when he would "slingshot" himself "into the distance, faster and faster" (1), as well as the amazement he felt later that he had lived to tell the tale.

Considering Topics for Your Own Essay

Bragg has focused on a particular incident that tells us something about himself both as an adolescent and as the man he would become by his mid-thirties. Think of incidents early in your life (before you were eleven or twelve years old) that are particularly revealing about you, both as a child and as a person of your present age. Try to think of incidents that tested or challenged you or incidents in which you behaved either typically or atypically in relation to the way you remember yourself to have been or think of yourself now. Perhaps you experienced a dreadful disappointment or an unexpected delight, or you accomplished something you now think you were unprepared for.

Purpose and Audience

Writing autobiography, writers relive moments of pleasure and pain, and they also gain insight, learning who they are now by examining who they used to be and the forces that shaped them. But because autobiographers write to be read, they are as much concerned with self-presentation as with self-discovery. Writers present themselves to readers in the way they want to be perceived. The rest they keep hidden, though readers may read between the lines.

We read about others' experiences for much the same reason that we write about our own—to learn how to live our lives. Reading autobiography can validate our sense of ourselves, particularly when we see our own experience reflected in another's life. Reading about others' lives can also challenge our complacency and help us appreciate other points of view.

Basic Features: Remembering Events

A Well-Told Story

Whatever else the writer may attempt to do, he or she must shape experience into a story that is entertaining and memorable. This is done primarily by building suspense, leading readers to wonder, for example, whether Jean Brandt will get caught for shoplifting, or what will happen to Rick Bragg and his sports car. The principal technique for propelling the narrative and heightening suspense is specific narrative action with its action verbs and verbals. Suspense increases, for instance, when the man gets out of his car and takes off after Dillard and her friends. Readers wonder whether he will catch them and, if so, what he will do next. In addition, writers use temporal transitions, as when Rick Bragg begins paragraphs with "In the summer of 1976," "That first weekend," and "On Saturday night." Finally, writers often use dialogue to convey immediacy and drama, as Brandt does to dramatize her confrontation with her mother on the phone.

A Vivid Presentation of Places and People

Skillful writers attempt to re-create the place where the event occurred and let us hear what people said. Vivid language and specific details make the writing memorable. A writer can name specific objects at a place, such as when Brandt catalogs the store's knickknacks, calendars, and buttons, or provide details about some of the objects, as when she describes the coveted "75-cent Snoopy button." Writers also use similes and metaphors to help readers understand the point. For example, when Brandt says she "felt like Hester Prynne being put on public display" (par. 17), readers familiar with *The Scarlet Letter* can imagine how embarrassed she must have felt.

To present people who played an important role in a remembered event, autobiographers often provide descriptive details and dialogue. They may detail the person's appearance, as Annie Dillard does by describing the man who chased her "in city clothes: a suit and tie, street shoes" as "a thin man, all action" (par. 10). Dialogue can be an especially effective way of giving readers a vivid impression of someone, as when Brandt reconstructs what her parents said to her over the phone.

An Indication of the Event's Significance

Writers can communicate an event's autobiographical significance in two ways: by showing us that the event was important or by telling us directly what it meant. Most writers do both. Showing is necessary because the event must be dramatized in order for readers to appreciate its importance and understand the writer's feelings about it. Seeing the important scenes and people from the writer's point of view naturally leads readers to identify with the writer. We can well imagine what that "unexpected tap on [the] shoulder" (par. 5) must have felt like for Brandt, how Dillard felt when the man chased her and Mikey "silently over picket fences, through thorny hedges, between houses, around garbage cans, and across streets" (13), and what Bragg was thinking as he hung upside down in his overturned car.

Telling also contributes to a reader's understanding, so most writers comment on the event's meaning and importance. They do not, however, typically begin their essays with the kind of thesis statement typical of argumentative writing. Instead, as the story moves along, they tell us how they felt at the time or how they feel now as they look back on the experience. Often writers do both. Dillard, for example, remembers that she wished "the glory" to "have lasted forever" (par. 20) and reflects that "nothing has required so much of me since" (21). Telling is the main way that writers interpret the event for readers, but skillful writers are careful not to append these reflections artificially, like a moral tacked on to a fable.

Remembering Events

Invention and Research

What are some events that have been important in your life, ones whose details you remember and would not mind sharing with your class? Think about several possible events, choose one of them, and do some more thinking and some writing about it. Then consider how you would express what it meant — and means — to you. . . . **See p. 33 for more.**

Planning and Drafting

As you look over what you have written so far, can you present the event vividly to readers and make them understand its importance to you? How can you engage their attention? What details and dialogue will bring the story to life? Make a plan for your narrative, and start drafting it. . . . **See p. 38 for more.**

Critical Reading Guide

What are your draft's strengths and weaknesses? Is the sequence of actions confusing? Is it unclear why the event was important to you? Ask a classmate, a friend, a writing tutor, or someone else to read and respond to your essay, especially the parts you are most unsure of. . . . **See p. 42 for more.**

Revising

As you consider your essay again in light of your reader's comments, how can you improve it? Did the beginning fail to engage the reader? Do you need more dialogue? Are you giving the wrong impression of how you felt at the time? Go through your draft systematically, making changes wherever necessary. . . . **See p. 43 for more.**

Editing and Proofreading

Have you checked for errors that are especially likely in essays about remembered events? Have you left out commas after introductory time references in sentences? Have you forgotten to use the past perfect tense to indicate a past action that was completed at the time of another one? Look for and correct these and any other errors. . . . **See p. 47 for more.**

☐ The Writing Assignment

Write an essay about an event in your life that will engage readers and that will, at the same time, help them understand the significance of the event. Tell your story dramatically and vividly.

■ Invention and Research

The following invention activities will help you choose an appropriate event, recall specific details, sketch out the story, test your choice, and explore the event's autobiographical significance.

Each invention activity is easy to complete and takes only a few minutes. If you can spread out the activities over several days, it will be easier to recall details and to reflect deeply on the event's meaning. Keep a written record of your invention work to use when you draft the essay and later when you revise it. Also, by never being without a small notebook and pencil or your laptop computer, you can write down some of the relevant details and ideas that will inevitably arise in your inner speech.

Finding an Event to Write About

To find the best possible event to write about, consider several possibilities rather than automatically choosing the first event that comes to mind.

Listing Remembered Events.   *Make a list of significant events from your past that you would feel comfortable sharing with your instructor and classmates.* For this assignment, an event is something that happened on *one day or just a part of a day.* Begin your list now, and add to it over the next few days. Include possibilities suggested by the Considering Topics activities following the readings in addition to these categories:

- An incident you know you will never forget
- A difficult situation, such as when you made a tough choice, when someone you admired let you down (or you let someone down), or when you struggled to learn or do something hard
- An occasion when things did not turn out as expected, such as when you expected to be praised but were criticized or ignored, or when you were convinced you would fail but succeeded
- An incident charged with strong emotion
- An occasion when you realized you had a special skill, ambition, or problem
- A time when you became aware of injustice, selflessness, or heroism

■ *Listing Events Relating to Identity and Community.* These suggestions will help you recall events that reveal important aspects of your sense of identity and your relationships with others:

- An event that revealed an aspect of your personality you had not seen before, such as your independence, ambitiousness, or jealousy
- An incident that made you reexamine a basic value or belief, such as when you were expected to do something against your better judgment
- An occasion when others' actions led you to consider seriously a new idea or point of view
- An incident that made you feel the need to identify yourself with a particular community, such as an ethnic group, a political or religious group, or a group of coworkers
- An event that made you realize that you were playing a role you were uncomfortable with
- An incident in which an encounter with another person changed the way you view yourself

■ *Listing Events Related to Work and Career.* Think of events involving your work experiences and career aspirations:

- An event that made you aware of your interest in a particular kind of career or that convinced you that you were not cut out for one
- An incident of great achievement, insight, or harassment at work
- An event that revealed to you other people's assumptions or attitudes about you as a worker, your fitness for a particular job, or your career goals
- An incident of conflict or serious misunderstanding at work

An Online Activity:
Finding an Event
to Write About

Exploring Web sites that collect personal narratives will give you a broad view of the importance of autobiography in American life. Not all of the narratives at the sites we recommend here focus on a single remembered event, as your essay will, but any one of them might nevertheless suggest to you an event from your own life you might want to write about:

American Life Histories: Manuscripts from the Federal Writers' Project, 1936–1940 (rs6.loc. gov/wpaintro/wpahome.html). You might want to focus on stories from your own state.

First-Person Narratives of the American South, Written between 1860 and 1920 (docsouth.unc. edu/fpn). A project of the University of North Carolina at Chapel Hill.

Sixties Personal Narrative Project (www3.iath.Virginia.edu/sixties/HTML_docs/Narrative. html). This site, a project of the University of Virginia, collects personal narratives by men and women who came of age during the decade of the Vietnam War.

Add to your list of possibilities any events suggested by your online research.

Choosing an Event.   *Look over your list of possibilities, and choose one event that you think will make an interesting story.* Your event should be limited to one day or part of a day. You should be eager to explore its significance and comfortable about sharing it with your instructors and classmates. You may find the choice easy to make, or you may have several equally promising possibilities from which to choose.

Make the best choice you can now. If this event does not work out, you can try a different one later.

Describing the Place

The following activities will help you decide which places are important to your story and generate descriptive language you may be able to use in your essay.

Listing Key Places.   *Make a list of all the places where the event occurred, skipping some space after each entry on your list.* List all the places you remember without worrying about whether they should be included in your story.

Describing Key Places.   *In the space after each entry on your list, make some notes describing each place.* What do you see (excluding people for the moment)? What objects stand out? Are they large or small, green or brown, square or oblong? What sounds do you hear? Do you detect any smells? Does any taste come to mind? Do you recall anything soft or hard, smooth or rough?

Recalling Key People

These activities will help you remember the people who played a role in the event — what they looked like, did, and said.

Listing Key People.   *List the people who played more than a casual role in the event.* You may have only one person to list, or you may have several.

Describing a Key Person.   *Write a brief description of a person other than yourself who played a major role in the event.* For this person, name and detail a few distinctive physical features or items of dress. Briefly describe this person's way of moving and gesturing.

Re-creating a Conversation.   *Reconstruct one important conversation you had during the event.* It could have lasted only a moment or several minutes. Try to recall any telling remarks that you made or were made to you. You will not remember exactly what was said during an entire conversation, but try to re-create it so that readers can imagine what was going on and how what was said and the way you each talked reveal who you were and your relationship.

Sketching the Story

Write for a few minutes, telling what happened. You may find it easier to outline what happened rather than writing complete sentences. Any way you can put the main activities or actions into words is fine.

Filling Out Your Invention Notes

Over the next few days, add newly remembered details to your notes in each invention category.

Testing Your Choice

Now you need to decide whether you recall enough of the event and care enough about it to write a good story. Test your choice using the questions below. If you lose confidence in your choice, return to your list of possible events, and choose another event.

- Do I recall enough of what happened during the event to narrate a complete and coherent story?

- Do I vividly remember feelings associated with the event?

- Have I been able to reconstruct conversations and recall details of the appearance, gestures, etc., of people involved?

- *Do I feel drawn toward understanding what this event meant to me then and means to me now?* You need not yet know the significance or feel entirely confident about your remembered feelings and present perspective, but you have to feel compelled to discover them — keeping in mind that you will decide what you want to disclose.

- *Do I feel comfortable writing about this event?* You are not writing a diary entry. Rather, you are writing a public document to be shared with classmates and your instructor, a fact that may give you pause, but can also inspire you.

A Collaborative Activity: Testing Your Choice

Get together with two or three other students to try out your story. Your classmates' reactions will help you determine whether you have chosen an event you can present in an interesting way.

Storytellers: Take turns telling your story, describing the place and key people. Try to pique your listeners' curiosity and build suspense.

Listeners: Briefly tell each storyteller what you found most intriguing about the story. For example, were you eager to know how the story would turn out? Were you curious about any of the people? Were you able to identify with the storyteller? Could you understand why the event was significant for the storyteller?

Exploring Memorabilia

Memorabilia are images, sounds, and objects that can help you remember details and understand the significance of an event. Examples include photographs, newspaper clippings, music, and ticket stubs. Memorabilia are not a requirement for success with this assignment, but they may prove helpful in stimulating your memory. *Look for memorabilia relevant to the remembered event you will write about, and add to your invention notes any details about the period, places, or people the memorabilia suggest.*

Also consider including memorabilia in your essay by appending items to your printed-out essay, or scanning or downloading images into your electronic document. Label and number them as Figure 1, Figure 2, and so on, and include captions identifying them.

Reflecting on the Event's Significance

The following activities will help you understand the meaning the event holds in your life and develop ways to convey this significance to your readers.

Recalling Your Remembered Feelings and Thoughts.   *Write for a few minutes about your feelings and thoughts during and immediately after the event,* using these questions to stimulate your memory:

- What were my expectations before the event?
- What was my reaction to the event as it was happening and right after?
- How did I show my feelings? What did I say?
- What did I want the people involved to think of me? Why did I care?
- What did I think of myself at the time?
- What were the immediate consequences of the event for me?

Pause now to reread what you have written. *Then write another sentence or two about the event's significance to you at the time it occurred.*

Exploring Your Present Perspective.   *Write for a few minutes about your current feelings and thoughts as you look back on the event.* These questions may help you get started:

- How do I feel now about this event? If I understand it differently now than I did then, what is the difference?
- What do my actions at the time of the event say about the person I was then? How would I respond to the same event if it occurred today?
- Can looking at the event historically or culturally help explain what happened? For example, did I upset gender expectations or feel torn between two cultures or ethnic identities?

- Do I now see that there was a conflict underlying the event? For example, did I struggle with contradictory desires within myself? Were my desires and rights in conflict with someone else's? Was the event about power, asserting myself, pleasing or being pressured by someone else?

Pause now to reflect on what you have written about your present perspective. *Then write another sentence or two, commenting on the event's significance as you look back on it.*

Defining Your Purpose for Your Readers

In a few sentences, define your purpose in writing about this event for your readers. Use these questions to focus your thoughts:

- Who are my readers?
- What do they know about me?
- What in my story is likely to surprise my readers?
- How do I expect my readers to understand or react to the event?
- How do I want my readers to feel about what happened? What is the dominant impression or mood I want my story to create?
- What do I want my readers to think of me? What do I expect or fear?

It is unlikely, but you may decide at this point that you feel uncomfortable disclosing this event. If so, choose another event to write about.

Formulating a Tentative Thesis Statement

Review what you wrote for Reflecting on the Event's Significance, and add another two or three sentences extending your insights. These sentences must necessarily be speculative and tentative because you may not yet fully understand the event's significance yourself.

Keep in mind that readers do not expect you to begin your essay with the kind of explicit thesis statement typical of argumentative or explanatory writing. You are not obliged to announce the significance, but you must convey it to readers through the way you present the story.

■ Planning and Drafting

This section will help you review your invention writing and get started on your first draft.

Seeing What You Have

You have now done a lot of thinking and writing about the basic elements of a remembered-event essay: what happened, where it happened, who was involved, what was said, and how you felt. You have also begun to develop your understanding of why the event is important to you. Reread what you have written so far to see what you have. Watch for specific narrative actions, vivid descriptive details, and choice bits of dialogue. Note also any language that resonates with feeling or that seems especially insightful. Highlight any writing you think could be used in your draft.

Then ask yourself the following questions:

- Do I remember enough specific details about the event to describe it vividly and to create a dominant impression?

- Does my invention material provide what I need to convey the event's significance to my readers?

If you find little that seems promising, you are not likely to be able to write a good draft. Consider starting over with another event. If, however, your invention writing offers some promising material, the following activities may help you develop more:

- To remember more of what actually happened, discuss the event with someone who was there or who remembers having heard about it at the time.

- To recall additional details about a person who played an important role in the event, look at any available photographs or letters, talk with the person or people who played an important role, or talk with someone who remembers them. If that is impossible, you might imagine having a conversation with them today: What would you say? How do you think they would respond?

- To remember how you felt at the time of the event, try to recall what else was happening in your life during that period. What music, movies, sports, books did you like? What concerns did you have at home, school, work, play?

- To develop your present perspective on the event, try viewing your experience as a historical occurrence. If you were writing a news story about the event, what would you want people to know?

- To decide on the dominant impression you want your story to have on readers, imagine that you are making a film based on this event. What mood or atmosphere would you try to create? Alternatively, imagine writing a song or poem about the event. Think of an appropriate image or refrain. What kind of song would you write—blues, hip-hop, rock?

Setting Goals

Before starting to draft, set goals. Here are some questions that will help you:

Your Purpose and Readers

- What do I want my readers to think of me and my experience? Should I tell them how I felt and what I thought at the time of the event, as Dillard does? Should I tell them how my perspective has changed, as Bragg does?

- If my readers are likely to have had a similar experience, how can I convey the uniqueness of my experience or its special importance in my life? Should I tell them more about my background or the particular context of the event, as Bragg does? Should I give them a glimpse, as Dillard does, of its impact years later?

- If my readers are not likely to have had a similar experience, how can I help them understand what happened? Should I reveal the cultural influences acting on me, as Bragg does?

The Beginning

- What can I do in the opening sentences to arouse readers' curiosity? Should I begin with a surprising announcement, as Bragg does, or should I establish the setting and situation, as Dillard and Brandt do?

- How can I get my readers to identify with me? Should I tell them a few things about myself, as Bragg does?

- Should I do something unusual, such as begin in the middle of the action or with a funny bit of dialogue?

The Story

- What should be the climax of my story—the point that readers anticipate with trepidation or eagerness?

- What narrative actions or dialogue would intensify the drama of the story?

- Should I follow strict chronological order? Or would flashback (referring to an event that occurred earlier) or flashforward (referring to an event that will occur later) make the narrative more interesting?

- How can I use vivid descriptive detail to dramatize the story?

The Ending

- If I conclude with some reflections on the meaning of the experience, how can I avoid tagging on a moral or being too sentimental?

- If I want readers to think well of me, should I end with a paradoxical statement, like Dillard? Should I be satirical? Should I be self-critical to avoid seeming smug?

- If I want to underscore the event's continuing significance in my life, can I show that the conflict was never fully resolved, as Brandt does? Could I contrast my remembered and current feelings and thoughts?

- Should I frame the essay by echoing something from the beginning to give readers at least a superficial sense of closure, as Brandt does by setting the last scene, like the first, in a car?

Outlining

The goals you have set should help you draft your essay, but first you might want to make a quick scratch outline. In your outline, list the main actions in order, noting where you plan to describe the place, introduce particular people, present dialogue, and insert remembered or current feelings and thoughts. Use this outline to guide your drafting, but do not feel tied to it. As you draft, you may find a better way to sequence the action and integrate these features.

For an example of a paragraph scratch outline, turn to the Commentary following Annie Dillard's essay on p. 22. For more information on scratch outlining, see Chapter 9, p. 315.

Drafting

General Advice.   Keep in mind the goals you have set for yourself, especially the goal of telling the story dramatically. Turn off your grammar checker and spelling checker at this stage if you find them distracting. Don't be afraid to skip around in your story. Jump back and fill in a spontaneous idea, or leap ahead and write a later section first if you find that easier. Refer to your outline to help you sequence the action. If you get stuck while drafting, either make a note of what you need to fill in later or see if you can use something from your invention writing.

As you read over your first draft, you may see places where you can add new material to make the story dramatic. Or you may even decide that after this first draft you can finally see the story you want to write and set out to do so in a second draft.

A Sentence Strategy: Short Sentences.   As you draft a remembered-event essay, you will be trying to help readers feel the suspense of your story and recognize its significance. In thinking about how to achieve this goal, you can benefit by paying attention to how long your sentences are.

Use short sentences to heighten the drama or suspense, point out autobiographical significance, and summarize action.

> Finally, I felt a hand on my collar. (Bragg, par. 13)
>
> He caught us and we all stopped. (Dillard, 15)
>
> I wanted the glory to last forever. (Dillard, 19)
>
> The humiliation at that moment was overwhelming. (Brandt, 17)

Note that experienced writers of autobiography use short sentences infrequently. Because short sentences are infrequent, they seem to say, "Pay close attention here." But they achieve this effect only in relation to long sentences. See how Dillard uses a series of longer sentences to build suspense that she brings to a peak with a short one:

> On one weekday morning after Christmas, six inches of new snow had just fallen. We were standing up to our boot tops in snow on a front yard on trafficked Reynolds Street, waiting for cars. The cars traveled Reynolds Street slowly and evenly; they were targets all but wrapped in red ribbons, cream puffs. We couldn't miss. (par. 3)

For more on using short sentences, go to **bedfordstmartins.com/conciseguide** and click on Sentence Strategies.

Critical Reading Guide

Now is the time to get a good critical reading of your draft. Your instructor may schedule readings of drafts as part of your coursework—in class or online. If not, ask a classmate or a friend to read your draft. You could also seek comments from a tutor at your campus writing center. The guidelines in this section can be used by anyone reviewing an essay about a remembered event. (If you are unable to have someone read your draft, turn ahead to the Revising section, where you will find guidelines for reading your own draft critically.)

▶ **If You Are the Writer.** To provide focused, helpful comments, your reader must know your essay's intended audience, your purpose, and a problem in the draft that you need help solving. Briefly write out this information at the top of your draft.

- *Audience:* Identify the intended audience of your essay.
- *Purpose:* What do you hope will most interest readers? What do you want to disclose about yourself?
- *Problem:* Describe the single most important problem with your draft.

▶ **If You Are the Reader.** Use the following guidelines to help you give critical comments to others on remembered-event essays.

1. *Read for a First Impression.* Begin by reading the draft quickly, to enjoy the story and to get a sense of its significance. Then, in just a few sentences, describe your first impression. If you have any insights about the meaning or importance of the event, share your thoughts.

   Next, consider the problem the writer identified, and respond briefly to that concern now. (If you find that the problem is covered by one of the other items listed below, respond to it in more detail there if necessary.)

2. *Analyze the Effectiveness of the Storytelling.* Review the story, looking at the way the suspense builds and resolves itself. Point to any places where the drama loses intensity—perhaps where the suspense slackens, where specific narrative action is sparse or action verbs are needed, where narrative transitions would help readers, or where dialogue could be added to dramatize people's interactions.

> **Making Comments Electronically**
> Most word processing software offers features that allow you to insert comments directly into the text of someone else's document. Many readers prefer to make their comments in this way because it tends to be faster than writing on a hard copy and space is virtually unlimited; it also eliminates the problem of deciphering handwritten comments. Where such special comment features are not available, simply typing comments directly into a document in a contrasting color can provide the same advantages.

3. *Consider How Vividly the Places and People Are Described.* Point to any descriptive details, similes, or metaphors that are especially effective. Note any places or people that need more specific description. Also indicate any descriptive details that seem unnecessary. Identify any quoted dialogue that might be summarized or any dialogue that does not seem relevant.

4. *Assess Whether the Autobiographical Significance Is Clear.* Explain briefly what you think makes this event significant for the writer. Point out any places in the draft where the significance seems so overstated as to be sentimental or so understated as to be vague or unclear. If the event seems to lack significance, speculate about what you think the significance could be. Then point to one place in the draft where you think the writer could make the significance clearer by telling the story more fully or dramatically or by stating the significance.

5. *Assess the Use of Memorabilia.* If the writer makes use of memorabilia, evaluate how successfully each item is used. How is it relevant? Does it seem integrated into the narrative or merely appended? Is it placed in the most appropriate location? Does it make a meaningful contribution to the essay?

6. *Analyze the Effectiveness of the Organization.* Consider the overall plan, perhaps by making a scratch outline. Pay special attention to temporal transitions and verb tenses so that you can identify any places where the order of the action is unclear. Also indicate any places where you think the description or background information interrupts the action. If you can, suggest other locations for this material.

   - Look at the beginning. If it does not arouse curiosity, point to language elsewhere in the essay that might serve as a better opening—for example, a bit of dialogue, a striking image, or a remembered feeling.
   - Look at the ending. Indicate whether the conflict in the story is too neatly resolved at the end, whether the writer has tacked on a moral, or whether the essay abruptly stops without really coming to a conclusion. If there is a problem with the ending, try to suggest an alternative ending, such as framing the story with a reference to something from the beginning or projecting into the future.

7. *Give the Writer Your Final Thoughts.* What is the draft's strongest part? What part is most in need of further work?

For a printable version of this critical reading guide, go to **bedfordstmartins.com/conciseguide.**

■ Revising

This section will help you get an overview of your draft and revise it accordingly.

Working with Sources

Using references to time to keep readers oriented to the stages of the event In the essays you will write in later chapters of this book, you will rely on interviews and observation and on print or visual sources to support your explanations or arguments. In writing about a remembered event, however, you will rely almost entirely on your memory. Because you cannot refer your readers to your memory the way you can to a book, Web site, or other source they could consult, you'll need to work especially hard to recount your remembered event vividly, clearly, and persuasively.

One way to keep your readers oriented to the story you tell is by giving them frequent, explicit cues about time. Without these cues, readers may not know in which decade, year, or season the event occurred; whether it unfolded slowly or quickly; or in what sequence the various actions took place.

When experienced writers of autobiography use these cues, they nearly always place them at the beginnings of sentences (or main clauses), as Annie Dillard does in this sentence from *An American Childhood*:

> *On one weekday morning after Christmas,* six inches of new snow had just fallen. (par. 3)

Placing these two important time cues—day of the week and time of the year—at the beginning of a sentence may not seem noteworthy, but in fact time cues can usually be placed nearly anywhere in a sentence. Dillard might have written

> Six inches of new snow had just fallen *on one weekday morning after Christmas.*

Why might Dillard decide to locate these time cues at the beginning of the sentence, as she does with nearly all the time cues in her essay? The answer is that this placement gives the greatest possible emphasis to time cues. Experienced writers of autobiography give highest priority to keeping readers oriented to time. To do so, they can rely on words, phrases, or clauses:

> Slowly, . . . (Brandt, par. 36)

> A few seconds later, . . . (Brandt, 3)

> As we drove away, . . . (Bragg, 16)

As you draft and revise, try to locate your time cues at the beginnings of your sentences. It is easy to do, and your readers will be grateful.

Getting an Overview

Consider the draft as a whole, following these two steps:

1. **Reread.** If at all possible, put the draft aside for a day or two. When you do reread

it, start by reconsidering your purpose. Then read the draft straight through, trying to see it as your intended readers will.

2. *Outline.* Make a quick scratch outline on paper, or use the headings and outline or summary functions of your word processor.

Planning for Revision.   Resist the temptation to dive in and start changing your text until you have a comprehensive view of what needs to be done. Using your outline as a guide, move through the document and note comments received from others and problems you want to solve.

Analyzing the Basic Features of Your Own Draft.   Turn to the Critical Reading Guide on the preceding pages (pp. 42–43). Using this guide, reread the draft to identify problems you need to solve. Note the problems on your draft.

Turn to pp. 30–31 to review the basic features.

Studying Readers' Comments.   Review all of the comments you have received from other readers and add to your notes any that you intend to act on. For each comment, refer to the draft to see what might have led the reader to make that particular point. Try to be objective about any criticism. Ideally, these comments will help you to see your draft as others see it (rather than as you hoped it would be) and to identify specific problems.

Carrying Out Revisions

Having identified problems in your draft, you now need to figure out solutions and—most important—to carry them out. Basically, there are three ways to find solutions:

1. Review your invention and planning notes for material you can add to your draft.
2. Do additional invention writing to provide material you or your readers think is needed.
3. Look back at the readings in this chapter to see how other writers have solved similar problems.

The following suggestions, which are organized according to the basic features of remembered-event essays, will get you started solving some writing problems that are common in them.

A Well-Told Story

- *Is the climax difficult to identify?* Check to be sure your story has a climax. Perhaps it is the point when you get what you were striving for (Dillard), when something frightening happens (Bragg), or when you get caught (Brandt). If you cannot find a climax in your story or reconstruct your story so that it has one, then you may have a major problem. If this is the case, you should discuss with your instructor the possibility of starting over with another event.

- *Does the suspense slacken instead of building to the climax?* Try showing people moving or gesturing, adding narrative transitions to propel the action, or substituting quoted dialogue for summarized dialogue. Remember that writers of autobiography often use short sentences to summarize action and heighten suspense, as when Dillard writes "We couldn't miss." and "He didn't even close the car door."

A Vivid Presentation of Places and People

- *Do any places or people need more specific description?* Try naming objects and adding sensory details to help readers imagine what the objects look, feel, smell, taste, or sound like. For people, describe a physical feature or mannerism that shows the role the person plays in your story.

- *Does any dialogue seem irrelevant or poorly written?* Eliminate any unnecessary dialogue, or summarize quoted dialogue that has no distinctive language or dramatic purpose. Liven up quoted dialogue with faster repartee to make it more dramatic. Instead of introducing each comment with the dialogue cue "he said," describe the speaker's attitude or personality with phrases like "she gasped" or "he joked."

- *Do any descriptions weaken the dominant impression?* Omit extraneous details or reconsider the impression you want to make. Add similes and metaphors that strengthen the dominant impression you want your story to have.

- *Do readers question any visuals you used?* Might you move a visual to a more appropriate place or replace an ineffective visual with a more appropriate one? Could you make clear the relevance of a visual by mentioning it in your text?

An Indication of the Event's Significance

- *Are readers getting a different image of you from the one you want to create?* Look closely at the language you use to express your feelings and thoughts. If you project an aspect of yourself you did not intend, reconsider what the story reveals about you.

- *Are your remembered or current feelings and thoughts about the event coming across clearly and eloquently?* If not, look in your invention writing for more expressive language. If your writing seems too sentimental, try to express your feelings more directly and simply, or let yourself show ambivalence or uncertainty.

- *Do readers appreciate the event's uniqueness or special importance in your life?* If not, consider giving them more insight into your background or cultural heritage or telling what has happened since the event took place.

The Organization

- *Is the overall plan ineffective or the story hard to follow?* Look carefully at the way the action unfolds. Fill in any gaps. Add or clarify temporal transitions. Fix confusing verb tenses. Remember that writers of autobiography tend to place references to time at the beginnings of sentences — *"When a car came,* we all popped it one" — to keep readers on track as the story unfolds.

- *Does description or other information disrupt the flow of the narrative?* Try integrating this material by adding smoother transitions. Or consider removing the disruptive parts or placing them elsewhere.

- *Is the beginning weak?* See whether there is a better way to start. Review the draft and your notes for an image, a bit of dialogue, or a remembered feeling that might catch readers' attention or spark their curiosity.

- *Does the ending work?* If not, think about a better way to end — with a memorable image, perhaps, or a provocative assertion. Consider whether you can frame the essay by referring back to something in the beginning.

For a revision checklist, go to **bedfordstmartins.com/conciseguide**.

■ Editing and Proofreading

Now is the time to check your revised draft for errors in grammar, punctuation, and mechanics and to consider matters of style. Our research has identified several errors that occur often in essays about remembered events: missing commas after introductory elements, fused sentences, and misused past-perfect verbs. The following guidelines will help you check your essay for these common errors.

> **A Note on Grammar and Spelling Checkers**
> These tools are good at catching certain types of errors, but currently there is no replacement for a good human proofreader. Grammar checkers in particular are extremely limited in what they can find. They also tend to give faulty advice for fixing problems and to flag correct items as wrong. Spelling checkers cause fewer problems but cannot catch misspellings that are themselves words, such as *to* for *too*.

Checking for Missing Commas after Introductory Elements.   Introductory elements in a sentence can be words, phrases, or clauses. A comma tells readers that the introductory information is ending and the main part of the sentence is about to begin. If there is no danger of misreading, you can omit the comma after single words or short phrases or clauses, but you will never be wrong to include the comma. Remembered-event essays require introductory elements, especially those showing time passing. The following sentences, taken from drafts written by college students using this book, show several kinds of introductory sentence elements that should have a comma after them.

▶ Through the nine-day run of the play ⌃ the acting just kept getting better and better.

▶ Knowing that the struggle was over ⌃ I felt through my jacket to find tea bags and cookies the robber had taken from the kitchen.

▶ As I stepped out of the car ⌃ I knew something was wrong.

For practice, go to **bedfordstmartins.com/conciseguide/exercisecentral** and click on
Commas after Introductory Elements.

Checking for Fused Sentences.   Fused sentences occur when two independent
clauses are joined with no punctuation or connecting word between them. When you
write about a remembered event, you try to re-create a scene. In so doing, you might
write a fused sentence like this one:

> **Sleet glazed the windshield the wipers were frozen stuck.**

There are several ways to edit fused sentences:

- Make the clauses separate sentences.

  > ► **Sleet glazed the windshield. ~~the~~ The wipers were frozen stuck.**

- Join the two clauses with a comma and *and, but, or, nor, for, so,* or *yet.*

  > ► **Sleet glazed the windshield , and the wipers were frozen stuck.**

- Join the two clauses with a semicolon.

  > ► **Sleet glazed the windshield ; the wipers were frozen stuck.**

- Rewrite the sentence, subordinating one clause.

  > ► **~~Sleet~~ As sleet glazed the windshield , the wipers ~~were~~ became frozen stuck.**

For practice, go to **bedfordstmartins.com/conciseguide/exercisecentral** and click on
Fused Sentences.

Checking Your Use of the Past Perfect.   Verb tenses indicate the time an action
takes place. As a writer, you will generally use the present tense for actions occurring at
the time you are writing (we *see*), the past tense for actions completed in the past (we
saw), and the future tense for actions that will occur in the future (we *will see*). When
you write about a remembered event, you will often need to use various forms of the
past tense: the past perfect to indicate an action that was completed at the time of
another past action (she *had finished* her work when we saw her) and the past progres-
sive to indicate a continuing action in the past (she *was finishing* her work). One common problem in writing about a remembered event is the failure to use the past perfect
when it is needed. For example:

> ► **I had three people in the car, something my father had told me not to do on several occasions.**

In the following sentence, the meaning is not clear without the past perfect:

                       had run
▶ **Coach Kernow told me I ~~ran~~ faster than ever before.**

For practice, go to **bedfordstmartins.com/conciseguide/exercisecentral** and click on The Past Perfect.

A Common ESL Problem.   It is important to remember that the past perfect is formed with *had* followed by a past participle. Past participles usually end in *-ed, -d, -en, -n,* or *-t: worked, hoped, eaten, taken, bent.*

                                                  spoken
▶ **Before Tania went to Moscow last year, she had not really ~~speak~~ Russian.**

For practice, go to **bedfordstmartins.com/conciseguide/exercisecentral** and click on A Common ESL Problem: Forming the Past Perfect.

Thinking About
Document Design

Adding Visual and Textual Elements

As the student and rancher were working on the text of the local history project described earlier in this chapter (see p. 13), they considered visual and textual elements appropriate to writing about remembered events—including, for instance, photographs of the area—and quotations from the rancher's tape-recorded story.

Selecting Visuals

To begin, the student and rancher discussed what visuals might accompany the final written piece. The student found old snow-day photographs from the local newspaper's archives, and the rancher selected a compelling photo of his wife standing on the roof of the family home after the storm. The student and the rancher also considered including a painting of an isolated homestead and an early snapshot that the rancher had taken of his house in 1941, but decided that the painting was too abstract for a newspaper story, and the snapshot did not capture the snowstorm, which was the focus of the newspaper's special supplement. They narrowed their selection to two black-and-white photos—the photo of his wife standing on the house and the family photo taken in the spring, both of which emphasized the key points they wanted readers to pull from the story—the importance of family in the face of adversity.

Pulling Revealing Quotations

After reviewing the draft of their article, the student and the rancher chose two potential "pull- quotes" (inset or

The Rocky Valley Times

Special Supplement, Volume XCII, Number 2   January 14, 2006

This Sunday marks the 68th anniversary of the legendary "Storm of the Century" that blitzed the Rocky Valley area with up to 8 feet of snow in just a few hours.

In this era of cell phones and fax machines, it's all too easy to forget the danger and difficulties the regions' widely scattered settlers faced at that time.

In this special 6-page supplement, we salute the resourceful individuals who "made it through" and helped to establish our community as we know it today.
—The Editor

INSIDE
The General Store, 2
An Engineer's Tale, 2
Women Saved Lives, 2
Born During Storm, 3
Animals in Snowstorm, 4
Forecast Went Wrong, 5
Logger's Perspective, 5
Happen Today? 6

RANCHER REMEMBERS THE STORM OF THE CENTURY
By George Valentino

"It was only a few days, but it seemed like a lifetime."

Jim and Anne Austin were new to Rocky Valley, and when it became clear that a major blizzard was imminent, relatives urged the couple and their two young children to stay in town lest supplies become scarce. But Austin and Anne had lived off the land for years, and had weathered storms before.

Anne Austin standing on the roof of the Austin home after the 1938 snowstorm.

They felt safest returning to their ranch to tend their livestock. They were confident they had enough food, water, and candles at the ranch to carry them through any storm. Nothing in their past experience had prepared the couple, however, for the onslaught of what quickly came to be known as "the storm of the century." In a recent interview for the Times, Austin unfolded an inspiring tale of resourcefulness and courage in a desperate situation.

The date was January 1938. Young Jim Jr. was only two, and Mark was just a few months old. Austin remembered that, despite the frigid temperature, the children were happy and excited on the ride home from town as the first few flakes of snow started to fall—innocently enough, it seemed at first.

While Anne put the children to bed, Austin went about his usual evening chores. "Within the span of a few hours, the wind started to blow quite a bit harder," he recalls, "but the animals were calm and comfortable in their quarters. Anne and I retired for the night without suspicion about what was to come."

Anne checked on Mark "at about 2:45 in the morning," Austin recalls wryly," and when she came back down the hall, I knew something was wrong just from the look on her face. She said—and this is what I'll never forget—that Mark was crying because there were snowdrifts up to the windowsills." The snow was blocking the scant light from the moon, leaving the room in total darkness. SEE STORM, 4

otherwise highlighted quotations) from the story that they thought would capture readers' attention and convey some of the story's drama: "It was only a few days, but it seemed like a lifetime" and "I knew I had to make a decision—to continue on through the storm, or to head back to the house. Either way, I was unsure of my fate." The idea was not to summarize the rancher's story in these quotations, but to emphasize to readers the significance of the event as well as to leave them with a good understanding of the event as they finished reading the piece. The newspaper selected the first quotation as the story lead.

Reflecting on Your Writing

Now that you have worked extensively in autobiography—reading it, talking about it, writing it—take some time to reflect on what you have learned: What problems did you have while you were writing, and how did you solve them?

Write a page or so telling your instructor about a problem you encountered in writing your essay and how you solved it. Before you begin, gather all of your writing—invention and planning notes, outlines, drafts, critical comments, revision plans, and final revision. Review these materials as you complete this writing task.

1. ***Identify one problem you needed to solve as you wrote about a remembered event.*** Do not be concerned with grammar and punctuation; concentrate on problems unique to writing a story about your experience. For example: Did you puzzle over how to present a particular place or person? Was it difficult to structure the narrative so it held readers' interest? Did you find it hard (or uncomfortable) to convey the event's autobiographical significance?

2. ***Determine how you came to recognize the problem.*** When did you first discover it? What called it to your attention? Did you notice it yourself, or did another reader point it out? Can you now see hints of it in your invention writing, your planning notes, or an earlier draft? If so, where specifically?

3. ***Reflect on how you went about solving the problem.*** Did you work on a particular passage, cut or add details, or reorganize the essay? Did you reread one of the essays in the chapter to see how another writer handled similar material? Did you look back at the invention guidelines? Did you discuss the problem with another student, a tutor, or your instructor? If so, how did talking about it help, and how useful was the advice you got?

4. ***Write a brief explanation of the problem and your solution.*** Be as specific as possible in reconstructing your efforts. Quote from your invention notes or early drafts, from readers' comments, from your revision plan, and from your final revision to show the various changes your writing underwent as you worked to solve the problem. Taking the time now to think about how you recognized and solved a real writing problem will help you become more aware of what works and does not work. This will make you a more confident writer.

3

Writing
Profiles

IN COLLEGE COURSES To fulfill an important requirement for an upper-division education course, a student who plans to teach sixth grade decides to study collaborative learning (CL) in action. The student arranges to visit an elementary school class that is beginning an Internet project about immigration. On three separate visits, she observes a group of three students working together on the project and interviews them individually and as a group.

The student organizes her profile narratively, combining her observations over the course of three visits into the story of one meeting. She reports as a detached observer. From her profile emerges the central idea that sixth graders' collaborative work is unlikely to succeed unless the students, along with their teacher, frequently reflect on what they are learning and how they can work together more productively.

IN THE COMMUNITY A newspaper reporter profiles a local artist commissioned to paint a mural on a wall sheltering a section of the city's central park.

Having scheduled an appointment, he visits the artist's studio and talks with him about mural painting. The artist invites the reporter to spend the following day working on the mural.

The next day, the artist puts him to work alongside two volunteers. This firsthand experience helps the reporter describe the process of mural painting from a participant-observer's point of view.

The reporter organizes the profile around the main stages of this collaborative mural project, from conception to completion. As he describes each stage, he weaves in details about the artist, his helpers, and the mural itself, seeking to capture the civic spirit that pervades the entire project.

IN THE WORKPLACE For a company newsletter, a public-relations officer profiles a day in the life of the corporation's new chief executive officer (CEO). He follows the CEO from meeting to meeting, taking photographs and observing her interactions. Between meetings, he interviews her and, with her permission, records them. Immediately after the interviews he listens to the recordings, making notes and writing down questions to ask in a follow-up interview.

A day later, the CEO invites the writer to visit her at home. He stays for dinner, and then watches the CEO help her daughter with homework. He converses with her husband. He also takes more photographs.

The writer illustrates the profile with two images, one showing the CEO at a meeting and the other showing her with her daughter. As he reports on some of the immediate challenges she anticipates for the corporation, he tries to convey the ease and confidence she shows throughout a typical day of her life.

Profiles tell us about people, places, and activities. Some profile writers try to reveal the not-so-obvious workings of places or activities we consider familiar. Others introduce us to exotic places or people—peculiar hobbies, unusual places of business, bizarre personalities.

Whatever their subject, profile writers strive most of all to enable readers to imagine the person, place, or activity that is the focus of the profile. Writers succeed only through specific and vivid details: how the person dresses, gestures, and talks; what the place looks, sounds, and smells like; what the activity requires of those who participate in it. Not only must the details be vivid, but they also must help to convey a writer's perspective—some insight, idea, or interpretation—on the subject.

Because profiles share many features with essays about remembered events, you may use many of the strategies learned in Chapter 2 when you write your profile. Yet the differences are significant. To write about a remembered event, you look inside for memories in order to write about yourself and your intimate experiences. To write a profile, you look outside for observations of an unfamiliar subject in order to understand it better. Yet both remembered event and profile require you to strive for understanding, to recognize significance or uniqueness, to gain a new perspective.

The scope of your profile may be large or small. You could attend a single event such as a parade, dress rehearsal for a play, or city council meeting and write your observations. Or you might conduct an interview with a person who has an unusual occupation and write a profile based on your notes. If you have the time to do more research, you might write a more complete profile based on several visits and interviews.

Writing a profile will make you a more insightful consumer of the profiles you see on television or the Internet or read in newspapers and magazines. Observing and interviewing will give you confidence in observing, ordering, and reporting your own world. You will practice asking probing questions that produce revealing answers and discover that strangers will talk to you at length about their work and interests. You will learn how to get under the surface or go behind facades to better understand other people and your world. You may even learn some of the ways that businesses, institutions, and people are often not what they appear to be.

A Collaborative Activity: Practice Choosing a Profile Subject

Part 1. List three to five subjects you are curious about. Consider interesting people (for example, store owners, teachers, campus musicians or sports figures, public defenders, CEOs, radio talk show hosts), places (for example, a student newspaper office, day-care center, botanical garden, police department, zoo, senior citizen center, farmer's market, historic building, or garage), and businesses or activities (for example, a comic-book store, wrecking company, motorcycle dealer, commercial fishing boat, local brewery, homeless shelter, dance studio, or dog kennel).

Now get together with two or three other students, and take turns reading your lists of subjects to one another. The other group members will tell you which item on your list they find most interesting and ask you any questions they have about it.

Part 2. After you have all read your lists and received responses, discuss these questions as a group:

- What surprised you most about group members' choices of interesting subjects from your list?
- If you were choosing a subject from your list to write about, how would group members' comments and questions influence your choice?
- How might their comments and questions influence your approach to learning more about this subject?

Readings

BRIAN CABLE wrote the following selection when he was a first-year college student. As you read, notice how Cable manages to inform you about the business of a mortuary while taking you on a guided tour of the premises. Notice also how he expresses his sense of humor about a serious place, a place of death and grief.

The Last Stop
Brian Cable

1   More than a few people avert their eyes as they walk past the dusty-pink building that houses the Goodbody Mortuaries. It looks a bit like a church—tall, with Gothic arches and stained glass—and somewhat like an apartment complex—low, with many windows stamped out of red brick.

2   It wasn't at all what I had expected. I thought it would be more like Forest Lawn, serene with lush green lawns and meticulously groomed gardens, a place set apart from the hustle of day-to-day life. Here instead was an odd pink structure set in the middle of a business district. On top of the Goodbody Mortuaries sign was a large electric clock. "What the hell," I thought, "Mortuaries are concerned with time, too."

3   I was apprehensive as I climbed the stone steps to the entrance. I feared rejection or, worse, an invitation to come and stay. The door was massive, yet it swung open easily on well-oiled hinges. "Come in," said the sign. "We're always open." Inside was a cool and quiet reception room. Curtains

Because Cable must help readers imagine his subject, he immediately provides **visual details.**

Cable provides an impression of his subject: **not what he expected.**

Occasional notes of humor, starting with the title, provide readers relief from a somber subject.

From here through paragraph 9, Cable **describes** Mr. Deaver: his stature, skin, hair, dress, personality, way of speaking, work space, and nervous tics.

To fill out his presentation of Mr. Deaver, Cable **quotes** him extensively throughout the essay.

Cable begins providing **information about the mortuary business** from notes he made during this meeting with Mr. Deaver.

were drawn against the outside glare, cutting the light down to a soft glow.

I found the funeral director in the main lobby, adjacent to the reception room. Like most people, I had preconceptions about what an undertaker looked like. Mr. Deaver fulfilled my expectations entirely. Tall and thin, he even had beady eyes and a bony face. A low, slanted forehead gave way to a beaked nose. His skin, scrubbed of all color, contrasted sharply with his jet black hair. He was wearing a starched white shirt, gray pants, and black shoes. Indeed, he looked like death on two legs.

He proved an amiable sort, however, and was easy to talk to. As funeral director, Mr. Deaver ("Call me Howard") was responsible for a wide range of services. Goodbody Mortuaries, upon notification of someone's death, will remove the remains from the hospital or home. They then prepare the body for viewing, whereupon features distorted by illness or accident are restored to their natural condition. The body is embalmed and then placed in a casket selected by the family of the deceased. Services are held in one of three chapels at the mortuary, and afterward the casket is placed in a "visitation room," where family and friends can pay their last respects. Goodbody also makes arrangements for the purchase of a burial site and transports the body there for burial.

All this information Howard related in a well-practiced, professional manner. It was obvious he was used to explaining the specifics of his profession. We sat alone in the lobby. His desk was bone clean, no pencils or paper, nothing—just a telephone. He did all his paperwork at home; as it turned out, he and his wife lived right upstairs. The phone rang. As he listened, he bit his lips and squeezed his Adam's apple somewhat nervously.

"I think we'll be able to get him in by Friday. No, no, the family wants him cremated."

Cable conveys a **perspective** on Goodbody Mortuaries: though it provides a highly personal service to grieving family members, it operates like a business.

His tone was that of a broker conferring on the Dow Jones. Directly behind him was a sign announcing "Visa and Master Charge Welcome Here." It was tacked to the wall, right next to a crucifix.

"Some people have the idea that we are bereavement specialists, that we can handle the emotional problems which follow a death: Only a trained therapist can do that. We provide services for the dead, not counseling for the living."

10   Physical comfort was the one thing they did provide for the living. The lobby was modestly but comfortably furnished. There were several couches, in colors ranging from earth brown to pastel blue, and a coffee table in front of each one. On one table lay some magazines and a vase of flowers. Another supported an aquarium. Paintings of pastoral scenes hung on every wall. The lobby looked more or less like that of an old hotel. Nothing seemed to match, but it had a homey, lived-in look.

> Cable has been piling up **visual details** like these since the first paragraph—and will continue to do so.

11   "The last time the Goodbodys decorated was in '59, I believe. It still makes people feel welcome."

12   And so "Goodbody" was not a name made up to attract customers but the owner's family name. The Goodbody family started the business way back in 1915. Today, they do over five hundred services a year.

13   "We're in *Ripley's Believe It or Not*, along with another funeral home whose owners' names are Baggit and Sackit," Howard told me, without cracking a smile.

14   I followed him through an arched doorway into a chapel that smelled musty and old. The only illumination came from sunlight filtered through a stained glass ceiling. Ahead of us lay a casket. I could see that it contained a man dressed in a black suit. Wooden benches ran on either side of an aisle that led to the body. I got no closer. From the red roses across the dead man's chest, it was apparent that services had already been held.

> Readers may infer by this point that Cable's plan for his profile is **narrative:** he tells the story of one visit from beginning to end.

15   "It was a large service," remarked Howard. "Look at that casket—a beautiful work of craftsmanship."

16   I guess it was. Death may be the great leveler, but one's coffin quickly reestablishes one's status.

17   We passed into a bright, fluorescent-lit "display room." Inside were thirty coffins, lids open, patiently awaiting inspection. Like new cars on the showroom floor, they gleamed with high-gloss finishes.

18   "We have models for every price range."

19   Indeed, there was a wide variety. They came in all colors and various materials. Some were little more than cloth-covered cardboard boxes, others were made of wood, and a few were made of steel, copper, or bronze. Prices started at $400 and averaged about $1,800. Howard motioned toward the center of the room: "The top of the line."

> With attention to caskets from here through paragraph 20, Cable reminds readers that a mortuary is a business.

20   This was a solid bronze casket, its seams electronically welded to resist corrosion. Moisture-proof and air-tight, it could be hermetically sealed off from all outside elements. Its

handles were plated with 14-karat gold. The price: a cool $5,000.

A proper funeral remains a measure of respect for the deceased. But it is expensive. In the United States the amount spent annually on funerals is about $2 billion. Among ceremonial expenditures, funerals are second only to weddings. As a result, practices are changing. Howard has been in this business for forty years. He remembers a time when everyone was buried. Nowadays, with burials costing $2,000 a shot, people often opt instead for cremation—as Howard put it, "a cheap, quick, and easy means of disposal." In some areas of the country, the cremation rate is now over 60 percent. Observing this trend, one might wonder whether burials are becoming obsolete. Do burials serve an important role in society?

21

For Tim, Goodbody's licensed mortician, the answer is very definitely yes. Burials will remain in common practice, according to the slender embalmer with the disarming smile, because they allow family and friends to view the deceased. Painful as it may be, such an experience brings home the finality of death. "Something deep within us demands a confrontation with death," Tim explained. "A last look assures us that the person we loved is, indeed, gone forever."

22

Apparently, we also need to be assured that the body will be laid to rest in comfort and peace. The average casket, with its inner-spring mattress and pleated satin lining, is surprisingly roomy and luxurious. Perhaps such an air of comfort makes it easier for the family to give up their loved one. In addition, the burial site fixes the deceased in the survivors' memory, like a new address. Cremation provides none of these comforts.

23

Tim started out as a clerk in a funeral home but then studied to become a mortician. "It was a profession I could live with," he told me with a sly grin. Mortuary science might be described as a cross between pre-med and cosmetology, with courses in anatomy and embalming as well as in restorative art.

24

Tim let me see the preparation, or embalming, room, a white-walled chamber about the size of an operating room. Against the wall was a large sink with elbow taps and a draining board. In the center of the room stood a table with equipment for preparing the arterial embalming fluid, which consists primarily of formaldehyde, a preservative, and phenol,

25

The facts in this paragraph come from Cable's **Internet research.**

Cable **defines key terms** of the mortuary business: mortuary science and embalming fluid.

a disinfectant. This mixture sanitizes and also gives better color to the skin. Facial features can then be "set" to achieve a restful expression. Missing eyes, ears, and even noses can be replaced.

26 I asked Tim if his job ever depressed him. He bridled at the question: "No, it doesn't depress me at all. I do what I can for people and take satisfaction in enabling relatives to see their loved ones as they were in life." He said that he felt people were becoming more aware of the public service his profession provides. Grade-school classes now visit funeral homes as often as they do police stations and museums. The mortician is no longer regarded as a minister of death.

27 Before leaving, I wanted to see a body up close. I thought I could be indifferent after all I had seen and heard, but I wasn't sure. Cautiously, I reached out and touched the skin. It felt cold and firm, not unlike clay. As I walked out, I felt glad to have satisfied my curiosity about dead bodies, but all too happy to let someone else handle them.

Cable approaches one other person before he leaves, reinforcing his **participant role** in the profile.

JOHN T. EDGE directs the Southern Foodways Symposium at the University of Mississippi. Food writer for the national magazine *Oxford American,* he has also written for *Food & Wine, Gourmet,* and *Saveur* magazines. He has published several books, including *A Gracious Plenty: Recipes and Recollections from the American South* (1999); and *Southern Belly* (2000), a portrait of southern food told through profiles of people and places.

This reading first appeared in a 1999 issue of *Oxford American.* Edge profiles an unusual manufacturing business, Farm Fresh Food Supplier, in a small Mississippi town. He introduces readers to its pickled meat products, which include pickled pig lips. Like many other profile writers, Edge participates in his subject, in his case by attempting to eat a pig lip at Jesse's Place, a nearby "juke" bar.

As you read, notice how much you are learning about this bar snack food as Edge details his discomfort in trying to eat it. Be equally attentive to the information he offers about the history and manufacturing of pig lips at Farm Fresh.

I'm Not Leaving Until I Eat This Thing

John T. Edge

1 It's just past 4:00 on a Thursday afternoon in June at Jesse's Place, a country juke 17 miles south of the Mississippi line and three miles west of Amite, Louisiana. The

air conditioner hacks and spits forth torrents of Arctic air, but the heat of summer can't be kept at bay. It seeps around the splintered doorjambs and settles in, transforming the squat particleboard-plastered roadhouse into a sauna. Slowly, the dank barroom fills with grease-smeared mechanics from the truck stop up the road and farmers straight from the fields, the soles of their brogans thick with dirt clods. A few weary souls make their way over from the nearby sawmill. I sit alone at the bar, one empty bottle of Bud in front of me, a second in my hand. I drain the beer, order a third, and stare down at the pink juice spreading outward from a crumpled foil pouch and onto the bar.

I'm not leaving until I eat this thing, I tell myself.

Half a mile down the road, behind a fence coiled with razor wire, Lionel Dufour, proprietor of Farm Fresh Food Supplier, is loading up the last truck of the day, wheeling case after case of pickled pork offal out of his cinder-block processing plant and into a semitrailer bound for Hattiesburg, Mississippi.

His crew packed lips today. Yesterday, it was pickled sausage; the day before that, pig feet. Tomorrow, it's pickled pig lips again. Lionel has been on the job since 2:45 in the morning, when he came in to light the boilers. Damon Landry, chief cook and maintenance man, came in at 4:30. By 7:30, the production line was at full tilt: six

women in white smocks and blue bouffant caps, slicing ragged white fat from the lips, tossing the good parts in glass jars, the bad parts in barrels bound for the rendering plant. Across the aisle, filled jars clatter by on a conveyor belt as a worker tops them off with a Kool-Aid-red slurry of hot sauce, vinegar, salt, and food coloring. Around the corner, the jars are capped, affixed with a label, and stored in pasteboard boxes to await shipping.

Unlike most offal—euphemistically called "variety meats"—lips belie their provenance. Brains, milky white and globular, look like brains. Feet, the ghosts of their cloven hoofs protruding, look like feet. Testicles look like, well, testicles. But lips are different. Loosed from the snout, trimmed of their fat, and dyed a preternatural pink, they look more like candy than like carrion.

At Farm Fresh, no swine root in an adjacent feedlot. No viscera-strewn killing floor lurks just out of sight, down a darkened hallway. These pigs died long ago at some Midwestern abattoir. By the time the lips arrive in Amite, they are, in essence, pig Popsicles, 50-pound blocks of offal and ice.

"Lips are all meat," Lionel told me earlier in the day. "No gristle, no bone, no nothing. They're bar food, hot and vinegary, great with a beer. Used to be the lips ended up in sausages, headcheese, those sorts of things. A lot of them still do."

Lionel, a 50-year-old father of three with quick, intelligent eyes set deep in a face the color of cordovan, is a veteran of nearly 40 years in the pickled pig lips business. "I started out with my daddy when I wasn't much more than 10," Lionel told me, his shy smile framed by a coarse black mustache flecked with whispers of gray. "The meatpacking business he owned had gone broke back when I was 6, and he was peddling out of the back of his car, selling dried shrimp, napkins, straws, tubes of plastic cups, pig feet, pig lips, whatever the bar owners needed. He sold to black bars, white bars, sweet shops, snowball stands, you name it. We made the rounds together after I got out of school, sometimes staying out till two or three in the morning. I remember bringing my toy cars to this one joint and racing them around the floor with the bar owner's son while my daddy and his father did business."

For years after the demise of that first meatpacking company, the Dufour family sold someone else's product. "We used to buy lips from Dennis Di Salvo's company down in Belle Chasse," recalled Lionel. "As far as I can tell, his mother was the one who came up with the idea to pickle and pack lips back in the '50s, back when she was working for a company called Three Little Pigs over in Houma. But pretty soon, we were selling so many lips that we had to almost beg Di Salvo's for product. That's when we started cooking up our own," he told me, gesturing toward the cast-iron kettle that hangs from the rafters by the front door of the plant. "My daddy started cooking lips in that very pot."

Lionel now cooks lips in 11 retrofitted milk tanks, dull stainless-steel cauldrons shaped like oversized cradles. But little else has changed. Though Lionel's father has passed away, Farm Fresh remains a family-focused company. His wife, Kathy, keeps the books. His daughter, Dana, a button-cute college student who has won

numerous beauty titles, takes to the road in the summer, selling lips to convenience stores and wholesalers. Soon, after he graduates from business school,
Lionel's younger son, Matt, will take over operations at the plant. And his older
son, a veterinarian, lent his name to one of Farm Fresh's top sellers, Jason's Pickled
Pig Lips.

"We do our best to corner the market on lips," Lionel told me, his voice tinged with   11
bravado. "Sometimes they're hard to get from the packing houses. You gotta kill a lot
of pigs to get enough lips to keep us going. I've got new customers calling every day;
it's all I can do to keep up with demand, but I bust my ass to keep up. I do what I can
for my family—and for my customers.

"When my customers tell me something," he continued, "just like when my daddy   12
told me something, I listen. If my customers wanted me to dye the lips green, I'd ask,
'What shade?' As it is, every few years we'll do some red and some blue for the
Fourth of July. This year we did jars full of Mardi Gras lips—half purple, half gold,"
Lionel recalled with a chuckle. "I guess we'd had a few beers when we came up with
that one."

Meanwhile, back at Jesse's Place, I finish my third Bud, order my fourth. *Now,* I   13
tell myself, my courage bolstered by booze, *I'm ready to eat a lip.*

They may have looked like candy in the plant, but in the barroom they're carrion   14
once again. I poke and prod the six-inch arc of pink flesh, peering up from my rev-
erie just in time to catch the barkeep's wife, Audrey, staring straight at me. She fixes
me with a look just this side of pity and asks, "You gonna eat that thing or make love
to it?"

Her nephew, Jerry, sidles up to a bar stool on my left. "A lot of people like 'em with   15
chips," he says with a nod toward the pink juice pooling on the bar in front of me. I
offer to buy him a lip, and Audrey fishes one from a jar behind the counter, wraps it in
tinfoil, and places the whole affair on a paper towel in front of him.

I take stock of my own cowardice, and, following Jerry's lead, reach for a bag of   16
potato chips, tear open the top with my teeth, and toss the quivering hunk of hog flesh
into the shiny interior of the bag, slick with grease and dusted with salt. Vinegar vapors
tickle my nostrils. I stifle a gag that rolls from the back of my throat, swallow hard, and
pray that the urge to vomit passes.

With a smash of my hand, the potato chips are reduced to a pulp, and I feel the   17
cold lump of the lip beneath my fist. I clasp the bag shut and shake it hard in an effort
to ensure chip coverage in all the nooks and crannies of the lip. The technique that
Jerry uses—and I mimic—is not unlike that employed by home cooks mixing up a
mess of Shake 'n Bake chicken.

I pull from the bag a coral crescent of meat now crusted with blond bits of potato   18
chips. When I chomp down, the soft flesh dissolves between my teeth. It tastes like a
flaccid cracklin', unmistakably porcine, and not altogether bad. The chips help, providing texture where there was none. Slowly, my brow unfurrows, my stomach ceases
its fluttering.

Sensing my relief, Jerry leans over and peers into my bag. "Kind of look like   19
Frosted Flakes, don't they?" he says, by way of describing the chips rapidly turning to
mush in the pickling juice. I offer the bag to Jerry, order yet another beer, and turn to
eye the pig feet floating in a murky jar by the cash register, their blunt tips bobbing up
through a pasty white film.

Making Connections to Personal and Social Issues: Gaining Firsthand Experience

Edge decided to experience pigs' lips firsthand by handling, smelling, and tasting them. Except for his own squeamishness, nothing prevented him from doing this. Think about times when you have sought to gain firsthand experience and either succeeded or failed. Perhaps you challenged yourself to go beyond watching basketball or soccer on television and won a spot on a school team, or, on the other hand, you dreamed of an internship at a certain workplace but never could find the time to arrange it.

Identify in writing one longed-for personal experience you missed out on and one you achieved, and think about why you failed in one case and succeeded in the other. What part did your personal decisiveness and effort play? What roles did other people play?

With two or three other students, discuss your attempts to gain personal experience. Begin by telling each other about one experience, explaining briefly what drew you to it, what happened, how you felt about the outcome, and why you think you succeeded or failed. Then, as a group, discuss what your stories reveal about what motivates and helps young Americans and what frustrates them as they try to gain experiences that may open new opportunities to them.

Analyzing Writing Strategies

1. Edge focuses on one of Farm Fresh's products, pickled pig lips. He probably assumes that most of his readers have never seen a pickled pig lip, much less eaten one. Therefore, he **describes** this product carefully. Underline or highlight in paragraphs 4, 5, 7, 14, and 18 every detail of a pickled pig lip's appearance, size, texture or consistency, smell, and taste. *Then write a few sentences on Edge's description.* If you have never seen a pickled pig lip, what more do you need to know to imagine it? Which details make a lip seem appealing to you? Which ones make it seem unappealing?

2. The scene in the bar begins in the first two paragraphs, then picks up again in paragraph 13 and continues to the end of the profile. In these paragraphs Edge **narrates** the story of his attempt to eat a pig lip. Three strategies dominate: reconstructed conversation or dialogue, narrative action, and suspense. Begin by putting brackets around the dialogue so that you can see it more clearly at a glance. Then

underline the action, instances of people physically moving or gesturing. *Finally, at the end of the essay write a few brief notes in the margin explaining how Edge creates suspense to keep you reading.*

3. To present their subjects, profile writers occasionally make use of a strategy that relies on a sentence structure known as an **absolute phrase**. To discover what absolute phrases contribute, underline these absolutes in Edge's profile: in paragraph 1, sentence 4, from "the soles" to the end of the sentence, and sentence 6, from "one empty bottle" to the end; in paragraph 8, sentence 2, from "his shy smile" to the end; and in paragraph 19, sentence 3, from "their blunt tips" to the end. Make notes in the margin about how the absolute phrase seems to be related to what comes before it in the sentence. Given that Edge's goal is to help readers imagine what he observes, what does each absolute contribute toward that goal? How are these four absolutes alike and different in what they add to their sentences? *Write several sentences about your insights.*

Commentary: A Topical Plan

A profile may be presented **narratively,** as a sequence of events observed by the writer during an encounter with the place, person, or activity; or it may be presented **topically,** as a series of topics of information gathered by the writer about the person, place, or activity. Though Edge **frames** (begins and ends) his profile with the narrative or story about attempting to eat a pig lip, he presents the basic information about Farm Fresh topically.

The following scratch outline of Edge's profile shows at a glance the topics he chose and how they are sequenced:

loading meat products on a truck (par. 3)

an overview of the production process, with a focus on that day's pig lips (4)

pig lips' peculiarity in not looking like where they come from on the pig (5)

the origin of Farm Fresh's materials — shipped frozen from the Midwest (6)

some characteristics of a pig lip (7)

Lionel's introduction to marketing food products and services (8)

Lionel's resurrection of the family meatpacking business (9)

family involvement in the business (10)

Lionel's marketing strategy (11)

Lionel's relations with customers (12)

Reviewing his interview and observation notes taken while he was at Farm Fresh, Edge apparently decided to organize them not in the order in which he took them but as topics sequenced to be most informative for readers. He begins with the finished product, with Lionel loading the truck for shipment. Then he outlines the production process and mentions the various products. From there, he identifies the source of the products and briefly describes a pig lip, his main interest. Then he offers a history of Farm Fresh and concludes with Lionel's approach to his business. When you plan your profile essay, you will have to decide whether to organize your first draft topically or narratively.

Considering Topics for Your Own Essay

Consider writing about a place that serves, produces, or sells something unusual, perhaps something that, like Edge, you could try yourself. If such places do not come to mind, browse the Yellow Pages of your local phone directory. There are many possibilities: acupuncture clinic, talent agency, bead store, nail salon, tattoo parlor, scrap metal recycler, dog or cat sitting service, burglar alarm installer, wedding planner, reweaving specialist. You need not evaluate the quality of the work provided at a place as part of your essay. Instead, keep the focus on informing readers about the service or product the place offers. Relating a personal experience with the service or product is a good idea but not a requirement.

JOHN McPHEE (b. 1931) lives in Princeton, New Jersey, where he occasionally teaches a writing workshop in the "literature of fact" at Princeton University. He is highly regarded as a writer of profiles, in which he integrates information from observations, interviews, and research into engaging, readable prose, explaining clearly such complex subjects as experimental aircraft or modern physics and the complexities of such ordinary subjects as bears or oranges. Among his books are *Oranges* (1967); *The Control of Nature* (1989); *Annals of the Former World* (1998), for which he was awarded the Pulitzer Prize; *The Founding Fish* (2002); and *Uncommon Carriers* (2006). In a recent interview, McPhee spoke frankly about his struggles with writing: "When I start work on a piece, I start at a zero level of confidence. . . . I have a very mild form of writer's block that I have to break through each day. . . . [O]ver time I've learned to be alone and to work alone and to enjoy it."

As you read, notice how McPhee introduces pickpockets and their crimes. A sociologist would offer statistics on petty crimes in Brooklyn. McPhee instead offers strikingly different individual criminals, describing different kinds of pickpocketing and other theft, all in an outdoor farmers' market. Notice from what single perspective he views all of this activity.

The New York Pickpocket Academy
John McPhee

Brooklyn, and the pickpocket in the burgundy jacket appears just before noon. Melissa Mousseau recognizes him much as if he were an old customer and points him out to Bob Lewis, who follows him from truck to truck. Aware of Lewis, he leaves the market.

1

By two, he will have made another run. A woman with deep-auburn hair and pale, nervous hands clumsily attracts the attention of a customer whose large white purse she is rifling. Until a moment ago, the customer was occupied with the choosing of apples and peppers, but now she shouts out, "Hey, what are you doing? Your hand is in my purse. What are you doing?" The auburn-haired woman not only has her hand in the purse but most of her arm as well. She withdraws it, and with intense absorption begins to finger the peppers. "How much are the peppers? Mister, give me some of these!" she says, looking up at me with a gypsy's dark, starburst eyes. "Three pounds for a dollar," I tell her, with a swift glance around for Lewis or a cop. When I look back, the pickpocket is gone. Other faces have filled in—people unconcernedly examining the fruit. The woman with the white purse has returned her attention to the apples. She merely seems annoyed. Lewis once sent word around from truck to truck that we should regularly announce in loud voices that pickpockets were present in the market, but none of the farmers complied. Hodgson shrugged and said, "Why distract the customers?" Possibly Fifty-ninth Street is the New York Pickpocket Academy. Half a dozen scores have been made there in a day. I once looked up and saw a well-dressed gentleman under a gray fedora being kicked and kicked again by a man in a green polo shirt. He kicked him in the calves. He kicked him in the thighs. He kicked him in the gluteal bulge. He kicked him from the middle of the market out to the edge, and he kicked him into the street. "Get your ass out of here!" shouted the booter, redundantly. Turning back toward the market, he addressed the curious. "Pickpocket," he explained. The dip did not press charges.

People switch shopping carts from time to time. They make off with a loaded one and leave an empty cart behind. Crime on such levels is a part of the background here, something in the urban air, so many parts per million. The condition is accepted with a resignation that approaches nonchalance. 2

Most thievery is petty and is on the other side of the tables. As Rich describes it, "Brooklyn, Fifty-ninth Street, people rip off stuff everywhere. You just expect it. An old man comes along and puts a dozen eggs in a bag. Women choosing peaches steal one for every one they buy—a peach for me, a peach for you. What can you do? You stand there and watch. When they take too many, you complain. I watched a guy one day taking nectarines. He would put one in a plastic bag, then one in a pocket, then one in a pile on the ground. After he did that half a dozen times, he had me weigh the bag." 3

"This isn't England," Barry Benepe informed us once, "and a lot of people are pretty dishonest." 4

Now, in Brooklyn, a heavyset woman well past the middle of life is sobbing pitifully, flailing her arms in despair. She is sitting on a bench in the middle of the market. She is wearing a print dress, a wide-brimmed straw hat. Between sobs, she presents in a heavy Russian accent the reason for her distress. She was buying green beans from Don Keller, and when she was about to pay him she discovered that someone had opened her handbag—even while it was on her arm, she said—and had removed 5 several books of food stamps, a telephone bill, and eighty dollars in cash. Lewis, in his daypack, stands over her and tells her he is sorry. He said, "This sort of thing will happen wherever there's a crowd."

Another customer breaks in to scold Lewis, saying, "This is the biggest rip-off place in Brooklyn. Two of my friends were pick-pocketed here last week and I had to give them carfare home." | 6

Lewis puts a hand on his forehead and, after a pensive moment, says, "That was very kind of you." | 7

The Russian woman is shrieking now. Lewis attends her like a working dentist. "It's all right. It will be O.K. It may not be as bad as you think." He remarks that he would call the police if he thought there was something they could do. | 8

Jeffrey Mack, eight years old, has been listening to all this, and he now says, "I see a cop." | 9

Jeffrey has an eye for cops that no one else seems to share. (A squad car came here for him one morning and took him off to face a truant officer. Seeing his fright, a Pacific Street prostitute got into the car and rode with him.) | 10

"Where, Jeffrey?" | 11

"There," Jeffrey lifts an arm and points. | 12

"Where?" | 13

"There." He points again—at trucks, farmers, a falafel man. | 14

"I don't see a policeman," Lewis says to him. "If you see one, Jeffrey, go and get him." | 15

Jeffrey goes, and comes back with an off-duty 78th Precinct cop who is wearing a white apron and has been selling fruits and vegetables in the market. The officer speaks sternly to the crying woman. "Your name?" | 16

"Catherine Barta." | 17

"Address?" | 18

"Eighty-five Eastern Parkway." | 19

Every Wednesday, she walks a mile or so to the Greenmarket. She has lived in Brooklyn close to half her life, the rest of it in the Ukraine. Heading back to his vegetables, the officer observes that there is nothing he can do. | 20

Out from behind her tables comes Joan Benack, the baker, of Rocky Acres Farm, Milan, New York—a small woman with a high, thin voice. Leaving her tropical carrot bread, her zucchini bread, her anadama bread, her beer bread, she goes around with a borrowed hat collecting money from the farmers for Catherine Barta. Bills stuff that hat, size 7—the money of Alvina Frey and John Labanowski and Cleather Slade and Rich Hodgson and Bob Engle, who has seen it come and go. He was a broker for Merrill Lynch before the stock market imploded, and now he is a blond-bearded farmer in a basketball shirt selling apples that he grows in Clintondale, New York. Don Keller offers a dozen eggs, and one by one the farmers come out from their trucks to fill Mrs. Barta's shopping cart with beans and zucchini, apples, eggplants, tomatoes, peppers, and corn. As a result, her wails and sobs grow louder. | 21

A man who gave Rich Hodgson a ten-dollar bill for a ninety-five-cent box of brown eggs asks Rich to give the ten back after Rich has handed him nine dollars and five cents, explaining that he has smaller bills that he wants to exchange for a twenty. Rich hands him the ten. Into Rich's palm he counts out five ones, a five, and the ten for a twenty and goes away satisfied, as he has every reason to be, having conned Rich out of nine dollars, five cents, and a box of brown eggs. Rich smiles at his foolishness, shrugs, and sells some cheese. If cash were equanimity, he would never lose a cent. One day, a gang of kids began taking Don Keller's vegetables and throwing them at the Hodgson truck. Anders Thueson threw an apple at the kids, who then picked up rocks. Thueson reached into the back of the truck and came up with a machete. While Hodgson told him to put it away, pant legs went up, switchblades came into view. Part of the gang bombarded the truck with debris from a nearby roof. Any indication of panic might have been disastrous. Hodgson packed deliberately, and drove away.

22

Todd Jameson, who comes in with his brother Dan from Farmingdale, New Jersey, weighed some squash one day, and put it in a brown bag. He set the package down while he weighed something else. Then, reaching for the squash, he picked up an identical bag that happened to contain fifty dollars in rolled coins. He handed it to the customer who had asked for the squash. Too late, Todd discovered the mistake. A couple of hours later, though, the customer — "I'll never forget him as long as I live, the white hair, the glasses, the ruddy face" — came back. He said, "Hey, this isn't squash. I didn't ask for money, I asked for squash." Whenever that man comes to market, the Jamesons give him a bag full of food. "You see, where I come from, that would never, never happen," Todd explains. "If I made a mistake like that in Farmingdale, no one — no one — would come back with fifty dollars' worth of change."

23

Dusk comes down without further crime in Brooklyn, and the farmers are packing to go. John Labanowski — short, compact, with a beer in his hand — is expounding on his day. "The white people are educating the colored on the use of beet greens," he reports. "A colored woman was telling me today, 'Cut the tops off,' and a white woman spoke up and said, 'Hold it,' and told the colored woman, 'You're throwing the best part away.' They go on talking, and pretty soon the colored woman is saying, 'I'm seventy-three on Monday,' and the white says, 'I don't believe a word you say.' You want to know why I come in here? I come in here for fun. For profit, of course, but for relaxation, too. I like being here with these people. They say the city is a rat race, but they've got it backwards. The farm is what gets to be a rat race. You should come out and see what I —." He is interrupted by the reappearance in the market of Catherine Barta, who went home long ago and has now returned, her eyes hidden by her wide-brimmed hat, her shopping cart full beside her. On the kitchen table, at 85 Eastern Parkway, she found her telephone bill, her stamps, and her cash. She has come back to the farmers with their food and money.

24

Making Connections to Personal and Social Issues: Petty Crime

Petty crime takes its name from a word meaning small, trivial, or unimportant. It is rarely violent, yet it can contribute to a sense of social or public insecurity. Petty crimes include pickpocketing, purse snatching, car break-ins, tire slashing, shoplifting, and vandalism. Most are never reported to the police.

Write a few sentences about a time when you were a victim of a petty crime, observed one, or heard about one from the victim. With two or three other students, take turns describing what happened. Then, discuss these questions: How has petty crime influenced your feelings about your community? Has it placed any constraints on your public activities? Has it influenced your attitudes toward law enforcement? Some cities have tried to take a "zero tolerance" approach to petty crime. This strategy requires high-visibility police patrols. Do you think this strategy could work in your community? Would you be willing to pay the taxes to support it? Would you support a higher arrest rate for petty crimes even if prison and court costs would rise sharply?

Analyzing Writing Strategies

1. The activity McPhee describes at the market is so entertaining that readers may underestimate on first reading the sheer quantity of **information** the essay offers. For example, McPhee classifies the petty thefts he observed over the course of a day at the market. Reread paragraphs 1–3 and 22 and underline a phrase or sentence that best defines each crime. Then list and describe each in a phrase or two. *Finally, write two or three sentences explaining what surprised you most about these crimes.*

2. In spite of the pickpockets, the market seems a peaceful place. In this quiet context, a writer might report noise to dramatize key scenes, and that is what McPhee does. He mentions shouting (par. 1, twice), sobbing (5 and 21), shrieking (8), and wailing (21). Find and highlight or underline these words. *Then write two or three sentences about how your imagining of these loud noises within a relatively quiet scene influences your response to what is going on.*

Commentary: A Narrative Plan

McPhee profiles his subject primarily through telling stories about it. His profile opens with three brief narratives relating attempts at thievery by the man in the burgundy jacket, the woman with the starburst eyes, and the man wearing the gray fedora. The longest narrative tells the story of Catherine Barta, who thought someone had stolen her food stamps and money. Reread this part of the profile, paragraphs 8–20. Notice the importance of dialogue and description, and the way McPhee introduces background information about the characters.

Both Edge and McPhee begin and end their profiles with narratives, a common strategy in a genre where writers aim to entertain as much as inform. A profile writer, like a novelist or filmmaker, attempts to create a scene with action, showing individuals moving, talking, gesturing, and weaving information about the subject into and around it.

Considering Topics for Your Own Essay

Crowds offer good material for profiles, but they also present problems for profile writers, mainly because of their size and scope: So many people are present and so much is happening at once that the observer may not be able to decide where to focus. McPhee solves this problem by remaining in one location, the stall where he is selling vegetables. The action focuses on only a few people and events.

You could likewise find a focus for a profile in a large, crowded public place: for example, a lifeguard station at the beach, one car dealer at an auto show, a musician playing for donations in a subway station, one librarian at work in your college library, a coach supervising a team at a sporting event. In each of these situations, you would not limit your observations to one or two individuals but would also survey the larger scene and observe the individual's interactions with the other people there.

Throughout his profile McPhee assumes the role of **detached observer**. He positions himself at the site where he makes his observations and participates in that he helps the farmers sell vegetables, but he never shifts the focus to himself. When you visit a place to profile, you can usually choose whether to remain detached or to participate.

■ Purpose and Audience

A profile writer's primary purpose is to inform readers about the subject of the profile. Readers expect a profile to present information in an engaging way, however. Readers of profiles expect to be surprised by unusual subjects. If they read about a familiar subject, they expect it to be presented from an unusual perspective. When writing a profile, you will have an immediate advantage if your subject is a place, an activity, or a person that is likely to surprise and intrigue your readers. For example, in "I'm Not Leaving Until I Eat This Thing" (pp. 59–63), Edge has the triple advantage of being able to describe an unusual snack food, a little-known production process, and a colorful bar in which he can try out the unusual snack. Even when your subject is familiar, however, you can still engage your readers by presenting it in a way they have never before considered. For example, in "The Last Stop" (pp. 55–59), Brian Cable describes a mortuary owner as an ordinary, efficient businessman and not a "bereavement specialist."

A profile writer has one further concern: to be sensitive to what readers are likely to know already about a subject. For a profile of a pig-products processor, the decisions of a writer whose readers have likely never seen a pickled pig lip will be quite different from those of a writer whose readers occasionally hang out in bars where pickled pig products abound. Given Edge's attention to detail, he is clearly writing for an audience that has never before seen a pickled pig lip, much less considered eating one.

Basic Features: Profiles

Description of People and Places

Successful profile writers master the strategies of description. The profiles in this chapter, for example, evoke all the senses: **sight** ("the pink juice pooling on the bar in front of me," Edge, par. 15; "switchblades came into view," McPhee, 22); **touch** ("slick with grease," Edge, 16; "the skin . . . felt cold and firm, not unlike clay," Cable, 27); **smell** and **taste** ("hot and vinegary," Edge, 7); **hearing** ("woman is shrieking now," McPhee, 8); and **physical sensation** ("a gag that rolls from the back of my throat," Edge, 16; "my stomach ceases its fluttering," Edge, 18). **Similes** ("Lewis attends her like a working dentist," McPhee, 8), and **metaphors** ("the air conditioner hacks and spits forth torrents of Arctic air," Edge, 1) appear occasionally.

Profile writers often describe people in graphic detail ("his shy smile framed by a coarse black mustache," Edge, 8; "beady eyes and a bony face," Cable, 4; "deep-auburn hair and pale, nervous hands," McPhee, 1). They show people moving and gesturing ("he bit his lips and squeezed his Adam's apple," Cable, 6; "I poke and prod the six-inch arc of pink flesh," Edge, 14). These writers also rely on dialogue to reveal character ("Look at that casket—a beautiful work of craftsmanship," Cable, 15; "You gonna eat that thing or make love to it?" Edge, 14).

Information about the Subject

Profile writers give much thought to how and where to introduce information to their readers. After all, readers expect to learn something surprising or useful. Most profile writers interweave information either with descriptions of the subject (as Cable does profiling a mortuary) or with narratives of events (as Edge does when he struggles to eat a pig lip). Throughout their profiles, writers make good use of several strategies relied on by all writers: classification, example or illustration, comparison and contrast, definition, process narration, and cause and effect.

Edge **classifies** information about Farm Fresh into four categories: rebirth of the family business, family involvement, marketing strategies, and customer relations. McPhee gives many **examples** of pickpocketing. Cable **compares** the mortuary's exterior to that of a church and an apartment complex. He later **defines** the terms "mortuary science" and "embalming fluid." Edge **narrates** the process of preparing and bottling pig lips and, after receiving instruction, of eating one. Edge presents the **causes** of Farm Fresh's failure as a business and of its rebirth, and he discloses frankly the effects of his attempts to eat a pig lip. McPhee **illustrates** the **effects** on farmers of their regular trips into the big city.

A Topical or Narrative Plan

Profile writers rely on two basic plans for reporting their observations: **topical**, with the information grouped into topics; and **narrative**, with the information interwoven with elements of a story. The profiles by Cable and McPhee are organized narratively. In both, the narrative is a story of a single visit to a place. For Cable, the visit is one of probably two or three hours, to Goodbody Mortuaries. McPhee's visit lasts all or most of a day.

In the central segment of his profile, Edge organizes the information topically: He creates topics out of the many bits of information he gathers on the tour of Farm Fresh and then sequences them in the profile in a way that he thinks will be most informative to readers. Yet Edge frames the information about Farm Fresh with a narrative of his attempts to eat one of its products, illustrating that a profile can be organized topically in some parts and narratively in others. Usually, however, one plan or the other predominates. Which plan you adopt will depend on your subject, the kinds of information you collect, and your assessment of what might be most engaging and informative for your readers.

A Role for the Writer

Profile writers must adopt a role or stance for themselves when they present their subjects. There are two basic options: **detached observer** and **participant observer**. McPhee is a detached observer of pickpockets and the swirl of activity at the outdoor market. In the central part of his profile, where he presents what he learned on his visit to Farm Fresh, Edge, too, is a detached observer. We can easily infer that he asked questions and made comments, but he decides not to report any of them; instead, he focuses unwaveringly on the equipment, canning process, workers, and Dufour family members. By contrast, Cable adopts a participant-observer role. Even before he enters the mortuary, he inserts himself personally into the profile, reflecting on death, expressing his disappointment in the appearance of the place, admitting his apprehension about entering, revealing his sense of humor. Readers know where he is at all times as his tour of the building proceeds, and he seems as much a participant in the narrative of his visit as Deaver and Tim are. Before he leaves the mortuary, he touches a corpse to satisfy his curiosity. Edge participates briefly when he tries to eat a pig's lip in the juke.

A Perspective on the Subject

Profile writers do not simply present their observations of a subject; they also offer insights into the person, place, or activity being profiled. They may convey a perspective by stating it explicitly, by implying it through the descriptive details and other information they include, or both. Cable shares his realization that Americans seem to capitalize on death as a way of coping with it. McPhee seems resigned to the petty crime that he observes but also emphasizes the sense of community shared by many at the farmers market. Edge's perspective on pig products is less explicit, but perhaps, as a specialist in southern cooking, he hopes to convey the impression that regional foods remain important, however unappetizing they may seem to some.

Writing Profiles

Invention and Research

What is a person, place, or activity you are curious about and could interview or observe? A campus personality? A local hangout? An online community? Set up your interview or observation, take good notes, and do some thinking and writing about your subject. Then come up with a possible approach for presenting it to readers. . . . **See p. 75 for more.**

Planning and Drafting

As you look over what you have written about your subject so far, how can you describe it in an interesting, informative way? Should you present your profile as a narrative? Should you mention yourself? What perspective on the subject have you developed? Make a plan for your profile, and start drafting it. . . . **See p. 83 for more.**

Critical Reading Guide

What are your draft's strengths and weaknesses? Are there key aspects of your subject that seem vague? Does the profile seem to ramble, with no shape or point? Get a classmate, a friend, a writing tutor, or someone else to read and respond in detail to your essay, especially the parts you are most unsure of. . . . **See p. 87 for more.**

Revising

As you consider your essay again in light of your reader's comments, how can you improve it? Do you provide too little information about the subject? Too much? Is your own presence in the profile too prominent? Does the ending seem weak? Go through your draft systematically, making changes wherever necessary. . . . **See p. 89 for more.**

Editing and Proofreading

Have you checked for errors that are especially likely in profiles? For example, have you forgotten to include quotation marks around someone's exact words? Have you put commas and periods outside rather than inside closing quotation marks? Look for and correct these and any other errors. . . . **See p. 94 for more.**

☐ The Writing Assignment

Write an essay about an intriguing person, place, or activity in your community. Observe your subject closely, and then present what you have learned in a way that both informs and engages readers.

▓ Invention and Research

Preparing to write a profile involves finding a subject, exploring your preconceptions about it, planning your project, and posing some preliminary questions. Each step takes no more than a few minutes, yet together these activities will enable you to anticipate problems likely to arise, to arrange and schedule your interviews wisely, and to take notes and gather materials productively.

To learn about using the *Concise Guide* e-book for invention and drafting, go to bedfordstmartins.com/conciseguide.

Finding a Subject to Write About

When you choose a subject, you consider various possibilities, select a promising one, and check that particular subject's accessibility.

Listing Subjects. *Make a list of subjects you might consider for your profile.* Even if you already have a subject in mind, take a few minutes to consider some other possibilities. The more you consider, the more confident you can be about your choice. You might start with subjects suggested by the Considering Topics for Your Own Essay activities on pp. 65 and 70, or consider one we suggest below.

As you list possible subjects, consider realistically the time you have available. Whether you have a week or a month will determine what kinds of subjects will be appropriate for you. Consult with your instructor if you need help defining the scope of your profile project.

People

- Anyone with an unusual or intriguing job or hobby—a private detective, beekeeper, or dog trainer
- A prominent local personality—a parent of the year, politician, television or radio personality, or community activist
- A campus personality—a coach, distinguished teacher, or ombudsman
- Someone recently recognized for outstanding service or achievement—a volunteer, mentor, or therapist

Places

- A weight-reduction clinic, martial arts studio, or health spa
- A small-claims court, juvenile court, or consumer fraud office

- A used-car lot, used-book store, antique shop, historic site, auction hall, gun show, or flea market
- A hospital emergency room, hospice, birthing center, or psychiatric unit
- A local diner; the oldest, biggest, or quickest restaurant in town; or a coffeehouse
- A campus radio station, computer center, student center, faculty club, museum, or health center
- A book, newspaper, or Internet publisher; florist shop or greenhouse; pawnshop; or automobile wrecking yard
- A recycling center; fire station; airport control tower; theater box office; refugee center; orphanage; or monastery

Activities

- A citizens' volunteer program—a voter registration service, meals-on-wheels project, tutoring program, or election campaign
- A sports event—a marathon, a Frisbee tournament, chess match, or wrestling meet
- The activities of a particular group of hobbyists—folk dancers, rock climbers, poetry readers, comic book collectors or investors

Listing Subjects Related to Identity and Community.   By *community* we mean both geographic communities, such as towns and neighborhoods, and institutional and temporary communities, such as religious congregations, college students majoring in the same subject, volunteer organizations, and sports teams. Writing a profile about a person or a place in your community can help you learn more about individuals and about institutions and activities fundamental to community life. The following suggestions will enable you to list several possible subjects.

People

- A prominent member of one of the communities you belong to
- Someone in a community who is generally tolerated but is not liked or respected, such as a homeless person, a gruff store owner, or an eccentric church member
- Someone who has built a successful business, overcome a disability or setback, supported a worthy cause, served as a role model, or won respect from coworkers or neighbors

Places

- A facility that provides a needed service in a community, such as a legal advice bureau, child-care center, medical clinic, or shelter
- A place where people of different ages, genders, ethnic groups, or some other attribute have formed a community, such as a chess table in the park, political action headquarters, computer class, coffeehouse, or barber or beauty shop

- A place where people come together because they are of the same age, gender, or ethnic group, such as a seniors-only housing complex, a campus women's center, or an African American or Asian American student center

Activities

- A team practicing a sport or other activity
- A community improvement project, such as graffiti cleaning, tree planting, house repairing, or highway litter pickup
- A group of researchers working collaboratively on a project and meeting regularly

Listing Subjects Related to Work and Career.   The following categories will help you consider work- and career-related subjects. Writing a profile on one of these possibilities can help you learn more about your attitudes toward your own work and career goals.

People

- A college senior or graduate student in a major you are considering
- Someone working in the career you are thinking of pursuing
- Someone who trains people to do the kind of work you would like to do

Places

- A place on campus where students work part-time at some well-defined job — the library, computer center, cafeteria, bookstore, or tutoring center
- A place where you could learn more about the kind of career you would like to pursue — a law office, medical center, television station, newspaper, school, software manufacturer, or engineering firm
- A place where people do a kind of work you would like to know more about — a clothing factory, coal mine, dairy farm, racetrack, bakery, nursing home, or delicatessen
- A place where people are trained for a certain kind of work — a police academy, cosmetology program, or truck drivers' school

Activities

- The activities actually performed by someone doing a kind of work represented on television, such as that of a police detective, attorney, newspaper reporter, taxi driver, or emergency room doctor
- The activities involved in preparing for a particular kind of work, such as a boxer preparing for a fight, an attorney preparing for a trial, an actor rehearsing a role, or a musician practicing a new piece for the first time

Choosing a Subject.　*Look over your list of possibilities, and choose a subject that you find you want to know more about and that your readers will find interesting.* Note that most profile writers report the greatest satisfaction and the best results when they profile an *unfamiliar* person, place, or activity. If you choose a subject with which you are some-what familiar, try to study it in an unfamiliar setting. For example, if you are a rock climber and decide to write a profile on rock climbing, interview some critics of the sport to get another perspective, or visit a rock-climbing event where you can observe without participating. By adopting an *outsider's perspective* on a familiar subject, you can make writing your profile a process of discovery for yourself as well as for your readers.

Stop now to focus your thoughts. *In a sentence or two, identify the subject you have chosen, and explain why you think it is a good choice for you and your readers.*

Checking on Accessibility.　*Take steps to ensure that your subject will be accessible* to you. Having chosen a subject, you need to be certain you will be able to make observations and conduct interviews to learn more about it. (Keep in mind your deadline for completing the first draft of your profile.) Find out who might be able to give you information by making some preliminary phone calls. If you are unable to contact knowledgeable people or get access to the place you need to observe, you may not be able to write on this subject. Therefore, try to make these initial contacts early.

Exploring Your Preconceptions

Explore your initial thoughts and feelings about your subject in writing before you begin observing or interviewing. Write for a few minutes about your thoughts, using the following questions as a guide:

What I already know about this subject

- How can I define or describe it?
- What are its chief qualities or parts?
- Do I associate anyone or anything with it?
- What is its purpose or function?
- How does it compare with other, similar subjects?

My attitude toward this subject

- Why do I consider it intriguing?
- What about it most interests me?
- Do I like it? Respect it?

My own and my classmates' expectations

(For now, consider your classmates as your readers.)

- What attitudes and expectations about this subject do I share with my class-mates?
- What might be unique about my attitudes?
- How is this subject represented in the media?
- What values and ideas are associated with subjects of this kind?

Testing Your Choice

Decide whether you should proceed with this particular subject. Giving up on a profile subject is bound to be frustrating, but if, after some work on it, the subject does not seem a strong possibility for you to research and write about, starting over may be the wisest course of action. The questions that follow may help you decide whether to go on with this subject or begin looking for an alternative.

- After reviewing my first list of possible subjects, do I still feel that I have made the best choice?
- Do any of the subjects chosen by other students in my class suggest one I might like to change to?
- Do I still feel curious about the subject?
- Am I looking forward to presenting my subject to readers?
- Do I believe that I can fulfill my profile subjects' expectations that I will be serious and responsible, thorough and fair?

A Collaborative Activity:
Testing Your Choice

Get together with two or three other students and describe the subject you have chosen to profile.

Presenters: Take turns identifying your subjects. Explain your interest in the subject, and speculate about why you think it will interest readers.

Listeners: Briefly tell each presenter what you already know about his or her subject, if anything, and what might make it interesting to you.

Planning Your Project

Set up a tentative schedule for your observational and interview visits. Whatever the scope of your project—a single observation, an interview with one follow-up exchange, or multiple observations and interviews—you will want to get the most out of your time with your subject.

Figure out the amount of time you have to complete your essay, and then decide what visits you will need to make, whom you will need to interview, and what library or Internet research you might want to do, if any. Estimate the time necessary for each. You might use a chart like the following one:

Date	Time Needed	Purpose	Preparation
10/23	1 hour	Observe	Bring map, directions, paper
10/25	2 hours	Library research	Bring references, change or copy-card for copy machine
10/26	45 minutes	Interview	Read brochure and prepare questions
10/30	3 hours	Observe and interview	Confirm appointment; bring questions and extra pens/paper

You will probably have to modify your plan once you actually begin work, but it is a good idea to keep some sort of schedule in writing.

If you are developing a full profile, your first goal is to get your bearings. Some writers begin by observing; others start with an interview. Many read up on the subject before doing anything else to get a sense of its main elements. You may also want to read about other subjects similar to the one you have chosen. Save your notes.

An Online Activity: Researching Your Profile Subject

One way to get a quick initial overview of the information available on the subject of your profile is to search for the subject online. Use Google (http://www.google.com) or Yahoo! Directory (http://dir.yahoo .com) to discover possible sources of information about the subject:

- For example, if you are profiling a beekeeper, you could get some useful background information to guide you in planning your interview by entering "beekeeping."
- If you are profiling a person, enter the full name to discover whether he or she has a personal Web site. If you are profiling a business or institution, see if it offers a site. Either kind of site would orient you prior to your interview or first visit. Bookmark or keep a record of promising sites. Download any materials, including visuals, you might consider including in your own essay.

Posing Some Preliminary Questions

Write questions to prepare for your first visit. Before beginning your observations and interviews, try writing some questions for which you would like to find answers. These questions will orient you and allow you to focus your visits. Add to this list as new questions occur to you, and delete any that come to seem irrelevant.

Each subject invites its own special questions, and every writer has particular concerns. Consider, for example, how one student prepares interview questions for her profile of a local office of the Women's Health Initiative, a long-term, nationwide study of women's health established by the National Institutes of Health in 1991. After reading about the study in her local newspaper, the student calls the local WHI office to get further information. The administrator faxes her a fact sheet on the study and her office's special part in it. The student knows that she will need to mention the study and its findings in her profile of the local office and the people who work there. She also hopes to interview women who volunteered to participate in the research. Consequently, she devises the following questions to launch her research:

- Why has so little research been done on women's health until recently?
- How did the study come about, and what is the role of the National Institutes of Health?
- Why does the study focus only on women between the ages of fifty and eighty?
- Are women from all income levels involved?
- When was this office established, and what role does it play in the national study?
- Does the office simply coordinate the study, or does it also provide health and medical advice to women participating in the study?
- Who works at the office, and what are their qualifications?
- Will I be able to interview women who volunteer to participate in the research?
- Will I be permitted to take photographs in the office?
- Would it be appropriate to take photographs of the researchers and participants, if they give their consent?

Discovering a Perspective

After you have completed your observations and interviews, write for a few minutes, reflecting on what you now think about the person, place, or activity you have chosen for your profile. Consider how you would answer these questions about your subject:

- What visual or other sensory impression is most memorable?
- What does this impression tell me about the person, place, or activity?
- What mood do I associate with my subject?
- What about my subject is most likely to surprise or interest my readers?
- What is the most important thing I have learned about my subject? Why is it important?
- If I could find the answer to one more question about my subject, what would that question be? Why is this question important?
- What about my subject says something larger about our culture and times?
- Which of my ideas, interpretations, or judgments do I most want to share with readers?

Considering Your Own Role

Decide tentatively whether you will adopt a detached-observer or participant-observer role to present your profile. As a detached observer, you would focus solely on the place, people, and activities, keeping yourself invisible to readers. As a participant observer, you would insert yourself into the profile by reporting what you said or thought during interviews and commenting on the activities you observed.

Defining Your Purpose for Your Readers

Write a few sentences defining your purpose in writing about this particular person, place, or activity for your readers. Use these questions to focus your thoughts:

- Who are my readers? Who would be interested in reading an essay about this particular subject? If I were to try to publish my essay, what kind of magazine, newspaper, newsletter, or Web site might want a profile on this particular subject?
- What do I want my readers to learn about the subject from reading my essay?
- What insight can I offer my readers about the subject?

Formulating a Tentative Thesis Statement

Review what you wrote for Discovering a Perspective (p. 81), and add another two or three sentences that will help you tell readers what you understand about the subject. Try to write sentences that extend your insights and interpretations and that do not simply summarize what you have already written.

Keep in mind that readers do not expect you to begin a profile essay with the kind of explicit thesis statement typical of argumentative essays. If you decide to spell out your perspective on the subject, you can do so. You may, however, decide to convey your perspective only through the ways in which you describe people and places, present dialogue, and narrate what you observed.

Designing Your Document

Think about whether visual or audio elements — photographs, postcards, menus, or snippets from films, television programs, or songs — would strengthen your profile. These are not a requirement of an effective profile, but they can be helpful. Consider also whether your readers might benefit from design features such as headings, bulleted or numbered lists, or other typographic elements that can make an essay easier to follow.

Think of the profiles you have seen in a magazine or on a Web page or television show. What visual or audio elements, if any, were used to create a strong sense of the subject being profiled? Photographs? Postcards? Menus? Signs? Song lyrics?

As you review the questions on the next few pages, especially those in the "Setting Goals" section on pp. 83–84, think about the ways in which you might show as well as tell readers about your object of study. (Remember that you must cite the source of any visual or audio element you do not create yourself, and you should also request permission from the source if your essay is going to be posted on a Web site that is not password-protected.)

■ Planning and Drafting

This section will help you review your invention writing and research notes and get started on your first draft.

Seeing What You Have

Read over your invention materials to see what you have. You probably have a great deal of material—notes from observational and interview visits or from library research, some idea of your preconceptions, a list of questions, and perhaps even some answers. You should also have a tentative perspective on the subject, some idea about it or insight into it. Your goals at this point are to digest all of the information you have gathered; to pick out the promising facts, details, anecdotes, and quotations; and to see how it all might come together to present your subject and your perspective on it to readers.

As you sort through your material, try asking yourself the following questions to help clarify your focus and interpretation:

- How do my preconceptions of the subject contrast with my findings about it?
- Can I compare or contrast what different people say about my subject?
- How do my reactions compare with those of the people directly involved?
- If I examine my subject as an anthropologist or archaeologist would, what evidence could explain its role in society at large?
- Could I use a visual or other graphic to complement the text?

Setting Goals

The following questions will help you establish goals for your first draft. Consider each question briefly now, and then return to them as necessary as you draft and revise.

Your Purpose and Readers

- Are my readers likely to be familiar with my subject? If not, what details do I need to provide to help them understand and visualize it?
- If my readers are familiar with my subject, how can I present it to them in a new and engaging way?
- What design elements might make my writing more interesting or easier for readers to understand?

The Beginning

The opening is especially important in a profile. Because readers are unlikely to have any particular reason to read a profile, the writer must arouse their curiosity and interest. The best beginnings are surprising and specific; the worst are abstract. Here are some strategies you might consider:

- Should I open with a brief anecdote, as Edge does; action, as McPhee does; or description, as Cable does?
- Can I start with a fact, anecdote, or question that would catch readers' attention?

Description of People and Places

- How might I give readers a strong visual image of people and places?
- Can I think of a simile or metaphor that would help me present an evocative image?
- Which bits of dialogue would convey information about my subject as well as a vivid impression of the speaker?
- What narrative actions can I include?

Information about the Subject

- How can I satisfy readers' need for information about my subject?
- How can I manage the flow of information so that readers do not lose interest?
- What terms will I need to define for my readers?
- What comparisons or contrasts might make the information clearer and more memorable?

A Narrative or Topical Plan

Profile writers use two basic methods of organizing information: arranging it narratively, like a story, or topically by grouping related materials.

If You Use a Narrative Plan

- How can I make the narrative interesting, perhaps even dramatic?
- What information should I present through dialogue, and what information should I interrupt the narrative to present?
- How much space should I devote to describing people and places and to telling what happened during a visit?
- If I have the option of including images or other design elements, how might I use them effectively—to clarify the sequence of events, highlight a dramatic part of the narrative, or illustrate how the people and places in the profile changed over time?

If You Use a Topical Plan

- Which topics will best reflect the information I have gathered, inform my readers, and hold their interest?
- How can I sequence the topics to bring out significant comparisons or contrasts?
- What transitions will help readers make connections between topics?
- If I have the option of including design elements, are there ways I can use them effectively to illustrate topics and reinforce the topical organization?

A Perspective on the Subject

- How can I convey a fresh perspective on the subject?
- Should I state my perspective or leave readers to infer it from the details of my presentation?

The Ending

- Should I frame the essay by repeating an image or phrase from the beginning or by completing an action begun earlier in the profile?
- Would it be effective to end by stating or restating my perspective?
- Should I end with a telling image, anecdote, or bit of dialogue or with a provocative question or connection?

Outlining

If you plan to arrange your material *narratively*, plot the key events on a timeline. If you plan to arrange your material *topically*, use clustering or outlining to help you divide and group related information.

The following suggests one possible way to organize a *narrative profile* of a place:

Begin by describing the place from the outside.

Present background information.

Describe what you see as you enter.

Introduce the people and activities.

Tour the place, describing what you see as you move from one part to the next.

Fill in information wherever you can, and comment about the place or the people.

Conclude with reflections on what you have learned about the place.

Here is a suggested outline for a *topical profile* about a person:

Begin with a vivid image of the person in action.

Use dialogue to present the first topic. (A topic could be a characteristic of the person or one aspect of his or her work.)

Narrate an anecdote or a procedure to illustrate the first topic.

Present the second topic.

Describe something related to it.

Evaluate or interpret what you have observed.

Present the third topic, etc.

Conclude with a bit of action or dialogue.

The tentative plan you choose should reflect the possibilities in your material as well as your purpose and readers. As you begin drafting, you will almost certainly discover new ways of organizing your material.

Drafting

General Advice.   Start drafting your essay, keeping in mind the goals you set while you were planning. As you write, try to describe your subject in a way that conveys your perspective on it. Turn off your grammar checker and spelling checker at this stage if you find them distracting. Don't be afraid to skip around in your draft. Jump back and fill in a spontaneous idea, or leap ahead and write a later section first if you find that easier. If you get stuck while drafting, explore the problem by using some of the writing activities in the Invention and Research section of this chapter (pp. 75–83).

As you read over your first draft, you may see places where you can add new material to reveal more about the person, place, or activity.

A Sentence Strategy: Absolute Phrases.   As you draft your profile, you will need to help your readers imagine your subject. A grammatical structure called an **absolute phrase** is useful for this purpose. This structure adds meaning to a sentence but does not modify any particular word in the rest of the sentence. (You need not remember its name or grammatical explanation to use the absolute phrase effectively.) Here is an example, with the absolute phrase in italics:

> I offer the bag to Jerry, order yet another beer, and turn to eye the pig feet floating in a murky jar by the cash register, *their blunt tips bobbing up through a pasty white film.* (Edge, par. 19)

Edge could have presented his observation of the pickled pig feet in a separate sentence, but the sentence he wrote brings together his turning and looking and what he actually saw, emphasizing the at-a-glance instant of another possible stomach flutter. Absolute phrases nearly always are attached to the end of a main clause, adding various kinds of details to it to create a more complex, informative sentence. They are usually introduced by a noun or a possessive pronoun like *his* or *their.* Here are two further examples of absolute phrases from this chapter's readings:

> This was a solid bronze casket, *its seams electronically welded to resist corrosion.* (Cable, par. 20)

He is interrupted by the reappearance in the market of Catherine Barta, who went home long ago and has now returned, *her eyes hidden by her wide-brimmed hat, her shopping cart full beside her.* (McPhee, 24)

Absolute phrases are certainly not required for a successful profile—experienced writers use them only occasionally—yet they do offer writers an effective sentence option. Try them out in your own writing.

You can strengthen your profile with other kinds of sentences as well: You may want to review the discussions of short sentences (p. 41) and sentences that place references to time at the beginning (pp. 44–45).

For more on using absolute phrases, go to **bedfordstmartins.com/conciseguide** and click on Sentence Strategies.

Critical Reading Guide

Now is the time to get a close reading of your draft. Writers usually find it helpful to have someone else read and comment on their drafts, and all writers know how much they learn about writing when they read other writers' drafts. Your instructor may schedule readings of drafts as part of your coursework—in class or online. If not, you can ask a classmate to read your draft. You could also seek comments from a tutor at your campus writing center. The guidelines in this section can be used by anyone reviewing a profile. (If you are unable to have someone else read your draft, turn ahead to the Carrying Out Revisions section on p. 92, where you will find guidelines for analyzing and evaluating your own draft.)

► **If You Are the Writer.** To provide comments that are focused and helpful, your reader must know your essay's intended audience, your purpose, and a problem in the draft that you need help solving. Briefly write out this information at the top of your draft.

- *Audience:* Identify the intended audience of your essay.
- *Purpose:* What do you hope your audience will learn about your subject?
- *Problem:* Describe the most important problem you see with your draft.

► **If You Are the Draft Reader.** The following guidelines can be useful for approaching a draft with a well-focused, questioning eye.

> **Making Comments Electronically**
> Most word processing software offers features that allow you to insert comments directly into the text of someone else's document. Many readers prefer to make their comments in this way because it tends to be faster than writing on a hard copy and space is virtually unlimited; it also eliminates the problem of deciphering handwritten comments. Where such features are not available, simply typing comments directly into a document in a contrasting color can provide the same advantages.

1. ***Read for a First Impression.*** Begin by reading the draft straight through to get a general impression. Ignore spelling, punctuation, and other kinds of errors for now. Try to imagine the subject and to understand the perspective that the profile offers on its subject.

   When you have finished this first quick reading, write a few sentences about your overall impression. State the profile's perspective on its subject or main insight into it, as you best understand it. Next, consider the problem the writer identified, and respond briefly to that concern now. (If you find that the problem is covered by one of the other guidelines listed below, respond to it in more detail there if necessary.)

2. ***Analyze the Effectiveness of the Organization.*** Consider the overall plan, perhaps by making a scratch outline. Keep in mind that the plan may be narrative or topical or a combination of the two. If the plan narrates a visit (or visits) to a place, point out passages where the narrative slows unnecessarily or shows gaps. Point out where time markers and transitions would help. Let the writer know whether the narrative arouses and holds your curiosity. Where does dialogue fall flat, and where does it convey immediacy and valuable information? If the plan is organized topically, note whether the writer presents too much or too little information and whether topics might be sequenced differently or connected more clearly. Finally, decide whether the writer might strengthen the profile by reordering any of the parts or the details.

   - ***Look again at the beginning*** of the essay to see whether it captures your attention. If not, is there a quotation, a fact, or an anecdote elsewhere in the draft that might make a better opening?
   - ***Look again at the ending*** to see whether it leaves you hanging, seems too abrupt, or oversimplifies the subject. If it does, suggest another way of ending, possibly by moving a part or a quotation from elsewhere in the essay.
   - ***Look again at any visuals.*** Tell the writer how well the visuals — headings, lists, tables, photographs, drawings, video — are integrated into the profile. Advise the writer about any visuals that seem misplaced or unnecessary.

3. ***Evaluate the Writer's Role.*** Decide whether the writer has adopted a participant-observer role, a detached-observer role, or a combination. If both roles are visibly present, evaluate whether the alternation between the two is confusing in any way. If the writer has adopted a participant-observer role, look for places where the writer is perhaps too prominent, dominating rather than featuring the subject. Point out where the writer-participant is most appealing and informative and also, perhaps, most distracting and tiresome. If the writer has taken a detached-observer role, notice whether the writer consistently directs you where and how to look at the subject.

4. *Analyze the Description of People and Places.* Begin by pointing out two or three places in the profile where the description of people, places, and activities or processes is most vivid for you, where your attention is held and you can readily imagine who or what is being described. Identify places where you would like more descriptive details. Also indicate where you need to see people in action — moving, talking, gesturing — to understand what is going on.

5. *Assess the Quality and Presentation of the Information about the Subject.* Show the writer where you learned something truly interesting, surprising, or useful. Point out where the information is too complex, coming at you too quickly, or incomplete. Ask for definitions of words you do not understand or clarification of definitions that do not seem immediately clear. Ask for a fuller description of any activity or process you cannot readily understand. Assess the clarity of all visuals and design features. If there are passages that you think could be better presented or complemented by visuals, let the writer know. Show the writer where the interweaving of description and information seems out of balance — too much of one or the other for too long.

6. *Question the Writer's Perspective on the Subject.* Begin by trying to state briefly what you believe to be the writer's perspective on the subject — some idea or insight the writer wants to convey. (This perspective statement may differ from the one you wrote at the beginning of your critical reading of this draft.) Then look for and underline one or two places where the writer explicitly states or implies a perspective. If the perspective is stated, tell the writer whether you fully understand or would welcome some elaboration. If the perspective is only implied, let the writer know whether you are content with t he implication or whether you would prefer to have the perspective explicitly stated. With the writer's perspective in mind, skim the draft one last time looking for unneeded or extraneous description and information.

7. *Give the Writer Your Final Thoughts.* What is the draft's strongest part? What part is most memorable? What part is weakest or most in need of further work?

For a printable version of this critical reading guide, go to **bedfordstmartins.com/conciseguide**.

■ Revising

This section will help you get an overview of your draft and revise it accordingly.

Working with Sources

Integrating quotations from your interviews   In addition to describing people, your profile will also quote them. These quotations can be especially revealing because they let readers hear different people speaking for themselves, rather than being presented only through your eyes. Nevertheless, it is the writer who decides which quotations to use and how. Therefore, one major task you face in drafting and revising your essay is to choose quotations from your notes, present the quotations in a timely way to reveal the style and character of people you interviewed, and integrate these quotations smoothly into your sentences.

When you directly quote (rather than paraphrase or summarize) what someone has said, you will usually need to identify the speaker. The principal way to do so is to create what is called a **speaker tag**. You may rely on a *general* or all-purpose speaker tag, using the forms of *say* and *tell*:

> "I don't see a policeman," Lewis *says* to him. (McPhee, par. 15)

> "Three pounds for a dollar," I *tell* her. (McPhee, 1)

Other speaker tags are more *specific* or precise:

> "It was a large service," *remarked* Howard. (Cable, 16)

> "Something deep within us demands a confrontation with death," Tim *explained*. (Cable, 22)

As you draft your profile, consider using specific speaker tags. They give readers more help with imagining speakers' attitudes and personal styles. Nevertheless, keep in mind that experienced writers rely on general speaker tags using forms of *say* and *tell* for most of their sentences with quotations.

In addition, you may add a word or phrase to any speaker tag to identify or describe the speaker or to reveal more about *how, where, when,* or *why* the speaker speaks:

> "It was a profession I could live with," he told me *with a sly grin*. (Cable, 24)

> "We do our best to corner the market on lips," Lionel told me, *his voice tinged with bravado*. (Edge, 11)

> "How much are the peppers? Mister, give me some of these!" she says, *looking up at me with a gypsy's dark starburst eyes*. (McPhee, 1)

In addition to being carefully introduced, quotations must be precisely punctuated, and fortunately there are only two general rules:

1. Enclose all quotations in quotation marks. These always come in pairs, one at the beginning, one at the end of the quotation. Be especially careful not to forget to include the one at the end.

2. Separate the quotation from its speaker tag with appropriate punctuation, usually a comma.

You can readily see how these rules apply by glancing over each of the examples in this section. In special situations other rules apply. For details, see the Editing and Proofreading section of this chapter on pp. 94–95 and the sections on quotations in Chapter 14, pp. 406–14.

For more help integrating quotations, go to **bedfordstmartins.com/conciseguide** and click on Bedford Research Room.

Getting an Overview

Consider your draft as a whole, following these two steps:

1. *Reread.* If at all possible, put the draft aside for a day or two. When you do reread it, start by reconsidering your purpose. Then read the draft straight through, trying to see it as your intended readers will.

2. *Outline.* Make a quick scratch outline on paper, or use the headings and outline/ summary function of your word processor.

Planning for Revision. Resist the temptation to dive in and start changing your text until after you have a comprehensive view of what needs to be done. Using your outline as a guide, move through the document and note comments received from others and problems you want to solve.

Analyzing the Basic Features of Your Own Draft. Turn to the Critical Reading Guide on pp. 87–89. Using this guide, reread the draft to identify problems you need to solve. Note the problems on your draft.

Studying Readers' Comments. Review all of the comments you have received from other readers. For each comment, look at the draft to determine what might have led the reader to make that particular point. Try to be open-minded about any criticism. Ideally, these comments will help you see your draft as others see it (rather than as you hoped it would be) and identify specific problems. Add to your notes any problems readers have identified.

Carrying Out Revisions

Having identified problems in your draft, you now need to figure out solutions and carry them out. Basically, you have three options for finding solutions:

1. Review your observation or interview notes for other information and ideas.
2. Do additional observations or interviews to answer questions that you or other readers raised.
3. Look back at the readings in this chapter to see how other writers have solved similar problems.

The following suggestions, which are organized according to the basic features of profiles, will get you started.

A Description of People and Places

- **Can your descriptions be improved?** Add details to help readers see them. Think, for example, of McPhee's description of a distraught woman: "She is wearing a print dress, a wide-brimmed straw hat" (par. 5) or of how Edge describes Lionel Dufour: "his shy smile framed by a coarse black mustache flecked with whispers of gray" (8). Consider adding comparisons, as Cable does when he says Howard Deaver "looked like death on two legs" (4). Also consider adding specific narrative action. Think of Deaver again, on the phone: "As he listened, he bit his lips and squeezed his Adam's apple" (6).

- **Can you enliven the description of the place?** Add other senses to visual description. Recall, for example, these sensory descriptions from the readings: sound (the clattering of a conveyer belt, a door creaking open), texture (the soft flesh of a pig lip, a cold and firm cadaver), smell and taste (the "hot and vinegary" taste of the pigs' lips).

- **Do readers have difficulty seeing people in action or imagining what is involved in the activity?** Add specific narrative actions to show people moving, gesturing, or talking. For example, recall from Edge's profile how he smashes the bag of potato chips, from Cable's how he reaches out to touch the cadaver's skin, from McPhee's how and where the man in the green polo shirt kicks the well-dressed pickpocket.

Information about the Subject

- **Do readers feel bogged down by information?** Look for ways to reduce information or to break up long blocks of informational text with description of scenes or people, narration of events, lists, or other design elements. Consider presenting information through dialogue, as Edge and Cable do.

A Topical or Narrative Plan

- **Does your narratively arranged essay seem to drag or ramble?** Try adding drama through dialogue or specific narrative action, as Edge does in the bar.

- *Does your topically arranged essay seem disorganized or out of balance?* Try re-arranging topics to see whether another order makes more sense. Add clearer, more explicit transitions or topic sentences. Move or condense information to restore balance.

- *Does the opening fail to engage readers' attention?* Consider alternatives. Think of questions you could open with, or look for an engaging image or dialogue later in the essay to move to the beginning. Go back to your notes for other ideas. Recall how the writers in this chapter open their profile essays: Cable stands on the street in front of the mortuary, Edge sits at a bar staring at a pig lip, McPhee shows you a pickpocket at work.

- *Are transitions between stages in the narrative or between topics confusing or abrupt?* Add appropriate words or phrases, or revise sentences to make transitions clearer or smoother.

- *Does the ending seem weak?* Consider ending at an earlier point or moving something striking to the end. Review your invention and research notes to see if you overlooked something that would make for a strong ending. Cable touches the cold, firm flesh of a cadaver. Edge stares at floating pig feet. McPhee returns to the Barta story introduced earlier.

- *Are the visual features effective?* Use an image, as Edge does. Consider adding textual references to any images in your essay or positioning images more effectively. Think of other possible design features—drawings, lists, tables, graphs, cartoons, headings—that might make the place and people easier to imagine or the information more understandable.

A Role for the Writer

- *Do readers want to see more of you in the profile?* Consider revealing yourself in some part of the activity. For example, add your contributions to one of the conversations you participated in.

- *Do readers find your participation so dominant that you seem to eclipse other participants?* Bring other people forward by adding material about them, reducing the material about yourself, or both.

A Perspective on the Subject

- *Are readers unsure what your perspective is?* Try stating it more directly. Be sure that the descriptive and narrative details reinforce the perspective you want to convey.

- *Are your readers' ideas about the person, place, or activity being profiled different from yours?* Consider

A Note on Grammar and Spelling Checkers
These tools are good at catching certain types of errors, but currently there is no replacement for a good human proofreader. Grammar checkers in particular are extremely limited in what they can find. They also tend to give faulty advice for fixing problems and to flag correct items as wrong. Spelling checkers cause fewer problems but cannot catch misspellings that are themselves words, such as *to* for *too*.

whether you can incorporate any of their ideas into your essay or use them to develop your own ideas.

- ***Do readers point to any details that seem especially meaningful?*** Consider what these details suggest about your own perspective on the subject.

For a revision checklist, go to **bedfordstmartins.com/conciseguide**.

■ Editing and Proofreading

Now is the time to check your revised draft for errors in grammar, punctuation, and mechanics. Our research has identified several errors that occur often in profiles, including problems with the punctuation of quotations and the order of adjectives. The following guidelines will help you check your essay for these common errors.

Checking the Punctuation of Quotations.　Because most profiles are based in part on interviews, you probably have quoted one or more people in your essay. When you quote someone's exact words, you must enclose those words in quotation marks and observe strict conventions for punctuating quotations.

All quotations should have quotation marks at the beginning and the end.

▶ "What exactly is civil litigation?" I asked.

Commas and periods go *inside* quotation marks.

▶ "I'm here to see Anna Post ," I replied nervously.

▶ Tony explained, "Fraternity boys just wouldn't feel comfortable at the Chez Moi Café."

Question marks and exclamation points go *inside* closing quotation marks if they are part of the quotation, *outside* if they are not.

▶ After a pause, the patient asked, "Where do I sign?"

▶ Willie insisted, "You can *too* learn to play Super Mario!"

▶ When was the last time someone you just ticketed said to you, "Thank you, Officer, for doing a great job?"

Use commas with speaker tags (*he said, she asked,* etc.) that accompany direct quotations.

▶ "This sound system costs only four thousand dollars ," Jorge said.

▶ I asked , "So where were these clothes from originally?"

For practice, go to **bedfordstmartins.com/conciseguide/exercisecentral** and click on Punctuation of Quotations.

A Common ESL Problem: Adjective Order.   In trying to present the subject of your profile vividly and in detail, you probably have included many descriptive adjectives. When you include more than one adjective in front of a noun, you may have difficulty sequencing them. For example, do you write *a large old ceramic pot* or *an old large ceramic pot?* The following list shows the order in which adjectives are ordinarily arranged in front of a noun.

1. *Amount:* a/an, the, a few, six
2. *Evaluation:* good, beautiful, ugly, serious
3. *Size:* large, small, tremendous
4. *Shape, length:* round, long, short
5. *Age:* young, new, old
6. *Color:* red, black, green
7. *Origin:* Asian, Brazilian, German
8. *Material:* wood, cotton, gold
9. *Noun used as an adjective:* computer (as in *computer program*), cake (as in *cake pan*)
10. *The noun modified*

For practice, go to **bedfordstmartins.com/conciseguide/exercisecentral** and click on A Common ESL Problem: Adjective Order.

Thinking About Document Design

◼ Creating Web-Based Essays

The education student writing on collaborative learning principles (see p. 53) published her essay as a Web site so that classmates and other interested people could read her work. Web-based publishing allowed her not only to include photographs and materials from her research, but also to show her final product to the sixth graders and the teacher she had profiled.

Web documents can be more visually complex and interactive than essays written for print. In her Web-based essay, the education student incorporated photographs, links, and color highlights to make the material both more interesting and helpful to her readers. As the screen shot on this page shows, she embedded links on the left side of the page so readers could easily move through her essay and used a graphic (the dark blue circle) to mark the current page. Since Web readers tend to skim, surf, and bounce around, the student provided several different points of entry into her site: a table of contents ("Contents"); an introduction with information about the assignment and some context for the site ("Introduction"); a page summarizing the work she researched, read, and reviewed for the project ("Background Reading"); a section reporting on her research ("Findings"); and a page including photos taken during the project ("Gallery"). She also included a page with her works cited ("Bibliography") — the list of scholarly essays that served as back-ground reading, with links to material available online. In addition, the student writer included links to the sixth-grade class's Web site, which contained the final projects that resulted from the Internet research she had watched the children engage in. She encouraged readers to view these projects as evidence of the advantages of collaborative learning.

Because her topic was collaboration, she wanted a photograph showing children working together. However, since the children were minors, she would have needed parent and teacher (and perhaps even school board) permission to take and include their photographs. Instead, she used graphic software to alter a picture of four children so that the children's faces were not identifiable. At key points in her essay, the student writer also included quotes from the sixth graders. She used these quotes as subtitles for individual sections of her essay, and to draw more attention to the quotes, she used a font larger than the body of the essay — a technique borrowed from print publishing.

Reflecting on Your Writing

Now that you have spent several days discussing profiles and writing one of your own, take some time to reflect on what you have learned about this genre. What problems did you encounter while you were writing your profile, and how did you solve them?

Write a one-page explanation, telling your instructor about a problem you encountered in writing your profile and how you solved it. Before you begin, gather all of your written invention material, planning and interview notes, drafts, advice on improving your draft, revision notes and plans, and final revision. Review these materials as you complete this writing task.

1. ***Identify one writing problem you needed to solve as you worked on your profile.*** Do not be concerned with grammar or punctuation; concentrate instead on problems unique to developing a profile. For example: Did you puzzle over how to organize your diverse observations into a coherent essay? Was it difficult to convey your own perspective? Did you have any concerns about presenting your subject vividly or controlling the flow of information?

2. ***Determine how you came to recognize the problem.*** When did you first discover it? What called it to your attention? If someone else pointed out the problem to you, can you now see hints of it in your invention writings? If so, where specifically? When you first recognized the problem, how did you respond?

3. ***Reflect on how you went about solving the problem.*** Did you work on the wording of a passage, cut or add details about your subject, or move paragraphs or sentences around? Did you reread one of the essays in this chapter to see how another writer handled a similar problem, or did you look back at the invention suggestions? If you talked about the problem with another student, your instructor, or someone else, what specific help did you receive?

4. ***Write a brief explanation of the problem and your solution.*** Reconstruct your efforts as specifically as possible. Quote from your invention notes or draft essay, others' advice, your revision plan, or your revised essay to show the various changes your writing underwent as you tried to solve the problem. When you have finished, consider how explaining what you have learned about solving this writing problem can help you solve future writing problems.

4

Explaining
a Concept

IN COLLEGE COURSES For a linguistics course, a student writes a term paper tracing the development in children's control of sentences, or *syntax*. To get started, she goes to the library and finds some sources that were listed in her linguistics textbook. She then goes to her professor's office hours and asks for other articles or books she should consult. These sources become the basis of the first section of her paper.

From one of the books her professor recommends, she learns about stages that children go through as they gain control of syntax, beginning with the one-word or holophrastic stage (such as *mommy*) and progressing through the two-word or duose stage (*baby sleep* or *want toy*), and multiword or telegraphic stages (*no sit there*). She decides to organize her essay around these stages. Even though she writes for her professor, who is an expert in child language development, she carefully defines key terms to show that she understands what she is writing about.

IN THE WORKPLACE Returning from a seminar on the national security implications of satellite photography, the CEO of a space-imaging company prepares a report to his employees on the debate about *symmetrical transparency*, which involves using satellite photography to make everything on the planet visible at one-meter resolution—enough detail to reveal individual cars in parking lots and individual shrubs and trees planted in parks. Aware of the financial implications for his company, the executive prepares a written text to read aloud to his employees and a PowerPoint presentation to project on a large screen during his talk.

He begins by reminding employees that the company's cameras already provide high-resolution images to government and corporate purchasers and then gives a brief overview of key issues in the debate. These issues include the impact of changing technologies and the politics of global terrorism.

IN THE COMMUNITY A manager at a marketing research firm has been tutoring fifth-grade students in math for a few hours each month. Learning about the manager's market research expertise, the teacher asks her to plan a presentation to the class about *surveying*, an important research method in the social sciences.

She begins the presentation by having students fill out a brief questionnaire on their television-watching habits. When they are done, she discusses with them how such data could be used for purposes such as deciding where to place commercials. Then, with the students' help, she separates the results into three categories: the viewer's gender, the time of the show, and the type of show. Using a PowerPoint program, she projects the data onto a large screen.

She concludes by giving examples of questions from other surveys and explaining who does them, what they hope to learn, and how they report and use the results. Finally, she passes out a quiz so that she and each student can find out how much has been learned about surveys.

Concept explanations inform readers about processes, phenomena, theories, principles, or ideas. The scenarios that open this chapter illustrate a variety of concepts and situations in which they may be explained.

Every student entering a new academic field is introduced to an array of new concepts. Introductory courses and their textbooks teach a whole new vocabulary of technical terms and specialized jargon. The opening chapter of this textbook, for example, introduced concepts such as *genre, critical thinking, recursiveness,* and *invention.* Every field of study has concepts that students must learn and be able to explain and apply. Physics has *entropy, mass,* and *quantum mechanics;* music has *harmonics, counterpoint,* and *sonata form;* mathematics has *probability, proportionality,* and *geometric progression;* psychology has *subconscious, transference, attachment disorder,* and so on.

In this chapter, you will read essays explaining the concepts of *cannibalism* (an anthropological concept), *romantic love* (a cultural concept), and *contemporary evolution* (a biological concept dealing with the kinds of changes in species that happen quickly, often as a result of environmental change). One of these essays was written by an expert on the subject — the explanation of contemporary evolution by evolutionary biologist Bob Holmes. The other essays were written by student Linh Kieu Ngo and science reporter Anastasia Toufexis, both of whom explain concepts they have learned about from researching what experts have discovered.

Your instructor may encourage you to explain a concept related to a subject on which you are an expert. For example, if you are knowledgeable about music, you might choose to explain a phenomenon like *hip hop* or a theory like *counterpoint.* If you are an avid video game player, you could explain *game mechanics, mods,* or *real-time strategy* games. If you are a sports enthusiast, you could write about the *curve ball* in baseball or the *Wing-T offense* in football. Or your instructor may ask you to write about an academic concept you are just now learning in your English or other courses.

Learning to explain a concept is especially important for you as a college student. It will help you read critically; it will prepare you to write a common type of exam and paper assignment; it will acquaint you with the basic strategies common to all types of explanatory writing — definition, classification, comparison and contrast, cause and effect, and process narration; and it will sharpen your skill in researching and using sources, abilities essential for success in college, whatever your major.

A Collaborative Activity: Practice Explaining a Concept

Part 1. Choose one concept to explain to two or three other students. When you have chosen your concept, think about what others in the group are likely to know about it and how you can inform them about it in two or three minutes. Consider how you will define the concept and what strategies you might use — description, comparison, and so on — to explain it in an interesting, memorable way.

Get together with two or three other students, and explain your concepts to one another. You might begin by indicating where you learned the concept and in what area of study or work or leisure it is usually used.

Part 2. When all group members have explained their concepts, discuss what you learned from the experience. Begin by asking one another a question or two that elicits further information. Then consider these questions:

- How did you decide what to include in your explanation and what to leave out?
- What surprised you in the questions that readers asked about your presentation?
- If you were to repeat your explanation to a similar group of listeners, what would you add, subtract, or change?

Readings

LINH KIEU NGO wrote this essay as a first-year college student. In it, he explains the concept of cannibalism, the eating of human flesh by other humans. Most Americans know about survival cannibalism — eating human flesh to avoid starvation — but Ngo also explains the historical importance of dietary and ritual cannibalism in his essay. As you read, notice how he relies on examples to illustrate the three types of cannibalism.

Cannibalism: It Still Exists

Linh Kieu Ngo

1   Fifty-five Vietnamese refugees fled to Malaysia on a small fishing boat to escape communist rule in their country following the Vietnam War. During their escape attempt, the captain was shot by the coast guard. The boat and its passengers managed to outrun the coast guard to the open sea, but they had lost the only person who knew the way to Malaysia, the captain.

2   The men onboard tried to navigate the boat, but after a week fuel ran out, and they drifted farther out to sea. Their supply of food and water was gone; people were starving, and some of the elderly were near death. The men managed to produce a small amount of drinking water by boiling salt water, using dispensable wood from the boat to create a small fire near the stern. They also tried to fish but had little success.

3   A month went by, and the old and weak died. At first, the crew threw the dead overboard, but later, out of desperation, they turned to human flesh as a source of food. Some people vomited as they attempted to eat it, while others refused to

By beginning with a dramatic anecdote (pars. 1–4), Ngo tries to interest readers and make the concept seem less abstract. As you read, notice how much you are learning about the concept even before he gives it a name.

resort to cannibalism and see the bodies of their loved ones sacrificed for food. Those who did not eat died of starvation, and their bodies in turn became food for others. Human flesh was cut out, washed in salt water, and hung to dry for preservation. The liquids inside the cranium were drunk to quench thirst. The livers, kidneys, hearts, stomachs, and intestines were boiled and eaten.

Five months passed before a whaling vessel discovered the drifting boat, looking like a graveyard of bones. There was only one survivor. [4]

Cannibalism, the act of human beings eating human flesh (Sagan 2), has a long history and continues to hold interest and create controversy. Many books and research reports offer examples of cannibalism, but a few scholars have questioned whether it actually was ever practiced anywhere, except in cases of ensuring survival in times of famine or isolation (Askenasy 43-54). Recently, some scholars have tried to understand why people in the West have been so eager to attribute cannibalism to non-Westerners (Barker, Hulme, and Iversen). Cannibalism has long been a part of American popular culture. For example, Mark Twain's "Cannibalism in the Cars" tells a humorous story about cannibalism by well-to-do travelers on a train stranded in a snowstorm, and cannibalism is still a popular subject for jokes ("Cannibal Jokes"). [5]

If we assume there is some reality to the reports about cannibalism, how can we best understand this concept? Cannibalism can be broken down into two main categories: exocannibalism, the eating of outsiders or foreigners, and endocannibalism, the eating of members of one's own social group (Shipman 70). Within these categories are several functional types of cannibalism, three of the most common being survival cannibalism, dietary cannibalism, and religious and ritual cannibalism. [6]

Survival cannibalism occurs when people trapped without food have to decide "whether to starve or to eat fellow humans" (Shipman 70). In the case of the Vietnamese refugees, the crew and passengers on the boat ate human flesh to stay alive. They did not kill people to get human flesh for nourishment but instead waited until the people had died. Even after human carcasses were sacrificed as food, the boat people ate only enough to survive. Another case of survival cannibalism occurred in 1945, when General Douglas MacArthur's forces cut supply lines to Japanese troops stationed in the Pacific Islands. In one incident, Japanese troops were reported to have sacrificed the [7]

Here Ngo shifts from narrating to explaining what experts have written about cannibalism. The parenthetical citations are keyed to the Works Cited list at the end of the essay. Ngo cites a range of sources, showing readers that the information he presents is well established.

Ngo poses a rhetorical question that anticipates what his readers may be thinking.

Ngo's thesis statement names the three types of cannibalism he will discuss, forecasting his essay's plan.

Ngo uses topic sentences to announce what he is about to discuss because readers expect essays explaining a concept to be clear and easy to follow.

Ngo refers to the opening anecdote and then presents additional examples to illustrate survival cannibalism.

Arapesh people of northeastern New Guinea for food in order to avoid death by starvation (Tuzin 63). The most famous example of survival cannibalism in American history comes from the diaries, letters, and interviews of survivors of the California-bound Donner Party, who in the winter of 1846 were snowbound in the Sierra Nevada Mountains for five months. Thirty-five of eighty-seven adults and children died, and some of them were eaten (Hart 116-117; Johnson).

8   Unlike survival cannibalism, in which human flesh is eaten as a last resort after a person has died, in dietary cannibalism humans are purchased or trapped for food and then eaten as a part of a culture's traditions. In addition, survival cannibalism often involves people eating other people of the same origins, whereas dietary cannibalism usually involves people eating foreigners.

> Another topic sentence cues readers that Ngo is making a transition to the second category of cannibalism.

9   In the Miyanmin society of the west Sepik interior of Papua, New Guinea, villagers do not value human life over that of pigs or marsupials because human flesh is part of their normal diet (Poole 7). The Miyanmin people observe no differences in "gender, kinship, ritual status, and bodily substance"; they eat anyone, even their own dead. In this respect, then, they practice both endocannibalism and exocannibalism; and to ensure a constant supply of human flesh for food, they raid neighboring tribes and drag their victims back to their village to be eaten (Poole 11). Perhaps, in the history of this society, there was at one time a shortage of wild game to be hunted for food, and because people were more plentiful than fish, deer, rabbits, pigs, or cows, survival cannibalism was adopted as a last resort. Then, as their culture developed, the Miyanmin may have retained the practice of dietary cannibalism, which has endured as a part of their culture.

> Ngo presents examples to illustrate dietary cannibalism.

10   Similar to the Miyanmin, the people of the Leopard and Alligator societies in South America eat human flesh as part of their cultural tradition. Practicing dietary exocannibalism, the Leopard people hunt in groups, with one member wearing the skin of a leopard to conceal the face. They ambush their victims in the forest and carry their victims back to their village to be eaten. The Alligator people also hunt in groups, but they hide themselves under a canoelike submarine that resembles an alligator, then swim close to a fisherman's or trader's canoe to overturn it and catch their victims (MacCormack 54).

11   Religious or ritual cannibalism is different from survival and dietary cannibalism in that it has a ceremonial purpose rather than one of nourishment. Sometimes only a single victim

> Another topic sentence cues readers that Ngo is making a transition to the third category of cannibalism.

is sacrificed in a ritual, while at other times many are sacrificed. For example, the Bangala tribe of the Congo River in central Africa honors a deceased chief or leader by purchasing, sacrificing, and feasting on slaves (Sagan 53). The number of slaves sacrificed is determined by how highly the tribe members revered the deceased leader.

Ritual cannibalism among South American Indians often   12
serves as revenge for the dead. Like the Bangalas, some South American tribes kill their victims to be served as part of funeral rituals, with human sacrifices denoting that the deceased was held in high honor. Also like the Bangalas, these tribes use outsiders as victims. Unlike the Bangalas, however, the Indians sacrifice only one victim instead of many in a single ritual. For example, when a warrior of a tribe is killed in battle, the family of the warrior forces a victim to take the identity of the warrior. The family adorns the victim with the deceased warrior's belongings and may even force him to marry the deceased warrior's wives. But once the family believes the victim has assumed the spiritual identity of the deceased warrior, the family kills him. The children in the tribe soak their hands in the victim's blood to symbolize their revenge of the warrior's death. Elderly women from the tribe drink the victim's blood and then cut up his body for roasting and eating (Sagan 53-54). The people of the tribe believe that by sacrificing a victim, they have avenged the death of the warrior and the soul of the deceased can rest in peace.

In the villages of certain African tribes, only a small part of   13
a dead body is used in ritual cannibalism. In these tribes, where the childbearing capacity of women is highly valued, women are obligated to eat small, raw fragments of genital parts during fertility rites. Elders of the tribe supervise this ritual to ensure that the women will be fertile. In the Bimin-Kuskusmin tribe, for instance, a widow eats a small, raw fragment of flesh from the penis of her deceased husband in order to enhance her future fertility and reproductive capacity. Similarly, a widower may eat a raw fragment of flesh from his deceased wife's vagina along with a piece of her bone marrow; by eating her flesh, he hopes to strengthen the fertility of his daughters borne by his dead wife, and by eating her bone marrow, he honors her reproductive capacity. Also, when an elder woman of the village who has shown great reproductive capacity dies, her uterus and the interior parts of her vagina are eaten by other women who hope to benefit from her reproductive power (Poole 16-17).

Ngo presents examples to illustrate religious or ritual cannibalism.

14   Members of developed societies in general practice none of these forms of cannibalism, with the occasional exception of survival cannibalism when the only alternative is starvation. It is possible, however, that our distant-past ancestors were cannibals who through the eons turned away from the practice. We are, after all, descended from the same ancestors as the Miyanmin, the Alligator, and the Leopard people, and survival cannibalism shows that people are capable of eating human flesh when they have no other choice.

> Ngo's conclusion anticipates another likely question readers may have: Why should I be interested in this concept?

Works Cited

Askenasy, Hans. *Cannibalism: From Sacrifice to Survival.* Amherst, NY: Prometheus, 1994. Print.

Barker, Francis, Peter Hulme, and Margaret Iversen, eds. *Cannibalism and the New World.* Cambridge: Cambridge UP, 1998. Print.

Brown, Paula, and Donald Tuzin, eds. *The Ethnography of Cannibalism.* Washington: Society of Psychological Anthropology, 1983. Print.

"Cannibal Jokes." *Bored.com.* N.p., n.d. Web. 22 Sept. 2008.

Hart, James D. *A Companion to California.* Berkeley: U of California P, 1987. Print.

Johnson, Kristin. "New Light on the Donner Party." Kristin Johnson, 5 Nov. 2006. Web. 28 Sept. 2008.

MacCormack, Carol. "Human Leopard and Crocodile." Brown and Tuzin 54-55.

Poole, Fitz John Porter. "Cannibals, Tricksters, and Witches." Brown and Tuzin 16-17.

Sagan, Eli. *Cannibalism.* New York: Harper, 1976. Print.

Shipman, Pat. "The Myths and Perturbing Realities of Cannibalism." *Discover* Mar. 1987: 70+. Print.

Tuzin, Donald. "Cannibalism and Arapesh Cosmology." Brown and Tuzin 61-63.

Twain, Mark. "Cannibalism in the Cars." *The Complete Short Stories of Mark Twain.* Ed. Charles Neider. New York: Doubleday, 1957. 9-16. Print.

> In his Works Cited, Ngo uses MLA documentation style with the title centered, the entries in alphabetical order, and subsequent lines of the same entry indented one-half inch.

ANASTASIA TOUFEXIS has been an associate editor of *Time,* senior editor of *Discover,* and editor in chief of *Psychology Today.* She has written on subjects as diverse as medicine, health and fitness, law, environment, education, science, and national and world news. Toufexis has won a number of awards for her writing, including a Knight-Wallace Fellowship at the University of Michigan and an Ocean Science Journalism Fellowship at Woods Hole Oceanographic Institution. She has also lectured on science writing at Columbia University, the University of North Carolina, and the School of Visual Arts in New York.

The following essay was originally published in 1993 in *Time* magazine. As you read, notice how Toufexis brings together a variety of sources to present a neurochemical perspective on love.

Love: The Right Chemistry

Anastasia Toufexis

Love is a romantic designation for a most ordinary biological—or, shall we say, chemical?—process. A lot of nonsense is talked and written about it.
—GRETA GARBO TO MELVYN DOUGLAS IN *NINOTCHKA*

O.K., let's cut out all this nonsense about romantic love. Let's bring some scientific precision to the party. Let's put love under a microscope.

When rigorous people with Ph.D.s after their names do that, what they see is not some silly, senseless thing. No, their probe reveals that love rests firmly on the foundations of evolution, biology and chemistry. What seems on the surface to be irrational, intoxicated behavior is in fact part of nature's master strategy—a vital force that has helped humans survive, thrive and multiply through thousands of years. Says Michael Mills, a psychology professor at Loyola Marymount University in Los Angeles: "Love is our ancestors whispering in our ears."

It was on the plains of Africa about 4 million years ago, in the early days of the human species, that the notion of romantic love probably first began to blossom or at least that the first cascades of neurochemicals began flowing from the brain to the bloodstream to produce goofy grins and sweaty palms as men and women gazed deeply into each other's eyes. When mankind graduated from scuttling around on all fours to walking on two legs, this change made the whole person visible to fellow human beings for the first time. Sexual organs were in full display, as were other characteristics, from the color of eyes to the span of shoulders. As never before, each individual had a unique allure.

When the sparks flew, new ways of making love enabled sex to become a romantic encounter, not just a reproductive act. Although mounting mates from the rear was, and still is, the method favored among most animals, humans began to enjoy face-to-face couplings; both looks and personal attraction became a much greater part of the equation.

Romance served the evolutionary purpose of pulling males and females into long-term partnership, which was essential to child rearing. On open grasslands, one parent would have a hard—and dangerous—time handling a child while foraging for food. "If a woman was carrying the equivalent of a 20-lb. bowling ball in one arm and a pile of sticks in the other, it was ecologically critical to pair up with a mate to rear the young," explains anthropologist Helen Fisher, author of *Anatomy of Love*.

While Western culture holds fast to the idea that true love flames forever (the movie *Bram Stoker's Dracula* has the Count carrying the torch beyond the grave), nature apparently meant passions to sputter out in something like four years. Primitive pairs stayed together just "long enough to rear one child through infancy," says Fisher. Then each would find a new partner and start all over again.

What Fisher calls the "four-year itch" shows up unmistakably in today's divorce statistics. In most of the 62 cultures she has studied, divorce rates peak around the fourth year of marriage. Additional youngsters help keep pairs together longer. If, say, a couple have another child three years after the first, as often occurs, then their union can be expected to last about four more years. That makes them ripe for the more familiar phenomenon portrayed in the Marilyn Monroe classic *The Seven-Year Itch*.

If, in nature's design, romantic love is not eternal, neither is it exclusive. Less than 5% of mammals form rigorously faithful pairs. From the earliest days, contends Fisher, the human pattern has been "monogamy with clandestine adultery." Occasional flings upped the chances that new combinations of genes would be passed on to the next generation. Men who sought new partners had more children. Contrary to common assumptions, women were just as likely to stray. "As long as prehistoric females were secretive about their extramarital affairs," argues Fisher, "they could garner extra

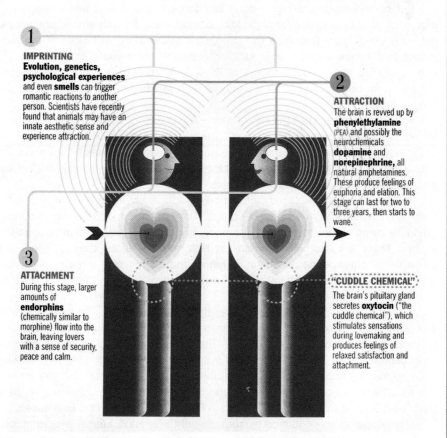

1 IMPRINTING
Evolution, genetics, psychological experiences and even **smells** can trigger romantic reactions to another person. Scientists have recently found that animals may have an innate aesthetic sense and experience attraction.

2 ATTRACTION
The brain is revved up by **phenylethylamine** (PEA) and possibly the neurochemicals **dopamine** and **norepinephrine,** all natural amphetamines. These produce feelings of euphoria and elation. This stage can last for two to three years, then starts to wane.

3 ATTACHMENT
During this stage, larger amounts of **endorphins** (chemically similar to morphine) flow into the brain, leaving lovers with a sense of security, peace and calm.

"CUDDLE CHEMICAL"
The brain's pituitary gland secretes **oxytocin** ("the cuddle chemical"), which stimulates sensations during lovemaking and produces feelings of relaxed satisfaction and attachment.

resources, life insurance, better genes and more varied DNA for their biological futures. . . ."

Lovers often claim that they feel as if they are being swept away. They're not mistaken; they are literally flooded by chemicals, research suggests. A meeting of eyes, a touch of hands or a whiff of scent sets off a flood that starts in the brain and races along the nerves and through the blood. The results are familiar: flushed skin, sweaty palms, heavy breathing. If love looks suspiciously like stress, the reason is simple: the chemical pathways are identical.

Above all, there is the sheer euphoria of falling in love — a not-so-surprising reaction, considering that many of the substances swamping the newly smitten are chemical cousins of amphetamines. They include dopamine, norepinephrine and especially phenylethylamine (PEA). Cole Porter knew what he was talking about when he wrote, "I get a kick out of you." "Love is a natural high," observes Anthony Walsh, author of *The Science of Love: Understanding Love and Its Effects on Mind and Body.* "PEA gives you that silly smile that you flash at strangers. When we meet someone who is attractive to us, the whistle blows at the PEA factory."

But phenylethylamine highs don't last forever, a fact that lends support to arguments that passionate romantic love is short-lived. As with any amphetamine, the body builds up a tolerance to PEA; thus it takes more and more of the substance to produce love's special kick. After two to three years, the body simply can't crank up the needed amount of PEA. And chewing on chocolate doesn't help, despite popular belief. The candy is high in PEA, but it fails to boost the body's supply.

Fizzling chemicals spell the end of delirious passion; for many people that marks the end of the liaison as well. It is particularly true for those whom Dr. Michael Liebowitz of the New York State Psychiatric Institute terms "attraction junkies." They crave the intoxication of falling in love so much that they move frantically from affair to affair just as soon as the first rush of infatuation fades.

Still, many romances clearly endure beyond the first years. What accounts for that? Another set of chemicals, of course. The continued presence of a partner gradually steps up production in the brain of endorphins. Unlike the fizzy amphetamines, these are soothing substances. Natural pain-killers, they give lovers a sense of security, peace and calm. "That is one reason why it feels so horrible when we're abandoned or a lover dies," notes Fisher. "We don't have our daily hit of narcotics."

Researchers see a contrast between the heated infatuation induced by PEA, along with other amphetamine-like chemicals, and the more intimate attachment fostered and prolonged by endorphins. "Early love is when you love the way the other person makes you feel," explains psychiatrist Mark Goulston of the University of California, Los Angeles. "Mature love is when you love the person as he or she is." It is the difference between passionate and compassionate love, observes Walsh, a psychobiologist at Boise State University in Idaho. "It's Bon Jovi vs. Beethoven."

Oxytocin is another chemical that has recently been implicated in love. Produced by the brain, it sensitizes nerves and stimulates muscle contraction. In women it helps uterine contractions during childbirth as well as production of breast milk, and seems to inspire mothers to nuzzle their infants. Scientists speculate that oxytocin might encourage similar cuddling between adult women and men. The versatile chemical may also enhance orgasms. In one study of men, oxytocin increased to three to five times its normal level during climax, and it may soar even higher in women. . . .

Chemicals may help explain (at least to scientists) the feelings of passion and compassion, but why do people tend to fall in love with one partner rather than a myriad of others? Once again, it's partly a function of evolution and biology. "Men are looking for maximal fertility in a mate," says Loyola Marymount's Mills. "That is in large part why females in the prime childbearing ages of 17 to 28 are so desirable." Men can size up youth and vitality in a glance, and studies indeed show that men fall in love quite rapidly. Women tumble more slowly, to a large degree because their requirements are more complex; they need more time to check the guy out. "Age is not vital," notes Mills, "but the ability to provide security, father children, share resources and hold a high status in society are all key factors."   16

Still, that does not explain why the way Mary walks and laughs makes Bill dizzy with desire while Marcia's gait and giggle leave him cold. "Nature has wired us for one special person," suggests Walsh, romantically. He rejects the idea that a woman or a man can be in love with two people at the same time. Each person carries in his or her mind a unique subliminal guide to the ideal partner, a "love map," to borrow a term coined by sexologist John Money of Johns Hopkins University.   17

Drawn from the people and experiences of childhood, the map is a record of whatever we found enticing and exciting—or disturbing and disgusting. Small feet, curly hair. The way our mothers patted our head or how our fathers told a joke. A fireman's uniform, a doctor's stethoscope. All the information gathered while growing up is imprinted in the brain's circuitry by adolescence. Partners never meet each and every requirement, but a sufficient number of matches can light up the wires and signal, "It's love." Not every partner will be like the last one, since lovers may have different combinations of the characteristics favored by the map.   18

O.K., that's the scientific point of view. Satisfied? Probably not. To most people—with or without Ph.D.s—love will always be more than the sum of its natural parts. It's a commingling of body and soul, reality and imagination, poetry and phenylethylamine. In our deepest hearts, most of us harbor the hope that love will never fully yield up its secrets, that it will always elude our grasp.   19

Making Connections to Personal and Social Issues: Love Maps

The chemistry of love is easily summarized: Amphetamines fuel romance; endorphins and oxytocin sustain lasting relationships. As Toufexis makes clear, however, these chemical reactions do not explain why specific people are initially attracted to each other. Toufexis observes that an initial attraction occurs because each of us carries a "unique subliminal guide" or "love map" (par. 17) that leads us unerringly to a partner.

In writing or conversation with two or three other students, consider where your love map comes from. How much can it be influenced by family traditions, friends and community, or images in the media and advertising? Consider also whether it is possible for an individual's love map to change over time—and whether your own has changed. What might contribute to such changes?

Analyzing Writing Strategies

1. What does Toufexis do to **catch readers' attention**? Look, for example, at the title and the epigraph quoting from the film *Ninotchka*. What appeal might these features have for readers?

   Reread the opening paragraph, paying special attention to its tone. Note the conversational "O.K." with which it begins and the use of a contraction (*let's*) instead of the more formal (*let us*). *In a few sentences, consider what other characteristics of Toufexis's language seem designed to entice readers to read on.*

2. Toufexis's essay includes a **visual** that combines words with drawings. *In writing or with a few classmates, discuss what this visual contributes to your understanding of her concept explanation.* Begin by examining how you read it. Do you start with the words, the images, or some combination of the two? Do you read from left to right and top to bottom, as you would a written text in English, or do you follow some other path? How do the numbers together with the colored and dotted lines guide your eye?

   There is no title or caption to explain the role the visual plays in the essay. What seems to you to be its role? Does it illustrate something already discussed in the essay, add new information, do both, or do something else altogether?

Commentary: A Focused Concept, Logical Plan, and Careful Use of Sources

Toufexis's article resembles the essay by student Linh Kieu Ngo in that both authors obviously thought a lot about their readers when planning their essays. Neither Ngo nor Toufexis tries to present everything there is to know about the concept; instead, each focuses the explanation on aspects that are likely to be new and interesting to readers. Both authors carefully plan the essay and provide cues that make it easy to follow. Moreover, to reassure readers that the information is trustworthy, both Ngo and Toufexis cite authoritative sources.

Writers of essays explaining concepts must limit the scope of their explanations. In her relatively brief magazine article, Toufexis writes about a narrowly **focused concept**: the evolutionary biology and neurochemistry of love between adult human heterosexual mates. She excludes other love relationships such as romantic love between members of the same gender as well as platonic or nonsexual love, and she chooses not to discuss views on love held by various cultures and religions, or dozens of other possible subjects related to love. When readers finish the essay, they are well informed about the evolutionary biology and chemistry of love.

The unfamiliarity of the information in concept explanations makes it imperative that writers develop a **logical plan**. Toufexis gives readers cues to help them anticipate how the essay will unfold: a *thesis statement* that identifies the focused concept that is the subject of the essay and a *forecast* of the topics that will be addressed in the essay. In paragraph 1, Toufexis announces that she is writing about "romantic love," a concept she will address with "scientific precision." In paragraph 2, she states the essay's thesis ("What seems on the surface to be irrational, intoxicated behavior is in fact part of nature's master strategy—a vital force that has helped humans survive, thrive and multiply through thousands of years"). She also forecasts the topics she will discuss in the essay ("love rests firmly on the foundations of evolution, biology and chemistry"). Here's a simple scratch outline of the topics she goes on to develop, showing that she delivers on the promise of this forecast:

introduction (epigraph and pars. 1–2)

evolutionary biology (3–8)

neurochemistry (9–15)

love maps (16–18)

conclusion (19)

By using transitions, Toufexis also lets readers know when she is leaving one topic and beginning the next. For example, at the beginning of paragraph 9, where she moves from discussing evolutionary biology to neurochemistry, Toufexis writes: "Lovers often claim that they feel as if they are being swept away. They're not mistaken; they are literally flooded by chemicals, research suggests." Similarly, when the topic shifts to love maps, Toufexis uses the whole paragraph (17) to make the transition. She also uses transitions within her discussion of each topic. Look, for example, at the way she introduces each neurochemical involved in romantic feelings:

Above all, there is the sheer euphoria of falling in love—a not-so-surprising reaction, considering that many of the substances swamping the newly smitten are chemical cousins of amphetamines. They include dopamine, norepinephrine and especially phenylethylamine (PEA). (par. 10)

Still, many romances clearly endure beyond the first years. What accounts for that? Another set of chemicals, of course. (13)

Oxytocin is another chemical that has recently been implicated in love. (15)

To learn more about cueing readers, see Chapter 10.

In addition to giving readers a focused concept and a logical plan, writers have to convince readers that the information they've used to explain the concept is reliable. They do this by acknowledging their expert **sources**. Like most journalists, Toufexis relies primarily on interviews, although it appears that she also read at least parts of the two books she names in paragraphs 5 and 10. She arranged interviews with six different professors specializing in diverse academic disciplines: psychology, anthropology, psychiatry, and sexology. Identifying her sources by their specialization, academic institution, and books or articles on the subject helps to establish that they are indeed credible authorities.

What is most notable about Toufexis's use of sources is that she does not indicate precisely where she obtained all the information she includes. For example, she does not cite the source of the anthropological information in paragraphs 3–5, although a reader might guess that she summarized it from *Anatomy of Love*, cited at the end of paragraph 5. We cannot be certain whether the quote at the end of paragraph 5 comes from the book or from an interview with its author. Because she is writing for a respected publication, *Time* magazine, Toufexis can probably assume that her readers will not fault her for failing to provide exact bibliographical citations. Readers would be surprised to find footnotes or works cited lists in popular publications.

In college writing, however, sources must be cited. Moreover, college writers—whether students or professors—are expected to follow certain styles for source citations, such as MLA style in English and APA style in psychology.

Considering Topics for Your Own Essay

Like Toufexis, you could write an essay about love or romance, but you could choose a different focus: its history (how and when did romantic love develop as an idea in the West?), its cultural characteristics (how is love regarded currently among different American ethnic groups or world cultures?), its excesses or extremes, or the phases of falling in and out of love. Also consider writing about other concepts involving personal relationships, such as jealousy, codependency, idealization, stereotyping, or homophobia.

BOB HOLMES has a B.S. in zoology from the University of Alberta and a Ph.D. in ecology and evolutionary biology from the University of Arizona. After obtaining a certificate in science writing from the University of California, Santa Cruz, Holmes taught in UCSC's writing program for several years. He has been a science writer for over a decade and has written about 600 magazine articles, mostly for *New Scientist*, a popular science magazine published in England. Holmes writes on a wide range of topics in a variety of genres, including profiles and interviews, book reviews, and concept explanations. "In the Blink of an Eye" originally appeared in the *New Scientist* in July 2005.

In the Blink of an Eye
Bob Holmes

Every weekend angler knows to throw back the tiddlers. Likewise, commercial fishermen use large-meshed nets to spare smaller fish. Both are working on the principle that by reducing their haul this way, they can keep fish populations vigorous and healthy. But they could be making a terrible mistake. It is becoming increasingly clear that such well-meaning strategies may actually have the opposite effect to what the fishermen intend.

What they and most of the rest of us have overlooked is evolution—not the familiar glacier-slow process found in textbooks, which takes millennia to work its wonders, but a burbling freshet of evolutionary change that can occur in a matter of years or decades. By leaving the smaller fish, fishermen may be shifting the evolutionary goalposts, reshaping fish species as they go. In fact, biologists are starting to suspect that this phenomenon, which they have dubbed contemporary evolution, is happening all around us. Besides emptying fishing nets, rapid evolutionary change cripples the efforts of doctors and farmers, thwarts trophy hunters in search of the big prize, and frustrates conservation biologists trying to rescue endangered species.

What's more, in the decades to come, the pace of evolution may quicken still further, as human activities transform the Earth, forcing species to adapt or die. That makes our need to understand the forces at work even more compelling. If we know what's going on, we may be able to find ways to control evolution, and even shape it for our benefit and that of the world around us.

Evolutionary biologists have long known that the process can happen rapidly—Charles Darwin himself pointed out the observable changes wrought by pigeon fanciers and dog breeders. A century later biologists showed that peppered moths in England's industrial heartland had evolved darker colours to camouflage themselves against soot-blackened trees. And by the end of the 20th century everyone knew that bacteria, insects and weeds were able to evolve resistance to antibiotics and pesticides

By taking only the biggest cod, fishermen favour fish that grow slowly and stay small.

within a few years. But few thought such speedy evolution was more than just a special case.

"When I was a graduate student in the 1970s, the prevailing idea was that evolution was this gradual, slow process," says David Reznick of the University of California, Riverside. "We already knew there were instances of evolution that people had witnessed, but it was considered to be exceptional, not the usual pattern."

5

The experts had good reason to be sceptical that evolution could happen quickly. After all, evolution is driven by a mismatch between an organism's needs and its abilities to meet them. The prevailing wisdom was that most organisms were already well adapted to their circumstances. Although there would be genetic variation between individuals within a population, no combination of genes would be particularly better adapted than any other, so there would be little pressure for natural selection to favour the survival and reproduction of some individuals over others. In other words, selection would generally be low and evolution slow—except where humans used antibiotics or pesticides to wipe out all but the one-in-a-million resistant individuals, or allowed only the gaudiest pigeons to breed.

6

All Change

But in the 1980s biologists began to realise that adaptation might be a more dynamic process than they had thought. For example, on one of the Galapagos Islands, Peter and Rosemary Grant of Princeton University discovered that among one species of finch, individuals with small beaks do best in wet years, when small-seeded plants thrive, while their larger-beaked nestmates have the edge in drier years, when larger-seeded plants predominate. As a result, beak size see-saws back and forth rapidly.

7

More recently, a team led by Barry Sinervo of the University of California, Santa Cruz, has found the same kind of rapid change in the side-blotched lizard in the southwestern U.S. Male lizards pursue one of three different genetically determined mating strategies, each corresponding with a different throat colour. Orange-throated males are big and aggressive, and easily bully the more timid blue-throated males into ceding their females. Yellow-throated males, which sneak in disguised as females, can steal mating opportunities from the orange males while they are busy blustering, but fail to fool the blue males as these pay close attention to their precious mates. The result is a game of evolutionary rock-paper-scissors, with each strategy becoming dominant every four to five years.

8

No one knows how common this sort of contemporary evolution is, because it is hard to spot in the wild. The change happens so fast that biologists are likely to miss it unless they keep very detailed records of exactly the right characters—a complete reversal of the old view that evolution is too slow to see in real time. "There's no reason this couldn't be going on all the time in organisms all over the place," says Reznick.

9

Nor is rapid evolution confined to the cycling of different versions of the same trait. Sometimes evolution drives steadily in one direction. This may be crucial to our understanding of the biology of invasive species. Biologists have often noted that introduced species, such as zebra mussels or garlic mustard in the U.S., can lurk inconspicuously in

10

Adaptation is a dynamic process for Galapagos finches and side-blotched lizards.

their new home for decades or even centuries before suddenly exploding into problem pests. One possible, though not yet well tested, explanation is that the invaders are at first poorly adapted to their new setting, and cannot take off until they evolve a better match. And once that happens, the result can be dramatic. "Many of these invasions may reflect a genetic shift in the invading population," says Donald Waller from the University of Wisconsin–Madison. "A lot of [organisms] are just a couple of percentage points above or below break-even, so it only takes a little change to make a big difference."

Human activity is changing some ecosystems faster, and more dramatically, than ever before, and strong directional selection may be especially common in these cases. "It's possible these human-induced changes are not just greater, but more consistent and more permanent. They may be resulting in evolutionary changes that are rapid, but may also be persistent as well," says Andrew McAdam from Michigan State University in East Lansing. For example, ivory hunting has favoured the evolution of tuskless elephants in parts of Africa and Asia.

One of the best places to see evolution in action is high in the Rocky Mountains of Alberta, Canada, home of the largest bighorn sheep in North America. Hunters can pay six-figure sums for the right to shoot a big ram, the massive, curling horns of which make it the continent's most highly prized hunting trophy. On one peak, aptly named Ram Mountain, hunting has been so intense that rams can expect to live only a year or two after their horns reach the almost-360-degree curl that makes them a legal target for hunters. Not surprisingly, this has led to intense selection in favour of males whose horns never grow to reach trophy status. 12

Sure enough, a study led by Dave Coltman, now at the University of Alberta in Edmonton, found that average horn size has declined by about 25 per cent over the past 30 years (Nature, vol 426, p 655). And the genetic erosion doesn't end there because larger-horned rams tend to have better genes in general. "You start taking out the prime-quality rams and the next generation will be missing those genes, because their fathers will be lower quality," says Coltman. In other words, every time they pull the trigger, hunters are working against their own long-term interests. "It's a form of artificial selection where instead of getting more of what you want you're actually going to end up with less," he says. 13

The same thing happens at sea, where fishermen are typically only allowed to keep fish larger than a particular size. Three years ago, David Conover from Stony Brook University in New York showed just how counterproductive this might be. 14

Hunting has reduced horn size by a quarter among Canada's bighorn sheep.

Conover and his colleague Stephan Munch simulated intense size-selective fishing on lab populations of a small commercial fish called the Atlantic silverside. After just four generations, fish from the "fished" populations—in which the largest 90 per cent of fish were removed before breeding—averaged barely half the size of fish in the "anti-fished" populations, in which the smallest 90 per cent were removed. As a result of the size difference, the total weight of fish removed (analogous to the fishery harvest) in the fifth generation of the fished population was barely half that of the anti-fished one (Science, vol 297, p 94).

Since then other researchers have shown that cod off the coast of Newfoundland, Canada, have also evolved toward maturing at smaller sizes—presumably as a result of the capture of the largest fish. As well as contributing to the crash of the area's fishery, this shift may also hinder the cod's ability to recover, since small fish produce many fewer eggs than large fish. This could help explain why cod populations have failed to bounce back on the Grand Banks, off south-east Newfoundland, despite closure of the fishery there for the past 13 years.

If contemporary evolution really is a dominant force in heavily fished populations, then fisheries managers may unwittingly be doing just the opposite of what they should to maintain healthy stocks. Instead of catching the biggest fish and letting the rest go, we need to treasure the big fish as bearers of the best genes. One solution, says Conover, would be to let fishers take only medium-sized fish. If we did that, he says, a fish's best strategy would then be to grow through that window as fast as possible. Such a scheme would select for fast growth rates—a big improvement over the present system, which selects for scrawny fish that never reach the minimum catch size.

Turning evolution back from the "dark side" in fisheries can be done, but it won't be easy. "If you had a maximum size limit, under present trawl technology there wouldn't be a way to let the large ones go

15

16

17

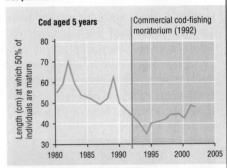

EVOLVING FAST

The adult body size of cod off the Atlantic coast of Labrador, Canada, shrank progressively over the time commercial fishing was permitted

Cod aged 5 years

Commercial cod-fishing moratorium (1992)

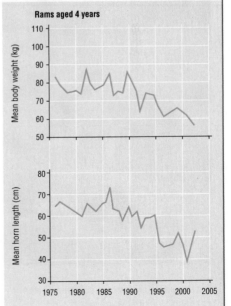

Mature bighorn rams weigh less and have much smaller horns than they did 30 years ago

Rams aged 4 years

except by picking them out on your deck and throwing them back, and a lot of them wouldn't survive," says Conover. But, he notes, modern trawls often use large-mesh metal grates to shunt sea turtles away from the net mouth while allowing fish through, and these might be adapted to exclude large fish as well.

But there is another, more drastic way to put the brakes on evolution: introduce no-fishing zones before stocks become too depleted. Such protected areas provide a refuge where larger fish can survive and continue to produce disproportionate numbers of eggs, so diluting the selection that would otherwise drive fish toward smaller sizes. No-hunting zones for bighorn sheep—or regulations that allow hunters to take a small number of sheep, but of any size—would similarly blunt selection for smaller horns. | 18

Contemporary evolution is not always a bad thing, though. It is already being used to fit microbes for useful work. . . . And with man-made climate change looming, plants and animals will need the ability to adapt quickly. Biologists have noticed that several species have already responded to the warmer temperatures, and hence earlier springs, of the past few years by migrating or breeding earlier. For example, Stan Boutin and his colleagues at the University of Alberta found that red squirrels in Canada's Yukon territory now give birth about 18 days earlier than they did just a decade ago. Using tissue samples to determine each squirrel's parentage, the researchers could see how much of the variation in birth date ran in families. From this they calculated that at least 13 percent of the change—representing a shift of almost a full day per generation—was due to evolution and not behavioural flexibility. | 19

Red squirrels are among several species adapting to global warming.

Fast Forward

Whether evolution can move fast enough to cope with the unprecedented rates of climate change expected over the next century remains to be seen. Clearly though, a species cannot evolve a new adaptation unless it has the right genes—and larger populations are more likely to possess this genetic capital than small ones. This means the losers in the climate-change shuffle are likely to be the species that are already rare. Conservationists might even need to consider abandoning some marginal populations and concentrating on those with the genetic resources to evolve successfully, says Boutin. "That means we maybe don't save every caribou herd in Alberta, but we focus on the ones with the highest probability of success." | 20

And if rapid contemporary evolution really is as widespread as some researchers are beginning to suspect, it has one more unsettling implication: we may have to modify our notion of "preserving" rare species because every effort to rescue a species through captive breeding, founding new wild populations, or modifying existing habitats may cause it to evolve away from its starting point.

"This brings up an interesting philosophical question," says McAdam. "What is it that we're hoping to conserve? Is it particular species, or is it something about those species? Would we be happy if we were able to maintain all the species we have today, but human-induced evolutionary changes were so great that they essentially became functionally domesticated? Would we be satisfied with that? I would say no, that's not satisfying—at least to me."

Making Connections to Personal and Social Issues: Implications of Scientific Research

If it is true, as Holmes explains in paragraph 3, that "human activities transform the Earth, forcing species to adapt or die," then what are our moral responsibilities as individuals and as nations? What can people do to prevent or reverse the climate change that apparently is causing rapid contemporary evolution? *In writing or conversation with two or three other students, discuss your views on these issues:*

- **How can individuals make a difference?** If you drive a gas-guzzling SUV, would you trade it in for a hybrid? Would you take public transportation to school or to work? What do you think your family and friends would be willing to do?

- **What role should government and business play?** Should government provide incentives and/or fines to encourage industry and individuals to adopt "greener" practices? Should the United States join the 175 nations that signed the 1997 Kyoto Protocol designed to reduce emissions of carbon dioxide and other greenhouse gases?

Analyzing Writing Strategies

1. We have said that essays explaining concepts present a **focused concept**. That is, writers do not try to explain everything that is known about the concept, but focus on certain aspects of it that they think will interest readers. Reread the opening paragraphs of Holmes's article to find where he first names the concept he will explain. *In a few sentences, consider:* What is the concept Holmes explains, and how does he focus his explanation?

2. Reread paragraphs 14–17 where Holmes discusses the effects of efforts to protect fish by restricting fishing. *In writing or in discussion with classmates, consider the following:*
   - In paragraph 15, Holmes presents the **problem** of Newfoundland cod. What exactly is the problem with the cod population?

- In paragraphs 16–18, Holmes discusses various **solutions** that have been proposed. Why do you think he devotes so much space to solutions in this relatively brief essay?
- Notice that Holmes first introduced the general problem in paragraph 1. How well does the specific Newfoundland cod problem illustrate the general problem?

Commentary: Explaining Concepts through Illustration

Concepts typically are abstract. They name ideas, not things; therefore, they are often hard to grasp. Among the strategies writers use to bring concepts down to earth is to provide illustrations, as Holmes does in his essay. Holmes uses two kinds of illustration: examples and visuals.

Examples provide specific, often vivid illustrations that help readers understand and remember abstract concepts. Writers explaining concepts may give several brief examples or they may focus on an extended example; often, like Holmes, they do both. Paragraph 4 shows how a writer might sprinkle an explanation with multiple, brief examples. In this short paragraph, Holmes refers to examples of rapid evolutionary changes in pigeons, dogs, peppered moths, bacteria, insects, and weeds. Holmes also develops several paragraph-long examples such as his discussion in paragraph 7 of how Galapagos finches adapt and in paragraph 10 of how invasive species like zebra mussels and garlic mustard can suddenly become "problem pests." Finally, Holmes uses two multiparagraph extended examples: showing how hunting bighorn sheep for their "trophy" horns has led to a reduction in the size of the horns (pars. 12–13) and how catching big Newfoundland cod has endangered the health of the species (15–18). All of these examples help to establish the fact that rapid contemporary evolution exists and that it represents a potential problem for conservationists.

Holmes also illustrates the concept with two kinds of **visuals**: photographs and graphs. The article includes photographs of some of the species used as examples: cod, Galapagos finches, side-blotched lizards, bighorn sheep, and red squirrels. Holmes adds captions, carefully composed to state how these species are affected by the evolutionary process.

Holmes adds a second type of visual—graphs—to emphasize the rapidity of the process of contemporary evolution. Under the heading "Evolving Fast," three graphs are presented with captions. The first graph shows the effect of fishing on the size of Atlantic cod over the last twenty-five years. The caption tells the story that the graph illustrates visually. The next two graphs show how over a thirty-year period hunting has affected both the bighorn rams' weight and the size of their horns. These graphs show at a glance the significant change that has occurred over a relatively short time.

When you are planning your essay, you will undoubtedly want to include examples—every essay in this chapter relies on examples. But you should also consider whether visuals might be added to illustrate and clarify your concept.

Considering Topics for Your Own Essay

Holmes refers to several concepts you might consider explaining, such as conservation, endangered species, natural and artificial selection, ecosystems, and global warming. You may also be interested in exploring related concepts like biodiversity, genetic drift, creationism, and intelligent design. Concepts related to global warming include the greenhouse effect, ozone depletion, renewable energy, fuel cells, and hybrid technology.

■ Purpose and Audience

Though it seeks to engage readers' interests, explanatory writing gives prominence to facts about a subject. It aims to engage readers' intellect rather than their imagination, to instruct rather than entertain or argue.

Setting out to teach readers about a concept is no small undertaking. To succeed, you must know the concept so well that you can explain it simply, with a minimum of jargon or other potentially off-putting language. You must also estimate what your readers already know about the concept. You need to define unfamiliar words and pace the information carefully so that your readers are neither bored nor overwhelmed.

This assignment requires a willingness to cast yourself in the role of expert. Like Toufexis and Holmes, you could assume a general audience of informed adults, people who regularly read a newspaper, magazines, or Internet sites. If your readers are unfamiliar with the concept, you will be introducing it to them. If they know something about the concept, the particular focus you have chosen may broaden their knowledge. If you choose a concept in a course you are currently taking, explaining it may help you understand it better and make it more interesting and comprehensible to other students as well. Even if you are told to consider your instructor your sole reader, you can assume that your instructor will be eager to be informed.

Basic Features: Explaining a Concept

A Focused Concept

The primary purpose for explaining a concept is to inform readers, but writers of explanatory essays do not hope to communicate everything that is known about a concept. Instead, they make choices about what to include and what to emphasize. Most writers focus their explanations by discussing a particular aspect of the concept. Linh Kieu Ngo, for example, focuses on three specific types of cannibalism. Anastasia Toufexis centers her explanation of love on evolutionary biology and neurochemistry. Bob Holmes's explanation of rapid contemporary evolution zeroes in on the role humans play in it and whether that role should change.

An Appeal to Reader's Interests

Because most people read explanations of concepts for work or study, they expect the writing to be informative, but not necessarily entertaining. Yet readers appreciate explanations that engage them with lively writing and vivid detail. The essays in this chapter show some of the ways in which writers may appeal to readers. For example, Toufexis uses everyday language and humor, opening her essay with this direct address to readers: "O.K., let's cut out all this nonsense about romantic love." Ngo opens his essay with a dramatic anecdote about a horrendous situation in which a group of refugees found themselves. Holmes tries to surprise readers by telling them that what fishermen typically do to "keep fish populations vigorous and healthy" actually may endanger these populations. Strategies like these can do much to interest readers in the concept.

A Logical Plan

Since concept explanations present information that is new to readers, writers need to develop a plan that presents material clearly and logically. The most effective explanations give readers all the obvious cues they need, such as forecasting statements, topic sentences, transitions, and summaries. In addition, the writer may try to frame the essay for readers by relating the ending to the beginning. We see these features in the readings in this chapter. For example, Toufexis frames her essay with references to Ph.D.s, forecasts the three sciences from which she has gleaned her information about the neurochemistry of love, and begins nearly all of her paragraphs with a transition sentence. Following the opening anecdote, Ngo organizes his essay around the three kinds of cannibalism he introduces in paragraph 6. After discussing the first type, survival cannibalism (par. 7), his topic sentences make a transition from one type to another: "Unlike survival cannibalism, in which . . ., in dietary cannibalism humans are . . ." (8); and "Religious or ritual cannibalism is different from survival and dietary cannibalism in that it . . ." (11).

Clear Definitions

Essays explaining concepts depend on clear definitions. Any key terms that are likely to be unfamiliar or misunderstood must be explicitly defined, as Toufexis defines *attraction junkies* (par. 12) and *endorphins* (13), as Ngo defines the categories of cannibalism (6), and as Holmes defines *rapid contemporary evolution.*

Careful Use of Sources

To explain concepts, writers often draw on their own experiences and observations, but they almost always do additional research into what others have to say about their subject. Referring to expert sources lends authority to an explanation.

How writers treat sources depends on the writing situation. Certain formal situations, such as college assignments or scholarly papers, have rules for citing and documenting sources. Students and scholars are expected to cite their sources formally because readers judge their work in part by what the writers have read and how they have used their reading. Ngo's essay illustrates this academic form of citing sources. For more informal writing — magazine articles, for example — readers do not expect or want page references or publication information, but they do expect sources to be identified. This identification often appears within the text of the article, for example, when Holmes quotes several authorities and summarizes the findings of their research, being careful to identify each source by name and university affiliation. In two instances (pars. 13 and 14), he also gives a parenthetical citation with the journal name, volume number, and page number in case readers want to look up the research themselves.

Explaining a Concept

Invention and Research

What is a concept that you enjoy explaining to other people — or would like to learn more about? How much do you already know about it? Do some library or online research if necessary, and do some thinking and writing about the concept. Then consider how you'd interest readers in it and explain it clearly to them. . . . **See p. 125 for more.**

Planning and Drafting

As you look over what you have written so far, how can you present the concept clearly to readers and engage their interest? How much do they already know about it? What terms do you need to define? What organization would be easiest to follow? Make a plan for your explanation, and start drafting it. . . . **See p. 131 for more.**

Critical Reading Guide

What are your draft's strengths and weaknesses? For example, does your focus seem too broad? Would visuals or better transitions make your explanation clearer? Get a classmate, a friend, a writing tutor, or someone else to read and respond in detail to your essay, focusing especially on the parts you are most unsure of. . . . **See p. 135 for more.**

Revising

As you consider your essay again in light of your reader's comments, how can you improve it? If the beginning failed to engage the reader's interest, how else could you begin? How could you integrate quotations more smoothly into your own text? Go through your draft systematically, making changes wherever necessary. . . . **See p. 136 for more.**

Editing and Proofreading

Have you checked for errors that are especially likely in explanations of concepts? Have you forgotten to include commas around adjective clauses that are not essential to the meaning or around phrases that interrupt the flow of a sentence? Look for and correct these and any other errors. . . . **See p. 140 for more.**

☐ The Writing Assignment

Write an essay about a concept that interests you and that you want to study further. When you have a good understanding of the concept, explain it to your readers, considering carefully what they already know about it and how your essay might add to what they know.

▦ Invention and Research

The following guidelines will help you find a concept, understand it fully, select a focus that is appropriate for your readers, test your choice, and devise strategies for presenting your discoveries in a way that will be truly informative for your particular readers. Keep a written record of your invention work to use when you draft the essay and later when you revise it.

Finding a Concept to Write About

Even if you already have a concept in mind, completing the following activities will help you to be certain of your choice.

Listing Concepts.   *Make a list of concepts you could write about.* The longer your list, the more likely you are to find the right concept, and should your first choice not work out, you will have a ready list of alternatives. Your courses cover many concepts you will want to consider, so take a look at your class notes or textbooks for some ideas. Include concepts you already know something about as well as some that are entirely new to you. Also include concepts suggested by the Considering Topics for Your Own Essay activities following the readings in this chapter.

■ *Listing Concepts Related to Coursework.* Here are some suggestions organized by subject:

- *Literature:* irony, semiotics, hero, utopia and dystopia, picaresque, canon, identity politics
- *Philosophy:* existentialism, nihilism, determinism, ethics, natural law, Zeno's paradox, ideology
- *Business management:* quality circle, cybernetic control system, management by objectives, zero-based budgeting, liquidity gap
- *Psychology:* Hawthorne effect, social cognition, intelligence, divergent/convergent thinking, operant conditioning, the Stroop effect
- *Government:* majority rule, minority rights, federalism, political party, political machine, interest group, hegemony
- *Biology:* photosynthesis, mitosis, morphogenesis, plasmolysis, phagocytosis, homozygosity

125

- *Art:* cubism, Dadaism, surrealism, expressionism
- *Math:* boundedness, null space, factoring, Rolle's theorem, continuity, indefinite integral
- *Physical sciences:* matter, gravity, atomic theory, osmotic pressure, first law of thermodynamics, entropy
- *Public health:* alcoholism, seasonal affective disorder, contraception, lead poisoning, prenatal care, glycemic index
- *Environmental studies:* acid rain, recycling, ozone depletion, toxic waste, sustainability
- *Sports:* squeeze play, hit and run (baseball); power play (hockey); nickel defense, wishbone offense (football); pick and roll, inside game (basketball)
- *Personal finance:* reverse mortgage, budget, revolving credit, interest rates, bankruptcy, socially conscious investing
- *Law:* garnishment, double indemnity, reasonable doubt, class-action suits, product liability
- *Sociology:* norm, deviance, ethnocentrism, class, conflict theory, action theory, Whorf-Sapir hypothesis, machismo

■ *Listing Concepts Related to Identity and Community.* If you decide to focus on identity and community, consider the following concepts: self-esteem, character, personality, autonomy, narcissism, multiculturalism, ethnicity, race, racism, social contract, social Darwinism, colonialism, the other, yuppie, generation Y.

■ *Listing Concepts Related to Work and Career.* Concepts like the following enable you to gain a deeper understanding of your work experiences and career aspirations: free enterprise, affirmative action, sweatshop, glass ceiling, downsizing, collective bargaining, service sector, entrepreneur, monopoly, automation, management style, deregulation, multinational corporation.

Choosing a Concept. *Look over your list of possibilities and select one concept to explore.* Pick a concept that you feel eager to learn more about. Consider also whether it might interest others. You may know very little about the concept now, but the guidelines that follow will help you research it and understand it better.

Gaining an Overview of the Concept

Your research efforts for a concept essay must be divided into two stages. First, you want to gain an overview of the concept you have chosen. Your goal in this first stage is to learn as much as you can from diverse sources so that you may decide whether you want to write about this topic and, if so, identify an aspect of it to focus on.

In the second stage, when you know what your focus will be, you begin in-depth research for information.

The activities that follow will guide you through this two-stage research process.

Discovering What You Already Know. *Before doing any research on your concept, take a few minutes to write about what you already know about the concept.* Also explain why you have chosen the concept and why you find it interesting. Write quickly, without planning or organizing. Note whatever you know as well as questions about the concept. You could even add drawings.

Sorting Through Your Personal Resources. *Check any materials you already have at hand that explain your concept.* If you are considering a concept from one of your academic courses, you will likely find explanatory material in your textbook or your lecture notes.

To acquire a comprehensive, up-to-date understanding of your concept, however, you will need to know how other experts define and illustrate it. To find this information, you might locate relevant articles and books in the library, search for resources or make inquiries on the Internet, or consult experts on campus or in the community.

Going to the Library. To learn about your concept and explore aspects that you could focus on, you may want to do some research in the library. Ask the librarian for help finding relevant encyclopedias, disciplinary guides, databases, or online resources available through the library. While at the library, look for your concept name in the subject headings of the Library of Congress Subject Headings and search the book catalog, using the keyword search option. Chapter 13, Library and Internet Research, has general information that will help you use your college library productively. Be sure to take notes of any potentially useful information or make a photocopy and write down the exact source information for your Works Cited list.

Going Online. An Internet search could turn up interesting information about your concept and help you find a focus for your essay. Bookmark Web sites you find that invite more than a quick glance, and copy into a word processing document any potentially useful information—making sure to include the URL, the title of the site, the date the information was posted (if available), and the date you accessed the site. Remember, your goal at this stage is to educate yourself quickly about the concept and look for a possible focus for your essay, so it is too early to begin printing or downloading a lot of material.

An Online Activity:
Researching
Concepts

One way to get a quick initial overview of the information available on a concept is to search for the concept online. Enter the name of your concept in a search tool such as Google (http://www.google.com) or Yahoo! Directory (http://dir.yahoo.com).

You might want to try entering the word "overview" or "definition" together with the name of your concept, in order to confine your results to introductions and overviews.

Bookmark or keep a record of promising sites. As always, if your first searches don't turn up much of use, be sure to try variations on the search terms you use.

Focusing the Concept

Once you have an overview of your concept, you must choose a focus for your essay. Concepts can be approached from many perspectives (for example, history, definition, known causes or effects), so you must limit your explanation. Because the focus must reflect both your special interest in the concept and your readers' likely knowledge and interest, you will want to explore both.

Exploring Your Own Interests.   *Make a list of two or three aspects of the concept that could become a focus for your essay, and evaluate what you know about each focus.* Leave some space after each item in the list. Under each possible focus in your list, make notes about why it interests you, what you know about it already, and what questions you want to answer about it.

Analyzing Your Readers.   *Take a few minutes to analyze your readers in writing.* Think about who your prospective readers are likely to be and speculate about their knowledge of and interest in the concept. Even if you are writing only for your instructor, you should give some thought to what he or she knows and thinks about the concept.

The following questions are designed to help you with your analysis:

- Who are my readers, and what are they likely to know about this concept?
- What, if anything, might they know about related concepts?
- What would be useful for them to know about this concept, perhaps something that could relate to their life or work?

Choosing a Focus.   *With your interests and those of your readers in mind, choose an aspect of your concept on which to focus, and write a sentence justifying its appropriateness.*

Testing Your Choice

Decide whether you should proceed with this particular concept and focus. As painful as it may be to consider, starting over with a new concept is better than continuing with an unworkable one. The questions and the collaborative activity that follow will help you test your choice.

- *Can I learn what I need to know in the time I have available to write a concept explanation with this focus?*
- *Am I likely to understand the concept well enough to make it clear to my readers?*
- *Do I feel a personal interest in the concept and the particular focus I have chosen?* If so, what is the basis for this interest? Is the concept so interesting to me that I am willing to spend the next two or three weeks on an essay explaining it?
- *Do I think I can make the concept and the focus I have chosen interesting to readers?* Can I relate the concept to something readers already know? Can I think of any anecdotes or examples that will make the concept more meaningful to them?

A Collaborative Activity: Testing Your Choice	Get together with two or three other students to find out what your readers are likely to know about your subject and what might interest them about it.

Presenters: Take turns briefly explaining your concept, describing your intended readers, and identifying the aspect of the concept that you will focus on.

Listeners: Briefly tell the presenter whether the focus sounds appropriate and interesting for the intended readers. Share what you think readers are likely to know about the concept and what information might be especially interesting to them.

Researching Your Topic Focus

Now begins stage two of your research process. With a likely focus in mind, you are ready to mine both the Internet and the library for information. You will now want to keep careful records of all sources you believe will contribute in any way to your essay. If possible, make photocopies of print sources, and print out sources you download from CD-ROMs or the Internet. If you must rely on notes, be sure to copy any quotations exactly and enclose them in quotation marks.

Since you do not know which sources you will ultimately use, keep a careful record of the author, title, publication information, page numbers, and other required information for each source you gather. Check with your instructor about whether you should follow the documentation style of the Modern Language Association (MLA), the American Psychological Association (APA), or a different style. In this chapter, the Ngo essay follows the MLA style.

Going Online.   *Return to online searching, with your focus in mind.* Download and print out essential material if possible, or take careful notes. Record all of the details you will need in order to acknowledge sources in your essay.

Going to the Library.   *Return to the library to search for materials relevant to your focus.* Photocopy, print out, or take notes on promising print and electronic materials. Keep careful records so that you can acknowledge your sources.

Considering Explanatory Strategies

Before you move on to plan and draft your essay, consider some possible ways of presenting the concept. Try to answer each of the following questions in a sentence or two. Questions that you can answer readily may identify the best strategies for presenting your focus.

- What term is used to name the concept, and what does it mean? (definition)
- How is this concept like or unlike related concepts? (comparison and contrast)
- How can an explanation of this concept be divided into parts? (classification)

- How does this concept happen, or how does one go about doing it? (process narration)
- What are this concept's known causes or effects? (cause and effect)
- What examples can make the concept less abstract and more memorable? (example)

Designing Your Document

Think about whether visual elements—tables, graphs, drawings, photographs—would make your explanation clearer. These are not a requirement, but they could be helpful. Consider also whether your readers might benefit from design features such as headings, bulleted or numbered lists, or other elements that would present information efficiently or make your explanation easier to follow. You could construct your own graphic elements (using word processing software to create bar graphs or pie charts, for example), download materials from the Internet, copy images from television or DVDs, or scan visuals from books and magazines. Remember that you must cite the source of any visual you do not create yourself, and you should also request permission from the source of the visual if your paper is going to be posted on a Web site that is not password-protected.

Defining Your Purpose for Your Readers

Write a few sentences that define your purpose in writing about this particular concept for your readers. Remember that you have already identified and analyzed your readers and that you have begun to research and develop your explanation with these readers in mind. Try now to define your purpose in explaining the concept to them. Use these questions to focus your thoughts:

- Are my readers familiar with the concept? If not, how can I relate it to what they already know? If so, will my focus allow my readers to see the familiar concept in a new light?
- If I suspect that my readers have misconceptions about the concept, how can I correct the misconceptions without offending readers?
- Will I need to arouse readers' interest in information that may seem at first to be less than engaging?
- Do I want readers to see that the information I have to report is relevant to their lives, families, communities, work, or studies?

Formulating a Tentative Thesis Statement

Write one or more sentences, stating your concept and focus, that could serve as a thesis statement. You might also want to forecast the topics you will use to explain the concept.

Anastasia Toufexis begins her essay with this thesis statement:

O.K., let's cut out all this nonsense about romantic love. Let's bring some scientific precision to the party. Let's put love under a microscope.

When rigorous people with Ph.D.s after their names do that, what they see is not some silly, senseless thing. No, their probe reveals that love rests firmly on the foundations of evolution, biology and chemistry.

Toufexis's concept is love, and her focus is the scientific explanation of love — specifically the evolution, biology, and chemistry of love. In announcing her focus, she forecasts the order in which she will present information from the three most relevant academic disciplines — anthropology (which includes the study of human evolution), biology, and chemistry. These discipline names become her topics.

In his essay on cannibalism, Linh Kieu Ngo offers his thesis statement in paragraph 6:

Cannibalism can be broken down into two main categories: exocannibalism, the eating of outsiders or foreigners, and endocannibalism, the eating of members of one's own social group (Shipman 70). Within these categories are several functional types of cannibalism, three of the most common being survival cannibalism, dietary cannibalism, and religious and ritual cannibalism.

Ngo's concept is cannibalism, and his focus is on three common types of cannibalism. He carefully forecasts how he will divide the information to create topics and the order in which he will explain each of the topics.

As you draft your own tentative thesis statement, take care to make the language clear. Although you may want to revise your thesis statement as you draft your essay, trying to state it now will give your planning and drafting more focus and direction. Keep in mind that the thesis in an explanatory essay merely announces the subject; it never asserts a position that requires an argument to defend it.

■ Planning and Drafting

The following guidelines will help you get the most out of your invention notes, determine specific goals for your essay, and write a first draft.

Seeing What You Have

Reread everything you have written so far. This is a critically important time for reflection and evaluation. Before beginning the actual draft, you must decide whether your subject is worthwhile and whether you have sufficient information for a successful essay.

It may help, as you read, to annotate your invention writings. Look for details that will help you explain the concept in a way that your readers can grasp. Highlight key words, phrases, or sentences; make notes on any material you think could be useful.

Be realistic. If at this point your notes do not look promising, you may want to choose a different focus or even a different concept. If your notes seem thin but promising, do further research to find more information before continuing.

Setting Goals

Successful writers are always looking beyond the next sentence to larger goals. Indeed, the next sentence is easier to write if you keep larger goals in mind. The following questions can help you set these goals. Consider each one now, and then return to them as necessary while you write.

Your Purpose and Readers

- How can I build on my readers' knowledge?
- What new information can I present to them?
- How can I organize my essay so that my readers can follow it easily?
- What tone would be most appropriate? Would an informal tone like Toufexis's or a formal one like Ngo's be more appropriate to my purpose?

The Beginning

- Can I begin in a way that will interest readers? Should I open with a provocative quotation, as Toufexis does? With an anecdote illustrating the concept, as Ngo does? With a startling example, as Holmes does?
- How can I orient readers? Should I forecast the topics I will address, as Toufexis and Ngo do?

Presentation of the Information

- Should I name and define my concept early in the essay, as Ngo, Toufexis, and Holmes do?
- Could I develop my explanation by dividing my concept into different categories, as Ngo does? By giving a series of examples, like Holmes?
- How can I establish the authority of my sources? Should I give their names and credentials, as Toufexis and Holmes do? Refer to specific publications or research, as Ngo, Toufexis, and Holmes do? Will my instructor require me to use the MLA, APA, or some other documentation style, as Ngo's instructor did?
- How can I make it easy for readers to follow my explanation? Should I simply use clear and explicit transitions when I move from one topic to another, as Ngo does? Should I use headings and visuals, like Holmes?

The Ending

- Should I frame the essay by relating the ending to the beginning, as Toufexis and Holmes do?
- Should I end with a speculation, as Ngo does?
- Should I end by formulating a question suggested by the concept, as Holmes does?

Outlining

The goals that you have set should help you draft your essay, but first you might want to make a quick scratch outline. In your outline, list the main topics into which you have divided the information about your concept. Use this outline to guide your drafting, but do not feel tied to it. As you draft, you may find a better way to sequence the action and integrate these features.

An essay explaining a concept is made up of four basic parts:

- An attempt to engage readers' interest
- The thesis statement, announcing the concept, its focus, and its topics
- An orientation to the concept, which may include a description or definition of the concept
- Information about the concept

Here is a possible outline for an essay explaining a concept:

An attempt to gain readers' interest in the concept

Thesis statement

Definition of the concept

Topic 1 with illustration

Topic 2 with illustration

(etc.)

Conclusion

An attempt to gain readers' interest could take as little as two or three sentences or as much as four or five paragraphs. The thesis statement and definition are usually quite brief—sometimes only a few sentences. A topic illustration may occupy one or several paragraphs, and there can be few or many topics, depending on how the information has been divided up. A conclusion might summarize the information presented, give advice about how to use or apply the information, or speculate about the future of the concept.

Drafting

General Advice.   Start drafting your essay, keeping in mind the goals you set while you were planning. Remember also the needs and expectations of your readers; organize, define, and explain with them in mind. Work to increase readers' understanding of your concept. Turn off your grammar checker and spelling checker at this stage if you find them distracting. Do not be afraid to skip around in your document. Jump back and fill in a spontaneous idea, or leap ahead and write a later section first if you find that easier. If you get stuck while drafting, try using some of the writing activities in the Invention and Research section of this chapter.

A Sentence Strategy: Appositives.   As you draft an essay explaining a concept, you have a lot of information to present, such as definitions of terms and credentials of experts. **Appositives** provide an efficient, clear way to integrate these kinds of information into your sentences. An appositive can be defined as a noun or pronoun, that, along with modifiers, gives more information about another noun or pronoun. Here is an example from Linh Kieu Ngo's concept essay (the appositive is in italics and the noun it refers to is underlined):

> Cannibalism, *the act of human beings eating human flesh* (Sagan 2), has a long history and continues to hold interest and create controversy. (par. 5)

By placing the definition in an appositive phrase right after the word it defines, this sentence locates the definition exactly where readers need it.

Not only are they a precise way to present information, but appositives are efficient. By using an appositive, Ngo merges two potential sentences into one or shrinks a potential clause to a phrase:

> Cannibalism can be defined as the act of human beings eating human flesh. It has a long history and continues to hold interest and create controversy.

> Cannibalism, which can be defined as the act of human beings eating human flesh, has a long history and continues to hold interest and create controversy.

Appositives serve many different purposes in concept essays, as the following examples demonstrate. (Again, the appositive is in italics and the noun it refers to is underlined.)

Defining a New Term

> Cannibalism can be broken down into two main categories: exocannibalism, *the eating of outsiders or foreigners,* and endocannibalism, *the eating of members of one's own social group* (Shipman 70). (Ngo, par. 6)

Introducing a New Term

> Each person carries in his or her mind a unique subliminal guide to the ideal partner, *a "love map."* (Toufexis, 17)

Giving Credentials of Experts

> "Love is a natural high," observes Anthony Walsh, *author of The Science of Love: Understanding Love and Its Effects on Mind and Body.* (Toufexis, 10)

Identifying People and Things

> One of the best places to see evolution in action is high in the Rocky Mountains of Alberta, Canada, *home of the largest bighorn sheep in North America.* (Holmes, 12)

Giving Examples or Specifics

> . . . they had lost *the only person who knew the way to Malaysia,* the captain. (Ngo, 1)

For more on using appositives, go to **bedfordstmartins.com/conciseguide** and click on Sentence Strategies.

Critical Reading Guide

Now is the time to get a good critical reading of your draft. Your instructor may arrange such a reading as part of your coursework—in class or online. If not, you can ask a classmate to read your draft using this guide. If your campus has a writing center, you might ask a tutor there to read and comment on your draft. (If you are unable to have someone else review your draft, turn ahead to the Revision section for help reading your own draft with a critical eye.)

▶ **If You Are the Writer.** To provide focused, helpful comments, your reader must know your essay's intended audience, your purpose, and a problem in the draft that you need help solving. Briefly write out this information at the top of your draft.

> **Making Comments Electronically**
> Most word processing software allows you to insert comments directly into the text of a document. Many readers prefer to make their comments in this way because it tends to be faster than writing on a hard copy and space is virtually unlimited; it also eliminates the problem of deciphering handwritten comments. Where such features are not available, simply typing comments directly into a document in a contrasting color can provide the same advantages.

- *Audience:* To whom are you directing your concept explanation? What do you assume they know about the concept? How do you plan to engage and hold their interest?
- *Purpose:* What do you hope to achieve with your essay?
- *Problem:* Describe the most important problem you see in the draft.

▶ **If You Are the Reader.** Use the following guidelines for giving constructive, helpful comments on essays explaining concepts.

1. *Read for a First Impression.* Read first to get a sense of the concept. Then briefly write out your impressions. What in the draft do you think will especially interest the intended readers? Where might they have difficulty in following the explanation? Next, consider the problem the writer identified, and respond briefly to that concern. (If you find that the problem is covered by one of the other guidelines listed below, respond to it in more detail there if necessary.)

2. *Assess Whether the Concept Is Clearly Explained and Focused.* Restate, in one sentence, what you understand the concept to mean. Indicate any confusion or uncertainty you have about its meaning. Does the focus seem appropriate, too broad, or too narrow for the intended readers? Can you think of a more interesting focus?

3. *Consider Whether the Content Is Appropriate for the Intended Readers.* Does it tell them all that they are likely to want to know about the concept?

Can you suggest additional information that should be included? Point out any information that seems either superfluous or too predictable.

4. ***Evaluate the Organization.***   Look at the way the essay is organized by making a scratch outline. Does the information seem to be logically divided? If not, suggest a better way to divide it. Also consider the order or sequence of information. Can you suggest a better way of sequencing it?

   - Look at the *beginning*. Does it pull readers into the essay and make them want to continue? Does it adequately forecast the direction of the essay? If possible, suggest a better way to begin.
   - Look for obvious *transitions* in the draft. Tell the writer how they are helpful or unhelpful. Try to improve one or two of them. Look for additional places where transitions would be helpful.
   - Look at the *ending*. Explain what makes it particularly effective or less effective than it might be, in your opinion. If you can, suggest a better way to end.

5. ***Assess the Clarity of Definitions.***   Point out any definitions that may be unclear or confusing to the intended readers. Identify any other terms that may need to be defined.

6. ***Evaluate the Use of Sources.***   If the writer has used sources, review the list of sources cited. Given the purpose, readers, and focus of the essay, does the list seem balanced and appropriate? Then consider the use of sources within the essay. Are there places where summary or paraphrase would be preferable to quoted material or vice versa? Note any places where the writer has placed quotations awkwardly into the text, and recommend ways to smooth them out.

7. ***Evaluate the Effectiveness of Visuals.***   If charts, graphs, tables, or other visuals are included, let the writer know whether they help you understand the concept. Suggest ideas you have for changing, adding, moving, or deleting visuals.

8. ***Give the Writer Your Final Thoughts.***   Which part needs the most work? What do you think the intended readers will find most informative or memorable? What do you like best about the draft essay?

For a printable version of this critical reading guide, go to **bedfordstmartins.com/ conciseguide.**

■ Revising

This section will help you get an overview of your draft and revise it accordingly.

Getting an Overview

Consider your draft as a whole. It may help to do so in two steps:

1. *Reread.*   If at all possible, put the draft aside for a day or two before rereading it. When you return to it, start by reconsidering your readers and purpose. Then read the draft straight through, trying to see it as your intended readers will.

2. *Outline.*   Make a scratch outline to get an overview of the essay's development.

Planning for Revision.   Resist the temptation to dive in and start changing your text until after you have a clear view of the big picture. Using your outline as a guide, move through the document, noting comments received from others and problems you want to solve.

Analyzing the Basic Features of Your Own Draft.   Using the Critical Reading Guide on the preceding pages, reread the draft to identify problems you need to solve. Note the problems on your draft.

Studying Readers' Comments. Review all of the comments you have received from other readers, and add to your notes any that you intend to act on. Try not to react defensively. For each comment, look at the draft to determine what might have led the reader to make the comment. By letting you see how others respond to your draft, these comments provide valuable information about how you might improve it.

Working with Sources

Using descriptive verbs to introduce information from sources

When explaining concepts, writers usually need to present information from different sources. There are many verbs writers can choose to introduce the information they quote or summarize. Here are a few examples from the concept essays in this chapter (the verbs are in italics):

"When I was a graduate student in the 1970s, the prevailing idea was that evolution was this gradual, slow process," *says* David Reznick of the University of California, Riverside. (Holmes, par. 5)

"That is one reason why it feels so horrible when we're abandoned or a lover dies," *notes* Fisher. (Toufexis, 13)

In one incident, Japanese troops *were reported* to have sacrificed the Arapesh people of northeastern New Guinea for food in order to avoid death by starvation (Tuzin 63). (Ngo, 7)

By using the verb *says*, Holmes takes a neutral stance toward the information he got from Reznick. Similarly, Toufexis's *notes* and Ngo's *were reported* indicate that they are not characterizing or judging their sources, but simply reporting them.

Often, however, writers are more descriptive — even evaluative — when they introduce information from sources, as these examples demonstrate:

> For example, on one of the Galapagos Islands, Peter and Rosemary Grant of Princeton University *discovered* that among one species of finch, individuals with small beaks do best in wet years, when small-seeded plants thrive, while their larger-beaked nestmates have the edge in drier years, when larger-seeded plants predominate. (Holmes, 7)

> "As long as prehistoric females were secretive about their extramarital affairs," *argues* Fisher, "they could garner extra resources, life insurance, better genes and more varied DNA for their biological futures. . . ." (Toufexis, 8)

> Lovers . . . are literally flooded by chemicals, research *suggests*. (Toufexis, 9)

The verbs in these examples — *discovered, argues,* and *suggests* — do not neutrally report the source material but describe the particular role played by the source in explaining the concept. Verbs like *found, showed,* and *discovered* are used to introduce information resulting from scientific research. When Holmes explains what Peter and Rosemary Grant *discovered* about finches, he is demonstrating that the concept of rapid contemporary evolution has been supported by research. In contrast, verbs like *contends* and *argues* emphasize that what is being reported is an interpretation that others may disagree with. *Suggests* indicates that in this case Toufexis is referring to broad implications of research rather than to specific findings.

As you refer to sources in your concept explanation, you will want to choose carefully among a wide variety of precise verbs. Every writer in this chapter uses many different verbs in an effort to help readers better understand how he or she is using each source. You may find these additional verbs helpful in introducing your sources: *reveals, recalls, looks at, questions, brings into focus, pulls together, tries to understand, documents, finds, notices, observes, emphasizes.* When you are introducing sources in an argumentative essay, you will want to draw from verbs such as *argues, contends, asserts, claims, supports, refutes, repudiates, advocates, contradicts, rejects, corroborates, acknowledges.* You can find more information about integrating sources into your sentences and constructing signal phrases in Chapter 14, Using Sources.

Notice that except for one quote in paragraph 7, Ngo does not introduce his sources in the body of his essay. Here is an example from paragraph 9:

> The Miyanmin people observe no differences in "gender, kinship, ritual status, and bodily substance"; they eat anyone, even their own dead. In this respect, then, they practice both endocannibalism and exocannibalism; and to ensure a constant supply of human flesh for food, they raid neighboring tribes and drag their victims back to their village to be eaten (Poole 11).

This strategy of integrating but not introducing source material allows Ngo to emphasize the information and play down the source.

For help working with sources, go to **bedfordstmartins.com/conciseguide**.

Carrying Out Revisions

Having identified problems in your draft, you now need to come up with solutions and—most important—to carry them out. Basically, there are three ways to find solutions:

1. Review your invention and planning notes and your sources for information and ideas to add to the draft.

2. Do further invention or research to answer questions your readers raised.

3. Look back at the readings in this chapter to see how other writers have solved similar problems.

The following suggestions, which are organized according to the basic features of explanatory essays, will get you started solving some common writing problems.

A Focused Concept

- *Is the focus too broad?* Consider limiting it further so that you can explain one part of the concept in more depth. If readers were uninterested in the aspect you focused on, consider focusing on some other aspect.

- *Is the focus too narrow?* You may have isolated too minor an aspect. Go back to your invention and research notes, and look for larger or more significant aspects.

An Appeal to Readers' Interests

- *Do you fail to connect to readers' interests and engage their attention throughout the essay?* Help readers see the significance of the information to them personally. Eliminate superfluous or too-predictable content. Open with an unusual piece of information that catches readers' interest.

- *Do you think readers will have unanswered questions?* Review your invention writing and sources to answer them.

A Logical Plan

- *Does the beginning successfully orient readers to your purpose and plan?* Try making your focus obvious immediately. Forecast the plan of your essay.

- *Is the explanation difficult to follow?* Look for a way to reorder the parts so that the essay is easier to follow. Add transitions or summaries to help keep readers on track. Or consider ways you might classify and divide the information to make it easier to understand or provide a more interesting perspective.

- *Is the ending inconclusive?* Consider moving important information there. Try summarizing highlights of the essay or framing it by referring to something in the beginning. Or you might speculate about the future of the concept or assert its usefulness.

Clear Definitions

- *Do readers need a clearer or fuller definition of the concept?* Add a concise definition early in your essay, or consider adding a brief summary that defines the concept later in the essay (in the middle or at the end). Remove any information that may blur readers' understanding of the concept.

- *Are other key terms inadequately defined?* Supply clear definitions, searching your sources or checking a dictionary if necessary.

Careful Use of Sources

- *Do readers find your sources inadequate?* Return to the library or the Internet to find additional ones. Consider dropping weak or less reliable sources. Make sure that your sources provide coverage in a comprehensive, balanced way.

- *Do you rely too much on quoting, summarizing, or paraphrasing?* Change some of your quotations to summaries or paraphrases, or vice versa.

> **A Note on Grammar and Spelling Checkers**
> These tools are good at catching certain types of errors, but currently there is no replacement for a good human proofreader. Grammar checkers in particular are extremely limited in what they can find. They also tend to give faulty advice and flag correct items as wrong. Spelling checkers cause fewer problems but cannot catch misspellings that are themselves words, such as *to* for *too*.

- *Does quoted material need to be more smoothly integrated into your own text?* Revise to make it so. Remember to use precise verbs to introduce sources and authors.

- *Are there discrepancies between your in-text citations and the entries in your list of sources?* Compare each citation and entry against the examples given in Chapter 14 for the documentation style you are using. Be sure that all of the citations and entries follow the style exactly. Check to see that your list of sources has an entry for each source that you cite in the text.

For a revision checklist, go to **bedfordstmartins.com/conciseguide.**

■ Editing and Proofreading

Now is the time to check your revised draft carefully for errors in usage, punctuation, and mechanics and to consider matters of style. Our research on students' writing has identified several errors that are especially common in writing that explains concepts. The following guidelines will help you check and edit your essay for these errors.

Checking the Punctuation of Adjective Clauses.   Adjective clauses include both a subject and a verb. They give information about a noun or a pronoun. They often begin with *who, which,* or *that.* Here is an example from a student essay explaining the concept of schizophrenia, a type of mental illness:

> **It is common for schizophrenics to have delusions** *that they are being persecuted.*

Because adjective clauses add information about the nouns they follow — defining, illustrating, or explaining — they can be useful in writing that explains a concept.

Adjective clauses may or may not need to be set off with a comma or commas. To decide, first you have to determine whether the clause is essential to the meaning of the sentence. Clauses that are essential to the meaning of a sentence should not be set off with a comma; clauses that are not essential to the meaning must be set off with a comma. Here are two examples from the student essay about schizophrenia:

ESSENTIAL   **It is common for schizophrenics to have delusions** *that they are being persecuted.*

The adjective clause defines and limits the word *delusions.* If the clause were removed, the basic meaning of the sentence would change, saying that schizophrenics commonly have delusions of all sorts.

NONESSENTIAL   **Related to delusions are hallucinations,** *which are very common in schizophrenics.*

The adjective clause gives information that is not essential to understanding the main clause (*Related to delusions are hallucinations*). Taking away the adjective clause (*which are very common in schizophrenics*) in no way changes the basic meaning of the main clause.

     To decide whether an adjective clause is essential or nonessential, mentally delete the clause. If taking out the clause changes the basic meaning of the sentence or makes it unclear, the clause is probably essential and should not be set off with commas. If the meaning of the main part of the sentence or the main clause does not change enormously, the clause is probably nonessential and should be set off with commas.

▶ **Postpartum neurosis, which can last for two weeks or longer, can adversely affect a mother's ability to care for her infant.**

▶ **The early stage starts with memory loss, which usually causes the patient to forget recent life events.**

▶ **Seasonal affective disorders are mood disturbances, that occur with a change of season.**

▶ **The coaches, who do the recruiting should be disciplined.**

Adjective clauses following proper nouns always require commas.

▶ **Nanotechnologists defer to K. Eric Drexler, who speculates imaginatively about the uses of nonmachines.**

For practice, go to **bedfordstmartins.com/conciseguide/exercisecentral** and click on Adjective Clauses.

Checking for Commas around Interrupting Phrases.   When writers are explaining a concept, they need to supply a great deal of information. They add much of this information in phrases that interrupt the flow of a sentence. Words that interrupt are usually set off with commas, one at the beginning of the phrase and one at the end:

▶ People on the West Coast, especially in Los Angeles ‸ have always been receptive to new ideas.

▶ Alzheimer's disease ‸ named after the German neuropathologist Alois Alzheimer, is a chronic degenerative illness.

▶ These examples ‸ though simple, present equations in terms of tangible objects.

For practice, go to **bedfordstmartins.com/conciseguide/exercisecentral** and click on Commas around Interrupting Phrases.

Thinking About
Document Design

■ Designing Surveys and Presenting Results

Effective document design is an important factor for the marketing manager who volunteers to teach fifth graders about surveys (see p. 99). Because the marketer is teaching students about surveys by having them take one, she knows that the design of the survey will be crucial to the students' understanding.

She recognizes that students need to be interested in the questionnaire and able to fill it out quickly; she also knows that it is important that they not feel intimidated by its appearance. After first drafting the questionnaire, she realizes that although the questions all fit on one page (cutting down on paper and photocopying costs), the page is very cluttered and difficult to read.

First Draft of Survey (excerpt)

1. What is your gender? _____
2. Where do you fall in terms of birth order in your family—youngest, oldest, in the middle, or only child? _____
3. How frequently are you able to watch the television programming you want to watch—all of the time, most of the time, some of the time, hardly ever, or never? _____

Before getting started on the redesign, she considers her audience—10- and 11-year-olds—and refers to workbooks and other print material designed for this age group. In this case, the convenience to her audience (their ability to easily read and answer the questions) outweighs the time and expense of photocopying multiple pages. She thinks that the students will be able to fill out the survey more easily if each question has more space around it.

Final Draft of Survey (excerpt)

1. I am

    ☐ male
    ☐ female

2. In my family, I am

    ☐ the youngest child
    ☐ a middle child
    ☐ the oldest child
    ☐ the only child

3. When I'm at home, I can watch the TV shows I want to watch

    ☐ all of the time
    ☐ most of the time
    ☐ some of the time
    ☐ hardly ever
    ☐ never

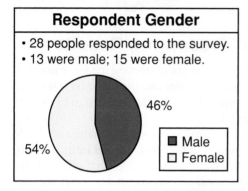

Respondent Gender

• 28 people responded to the survey.
• 13 were male; 15 were female.

46%

54%

■ Male
☐ Female

The appearance of the survey is only her initial design consideration, however. After the students complete the survey, she guides the class in tabulating the survey results. Knowing that the information from the questionnaire has to be easy to represent graphically so that the viewers will understand the results when they are projected, she then discusses with the class which information best fits in a pie chart (such as information broken into percentages) and which in a bar graph (such as hours of television watched by day). She creates the data displays using a PowerPoint program. Two of the slides are shown here.

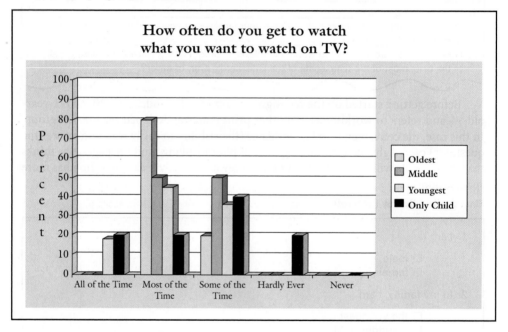

How often do you get to watch what you want to watch on TV?

Percent

100
90
80
70
60
50
40
30
20
10
0

All of the Time   Most of the Time   Some of the Time   Hardly Ever   Never

☐ Oldest
▨ Middle
☐ Youngest
■ Only Child

Reflecting on Your Writing

Now that you have read and discussed several essays that explain concepts and written one of your own, take some time to reflect on the act of writing concept essays.

Write a one-page explanation, telling your instructor about a problem you encountered in writing your essay and how you solved it. Before you begin, gather all of your writing—invention and planning notes, drafts, critical comments, revision notes and plans, and final revision. Review these materials, and refer to them as you complete this writing task.

1. *Identify one writing problem you had to solve as you worked to explain the concept in your essay.* Do not be concerned with grammar and punctuation; concentrate instead on problems unique to developing a concept explanation. For example: Did you puzzle over how to focus your explanation? Did you worry about how to appeal to your readers' interests or how to identify and define the terms that your readers would need explained? Did you have trouble integrating sources smoothly?

2. *Determine how you came to recognize the problem.* When did you first discover it? What called it to your attention? If you did not become aware of the problem until someone else pointed it out, can you now see hints of it in your invention writings? If so, where specifically? How did you respond when you first recognized the problem?

3. *Reflect on how you went about solving the problem.* Did you work on the wording of a particular passage, cut or add information, move paragraphs or sentences around, add transitions or forecasting statements, experiment with different writing strategies? Did you reread one of the essays in this chapter to see how another writer handled the problem, or did you look back at the invention suggestions? If you talked about the writing problem with another student, a tutor, or your instructor, did talking about it help? How useful was the advice you received?

4. *Write a brief explanation of how you identified the problem and how you solved it.* Be as specific as possible in reconstructing your efforts. Quote from your invention notes and draft essay, others' critical comments, your revision plan, or your revised essay to show the various changes your writing underwent as you tried to solve the problem. If you are still uncertain about your solution, say so. Thinking in detail about how you identified a particular problem, how you went about solving it, and what you learned from this experience can help you solve future writing problems more easily.

5

Arguing
a Position

IN COLLEGE COURSES   For a business course, a student writes an essay arguing that a "glass ceiling" still prevents women in the United States from advancing up the corporate ladder or being elected to national office.

She begins her essay by explaining that the term "glass ceiling" was first used by writers in the 1980s, and she takes the position that since then women's opportunities have not measurably improved. She cites statistics that in 2006 only 11 percent of corporate officers were women and that in 2004 only 15 percent of the members of the U.S. Congress were women, whereas in Sweden 45 percent of the members of Parliament were women. Among chief executives of corporations, she finds, women make up only 0.7 percent of the total in the United States; they are 5 percent in France. While conceding that some ambitious women decide to give their families priority, she insists that more women would claim top jobs if the climb were not such a struggle.

IN THE COMMUNITY   In a letter to the school board, a group of parents protest a new Peacekeepers program that is being implemented at the local middle school.

The writers acknowledge that the aim of the program—to teach students to avoid conflict—is worthwhile. But they argue that its methods unduly restrict students' freedom and may teach children to become passive and submissive. To support their argument, they list some of the rules that have been instituted at the middle school: Students must wear uniforms, must keep their hands clasped behind their backs when walking down the halls, may not raise their voices or use obscenities, and cannot play contact sports like basketball and football. Although the parents plan to propose that the school board drop Peacekeepers and institute a different program, they focus this first letter on critiquing Peacekeepers in order to understand how resolved the board is to keep it and why.

IN THE WORKPLACE   For a trade magazine, an executive writes an article arguing that protecting the environment can be good business. Environmentally friendly technologies, he acknowledges, initially incurred some costs for his company. Gradually, however, they began to save the company money by reducing heating and cooling costs. Recently, in fact, the company added rooftop solar cells to generate electricity. The executive supports his argument with a table showing that after the first five years, the costs of the equipment declined steadily in relation to profits.

Because the writer knows it will take more than his own experience to convince readers to spend money to make their business practices environmentally friendly, he supports his position with examples of two other companies. He also points out that the eight deciding factors in *Fortune* magazine's annual ranking of America's Most Admired Corporations include community and environmental responsibility.

To his surprise, the article produces several e-mails of thanks as well as a dozen requests to visit his company to see its environmental efforts firsthand.

You may associate arguing with quarreling or with the in-your-face debating we hear so often on radio and television talk shows. These ways of arguing may let us vent strong feelings, but they seldom lead us to consider seriously other points of view or to reflect on our own thinking.

This chapter presents a more deliberative way of arguing that we call **reasoned argument** because it depends on giving reasons rather than raising voices. It demands that positions be supported rather than merely asserted. It also commands respect for the right of others to disagree. Reasoned argument requires more planning and knowledge than quarreling but no less passion or commitment.

Controversial issues are, by definition, issues about which people may have strong feelings. The issue may involve an established practice, like allowing college athletes to register for their courses before other students to accommodate the athletes' practice and travel schedules. Or it may concern a new policy, like the U.S. military's use of torture. People may agree about goals but disagree about the best way to achieve them, as in the continuing debate over how to make college education affordable. Or they may disagree about fundamental values, as in the debate over gay marriage.

As you can see from these examples, controversial issues have no obvious right answer: they are matters of opinion and judgment. Although it is not possible to prove that a position on a controversial issue is right or wrong, it is possible through reasoned argument to convince others to accept or reject it. To be convincing, not only must an argument present convincing reasons and plausible support for its position, but it also should anticipate readers' likely objections and opposing arguments, conceding those that are reasonable and refuting those that are not.

Learning to make and evaluate reasoned arguments is a necessity if our form of government is to survive and flourish. As citizens in a democracy, we have a duty to inform ourselves about issues and to participate constructively in the public debate. Improving our research and argument strategies also has practical advantages in school, where we often are judged by our ability to write convincingly, and in the workplace, where we may want to take a stand on issues concerning working conditions or pay and promotional policies.

A Collaborative Activity: Practice Arguing a Position

Part 1. Get together with two or three other students and choose an issue from the following list.

- Should community service be a requirement for graduation from high school or college?
- Should the U.S. government ignore international laws that forbid torture?
- Should the primary purpose of a college education be job training?
- Should the racial, ethnic, or gender makeup of a local police force parallel the community it serves?
- Should U.S. state governments continue to sponsor lotteries?

Then complete the following activities:

- Choose someone in your group to take notes.
- Exchange opinions on the issue you have chosen. Then agree to support the same position on the issue, whether you personally agree with it or not.
- Define the key term in your position statement—for example, *community service* or *torture*.
- Imagine that you plan to send your argument to a group or agency that could take action, and identify that audience (your state governor's office, a committee of the U.S. Senate, or your local city council, for example).
- List three reasons why you support the position and briefly discuss how you would support each. Also list three likely objections your readers would make.

Part 2. Discuss your efforts at constructing an argument. What part of the task was easiest, and what part hardest? What most surprised you?

Readings

JESSICA STATSKY wrote the following essay about children's competitive sports for her college composition course. Before you read, recall your own experiences as an elementary school student playing competitive sports, either in or out of school. If you were not actively involved yourself, did you know anyone who was? Looking back, do you think that winning was unduly emphasized? What value was placed on having a good time? On learning to get along with others? On developing athletic skills and confidence?

Children Need to Play, Not Compete
Jessica Statsky

1 Over the past three decades, organized sports for children have increased dramatically in the United States. And though many adults regard Little League Baseball and Peewee Football as a basic part of childhood, the games are not always joyous ones. When overzealous parents and coaches impose adult standards on children's sports, the result can be activities that are neither satisfying nor beneficial to children.

2 I am concerned about all organized sports activities for children between the ages of six and twelve. The damage I see results from noncontact as well as contact sports, from sports organized locally as well as those organized nationally.

Statsky immediately **identifies the issue**— whether organized competitive sports benefit children—and **takes a clear position** on it, using precise language that makes her seem knowledgeable and thoughtful.

Highly organized competitive sports such as Peewee Football and Little League Baseball are too often played to adult standards, which are developmentally inappropriate for children and can be both physically and psychologically harmful. Furthermore, because they eliminate many children from organized sports before they are ready to compete, they are actually counterproductive for developing either future players or fans. Finally, because they emphasize competition and winning, they unfortunately provide occasions for some parents and coaches to place their own fantasies and needs ahead of children's welfare.

3

One readily understandable danger of overly competitive sports is that they entice children into physical actions that are bad for growing bodies. Although the official Little League Web site acknowledges that children do risk injury playing baseball, it insists that "severe injuries . . . are infrequent," the risk "far less than the risk of riding a skateboard, a bicycle, or even the school bus" ("What about My Child?"). Nevertheless, Leonard Koppett in *Sports Illusion, Sports Reality* claims that a twelve-year-old trying to throw a curve ball, for example, may put abnormal strain on developing arm and shoulder muscles, sometimes resulting in lifelong injuries (294). Contact sports like football can be even more hazardous. Thomas Tutko, a psychology professor at San Jose State University and coauthor of the book *Winning Is Everything and Other American Myths,* writes:

> I am strongly opposed to young kids playing tackle football. It is not the right stage of development for them to be taught to crash into other kids. Kids under the age of fourteen are not by nature physical. Their main concern is self-preservation. They don't want to meet head on and slam into each other. But tackle football absolutely requires that they try to hit each other as hard as they can. And it is too traumatic for young kids. (qtd. in Tosches A1)

As Tutko indicates, even when children are not injured, fear of being hurt detracts from their enjoyment of the sport. The Little League Web site ranks fear of injury as the seventh of seven reasons children quit ("What about My Child?"). One mother of an eight-year-old Peewee Football player explained, "The kids get so scared. They get hit once and they don't want anything to do with football anymore. They'll sit on the bench and pretend

4

In the last three sentences of paragraph 2, Statsky **forecasts her argument,** identifying the order of her main reasons for taking the position she does. To keep readers on track and introduce the argument supporting these four reasons, she begins paragraphs 3, 5, 7, and 8 with topic sentences that echo the language she uses in this paragraph.

In paragraphs 3 and 4, Statsky **supports** her first **reason:** that competitive sports can physically harm young children.

their leg hurts . . ." (qtd. in Tosches A1). Some children are driven to even more desperate measures. For example, in one Peewee Football game, a reporter watched the following scene as a player took himself out of the game:

> "Coach, my tummy hurts. I can't play," he said. The coach told the player to get back onto the field. "There's nothing wrong with your stomach," he said. When the coach turned his head the seven-year-old stuck a finger down his throat and made himself vomit. When the coach turned back, the boy pointed to the ground and told him, "Yes there is, coach. See?" (Tosches A33)

5 Besides physical hazards and anxieties, competitive sports pose psychological dangers for children. Martin Rablovsky, a former sports editor for the *New York Times,* says that in all his years of watching young children play organized sports, he has noticed very few of them smiling. "I've seen children enjoying a spontaneous pre-practice scrimmage become somber and serious when the coach's whistle blows," Rablovsky says. "The spirit of play suddenly disappears, and sport becomes joblike" (qtd. in Coakley 94). The primary goal of a professional athlete—winning—is not appropriate for children. Their goals should be having fun, learning, and being with friends. Although winning does add to the fun, too many adults lose sight of what matters and make winning the most important goal. Several studies have shown that when children are asked whether they would rather be warming the bench on a winning team or playing regularly on a losing team, about 90 percent choose the latter (Smith, Smith, and Smoll 11).

6 Winning and losing may be an inevitable part of adult life, but they should not be part of childhood. Too much competition too early in life can affect a child's development. Children are easily influenced, and when they sense that their competence and worth are based on their ability to live up to their parents' and coaches' high expectations—and on their ability to win—they can become discouraged and depressed. Little League advises parents to "keep winning in perspective" ("Your Role"), noting that the most common reasons children give for quitting, aside from change in interest, are lack of playing time, failure and fear of failure, disapproval by significant others, and psychological stress ("What about My Child?"). According to Dr. Glyn C. Roberts, a professor of kinesiology at the Institute of Child Behavior and Development at the University of Illinois,

To **support** her second reason—**psychological damage**—Statsky cites authoritative sources, quoting, summarizing, and commenting on them.

80 to 90 percent of children who play competitive sports at a young age drop out by sixteen (Kutner).

Statsky makes a smooth transition to her third reason.

This statistic illustrates another reason I oppose competitive sports for children: because they are so highly selective, very few children get to participate. Far too soon, a few children are singled out for their athletic promise, while many others, who may be on the verge of developing the necessary strength and ability, are screened out and discouraged from trying out again. Like adults, children fear failure, and so even those with good physical skills may stay away because they lack self-confidence. Consequently, teams lose many promising players who with some encouragement and experience might have become stars. The problem is that many parent-sponsored, out-of-school programs give more importance to having a winning team than to developing children's physical skills and self-esteem. [7]

In this paragraph, which introduces Statsky's fourth reason, Statsky risks losing some of her readers by offending them, but she tries to keep them aboard by promising specific horror stories as support.

Indeed, it is no secret that too often scorekeeping, league standings, and the drive to win bring out the worst in adults who are more absorbed in living out their own fantasies than in enhancing the quality of the experience for children (Smith, Smith, and Smoll 9). Recent newspaper articles on children's sports contain plenty of horror stories. *Los Angeles Times* reporter Rich Tosches, for example, tells the story of a brawl among seventy-five parents following a Peewee Football game (A33). As a result of the brawl, which began when a parent from one team confronted a player from the other team, the teams are now thinking of hiring security guards for future games. Another example is provided by an *L.A. Times* editorial about a Little League manager who intimidated the opposing team by setting fire to one of their team's jerseys on the pitching mound before the game began. As the editorial writer commented, the manager showed his young team that "intimidation could substitute for playing well" ("The Bad News"). [8]

The argument takes a new direction as, in paragraphs 9 and 11, Statsky describes two practical, tested alternatives to overly competitive children's sports teams.

Although not all parents or coaches behave so inappropriately, the seriousness of the problem is illustrated by the fact that Adelphi University in Garden City, New York, offers a sports psychology workshop for Little League coaches, designed to balance their "animal instincts" with "educational theory" in hopes of reducing the "screaming and hollering," in the words of Harold Weisman, manager of sixteen Little Leagues in New York City (Schmitt). In a three-and-one-half-hour Sunday morning workshop, coaches learn how to make practices more fun, treat injuries, deal with irate parents, and be "more sensitive to their young players' fears, emotional [9] frailties, and need for recognition." Little League is to be credited with recognizing the need for such workshops.

10   Some parents would no doubt argue that children cannot start too soon preparing to live in a competitive free-market economy. After all, secondary schools and colleges require students to compete for grades, and college admission is extremely competitive. And it is perfectly obvious how important competitive skills are in finding a job. Yet the ability to cooperate is also important for success in life. Before children are psychologically ready for competition, maybe we should emphasize cooperation and individual performance in team sports rather than winning.

11   Many people are ready for such an emphasis. In 1988, one New York Little League official who had attended the Adelphi workshop tried to ban scoring from six- to eight-year-olds' games—but parents wouldn't support him (Schmitt). An innovative children's sports program in New York City, City Sports for Kids, emphasizes fitness, self-esteem, and sportsmanship. In this program's basketball games, every member on a team plays at least two of six eight-minute periods. The basket is seven feet from the floor, rather than ten feet, and a player can score a point just by hitting the rim (Bloch). I believe this kind of local program should replace overly competitive programs like Peewee Football and Little League Baseball. As one coach explains, significant improvements can result from a few simple rule changes, such as including every player in the batting order and giving every player, regardless of age or ability, the opportunity to play at least four innings a game (Frank).

12   Authorities have clearly documented the excesses and dangers of many competitive sports programs for children. It would seem that few children benefit from these programs and that those who do would benefit even more from programs emphasizing fitness, cooperation, sportsmanship, and individual performance. Thirteen- and fourteen-year-olds may be eager for competition, but few younger children are. These younger children deserve sports programs designed specifically for their needs and abilities.

Works Cited

"The Bad News Pyromaniacs?" Editorial. *Los Angeles Times* 16 June 1990: B6. *LexisNexis*. Web 16 May 1999.

Bloch, Gordon B. "Thrill of Victory Is Secondary to Fun." *New York Times* 2 Apr. 1990, late ed.: C12. *LexisNexis*. Web. 14 May 1999.

Sidebar notes:

Statsky acknowledges the value many parents place on training their children for a life of competition and struggle. After conceding some wisdom in this value, however, she suggests that it is one-sided and short-sighted for children in this age range.

In her **conclusion,** Statsky firmly **reasserts** her position and reasons for it, while again limiting its scope to younger children and conceding that it may not apply to older ones.

In her Works Cited, Statsky lists eleven sources, all of which are cited in her essay. The sources not only provide material for her argument, but also contribute to her authority.

Coakley, Jay J. *Sport in Society: Issues and Controversies.* St. Louis: Mosby, 1982. Print.

Frank, L. "Contributions from Parents and Coaches." *CYB Message Board.* AOL, 8 July 1997. Web. 14 May 1999.

Koppett, Leonard. *Sports Illusion, Sports Reality.* Boston: Houghton, 1981. Print.

Kutner, Lawrence. "Athletics, through a Child's Eyes." *New York Times* 23 Mar. 1989, late ed.: C8. *LexisNexis.* Web. 15 May 1999.

Schmitt, Eric. "Psychologists Take Seat on Little League Bench." *New York Times* 14 Mar. 1988, late ed.: B2. *LexisNexis.* Web. 14 May 1999.

Smith, Nathan, Ronald Smith, and Frank Smoll. *Kidsports: A Survival Guide for Parents.* Reading: Addison, 1983. Print.

Tosches, Rich. "Peewee Football: Is It Time to Blow the Whistle?" *Los Angeles Times* 3 Dec. 1988: A1+. *LexisNexis.* Web. 22 May 1999.

"What about My Child?" *Little League Online.* Little League Baseball, Incorporated, 1999. Web. 30 May 1999.

"Your Role as a Little League Parent." *Little League Online.* Little League Baseball, Inc., 1999. Web. 30 May 1999.

AMITAI ETZIONI (b. 1929), professor of sociology at George Washington University, has written numerous articles and books including, most recently, *My Brother's Keeper: A Memoir and a Message* (2003) and *From Empire to Community: A New Approach to International Relations* (2004). The following essay was originally published in 1986 in the *Miami Herald.*

Before you read, think about the part-time jobs you held during high school. Recall the pleasures and disappointments of these jobs. In particular, think about what you learned that might have made you a better student and prepared you for college — or, alternatively, think about any negative effects your job(s) might have had on your schooling.

Working at McDonald's
Amitai Etzioni

McDonald's is bad for your kids. I do not mean the flat patties and the white-flour buns; I refer to the jobs teen-agers undertake, mass-producing these choice items.   1

As many as two-thirds of America's high school juniors and seniors now hold down part-time paying jobs, according to studies. Many of these are in fast-food chains, of which McDonald's is the pioneer, trend-setter and symbol.   2

At first, such jobs may seem right out of the Founding Fathers' educational manual for how to bring up self-reliant, work-ethic-driven, productive youngsters.   3

But in fact, these jobs undermine school attendance and involvement, impart few skills that will be useful in later life, and simultaneously skew the values of teen-agers—especially their ideas about the worth of a dollar.

It has been a longstanding American tradition that youngsters ought to get paying jobs. In folklore, few pursuits are more deeply revered than the newspaper route and the sidewalk lemonade stand. Here the youngsters are to learn how sweet are the fruits of labor and self-discipline (papers are delivered early in the morning, rain or shine), and the ways of trade (if you price your lemonade too high or too low . . .).

Roy Rogers, Baskin Robbins, Kentucky Fried Chicken, *et al.* may at first seem nothing but a vast extension of the lemonade stand. They provide very large numbers of teen jobs, provide regular employment, pay quite well compared to many other teen jobs and, in the modern equivalent of toiling over a hot stove, test one's stamina.

Closer examination, however, finds the McDonald's kind of job highly uneducational in several ways. Far from providing opportunities for entrepreneurship (the lemonade stand) or self-discipline, self-supervision and self-scheduling (the paper route), most teen jobs these days are highly structured—what social scientists call "highly routinized."

True, you still have to have the gumption to get yourself over to the hamburger stand, but once you don the prescribed uniform, your task is spelled out in minute detail. The franchise prescribes the shape of the coffee cups; the weight, size, shape and color of the patties; and the texture of the napkins (if any). Fresh coffee is to be made every eight minutes. And so on. There is no room for initiative, creativity, or even elementary rearrangements. These are breeding grounds for robots working for yesterday's assembly lines, not tomorrow's high-tech posts.

There are very few studies on the matter. One of the few is a 1984 study by Ivan Charper and Bryan Shore Fraser. The study relies mainly on what teen-agers write in response to questionnaires rather than actual observations of fast-food jobs. The authors argue that the employees develop many skills such as how to operate a food-preparation machine and a cash register. However, little attention is paid to how long it takes to acquire such a skill, or what its significance is.

What does it matter if you spend 20 minutes to learn to use a cash register, and then—"operate" it? What "skill" have you acquired? It is a long way from learning to work with a lathe or carpenter tools in the olden days or to program computers in the modern age.

A 1980 study by A. V. Harrell and P. W. Wirtz found that, among those students who worked at least 25 hours per week while in school, their unemployment rate four years later was half of that of seniors who did not work. This is an impressive statistic. It must be seen, though, together with the finding that many who begin as part-time employees in fast-food chains drop out of high school and are gobbled up in the world of low-skill jobs.

Some say that while these jobs are rather unsuited for college-bound, white, middle-class youngsters, they are "ideal" for lower-class, "non-academic," minority youngsters. Indeed, minorities are "over-represented" in these jobs (21 percent of fast-food employees). While it is true that these places provide income, work and even some training to such youngsters, they also tend to perpetuate their disadvantaged status. They provide no career ladders, few marketable skills, and undermine school attendance and involvement.

The hours are often long. Among those 14 to 17, a third of fast-food employees (including some school dropouts) labor more than 30 hours per week, according to the Charper-Fraser study. Only 20 percent work 15 hours or less. The rest: between 15 and 30 hours. | 12

Often the stores close late, and after closing one must clean up and tally up. In affluent Montgomery County, Md., where child labor would not seem to be a widespread economic necessity, 24 percent of the seniors at one high school in 1985 worked as much as five to seven days a week; 27 percent, three to five. There is just no way such amounts of work will not interfere with school work, especially homework. In an informal survey published in the most recent yearbook of the high school, 58 percent of seniors acknowledged that their jobs interfere with their school work. | 13

The Charper-Fraser study sees merit in learning teamwork and working under supervision. The authors have a point here. However, it must be noted that such learning is not automatically educational or wholesome. For example, much of the supervision in fast-food places leans toward teaching one the wrong kinds of compliance: blind obedience, or shared alienation with the "boss." | 14

Supervision is often both tight and woefully inappropriate. Today, fast-food chains and other such places of work (record shops, bowling alleys) keep costs down by having teens supervise teens with often no adult on the premises. | 15

There is no father or mother figure with which to identify, to emulate, to provide a role model and guidance. The work-culture varies from one place to another: Sometimes it is a tightly run shop (must keep the cash registers ringing); sometimes a rather loose pot party interrupted by customers. However, only rarely is there a master to learn from, or much worth learning. Indeed, far from being places where solid adult work values are being transmitted, these are places where all too often delinquent teen values dominate. Typically, when my son Oren was dishing out ice cream for Baskin Robbins in upper Manhattan, his fellow teen-workers considered him a sucker for not helping himself to the till. Most youngsters felt they were entitled to $50 severance "pay" on their last day on the job. | 16

The pay, oddly, is the part of the teen work-world that is most difficult to evaluate. The lemonade stand or paper route money was for your allowance. In the old days, apprentices learning a trade from a master contributed most, if not all, of their income to their parents' household. Today, the teen pay may be low by adult standards, but it is often, especially in the middle class, spent largely or wholly by the teens. That is, the youngsters live free at home ("after all, they are high school kids") and are left with very substantial sums of money. | 17

Where this money goes is not quite clear. Some use it to support themselves, especially among the poor. More middle-class kids set some money aside to help pay for college, or save it for a major purchase—often a car. But large amounts seem to flow to pay for an early introduction into the most trite aspects of American consumerism: flimsy punk clothes, trinkets and whatever else is the last fast-moving teen craze. | 18

One may say that this is only fair and square; they are being good American consumers and spend their money on what turns them on. At least, a cynic might add, these funds do not go into illicit drugs and booze. On the other hand, an educator might bemoan that these young, yet unformed individuals, so early in life driven to buy objects of no intrinsic educational, cultural or social merit, learn so quickly the dubious merit of keeping up with the Joneses in ever-changing fads, promoted by mass merchandising.

Many teens find the instant reward of money, and the youth status symbols it buys, much more alluring than credits in calculus courses, European history or foreign languages. No wonder quite a few would rather skip school—and certainly home-work—and instead work longer at a Burger King. Thus, most teen work these days is not providing early lessons in the work ethic; it fosters escape from school and respon-sibilities, quick gratification and a short cut to the consumeristic aspects of adult life.

Thus, parents should look at teen employment not as automatically educational. It is an activity—like sports—that can be turned into an educational opportunity. But it can also easily be abused. Youngsters must learn to balance the quest for income with the needs to keep growing and pursue other endeavors that do not pay off instantly—above all, education.

Go back to school.

Making Connections to Personal and Social Issues: Job Skills

Etzioni argues that working at McDonald's or similar places does not teach the skills and habits required for success. He points out that at McDonald's workers never get to practice "entrepreneurship [initiative, risk-taking, speculation, self-promotion] . . . or self-discipline, self-supervision and self-scheduling" (par. 6). He asserts that there is "no room for initiative, creativity, or even elementary rearrangements" (7).

With two or three other students, describe the most McDonald's-like job you have held. Then describe a job (if you have had one) that gave you practice in even one of the work virtues Etzioni mentions and explain how it did so. (If you have never held a job, talk about why you have focused your priorities elsewhere.) Finally, describe your ideal job or career and how you think your work or other out-of-school experience has—or has not—helped prepare you for it.

Analyzing Writing Strategies

1. To see how Etzioni makes use of statistics to **support** his argument, underline the statistics in paragraphs 2, 10, 11, 12, and 13. Underline also any references to the sources of these statistics. How would you explain Etzioni's repeated reliance on

statistics? How might his intended readers, parents of teenagers reading the *Miami Herald* newspaper, have been influenced by the statistics? *Write a few sentences about your insights.*

2. An argument for a position does not begin until **reasons** are given, and Etzioni gives several. Underline the most direct statements of Etzioni's reasons, the first sentence in paragraphs 6, 15, and 16, and the last sentence in paragraph 20. Then make a concise list of these reasons, reducing each one to no more than four or five words. Identify the one reason likely to be most convincing and the one likely to be least convincing. *Write a few sentences explaining why you made these choices.*

Commentary: Building a Strong Argument

Strong arguments present both a **focused presentation of an issue** and a **clear position** on it. Etzioni's piece does both. Its title, "Working at McDonald's," identifies the issue very visibly for readers. Within two sentences, Etzioni focuses on the issue of the impact such work has on teenagers. A few sentences later, he makes clear how many people this kind of low-wage work impacts (many of the "two-thirds of America's high school juniors and seniors [who] now hold down part-time paying jobs"— and, of course, their parents, to whom the article is addressed). In the last sentence in his third paragraph, he makes his position clear: "[T]hese jobs undermine school attendance and involvement, impart few skills that will be useful in later life, and simultaneously skew the values of teen-agers."

Presenting the issue and clearly stating a position is just the beginning. To convince readers, Etzioni has to give the **reasons** that he believes working at fast-food restaurants is detrimental. He gives several: the jobs are not educational; supervision is inadequate, with no role models or useful guidance offered; the work tends to skew values in the direction of "making a quick buck." In order to make these reasons seem plausible to readers, Etzioni provides convincing support in two forms: facts and statistics from two published studies, and references to the experience of his own teenage son, Oren.

Etzioni has his readers very much in mind as he writes this essay. He anticipates how they might object to his argument. Writers have three options in **counterarguing** readers' objections: They can simply acknowledge readers' concerns, they can accommodate them by making concessions, or they can try to refute them. Etzioni chooses the third option.

In paragraph 10, for example, Etzioni acknowledges as "impressive" Harrell and Wirtz's statistic showing that students who work twenty-five hours or more per week in high school are employed four years later at a higher rate than those who do not. He then counterargues, however, by noting that "many who begin as part-time employees in fast-food chains drop out of high school and are gobbled up in the world of low-skill jobs." He concludes this refutation by implicitly comparing McDonald's-type jobs to the school tracking system that separates "(non-academic)" and "college-bound" students (par. 11). Instead of providing minority youngsters with an opportunity to advance, he argues, such jobs "perpetuate their disadvantaged status" because they "provide no career ladders, few marketable skills, and undermine school attendance and involvement."

Considering Topics for Your Own Essay

Etzioni focuses on a single kind of part-time work, takes a position on whether it is worthwhile, and recommends against it. You could write a very similar kind of essay. For example, you could take a position for or against students partici-pating in other kinds of part-time work or recreation during the high school or college academic year. Possibilities include playing on an interscholastic or col-legiate sports team, doing volunteer work, or taking an extra class in art or music. If you have taken or must take the best-paying job you can find to support your-self and pay for college, you could focus on why the job either strengthens or weakens you as a person, given your life and career goals. Writing for other stu-dents, you would either recommend the job or activity to them or discourage them from pursuing it, giving reasons for your position. Like Etzioni, you might refer to studies of students engaging in the activity during their high school or college years.

KAREN STABINER is a journalist specializing in health, women's, and family issues. Her reports have been published in *Vogue,* the *New Yorker,* the *Los Angeles Times,* and the *New York Times.* Stabiner is the author of six books, the most recent being *All Girls: Single-Sex Education and Why It Matters* (2002) and *My Girl: Adventures with a Teen in Training* (2005). This essay was first published in 2002 in the *Washington Post.*

Boys Here, Girls There: Sure, If Equality's the Goal
Karen Stabiner

Many parents may be wondering what the fuss was about this past week, when the Bush administration endorsed single-sex public schools and classes. Separating the sexes was something we did in the days of auto shop and home ec, before Betty Friedan, Gloria Steinem and Title IX.[1] How, then, did an apparent return to the Fifties come to symbolize educational reform?   1

Here's how: By creating an alternate, parallel universe where smart matters more than anything, good looks hold little currency and a strong sense of self trumps a date   2

---

[1]Friedan and Steinem were pioneers in the feminist movement that began in the 1960s. Title IX of the Education Amendments of 1972 is the federal legislation that bans sexual discrimination in public schools, whether in academics or athletics.

on Saturday night—a place where "class clown" is a label that young boys dread and "math whiz" is a term of endearment for young girls.

I have just spent three years working on a book about two all-girls schools, the private Marlborough School in Los Angeles, and The Young Women's Leadership School of East Harlem (TYWLS), a six-year-old public school in New York City. I went to class, I went home with the girls, I went to dances and basketball games and faculty meetings, and what I learned is this: Single-sex education matters, and it matters most to the students who historically have been denied access to it. 3

Having said that, I do not intend to proselytize. Single-sex education is not the answer to everyone's prayers. Some children want no part of it and some parents question its relevance. The rest of us should not stop wondering what to do with our coeducational public schools just because of this one new option. 4

But single-sex education can be a valuable tool—if we target those students who stand to benefit most. For years, in the name of upholding gender equity, we have practiced a kind of harsh economic discrimination. Sociologist Cornelius Riordan says that poor students, minorities and girls stand to profit most from a single-sex environment. Until now, though, the only students who could attend a single-sex school were the wealthy ones who could afford private tuition, the relatively few lucky students who received financial aid or those in less-expensive parochial schools. We denied access to the almost 90 percent of American students who attend public schools. 5

For the fortunate ones—like the girls at Marlborough—the difference is one of attitude, more than any quantifiable measure; their grades and scores may be similar to the graduates of coed prep schools, but they perceive themselves as more competent, more willing to pursue advanced work in fields such as math and science. 6

At TYWLS, though, the difference is more profound. Students there are predominantly Latina and African American, survivors of a hostile public system. Half of New York's high school students fail to graduate on time, and almost a third never graduate. Throughout the nation, one in six Latina and one in five African American teens become pregnant every year. But most of the members of TYWLS's two graduating classes have gone on to four-year colleges, often the first members of their families to do so, and pregnancy is the stark exception. 7

There are now 11 single-sex public schools in the United States, all of which serve urban students, many of them in lower-income neighborhoods. Most are side-by-side schools that offer comparable programs for boys and girls in the same facility. The stand-alone girls' schools say that they are compensating for years of gender discrimination; several attempts at similar schools for boys have failed, however, casualties of legal challenges. 8

Now, thanks to a bipartisan amendment to President Bush's education reform bill, sponsored by Sens. Kay Bailey Hutchison (R-Tex.) and Hillary Rodham Clinton (D-N.Y.), the administration is about to revise the way it enforces Title IX, to allow for single-sex schools and classes. 9

The first objections last week came from the National Organization for Women   10
and the New York Civil Liberties Union, both of which opposed the opening of TYWLS
in the fall of 1996. The two groups continue to insist—as though it were 1896 and they
were arguing *Plessy v. Ferguson*[2]—that separate can never be equal. I appreciate
NOW's wariness of the Bush administration's endorsement of single-sex public
schools, since I am of the generation that still considers the label "feminist" to be a
compliment—and many feminists still fear that any public acknowledgment of differences between the sexes will hinder their fight for equality.

But brain research has shown us that girls and boys develop and process infor-   11
mation in different ways; they do not even use the same region of the brain to do their
math homework. We cannot pretend that such information does not exist just because
it conflicts with our ideology. If we hang on to old, quantifiable measurements of equality, we will fail our children. If we take what we learn and use it, we have the chance to
do better.

Educators at single-sex schools already get it: Equality is the goal, not the   12
process. There may be more than one path to the destination—but it is the arrival,
not the itinerary, that counts.

Some researchers complain that we lack definitive evidence that single-sex   13
education works. There are so many intertwined variables; the students at TYWLS
might do well because of smaller class size, passionate teachers and an aggressively
supportive atmosphere. Given that, the absence of boys might be beside the point.

The American Association of University Women called for more research even   14
after publishing a 1998 report that showed some girls continued to suffer in the coed
classroom. But it is probably impossible to design a study that would retire the question permanently, and, as TYWLS's first principal, Celenia Chevere, liked to say, "What
am I supposed to do with these girls in the meantime?"

What is this misplaced reverence for the coed school? Do not think that it was   15
designed with the best interests of all children at heart. As education professors David
and Myra Sadker explained in their 1994 book, *Failing at Fairness: How America's
Schools Cheat Girls,* our schools were originally created to educate boys. In the late
1700s, girls went to class early in the morning and late in the day—and unlike the
boys, they had to pay for the privilege. When families demanded that the public
schools do more for their girls, school districts grudgingly allowed the girls into existing
classrooms—not because it was the best way to teach children but because no one
had the money to build new schools just for girls. Coed classrooms are not necessarily
better. They just are.

For those who like hard data, here is a number: 1,200 girls on the waiting list for a   16
handful of spaces in the ninth grade at TYWLS. There is a growing desire for public
school alternatives, for an answer more meaningful than a vague if optimistic call for

---

[2]A U.S. Supreme Court decision upholding racial segregation: "Separate" facilities for
blacks and whites were constitutional as long as they were "equal." This ruling was not struck
down until 1954.

system-wide reform. The demand for single-sex education exists—and now the Bush administration must figure out how to supply it.

Implementation will not be easy. Girls may learn better without boys, but research and experience show that some boys seem to need the socializing influence of girls: Will there be a group of educational handmaidens, girls who are consigned to coed schools to keep the boys from acting out? Who will select the chosen few who get to go to single-sex schools, and how will they make that choice? Will they take students who already show promise or those who most need help? Or perhaps the philosophy of a new pair of boys' and girls' schools in Albany, N.Y., provides the answer: Take the poorest kids first.   17

Whatever the approach, no one is calling for a wholesale shift to segregation by gender, and that means someone will be left out. Single-sex public schools perpetuate the kind of two-tiered system that used to be based solely on family income, even if they widen the net. But that has always been true of innovative public schools, and it is no reason to hesitate.   18

The most troubling question about single-sex public education—Why now?—has nothing to do with school. When support comes so readily from opposite ends of the political spectrum, it is reasonable to ask why everyone is so excited, particularly given the political debate about vouchers and school choice.   19

If the intention is to strengthen the public school system by responding to new information about how our children learn, then these classes can serve as a model of innovative teaching techniques, some of which can be transported back into existing coed classrooms. Single-sex public schools and classes, as odd as it may sound, are about inclusion; any school district that wants one can have one and everyone can learn from the experience.   20

But if this is about siphoning off the best and potentially brightest, and ignoring the rest, then it is a cruel joke, a warm and fuzzy set-up for measures like vouchers. If single-sex becomes a satisfying distraction from existing schools that desperately need help, then it only serves to further erode the system. The new educational reform law is called the No Child Left Behind Act, an irresistible sentiment with a chilling edge to it—did we ever actually intend to leave certain children behind? The challenge, in developing these new schools and programs, is to make them part of a dynamic, ongoing reform, and not an escape hatch from a troubled system.   21

Making Connections to Personal and Social Issues: Paradoxes

Stabiner's argument for same-sex education presents a series of paradoxes. (A paradox is a seeming contradiction, something contrary to expectation, hard to believe at first.) Perhaps the most important one is the idea that girls learn math differently from the way boys learn it. Another is the possibility that girls' greatest chance for high achievement and full equality of opportunity with boys requires that girls be segregated from boys during their schooling. The first seems like a paradox because we are used to thinking of the human brain as functioning similarly among women and men. The latter seems like a paradox perhaps because of the long-standing belief that "separate" can never truly be "equal." Stabiner argues that observation, research, and science can and should contradict or overturn such traditional thinking.

With two or three other students, discuss paradoxes in your lives. First, list two or three situations where your own observations, experiences, or learning have contradicted what you were taught when you were younger either at home, in school, or in your religious (or another kind of) community. Then, present your paradoxes to each other and discuss whether you have resolved them.

Analyzing Writing Strategies

1. Stabiner gives three **reasons** for her position. First, underline the position they support: the last sentence, following the colon, at the end of paragraph 3. (Notice that Stabiner reiterates this position at the beginning of paragraph 5.) Then underline the reasons, found in the first sentence of paragraphs 5, 11, and 16. *Finally, write a sentence or two explaining the connection, as you see it, between the three reasons and the position they support.*

2. Stabiner provides **support** for each of her reasons. To see how she supports her first reason — that single-sex education has value — underline a phrase or sentence in each of paragraphs 5, 6, and 7 that identifies a benefit she asserts for it. *Then write a sentence or two explaining how this support is relevant to the reason. Finally, evaluate how convincing it is likely to be to readers who may resist her argument.*

Commentary: Establishing Authority

Stabiner **establishes her authority** with readers primarily by counterarguing their likely objections and anticipating their questions. After she asserts her position (in paragraph 3), she immediately (in the first sentence of paragraph 4) addresses readers' likely concern that she will attempt to "proselytize" — that is, convert them to a belief that single-sex schools are "the answer to everyone's prayers." As proof that she will not do so, she quickly lists three reasons why readers may want to resist her argument: some children would not like single-sex schools, some parents would question their relevance, and other people would prefer to focus on improving coed schools. It may seem odd or even reckless of Stabiner to give readers reasons so early in the essay to resist her argument, but actually it increases her authority. And she needs all the authority and trust she can muster, because she is asking readers to consider a radical social change.

Stabiner may seem to take an even bigger risk by acknowledging that three powerful and respected groups oppose her position: the National Organization for Women (NOW), the New York Civil Liberties Union, and the American Association of University Women (AAUW). She attempts to refute the reasons for the AAUW's caution (par. 14) and takes a more subtle approach to NOW's resistance (10–11). She concedes that she can sympathize with NOW's reasons for refusing to acknowledge gender differences, but she then insists that NOW is negligent in ignoring brain research showing that girls and boys learn math differently.

Stabiner's reference to brain research is just one instance of the **convincing support** she provides for her position. In addition, in paragraph 3, she states that she has spent three years studying two all-girls' schools; in paragraphs 6 and 7, she claims that students at these schools benefit in terms of attitude, graduation rates, and other significant factors. Stabiner cites experts (sociologist Cornelius Riordan in paragraph 5; the American Association of University Women in paragraph 14; education scholars David and Myra Sadker in paragraph 15) and statistics (for example, in paragraphs 5, 8, and 16).

Stabiner shows that she is mindful of her readers in every stage of her argument, yet this mindfulness does not weaken her argument or make her unassertive: She boldly asserts her position in the debate about same-sex schooling, and she is unequivocal about her reasons for taking the position she does. When you write your essay taking a position, you will want to strive for this clarity while at the same time you acknowledge, concede, or refute your readers' likely questions and objections.

Considering Topics for Your Own Essay

Every community frequently debates issues of schooling. These issues range from closing a school because its enrollment has dropped to deciding whether a certain book should be required reading. List further issues you are aware of. (You can be more certain it's a debatable issue if you can phrase it as a *should* question.) You can broaden your list by including issues related to any kind of training or coaching in school or the workplace.

■ Purpose and Audience

Most writers compose essays arguing for a position because they care deeply about the issue. As they develop an argument with their readers in mind, however, writers usually feel challenged to think about their own as well as their readers' feelings and thoughts about the issue.

Writers with strong convictions seek to influence their readers. Assuming that reasoned argument can prevail over prejudice, they try to change readers' minds by presenting compelling reasons and support based on shared values and principles. Nevertheless, they also recognize that in cases where disagreement is profound, it is highly unlikely that a single essay will be able to change readers' minds. When they are addressing an audience that is completely opposed to their position, most writers are satisfied if they can simply win their readers' respect for a different point of view.

Basic Features: Arguing Positions

A Focused Presentation of the Issue

Writers use a variety of strategies to present the issue and prepare readers for their argument. Statsky, for example, gives a brief history of the debate about competitive sports for children and provides concrete examples (Peewee Football and Little League Baseball) early on to make sure that readers can understand the issue.

Of course, writers also try to define the issue in a way that promotes their position. Stabiner, for example, presents the issue of single-sex education in terms of how it can improve the lives of girls—especially disadvantaged girls—and the opportunities available to them.

A Clear Position

Very often writers declare their position in a thesis statement early in the essay. Statsky places her thesis in the opening paragraph. Etzioni announces his thesis in the first sentence, using a provocative statement ("McDonald's is bad for your kids") that he restates with reasons at the end of his third paragraph ("[Fast-food] jobs undermine school attendance and involvement, impart few skills that will be useful in later life, and simultaneously skew the values of teen-agers"). All of the writers in this chapter restate the thesis at places in the argument where readers could lose sight of the central point, and they reiterate the thesis at the end.

In composing a thesis statement, writers try to make their position unambiguous, appropriately qualified, and clearly arguable.

Plausible Reasons and Convincing Support

To argue for a position, writers must give reasons. Even in relatively brief essays, writers sometimes give more than one reason and state their reasons explicitly. Statsky, for instance, gives four reasons for her opposition to competitive sports for children: They are harmful to the children both physically and psychologically, discourage most from participating, and encourage adults to behave badly.

Writers know they cannot simply assert their reasons. They must support them with examples, statistics, authorities, or anecdotes. We have seen all of these kinds of support used in this chapter. Statsky uses all of them in her essay—giving examples of common sports injuries that children incur, citing statistics indicating the high percentage of children who drop out of competitive sports, quoting authorities on the physical and psychological hazards of competitive sports for young children, and relating an anecdote of a child vomiting to show the enormous psychological pressure competitive sports put on some children. Stabiner supports one reason why she so favors single-sex education—that it benefits poor students and minorities the most—by pointing out the facts that Latina and African American girls at a single-sex New York City high school go on to four-year colleges at a much higher rate than their counterparts at coed schools.

Anticipating Opposing Positions and Objections

Writers also try to anticipate other widely held positions on the issue as well as objections and questions readers might raise to an argument. The writers in this chapter counterargue by either accommodating or refuting opposing positions and objections. Stabiner refutes the objections of several national organizations to her position that now is the time to try single-sex schooling. Etzioni refutes parents' and students' belief in the benefits of working at McDonald's by arguing that such work does nothing more than train "robots" for "yesterday's assembly lines."

Anticipating readers' positions and objections can enhance the writer's credibility and strengthen the argument. When readers holding an opposing position recognize that the writer takes their position seriously, they are more likely to listen to what the writer has to say. It can also reassure readers that they share certain important values and attitudes with the writer, building a bridge of common concerns among people who have been separated by difference and antagonism.

Arguing a Position

Invention and Research

What is a controversial issue that you have strong feelings about—or that just interests or puzzles you? Gay marriage? A community-service requirement for college graduation? Do some thinking and writing about the issue and some online research if necessary. Then come up with a tentative argument for your position. . . . **See p. 169 for more.**

Planning and Drafting

As you look over what you have written and found out about your subject so far, how can you make a convincing case for your position? How sympathetic are your readers to your point of view? What objections and questions are they likely to raise? Make a plan for your argument, and start drafting it. . . . **See p. 176 for more.**

Critical Reading Guide

What are your draft's strengths and weaknesses? Have you stated your position clearly enough? Does it need to be qualified? Have you provided enough support for all of your reasons? Get a classmate, a friend, a writing tutor, or someone else to read and respond to your essay, especially the parts you are most unsure of. . . . **See p. 181 for more.**

Revising

As you consider your essay again in light of your reader's comments, how can you improve it? Can you assert your position more confidently? Have you ignored a strong opposing argument that you need to address? Go through your draft systematically, making changes wherever necessary. . . . **See p. 182 for more.**

Editing and Proofreading

Have you checked for errors that are especially likely in writing that argues a position? Have you left out any commas that are needed before conjunctions like *and* or *but*? Any commas or semicolons that are needed with conjunctive adverbs like *however* or *consequently*? Look for and correct these and any other errors. . . . **See p. 187 for more.**

☐ The Writing Assignment

Write an essay on a controversial issue. Learn more about the issue, and take a position on it. Present the issue to readers, and develop an argument for the purpose of confirming, challenging, or changing your readers' views on the issue.

▮ Invention and Research

The following activities will help you find an issue, explore what you know about it, and do any necessary research to develop an argument and counterargument. Keep a written record of your invention and research to use when you draft and revise your essay.

Finding an Issue to Write About

To find the best possible issue for your essay, list as many possibilities as you can. The following activities will help you make a good choice.

Listing Issues. *Make a list of issues you might consider writing about.* Include issues on which you already have a position and ones you do not know much about but would like to explore further. Think about issues that you have become aware of in the subject matter of other college courses you are taking. Also, consider the issues suggested by the Considering Topics for Your Own Essay activities following the readings in this chapter.

Put the issues you list in the form of questions, like the following examples:

- Should teenagers be required to get their parents' permission to obtain birth-control information and contraceptives?
- Should public libraries and schools be allowed to block access to selected Internet sites?
- Should colleges be required to provide child-care facilities for children of students taking classes?
- Should elected state or national representatives vote primarily on the basis of their individual conscience, their constituents' interests, or the general welfare?
- Should scientists attempt to clone human beings as they have done with animals?
- Should more money be directed into research to cure [any disease you want to name]?

▪ *Listing Issues Related to Identity and Community.* As the following suggestions indicate, many controversial issues will enable you to explore your personal interests and needs and the expectations of various communities you belong to. List issues that interest you.

169

- Should parents be held responsible legally and financially for crimes committed by their children under age eighteen?

- Should high schools or colleges require students to perform community service as a condition for graduation?

- Should all materials related to voting, driving, and income-tax reporting be written only in English or in other languages read by members of the community?

- Should the racial, ethnic, or gender makeup of a police force parallel the makeup of the community it serves?

■ *Listing Issues Related to Work and Career.*   Many current controversial issues will allow you to explore work and career topics. Identify issues that you would consider writing about.

- Should businesses remain loyal to their communities, or should they move wherever labor costs, taxes, or other conditions are more favorable?

- Should the state or federal government provide job training or temporary employment to people who are unemployed but willing to work?

- Should the primary purpose of a college education be job training?

- Should drug testing be mandatory for people in high-risk jobs such as bus drivers, heavy-equipment operators, and airplane pilots?

Choosing an Interesting Issue.   *Select an issue from your list that you think would be interesting to explore further.* Your choice may be influenced by whether you have time for research or whether your instructor requires you to do research. Issues that have been written about extensively make excellent topics for extended research projects. In contrast, you may feel confident writing about a local community or campus issue without doing much, if any, research.

Exploring the Issue

To explore the issue, you need to define it, determine whether you need to do research, and decide tentatively on your position.

Defining the Issue.   *To begin thinking about the issue, write for a few minutes explaining how you currently understand it.* If you have strong feelings about the issue, briefly explain why, but do not try to present your argument at this time. Focus on clarifying the issue by considering questions like these:

- Who has taken a position on this issue, and what positions have they taken?

- How does the issue affect different groups of people? What is at stake for them?

- What is the issue's history? How long has it been an issue? Has it changed over time? What makes it important now?

- How broad is the issue? What other issues are related to it?

Confirming Your Interest in the Issue. *If you do not know very much about the issue or the different views people have taken on it, do some research before continuing.* This brief initial period of research should enable you to learn how the issue is being defined, orient you to the debate on it, and help you decide whether you want to learn more and write about it. Talk to other people about the issue. Gather some information online, using a keyword search in Google or Yahoo!, and do a catalog search to find out what useful material your school library might have. As you are learning about the issue and confirming your interest in it, keep a list of the most promising materials you discover.

If you find that you are not interested in an issue or encounter difficulty defining it, you should switch to another one. Return to your list of possible issues, and make another choice.

Exploring Your Opinion. *Write for a few minutes exploring your current thinking on the issue.* What is your current position? Why do you hold it? What are other possible positions? As you develop your argument and learn more about the issue, you may change your mind, but do not worry. Your aim now is merely to record your thinking as of this moment.

Analyzing Potential Readers

Write several sentences describing the readers to whom you will be addressing your argument. Begin by briefly identifying your readers; then use the following questions to help you describe them.

- What position or positions will my readers take on this issue? How entrenched are these positions likely to be?

- What do my readers know about the issue? In what contexts are they likely to have encountered it? In what ways might the issue affect them personally or professionally?

- How far apart on the issue are my readers and I likely to be? What fundamental differences in worldview or experience might keep us from agreeing? Which of my readers' values might most influence their view of the issue?

- Why would I want to present my argument to these particular readers? What could I realistically hope to achieve—convincing them to adopt my point of view, getting them to reconsider their own position, confirming or challenging some of their underlying beliefs and values?

Testing Your Choice

Use the questions below to help you decide whether you should proceed with this particular issue. Giving up on a topic after you have worked on it is bound to be frustrating, but if the issue has not come into focus for you, starting over may be the wisest course of action. (The collaborative activity on page 172 may also help you decide whether to go on with this issue or begin looking for an alternative.)

- *Do I now know enough about the issue or can I learn what I need to know in the time I have remaining?*

- *Have I begun to understand the issue well enough to describe it and explain its importance or significance?* (You need not be certain at this point how your entire argument will develop.)

- *Do I feel impelled to write about the issue?* What do I think I might gain by writing about it? Is it so important to me that I am willing to arrange my schedule over the next two or three weeks to spend the time and attention needed to produce an informed, thoughtful draft of my argument?

- *Am I interested enough in the issue to want to learn about other people's points of view on it and to develop an argument that addresses their concerns and questions?* What could I say at this point about the social or political significance of the issue? Does it matter to anyone but me? If I suspect that the issue is not one of current widespread concern, do I think I might be able to argue convincingly at the beginning of my essay that it ought to be of concern?

A Collaborative Activity: Testing Your Choice

Get together with two or three other students to discuss the issue you have tentatively chosen.

Arguers: Identify the issue you are planning to write about. Explain briefly why you care about it and why you think your intended readers might see it as important. Then explain the key reason you have for the position you have taken on the issue.

Listeners: Tell the arguer what you know about the issue and what you think makes it worth arguing about. Then suggest one thing the arguer could say to make his or her key reason most convincing to the intended readers.

Developing Your Argument

To construct a convincing argument, you need to list reasons for your position, choose the most plausible ones, and support them.

Listing Reasons.   *Write down every reason you can think of for why you have taken your position.* You can discover reasons for your position by trying to come up with "because" statements—for example, "I believe that my college should provide day care for the young children of full-time students **because these students are most likely to drop out if they cannot count on reliable day care.**" Given that few convincing arguments rely on only one reason, try to come up with at least two or three.

Choosing the Most Plausible Reasons. *Write several sentences on each reason to determine which reasons seem most plausible—that is, most likely to be convincing to* *your readers.* If you decide that none of your reasons seems very plausible, you might need to reconsider your position, do some more research, or choose another issue.

Anticipating Readers' Objections and Questions

To construct a convincing argument, you also need to decide how you will counterargue readers' objections and questions.

Listing Your Most Plausible Reasons. *Review the choices you made at the end of the preceding activity, and list your two or three most plausible reasons.*

Listing Objections and Questions. *Under each reason, list one or more objections or questions that readers could raise.* Imagining yourself as the reader, look for places where your argument is vulnerable. For example, think of an assumption that you are making that others might not accept or a value others might not share. Imagine how people in different situations—different neighborhoods, occupations, age groups, living arrangements—might react to your argument.

Accommodating a Legitimate Objection or Question. *Choose one objection or question that makes sense to you, and write for a few minutes on how you could accommodate it in your argument.* You may be able simply to acknowledge an objection or answer a question and explain why you think it does not negatively affect your argument. If the criticism is more serious, try not to let it shake your confidence. Instead, consider how you can accommodate it, perhaps by conceding the point and qualifying your position or changing the way you argue for it.

If the criticism seems so damaging that you cannot accommodate it into your argument, however, you may need to rethink your position or even consider writing on a different issue. If you arrive at such an impasse, discuss the problem with your instructor; do not abandon your issue unless absolutely necessary.

Refuting an Illegitimate Objection or Question. *Choose one objection or question that seems to challenge or weaken your argument, and write for a few minutes on how you could refute it.* Do not choose to refute only the weakest objection while ignoring the strongest one. Consider whether you can show that an objection is based on a misunderstanding or that it does not really damage your argument.

Anticipating Opposing Positions

Now that you have planned your argument and counterargument, you need to consider how you can respond to the arguments for other positions on the issue.

Considering Other Positions. *Identify one or more widely held positions other than your own that people take on the issue.* If you can, identify the individuals or groups who support the positions you list.

An Online Activity: Researching Opposing Positions   To learn more about opposing positions, search for your issue online. To do so, enter a word or brief phrase describing your issue into a search tool such as Google (http://www.google.com) or Yahoo! Directory (http://dir.yahoo.com). If possible, identify at least two positions different from your own.

Bookmark or keep a record of promising sites. Download any materials that may help you represent and counterargue opposing positions.

Listing Reasons for the Opposing Position.   *Choose the opposing position you think is likely to be most attractive to your particular readers, and list the reasons people give for taking this position.* Given what you now know, try to represent the argument accurately and fairly. Later, you may need to do some research to find out more about this opposing position.

Accommodating a Plausible Reason.   *Choose one reason that makes sense to you, and write for a few minutes on how you could accommodate it into your argument.* Consider whether you can accommodate the point and put it aside as not really damaging to your central argument. You may also have to consider qualifying your position or changing the way you argue for it.

Refuting an Implausible Reason.   *Choose one reason that you do not accept, and write for a few minutes on how you will plan your refutation.* Do not choose to refute a position no one really takes seriously. Also be careful not to misrepresent other people's positions or to criticize people personally. Instead, try to get at the heart of your disagreement.

You may want to argue that the values on which the opposing argument is based are not widely shared or are just plain wrong. Or perhaps you can point out that the reasoning is flawed (for instance, showing that an example applies only to certain people in certain situations). Or maybe you can show that the argument lacks convincing support (for instance, that the opposition's statistics can be interpreted differently or that quoted authorities do not qualify as experts). If you do not have all the information you need, make a note of what you need and where you might find it. Later, you can do more research to develop this part of your argument.

Designing Your Document

Think about whether including visual or audio elements—cartoons, photographs, tables, graphs, or clips from films, television programs, or songs—would strengthen your argument. These are not a requirement of an effective essay arguing a position, but they could be helpful. Consider also whether your readers might benefit from design features such as headings, bulleted or numbered lists, or other elements that would make your essay easier to follow. Remember, if you do use visual or audio materials you did not create yourself, you must acknowledge your sources in your essay, and you should request permission from the sources if your essay will be posted on a Web site that is not password-protected.

In thinking about possible visual aids to your argument, consider the ways in which effective speakers and writers draw upon visual information and evidence to support their claims. You might think back to compelling speeches—or even sermons—you've heard, or to interesting debates, slide shows, or campaign ads.

Defining Your Purpose for Your Readers

Write a few sentences that define your purpose in writing about your position on this issue for your readers. Remember that you already have analyzed your potential readers and developed your argument with these readers in mind. Try now to define your purpose by considering the following possibilities:

- If my readers are likely to be sympathetic to my point of view, what do I hope to achieve—to give them reasons to commit to my position, arm them with ammunition to make their own arguments, or win their respect and admiration?

- If my readers are likely to be hostile to my point of view, what do I hope to accomplish—to get them to concede that other points of view must be taken seriously, make them defend their reasons, show them how knowledgeable and committed I am to my position, or show them how well I can argue?

- If my readers are likely to take an opposing position but are not staunchly committed to it, what should I try to do—make them question or doubt the reasons and the kinds of support they have for their position, show them how my position serves their interests better, appeal to their values and sense of responsibility, or disabuse them of their preconceptions and prejudices against my position?

Formulating a Tentative Thesis Statement

Write a few sentences that could serve as a thesis statement. Draft a thesis statement that tells your readers simply and directly what you want them to think about the issue and why. Assert your position carefully. You might also forecast your reasons, mentioning them in the order in which you will take them up in your argument.

Statsky asserts her thesis at the end of the first paragraph and then qualifies it and forecasts her reasons in the second paragraph:

> When overzealous parents and coaches impose adult standards on children's sports, the result can be activities that are neither satisfying nor beneficial to children.
>
> I am concerned about all organized sports activities for children between the ages of six and twelve. The damage I see results from noncontact as well as contact sports, from sports organized locally as well as those organized nationally. Highly organized competitive sports such as Peewee Football and Little League Baseball are too often played to adult

standards, which are developmentally inappropriate for children and can be both physically and psychologically harmful. Furthermore, because they eliminate many children from organized sports before they are ready to compete, they are actually counterproductive for developing either future players or fans. Finally, because they emphasize competition and winning, they unfortunately provide occasions for some parents and coaches to place their own fantasies and needs ahead of children's welfare.

As you formulate your own tentative thesis statement, pay attention to the language you use. It should be clear and unambiguous, and emphatic but appropriately qualified. Although you will most probably refine this thesis statement as you work on your essay, trying now to articulate it will help give your planning and drafting direction and impetus.

■ Planning and Drafting

You should now review what you have learned about the issue, do further research if necessary, and plan your first draft by setting goals and making an outline.

Seeing What You Have

Pause now to reflect on your invention and research notes. Reread everything carefully to decide whether you have enough plausible reasons and convincing support to offer readers and whether you understand the debate well enough to anticipate and respond to your readers' likely objections. It may help, as you read, to annotate your invention writings. Look for details that will help you clarify the issue for readers, present a strong argument for your position, and counterargue possible objections and alternative positions.

If your invention notes are skimpy, you may not have given enough thought to the issue or know enough at this time to write a convincing argument about it. You can do further research at this stage or begin drafting and later do research to fill in the blanks.

If you fear that you are in over your head, consult your instructor to determine whether you should make a radical change. For example, your instructor might suggest that you tackle a smaller, more feasible aspect of the issue, perhaps one with which you have firsthand experience. It is also possible that your instructor will advise you to give up on this topic for the time being and to try writing on a different issue.

Doing Further Research

If you think you lack crucial information that you will need to plan and draft your essay, this is a good time to do some further research. Consider all possible sources, including people you could interview as well as library materials and Internet sites. Then do your research, making sure to record all the information you will need to cite your sources.

Setting Goals

Your draft will be easier to write and more focused if you have some clear goals in mind as you write it. Use the following questions to help you set your goals:

Your Purpose and Readers

- Who are my readers, and what can I realistically hope to accomplish by addressing them?
- Should I write primarily to change readers' minds, to get them to consider my arguments seriously, to confirm their opinions, to urge them to do something about the issue, or to accomplish some other purpose?
- How can I present myself so that my readers will consider me informed, knowledgeable, and fair?

The Beginning

- What opening would capture readers' attention?
- Should I begin as if I were telling a story, with phrases like "Over the past three decades" (Statsky)?
- Should I make clear at the outset exactly what my concerns are and how I see the issue, as Statsky does?

Presentation of the Issue

- Should I place the issue in a historical context, as Stabiner does, or in a personal context?
- Should I use examples—real or hypothetical—to make the issue concrete for readers, as Etzioni does?
- Should I try to demonstrate that the issue is important by citing statistics, quoting authorities, or describing its negative effects, as Statsky does?
- Should I present the issue as a paradox, something hard to believe at first, as Etzioni and Stabiner do?

Your Argument and Counterargument

- How can I present my reasons so that readers will see them as plausible, leading logically to my position, as Stabiner does?
- If I have more than one reason, how should I sequence them?
- Should I forecast my reasons or counterarguments early in the essay, as Statsky does?

- Which objections should I anticipate? Can I concede any objections without undermining my argument, as Stabiner does?
- Should I refute any objections, as Etzioni and Stabiner do?
- Which opposing positions should I anticipate? Can I counterargue by showing that the statistics offered by others are not relevant, as Etzioni does?
- Can I support my reasoning by narrating anecdotes (Etzioni), pointing out benefits (Stabiner), stressing consequences and losses (Etzioni, Statsky), or quoting research (Statsky, Stabiner, Etzioni)?

The Ending

- How can I conclude my argument effectively? Should I reiterate my thesis, as Etzioni does?
- Should I try to unite readers with different allegiances by reminding them of values we share, as Stabiner does?
- Could I conclude by looking to the future or by urging readers to take action or make changes, as Statsky does?
- Should I conclude with a challenge, as Etzioni and Stabiner do?

Outlining

An essay arguing a position on a controversial issue contains as many as four basic parts:

1. Presentation of the issue
2. A clear position
3. Reasons and support
4. Anticipating opposing positions and objections

These parts can be organized in various ways. If you expect some of your readers to oppose your argument, you might try to redefine the issue so that these readers can see that they share some common values with you. To reinforce your connection to readers, you could concede the wisdom of an aspect of their position before presenting the reasons and support for your position. You would conclude by reiterating the shared values on which you hope to build agreement. In this case, an outline might look like this:

Presentation of the issue

Accommodation of some aspect of an opposing position

Thesis statement

First reason with support

Second reason with support

(etc.)

Conclusion

If you have decided to write primarily for readers who agree rather than disagree with you, then you might choose to organize your argument as a refutation of opposing arguments. Begin by presenting the issue, stating your position, and reminding readers of your most plausible reasons. Then take up each opposing argument, and try to refute it. You might conclude by calling your supporters to arms. Here is an outline showing what this kind of essay might look like:

Presentation of the issue

Thesis statement

Your most plausible reasons

First opposing argument with refutation

Second opposing argument with refutation

(etc.)

Conclusion

There are, of course, many other ways to organize an essay arguing for a position on a controversial issue, but these outlines should help you start planning your own essay.

Consider tentative any outlining you do before you begin drafting. As you draft, you will usually see ways to improve on your original plan. Be ready to revise your outline, shift parts around, or drop or add parts as you draft.

Drafting

General Advice.   Start drafting your essay, keeping in mind the goals you set while you were planning. Remember also the needs and expectations of your readers; organize, define, and explain with them in mind. Turn off your grammar checker and spelling checker at this stage if you find them distracting. Don't be afraid to skip around in your draft; jump back and fill in a spontaneous idea, or leap ahead and write a later section first if you find that easier. If, as you draft, you find that you need more information, make a note of what you have to find out and go on to the next point. If you get stuck while drafting, explore the problem by using some of the writing activities in the Invention and Research section of this chapter.

As you draft, keep in mind that the basis for disagreement about controversial issues often depends on values as much as on credible support. Also keep in mind the values underlying your own as well as others' views so that your argument can take these values into account.

A Sentence Strategy: Concession Followed by Refutation.   As you draft, you will need to move back and forth smoothly between direct arguments for your position and counterarguments for your readers' likely objections, questions, and preferred positions on the issue. One useful strategy for making this move is to concede the value of a likely criticism and then to attempt to refute it immediately, either in the same sentence or in the next one.

How do you introduce a brief concession followed by refutation into your argument? The following sentences from Jessica Statsky's essay illustrate several ways to do so (the concessions are in italics, the refutations in bold):

The primary goal of a professional athlete—winning—is not appropriate for children. Their goals should be having fun, learning, and being with friends. *Although winning does add to the fun,* **too many adults lose sight of what matters and make winning the most important goal.** (par. 5)

And it is perfectly obvious how important competitive skills are in finding a job. **Yet the ability to cooperate is also important for success in life.** (10)

In both these examples from different stages in her argument, Statsky concedes the value of some of her readers' likely objections, but then firmly refutes them. The following examples come from other readings in the chapter:

The authors argue that the employees develop many skills such as how to operate a food-preparation machine and a cash register. **However, little attention is paid to how long it takes to acquire such a skill, or what its significance is.** (Etzioni, 8)

[M]any feminists still fear that any public acknowledgment of differences between the sexes will hinder their fight for equality.

But brain research has shown us that girls and boys develop and process information in different ways; they do not even use the same region of the brain to do their math homework. (Stabiner, 10, 11)

The concession-refutation move, sometimes called the "yes-but" strategy, is important in most arguments. Following is an outline of some other kinds of language authors rely on to introduce their concession-refutation moves:

Introducing the concession	*Introducing the refutation that follows*
I understand that ____.	What I think is ____.
I can't prove ____.	But I think ____.
X claims that ____.	As it happens ____.
It is true that ____.	But my point is ____.
Another argument ____.	But ____.
It has been argued that ____.	Nevertheless, ____.
We are told that ____.	My own belief is ____.
Proponents argue that ____.	This argument, however, ____.
This argument seems plausible ____.	But experience and evidence show ____.
One common complaint is ____.	In recent years, however, ____.
I'm not saying. . . . Nor am I saying ____.	But I am saying ____.
Activists insist ____.	Still, in spite of their good intentions ____.
A reader might ask ____.	But the real issue ____.

For more on concession followed by refutation, go to **bedfordstmartins.com/conciseguide** and click on Sentence Strategies.

Critical Reading Guide

Now is the time to get a good critical reading of your draft. Your instructor may arrange such a reading as part of your coursework; if not, you can ask a classmate to read it over. If your campus has a writing center, you might ask a tutor there to read and comment on your draft using this guide to critical reading. (If you are unable to have someone else review your draft, turn ahead to the Revising section for help reading your own draft with a critical eye.)

▶ **If You Are the Writer.** To provide focused, helpful comments, your reader must know your essay's intended audience, your purpose, and a problem in the draft that you need help solving. Briefly write out this information at the top of your draft.

- *Audience:* To whom are you directing your argument? What do you assume they think about this issue? Do you expect them to be receptive, skeptical, resistant, antagonistic?
- *Purpose:* What effect do you realistically expect your argument to have on this audience?
- *Problem:* Describe the most important problem you see in your draft.

▶ **If You Are the Reader.** Use the following guidelines for giving constructive comments to others on their position papers.

> **Making Comments Electronically**
>
> Most word processing software offers features that allow you to insert comments directly into the text of someone else's document. Many readers prefer to make their comments in this way because it tends to be faster than writing on a hard copy and space is virtually unlimited; it also eliminates the problem of deciphering handwritten comments. Where such features are not available, simply typing comments directly into a document in a contrasting color can provide the same advantages.

1. *Read for a First Impression.* Tell the writer what you think the intended audience would find most and least convincing. If you think the argument is seriously flawed, try to help the writer improve the argument.

   Next, consider the problem the writer identified, and respond briefly to that concern. (If you find that the problem is covered by one of the other guidelines listed below, respond to it in more detail there if necessary.)

2. *Analyze the Way the Issue Is Presented.* Look at the way the issue is presented, and indicate whether you think that most readers would understand the issue differently. If you think that readers will need more information to grasp the issue and appreciate its importance, ask questions to help the writer fill in whatever is missing.

3. *Assess Whether the Position Is Stated Clearly.* Write a sentence or two summarizing the writer's position as you understand it from reading the draft. Then identify the sentence or sentences in the draft where the thesis is stated

explicitly. (It may be restated in several places.) If you cannot find an explicit statement of the thesis, let the writer know. Given the writer's purpose and audience, consider whether the thesis statement is too strident or too timid and whether it needs to be more qualified, more sharply focused, or more confidently asserted. If you think that the thesis, as presented, is not really arguable—for example, if it asserts a fact no one questions or a matter of personal belief—let the writer know.

4. *Evaluate the Reasons and Support.*   Identify the reasons given for the writer's position. Have any important reasons been left out or any weak ones overemphasized? Indicate any contradictions or gaps in the argument. Point to any reasons that do not seem plausible to you, and briefly explain why. Then note any places where support is lacking or unconvincing. Help the writer think of additional support or suggest sources where more or better support might be found.

5. *Assess How Well Opposing Positions and Likely Objections Have Been Handled.*   Identify places where opposing arguments or objections are mentioned, and point to anywhere the refutation could be strengthened or where shared assumptions or values offer the potential for accommodation. Also consider whether the writer has ignored any important opposing arguments or objections.

6. *Consider Whether the Organization Is Effective.*   Get an overview of the essay's organization, perhaps by making a scratch outline. Point to any parts that might be more effective earlier or later in the essay. Point out any places where more explicit cueing—transitions, summaries, or topic sentences—would clarify the relationship between parts of the essay.

   - Reread the *beginning*. Will readers find it engaging? If not, see whether you can recommend something that might work better as an opening.
   - Study the *ending*. Does the essay conclude decisively and memorably? If not, suggest an alternative. Could something be moved to the end?
   - Assess the *design features and visuals*. Comment on the contribution of any headings, tables, or other design features and illustrations. Help the writer think of additional features that could make a contribution to the essay.

7. *Give the Writer Your Final Thoughts.* What is this draft's strongest part? What part is most in need of further work?

For a printable version of this critical reading guide, go to **bedfordstmartins.com/ conciseguide.**

■ Revising

This section will help you get an overview of your draft and revise it accordingly.

Getting an Overview

Consider your draft as a whole, following these two steps:

1. *Reread.* If at all possible, put the draft aside for a day or two before rereading it. When you return to it, start by reconsidering your purpose. Then read the draft straight through, trying to see it as your intended readers will.

2. *Outline.* Make a scratch outline, indicating the basic features as they appear in the draft.

Planning for Revision.   Resist the temptation to dive in and start changing your text until after you have a clear view of the big picture. Using your outline as a guide, move through the document, noting comments received from others and problems you want to solve.

Analyzing the Basic Features of Your Own Draft.   Using the questions presented in the Critical Reading Guide on pp. 181–82, reread your draft to identify specific problems you need to solve. Note the problems on your draft.

Studying Readers' Comments.   Review all of the comments you have received from other readers, and add to your notes any suggestions you intend to act on. For each comment, look at the draft to see what might have led the reader to make that particular point. Try to be receptive to any criticism. By letting you see how other readers respond to your draft, these comments provide valuable information about how you might improve it.

Working with Sources

Support your counterargument by quoting key words when summarizing opposing views   How you represent the views of those who disagree with your position is especially important because it affects your credibility with readers. If you do not represent your opponents' views fairly and accurately, readers very likely will—and probably should—question your honesty. One useful strategy is to quote your sources.

Compare the sentence from paragraph 3 of Statsky's essay to the passage from her source, the Little League Web site. The words Statsky quotes are highlighted.

Quote: Although the official Little League Web site acknowledges that children do risk injury playing baseball, it insists that "severe injuries . . . are infrequent," the risk "far less than the risk of riding a skateboard, a bicycle, or even the school bus" ("What about My Child?").

Source: (1) We know that injuries constitute one of parents' foremost concerns, and rightly so. (2) Injuries seem to be inevitable in any rigorous activity, especially if players are new to the sport and unfamiliar with its demands. (3) But because of the safety precautions taken in Little League, severe injuries such as bone fractures are infrequent. (4) Most injuries are sprains and strains, abrasions and cuts and bruises. (5) The risk of serious injury in Little League Baseball is far less than the risk of riding a skateboard, a bicycle, or even the school bus.

Statsky accurately condenses her source's second sentence ("Injuries seem to be inevitable in any rigorous activity, especially if players are new to the sport and unfamiliar with its demands.") into one clause ("children do risk injury playing baseball"). She makes clear in the second part of her sentence that although the Little League agrees with her on the risk of injury, it disagrees about the seriousness of that risk. By quoting ("it insists that 'severe injuries . . . are infrequent,' 'far less than the risk of riding a skateboard, a bicycle, or even the school bus'"), she assures readers she has not distorted the Little League's position.

Quoting Appropriately to Avoid Plagiarism

In an earlier, rough draft, Statsky omitted the quotation marks in her sentence. Below is part of her draft sentence, followed by the source with the quoted words highlighted.

> . . . it insists that severe injuries are infrequent, the risk far less than the risk of riding a skateboard, a bicycle, or even the school bus ("What about My Child?").

> . . . severe injuries such as bone fractures are infrequent. Most injuries are sprains and strains, abrasions and cuts and bruises. The risk of serious injury in Little League Baseball is far less than the risk of riding a skateboard, a bicycle, or even the school bus.

Even though Statsky cites the source, this failure to use quotation marks around language that is borrowed amounts to plagiarism. When you cite sources in a position paper, use quotation marks whenever you use phrases from your source *and* indicate your source. Doing one or the other is not enough; you must do both. For more information on integrating language from sources into your own sentences, see pp. 406–14 in Chapter 14.

For more help avoiding plagiarism, go to **bedfordstmartins.com/conciseguide** and click on Avoiding Plagiarism Tutorial.

Carrying Out Revisions

Having identified problems in your draft, you now need to come up with solutions and—most important—to carry them out. Basically, you have three ways of finding solutions:

1. Review your invention and planning notes for information and ideas to add to your draft.

2. Do additional invention and research to provide material you or your readers think is needed.

3. Look back at the readings in this chapter to see how other writers have solved similar problems.

The following suggestions will help you get started solving some problems common to position papers.

Presentation of the Issue

- **Do readers have difficulty summarizing the issue, or do they see it differently from the way you do?** Try to anticipate possible misunderstandings or other ways of seeing the issue.

- **Do readers need more information?** Consider adding examples, quoting authorities, or simply explaining the issue further.

- **Does the issue strike readers as unimportant?** State explicitly why you think it is important and why you think your readers should think so, too. Try to provide an anecdote, facts, or a quote from an authority that would demonstrate its importance.

A Clear Position

- **Do readers have difficulty summarizing your position or finding your thesis statement?** You may need to announce your thesis statement more explicitly or rewrite it to prevent misunderstanding.

- **Do any words seem unclear or ambiguous?** Use other words, explain what you mean, or add an example to make your position more concrete.

- **Do you appear to be taking a position that is not really arguable?** Consider whether your position is arguable. If you believe in your position as a matter of faith and cannot provide reasons and support, then your position probably is not arguable. Consult your instructor about writing about a different issue.

- **Could you qualify your thesis to account for exceptions or strong objections to your argument?** Add language that specifies when, where, under what conditions, or for whom your position applies.

Plausible Reasons and Convincing Support

- **Do readers have difficulty identifying your reasons?** Announce each reason explicitly, possibly with topic sentences. Consider adding a forecast early in the essay so readers know what reasons to expect.

- **Have you left out any reasons?** Consider whether adding particular reasons would strengthen your argument. To fit in new reasons, you may have to reorganize your whole argument.

- *Do any of your reasons seem implausible or contradictory?* Either delete such reasons, or show how they relate logically to your position or to your other reasons.

- *Does your support seem unconvincing or scanty?* Where necessary, explain why you think the support should lead readers to accept your position. Review your invention notes, or do some more research to gather additional examples, statistics, anecdotes, or quotations from authorities.

Anticipation of Opposing Arguments or Objections

Checking Sentence Strategies Electronically
Use your word processor's highlighting function to mark places in your draft where you are either making concessions to or trying to refute opposing arguments or objections that readers might have to your argument. Then look at each place, and think about whether you could strengthen your argument at that point by combining concession and refutation. For more on the concession-refutation strategy, see p. 180.

- *Do readers have difficulty finding your responses to opposing arguments or objections?* Add transitions that call readers' attention to each response.

- *Do you ignore any important objections or arguments?* Consider adding to your response. Determine whether you should replace a response to a relatively weak objection with a new response to a more important one.

- *Are there any concessions you could make?* Consider whether you should acknowledge the legitimacy of readers' concerns or accommodate particular objections. Show on what points you share readers' values, even though you may disagree on other points. Remember that all of the authors in this chapter concede and then attempt to refute, relying on useful sentence openers like *I understand that . . ., What I think is,* and *It is true that . . . , but my point is . . . .*

- *Do any of your attempts at refutation seem unconvincing?* Try to strengthen them. Avoid attacking your opponents. Instead, provide solid support—respected authorities, accepted facts, or statistics from reputable sources—to convince readers that your argument is credible.

The Organization

- *Do readers have trouble following your argument?* Consider adding a brief forecast of your main reasons at the beginning of your essay and adding explicit topic sentences and transitions to announce each reason as it is developed. As all the authors do in this chapter, consider signaling explicitly the logical relations between steps and sentences in your argument.

- *Does the beginning seem vague and uninteresting?* Consider adding a striking anecdote or surprising quotation to open the essay, or find something in the essay you could move to the beginning.

- *Does the ending seem indecisive or abrupt?* Search your invention notes for a strong quotation, or add language that will reach out to readers. Try moving your strongest point to the ending.

- *Can you add illustrations or any other design features to make the essay more interesting to read and to strengthen your argument?* Consider incorporating a visual you came across in your research or one you can create on your own.

For a revision checklist, go to **bedfordstmartins.com/conciseguide**.

Editing and Proofreading

Now is the time to edit your revised draft for errors in grammar, punctuation, and mechanics and to consider matters of style. Our research has revealed several errors that are especially likely to occur in student essays arguing a position. The following guidelines will help you check and edit your draft for these common errors.

> **A Note on Grammar and Spelling Checkers**
> These tools are good at catching certain types of errors, but currently there is no replacement for a good human proofreader. Grammar checkers in particular are extremely limited in what they can find. They also tend to give faulty advice for fixing problems and to flag correct items as wrong. Spelling checkers cause fewer problems but cannot catch misspellings that are themselves words, such as *to* for *too*.

Checking for Commas before Coordinating Conjunctions. An independent clause is a group of words that can stand alone as a complete sentence. Writers often join two or more such clauses with coordinating conjunctions (*and, but, for, or, nor, so, yet*) to link related ideas in one sentence. Look at one example from Jessica Statsky's essay:

> Winning and losing may be an inevitable part of adult life, but they should not be part of childhood. (par. 6)

In this sentence, Statsky links two ideas: (1) that winning and losing may be part of adult life and (2) that they should not be part of childhood. In essays that argue a position, writers often join ideas in this way as they set forth the reasons and support for their positions.

When you join independent clauses, use a comma before the coordinating conjunction so that readers can easily see where one idea stops and the next one starts:

> ▶ The new immigration laws will bring in more skilled people‚ but their presence will take jobs away from other Americans.

> ▶ Sexually transmitted diseases are widespread‚ and many students are sexually active.

Do not use a comma when the coordinating conjunction joins phrases that are not independent clauses:

> ▶ Newspaper reporters have visited pharmacies and observed pharmacists selling steroids illegally.

▶ We need people with special talents, and diverse skills to make the United States a stronger nation.

For practice, go to **bedfordstmartins.com/conciseguide/exercisecentral** and click on Commas before Coordinating Conjunctions.

Checking the Punctuation of Conjunctive Adverbs.   When writers take a position, the reasoning they need to employ seems to invite the use of conjunctive adverbs (*consequently, furthermore, however, moreover, therefore, thus*) to connect sentences and clauses. Conjunctive adverbs that open a sentence should be followed by a comma:

▶ Consequently, many local governments have banned smoking.

▶ Therefore, talented teachers will leave the profession because of poor working conditions and low salaries.

If a conjunctive adverb joins two independent clauses, it must be preceded by a semicolon and followed by a comma:

▶ The recent vote on increasing student fees produced a disappointing turnout; moreover, the presence of campaign literature on ballot tables violated voting procedures.

▶ Children watching television recognize violence but not its intention; thus, they become desensitized to violence.

Conjunctive adverbs that fall in the middle of an independent clause are set off with commas:

▶ Due to trade restrictions, however, sales of Japanese cars did not surpass sales of domestic cars.

For practice, go to **bedfordstmartins.com/conciseguide** and click on Punctuation of Conjunctive Adverbs.

A Common ESL Problem: Subtle Differences in Meaning.   Because the distinctions in meaning among some common conjunctive adverbs are subtle, nonnative speakers often have difficulty using them accurately. For example, the difference between *however* and *nevertheless* is small; each is used to introduce a statement that contrasts with what precedes it. But *nevertheless* emphasizes the contrast, whereas *however* softens it. Check usage of such terms in an English dictionary rather than a bilingual one. *The American Heritage Dictionary of the English Language* has special usage notes to help distinguish frequently confused words.

For practice, go to **bedfordstmartins.com/conciseguide** and click on A Common ESL Problem: Subtle Differences in Meaning.

Thinking About Document Design

Adding Tables and Charts

In her report arguing that the glass ceiling still exists for women in the corporate world (see the business course scenario described on p. 147), the student decides to reinforce her written argument with graphics because she believes her readers may have difficulty absorbing information from text that is densely packed with numerical data.

First, she considers downloading visuals from educational and governmental Web sites (such as from the Federal Glass Ceiling Commission Report, available online) but decides that the available charts and tables are too detailed to make a strong visual impact. Eventually, she locates an article in *Business Week* (July 26, 2004) that reports on women in executive management positions at major firms. The article includes a compelling table that she decides to reproduce in her report.

In another issue of *Business Week* (November 22, 1999), she locates several easy-to-read pie charts. She decides to include charts showing the percentages of female and male corporate officers, corporate officers with line jobs, and top earners. The charts are simple because each compares only two items, women and men. The *Business Week* graphics are also appealing because they indicate the actual numbers of women and men so that readers can see at a glance the relatively small numbers of women who have made it into the upper echelons.

WALL STREET'S GLASS CEILING

Few women ever make it on to the executive management committees of their firms:

FIRM	PERCENT OF WOMEN ON EMC
J.P. MORGAN	20%
MERRILL LYNCH	13
AVERAGE	12
CITIGROUP	11
GOLDMAN SACHS	8
MORGAN STANLEY	7
BEAR STEARNS	0
LEHMAN BROTHERS	0

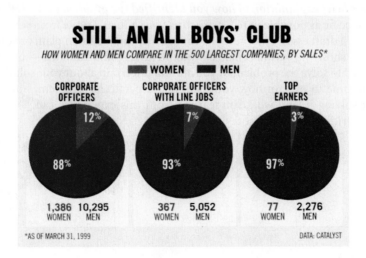

STILL AN ALL BOYS' CLUB
HOW WOMEN AND MEN COMPARE IN THE 500 LARGEST COMPANIES, BY SALES*
■ WOMEN ■ MEN

CORPORATE OFFICERS: 12% / 88% — 1,386 WOMEN / 10,295 MEN

CORPORATE OFFICERS WITH LINE JOBS: 7% / 93% — 367 WOMEN / 5,052 MEN

TOP EARNERS: 3% / 97% — 77 WOMEN / 2,276 MEN

*AS OF MARCH 31, 1999   DATA: CATALYST

Reflecting on Your Writing

Now that you have read and discussed several essays that argue a position on a contro-versial issue and written one of your own, take some time to reflect on what you have learned. What problems did you encounter as you were writing your essay, and how did you solve them?

Write a one-page explanation, telling your instructor about a problem you encoun-tered in writing your essay and how you solved it. Before you begin, gather your inven-tion and planning notes, drafts, readers' comments, revision plan, and final revision. Review these materials as you complete this writing task.

1. ***Identify one writing problem you needed to solve as you worked on the essay.*** Do not be concerned with grammar and punctuation; concentrate instead on prob-lems unique to developing an essay arguing for a position. For example: Did you puzzle over how to convince your readers that the issue is important? Did you have trouble asserting your position forcefully while acknowledging other points of view? Was it difficult to refute an important objection you knew readers would raise?

2. ***Determine how you came to recognize the problem.*** When did you first discover it? What called it to your attention? If you did not become aware of the problem until someone pointed it out to you, can you now see hints of it in your invention writings? If so, where specifically?

3. ***Reflect on how you went about solving the problem.*** Did you work on the wording of a passage, cut or add reasons or refutations, conduct further research, or move paragraphs or sentences around? Did you reread one of the essays in this chapter to see how another writer handled a similar problem, or did you look back at your invention writing? If you talked about the problem with another student, a tutor, or your instructor, did talking about it help? How useful was the advice you received?

4. ***Write a brief explanation of how you identified the problem and tried to solve it.*** Be as specific as possible in reconstructing your efforts. Quote from your invention notes and draft essay, other readers' comments, your revision plan, or your revised essay to show the various changes your writing—and thinking—underwent as you tried to solve the problem. If you are still uncertain about your solution, say so. Taking time to explain how you identified a particular problem, how you went about solving it, and what you learned from this experience can help you solve future writing problems more easily.

6

Proposing a Solution

IN COLLEGE COURSES For an education class, a student develops a proposal that would require television networks to provide programming designed to help preschool children learn English. During a meeting with his professor, he learns about the Communications Act of 1934, which requires publicly owned airwaves to serve the public interest, and the Children's Television Act of 1990, which was supposed to encourage commercial stations to provide a minimum amount of educational children's programming. He decides to argue that these laws need to be more rigorously enforced.

Through library and Internet research, the student discovers that the national commercial networks offer little in the way of educational programming for children and nothing targeted to English-language learners. He uses statistics to establish the need for such programming and supports his proposal with early education and language acquisition theory. He counters possible objections by citing two model programs, public television's *Sesame Street* and cable's *Mi Casita* (*My Little House*), as evidence that his proposal can be implemented.

IN THE COMMUNITY A social services administrator in a large Northeastern city becomes increasingly concerned about the rise in the number of adolescents in jail. His observations and the studies he reads convince him that a partial solution to the problem would be to intervene at the first sign of delinquent behavior in eight- to twelve-year-olds. In developing a proposal to circulate among influential people in the local police department, juvenile justice system, school system, and business and religious communities, the administrator begins by describing the consequences of jailing young criminals, focusing on the costs of incarceration and the high rate of return to criminal activity by juveniles after their release.

He then discusses the major components of his early intervention program, which include assigning mentors to young people who are beginning to fail in school, placing social workers with troubled families to help out before and after school, and hiring neighborhood residents to work full-time on the streets to counter the influence of gangs. The administrator acknowledges that his proposal will require the cooperation of many city agencies, and offers to take the lead in bringing it about. He also acknowledges the costs of the program but points to lowered costs for incarceration if it is successful and suggests sources of grant money to fund it.

IN THE WORKPLACE A driver of a heavy diesel tractor-and-trailer truck writes a proposal for trucking company owners, who face a shortage of well-qualified drivers, suggesting that they recruit more women. As she plans her proposal, she talks to the owner of the company she drives for and to the few women drivers she knows. In trucking industry magazines, she finds statistics she can use to argue for a new training program aimed at recruiting women.

The program she describes would exceed the Professional Truck Driver Institute standard, which requires a minimum of forty-four hours of driving time. After an initial off-road training period, recruits would be assigned to experienced drivers serving as paid teacher/mentors. The students would not have to pay the $4,000-plus tuition normally required by truck-driving schools, but they would be required to sign a contract agreeing to drive for the company for a minimum number of months after the training period at a slightly reduced pay.

The driver argues that everyone benefits. The company gets a skilled workforce. The experienced drivers get additional income. The recruits get hands-on experience without the up-front cost of tuition. She gives her proposal to the company president and it is eventually published in an industry newsletter.

Proposals are vital to a democracy. By reading and writing proposals, citizens learn about problems affecting their well-being and explore possible actions to solve them. For example, one of the scenarios opening this chapter describes a concerned citizen's proposal for helping at-risk children before they get into trouble. Similarly, an essay later in this chapter by a policy researcher and senator's staffer tries to help families attain flexibility in their work schedules. Proposals, however, do not have to be about large social problems. Many concern business-related or local community problems such as the proposal to train women as truck drivers in the previous scenario and the reading later in this chapter about making bicycle riding a more viable means of transportation.

Even students write proposals. Like the student who proposes more children's educational television programming, you may be asked in a course you are taking to propose a solution to a problem revealed in the course. Or you may decide on your own to propose a solution to a campus problem, as Patrick O'Malley does in proposing a solution to the problem of "high-stakes exams."

As a special form of argument, proposals have much in common with position papers, described in Chapter 5. Both take a stand on a subject about which there is disagreement and both make a reasoned argument, acknowledging readers' likely objections. Proposals, however, go further: They urge readers to take specific action. They argue for a proposed solution to a problem, and they succeed or fail by the strength of that argument.

Good proposals are creative as well as convincing. Problem-solving depends on a questioning attitude—wondering about alternative approaches to bringing about change and posing challenges to the status quo. To solve a problem, you need to look at it from new angles and in new contexts.

Because a proposal tries to convince readers that its way of defining and solving the problem makes sense, proposal writers must be sensitive to readers' needs and expectations. Readers need to know details of the solution and to be convinced that it will solve the problem and can be implemented. If readers initially favor a different solution, knowing why the writer rejects it will help them decide whether to support or reject the writer's proposal. Readers may be wary of costs, demands on their time, and grand schemes.

As you plan and draft a proposal, you will have to determine whether your readers are aware of the problem and whether they recognize its seriousness, and you will have to consider their views on possible alternative solutions. Knowing what your readers know—their knowledge of the problem and willingness to make changes, their assumptions and biases, the kinds of arguments likely to appeal to them—is a central part of proposal writing.

A Collaborative Activity: Practice Proposing a Solution to a Problem

To get a sense of the complexities and possibilities involved in proposing solutions, think through a specific problem with two or three other students, and try to come up with a feasible proposal. Here are some guidelines to follow:

Part 1. Select one person to take notes during your discussion.

- First, select a problem within your college or community that you all agree needs to be solved.

- Next, identify one solution that you can all support. You need not all be equally enthusiastic about this solution.
- Finally, determine who has the authority to take action on your proposed solution and how to convince this audience that your proposed solution is feasible and should be supported. Make notes about what objections the audience might raise.

Part 2. As a group, discuss your efforts. What surprised or pleased you most about this activity? What difficulties did you encounter?

Readings

PATRICK O'MALLEY wrote the following proposal while he was a first-year college student frustrated by what he calls "high-stakes exams." O'Malley interviewed two professors (his writing instructor and the writing program director), talked with several students, and read published research on the subject of testing. As you read his essay, notice how he anticipates professors' likely objections to his proposed solution and evaluates their preferred solutions to the problem.

More Testing, More Learning
Patrick O'Malley

1   It's late at night. The final's tomorrow. You got a C on the midterm, so this one will make or break you. Will it be like the midterm? Did you study enough? Did you study the right things? It's too late to drop the course. So what happens if you fail? No time to worry about that now—you've got a ton of notes to go over.

2   Although this last-minute anxiety about midterm and final exams is only too familiar to most college students, many professors may not realize how such major, infrequent, high-stakes exams work against the best interests of students both psychologically and intellectually. They cause unnecessary amounts of stress, placing too much importance on one or two days in the students' entire term, judging ability on a single or dual performance. They don't encourage frequent study, and they fail to inspire students' best performance. If professors gave additional brief exams at frequent intervals, students

To help readers see the stress of high-stakes exams, O'Malley opens with a scenario showing students' anxiety.

O'Malley defines the problem by describing negative effects.

O'Malley announces his **proposed solution** in a thesis statement that also forecasts his reasons.

would be spurred to study more regularly, learn more, worry less, and perform better on midterms, finals, and other papers and projects.

To explain how to **implement** his solution, O'Malley uses words like *could* and *might* to suggest possibilities and *should* to set goals.

Ideally, a professor would give an in-class test or quiz after each unit, chapter, or focus of study, depending on the type of class and course material. A physics class might require a test on concepts after every chapter covered, while a history class could necessitate quizzes covering certain time periods or major events. These exams should be given weekly or at least twice monthly. Whenever possible, they should consist of two or three essay questions rather than many multiple-choice or short-answer questions. To preserve class time for lecture and discussion, exams should take no more than 15 or 20 minutes.

Turning to the **argument for his solution**, O'Malley echoes key words from his thesis/forecast to keep readers oriented.

To **support** his causal argument that frequent exams enable students to learn more, O'Malley cites research studies, using APA documentation style keyed to a References list at the end.

The main reason professors should give frequent exams is that when they do and when they provide feedback to students on how well they are doing, students learn more in the course and perform better on major exams, projects, and papers. It makes sense that in a challenging course containing a great deal of material, students will learn more of it and put it to better use if they have to apply or "practice" it frequently on exams, which also helps them find out how much they are learning and what they need to go over again. A recent Harvard study notes students' "strong preference for frequent evaluation in a course." Harvard students feel they learn least in courses that have "only a midterm and a final exam, with no other personal evaluation." They believe they learn most in courses with "many opportunities to see how they are doing" (Light, 1990, p. 32). In a review of a number of studies of student learning, Frederiksen (1984) reports that students who take weekly quizzes achieve higher scores on final exams than students who take only a midterm exam and that testing increases retention of material tested.

To introduce his next **reason**, O'Malley echoes the idea of the thesis/forecast but repeats only the word *study*.

Another, closely related argument in favor of multiple exams is that they encourage students to improve their study habits. Greater frequency in test taking means greater frequency in studying for tests. Students prone to cramming will be required—or at least strongly motivated—to open their textbooks and notebooks more often, making them less likely to resort to long, kamikaze nights of studying for major exams. Since there is so much to be learned in the typical course, it makes sense that frequent, careful study and review are highly beneficial. But students need motivation to study regularly, and nothing works like an exam. If students had frequent exams in all their courses, they would have to schedule study time each week and gradually would develop a habit of

3

4

5

frequent study. It might be argued that students are adults who have to learn how to manage their own lives, but learning history or physics is more complicated than learning to drive a car or balance a checkbook. Students need coaching and practice in learning. The right way to learn new material needs to become a habit, and I believe that frequent exams are key to developing good habits of study and learning. The Harvard study concludes that "tying regular evaluation to good course organization enables students to plan their work more than a few days in advance. If quizzes and homework are scheduled on specific days, students plan their work to capitalize on them" (Light, 1990, p. 33).

6   By encouraging regular study habits, frequent exams would also decrease anxiety by reducing the procrastination that produces anxiety. Students would benefit psychologically if they were not subjected to the emotional ups and downs caused by major exams, when after being virtually worry-free for weeks they are suddenly ready to check into the psychiatric ward. Researchers at the University of Vermont found a strong relationship among procrastination, anxiety, and achievement. Students who regularly put off studying for exams had continuing high anxiety and lower grades than students who procrastinated less. The researchers found that even "low" procrastinators did not study regularly and recommended that professors give frequent assignments and exams to reduce procrastination and increase achievement (Rothblum, Solomon, & Murakami, 1986, pp. 393–394).

> To introduce his last **reason**, O'Malley does not repeat the word *worry* from paragraph 2 but instead uses the synonym *anxiety*, making his writing less predictable yet still easy to follow.

7   Research supports my proposed solution to the problems I have described. Common sense as well as my experience and that of many of my friends support it. Why, then, do so few professors give frequent brief exams?

> Here O'Malley sums up the argument for his solution and uses a **rhetorical question** to make a smooth transition to **anticipating readers' likely objections**.

8   Some believe that such exams take up too much of the limited class time available to cover the material in the course. Most courses meet 150 minutes a week — three times a week for 50 minutes each time. A 20-minute weekly exam might take 30 minutes to administer, and that is one-fifth of each week's class time. From the student's perspective, however, this time is well spent. Better learning and greater confidence about the course seem a good trade-off for another 30 minutes of lecture. Moreover, time lost to lecturing or discussion could easily be made up in students' learning on their own through careful regular study for the weekly exams. If weekly exams still seem too time-consuming to some professors, their frequency could be reduced to every other week or their length to 5 or 10 minutes. In courses

> O'Malley **refutes** the first objection by trying to get the professor to see the student's point of view. He also tries to **accommodate it** by modifying his proposed solution.

where multiple-choice exams are appropriate, several questions could be designed to take only a few minutes to answer.

Another objection professors have to frequent exams is that they take too much time to read and grade. In a 20-minute essay exam, a well-prepared student can easily write two pages. A relatively small class of 30 students might then produce 60 pages, no small amount of material to read each week. A large class of 100 or more students would produce an insurmountable pile of material. There are a number of responses to this objection. Again, professors could give exams every other week or make them very short. Instead of reading them closely they could skim them quickly to see whether students understand an idea or can apply it to an unfamiliar problem; and instead of numerical or letter grades they could give a plus, check, or minus. Exams could be collected and responded to only every third or fourth week. Professors who have readers or teaching assistants could rely on them to grade or check exams. And the Scantron machine is always available for instant grading of multiple-choice exams. Finally, frequent exams could be given *in place of* a midterm exam or out-of-class essay assignment.

Since frequent exams seem to some professors to create too many problems, however, it is reasonable to consider alternative ways to achieve the same goals. One alternative solution is to implement a program that would improve study skills. While such a program might teach students how to study for exams, it cannot prevent procrastination or reduce "large test anxiety" by a substantial amount. One research team studying anxiety and test performance found that study skills training was not effective in reducing anxiety or improving performance (Dendato & Diener, 1986, p. 134). This team, which also reviewed other research that reached the same conclusion, did find that a combination of "cognitive/relaxation therapy" and study skills training was effective. This possible solution seems complicated, however, not to mention time-consuming and expensive. It seems much easier and more effective to change the cause of the bad habit rather than treat the habit itself. That is, it would make more sense to solve the problem at its root: the method of learning and evaluation.

Still another solution might be to provide frequent study questions for students to answer. These would no doubt be helpful in focusing students' time studying, but students would probably not actually write out the answers unless they were required to. To get students to complete the questions in a timely way, professors would have to collect and check the

9

10

11

O'Malley **refutes** the second objection by suggesting several ways to cut down on professors' work while testing students frequently.

Here O'Malley shifts from anticipating objections to **evaluating alternative solutions**. Paragraphs 10–12 counter three alternative solutions.

O'Malley rejects this alternative solution by giving reasons and citing research.

answers. In that case, however, they might as well devote the time to grading an exam. Even if it asks the same questions, a scheduled exam is preferable to a set of study questions because it takes far less time to write in class, compared to the time students would devote to responding to questions at home. In-class exams also ensure that each student produces his or her own work.

12   Another possible solution would be to help students prepare for midterm and final exams by providing sets of questions from which the exam questions will be selected or announcing possible exam topics at the beginning of the course. This solution would have the advantage of reducing students' anxiety about learning every fact in the textbook, and it would clarify the course goals, but it would not motivate students to study carefully each new unit, concept, or text chapter in the course. I see this as a way of complementing frequent exams, not as substituting for them.

13   From the evidence and from my talks with professors and students, I see frequent, brief in-class exams as the only way to improve students' study habits and learning, reduce their anxiety and procrastination, and increase their satisfaction with college. These exams are not a panacea, but only more parking spaces and a winning football team would do as much to improve college life. Professors can't do much about parking or football, but they can give more frequent exams. Campus administrators should get behind this effort, and professors should get together to consider giving exams more frequently. It would make a difference.

In responding to the next two alternative solutions, O'Malley acknowledges their benefits but also points out their shortcomings.

O'Malley **concludes** by reiterating his reasons. He tries for a light touch at the end in talking about other ways *to improve college life.*

References

Dendato, K. M., & Diener, D. (1986). Effectiveness of cognitive/ relaxation therapy and study skills training in reducing self-reported anxiety and improving the academic performance of test-anxious students. *Journal of Counseling Psychology, 33,* 131–135.

Frederiksen, N. (1984). The real test bias: Influences of testing on teaching and learning. *American Psychologist, 39,* 193–202.

Light, R. J. (1990). *Explorations with students and faculty about teaching, learning, and student life.* Cambridge, MA: Harvard University Graduate School of Education and Kennedy School of Government.

Rothblum, E. D., Solomon, L., & Murakami, J. (1986). Affective, cognitive, and behavioral differences between high and low procrastinators. *Journal of Counseling Psychology, 33,* 387–394.

APA style lists References by author's last name, puts publication date next in parentheses, and then the title and other publication information.

KAREN KORNBLUH has worked in the private sector as a management consultant and in the public sector as director of the office of legislative and intergovernmental affairs at the Federal Communications Commission and as the deputy chief of staff at the Treasury Department in the Clinton administration. Kornbluh serves currently as the policy director for Senator Barack Obama.

As director of the Work and Family Program of the New America Foundation, a nonprofit, nonpartisan institute that sponsors research on public policy issues, Kornbluh led an effort to change the American workplace to accommodate what she calls the new "juggler family," in which parents have to juggle their time for parenting and work. The policy proposal reprinted here, published in 2005 by the New America Foundation, reflects this effort.

As you read, think about your own experiences and how they affect your response to Kornbluh's proposal. Have you had to juggle your time for parenting and work, or did your parents? If so, how did you/they manage it?

Win-Win Flexibility
Karen Kornbluh

Introduction

Today fully 70 percent of families with children are headed by two working parents or by an unmarried working parent. The "traditional family" of the breadwinner and home-maker has been replaced by the "juggler family," in which no one is home full-time. Two-parent families are working 10 more hours a week than in 1979 (Bernstein and Kornbluh).

To be decent parents, caregivers, and members of their communities, workers now need greater flexibility than they once did. Yet good part-time or flex-time jobs remain rare. Whereas companies have embraced flexibility in virtually every other aspect of their businesses (inventory control, production schedules, financing), full-time workers' schedules remain largely inflexible. Employers often demand workers be available around the clock. Moreover, many employees have no right to a minimum number of sick or vacation days; almost two thirds of all workers—and an even larger percentage of low-income parents—lack the ability to take a day off to care for a family member (Lovell). The Family and Medical Leave Act (FMLA) of 1993 finally guaranteed that workers at large companies could take a leave of absence for the birth or adoption of a baby, or for the illness of a family member. Yet that guaranteed leave is unpaid.

Many businesses are finding ways to give their most valued employees flexibility, but, all too often, workers who need flexibility find themselves shunted into part-time, temporary, on-call, or contract jobs with reduced wages and career opportunities—and, often, no benefits. A full quarter of American workers are in these jobs. Only 15 percent of women and 12 percent of men in such jobs receive health insurance from their employers (Wenger). A number of European countries provide workers the right to a part-time schedule, and all have enacted legislation to implement a European Union directive to prohibit discrimination against part-time workers.

In America, employers are required to accommodate the needs of employees with disabilities—even if that means providing a part-time or flexible schedule. Employers may also provide religious accommodations for employees by offering a part-time or flexible schedule. At the same time, employers have no obligation to allow parents or employees caring for sick relatives to work part-time or flexible schedules, even if the cost to the employer would be inconsequential.

In the 21st century global economy, America needs a new approach that allows businesses to gain flexibility in staffing without sacrificing their competitiveness and enables workers to gain control over their work-lives without sacrificing their economic security. This win-win flexibility arrangement will not be the same in every company, nor even for each employee working within the same organization. Each case will be different. But flexibility will not come for all employees without some education, prodding, and leadership. So, employers and employees must be required to come to the table to work out a solution that benefits everyone. American businesses must be educated on strategies for giving employees flexibility without sacrificing productivity or morale. And businesses should be recognized and rewarded when they do so.

America is a nation that continually rises to the occasion. At the dawn of a new century, we face many challenges. One of these is helping families to raise our next generation in an increasingly demanding global economy. This is a challenge America must meet with imagination and determination.

Background: The Need for Workplace Flexibility

Between 1970 and 2000, the percentage of mothers in the workforce rose from 38 to 67 percent (Smolensky and Gootman). Moreover, the number of hours worked by dual-income families has increased dramatically. Couples with children worked a full 60 hours a week in 1979. By 2000 they were working 70 hours a week (Bernstein and Kornbluh). And more parents than ever are working long hours. In 2000, nearly 1 out of every 8 couples with children was putting in 100 hours a week or more on the job, compared to only 1 out of 12 families in 1970 (Jacobs and Gerson).

In addition to working parents, there are over 44.4 million Americans who provide care to another adult, often an older relative. Fifty-nine percent of these caregivers either work or have worked while providing care ("Caregiving").

In a 2002 report by the Families and Work Institute, 45 percent of employees reported that work and family responsibilities interfered with each other "a lot" or "some" and 67 percent of employed parents report that they do not have enough time with their children (Galinksy, Bond, and Hill).

Over half of workers today have no control over scheduling alternative start and end times at work (Galinksy, Bond, and Hill). According to a recent study by the Institute for Women's Policy Research, 49 percent of workers—over 59 million Americans—lack basic paid sick days for themselves. And almost two-thirds of all workers—and an even larger percentage of low-income parents—lack the ability to take a day off to care for a family member (Lovell). Thirteen percent of non-poor workers with caregiving responsibilities lack paid vacation leave, while 28 percent of poor caregivers lack any paid vacation time (Heymann). Research has shown that flexible arrangements and benefits tend to be more accessible in larger and more profitable firms, and then to the most valued professional and managerial workers in those firms (Golden). Parents with young children and working welfare recipients—the workers who need access to paid leave the most—are the least likely to have these benefits, according to research from the Urban Institute (Ross Phillips).

In the US, only 5 percent of workers have access to a job that provides paid   11
parental leave. The Family and Medical Leave Act grants the right to 12 weeks of unpaid leave for the birth or adoption of a child or for the serious illness of the worker or a worker's family member. But the law does not apply to employees who work in companies with fewer than 50 people, employees who have worked for less than a year at their place of employment, or employees who work fewer than 1,250 hours a year. Consequently, only 45 percent of parents working in the private sector are eligible to take even this unpaid time off (Smolensky and Gootman).

Workers often buy flexibility by sacrificing job security, benefits, and pay. Part-   12
time workers are less likely to have employer-provided health insurance or pensions and their hourly wages are lower. One study in 2002 found that 43 percent of employed parents said that using flexibility would jeopardize their advancement (Galinksy, Bond, and Hill).

Children, in particular, pay a heavy price for workplace inflexibility (Waters Boots   13
2004). Almost 60 percent of child care arrangements are of poor or mediocre quality (Smolensky and Gootman). Children in low-income families are even less likely to be in good or excellent care settings. Full-day child care easily costs $4,000 to $10,000 per year—approaching the price of college tuition at a public university. As a result of the unaffordable and low quality nature of child care in this country, a disturbing number of today's children are left home alone: Over 3.3 million children age 6-12 are home alone after school each day (Vandivere et al.).

Many enlightened businesses are showing the way forward to a 21st century   14
flexible workplace. Currently, however, businesses have little incentive to provide families with the flexibility they need. We need to level the playing field and remove the competitive disadvantages for all businesses that do provide workplace flexibility.

This should be a popular priority. A recent poll found that 77 percent of likely vot-   15
ers feel that it is difficult for families to earn enough and still have time to be with their families. Eighty-four percent of voters agree that children are being shortchanged when their parents have to work long hours. . . .

Proposal: Win-Win Flexibility

A win-win approach in the US to flexibility . . . might function as follows. It would be   16
"soft touch" at first—requiring a process and giving business an out if it would be costly to implement—with a high-profile public education campaign on the importance of workplace flexibility to American business, American families, and American society. A survey at the end of the second year would determine whether a stricter approach is needed.

Employees would have the right to make a formal request to their employers for flexibility in the number of hours worked, the times worked, and/or the ability to work from home. Examples of such flexibility would include part-time, annualized hours,[1] compressed hours,[2] flex-time,[3] job-sharing, shift working, staggered hours, and telecommuting.

The employee would be required to make a written application providing details on the change in work, the effect on the employer, and solutions to any problems caused to the employer. The employer would be required to meet with the employee and give the employee a decision on the request within two weeks, as well as provide an opportunity for an internal appeal within one month from the initial request.

The employee request would be granted unless the employer demonstrated it would require significant difficulty or expense entailing more than ordinary costs, decreased job efficiency, impairment of worker safety, infringement of other employees' rights, or conflict with another law or regulation.

The employer would be required to provide an employee working a flexible schedule with the same hourly pay and proportionate health, pension, vacation, holiday, and FMLA benefits that the employee received before working flexibly and would be required thereafter to advance the employee at the same rate as full-time employees.

Who would be covered: Parents (including parents, legal guardians, foster parents) and other caregivers at first. Eventually all workers should be eligible in our flexible, 24x7 economy. During the initial period, it will be necessary to define nonparental "caregivers." One proposal is to define them as immediate relatives or other caregivers of "certified care recipients" (defined as those whom a doctor certifies as having three or more limitations that impede daily functioning—using diagnostic criteria such as Activities of Daily Living [ADL]/Instrumental Activities of Daily Living [IADL]—for at least 180 consecutive days). . . .

Public Education: Critical to the success of the proposal will be public education along the lines of the education that the government and business schools conducted in the 1980s about the need for American business to adopt higher quality standards to compete against Japanese business. A Malcolm Baldridge-like award[4] should be created for companies that make flexibility win-win. A public education campaign conducted by the Department of Labor should encourage small businesses to adopt best practices of win-win flexibility. Tax credits could be used in the first year to reward early adopters.

Works Cited

Bernstein, Jared, and Karen Kornbluh. *Running Faster to Stay in Place: The Growth of Family Work Hours and Incomes*. Washington: New America Foundation, 2005. Print.

---

[1] *Annualized hours* means working different numbers of hours a week but a fixed annual total.

[2] *Compressed hours* means working more hours a day in exchange for working fewer days a week.

[3] *Flex-time* means working on an adjustable daily schedule.

[4] The Malcolm Baldridge National Quality Award is given by the U.S. President to outstanding businesses.

Galinsky, Ellen, James Bond, and Jeffrey E. Hill. *Workplace Flexibility: What Is It? Who Has It? Who Wants It? Does It Make a Difference?* New York: Families and Work Inst., 2004. Print.

Golden, Lonnie. *The Time Bandit: What U.S. Workers Surrender to Get Greater Flexibility in Work Schedules.* Washington: Economic Policy Inst., 2000. Print.

Heymann, Jody. *The Widening Gap: Why America's Working Families Are in Jeopardy – and What Can Be Done About It.* New York: Basic, 2000. Print.

Jacobs, Jerry, and Kathleen Gerson. *The Time Divide: Work, Family and Gender Inequality.* Cambridge: Harvard UP, 2004. Print.

Lovell, Vicky. *No Time to Be Sick: Why Everyone Suffers When Workers Don't Have Paid Sick Leave.* Washington: Inst. for Women's Policy Research, 2004. Print.

National Alliance for Caregiving and AARP. *Caregiving in the U.S.* Bethesda: NAC, 2004. *National Alliance for Caregiving.* Web. 20 May 2008.

Ross Phillips, Katherine. *Getting Time Off: Access to Leave among Working Parents.* Washington: Urban Inst., 2004. Print. New Federalism: National Survey of America's Families B-57.

Smolensky, Eugene, and Jennifer A. Gootman, eds. *Working Families and Growing Kids: Caring for Children and Adolescents.* National Research Council and Inst. of Medicine, Washington: National Academies P, 2004. Print.

Vandivere, Sharon, et al. *Unsupervised Time: Family and Child Factors Associated with Self-Care.* Washington: Urban Inst., 2003. Print. Assessing the New Federalism, Occasional Paper No. 71.

Waters Boots, Shelley. *The Way We Work: How Children and Their Families Fare in a 21st Century Workplace.* Washington: New America Foundation, 2004. Print.

Wenger, Jeffrey. *Share of Workers in "Nonstandard" Jobs Declines.* Washington: Economic Policy Inst., 2003. Print.

Making Connections to Personal and Social Issues: The Problem of Child Care

Many of you have probably grown up during the period Kornbluh is describing, and your family may have been configured more as a "juggler" than as a "traditional family" (par. 1). Kornbluh asserts in paragraph 13 that it is the children in juggler families who "pay a heavy price." She is particularly critical of child care, which she says is very expensive and of low quality, especially for low-income families. She cites Vandivere et al. to argue that more than "3.3 million children age 6–12 are home alone after school each day" (13).

With two or three other students, discuss how Kornbluh's argument compares with your experiences as a child. Who cared for you as a preschooler? When you were of school age, did you attend any after-school programs? Were you ever unsupervised at home while your parents were at work?

Consider also the quality of your preschool and after-school care. What lasting effects, if any, do you think this care had? From your experience, what kinds of child-care do you think would serve children and their parents best today?

Analyzing Writing Strategies

1. Writers of persuasive proposals **describe the proposed solution** simply and directly. Kornbluh, for example, announces her solution in the title of her essay and repeats it in the third heading. Notice that she also repeats the key word *flexibility* many times. Skim the essay, underlining every time *flexibility* (in one form or another) is used. *Write a few sentences explaining why she repeats the term so often, particularly in the first and last sections, and how well you think this strategy works.*

2. To **argue for her proposed solution**, Kornbluh describes how the solution can be **implemented**. Reread paragraph 5, where she sets out some general principles, and paragraphs 16–22, where she details the elements of her solution. *List the steps she recommends.* Notice that she includes guidelines for what employees as well as employers should do and includes a timetable and criteria. *Then write a few sentences speculating about why Kornbluh includes so many details. Which, if any, could be cut? What, if anything, do you think is missing?*

Commentary: Defining the Problem and Evaluating Alternative Solutions

Every proposal begins with a problem. How writers **define the problem** depends on what they assume their readers already know. Obviously, if readers are already immersed in discussing the problem and possible solutions, then the writer may not have to say much. Nevertheless, savvy proposal writers try to redefine even familiar problems in a way that leads logically to the writer's preferred solution. For problems that are new to readers, writers need not only to explain the problem but also to convince readers that it exists and is serious enough to justify the proposed solution. Kornbluh assumes readers will not be familiar with the problem she's discussing, so she spends the first part of her essay defining it and the second part establishing its seriousness. In the second part, she also begins to make the case for her proposed solution, in part by evaluating alternative solutions that readers might think are already in place.

Kornbluh uses the first section, headed "Introduction," to acquaint readers with the "juggler family" and to set the stage for her argument that businesses should accommodate the needs of their employees. She begins by establishing that the so-called "traditional family" is no longer the norm for many Americans. To support this claim, she cites statistics from *Running Harder to Stay in Place*, a book she coauthored, demonstrating that two-parent families are working more today than they were twenty-five years ago. She cites Lovell to substantiate the claim that employees today have little flexibility to take time off from work to care for loved ones. These two claims are the cornerstones of her argument that the problem does indeed exist and requires some kind of resolution.

In paragraph 3, Kornbluh adds another element to her argument about the problem's importance when she compares America to Europe. She demonstrates that European Union members understand the gravity of the problem better than Americans do and have already solved it. This comparison puts the United States in a negative light by suggesting that it is less advanced than other Western countries. It also implies a subtle threat to business leaders that if they do not help solve the problem, a solution may be imposed on them.

Finally, in the opening paragraphs of the second section, "Background: The Need for Workplace Flexibility," Kornbluh argues that the problem requires immediate attention, citing statistics to establish that the problem is worsening. She shows how much work time has increased over the last thirty years (par. 7), how many workers provide care for children or other adults (8), and how many people feel torn between work and family responsibilities (9). These three paragraphs demonstrate the urgency of her proposal.

In addition to introducing the problem, Kornbluh prepares readers for her proposed solution by **evaluating alternative solutions**. One such solution is that workers use their sick days and vacation time to care for family members. Kornbluh apparently sees nothing wrong with using sick leave this way, but she argues that it is just not available for enough people (10). She cites statistics revealing that many Americans, particularly the working poor, do not receive pay when they are sick or on vacation. Another solution—the Family and Medical Leave Act—also falls short, Kornbluh contends, because the law grants only "unpaid leave" and applies only to "45 percent of parents working in the private sector" (11). At the end of paragraph 10, Kornbluh anticipates readers in pointing out that some firms already provide flexible work arrangements; however, she reports the findings of two research studies that show only a few firms make these arrangements and only for those employees at the top. In contrast, Kornbluh's proposal is designed to help "[p]arents with young children and working welfare recipients—the workers who need access to paid leave the most" (10).

As you plan your proposal, remember that when you introduce the problem and evaluate alternative solutions, you are advancing the argument for your solution and attempting to earn the confidence of your readers. Kornbluh shows readers she has done her homework and can be trusted, in part by citing research and in part by making clear she understands the needs of both employees and employers. Kornbluh tries to convince readers her proposal is a "win-win" proposition, not a zero-sum game in which one side wins and the other loses.

Considering Topics for Your Own Essay

If you are interested in the problem Kornbluh describes, you might suggest other ways of helping parents juggle their parenting and work responsibilities. For example, consider writing a proposal for increasing opportunities for one or more parents to work at home via telecommuting. Alternatively, you might consider ways of improving preschool or after-school child-care arrangements. Would it be feasible, for instance, for high schools or community colleges to train interested students who could provide child care at supervised facilities on campus? You might interview people in your community to explore alternative ways of funding after-school programs. Perhaps you could propose that local businesses sponsor sports teams or offer after-school internships to students.

GIAN-CLAUDIA SCIARA, currently a Ph.D. candidate in the area of city and regional planning, was a writer on land-use and transportation issues and served as the bicycle program director for Transportation Alternatives, a New York City–area citizens' group working to support bicycling, walking, and public transit. Sciara is a member of the American Institute of Certified Planners. She has worked as senior transportation planner for Parsons Brinckerhoff, a worldwide engineering firm. Her writing has appeared in the *New York Times* as well as in scholarly journals such as the *Journal of Planning Education and Research, Journal of the American Planning Association,* and *Transportation Planning and Technology.* "Making Communities Safe for Bicycles" originally appeared in 2003 in *Access,* the official journal of the University of California Transportation Center.

As you read this proposal, notice the subheadings, photographs, and graph, and think about how they contribute to your understanding of the proposal. You may notice that Sciara uses neither APA nor MLA documentation styles, nor does she include parenthetical citations or a complete list of sources. Instead she follows the requirements of *Access* and ends her essay with "Further Reading." If you have the opportunity to publish your proposal, you too will be expected to use the journal's required format. When writing for your college courses, be sure to ask your instructor which documentation style you should follow.

Making Communities Safe for Bicycles
Gian-Claudia Sciara

To those who use a bicycle for transportation, it's a simple but important machine—cheap, flexible, reliable, and environmentally friendly. Moreover, bicycles are convenient. Someone traveling by bike can usually make a trip door to door, choose among various routes, and easily add stops along the way. [1]

In addition to practicality for local trips, bicycles yield measurable health benefits. Public health professionals are beginning to see bicycles and bicycle-oriented community design as part of the remedy for Americans' inactive lifestyles, obesity, and related chronic diseases. Yet despite their obvious advantages, and despite federal statutes that promote bicycle planning, bicycles account for but a tiny percentage of trips in the US, even in "bicycle friendly" communities. Less than half of one percent of Americans bicycled to work in 2000. Estimates of personal and recreational bicycle use suggest that somewhere between 65 and 100 million Americans cycle sometimes. Even so, bicycles are scarcely used for everyday trips. [2]

Bicycles do not belong to mainstream transportation culture here as they do in places like Holland. Today's planners and engineers inherit a legacy of transportation infrastructure built exclusively for motor vehicles. Design, redesign, and construction of bicycle-oriented infrastructure have only recently been acknowledged as public goals. Dispersed land use patterns put many trip origins and destinations too far apart for bicycle travel. But one of the biggest reasons bicycles are underused may be safety: fear of being struck by a motor vehicle discourages many would-be bicycle commuters. [3]

Thinking Big: Facility Design and Routine Accommodation

A policy of "routine accommodation" is one sweeping change that could effectively increase bicycle use and, potentially, safety. In *Accommodating Bicycle and Pedestrian Travel: A Recommended Approach*, USDOT[1] acknowledges that "ongoing investment in the nation's transportation infrastructure is still more likely to overlook . . . than integrate bicyclists." In response, DOT encourages transportation agencies "to make accommodation of bicycling and walking a routine part of planning, design, construction, operations and maintenance activities."

Whether with wide curb lanes or separate bicycle facilities, corridors that accommodate bicyclists will attract potential riders. New York City's Hudson River Greenway is one example. An off-street facility, this path provides a north-south route paralleling Route 9A (locally known as the West Side Highway). Opening a key connection in spring 2001 exposed the latent demand for continuous bicycle facilities among New Yorkers. As seen in Figure 1, the number of cyclists jumped dramatically after the link between 55th and 72nd Streets made the facility continuous from 125th Street in Harlem to the Battery. Already one of the most-used bike routes in the US, the Hudson River Greenway provides a direct, scenic, and virtually auto-free route to downtown Manhattan.

Bicycle facilities—whether dedicated off-street paths, on-street lanes, or bicycle-friendly shoulders—can be controversial, even among bike advocates. Indeed some bicycle planners have argued for decades against separate bicycle facilities. Most notable among them, John Forester argues that "cyclists fare best when they act as and are treated as drivers of vehicles," and that they "can travel with speed and safety almost everywhere a road system goes." He rejects the proposition that "special, safer facilities must be made for cyclists so they can ride

[1]the U.S. Department of Transportation

safely." However, his position ignores the range of ability and experience among cyclists. New bicyclists are more likely to ride where roads are designed with bicyclists in mind, and improvements designed to make potential bicyclists more welcome can have dramatic results. The city of Portland, for example, attributes steadily increasing ridership from 1991 to 2001 to continued investment in its comprehensive citywide bicycle network. Portland also reports that, even with increased ridership, numbers of bicycle-motor vehicle crashes during the 1990s remained constant, which suggests a drop in the collision rate.

As policy, "routine accommodation" promises a middle ground between inflexible requirements for specific bicycle facilities and complete neglect of bicycle improvements. Bicycle design manuals (e.g., AASHTO's[2] *Guide for the Development of Bicycle Facilities*) and professional planners throughout the country have identified numerous bicycle-facility designs for a range of circumstances. But designs must be duly considered and implemented, not just cursorily reviewed and shelved. Routine accommodation implies a deliberate approach to bicycle planning and safety.

Thinking Small: Bringing Planners' Tools Up to Speed

Transportation professionals are often at a disadvantage when trying to identify bicyclists' needs, particularly with regard to safety. When asked to plan for motorized traffic, they can tap authoritative sources with detailed information about roadway volumes, network models, travel habits, collisions, etc. However, data on bicyclists, bicycle trips, and bicycle collisions are sparse. To understand how best to serve bicyclists and reduce the number and severity of bicycle collisions, it is essential to have

---

[2]the American Association of State Highway and Transit officials

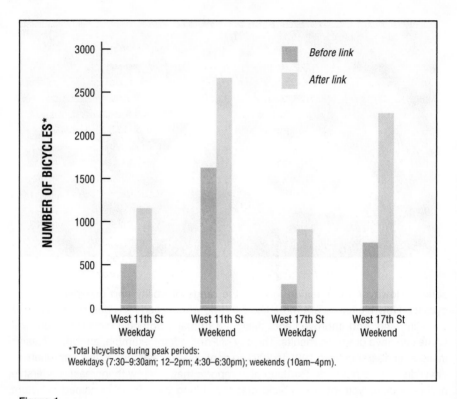

Figure 1
Route 9A Bikeway (Hudson River Greenway): Growth in bicycle use before and after Riverside South Link (2000–2001)

better data than currently exist about who rides, how often, how far, how long, on what routes, etc., and especially about the causes of collisions.

Bicyclists themselves are a latent source of valuable information. Regional travel surveys and revisions to transportation demand models should routinely draw on data solicited from them. In many places bicycle advocacy groups have grown increasingly involved in local planning efforts. Planners may find cyclists to be effective partners when seeking appropriate facilities and safety measures. 9

Planners should be able to consult motor-vehicle collision data to identify causes—and remedies—of bicycle collisions. However, collision data are collected in a system geared toward motor vehicles. Collision report forms often do not separately identify "bicycle" as a possible party to a collision. Also, damage thresholds keep police from reporting many bicycle collisions. Although $500 may truly represent minimal damage to a motor vehicle, equivalent damage to a bicycle could render it useless. One potential remedy would require officers to report any traffic collision involving a bicycle. We might then better understand nonfatal bicycle collisions. (Fatal collisions, as a rule, are well documented.) 10

Education and Enforcement

Analyses of vehicle collisions have led to safety improvements through vehicle rede- 11
sign, driver education, targeted enforcement, and modified vehicle codes. At the
1993 World Conference on Injury Control, Michael Brownlee pointed out that "over
the last ten years, the accomplishments in highway safety have overshadowed all
other periods in our history. About 40,000 people are alive today because of the
progress made in preventing drunk driving . . . An additional 30,000 lives were saved
due to increases in safety belt use." What if the safety of bicyclists were accorded
comparable priority? What if bicycle and motorist education campaigns were pursued on a scale equivalent to aggressive drunk driving and seatbelt campaigns?
Since 1932, the first year when estimates were recorded, over 47,000 cyclists have
been killed in traffic collisions, according to the National Highway Traffic Safety
Administration (NHTSA).
From 1995 to 2000, cyclist
fatalities trended down-
ward; nevertheless, an average of over 750 bicyclists
were killed each year.
NHTSA data do not capture
crashes not involving a
motor vehicle or not occurring on a public roadway,
but experts estimate an
additional 80 bicyclists die
each year, an annual total of
830 bicyclist deaths. Also,
51,000 cyclists were injured
in *reported* traffic collisions
in the year 2000, accounting for two percent of all
reported vehicular crash
injuries.

Sensors in the pavement can make crossings safer for bicyclists.

Some researchers sug- 12
gest that most bicycle
crashes involve only one
bike and its rider, but that is
not reason enough to ignore
bicycle-motor vehicle conflicts. Collisions with motor
vehicles can result in serious
injury. And because we know
many causes of bicycle-
motor vehicle collisions, we

also know what specific behavioral changes can reduce these conflicts. For example, at intersections and driveways, bicyclists and drivers need to make eye contact with each other. As bicyclists and motorists learn to coexist, each should be on guard for the other's bad habits. Motorists should learn to anticipate bicyclists coming from unexpected locations and directions. Also, bicyclists can actively prevent dooring (i.e., colliding with a vehicle door opening into the bicyclist's path) by riding a safe distance to the left of parked vehicles. A novice bicyclist might understandably be reluctant to do this, as it means moving into ("taking") the lane; and many motorists do not recognize the danger from dooring.

Safety instruction for bicyclists is important. Bicycle-safety education efforts, where they exist, most commonly target bicyclists. Essential rules of the road for bicyclists are to obey traffic signals and stop signs, be careful entering roadways at mid-block, and ride with the flow of traffic. However, motorist education is also important, though often more difficult and costly. In some states, driver education doesn't even mention bicycles. Aggressive public service campaigns are not within reach of many bicycle-planning budgets. Understandably, planners would rather use bicycle dollars to improve and build facilities than to fund costly and marginally effective advertising. Nevertheless, motorist education could save lives by emphasizing caution when pulling into the street and opening doors, consistent use of turn signals, safe speeds, and obedience to traffic signals and stop signs. 13

Making routine enforcement of traffic laws a priority would help. However, law enforcement officers who are knowledgeable about motor vehicle laws may be less informed about bicyclists' rights and responsibilities. Moreover, some officers are 14

unfamiliar with the infractions most often associated with bicycle-motor vehicle collisions. Some bicycle advocates contend that police are quick to assume the bicyclist caused the collision, or that officers are prone to cite bicyclists illegitimately because they themselves don't know the law. One bicyclist's attorney notes that bicyclists are often cited for speeding when they are not traveling any faster than motor vehicles in the same situation. A study of Los Angeles collision data found most bicycle citations were issued for failure to ride as close as practicable to the right-hand curb, suggesting ignorance of vehicle code provisions entitling cyclists to take the lane in circumstances where curb-hugging is unsafe or inadvisable.

Where to Go From Here

Bicycles are here to stay. Current trends suggest more commuters and recreational riders will turn to bikes for travel, particularly where the design of local transportation networks accommodates bicycles. So planners and policy makers face a choice. They can continue as they have, focusing on cars and considering bicycles only when compelled to. If so, we can expect things to remain as they are, with little support from law enforcement, marginal bicycle facilities, many bicycle injuries, and frustrated bicyclists and motorists.   15

Or, planners, engineers, and policy makers can acknowledge the benefits of bicycle riding and adopt a policy of routine accommodation. A 1995 survey conducted for Rodale Press queried respondents first about their current primary means of travel and second about their preferred means of travel, "all things being equal, and if good facilities [for each mode] existed." The percentage of people who chose to walk or bicycle increased from 5 to 13 percent under those hypothetical circumstances; those who chose driving alone dropped from 76 to 56 percent.   16

More and better facilities would enhance safety and encourage riding. More 17 bicyclists might accustom motorists to sharing the road and in turn might encourage still more cyclists. Both factors would increase bike safety. Enhanced bike safety might encourage some motorists to try riding; more people switching to bicycles might mean fewer cars on the road, less congestion, better public health, and safer conditions for bicyclists and pedestrians — and even less competition for parking.

Further Reading

Bruce Epperson, "Demographic and Economic Characteristics of Bicyclists Involved in Bicycle-Motor Vehicle Accidents," *Transportation Research Record*, 1502: pp. 56–64, Transportation Research Board, 1995.

John Forester, "Two Views in Cycling Transportation Engineering," *Bicycle Transportation: A Handbook for Cycling Transportation Engineers*, 2nd Edition. (Cambridge, MA: The MIT Press, 1994).

James O'Day, *Synthesis of Highway Practice 192: Accident Data Quality*. National Cooperative Highway Research Program, Transportation Research Board, National Research Council. (Washington, D.C.: National Academy Press, 1993).

Parkwood Research Associates. "Pathways for People II," Rodale Press, 1995.

John Pucher, "Cycling Safety on Bikeways vs. Roads," *Transportation Quarterly*, vol. 55, no. 4, Fall 2001.

Gregory B. Rodgers et al., *Bicycle Use and Hazard Patterns in the United States*. Study No. 344. (Washington, D.C.: US Consumer Product Safety Commission, June 1994). http://www.cpsc.gov/cpscpub/pubs/344.pdf

Jane C. Stutts and William W. Hunter, "Motor Vehicle and Roadway Factors in Pedestrian and Bicyclist Injuries: An Examination Based on Emergency Department Data," *Accident Analysis and Prevention*, vol. 31, pp. 505–514, 1999.

Robert G. Thom and Alan Clayton, "Accident Requirements for Improving Cycling Safety," *Transportation Research Record*, 1405: pp. 1–6, Transportation Research Board, 1993.

Making Connections to Personal and Social Issues: Experience with Bicycles

With two or three other students, discuss Sciara's proposal. Begin by telling the others in your group whether you use a bicycle for your everyday trips and, if not, why not.

Then discuss the kinds of changes that would need to be made to make bike riding part of your own and other people's "mainstream transportation culture" (par. 3). Would the kinds of infrastructure changes Sciara proposes make you more likely to commute by bike to work or school?

Analyzing Writing Strategies

1. To **define the problem**, proposal writers usually need to establish both that it exists and that it is important. Reread paragraphs 1–3 of Sciara's proposal to identify the problem. As you read, make notes about the kinds of information Sciara presents. *Then, explain the problem in a sentence or two.* How does Sciara convince readers that the problem exists and is important enough to be worth solving?

2. Writers of successful proposals **anticipate possible objections** to their proposed solution. Sciara does this in paragraph 6, where she discusses an objection raised by John Forester to her proposal that city planners should accommodate bicyclists by making "wide curb lanes or separate bicycle" paths. Reread paragraphs 4–7, and underline Forester's objection. Then make notes about how Sciara counterargues his objection. *Finally, write a brief evaluation of how successful her counterargument seems to be for its intended readers—city planners.* What seems most and least convincing?

Commentary: Describing and Arguing for the Proposed Solution

Like many solutions, Sciara's is multifaceted. Nevertheless, she makes every effort to describe her solution simply and clearly. She begins by announcing at the end of paragraph 3 that "one of the biggest reasons bicycles are underused may be safety." She then goes on to propose a tripartite approach to making bike riding safer, each part introduced by a heading:

1. "Thinking Big: Facility Design and Routine Accommodation" argues that constructing bicycle paths will ensure safety and attract riders (pars. 4–7);

2. "Thinking Small: Bringing Planners' Tools Up to Speed" argues that research will give planners important information to enhance safety (8–10);

3. "Education and Enforcement" argues that bicyclists and motorists need to be educated about safety and police need to enforce traffic laws (11–14).

In the first two paragraphs of the essay, Sciara presents several reasons why communities should be made safer for bicycle riders, condensing them in a few key words that she expects readers will be able to unpack for themselves: *cheap, flexible, reliable, environmentally friendly,* and *convenient.* The only reason that Sciara bothers to explain is *health benefits,* arguing that bicycling could provide a "remedy for Americans' inactive lifestyles, obesity, and related chronic diseases."

Sciara also gives reasons and support for each of the three parts of her proposed solution. For example, in "Thinking Big," she asserts that the "policy of 'routine accommodation' . . . could effectively increase bicycle use and, potentially, safety" (par. 4). She identifies three ways to carry out this policy:

"dedicated off-street paths, on-street lanes, or bicycle-friendly shoulders" (6). To support her argument that infrastructure redesign would make bicyclists feel safer and therefore encourage bike riding, Sciara cites two examples: "New York City's Hudson River Greenway" (5) and Portland's "comprehensive city-wide bicycle network" (6). To demonstrate that "the number of cyclists jumped dramatically" in New York with the completion of the auto-free bicycle corridor, she presents a bar graph showing the statistics at a glance (5). For the Portland example, she refers to "reports" of "steadily increasing ridership from 1991 to 2001." In addition, she suggests that because the number of accidents "remained constant" even though the number of bicyclists increased, there was actually "a drop in the collision rate" (6).

These examples allow Sciara not only to demonstrate that infrastructure changes can attract bicyclists and enhance safety, but also to show that such changes are feasible.

Considering Topics for Your Own Essay

Sciara's essay proposes changes that would affect conventional thinking and behavior regarding bicycle use. You might consider writing an essay proposing changes to conventional thinking and behavior of another sort. Think, for example, of the ways exams are administered, groups are instructed, graduation ceremonies are conducted, and so on, in high schools and colleges. Select one such practice that you believe needs to be improved or refined in some way. What changes would you propose? What individual or group might be convinced to take action on your proposal? What objections should you anticipate? Have others previously proposed improvements in the practice? Whom might you interview to learn more about the practice and the likelihood of changing it?

■ Purpose and Audience

Most proposals are calls to action. Because of this clear purpose, a writer must anticipate readers' needs and concerns more when writing a proposal than in any other kind of writing. The writer attempts not only to convince readers but also to inspire them to support or implement the proposed solution. What your readers know about the problem and what they are capable of doing to solve it determine how you address them.

If your readers are unaware of the problem, your task is clear: to present them with evidence that will convince them of its existence. This evidence may include statistics, testimony from witnesses or experts, and examples, including the personal experiences of people involved with the problem. You can also speculate about the cause of the problem and describe its ill effects.

Sometimes readers recognize the existence of a problem but fail to take it seriously. When readers are indifferent, you may need to connect the problem to their own concerns.

For instance, you might show how the problem affects them indirectly, or show them how much they have in common with the people directly affected by it.

Other readers may assume that someone or something else is taking care of the problem and that they need not become personally involved. In this situation, you might point out that the original solution has proved unworkable or that new, better solutions have become available.

In the best cases, your proposals will be addressed to parties who can take immediate action to remedy a problem. When you address readers who are in a position to take action, you want to assure them that it is wise to do so. You must demonstrate that the solution is feasible—that it can be implemented and that it will work.

Basic Features: Proposing Solutions

A Well-Defined Problem

A proposal is written to offer a solution to a problem. Before presenting the solution, the writer must be sure that readers know and understand what the problem is. Patrick O'Malley, for example, devotes the first three paragraphs of his essay to defining the problem of infrequent course exams. Similarly, Karen Kornbluh and Gian-Claudia Sciara describe the problem in their first few paragraphs.

Stating the problem is not enough, however; the writer also must establish the problem as serious enough to need solving. Occasionally a writer can assume that readers will recognize the problem and its seriousness, as does Sciara. Most often, writers assume readers will need to be convinced that the problem deserves their attention. For example, O'Malley assumes his intended readers—professors who can remedy the problem—will need to be convinced. To help them understand the students' point of view, he begins the proposal with a scenario and a series of rhetorical questions that dramatize the plight of students studying for a high-stakes exam. Similarly, Kornbluh provides a historical context and statistics to convince readers that the "juggler family" is a new and pressing problem that must be addressed.

In defining the problem, writers usually stress its negative consequences. O'Malley, for instance, describes students' stress and poor performance on high-stakes exams. Kornbluh shows how families are struggling to care for children and dependent parents.

A Clearly Described Solution

Once the problem is defined and its existence established, the writer must describe the solution so that readers can readily imagine it. Because O'Malley assumes that his readers know what brief exams are like, he runs little risk in not describing them. He does, however, identify their approximate lengths and possible forms—brief essay, short answer, or multiple choice. Kornbluh proposes leaving the details for a flexible work schedule up to employers to negotiate with their employees, but lists "examples" to illustrate how flexibility might be achieved: "part-time, annualized hours, compressed hours, flex-time, job-sharing, shift working, staggered hours, and telecommuting" (par. 17).

A Convincing Argument in Support of the Proposed Solution

The main purpose of a proposal is to convince readers that the writer's solution will help solve the problem. To this end, O'Malley gives three reasons why he thinks a greater number of brief exams will solve the problem and supports each reason with published research studies as well as his own experience. Kornbluh does not have to argue that a flexible work schedule will solve the problem she is discussing because it is obvious that workers need flexibility to spend more time with children and take care of sick relatives.

Writers must also argue that the proposed solution is feasible. Kornbluh points to the fact that her proposed solution has already been accomplished in Europe and that American business has already accommodated disabled workers in ways that workers with families also need. Similarly, Sciara asserts the feasibility of dedicated bicycle paths on the basis of the success of New York City's Hudson River Greenway and Portland's "citywide bicycle network" (pars. 5–6).

The easier a solution is to implement, the more likely it is to win readers' support. Therefore, writers sometimes set out the steps required to put the proposed solution into practice, an especially important strategy when the solution might seem difficult, time-consuming, or expensive. For example, O'Malley offers professors several ways to give their students frequent, brief exams. Similarly, Kornbluh recommends a plan and timetable to implement improvements in workplace flexibility. By not dictating a one-size-fits-all plan, she invests her proposal with the same flexibility she wants employers to make available to employees.

An Anticipation of Readers' Objections and Questions

The writer arguing for a proposal must anticipate and respond to objections and questions that readers may have about the proposed solution. O'Malley interviews people to discover what problems they might have with the proposed solution, presents three objections—that students should be treated like adults, that there is not enough class time for so many exams, and that exams take too much time to grade—and tries to refute all of them. Sciara also raises and refutes several objections. For example, she quotes John Forester's argument against separate bicycle facilities and counterargues that Forester "ignores the range of ability and experience among cyclists" (par. 6).

In addition to anticipating objections, proposal writers need to respond to likely questions readers may have. Kornbluh does this effectively when she asks, and answers, the question "Who would be covered?" in paragraph 21.

An Evaluation of Alternative Solutions

Proposal writers sometimes try to convince readers that the proposed solution is preferable to other possible solutions. O'Malley, for example, evaluates three alternative solutions to the problem of frequent exams—study-skills training, study questions, and sample exam questions—and demonstrates what is wrong with each one. He rejects study-skills training because it is overly complicated, time-consuming, and expensive. He rejects study questions because they would not save either students or professors any time or ensure that students each do their own individual work. He refutes the sample exam questions by arguing that they solve only part of the problem (pars. 10–12).

Like O'Malley, Kornbluh evaluates three alternative solutions—sick leave or vacation time, the Family and Medical Leave Act (FMLA), and firms already providing flexible work arrangements—and shows how they are not viable because many workers do not get sick leave or vacation time, the FMLA does not guarantee paid leave, and businesses only make arrangements for highly paid executives (2).

Proposing a Solution

Invention and Research

What is a problem that needs to be solved in a community or group you belong to? Is your dorm too noisy for you to study there? Is trash or tagging a problem in your neighborhood? Do some thinking, writing, and research about possible solutions. Then decide on a tentative proposal about what action to take and who should take it. . . . **See p. 221 for more.**

Planning and Drafting

As you look over what you have written and learned about your subject so far, can you make a convincing case for your proposal? How can you engage readers' interest in the problem? What questions are they likely to have about your proposed solution? Make a plan for your proposal essay, and start drafting it. . . . **See p. 228 for more.**

Critical Reading Guide

What are your draft's strengths and weaknesses? Have you defined the problem clearly enough? Have you neglected to discuss alternative solutions that have been proposed? Get a classmate, a friend, a writing tutor, or someone else to read and respond to your essay, especially the parts you are most unsure of. . . . **See p. 233 for more.**

Revising

As you consider your essay again in light of your reader's comments, how can you improve it? Can you define the problem more clearly? Do you need to explain more fully how your solution would be implemented or how much it would cost? Go through your draft systematically, making changes wherever necessary. . . . **See p. 235 for more.**

Editing and Proofreading

Have you checked for errors that are especially likely in writing that proposes a solution? Have you used *this* or *that* ambiguously, so that readers cannot tell what noun they refer to? Do any sentences about implementing the solution not indicate clearly who should be doing so? Look for and correct these and any other errors. . . . **See p. 238 for more.**

☐ The Writing Assignment

Write an essay proposing a solution to a problem. Choose a problem faced by a community or group to which you belong, and address your proposal to one or more members of the group or to outsiders who might help solve the problem.

▪ Invention and Research

The following activities will help you prepare to write a proposal. You will choose a problem you can write about, analyze and define the problem, identify your prospective readers, decide on and defend your proposed solution, test your choice, offer reasons and support for adopting your proposal, and consider readers' objections and alternative solutions, among other things. Be sure to keep a written record of your invention and research to use later when you draft and revise.

Finding a Problem to Write About

You may have already thought about a problem you could write about. Even so, you will want to consider several problems that need solving before making your final choice. The following activity will help you get started.

Listing Problems. *Make a list of problems you could write about.* Divide a piece of paper or your computer screen into two columns. In the left-hand column, list communities, groups, or organizations to which you belong. In the right-hand column, list any problems that exist within each group. Here is how such a chart might begin:

Community	*Problem*
My college	Poor advising or orientation
	No financial aid for part-time students
	Lack of enough sections of required courses
My neighborhood	Need for traffic light at dangerous intersection
	Megastores driving away small businesses
	Lack of safe places for children to play

▪ *Listing Problems Related to Identity and Community.* Writing a proposal can help you understand how members of a community negotiate their individual needs and concerns. The following categories may help you think of problems that you could add to your list:

- Problems with equity or fairness between men and women, rich and poor, different ethnic groups
- Lack of respect or trust among the members of the community
- Struggles for leadership of the community

■ *Listing Problems Related to Work and Career.* Proposals are frequently written about the work people do. Draw on your work experience to make a double-column chart like the following one. List the places you have worked in the left column and the problems you encountered on the job in the right column.

Workplace	*Problem*
Restaurant	Inadequate training
	Conflicts with supervisor
	Unfair shift assignments
Department store	Inadequate inventory
	Computer glitches
	Overcomplicated procedures
Office	Unfair workloads
	Inflexible work schedules
	Difficulty in scheduling vacations
	Outdated technology

Choosing a Problem. *Choose one problem from your list that is especially important to you, that concerns others in the group or community, and that seems solvable.* (You need not know how to solve it now.) The problem should also be one that you can explore in detail and are willing to discuss in writing.

Proposing to solve a problem in a group or community to which you belong gives you an important advantage: You can write as an expert. You know the history of the problem, have felt the urgency to solve it, and perhaps have already thought of possible solutions. Equally important, you will know to whom to address the proposal, and you can interview others in the group to get their views of the problem and your solution. From such a position of knowledge and authority comes confident, convincing writing.

Should you want to propose a solution for a problem of national scope, concentrate on one with which you have direct experience and for which you can suggest a detailed plan of action. Even better, focus on unique local aspects of the problem. For example, if you would like to propose a solution to the lack of affordable child care, you have a great advantage if you are a parent who has experienced this frustration, and if you can suggest a solution for your campus, business, or neighborhood.

Analyzing and Defining the Problem

Before you can begin to consider the best possible solution, you must analyze the problem and define it. Keep in mind that you will have to demonstrate to readers that the problem exists, that it is serious, and that you have a more than casual understanding of its causes and consequences. If you cannot do so, you will want to select some other problem to write about.

Analyzing.   *Start by writing a few sentences in response to these questions:*

- Does the problem really exist? How can I tell?
- What caused this problem? Is it caused by a flaw in the system, a lack of resources, individual misconduct or incompetence, or something else? How can I tell?
- What is the history of the problem?
- What are the effects of the problem? How does it harm members of the community or group? Does it raise any moral or ethical questions?
- Who is affected by the problem? Does anyone benefit from its existence?

Defining.   *Write a definition of the problem, being as specific as possible.* Identify who or what seems responsible for it.

Identifying Your Readers

In a few sentences, describe your readers, stating your reason for directing your proposal to them. Then take a few minutes to write about these readers. You want to address your proposal to the person or group who can help implement it. The following questions will help you develop a profile of your readers:

- How informed are my readers likely to be about the problem? Have they shown any awareness of it?
- Why would my readers care about solving this problem?
- Have my readers supported any other proposals to solve this problem? If so, what do those proposals have in common with mine?
- Do my readers and I share any values or attitudes that could bring us together to solve the problem?
- How have my readers responded to other problems? Do their past reactions suggest anything about how they might respond to my proposal?

Finding a Tentative Solution

Solving problems takes time. After all, a solution has to be both workable and acceptable to the community or group involved. Consequently, you should strive to come up with several possible solutions. You may notice that the best solutions sometimes occur to you only after you have struggled with a number of other possibilities.

Look back at the way you defined the problem and described your readers.

- What solutions to this problem have already been tried?
- What solutions have been proposed for related problems? Might they solve this problem as well?
- Is the problem too big to be solved all at once? Can I divide it into several related problems? What solutions might solve one or more of these problems?

- If a series of solutions is required, which should come first? Second?
- What might be a daring solution, arousing the most resistance but perhaps holding out the most promise?
- What would be the most conservative solution, acceptable to nearly everyone in the community or group?
- What solution would ultimately solve the problem?

Let your ideas percolate as you continue to add to your list of possible solutions and to consider the advantages and disadvantages of each one in light of your prospective readers. If possible, discuss your solutions with others who can help you consider the advantages and disadvantages of each one.

Choosing the Most Promising Solution.   *In a sentence or two, state what you consider the best possible way of solving the problem.*

Determining Specific Steps.   *Write down the major stages or steps necessary to carry out your solution.* This list of steps will provide an early test of whether your solution can, in fact, be implemented.

Defending Your Solution

Proposals have to be both reasonable and practical. Imagine that one of your readers strongly opposes your proposed solution and confronts you with the following statements. *Write a few sentences refuting each one.*

- It would not really solve the problem.
- I am comfortable with things as they are.
- We cannot afford it.
- It would take too long.
- People would not do it.
- Too few people would benefit.
- I do not even see how to get started on your solution.
- We already tried that, with unsatisfactory results.
- You support this proposal merely because it would benefit you personally.

Answering these questions should help you prepare responses to possible objections.

Testing Your Choice

Now test your choice by asking yourself the following questions:

- *Is this a significant problem?* Do other people in the community really care about it, or can they be persuaded to care?

- *Will my solution really solve the problem?* Have I worked out how it can be implemented in an affordable way?
- *Can I answer objections effectively enough to win support for my solution?*
- *Do I now know enough about the problem or can I learn what I need to know in the time remaining?*
- *Do I understand the problem well enough to convince my readers that it really exists and is serious?*
- *Do I feel a personal interest in the problem I have chosen?*
- *Can I make a convincing argument for my proposed solution?* Am I convinced that my solution is better than the alternative solutions my readers may prefer?

As you plan and draft your proposal, you will probably want to consider these questions again. If at any point you cannot answer them with a confident yes, you may want to consider proposing a different solution to the problem; if none exists, you may need to choose a different problem to write about.

A Collaborative Activity: Testing Your Choice   Get together with two or three other students and present your plans to one another.

Presenters: Take turns briefly defining the problem you hope to solve, identifying your intended readers, and describing your proposed solution.

Listeners: Tell the presenter whether the proposed solution seems feasible for the situation and intended readers. Suggest objections and reservations readers may have.

Offering Reasons for Your Proposal

To make a convincing case for your proposed solution, you must offer your readers good reasons for adopting it.

Listing Reasons.   *Write down every plausible reason you could give that might persuade readers to accept your proposal.* These reasons should answer your readers' key question: Why is this the best possible solution?

Choosing the Strongest Reasons.   *Put an asterisk next to the strongest reasons — the reasons most likely to be convincing to your intended readers.* If you do not consider at least two or three of your reasons strong, you will probably have difficulty developing a strong proposal and should reconsider your topic.

Evaluating Your Strongest Reasons.   *Now look at your strongest reasons and explain briefly why you think each one will be effective with your readers.*

Considering Alternative Solutions

List alternative solutions and consider the advantages and disadvantages of each. You might find it helpful to chart the information as follows:

Possible Solutions	*Advantages*	*Disadvantages*
My solution		
Alternative solution 1		
Alternative solution 2		
Etc.		

An Online Activity:
Researching
Alternative Solutions

Searching the Web can be a productive way of learning about solutions other people have proposed or tried out. If possible, use your online research to identify at least two alternative solutions. Your purpose is to gain information about these solutions that will help you evaluate them fairly. Here are some specific suggestions for finding information about solutions:

- Enter keywords—words or brief phrases related to the problem or a solution—into a search tool such as Google (www.google.com). For example, if you are concerned that many children in your neighborhood have no adult supervision after school, you could try keywords associated with the problem such as *latchkey kids* or keywords associated with possible solutions such as *after-school programs.*
- If you think solutions to your problem may have been proposed by a government agency, you could try adding the word *government* to your keywords or searching on FirstGov.gov, the U.S. government's official Web portal. For example, you might explore the problem of latchkey children by following links at the Web site of the U.S. Department of Health & Human Services (www.hhs.gov). If you want to see whether the problem has been addressed in your state or by local government, you can go to the Library of Congress Internet Resource Page on State and Local Governments (www.loc.gov/global/state/) and follow the links.

Add to your chart of the advantages and disadvantages of alternative solutions any information you find from your online research. Bookmark or keep a record of promising sites. You may want to download or copy information you could use in your essay, including visuals; if so, remember to record source information.

Doing Research

So far you have relied largely on your own knowledge and experience for ideas about solving the problem. *You may now need to do some research to learn more about the causes of the problem and to find more information about implementing the solution.*

If you are proposing a solution to a problem about which others have written, you will want to find out how they have defined the problem and what solutions they have proposed. If you are proposing a solution to a local problem, you will want to conduct interviews with people who are aware of or affected by the problem. Find out what they know about its history and current effects. Try out your solution on them. Discover whether they have other solutions in mind.

For guidelines on library and Internet research, see Chapter 13. For more on interviewing, see Chapter 12.

Designing Your Document

Think about whether your readers might benefit from design features such as headings or numbered or bulleted lists or from visuals such as drawings, photographs, tables, or graphs. Elements like these often make the presentation of a problem easier to follow and a solution more convincing. Earlier in this chapter, for example, Karen Kornbluh's proposal about flexibility in the workplace uses headings to introduce the major sections, and Gian-Claudia Sciara's proposal about making communities safe for bicyclists uses headings, photographs, and a bar graph.

Consider reviewing other published proposals to see how they use design elements and visuals to support and strengthen their arguments. Look back at the scenario on p. 193 about the truck driver making a proposal for recruiting more female truck drivers and "Thinking about Document Design" on p. 241 to see how she used visuals.

For more on document design, see Chapter 15. For guidelines on acknowledging the sources of visuals, see Chapter 14.

Defining Your Purpose for Your Readers

Write a few sentences defining your purpose. Remember that you have already identified your readers and developed your proposal with these readers in mind. Try now to define your purpose by considering the following questions:

- Do I seek incremental, moderate, or radical change? Am I being realistic about what my readers are prepared to do? How can I overcome their natural aversion to change of any kind?
- How can I ensure that my readers will not remain indifferent to the problem?
- Whom can I count on for support, and what can I do to consolidate that support? Who will oppose my solution? Shall I write them off or seek common ground with them?

- What exactly do I want my readers to do? To take my proposed solution as a starting point for further discussion? To take action immediately? To take preliminary steps, like seeking funding or testing the feasibility of the solution? To take some other action?

Formulating a Tentative Thesis Statement

Write one or more sentences to serve as your tentative thesis statement. In most essays proposing solutions to problems, the thesis statement is a concise announcement of the solution. Think about how emphatic you should make the thesis and whether you should include in it a forecast of your reasons.

Review the readings in this chapter to see how other writers construct their thesis statements. For example, recall that Patrick O'Malley states his thesis in paragraph 2: *If professors gave additional brief exams at frequent intervals, students would be spurred to study more regularly, learn more, worry less, and perform better on midterms, finals, and other papers and projects.* O'Malley's thesis announces his solution — brief, frequent exams — and lists the reasons students would benefit from the solution. A forecast is not a requirement, but it does enable readers to predict the stages of the argument, thereby increasing their understanding.

As you draft your own thesis, pay attention to the language you use. It should be clear and unambiguous, emphatic but appropriately qualified. Although you will probably refine your thesis as you draft and revise your essay, trying now to articulate it will help give your planning and drafting direction and impetus.

For more on thesis and forecasting statements, see Chapter 10. For more on asserting a thesis, see Chapter 11.

■ Planning and Drafting

This section will help you review your invention writing and research notes, determine specific goals for your essay, prepare a rough outline, and get started on your first draft.

Seeing What You Have

You have now produced a lot of writing for this assignment. Reread what you have written so far to identify the potentially useful material. Look for details that will help you present a convincing argument for your solution and a strong counterargument to readers' likely objections. Highlight key words, phrases, or sentences; make marginal notes or electronic annotations.

If at this point you doubt the significance of the problem or question the success of your proposed solution, you might want to consider a new topic.

If your invention material seems promising but a bit thin, you may be able to strengthen it with additional invention writing. Ask yourself the following questions:

- Can I make a stronger case for the seriousness of the problem?
- Can I think of additional reasons for readers to support my solution?
- Are there any other ways of refuting objections to my proposed solution or alternative solutions readers might prefer?

Setting Goals

Before beginning to draft, think seriously about the overall goals of your proposal. Not only will the draft be easier to write once you have clear goals, but it will be more convincing as well.

Here are some questions that will help you set goals now.

Your Purpose and Readers

- What do my readers already know about this problem? Should I assume, as O'Malley does, that my readers are unfamiliar with the problem? Or should I assume, as Kornbluh does, that my readers know about the problem but do not realize how serious it is?
- How can I gain readers' enthusiastic support? Can I convince them that solving the problem is in everyone's interest, as Kornbluh and Sciara try to do?
- How can I present myself so that I seem both reasonable and authoritative? Can I show that I am not dictating a one-size-fits-all solution but trying to get those involved to find solutions that work for them, as O'Malley and Kornbluh try to do?

The Beginning

- How can I immediately engage my readers' interest? Should I open, as O'Malley does, with a dramatic scenario and rhetorical questions? Or with a recitation of facts, as Sciara does?

Defining the Problem

- How can I demonstrate that the problem really exists? Can I present statistics, as Kornbluh and Sciara do?
- How can I show the seriousness and urgency of the problem? Should I stress negative consequences, as all the writers do? Can I use quotations or cite research to stress the problem's importance, as Kornbluh does?
- Will reporting or speculating about the problem's causes or history help readers understand why it needs attention? Can I use comparison and contrast, as Kornbluh does?
- How much space should I devote to defining the problem? Only a little space (like O'Malley and Sciara) or much space (like Kornbluh)?

Describing the Proposed Solution

- How can I describe my solution so that it will look like the best way to proceed? Should I give examples to show how it is feasible, as Sciara does? Or should I focus on my reasons to support it, as O'Malley does?

- Should I make the solution seem easy to implement, as O'Malley and Sciara do? Or should I acknowledge that the solution will require effort and compromise, as Kornbluh does?

Anticipating Readers' Objections or Questions

- How can I anticipate any specific objections or questions readers may have? Can I interview interested parties, as O'Malley does? Can I do library and Internet research, as all the writers do?

- How do I decide which objections to include? Has anyone already raised these objections? How can I name the source of the objection without criticizing the person?

- Should I accommodate or concede to certain objections by modifying my proposal, as O'Malley does?

- How can I support my refutation? Should I cite statistics or research studies, as Sciara does?

Evaluating Alternative Solutions

- How do I decide which alternative solutions to mention?

- How can I support my refutation of alternative solutions? Can I argue that they are too expensive and time-consuming, as O'Malley does, or that they will not really solve the problem, as Kornbluh does?

- How can I reject these other solutions without seeming to criticize their proponents? Can I provide reasons, as O'Malley does, or marshal statistics, as Kornbluh does?

The Ending

- How should I conclude? Should I end by summarizing my solution and its advantages, as O'Malley and Sciara do? Should I end with a scenario suggesting the consequences of a failure to solve the problem? Can I end with an inspiring call to action? Or might a shift to humor or satire provide an effective ending?

- Is there something special about the problem that I should remind readers of at the end, as Kornbluh does when she urges that an award be given to the companies that lead the way?

Outlining

After setting goals for your proposal, you are ready to make a working outline. The basic outline for a proposal is quite simple:

The problem

The solution

The reasons for accepting the solution

This simple plan is nearly always complicated by other factors, however. In outlining your material, you must take into consideration whether readers already recognize the problem, how much agreement exists on the need to solve the problem, how many alternative solutions are available, how much attention must be given to these other solutions, and how many objections should be expected.

Here is a possible outline for a proposal where readers may not understand the problem fully:

Presentation of the problem

    Its existence

    Its seriousness

    Its causes

Consequences of failing to solve the problem

Description of the proposed solution

List of steps for implementing the solution

Reasons and support for the solution

    Acknowledgment of objections

    Accommodation or refutation of objections

Consideration of alternative solutions and their disadvantages

Restatement of the proposed solution and its advantages

Your outline will of course reflect your own writing situation. Once you have a working outline, you should not hesitate to change it as necessary while drafting and revising. For instance, you might find it more effective to hold back on presenting your own solution until you have dismissed other possible solutions. Or you might find a better way to order the reasons for adopting your proposal. The purpose of an outline is to identify the basic features of your proposal and to help you organize them effectively, not to lock you into a particular structure.

For more on outlining, see Chapter 8.

Drafting

General Advice. Keep in mind the goals you set while you were planning and the needs and expectations of your readers; organize, define, and argue with them in mind. Also keep in mind the two main goals of proposals: (1) to establish that a problem exists and is serious enough to require a solution and (2) to demonstrate that your proposed solution is both feasible and the best possible alternative. Use your outline to guide you as you write, but do not hesitate to stray from it whenever you find that drafting takes you in an unexpected direction.

Turn off your grammar checker and spelling checker at this stage if you find them distracting. Don't be afraid to skip around in your document. Jump back and fill in a spontaneous idea, or leap ahead and write a later section first if you find that easier. If you get stuck while drafting, explore the problem by using some of the writing activities in the Invention and Research section of this chapter (p. 221).

A Sentence Strategy: Rhetorical Questions. As you draft an essay proposing a solution to a problem, you will want to connect with your readers. You will also want readers to become concerned with the seriousness of the problem and thoughtful about the challenge of solving it. Sentences that take the form of **rhetorical questions** can help you achieve these goals.

A rhetorical question is conventionally defined as a sentence posing a question to which the writer expects no answer from the reader. However, rhetorical questions do important rhetorical work—that is, they assist a writer in realizing a particular purpose and they influence readers in certain ways. Writers in this chapter use rhetorical questions for a number of different purposes:

- Engaging readers' attention to or interest in the problem or the proposed solution:

   Will it be like the midterm? Did you study enough? Did you study the right things? It's too late to drop the course. So what happens if you fail? (O'Malley, par. 1)

   What if the safety of bicyclists were accorded comparable priority? What if bicycle and motorist education campaigns were pursued on a scale equivalent to aggressive drunk driving and seatbelt campaigns? (Sciara, 11)

O'Malley uses his rhetorical questions to dramatize the plight of students studying for a high-stakes exam in order to engage his primary readers—professors capable of implementing his solution—and put them in a receptive frame of mind. Sciara presents her questions after reporting the number of lives saved by drunk driving and seatbelt education campaigns. Her objective is to get readers to recognize for themselves the life-saving potential of a bicycle safety campaign.

- Orienting readers to a proposal and forecasting the plan of the argument or parts of it:

   Why, then, do so few professors give frequent brief exams? (O'Malley, 7)

O'Malley uses this rhetorical question as a transition to his anticipating objections that professors are likely to have to his proposed solution.

Though rhetorical questions are useful, they are not a requirement for a successful proposal. They should be used for a specific purpose, and they should not be overused, because readers may begin to find them annoying.

Critical Reading Guide

Now is the time to get a good critical reading of your draft. Writers usually find it helpful to have someone else read and comment on their drafts, and all writers know how much they learn when they read other writers' drafts. Your instructor may arrange such a reading as part of your coursework—in class or online. If not, you can ask a classmate to read your draft. You could also seek comments from a tutor at your campus writing center. (If you are unable to have someone else read your draft, turn ahead to the Revising section on p. 235, where you will find guidelines for reading your own draft critically.)

▶ **If You Are the Writer.** To provide focused, helpful comments, your reader must know your essay's intended audience, your purpose, and a problem in the draft that you need help solving. Briefly write out this information at the top of your draft.

- *Audience:* Identify the intended audience of your essay. How much do they know about the problem? How will they react to your proposed solution?
- *Purpose:* What do you want your audience to do or think as a result of reading your proposal?
- *Problem:* Describe the single most important problem you see with your draft.

▶ **If You Are the Reader.** Use the following guidelines to help you give critical comments to others on essays that propose solutions to problems.

1. *Read for a First Impression.* Read first to get a basic understanding of the problem and the proposed solution. After reading the draft, write out your impressions. How convincing do you think the proposal will be for its audience? Next, consider the problem with the draft the writer identified, and respond briefly to that concern now. (If you find that the problem is covered by one of the other guidelines listed below, respond to it in more detail there.)

2. *Evaluate How Well the Problem Is Defined.* Decide whether the problem is stated clearly. Does the writer give enough information about its causes and consequences? What more might be done to establish its seriousness? Is there more that readers might need or wish to know about it?

3. *Consider Whether the Solution Is Described Adequately.* Is the solution presented clearly?

> **Making Comments Electronically**
>
> Most word processing software offers features that allow you to insert comments directly into the text of someone else's document. Many readers prefer to make their comments in this way because it tends to be faster than writing on a hard copy and space is virtually unlimited; it also eliminates the problem of deciphering handwritten comments. Where such features are not available, simply typing comments directly into a document in a contrasting color can provide the same advantages.

How could it be strengthened? Has the writer laid out steps for implementation? If not, might readers expect or require them? Does the solution seem practical? If not, why?

4. ***Assess Whether a Convincing Argument Is Advanced in Support of the Proposed Solution.*** Look at the reasons offered for advocating this solution. Are they sufficient? Which are likely to be most and least convincing to the intended audience? What kind of support does the writer provide for each reason? Has the writer argued forcefully for the proposal without offending readers?

5. ***Evaluate How Well the Writer Anticipates Readers' Objections and Questions.*** Which accommodations and refutations seem most convincing? Which seem least convincing? Are there other objections or reservations that the writer should acknowledge?

6. ***Assess the Writer's Evaluation of Alternative Solutions.*** Are alternative solutions discussed? Which are the most convincing reasons given against other solutions? Which are least convincing, and why? Has the writer sought out common ground with readers who may advocate alternative solutions? Are such solutions discussed without a personal attack on those who propose them? Try to think of other solutions that readers may prefer.

7. ***Consider the Effectiveness of the Organization.*** Evaluate the overall plan of the proposal, perhaps by outlining it briefly. Would any parts be more effectively placed earlier or later in the essay?

   • Look at the *beginning*. Is it engaging? If not, how might it be revised to capture readers' attention? Does it adequately forecast the main ideas and the plan of the proposal? Suggest other ways the writer might begin.

   • Look closely at the way the writer *orders the argument* for the solution—the presentation of the reasons and the accommodation or refutation of objections and alternative solutions. How might the sequence be revised to strengthen the argument? Point out any gaps in the argument.

   • Look at the *ending*. Does it frame the proposal by echoing or referring to something at the beginning? If not, how might it do so? Does the ending convey a sense of urgency? Suggest a stronger way to conclude.

   • Look at any *design elements and visuals* the writer has incorporated. Assess how well they are incorporated into the essay. Suggest additional design elements or visuals that might strengthen the proposal.

8. ***Give the Writer Your Final Thoughts.*** What is the draft's strongest part? What part is most in need of further work?

For a printable version of this critical reading guide, go to **bedfordstmartins.com/ conciseguide.**

■ Revising

This section will help you get an overview of your draft and revise it accordingly.

Getting an Overview

Consider your draft as a whole, following these two steps:

1. *Reread.* If at all possible, put the draft aside for a day or two before rereading it. When you do go back to it, start by reconsidering your audience and purpose. Then read the draft straight through, trying to see it as your intended readers will.
2. *Outline.* Make a scratch outline, indicating the basic features as they appear in the draft. Consider using the headings and outline or summary functions of your word processor.

Planning for Revision.   Resist the temptation to dive in and start changing your text until after you have a clear view of the big picture. Using your outline as a guide, move through the document, and note comments received from others and problems you want to solve.

Analyzing the Basic Features of Your Own Draft.   Turn to the Critical Reading Guide that begins on p. 233. Using this guide, reread the draft to identify problems you need to solve. Note the problems on your draft.

Studying Readers' Comments.   Review all of the comments you have received from other readers. For each comment, look at the draft to determine what might have led the reader to make that particular point. Try to be receptive to constructive criticism. Ideally, these comments will help you see your draft as others see it. Add to your notes any problems readers have identified.

Working with Sources

Citing statistics to establish the problem's existence and seriousness   Statistics can be helpful in establishing that the problem exists and is serious. For example, Karen Kornbluh cites statistics to demonstrate that the "juggler family," as she calls it, has taken the place of the "traditional family" that had a homemaker capable of taking care of children and dependent parents:

> Today fully 70 percent of families with children are headed by two working parents or by an unmarried working parent. The "traditional family" of the breadwinner and homemaker has been replaced by the "juggler family," in which no one is home full-time. (par. 1)

Kornbluh begins with an impressive statistic, "fully 70 percent." But what does it mean? Seventy percent of how many? She does not answer this question with a number, but she does make clear that she is talking about nearly three-quarters of all "families with children," a number that we can infer is very large. At other points in the essay, Kornbluh does provide the raw numbers along with statistics such as percentages. Here are a couple of examples:

> In addition to working parents, there are over 44.4 million Americans who provide care to another adult, often an older relative. Fifty-nine percent of these caregivers either work or have worked while providing care ("Caregiving"). (par. 8)

> Over half of workers today have no control over scheduling alternative start and end times at work (Galinksy, Bond, and Hill). According to a recent study by the Institute for Women's Policy Research, 49 percent of workers—over 59 million Americans— lack basic paid sick days for themselves. (10)

Because of the raw numbers, readers can see at a glance that the percentages Kornbluh cites are truly significant: 59 percent of 44.4 million people (who have worked while providing care to another adult) and 59 million people (who lack sick leave). Note that Kornbluh spells out some of the numbers she provides and uses numerals for others, depending on whether the number begins a sentence.

Kornbluh also compares different time periods to show that the problem has worsened over the last thirty years. Here are several examples from paragraph 7. Note that Kornbluh presents statistics in three different ways: percentages, numbers, and proportion.

> Between 1970 and 2000, the percentage of mothers in the workforce rose from 38 to 67 percent (Smolensky and Gootman). Moreover, the number of hours worked by dual-income families has increased dramatically. Couples with children worked a full 60 hours a week in 1979. By 2000 they were working 70 hours a week (Bernstein and Kornbluh). And more parents than ever are working long hours. In 2000, nearly 1 out of every 8 couples with children was putting in 100 hours a week or more on the job, compared to only 1 out of 12 families in 1970 (Jacobs and Gerson).

To establish that there is a widespread perception among working parents that the problem is serious, Kornbluh cites survey results:

> In a 2002 report by the Families and Work Institute, 45 percent of employees reported that work and family responsibilities interfered with each other "a lot" or "some" and 67 percent of employed parents report that they do not have enough time with their children (Galinksy, Bond, and Hill).

This example, from paragraph 9, shows that a large percentage, nearly half of all employees surveyed, are aware of interference between work and family responsibilities. The readers Kornbluh is addressing—employers—are likely to find this statistic important because it suggests that their employees are spending time worrying about or attending to family responsibilities instead of focusing on work.

For statistics to be persuasive, they must be from sources that readers consider reliable. Researchers' trustworthiness, in turn, depends on their credentials as experts in the field they are investigating and also on the degree to which they are disinterested, or free from bias.

Kornbluh provides a Works Cited list of sources that readers can follow up on to check whether the sources are indeed reliable. The fact that some of her sources are books published by major publishers (Harvard University Press and Basic Books, for example) helps establish their credibility. Other sources she cites are research institutes (such as New America Foundation, Economic Policy Institute, and Families and Work Institute) that readers can easily check out. Another factor that adds to the appearance of reliability is that Kornbluh cites statistics from a range of sources instead of relying on only one or two. Moreover, the statistics are current and clearly relevant to her argument.

Carrying Out Revisions

Having identified problems in your draft, you now need to find solutions and—most important—to carry them out. You have three ways of finding solutions:

1. Review your invention and planning notes for additional information and ideas.
2. Do further invention writing or research to provide material you or your readers think is needed.
3. Look back at the readings in this chapter to see how other writers have solved similar problems.

The following suggestions, which are organized according to the basic features of essays that propose solutions, will get you started solving some common writing problems. For now, focus on solving the problems identified in your notes. Avoid tinkering with grammar and punctuation; those tasks will come later, when you edit and proofread.

A Well-Defined Problem

- *Is the definition of the problem unclear?* Consider sketching out its history, including past attempts to deal with it, discussing its causes and consequences more fully, or comparing it to other problems that readers may be familiar with.
- *Have you failed to establish the problem's existence and seriousness?* Look for additional statistics, facts, and quotations to establish that the problem really exists. Try to dramatize its effect on people and to create a sense of urgency.

A Clearly Described Solution

- *Is the description of the solution inadequate?* Try outlining the steps or phases involved in its implementation. Help readers see how easy the first step will be, or acknowledge the difficulty of the first step. Give examples of similar solutions that have been implemented.

A Convincing Argument in Support of the Proposed Solution

- **Does the argument seem weak?** Try to think of more reasons for readers to support your proposal.

- **Is the argument hard to follow?** Try to put your reasons in a more convincing order—leading up to the strongest one rather than putting it first, perhaps.

- **Does the solution not seem feasible?** Show how your solution would really solve the problem, possibly by removing its causes. Provide additional statistical or expert support.

An Anticipation of Readers' Objections and Questions

- **Does your refutation of any objection or question seem unconvincing?** Consider accommodating it by modifying your proposal.

- **Have you left out any likely objections?** Acknowledge those objections and either accommodate or refute them.

An Evaluation of Alternative Solutions

- **Have you neglected to mention alternative solutions that some readers are likely to prefer?** Evaluate those alternatives. Consider whether you want to accommodate or refute them. For each one, try to acknowledge its good points, but argue that it is not as effective a solution as your own. You may in fact strengthen your own solution by incorporating into it some of the good points from alternative solutions.

The Organization

- **Is the beginning weak?** Think of a better way to start. Would an anecdote or an example of the problem engage readers more effectively?

- **Is the ending flat?** Consider framing your proposal by mentioning something from the beginning of your essay or ending with a call for action that expresses the urgency of implementing your solution.

- **Would design elements make the problem or proposed solution easier to understand?** Consider adding headings or visuals.

■ Editing and Proofreading

Now is the time to check your revised draft for errors in grammar, punctuation, and mechanics as well as to consider matters of style. Our research has identified several errors that are especially common in essays that propose solutions. The following guidelines will help you check and edit your essay for these common errors.

Checking for Ambiguous Use of *This* and *That*.   Using *this* and *that* vaguely to refer to other words or ideas can confuse readers. Because you must frequently refer to the problem and the solution in a proposal, you will often use pronouns to avoid the monotony or wordiness of repeatedly referring to them by name. Check your draft carefully for ambiguous use of *this* and *that*. Often the easiest way to edit such usage is to add a specific noun after *this* or *that*, as Patrick O'Malley does in the following example from his essay in this chapter:

> Another possible solution would be to help students prepare for midterm and final exams by providing sets of questions from which the exam questions will be selected or announcing possible exam topics at the beginning of the course. *This solution* would have the advantage of reducing students' anxiety about learning every fact in the textbook. . . . (par. 12)

> **A Note on Grammar and Spelling Checkers**
> These tools are good at catching certain types of errors, but currently there is no replacement for a good human proofreader. Grammar checkers in particular are extremely limited in what they can find. They also tend to give faulty advice for fixing problems and to flag correct items as wrong. Spelling checkers cause fewer problems but cannot catch misspellings that are themselves words, such as *to* for *too*.

O'Malley avoids an ambiguous *this* in the second sentence by repeating the noun *solution*. (He might just as well have used *preparation* or *action* or *approach*.)

The following sentences from proposals have been edited to avoid ambiguity:

▶ Students would not resist a reasonable fee increase of about $40 a year.

     increase
This would pay for the needed dormitory remodeling.
   ^

▶ Compared with other large California cities, San Diego has the weakest

           neglect
programs for conserving water. This and our decreasing access to Colorado
          ^

River water give us reason to worry.

                                      one
▶ Compared with other proposed solutions to this problem, that is clearly the most
                                                        ^

feasible.

For practice, go to **bedfordstmartins.com/conciseguide/exercisecentral** and click on Ambiguous Use of *This* and *That*.

Checking for Sentences That Lack an Agent.   A writer proposing a solution to a problem usually needs to indicate who exactly should take action to solve it. Such actors are called "agents." An agent is a person who is in a position to take action. Look at this sentence from O'Malley's proposal:

> To get students to complete the questions in a timely way, professors would have to collect and check the answers.

In this sentence, *professors* are the agents. They have the authority to assign and collect study questions, and they would need to take this action in order for this solution to be successfully implemented. Had O'Malley instead written "the answers would have to be collected and checked," the sentence would lack an agent. Naming an agent makes his argument convincing, demonstrating to readers that O'Malley has thought through one of the key parts of any proposal: who is going to take action.

The following sentences from student-written proposals illustrate how you can edit agentless sentences:

> *Your staff should plan a survey*
> ▶ ~~A survey could be planned~~ to find out more about students' problems in scheduling the courses they need.

> *The registrar should extend*
> ▶ ~~Extending~~ the deadline to mid-quarter~~ would make sense.~~

Sometimes it is appropriate to write agentless sentences, however. Study the following examples from O'Malley's essay:

These exams should be given weekly, or at least twice monthly.

Exams could be collected and responded to only every third or fourth week.

Still another solution might be to provide frequent study questions for students to answer.

Even though these sentences do not name explicit agents, they are all fine because it is clear from the larger context who will perform the action. In each case, it is obvious that the action will be carried out by a professor.

For practice, go to **bedfordstmartins.com/conciseguide/exercisecentral** and click on Sentences That Lack an Agent.

Thinking About
Document Design

■ Following Existing Formatting Conventions

The truck driver who wrote the proposal for recruiting and training more women (in the "In the Workplace" scenario described on p. 193) drafted and designed her document on her computer. She was familiar with some of the features of her word processing software, such as the ability to create headings, format lists, and include photographs. More important, she recognized that these elements could serve persuasive purposes in the document she wanted to produce. She searched the Web for similar proposals that she could use as models. After looking them over, she found they all contained some of the same formatting conventions: They were all single-spaced, had descriptive headings, and included some sort of visuals (tables, charts, and photographs).

The driver decided to format her document similarly, using single-spacing and headings and incorporating graphs and tables gathered from several trucking industry magazines and newsletters. To stress that carriers must increase their fleets to remain competitive within the industry, she used the line graph below showing how the skyrocketing demand for carriers over the next ten years would greatly exacerbate the current driver shortage. She used a second graph, the pie chart on the next page, to show that current projections indicate that women will remain an underutilized group in the truck driver workforce. And to show how the trucking industry can attract women on the basis of salary, she also included a table contrasting the amount of money a woman truck driver could earn after one year, after five years, and so on, with how much women in other fields could earn over the same periods of time.

She knew that the preferred hiring solution of many companies is to recruit from truck-driving schools. However, she also knew that the region's divorced and single-parent women would likely not be able to afford such training. Therefore, she included a list comparing truck-driving school tuition rates with income statistics for women in the region to illustrate their lack of access. As an alternative solution, she proposed that companies offer after-hours training programs at various community centers in the region, which she admitted would require the companies to spend some money up

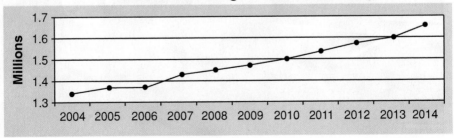

Projected Number of Heavy-duty Truck Drivers Needed in Long-distance Trucking

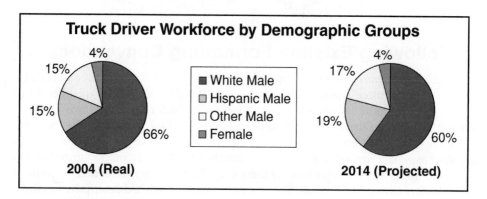

Truck Driver Workforce by Demographic Groups

Legend:
- ■ White Male
- ☐ Hispanic Male
- ☐ Other Male
- ■ Female

2004 (Real): 66%, 15%, 15%, 4%

2014 (Projected): 60%, 19%, 17%, 4%

front but would allow them to help the community, support the training of women, and recruit from the pool of qualified women in the region.

Finally, the proposal author used photographs as a framing device. She knew from her own experience that people respond to photographs and are compelled by appropriate images. Thus, toward the beginning of the proposal, she scanned in a snapshot showing herself in the double-bottom dump truck that she first learned to drive, which helped establish her authority as a trucker. Toward the end of the proposal, she included a variety of photographs like the one below, showing women truck drivers competently performing their jobs; each of these images attested to the feasibility of her proposed solution.

Reflecting on Your Writing

Now that you have worked extensively with essays that propose solutions to problems—reading them, talking about them, writing one of your own—take some time to reflect on what you have learned. What problems did you encounter while you were writing your essay, and how did you solve them?

Write a page or two telling your instructor about a problem you encountered in writing an essay that proposes a solution and how you solved it. Before you begin, gather all of your writing—invention and planning notes, drafts, critical comments, revision notes and plans, and final revision. Review these materials as you complete this writing task.

1. *Identify one writing problem you had to solve as you worked on your proposal essay.* Do not be concerned with grammar and punctuation; concentrate instead on problems unique to developing a proposal. For example: Did you puzzle over how to convince readers that your proposed solution would actually solve the problem you identified? Did you find it difficult to support the reasons you gave for recommending the solution? Did you have trouble coming up with alternative solutions that your readers might favor?

2. *Determine how you came to recognize the writing problem.* When did you first discover it? What called it to your attention? If someone else pointed out the problem to you, can you now see hints of it in your invention writings? If so, where specifically? When you first recognized the problem, how did you respond?

3. *Reflect on how you went about solving the problem.* Did you reword a passage, cut or add details about the problem or solution, or move paragraphs or sentences around? Did you reread one of the essays in this chapter to see how another writer handled a similar problem, or did you look back at the invention suggestions? If you discussed the writing problem with another student, a tutor, or your instructor, did talking about it help? How useful was the advice you received?

4. *Write a page or so explaining the problem and your solution.* Be as specific as possible in reconstructing your efforts. Quote from your invention notes, your draft essay, others' critical comments, your revision plan, and your revised essay to show the various changes your writing underwent as you tried to solve the problem. If you are still uncertain about your solution, say so. The point is not to prove that you have solved the problem perfectly but rather to show what you have learned about solving problems when writing proposals. Taking time to explain how you identified a particular problem, how you went about trying to solve it, and what you learned from this experience can help you solve future writing problems more easily.

243

7

Justifying an Evaluation

IN COLLEGE COURSES For a research paper in a literature in film course, a student sets out to evaluate the 1995 film *Clueless*, an adaptation of Jane Austen's novel *Emma* set in modern day Beverly Hills. While reading the novel, he reviews key scenes in the film and looks closely at differences in how the main characters are portrayed.

During an Internet search for reviews of *Clueless*, he discovers that there is a 1996 film called *Emma* set in early nineteenth-century England like the novel. He goes to his professor's office hours to see if there is any problem evaluating two film versions of a novel instead of one. His professor responds enthusiastically.

He then spends several days writing his essay and capturing stills from the two films to illustrate his argument that *Clueless* does a better job than *Emma* of presenting the novel's ironic social commentary for today's viewers. He gives two reasons: *Emma* emphasizes set design over action, and it doesn't allow viewers to identify with the main characters. In contrast, he argues that because the action and characters in *Clueless* are recognizable and realistic, contemporary viewers can better appreciate the social commentary.

IN THE COMMUNITY A motorcycle enthusiast rides to York, Pennsylvania, to tour the Harley-Davidson factory there. He intends to write a review of the tour to post on his blog. After arriving, he and about twenty other visitors wander through the Vaughn L. Beals Tour Center, marveling at the dozens of vintage motorcycles on display. He watches a short film that relates the history of the company, and then explores exhibits describing the manufacturing process he is about to observe.

The factory is housed in an immense building of more than 230 acres with over a thousand workers on each shift. He takes digital photos and makes notes describing the swift, orchestrated labor in which workers add a new part to each bike every three minutes as it moves along a conveyor belt and is ultimately rolled off the assembly line.

On the way home, he decides to title his review "Hog Heaven." He spends a couple of days writing, describing the tour as an exhilarating ride that is free, fun, and educational. He illustrates his review with his photographs and then posts it.

IN THE WORKPLACE For a conference panel on innovations in education, an elementary school teacher decides to give a talk on *Schoolhouse Rock!*, an animated television series developed in the 1970s and 1980s. She had recently started showing segments to her students, who seemed to enjoy them as much as she had.

To prepare her talk, she plays four songs for her class: two from "Grammar Rock" ("Conjunction Junction" and "A Noun Is a Person, Place or Thing") and two from "Multiplication Rock" ("Three Is a Magic Number" and "The Good 11"). Following each, she gives her students a quiz to see how well they have learned the lesson. Finally, she conducts a poll to see whether the kids enjoy this kind of learning.

In her panel presentation, she describes her research and gives two reasons why the series is an effective educational tool: the witty lyrics and catchy tunes make the information memorable, and the cartoon visuals make the lessons vivid and enjoyable. She supports her evaluation by screening and discussing the segments she played in class, presenting the results of the follow-up quizzes, and quoting from the opinion poll. She ends by expressing her hope that teachers and educational publishers will learn from the example of *Schoolhouse Rock!*

Evaluation involves making judgments. Many times each day, people make judgments about subjects as diverse as the weather, food, music, sports, politics, and films. In everyday conversation, you often express judgments casually ("I like it" or "I don't like it"), only occasionally giving your reasons (for example, "I hate cafeteria food because it is bland and overcooked") or supporting them with specific examples ("Take last night's spaghetti. That must have been a tomato sauce because it was red, but it didn't taste like tomatoes. And the noodles were mushy").

When you write an evaluation, however, readers expect you to provide reasons and support for your judgment. In the scenario about the Harley-Davidson tour, for example, the writer gives three reasons for recommending the tour, supporting them with description and photographs. Similarly, the student evaluating two film versions of Jane Austen's novel gives two reasons for thinking *Clueless* is a more effective adaptation than *Emma*, supporting his argument with examples from both films and the novel as well as with stills from the films. The teacher who gives a presentation on *Schoolhouse Rock!* uses the songs as well as her quiz grades and survey results to support her reasons for praising the series.

In addition, readers need to agree that your reasons are appropriate for evaluating the subject. For example, in an evaluation of a film like *Mission: Impossible III*, you would want to show that you are judging the film according to standards most people would use in evaluating action films, as James Berardinelli does in his *ReelViews* review (www.reelreviews.net/movies/m/mission3.html). Berardinelli first places the film in its general category ("a flashy, leave-your-brain-at-the-door summer movie"). Then he goes on to argue that even though it has all the characteristics of a summer blockbuster ("It's loud, raucous, frenetic, and blows things up real good"), he found the film disappointing because "it's testosterone without adrenaline, danger without suspense." Berardinelli understands that readers expect him to judge the film as an example of its genre, so he bases his judgment on qualities such as the film's special effects, action sequences, and most important, its ability to generate excitement. He even makes a point of saying that he is not criticizing the film's "plot contrivances" because "they go with the territory."

Showing readers you understand how your subject relates to other subjects in the same category demonstrates that your judgment is based on reasons and standards readers recognize as appropriate. Readers may disagree with you, but they will understand and respect your argument.

A Collaborative Activity: Practice Evaluating a Subject	**Part 1.** Get together with two or three other students to choose a reading from an earlier chapter that you have all already read. Review the reading, and decide whether you think the reading was helpful or unhelpful to you in learning to write well in that genre.

- First, take turns telling the group whether the reading was helpful and giving two reasons for that judgment. Do not try to convince the others that your judgment is right or your reasons are sound; simply state your judgment and reasons.

- Next, after everyone gives a judgment and reasons, discuss briefly as a group whether the reasons seem appropriate. Again, you do not have to agree about whether the reading was helpful or unhelpful; all you have to do is discover whether you can agree on the kinds of reasons that make sense when evaluating a reading in the context of a writing course.

Part 2. As a group, spend a few minutes discussing what happened:

- Begin by focusing on the reasons your group found easiest to agree on. Discuss why your group found these reasons so easy to agree on.
- Then focus on the reasons your group found hardest to agree on. Discuss why your group found these particular reasons so hard to agree on.

What can you conclude about group standards for judging readings in a writing course?

Readings

WENDY KIM immigrated to the United States from South Korea when she was eight years old. A business administration major, Kim plans to go to graduate school in business. For a composition course, she decided to research a Web site she uses regularly to decide which classes to take: RateMyProfessors.com. You may want to take a look at the Web site (which has been redesigned since Kim wrote her description) to see whether you think her judgment is sound.

Grading Professors

Wendy Kim

1 "Where the Students Do the Grading" is the tagline for the Web site www.RateMyProfessors.com (RMP). Users just choose their state and find their school among the more than 6,000 campuses listed, and they're ready to start grading their professors. The home page proudly displays the numbers: last I looked, there were more than 6,200,000 ratings, covering more than 770,000 professors in the United States and Canada. In fact, RMP has been so successful that it has expanded to Australia, Ireland, and the United Kingdom, and its sister-site for high school students, RateMyTeachers.com, already has a user base of 3 million students (RateMyProfessors). While not everyone agrees that these ratings provide an entirely accurate assessment,

Kim attracts readers with her title and use of RMP's tagline.

She piles up statistics to show the site's popularity.

Kim uses MLA style throughout to cite sources parenthetically.

Kim's thesis forecasts the reasons she will develop in subsequent paragraphs. She introduces her first reason—that the Web site is well designed—by focusing on its appearance and ease of use.

Kim takes readers on a tour of the home page, which she illustrate in Fig. 1 and analyzes here and in par. 3.

many students, like me, routinely consult RMP at the beginning of every term to decide which classes to take. Overall, the Web site is well designed, amusing, and extremely helpful.

The design of RateMyProfessors.com makes the site 2 attractive and easy to browse (see Fig. 1). In my senior year of high school, I took a class which taught me how to make a good Web site and learned that Web site design requires care in picking colors and in organizing the layout. The layout of RMP's home page is smart, with information grouped in clearly defined rectangular boxes. Across the top is a banner with the name in easy-to-read letters. Below the banner, the page is divided into boxes, three across and two down, with plenty of white space along the left and right borders and bottom so that the page looks neatly organized and uncluttered. The top box on the left has the main menu in blue lettering against a white background with links to "Hot or Not," "Funny Ratings," "Signup Now," "Recent Press," and "Forum," five areas likely to be of most use to users. The placement of the menu is smart because readers of English are used to reading from left to right as well as top to bottom. Below the menu a box titled "Statistics" (which I cited in the first paragraph) reveals how many students use the ratings.

3

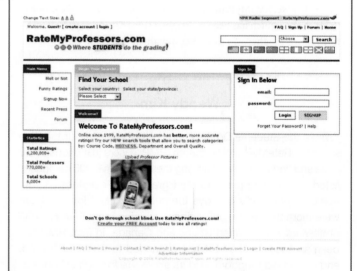

4

Figure 1. *Rate My Professors.com.* Home page. 26 Sept. 2006 <http://www.ratemyprofessors.com>.

The viewer's eye is drawn to the center box, which is twice as wide as the boxes on the sides and includes the all-important search function (set off against a distinctive yellow background). The box below this, which includes eye-catching graphics, serves as a portal to the Welcome page. The box in the top righthand portion of the screen allows users to sign in conveniently. Ads fill the space in the lower righthand portion of the screen; however, they coordinate in color with the rest of the elements on the page, so they're not too distracting. The placement of information seems just right.

The navigation system is smooth and fast. When you log in, you get the main member page; from there, you easily link to your school's page. On the member page, you can edit your ratings, go to the message board, or manage your account. Your school's page is the destination for checking out professors whose classes you are considering, entering your own rating of a professor, or adding a professor not already listed. Finding a particular professor is quick and easy because professors' names are listed in alphabetical order. The list is easy to skim and contains lots of valuable information. To the left of each name is a face icon (which I will explain in a minute) followed by a check icon that you can click on to add your own rating. To the right of the name is the professor's department, the date he or she was last rated, the number of ratings, and the vital average ratings for overall quality and ease. Clicking on a name takes you to the professor's page, which presents even more information: a box with averages in each rating category and a list of individual users' ratings, starting with the most recent. These ratings identify the class, give the student's rating in each category, and often include a comment. You can add your own rating of the professor or respond to other users' ratings. Every page displays the information clearly, without distractions. Even though there are ads, they do not flicker or get in the way. This is not the kind of Web site that takes minutes just to find what you need. Not only is it easy to browse, but it also doesn't lag because there are no large files or images to slow it down. For me, the longest it took to get to another page was two seconds using a cable modem.

Most important, RateMyProfessors.com is full of useful information that can help students make informed decisions when it comes to choosing teachers and preparing for a class they are about to take. A student debating whether to take a

5

Kim provides more support for her first reason, showing how fast RMP's navigation system is and how easy it is to find specific professors.

This topic sentence introduces the section on Kim's second reason—that RMP is extremely helpful.

history or a sociology class, for example, can go to the Web site, first look at the overall ratings of each professor and then find user ratings for the classes being considered. Assuming the professor has been graded by other students, a great deal can be learned about the professor and possibly also about the specific class.

6

Professors are rated in several categories on a scale of 1 (worst) to 5 (best). The scores on clarity and helpfulness are averaged for the "Overall Quality rating," the overall rating that determines which icon is placed next to the professor's name: A yellow smiley face indicates "good quality," a bluish-gray sad face "poor quality," and an indifferent-looking green face "average quality." The numerical rating in each category is displayed along with the face so that students and professors can see the breakdown. In addition to evaluating the professor's clarity and helpfulness, students also rate the difficulty of the course. This rating, however, has no effect on assigning the face icon because, as the site explains, "an Easiness rating of 5 may actually mean the teacher is TOO easy." Although RMP acknowledges that easiness is "definitely the most controversial" reason for judging a class, they still present it because "many students decide what class to take based on the difficulty of the teacher." Another category that is not included in the overall rating is "Rater Interest." To explain this category the Web site quotes from a study that found student "motivation correlated with the overall evaluation," meaning that the more motivated a student was to succeed in a course, the higher the professor's overall quality score. "Instructors," however, as RMP acknowledges, "usually have little control over student motivation" (RateMyProfessors).

> *Kim anticipates readers' concern about the Easiness rating. She counterargues by acknowledging the criticism and RMP's response.*

7

The faces and numbers are informative, but I think the comments help the most because they are so detailed. Not surprisingly, the comments on RateMyProfessors.com tend to address many of the same issues that my college's course evaluation forms do. For example, one question on my campus evaluation asks if the instructor presented the material in "an organized, understandable manner." Many of the RMP comments answer this question: from high praise ("lectures are interesting, and he's happy to answer whatever questions you could ask") to severe criticism ("lectures are BORING and POINTLESS" or "totally disorganized!! boring and reads off the power point!!"). Another question on my campus form asks if the instructor was "concerned about students learning and understanding the course material." This issue also draws many comments on RMP, from highly positive ("he wrote a personal whole-page

> *Kim uses the questions in her college course evaluation form to classify comments on the Web site.*

> *Kim quotes many comments such as these to help readers appreciate how informative the site is.*

response to each of my papers. So I knew exactly what he liked and how to improve on my writing") to slams ("Kinda scary and intimidating" or "He does not care if the students are learning the basic concepts. He teaches as if he were teaching a Graduate level class. This is an INTRO class, let us learn the basics 1st"). In addition to these kinds of comments, RMP also posts information that course evaluations do not include—advice on how to pass the course ("If you keep up w/ your notes and the reading, you should be fine. Pop quizzes every week." or "Has notes available online. Tests are extremely difficult and require a lot of reading from the book to be successful as well as attending class. Gives surprise quizzes"). The site also gives students warnings ("He's ****in' hard. Fails half his class." or "OMG, one of the worst teachers I've ever had . . . Does not know how to teach and wears the tightest pants ever . . . gross.")

> *Here Kim adds another category not found on course evaluations.*

8   And as this last comment suggests, we can't forget the last rating category: Is your professor hot or not? The answer to this question makes the Web site amusing. "Hot" professors are marked with a red chili pepper beside their names. Some students also include comments in this area: "good lookin guy, nice body" and "this chick [the professor] totally blew my mind. She was sooo hot. I'm serious take this class just to check her out. SEXY!!!!" In fact, this issue may not be just a sideline to ones that supposedly are more serious. Students give professors higher overall ratings if they are hot, according to a *New York Times* article, "The Hunk Differential," which the RMP site provides as the answer to its FAQ question "Why do you have the 'hot' category?" The article, written by a professor of business, economics, and information management, reports a study that found "good-looking professors got significantly higher teaching scores" than those who did not rate as high on a beauty scale (Varian). So it may be that a professor who is considered "hot" on the site may be judged on a more lenient scale of teaching effectiveness.

> *Here Kim introduces her third reason—that RMP is amusing.*

> *Kim anticipates a concern, refuting possible criticism with support from published research.*

9   This question about the possible effect of the teacher's appearance on student response and learning leads to a more basic question about the credibility of the evaluations on RateMyProfessors.com: Are the ratings statistically valid? The simple answer, the Web site itself admits, is "Not really. They are a listing of opinions and should be judged as such" (RateMyProfessors). The results are statistically invalid, as one psychology professor explained, because the users are self-selected and not selected randomly (Harmon). And the fewer student ratings an instructor has been given, the less reliable the overall evaluation. Nevertheless, RMP claims "we often

> *Here, Kim anticipates a fourth, and major criticism, which she concedes. Nevertheless, she defends her positive judgment with support from researchers and students.*

receive emails stating that the ratings are uncannily accurate, especially for schools with over 1000 ratings" (RateMyProfessors). RMP also refers readers to an article reporting a study at the University of Waterloo, Canada (UW), that found fifteen of the sixteen Distinguished Teacher Award winners at UW also had yellow smiley faces on RateMyProfessors.com (TRACE). While this correlation is reassuring, students should not approach the ratings uncritically. And evidence suggests most don't. As one college newspaper reporter put it, "students claim they do not blindly follow the comments" (Espach). A recent study of RMP published in the *Journal of Computer-Mediated Communication* found that students "are aware that ratings and comments on the site could reflect students exacting revenge or venting" (Kindred and Mohammed). As one student explained: "If half the ratings are bad, I will ask around about the professor. If every rating is poor I won't take the teacher" (Espach).

There are other Internet professor evaluation sites, but none is as widely used or as easy to use as RateMyProfessors. com. I compared RMP with three competitors: Professor Performance, Reviewum.com, and RatingsOnline. The user base of the first two sites looks too small to provide reliable information. Professor Performance has 73,040 evaluations at 1,742 colleges and universities, and Reviewum.com claims to have 20,098 records for 137 campuses. In addition, for the limited number of professors who are listed, there are only a small number of evaluations, not enough to enable students to make informed judgments.

Although RatingsOnline does not appear to display its statistics, it claims to have ratings for "thousands of professors." However, there are only nineteen professors from my campus listed compared to 1252 on RMP. Still, RatingsOnline is better designed and includes more helpful information than the other two competitors, and it may even be better than RMP in terms of helpfulness. Students not only identify the class and term it was taken, but also are asked to list the grade they received. Of course, this information about the grade is no more reliable than any other information a user gives, but it could help students judge the user's credibility. The ratings categories on RatingsOnline also seem more specific than on RMP: prepared, enthusiastic, focused, available, material, exam prep, quality. In addition, students are prompted to indicate the percentage given to homework, quizzes, and exams in determining the final grade. This information could be useful in helping

10

11

Kim compares RMP to competing Web sites.

She compares the different sites' statistics to argue for RMP's greater reliability.

Kim points out the relative strengths and weaknesses of RatingsOnline compared to RateMyProfessors.

students decide which classes to take, but only if there are enough reviews posted. In its design and potential helpfulness, RatingsOnline is a very good site but not likely to be as good as RMP because its user base appears to be smaller.

12   When you have the option of choosing a teacher, wouldn't you really like some information? RateMyProfessors.com allows you to see what other students have to say about professors and courses you may be considering as well as to voice your opinion. As a Web site, it is not only helpful and easy to use, but it is also amusing to read.

Kim concludes by reminding readers of her reasons.

Works Cited

Espach, Alison. "RateMyProfessors.com — Blessing or Bluffing?" *The Cowl.* Providence College, 27 Apr. 2006. Web. 15 May 2006.

Harmon, Christine. "Professors Rate Reliability of RateMyProfessors. com." *Daily Forty-Niner.* California State U, Long Beach, 2 May 2006. Web. 15 May 2006.

Kindred, Jeannette, and Shaheed N. Mohammed. "'He Will Crush You Like an Academic Ninja!': Exploring Teacher Ratings on RateMyProfessors.com." *Journal of Computer-Mediated Communication* 10.3 (2005): n. pag. Web. 15 May 2006.

Professor Performance. Professorperformance.com, n.d. Web. 19 May 2006.

RateMyProfessors. Ratemyprofessors.com, 2006. Web. 13 May 2006.

"ratemyprofessors.ca." *Teaching Matters Newsletter.* U of Waterloo Teaching Resources Office, Sept. 2001. Web. 13 May 2005.

RatingsOnline. Ratingsonline.com, n.d. Web. 19 May 2006.

Reviewum.com. Reviewum.com, 2006. Web. 19 May 2006.

Varian, Hal R. "The Hunk Differential." *New York Times.* New York Times, 28 Aug. 2003. Web. 14 May 2006.

A. O. SCOTT is a film reviewer for the *New York Times.* An occasional contributor to other publications such as *Slate* and *The New Yorker,* Scott has also edited several books, including *A Bolt from the Blue and Other Essays* (2002) and the *New York Times Guide to the Best 1,000 Movies Ever Made* (2004).

The 2005 film *Good Night, and Good Luck* was a critical as well as a popular success, receiving six Academy Award nominations, including ones for director, screenplay, and picture.

George Clooney, who cowrote, directed, and acted in the film, explained in a *Columbia Journalism Review* interview that he intended the film "to reflect a great moment in journalism" when newscaster Edward R. Murrow challenged U.S. Senator Joseph R. McCarthy's public attacks against alleged Communists among the U.S. populace. Clooney said he wanted the film to stir debate about the news media's responsibility to speak truth to power.

Notice that Scott judges the film for its cinematic qualities as well as for its ideas, which he seems especially to value because of their complexity, the "shades of gray" indicated in his title. Consider, as you read, whether these reasons seem appropriate to you or whether you would apply different standards.

News in Black, White and Shades of Gray

A. O. Scott

Shot in a black-and-white palette of cigarette smoke, hair tonic, dark suits and pale button-down shirts, *Good Night, and Good Luck* plunges into a half-forgotten world in which television was new, the cold war was at its peak, and the Surgeon General's report on the dangers of tobacco was still a decade in the future. Though it is a meticulously detailed reconstruction of an era, the film, directed by George Clooney from a script he wrote with Grant Heslov, is concerned with more than nostalgia. [1]

Burnishing the legend of Edward R. Murrow, the CBS newsman who in the 1940s and '50s established a standard of journalistic integrity his profession has scrambled to live up to ever since, *Good Night, and Good Luck* is a passionate, thoughtful essay on power, truth-telling and responsibility. . . . The title evokes Murrow's trademark sign-off, and I can best sum up my own response by recalling the name of his flagship program: See it now. [2]

And be prepared to pay attention. *Good Night, and Good Luck* is not the kind of historical picture that dumbs down its material, or walks you carefully through events that may be unfamiliar. Instead, it unfolds, *cinéma-vérité* style,[1] in the fast, sometimes frantic present tense, following Murrow and his colleagues as they deal with the petty annoyances and larger anxieties of news gathering at a moment of political turmoil. The story flashes back from a famous, cautionary speech that Murrow gave at an industry convention in 1958 to one of the most notable episodes in his career—his war of words and images with Senator Joseph R. McCarthy. [3]

While David Strathairn plays Murrow with sly eloquence and dark wit, Mr. Clooney allows the junior Senator from Wisconsin to play himself (thanks to surviving video clips of his hearings and public appearances), a jolt of documentary truth that highlights [4]

---

[1]*cinéma-vérité* style: In French, "films of truth." This style of filmmaking uses documentary film techniques to make the drama seem lifelike or realistic.

And that's the way it was: from left, George Clooney as Fred Friendly, Robert Downey, Jr. as Joe Wershba, and David Strathairn as Edward R. Murrow. (Photo credit: Melinda Sue Gordon)

some of the movie's themes. Television, it suggests, can be both a potent vehicle for demagoguery[2] and a weapon in the fight against it.

Mr. Clooney, who plays Murrow's producer and partner, Fred Friendly, has clearly   5
thought long and hard about the peculiar, ambiguous nature of the medium. It is a subject that comes naturally to him: his father, Nick, was for many years a local television newscaster in Cincinnati, and the younger Mr. Clooney's own star first rose on the small screen. Like *Good Night, and Good Luck*, his first film, *Confessions of a Dangerous Mind* (2002), used the biography of a television personality (Chuck Barris of *The Gong Show*) as a way of exploring the medium's capacity to show the truth, and also to distort and obscure it.

Indeed, these two movies can almost be seen as companion pieces. *Confessions*   6
of a Dangerous Mind suggests that a man with a hard time telling truth from fiction can find a natural home on the tube, while *Good Night, and Good Luck* demonstrates that a furiously honest, ruthlessly rational person may find it less comfortable. Murrow, as conceived by the filmmakers and incarnated by Mr. Strathairn, is a man of strong ideals and few illusions. He knows that McCarthy will smear him (and offers the Senator airtime to do so), and that sponsors and government officials will pressure his boss, William Paley (Frank Langella), to rein him in.

He is aware that his reports are part of a large, capitalist enterprise, and makes   7
some necessary concessions. In addition to his investigative reports—and, in effect,

---

[2]*demagoguery:* The tactic of appealing to people's fears and prejudices instead of their reason, usually as a way to gain or retain power.

to pay for them—Murrow conducts celebrity interviews, including one with Liberace,[3] which Mr. Clooney has lovingly and mischievously rescued from the archives.

From that odd encounter to the kinescopes[4] of the Army-McCarthy hearings,[5] *Good Night, and Good Luck* brilliantly recreates the milieu of early television. Robert Elswit's smoky cinematography and Stephen Mirrione's suave, snappy editing are crucial to this accomplishment. It also captures, better than any recent movie I can think of, the weirdly hermetic atmosphere of a news organization at a time of crisis.   8

Nearly all the action takes place inside CBS headquarters (or at the bar where its employees drink after hours), which gives the world outside a detached, almost abstract quality. A telephone rings, an image flickers on a screen, a bulldog edition[6] of the newspaper arrives . . . this is what it means for information to be mediated.   9

But its effects are nonetheless real. While the camera never follows Friendly or Murrow home from the office, and the script never delves into psychology, we see how the climate of paranoia and uncertainty seeps into the lives of some of their co-workers. Don Hollenbeck (Ray Wise), an anchor for the New York CBS affiliate, is viciously red-baited[7] by a newspaper columnist, and Joe and Shirley Wershba (Robert Downey Jr. and Patricia Clarkson) skulk around the office like spies (though for reasons that have more to do with office politics than with national security). When Murrow, in March 1954, prepares to broadcast his exposé of McCarthy's methods, the suspense is excruciating, even if we know the outcome.   10

Because we do, it is possible to view *Good Night, and Good Luck* simply as a reassuring story of triumph. But the film does more than ask us, once again, to admire Edward R. Murrow and revile Joseph R. McCarthy. That layer of the story is, as it should be, in stark black-and-white, but there is a lot of gray as well, and quite a few questions that are not so easily resolved. The free press may be the oxygen of a democratic society, but it is always clouded by particles and pollutants, from the vanity or cowardice of individual journalists to the impersonal pressures of state power and the profit motive.   11

And while Mr. Clooney is inclined to glorify, he does not simplify. The scenes between Murrow and Paley, taking place in the latter's cryptlike office, have an almost Shakespearean gravity, and not only because Mr. Strathairn and Mr. Langella perform their roles with such easy authority. McCarthy may serve as the hissable villain, but Paley is a more complicated foil for Murrow—at once patron, antagonist   12

---

[3]*Liberace:* A pianist who was popular in the 1950s. He never came out of the closet as a homosexual, but in the interview shown in the film he seems to be saying that, like England's Princess Margaret, he is looking for his "dream man, too."

[4]*kinescopes:* A method of recording television programs used in the 1950s.

[5]*Army-McCarthy hearings:* Nationally televised congressional hearings in 1954 to investigate Senator McCarthy's charges that the U.S. Army was harboring Communists. In the end, McCarthy was discredited by the hearings, whose high point was the army attorney Joseph Welch's exasperated comment: "Have you no sense of decency, sir, at long last? Have you left no sense of decency?"

[6]*bulldog edition:* The earliest morning edition of a newspaper.

[7]*red-baited:* To be accused and denounced as a Communist or Communist sympathizer.

and protector. (Addressed by everyone else, in hushed tones, as "Mr. Paley," he is "Bill" only to Murrow.)

Most of the discussion of this movie will turn on its content—on the history it investigates and on its present-day resonance. This is a testament to Mr. Clooney's modesty (as is the fact that, on screen, he makes himself look doughy and pale), but also to his skill. Over the years he has worked with some of the smartest directors around, notably Joel Coen and Steven Soderbergh (who is an executive producer of this film). And while he has clearly learned from them, the cinematic intelligence on display in this film is entirely his own. He has found a cogent subject, an urgent set of ideas and a formally inventive, absolutely convincing way to make them live on screen.

13

Making Connections to Personal and Social Issues: A Free Press and Democracy

Scott appears to agree with Clooney that journalism plays a crucial role in maintaining democracy, saying that a "free press may be the oxygen of a democratic society" (par. 11). But, as Scott also points out, there are many reasons the press fails to fulfill its obligations: "from the vanity or cowardice of individual journalists to the impersonal pressures of state power and the profit motive" (11). In today's society, there may also be problems on the receiving end. The number of newspapers in the United States has steadily declined in the last two decades, and only half of Americans today read a daily newspaper. Similarly, viewership of television news programs has declined, from 60 percent in 1993 to 30 percent in 2000. Whereas the median age of evening news show viewers is 60 years old, young people aged 18–29 reportedly are more likely to get their news from the Internet and TV comedy shows than from television or radio news programs, newspapers, or newsmagazines.

With two or three other students, discuss which of the news media—print, television, radio, or the Internet—you follow and how much time per day or week you typically spend reading or viewing it. What are your favorite sources of information and why?

Based on your own experience and those of people you know, do you think the decline in newspaper readership and television news viewing is a problem? Or do you think young people are sufficiently informed about important issues through the Internet, "fake news" shows, and other sources?

Analyzing Writing Strategies

1. In evaluating a film, writers often point out details from the film as examples to **support their argument**. Reread paragraphs 8–10 and underline the details Scott presents. *Explain briefly in writing what the details illustrate and how effectively they support the argument.*

2. Writers of evaluations often use comparison to **support their reasons**. One of the reasons Scott offers for his judgment of the film is that it is "a passionate, thoughtful essay on power, truth-telling and responsibility" (par. 2). At the beginning of paragraph 5, he observes that George Clooney "has clearly thought long and hard about the peculiar, ambiguous nature of the medium" of television, specifically its "capacity to show the truth, and also to distort and obscure it." *To see how Scott uses comparison to develop and support this reason, reread paragraphs 5 and 6 where he compares* Good Night, and Good Luck *to the first film Clooney directed,* Confessions of a Dangerous Mind, *and explain briefly in writing how the comparison supports Scott's argument.*

Commentary: Presenting the Subject, Overall Judgment, and Reasons

Film reviews, like other evaluations, usually begin by **presenting the subject** and conveying the writer's judgment. Scott identifies the movie by name in his first sentence, and in the first four paragraphs he categorizes it as a "historical picture" in "*cinéma-vérité* style" (par. 3), and associates it with "documentary" films (4). He indicates the time period in the first paragraph ("when the cold war was at its peak"), and in paragraph 10, he concisely explains the focus of the story: "When Murrow, in March 1954, prepares to broadcast his exposé of McCarthy's methods, the suspense is excruciating. . . ." Additionally, Scott tells who the main actors are and what characters they play.

Because film reviewers need to assume their readers are trying to decide whether to see the film, they have to think carefully about how much plot detail to reveal. In this case, because the film depicts historical events, Scott does not try to hide the outcome, but neither does he describe the climax.

In addition to presenting the subject, writers of evaluation usually **state their judgment** early on. In paragraph 2, Scott claims "*Good Night, and Good Luck* is a passionate, thoughtful essay on power, truth-telling and responsibility" and urges readers, "See it now." Throughout the essay, Scott makes other evaluative statements about the acting, the atmosphere the film creates, and the complexity with which the story is told. But he saves his overall judgment of the film, the thesis, until the end: "He [Clooney] has found a cogent subject, an urgent set of ideas and a formally inventive, absolutely convincing way to make them live on screen" (par. 13).

Because it comes at the end, instead of at the beginning, this thesis summarizes the main **reasons** instead of forecasting them. The key words "subject" and "ideas" refer to what Scott writes in paragraph 2 about the film being about "power, truth-telling and responsibility." He returns in paragraphs 6, 7, 11, and 12 to developing and supporting this reason. First, he makes the point that broadcast news is "part of a large, capitalist enterprise" that leads inevitably to the compromising of ideals. Then, he demonstrates that the film's idea that a "free press" is the "oxygen" needed for "a democratic society" is treated with some subtlety. Anticipating readers' possible objection to the film's apparent hero-worship of Murrow, he argues that it is not as simplistic as it might seem ("there is a lot of gray as well, and quite a few questions that are not so easily resolved" [par. 11]).

The second main reason for his high regard for the film relates to its being "formally inventive" (13). In talking about the film's form, Scott refers to its use of "*cinéma-vérité*," or "documentary" style. He shows that it is "a meticulously detailed reconstruction of an era" (1), but as he explains in paragraph 3, it is not a traditional "historical picture that dumbs down its material, or walks you carefully through events." Instead, he shows that it is fast paced and uses flashback to frame the events. In paragraphs 9 and 10, he provides additional support by showing how Clooney's direction and screenplay combine with the cinematography and the editing to create "the weirdly hermetic atmosphere of a news organization at a time of crisis" (8).

For more information on thesis statements, see Chapter 11.

Considering Topics for Your Own Essay

List several movies that you have seen recently, and choose one from your list that you recall especially well and about which you have a strong overall judgment. Then consider how you would argue for your judgment. Specifically, what reasons do you think you would give your readers? Why do you assume that your readers would accept these reasons as appropriate for evaluating this particular film?

CHRISTINE ROMANO wrote the following essay when she was a first-year college student. In it she evaluates an argument essay written by another student, Jessica Statsky's "Children Need to Play, Not Compete," which appears in Chapter 5 of this book (pp. 149–54). Romano focuses not on the writing strategies or basic features of an essay arguing a position but rather on its logic—on whether the argument is likely to convince its intended readers. She evaluates the logic of the argument according to the standards presented in Chapter 9. You might want to review these standards on pp. 326–28 before you read Romano's evaluation. Also, if you have not already read Statsky's essay, you might want to do so now, thinking about what seems most and least convincing to you about her argument that competitive sports can be harmful to young children.

"Children Need to Play, Not Compete," by Jessica Statsky: An Evaluation

Christine Romano

Parents of young children have a lot to worry about and to hope for. In "Children Need to Play, Not Compete," Jessica Statsky appeals to their worries and hopes in order to convince them that organized competitive sports may harm their children   1 physically and psychologically. Statsky states her thesis clearly and fully forecasts the reasons she will offer to justify her position: Besides causing physical and psychological harm, competitive sports discourage young people from becoming players and fans when they are older and inevitably put parents' needs and fantasies ahead of children's welfare. Statsky also carefully defines her key terms. By *sports*, for example, she means to include both contact and noncontact sports that emphasize competition. The sports may be organized locally at schools or summer sports camps or nationally, as in the examples of Peewee Football and Little League Baseball. She is concerned only with children six to twelve years of age.

In this essay, I will evaluate the logic of Statsky's argument, considering whether the support for her thesis is appropriate, believable, consistent, and complete. While her logic *is* appropriate, believable, and consistent, her argument also has weaknesses. I will focus on two: Her argument seems incomplete because she neglects to anticipate parents' predictable questions and objections and because she fails to support certain parts of it fully.

Statsky provides appropriate support for her thesis. Throughout her essay, she relies for support on different kinds of information (she cites eleven separate sources, including books, newspapers, and Web sites). Her quotations, examples, and statistics all support the reasons she believes competitive sports are bad for children. For example, in paragraph 3, Statsky offers the reason that "overly competitive sports" may damage children's growing bodies and that contact sports, in particular, may be especially hazardous. She supports this reason by paraphrasing Koppett's claim that muscle strain or even lifelong injury may result when a twelve-year-old throws curve balls. She then quotes Tutko on the dangers of tackle football. The opinions of both experts are obviously appropriate. They are relevant to her reason, and we can easily imagine that they would worry many parents.

Not only is Statsky's support appropriate, but it is also believable. Statsky quotes or summarizes authorities to support her argument in paragraphs 3–6, 8, 9, and 11. The question is whether readers would find these authorities credible. Since Statsky relies almost entirely on authorities to support her argument, readers must believe these authorities for her argument to succeed. I have not read Statsky's sources, but I think there are good reasons to consider them authoritative. First of all, the newspaper authors she quotes write for two of America's most respected newspapers, the *New York Times* and the *Los Angeles Times*. These newspapers are read across the country by political leaders and financial experts and by people interested in the arts and popular culture. Both have sports reporters who not only report on sports events but also take a critical look at sports issues. In addition, both newspapers have reporters who specialize in children's health and education. Second, Statsky gives background information about the authorities she quotes, which is intended to increase the person's believability in the eyes of parents of young children. In paragraph 3, she tells readers that Thomas Tutko is "a psychology professor at San Jose State University and coauthor of the book *Winning Is*

Everything and Other American Myths." In paragraph 5, she announces that Martin Rablovsky is "a former sports editor for the *New York Times*," and she notes that he has watched children play organized sports for many years. Third, she quotes from two Web sites—the official Little League site and an AOL message board. Parents are likely to accept the authority of the Little League site and be interested in what other parents and coaches (most of whom are also parents) have to say.

In addition to quoting authorities, Statsky relies on examples and anecdotes to support the reasons for her position. If examples and anecdotes are to be believable, they must seem representative to readers, not bizarre or highly unusual or completely unpredictable. Readers can imagine a similar event happening elsewhere. For anecdotes to be believable, they should, in addition, be specific and true to life. All of Statsky's examples and anecdotes fulfill these requirements, and her readers would find them believable. For example, early in her argument, in paragraph 4, Statsky reasons that fear of being hurt greatly reduces children's enjoyment of contact sports. The anecdote comes from Tosches's investigative report on Peewee Football as does the quotation by the mother of an eight-year-old player who says that the children become frightened and pretend to be injured in order to stay out of the game. In the anecdote, a seven-year-old makes himself vomit to avoid playing. Because these echo the familiar "I feel bad" or "I'm sick" excuse children give when they do not want to go somewhere (especially school) or do something, most parents would find them believable. They could easily imagine their own children pretending to be hurt or ill if they were fearful or depressed. The anecdote is also specific. Tosches reports what the boy said and did and what the coach said and did.

Other examples provide support for all the major reasons Statsky gives for her position:

- That competitive sports pose psychological dangers—children becoming serious and unplayful when the game starts (paragraph 5)

- That adults' desire to win puts children at risk—parents fighting each other at a Peewee Football game and a coach setting fire to an opposing team's jersey (paragraph 8)

- That organized sports should emphasize cooperation and individual performance instead of winning—a coach banning scoring but finding that parents would not support him and a New York City basketball league in which all children play an equal amount of time and scoring is easier (paragraph 11)

All of these examples are appropriate to the reason they support. They are also believable. Together, they help Statsky achieve her purpose of convincing parents that organized, competitive sports may be bad for their children and that there are alternatives.

If readers are to find an argument logical and convincing, it must be consistent and complete. While there are no inconsistencies or contradictions in Statsky's argument, it is seriously incomplete because it neglects to support fully one of its reasons,

5

6

7

it fails to anticipate many predictable questions parents would have, and it pays too little attention to noncontact competitive team sports. The most obvious example of this support comes in paragraph 11, where Statsky asserts that many parents are ready for children's team sports that emphasize cooperation and individual performance. Yet the example of a Little League official who failed to win parents' approval to ban scores raises serious questions about just how many parents are ready to embrace noncompetitive sports teams. The other support, a brief description of City Sports for Kids in New York City, is very convincing but will only be logically compelling to those parents who are already inclined to agree with Statsky's position. Parents inclined to disagree with Statsky would need additional evidence. Most parents know that big cities receive special federal funding for evening, weekend, and summer recreation. Brief descriptions of six or eight noncompetitive teams in a variety of sports in cities, rural areas, suburban neighborhoods—some funded publicly, some funded privately—would be more likely to convince skeptics. Statsky is guilty here of failing to accept the burden of proof, a logical fallacy.

Statsky's argument is also incomplete in that it fails to anticipate certain objections and questions that some parents, especially those she most wants to convince, are almost sure to raise. In the first sentences of paragraphs 6, 9, and 10, Statsky does show that she is thinking about her readers' questions. She does not go nearly far enough, however, to have a chance of influencing two types of readers: those who themselves are or were fans of and participants in competitive sports and those who want their six- to twelve-year-old children involved in mainstream sports programs despite the risks, especially the national programs that have a certain prestige. Such parents might feel that competitive team sports for young children create a sense of community with a shared purpose, build character through self-sacrifice and commitment to the group, teach children to face their fears early and learn how to deal with them through the support of coaches and team members, and introduce children to the principles of social cooperation and collaboration. Some parents are likely to believe and to know from personal experience that coaches who burn opposing team's jerseys on the pitching mound before the game starts are the exception, not the rule. Some young children idolize teachers and coaches, and team practice and games are the brightest moments in their lives. Statsky seems not to have considered these reasonable possibilities, and as a result her argument lacks a compelling logic it might have had. By acknowledging that she was aware of many of these objections—and perhaps even accommodating more of them in her own argument, as she does in paragraph 10, while refuting other objections—she would have strengthened her argument.

Finally, Statsky's argument is incomplete because she overlooks examples of noncontact team sports. Track, swimming, and tennis are good examples that some readers would certainly think of. Some elementary schools compete in track meets. Public and private clubs and recreational programs organize competitive swimming and tennis competitions. In these sports, individual performance is the focus. No one gets trampled. Children exert themselves only as much as they are able to. Yet individual performances are scored, and a team score is derived.

Because Statsky fails to mention any of these obvious possibilities, her argument is weakened.

The logic of Statsky's argument, then, has both strengths and weaknesses. 10 The support she offers is appropriate, believable, and consistent. The major weakness is incompleteness—she fails to anticipate more fully the likely objections of a wide range of readers. Her logic would prevent parents who enjoy and advocate competitive sports from taking her argument seriously. Such parents and their children have probably had positive experiences with team sports, and these experiences would lead them to believe that the gains are worth whatever risks may be involved. Many probably think that the risks Statsky points out can be avoided by careful monitoring. For those parents inclined to agree with her, Statsky's logic is likely to seem sound and complete. An argument that successfully confirms readers' beliefs is certainly valid, and Statsky succeeds admirably at this kind of argument. Because she does not offer compelling counterarguments to the legitimate objections of those inclined not to agree with her, however, her success is limited.

Making Connections to Personal and Social Issues: Competitive Team Sports and Social Cooperation

Romano reasons in paragraph 8 that some parents "feel that competitive team sports for young children create a sense of community with a shared purpose, build character through self-sacrifice and commitment to the group, teach children to face their fears early and learn how to deal with them through the support of coaches and team members, and introduce children to the principles of social cooperation and collaboration."

With two or three other students, discuss this view of the role that sports play in developing a child's sense of social cooperation. Begin by telling one another about your own, your siblings', or your children's experiences with team sports between the ages of six and twelve. Explain how participating in sports at this young age did or did not teach social cooperation. If you think team sports failed to teach cooperation or had some other effect, explain the effect it did have.

Analyzing Writing Strategies

1. In paragraph 2, Romano **presents her overall judgment**. *Underline the thesis statement, and explain briefly in writing how well it meets the three standards for a good thesis: that it be clear and unambiguous, arguable, and appropriately qualified.*

2. In addition to presenting her judgment in her thesis statement, Romano forecasts her reasons in paragraph 2. Reread Romano's essay, noting in the margin where she addresses each of these reasons. *Then explain in a few sentences what you learn from*

the way Romano presents her reasons. Are they clear and easy to follow? Do you think her intended readers—her instructor and parents of young children (the same audience Statsky is trying to convince)—are likely to consider her reasons plausible? In other words, are these reasons appropriate for evaluating an essay that argues a position, based on standards her readers are likely to share? If you see a potential problem with any of the reasons she uses, explain the problem you see.

Commentary: Providing Convincing Support and Anticipating Readers' Possible Objections

Writers of evaluation do not merely assert the reasons for their judgment; they also provide support to back up their argument. In addition, they often try to anticipate readers' likely objections.

Because she is writing about a text, Romano relies on textual evidence in the form of examples, summaries, and paraphrases to **support** her argument. She points to numerous examples from Statsky's essay throughout her evaluation:

> The other support, *a brief description of City Sports for Kids in New York City,* is very convincing but . . . (par. 7)

> *In the first sentences of paragraphs 6, 9, and 10,* Statsky does show that she is thinking about her readers' questions. (8)

> By acknowledging that she was aware of many of these objections—and perhaps even accommodating more of them in her own argument, *as she does in paragraph 10,* while refuting other objections—she would have . . . (8)

The first example (highlighted in italics) illustrates one kind of support Statsky presents in her essay. The second points to three sentences that demonstrate Statsky's use of a particular argumentative strategy. The third refers to a place where Statsky uses a different argumentative strategy. By using brief examples like these, Romano can provide many references to support her argument.

In paragraph 6, Romano presents a bulleted list of examples:

- That competitive sports pose psychological dangers—*children becoming serious and unplayful when the game starts*
- That adults' desire to win puts children at risk—*parents fighting each other at a Peewee Football game and a coach setting fire to an opposing team's jersey*
- That organized sports should emphasize cooperation and individual performance instead of winning—*a coach banning scoring but finding that parents would not support him and a New York City basketball league in which all children play an equal amount of time and scoring is easier*

Listing marshals evidence efficiently. Moreover, presenting the examples in a way that connects each example (highlighted in italics above) directly to the reason it supports helps make the examples clear and convincing.

These examples also show how Romano summarizes or paraphrases passages from Statsky's essay. A summary is a concise restatement of the original text in which only the main ideas or most important information is included. A paraphrase tends to include more details than does a summary and may be as long as or even longer than the original.

The following side-by-side comparison illustrates Romano's use of summarizing in paragraph 5:

Romano's Summary	*Statsky's Original (paragraph 4):*
"In the anecdote, a seven-year-old *makes himself vomit* to avoid playing."	"Coach, my tummy hurts. I can't play," he said. The coach told the player to get back onto the field. "There's nothing wrong with your stomach," he said. When the coach turned his head the seven-year-old stuck a finger down his throat and *made himself vomit.* When the coach turned back, the boy pointed to the ground and told him, "Yes there is, coach. See?" (Tosches A33)

This summary is significantly shorter than the version in Statsky's original. Romano does use some of Statsky's words (highlighted in italics), but she does so appropriately, changing Statsky's idiomatic phrase *made himself vomit* from past to present tense so that the phrase fits grammatically into her own sentence. Romano uses summary well here to relate the essential information.

A good illustration of paraphrasing appears in Romano's opening paragraph, where she represents Statsky's argument. Compare Romano's paraphrase to the original passage from Statsky's essay:

Romano's Paraphrase	*Statsky's Original (paragraph 2)*
Besides causing *physical and psychological harm, competitive sports* discourage young people from becoming *players* and *fans* when they are older and inevitably put parents' needs and fantasies ahead of children's welfare.	Highly organized *competitive sports* such as Peewee Football and Little League Baseball are too often played to adult standards, which are developmentally inappropriate for children and can be both *physically and psychologically harmful.* Furthermore, because they eliminate many children from organized sports before they are ready to compete, they are actually counterproductive for developing either future *players or fans.*

Romano's paraphrase does not condense Statsky's original language very much. Romano includes many of the details from the original, leaving out only the specific examples of competitive sports ("Peewee Football and Little League Baseball") and the characterization of "adult standards" as "developmentally inappropriate for children."

Writers choose summarizing over quoting when they want to emphasize the ideas rather than the language. They choose summarizing over paraphrasing when they want to stress the source's main ideas or information and skip the details. For additional information on using these strategies for presenting textual evidence see Chapter 11: Arguing, and Chapter 14: Using Sources.

In addition to providing convincing support, writers of evaluation also have to **anticipate readers' objections**. Romano was made aware by her classmates that readers might raise certain objections to Statsky's argument. Romano responded by revising her essay to include these objections. In paragraph 8, for example, Romano asserts that Statsky's argument "fails to anticipate certain objections and questions that some parents, especially those she most wants to convince, are almost sure to raise." She then goes on to discuss several positive effects of competitive team sports such as creating a sense of community, building character, and teaching students to face their fears. In addition, she acknowledges that for some kids "team practice and games are the brightest moments in their lives." As you plan your own evaluation, think about your readers and how you could anticipate their possible objections. In responding to these objections, consider whether you should merely acknowledge the objection, accommodate it by making it part of your argument, or refute it—three strategies for counterarguing.

For more on using textual evidence as support, see Chapter 11.

Considering Topics for Your Own Essay

List several written texts you would consider evaluating. For example, you might include in your list an essay from one of the chapters in this book, a children's book that you read when you were young or that you now read to your own children, a magazine for people interested in a particular topic like computers or cars, or a scholarly article you read for a research paper. You need not limit yourself to texts written on paper; also consider texts available online. Choose one possibility from your list, and come up with two or three reasons why it is a good or bad text.

Purpose and Audience

When you evaluate something, you seek to influence readers' judgments and possibly their actions. Your primary aim is to convince readers that your judgment is well informed and reasonable and therefore that they can feel confident in making decisions based on it. Readers do not simply accept reviewers' judgments, however, especially on important subjects. More likely they read reviews to learn more about a subject so that they can make an informed decision themselves. Consequently, most readers care less about the forcefulness with which you assert your judgment than about the reasons and support you give for it.

Effective writers develop an argument designed for their particular readers. Given what you can expect your readers to know about your subject and the standards they would apply when evaluating it, you decide which reasons to use as well as what support to give.

You may want to acknowledge directly your readers' knowledge of the subject, perhaps revealing that you understand how they might judge it differently. You might even let readers know that you have anticipated their objections to your argument. In responding to objections or different judgments, you could agree to disagree on certain points but try to convince readers that on other points you do share the same or at least similar standards.

Basic Features: Evaluations

A Well-Presented Subject

The subject must be clearly identified if readers are to know what is being evaluated. Most writers name it explicitly. When the subject is a film, an essay, or a Web site, naming it is easy. When it is something more general, naming may require more imagination.

Evaluations should provide only enough information to give readers a context for the judgment. However, certain kinds of evaluations—such as reviews of films, video games, television programs, and books—usually require more information than others because reviewers have to assume that readers will be unfamiliar with the subject and are reading in part to learn more about it. For example, in reviewing *Good Night, and Good Luck*, Scott tells readers the names of the director, screenwriters, and main characters and the actors who play them, as well as the place and time in which the film's story unfolds and generally what happens. For a recently released film, television program, or video game, the writer must decide how much of the plot to reveal—trying not to spoil the suspense while explaining how well or poorly the suspense is managed. In certain situations, such as when writing for your instructor and classmates, you usually do not need to worry about giving anything away.

A Clear Overall Judgment

Evaluation essays are built around an overall judgment—an assertion that the subject is good or bad or that it is better or worse than something else of the same kind. This judgment is the thesis of the essay. The thesis statement may be combined with a forecast of the reasons that will be discussed in the essay, as in Kim's essay ("Overall, the Web site is well designed, amusing, and extremely helpful."). It may also be repeated in the concluding paragraph, again as Kim does ("RateMyProfessors.com allows you to see what other students have to say about professors and courses you may be considering as well as to voice your opinion. As a Web site, it is not only helpful and easy to use, but it is also amusing to read."). Scott presents his judgment as advice to readers in the second paragraph: ("See it now."). He restates his overall judgment in the last paragraph and summarizes his reasons ("He has found a cogent subject, an urgent set of ideas and a formally inventive, absolutely convincing way to make them live on screen.").

Although readers expect a definitive judgment, they also appreciate a balanced one. Kim and Romano acknowledge both good and bad qualities of the subject they are evaluating. Kim acknowledges that RatingsOnline "may even be better than [RateMyProfessors.com] in terms of helpfulness" although it is not as helpful overall because of its apparently smaller user base (par. 11). Similarly, Romano praises the strengths and criticizes the weaknesses of Statsky's logic.

Appropriate Reasons and Convincing Support

Writers assert the reasons for their judgment, often explain their reasons in some detail, and provide support for their reasons. For example, one of Scott's reasons for liking the film *Good Night, and Good Luck* is that it is "formally inventive." To explain what he means by form, Scott uses the terms "*cinéma-vérité*" and "documentary," terms readers knowledgeable about film are likely to recognize as styles of filmmaking. He also specifies particular qualities of the film typical of these styles, such as "a meticulously detailed reconstruction of an era" (par. 1). He supports his point that the film is inventive by contrasting its fast pacing to the plodding way a traditional "historical picture . . . walks you carefully through events" (3).

For an argument to be convincing, readers have to accept the reasons as appropriate for evaluating the subject. Kim, for example, assumes that her audience will agree that her reasons are appropriate because they are based on standards that most Internet users apply when evaluating a Web site.

Evaluators not only give reasons but must also support their reasons. They may use various kinds of support. Romano, for example, relies primarily on textual evidence to support her reasons, presenting it in quotations, paraphrases, and summaries. Scott and Kim support their argument with examples and descriptions, but Kim also cites statistics and authorities.

Many writers also use comparisons to support an evaluative argument. For example, Scott compares *Good Night, and Good Luck* to Clooney's first film, *Confessions of a Dangerous Mind*. Similarly, Kim compares RateMyProfessors.com to three competitors: Professor Performance, Reviewum.com, and RatingsOnline. Comparisons like these both support the argument and help to convince readers that the writer is an expert who knows the standards that knowledgeable people normally apply when evaluating a subject of this kind.

Anticipation of Readers' Objections and Alternative Judgments

Counterarguing is not as crucial for evaluation as is arguing directly for a judgment by giving reasons and support. When reviewers do counterargue, they may simply acknowledge that others perhaps disagree, may accommodate into their argument points others have made, or may try to refute objections and alternative judgments. Kim anticipates three objections readers have raised to RateMyProfessors.com and uses all three ways of counterarguing: acknowledging objections to the "Easiness" rating; accommodating, or conceding that the site is not statistically valid; and refuting criticism of the "hot" rating. Romano did not anticipate objections, but her classmates helped her understand alternative judgments of competitive sports for children, leading her to modify her argument to accommodate other views. When you plan your essay, be sure to take into consideration objections and alternative judgments others have made. If you simply ignore others' views, your readers may think your evaluation is not balanced and fair.

Justifying an Evaluation

Invention and Research

What subject could you make a judgment about and then support that judgment with good reasons? A movie? A sports team? A job? Learn all you can about the subject (using online research if necessary), and do some thinking and writing about it. Then come up with a tentative overall judgment. . . . **See p. 271 for more.**

Planning and Drafting

As you look over what you have written and learned about your subject, can you make a convincing case for your evaluation? If your readers are not familiar with the subject, how can you interest them in it? Should you start off with your overall judgment or lead up to it? Make a plan for your evaluation and start drafting it. . . . **See p. 277 for more.**

Critical Reading Guide

What are your draft's strengths and weaknesses? Have you defined your standards for evaluation clearly? Does your judgment seem wishy-washy or too extreme? Get a classmate, a friend, a writing tutor, or someone else to read and respond to your essay, especially the parts you are most unsure of. . . . **See p. 281 for more.**

Revising

As you consider your essay again in light of your reader's comments, how can you improve it? Can you make the beginning more engaging? Do you need to present the subject in more detail? Are the reasons for your judgment unclear? Go through your draft systematically, making changes wherever necessary. . . . **See p. 283 for more.**

Editing and Proofreading

Have you checked for errors that are especially likely in evaluative writing? If you are comparing your subject to something else, have you left out any words necessary to make the comparison complete, logical, or clear? Look for and correct these and any other errors. . . . **See p. 288 for more.**

☐ The Writing Assignment

Write an essay evaluating a particular subject. Examine your subject closely, and make a judgment about it, with reasons based on widely recognized standards for evaluating a subject like yours. Support your reasons with examples and other details.

▮ Invention and Research

The following activities will help you choose and explore a subject, consider your judgment, and develop your argument. Keep a written record of your invention and research to use later when you draft and revise.

Finding a Subject to Write About

You may already have a subject in mind and some ideas on how you will evaluate it. Even so, it is wise to take a few minutes to consider some other possible subjects. That way you can feel confident not only about having made the best possible choice but also about having one or two alternative subjects in case your first choice does not work. The following activities will help you make a good choice.

Listing Subjects.   *Make a list of subjects you might be interested in evaluating.* Review the subjects suggested by the Considering Topics for Your Own Essay activity following the last two readings in this chapter, and consider, too, the subjects listed below:

- *Culture:* Television program, computer game, new music, film, dance club, coffeehouse, museum exhibit
- *Written work:* Poem, short story, novel, Web site, magazine article, newspaper column, textbook, autobiography, essay from this book
- *Education:* School, library, academic or psychological counseling service, writing center, campus publication, sports team
- *Government:* Government official, proposed or existing law, agency or program, candidate for public office
- *Leisure:* Amusement park, restaurant, sports team, national or state park

  ▪ *Listing Subjects Related to Identity and Community.*

- Evaluate how well one of the following meets the needs of residents of your town or city: a community center, public library, health clinic, neighborhood watch program, meals-on-wheels program, theater or symphony, school or school program.
- Evaluate how well one of the following serves the members of your religious community: a religious school, youth or senior group, religious leader, particular sermon, fund-raising activity, choir, building and grounds.

- Evaluate how well one of the following aspects of local government serves the needs of the community: mayor, city council, police, courts, social services, park system.

   ■ *Listing Subjects Related to Work and Career.*

- Evaluate a job you have had or currently have, or evaluate someone else you have observed closely, such as a coworker or supervisor.

- Evaluate a local job-training program, either one in which you have participated or one where you can observe and interview trainees.

Choosing a Subject.   *Review your list, and choose the one subject that seems most promising.* Your subject should be one that you can evaluate with some authority, either one that you already know quite well or one that you can study closely over the next week or two.

Exploring Your Subject and Possible Readers

Before you proceed to study your subject in depth, you need to review what you now know about it, become more familiar with it, make a tentative judgment about it, and think seriously about who your readers may be. You then will be in a good position to decide whether to stick with this subject for your essay or choose a different subject.

Reviewing What You Now Know about the Subject.   *Write for a few minutes about what you already know about your subject at this moment.* Focus your thinking by considering questions like these:

- Why am I interested in this subject?

- What do I like and dislike about this subject?

- What do I usually look for in evaluating a subject of this kind? What do other people look for?

- How can I arrange to become very familiar with my subject over the next week or two?

Familiarizing Yourself with the Subject.   *Take notes about what you observe and learn as you get acquainted with your subject, notes that include the kinds of details that make your subject interesting and special.* If you are evaluating a one-time performance, you must be exceedingly attentive to the one performance and take careful notes. If you plan to evaluate a film, it would be best if you could rent the DVD or video so that you can reexamine parts you need to refer to. If you are evaluating an agency, a service, or a program, observe and talk to people and make notes about what you see and hear.

Making a Tentative Judgment.   *Review what you have written as you have been getting to know your subject; then write a few sentences stating your best current overall judgment of the subject.* Your judgment may be only tentative at this stage, or you may feel quite confident in it. Your judgment may also be mixed: You may have a high regard for certain aspects of the subject and, at the same time, a rather low assessment of other aspects. As you consider your overall judgment, keep in mind that readers of evaluative essays expect writers not only to balance their evaluation of a subject (by pointing out things they like as well as things they dislike) but also to state a definitive judgment, not a vague, wishy-washy, or undecided judgment.

Identifying and Understanding Potential Readers. *Write several sentences about possible readers, with the following questions in mind:*

- For what particular kinds of readers do I want to write this evaluation?
- What are my readers likely to know about my subject? Will I be introducing the subject to them (as in a film or book review)? Or will they already be familiar with it, and if so, how expert on the subject are they likely to be?
- How are my readers likely to judge my subject? What about it might they like, and what might they dislike?
- What reasons might they give for their judgment?
- On what standards is their overall judgment likely to be based? Do I share these standards or at least recognize their appropriateness?

Testing Your Choice

Pause now to decide whether you have chosen a subject about which you can make a convincing evaluative argument. Reread your invention notes to see whether you know or can learn enough about your subject to write a convincing evaluation for the readers you have identified. Also consider whether you feel confident in your judgment.

As you develop your argument, you should become even more confident. If, however, you begin to doubt your choice, consider beginning again with a different subject. Before changing your subject, however, discuss your ideas with another student or your instructor.

A Collaborative
Activity:
Testing Your Choice

Get together with two or three other students to discuss your subjects and test ways of evaluating them.

Presenters: Briefly describe your subject without revealing your overall judgment.

Evaluators: Explain to each presenter how you would evaluate a subject of this kind. For example, would you judge a science-fiction film by the story, acting, ideas, special effects, or some other aspect of the film? Would you judge a lecture course by how interesting or entertaining the lectures are, how hard the tests are, how well the lectures are organized, or how successful some other aspect of the class is? (Presenters: Take notes about what you hear.)

Becoming an Expert on Your Subject

Now that you are confident about your choice of subject and have in mind some standards for judging it, you can confidently move ahead to become an expert on your subject by immersing yourself in it.

Immersing Yourself in Your Subject.   *Take careful notes as you gradually familiarize yourself with your subject.* If you are writing about a film, for example, you will need to view the film at least twice by attending screenings or renting a DVD or video. If you are evaluating the effectiveness of a public official, you will need to read recent public statements by the official and perhaps observe the official in action. If you decide to evaluate a local sports team, you will need to study the team, attend a game and if possible a practice, and review films of recent games. Consult with other students and your instructor about efficient strategies for becoming an expert on your subject. Your goal is to gather the details, facts, examples, or stories you will need to write an informative, convincing evaluation.

If you think you will need to do more research than time permits, or if you cannot view, visit, or research your subject to discover the details needed to support an evaluation of it, then you may need to consider choosing a different, more accessible subject.

Learning More about Standards for Judging Your Subject.   *Make a list of prominent, widely recognized standards for judging your subject.* If you do not know the standards usually used to evaluate your subject, do some research. For example, if you are reviewing a film, you could read a few recent film reviews online or in the library, noting the standards that reviewers typically use and the reasons they give for liking or disliking a film. If you are evaluating a soccer team or one winning (or losing) game, you could read a book on coaching soccer or talk to an experienced soccer coach to learn about what makes an excellent soccer team or winning game. If you are evaluating a civic, governmental, or religious program, look for information online or in the library about what makes a good program of its type. If you are evaluating an essay in this book, you will find standards in the Purpose and Audience section and in the Basic Features section of the chapter where the essay appears. If you are evaluating an argument essay from Chapters 5–7, you will find additional standards in Evaluating the Logic of an Argument, Recognizing Emotional Manipulation, and Judging the Writer's Credibility, pp. 326–30.

Developing Your Evaluation

Now you are ready to discover how you might proceed to make a convincing argument to justify your judgment. Each of the following activities requires only a few minutes of your time, and they are all essential to your success in organizing and drafting your evaluation.

Listing Reasons.   *Write down every reason you can think of to convince readers of your overall judgment.* Try stating your reasons like this: "My judgment is X because . . ." or

"A reason I like (or dislike) X is that. . . ." Then look over your list to consider which reasons you regard as most important and likely to be most convincing to your readers. Highlight these reasons.

Finding Support. *Make notes about how to support your most promising reasons.* From your invention notes made earlier, select a few details, facts, comparisons, contrasts, or examples about your subject that might help you support each reason.

Anticipating Readers' Alternative Judgments, Questions, and Objections. *List a few questions your particular readers would likely want to ask you or objections they might have to your argument. Write for a few minutes responding to at least two of these questions or objections.* Assume that some of your particular readers would judge your subject differently from the way you do. Remember that your responses—your counterargument—could simply acknowledge the disagreements, accommodate readers' views by conceding certain points, or refute readers' arguments as uninformed or mistaken.

An Online Activity: Researching Alternative Judgments

One way to learn more about different responses to your subject is to search for reviews or evaluations of it online. You may even decide to incorporate quotations from or references to these reviews, although you need not do so. Enter the name of your subject—movie title, restaurant name, compact disc title, title of a proposed law, name of a candidate for public office—in a search engine such as Google (www.google.com) or Yahoo! Directory (http://dir.yahoo.com). (Try narrowing the search by including the keyword *review*.) Of course, not all subjects are conveniently searchable online, and some subjects—a local concert, a college sports event, a campus student service, a neighborhood program—will likely not have been reviewed by anyone but you.

Bookmark or keep a record of promising sites. Download any materials you might wish to cite in your evaluation, making sure you have all the information necessary to document the source.

Designing Your Document

Think about whether visual or audio elements—cartoons, photographs, tables, graphs, or snippets from films, television programs, or songs—would strengthen your argument. Consider also whether your readers might benefit by such design features as headings, bulleted or numbered lists, or other elements that would make your essay easier to follow.

In trying to decide what to incorporate, consider what would help you make the most compelling analysis. In some cases, it is enough to *tell* readers, but in other cases, visuals help to *show* readers the points you are making. For instance, in evaluating the ways in which presidential candidates use body language and hand gestures to convey meaning and encourage trust, photos or video from the presidential debates would be invaluable. If tone of voice is being analyzed, audio snippets from a debate embedded in, for instance, a slideshow presentation would serve to illustrate the arguments made. As always, if you do use visual or audio elements you did not create yourself, remember to document the sources in your essay (and request permission from the sources if the essay will be posted on the Web).

Defining Your Purpose for Your Readers

Write a few sentences defining your purpose in writing this evaluation for your readers. Consider the following possibilities and any others that might apply to your writing situation:

- If my readers are likely to agree with my overall judgment, should I try to strengthen their resolve by giving them well-supported reasons, helping them refute others' judgments, or suggesting how they might respond to questions and objections?

- If my readers and I share certain standards for evaluating a subject of this kind but we disagree on our overall judgment of this particular subject, can I build a convincing argument based on these shared standards or at least get readers to acknowledge the legitimacy of my judgment?

- If my readers use different standards of judgment, what should I try to do—urge them to think critically about their own judgment, to consider seriously other standards for judging the subject, or to see certain aspects of the subject they might have overlooked?

Formulating a Tentative Thesis Statement

Write several sentences that could serve as your thesis statement. Think about how you should state your overall judgment—how emphatic you should make it, whether you should qualify it, and whether you should include in the thesis a forecast of your reasons and support. Remember that a strong thesis statement should be clear, arguable, and appropriately qualified.

Review the readings in this chapter to see how other writers construct thesis statements. For example, Romano uses the thesis statement to forecast her reasons as well as to express her overall judgment. "While [Statsky's] logic *is* appropriate, believable, and consistent, her argument also has weaknesses" (par. 2). Romano makes her thesis statement seem thoughtful and balanced. There is no ambivalence or confusion, however, about Romano's judgment.

As you draft your own tentative thesis statement, think carefully about the language you use. It should be clear and unambiguous, emphatic but appropriately qualified. Although you will most probably refine your thesis statement as you draft and revise your essay, trying now to articulate it will help give direction and impetus to your planning and drafting.

■ Planning and Drafting

This section will help you review what you have learned about evaluating your subject, determine specific goals for your essay, make a tentative outline, and get started on your first draft.

Seeing What You Have

Pause now to reread your invention and research notes. Watch for language that describes the subject vividly, states your judgment clearly, presents your reasons and support convincingly, and counterargues objections to your argument or readers' alternative judgments. Highlight key words, phrases, and sentences; make marginal notes or electronic annotations.

If your invention notes seem skimpy, you may need to do further research at this stage, or you could begin drafting now and later do research to fill in the blanks.

If your confidence in your judgment has been shaken or if you are concerned that you will not be able to write an argument to support your judgment, consult your instructor to determine whether you should try evaluating a different subject.

Setting Goals

Before you begin drafting, set some specific goals to guide the decisions you will make. The following questions will help you:

Your Purpose and Readers

- What do I want my readers to think about the subject after reading my evaluation? Do I want them to appreciate the subject's strengths and weaknesses, as Kim and Romano do? Or do I want them to see why it succeeds (as Scott does) or fails?

- Should I assume that my readers may have read other evaluations of my subject (perhaps like Scott)? Or should I assume that I am introducing readers to the subject, as Kim and Romano seem to do?

- How should I present myself to my readers—as someone who is an expert on the subject (perhaps like Scott) or as someone who has simply examined the subject closely (like Kim and Romano)? Should I convey enthusiasm (as Kim and Scott do) or strike a more balanced, distanced tone (as Romano does)?

The Beginning

- How can I capture readers' attention from the start? Should I begin by naming and describing the subject, as all the writers do?

- When should I state my judgment? At the beginning of the opening paragraph, in the middle like Romano, or at the end like Kim? Or should I wait until the second paragraph, as Scott does?

- Should I forecast the reasons for my judgment in the first couple of paragraphs, as Kim and Romano do?

The Presentation of the Subject

- How should I identify the subject? In addition to naming it, as all the writers do, should I place it in a recognizable category or genre, as Kim does when she talks about "Internet professor evaluation sites" (par. 10), or as Scott does when he describes the film as a "historical picture" in "*cinéma-vérité* style" (2)?
- What about the subject should I describe? Can I use visuals to illustrate? Should I place the subject historically, as Scott does?
- If the subject has a story, how much of it should I tell? Should I simply set the scene and identify the characters, or should I give details of the plot, as Scott does?

The Statement of Your Judgment

- How should I state my thesis? Should I forecast my reasons early in the essay, as Romano does? Should I place my thesis at the beginning or wait until after I have provided a context?
- How can I convince readers to consider my overall judgment seriously even if they disagree with it? Should I try to present a balanced judgment by praising some things and criticizing others, as Kim and Romano do?

Your Reasons and Support

- How can I present my reasons? Should I explain the standards on which I base my reasons, as Romano does, or can I assume that my readers will share my standards?
- If I have more than one reason, how should I order them? Should I begin with the ones I think are most important for judging a subject of this kind, or should I end with them?
- How can I support my reasons? With example, paraphrase, and summary, as all the writers do? Should I quote the text, as Kim and Romano do? Can I call on authorities and cite statistics, as Kim does?

Your Anticipation of Objections or Alternative Judgments

- What objections or alternative judgments should I anticipate? Should I acknowledge or accommodate legitimate objections and qualify my judgment, as Romano does? Are there any illegitimate objections or alternative judgments I should refute?

The Ending

- How should I conclude? Should I try to frame the essay by echoing something from the opening or from another part of the essay?

- Should I conclude by presenting or restating my overall judgment, as all the writers do?
- Should I include a rhetorical question at the end, as Kim does?

Outlining

An evaluative essay contains as many as four basic parts:

1. A presentation of the subject
2. A judgment of the subject
3. A presentation of reasons and support
4. A consideration of readers' objections and alternative judgments

These parts can be organized in various ways. If, for example, you expect readers to disagree with your judgment, you could show them what you think they have overlooked or misjudged about the subject. You could begin by presenting the subject; then you could assert your thesis, present your reasons and support, and anticipate and refute readers' likely objections.

Presentation of the subject

Thesis statement (judgment)

First reason and support

Anticipation and refutation of objection

Second reason and support

Anticipation and accommodation of objection

Conclusion

If you expect some of your readers to disagree with your negative judgment even though they base their judgment on the same standard on which you base yours, you could try to show them that the subject really does not satisfy the standard. You could begin by reinforcing the standard you share and then demonstrate how the subject fails to meet it.

Establish shared standard

Acknowledge alternative judgment

State thesis (judgment) that subject fails to meet shared standard

First reason and support showing how subject falls short of standard

Second reason and support

(etc.)

Conclusion

There are, of course, many other possible ways to organize an evaluative essay, but these outlines should help you start planning your own essay.

Consider tentative any outlining you do before you begin drafting. Be ready to revise your outline, shift parts around, or drop or add parts as you draft.

Drafting

General Advice. Start drafting your essay, keeping in mind the goals you set while you were planning. Turn off your grammar checker and spelling checker at this stage if you find them distracting. Don't be afraid to skip around in your draft; jump back and fill in a spontaneous idea, or leap ahead and write a later section first if you find that easier. If you get stuck while drafting, explore the problem by using some of the writing activities in the Invention and Research section of this chapter (pp. 271–76).

Keep in mind that in writing an evaluative argument, you must accept the burden of proof by offering reasons and support for your judgment. Remember, too, that the basis for judgment often depends on standards as much as reasons and support. Try to think critically about the standards on which you base your judgment as well as the standards that others apply to subjects of the kind you are evaluating.

Sentence Strategies: Comparing and Contrasting Your Subject with Similar Ones and Balancing Criticism and Praise. As you draft, you may want to compare or contrast your subject with similar subjects to establish for readers your authority to evaluate a subject like yours. In addition, you are likely to want to balance the evaluation of your subject—by criticizing one or more aspects of the subject if you generally praise it or by praising one or more aspects of it if you generally criticize it. To do either of these things, you will need to use sentences that clearly and efficiently express comparisons or contrasts.

Sentences comparing or contrasting one subject with similar subjects will often make use of key comparative terms like *more, less, most, least, as, than, like, unlike, similar,* or *dissimilar.*

Let us begin with three examples, all from paragraph 11 of Wendy Kim's essay:

Still, RatingsOnline is *better* designed and includes *more helpful* information than the other two competitors, and it may even be *better* than RMP in terms of helpfulness.

The ratings categories on RatingsOnline also seem *more specific* than on RMP. . . .

In its design and potential helpfulness, RatingsOnline is a very good site but likely *not* to be *as good as* RMP because its user base appears to be *smaller.*

In her first sentence, Kim compares RatingsOnline and three other sites, including RMP, the acronym for RateMyProfessors. In the second and third examples, she narrows the match-up to what she considers the two best Web sites, pointing out their relative strengths and weaknesses.

In the following examples, Scott contrasts *Good Night, and Good Luck* with other period or historical films. Notice that he leaves out the explicitly comparative term in both sentences:

> Though it is a meticulously detailed reconstruction of an era, the film . . . is concerned with *more than* nostalgia. (par. 1)

> *Good Night, and Good Luck* is *not the kind of historical picture* that dumbs down its material, or walks you carefully through events that may be unfamiliar. (3)

For more on using sentences of comparison and contrast in evaluations, go to bedfordstmartins.com/conciseguide and click on Sentence Strategies.

Sentences that balance criticism and praise rely on words expressing contrast, like *but, although, however, while,* and so on to set up the shift between the two responses.

Praise followed by criticism:

> This information could be useful in helping students decide which classes to take, *but* only if there are enough reviews posted. (Kim, par. 11)

> . . . Statsky does show that she is thinking about her readers' questions. She does not go nearly far enough, *however,* to have a chance of influencing two types of readers. . . . (Romano, 8)

Criticism followed by praise:

> And *while* Mr. Clooney is inclined to glorify, he does not simplify. (Scott, 12)

Of course, you can strengthen your evaluation with other kinds of sentences as well. You may want to review in particular the information about using appositives (pp. 133–34) and writing sentences introducing concession and refutation (pp. 179–80).

For more on using sentences that balance criticism and praise in evaluations, go to bedfordstmartins.com/conciseguide and click on Sentence Strategies.

Critical Reading Guide

Now is the time to get a good critical reading of your draft. Writers usually find it helpful to have someone else read and comment on their drafts, and all writers know how much they learn about writing when they read other writers' drafts. Your instructor may arrange such a reading as part of your course-work—in class or online. If not, you can ask a classmate to read your draft. You could also seek comments from a tutor at your campus writing center. (If you are unable to have someone else read your draft, turn ahead to the Revising section on p. 283, where you will find guidelines for reading your own draft critically.)

▶ **If You Are the Writer.** To provide focused, helpful comments, your reader must know your essay's intended audience, your purpose, and a problem in the draft that you need help solving. Briefly write out this information at the top of your draft.

- *Audience:* Identify the intended audience of your essay. What do you assume they think about your subject? Do you expect them to be receptive, skeptical, resistant, or antagonistic?

- *Purpose:* What effect do you realistically expect your argument to have on your audience?
- *Problem:* Describe the most important problem you see in your draft.

▶ **If You Are the Reader.**   Use the following guidelines to help you give constructive, critical comments to others on evaluation essays:

1. *Read for a First Impression.*   Tell the writer what you think the intended audience would find most and least convincing. If you think the evaluation is seriously flawed, try to help the writer improve it. Next, consider the problem the writer identified, and respond briefly to that concern. (If you find that the problem is covered by one of the other guidelines listed below, respond to it in more detail there if necessary.)

2. *Analyze How Well the Subject Is Presented.* If you are surprised by the way the writer has presented the subject, briefly explain how you usually think of this particular subject or subjects of this kind. Also indicate whether any of the information about the subject seems unnecessary. Finally, and most important, let the writer know whether any of the information about the subject seems to you possibly inaccurate or only partly true.

3. *Assess Whether the Judgment Is Stated Clearly.*   Write a sentence or two summarizing the writer's judgment as you understand it. Then identify the sentence or sentences in the draft where the judgment is stated explicitly. (It may be restated in several places.) If you cannot find an explicit statement of the judgment, let the writer know. Given the writer's purpose and audience, consider whether the judgment is arguable, clear, and appropriately qualified. If it seems indecisive or too extreme, suggest how the writer might make it clearer or might qualify it by referring at least occasionally to the strengths of a criticized subject or the weaknesses of a praised subject.

4. *Evaluate the Reasons and Support.*   Identify the reasons, and look closely at them and the support that the writer gives for them. If anything seems problematic, briefly explain what bothers you. For example, the reason may not seem appropriate for judging this kind of subject, you may not fully understand the reason or how it applies to this particular subject, the connection between a particular reason and its support may not be clear or convincing to you, the support may be too weak, or there may not be enough support to sustain the argument. Be as specific and constructive as you can, pointing out

---

Making Comments Electronically

Most word processing software offers features that allow you to insert comments directly into the text of someone else's document. Many readers prefer to make their comments in this way because it tends to be faster than writing on a hard copy and space is virtually unlimited; it also eliminates the problem of deciphering handwritten comments. Where such features are not available, simply typing comments directly into a document in a contrasting color can provide the same advantages.

what does not work and also suggesting what the writer might do to solve the problem. For example, if the reason seems inappropriate, explain why you think so, and indicate what kinds of reasons might work better. If the support is weak, suggest how it could be strengthened.

5. ***Assess How Well Readers' Objections, Questions, and Alternative Judgments Have Been Handled.***   Mark where the writer acknowledges, accommodates, or tries to refute readers' objections or alternative judgments, and point to any places where the counterargument seems superficial or dismissive. Suggest how it could be strengthened. Help the writer anticipate any important objections or questions that have been overlooked, providing advice on how to respond to them.

6. ***Consider the Effectiveness of the Organization.***   Get an overview of the essay's organization, and point out any places where more explicit cueing—transitions, summaries, or topic sentences—would clarify the relationship between parts of the essay.

   • Look at the *beginning*. Do you think readers will find it engaging? If not, propose an alternative.

   • Look at the *ending*. Does the essay conclude decisively and memorably? If not, suggest an alternative.

   • Look at the *design features*. Comment on the figures, headings, tables, and other design features. Indicate whether any visual or audio elements that have been included fail to support the evaluation effectively, and offer suggestions for improvement. Help the writer think of additional visual or audio elements that could strengthen the essay.

7. ***Give the Writer Your Final Thoughts.***   What is this draft's strongest part? What part is most in need of further work?

For a printable version of this critical reading guide, go to **bedfordstmartins.com/conciseguide**.

■ Revising

This section will help you get an overview of your draft and revise it accordingly.

Getting an Overview

Consider your draft as a whole, following these two steps:

1. ***Reread.*** If at all possible, put the draft aside for a day or two before rereading it. When you return to it, start by reconsidering your purpose. Then read the draft straight through, trying to see it as your intended readers will.

Working with Sources

Using summary to support your evaluative argument Writers of evaluation often use summary to support their argument. As the following examples show, evaluations may summarize an expert source (as Kim does in her Web site evaluation), the plot of a film or video game (as Scott does in his film review), or an aspect of an essay or story (as Romano does in her evaluation of another essay in this book), to name just a few of the more common uses of summary.

> The results are statistically invalid, as one psychology professor explained, because the users are self-selected and not selected randomly (Harmon). (Kim, par. 9)

> The story flashes back from a famous, cautionary speech that Murrow gave at an industry convention in 1958 to one of the most notable episodes in his career—his war of words and images with Senator Joseph R. McCarthy. (Scott, 3)

> In the anecdote, a seven-year-old makes himself vomit to avoid playing. (Romano, 5)

To get a better understanding of how summaries can support an evaluative argument, let us look closely at another example of summarizing, from paragraph 3 of Christine Romano's essay. This summary, highlighted in red, supports Romano's argument that Statsky provides "appropriate" support:

> Her quotations, examples, and statistics all support the reasons she believes competitive sports are bad for children. For example, in paragraph 3, Statsky offers the reason that "overly competitive" sports may damage children's fragile bodies and that contact sports, in particular, may be especially hazardous. She supports this reason by paraphrasing Koppett's claim that muscle strain or even lifelong injury may result when a twelve-year-old throws curve balls. She then quotes Tutko on the dangers of tackle football. The opinions of both experts are obviously appropriate. They are relevant to her reason, and we can easily imagine that they would worry many parents.

To understand how this summary works, compare it to the original:

Statsky's Original (paragraph 3)

One readily understandable danger of overly competitive sports is that they entice children into physical actions that are bad for growing bodies. Although the official Little League Web site acknowledges that children do risk injury playing baseball, they insist that severe injuries are infrequent, "far less than the risk of riding a skateboard, a bicycle, or even the school bus" ("What about My Child?"). Nevertheless, Leonard Koppett in *Sports Illusion, Sports Reality* claims that a twelve-year-old trying to throw a curve ball, for example, may put abnormal strain on developing arm and shoulder muscles, sometimes resulting in lifelong injuries (294). Contact sports like football can be even more hazardous. Thomas Tutko, a psychology professor at San Jose State University and coauthor of the book *Winning Is Everything and Other American Myths*, writes:

> I am strongly opposed to young kids playing tackle football. It is not the right stage of development for them to be taught to crash into other kids. Kids under the age

of fourteen are not by nature physical. Their main concern is self-preservation. They don't want to meet head on and slam into each other. But tackle football absolutely requires that they try to hit each other as hard as they can. And it is too traumatic for young kids. (qtd. in Tosches A1)

Romano not only repeats Statsky's main ideas in a condensed form (reducing 220 words to 105), but she also describes Statsky's moves as a writer:

Statsky offers the reason . . .

She supports this reason by paraphrasing Koppett's claim . . .

She then quotes Tutko . . .

Romano's description of each step in Statsky's argument shows readers exactly how Statsky uses her sources in constructing her argument.

Notice that in her summary, Romano puts quotation marks around only one of the phrases she borrows from Statsky ("overly competitive"). The most likely reason for this is that Romano considers the designation "overly competitive" debatable. She may have decided not to use quotation marks around other borrowed phrases such as *contact sports* and *tackle football* because they are common expressions and not specific to Statsky.

Because Romano makes it perfectly clear when she is re-presenting her source's language and ideas, and also includes careful citations to indicate where in the original text the material comes from, there is little concern about plagiarizing. Remember, though, that putting quotation marks around quoted words and phrases will eliminate any possible misunderstanding. If you are unsure about whether you need quotation marks, consult your instructor. (To learn more about Romano's use of summarizing together with quoting and paraphrasing, see the Commentary on p. 264. For additional information, see Chapter 11: Arguing, pp. 345–57, and Chapter 14: Using Sources, pp. 412–14.)

2. *Outline.* Make a scratch outline, indicating the basic features as they appear in the draft. Consider using the headings and outline/summary functions of your word processor.

Planning for Revision.   Resist the temptation to dive in and start changing your text until after you have a solid grasp of the big picture. Using your outline as a guide, move through the document and note useful comments received from others and problems you want to solve.

Analyzing the Basic Features of Your Own Draft.   Using the Critical Reading Guide that begins on p. 281, identify problems that you now see in your draft.

Studying Readers' Comments.   Review all of the comments you have received from other readers, and add to your revision plan any that you intend to act on. For each comment, look at the draft to determine what might have led the reader to make that particular point. Try to be objective about any criticism. Ideally, these comments will help you see your draft as others see it, providing valuable information about how you can improve it.

Carrying Out Revisions

Having identified problems in your draft, you now need to come up with solutions and—most important—to carry them out. Basically, you have three ways of finding solutions:

1. Review your invention and planning notes for information and ideas to add to your draft.
2. Do additional invention and research to provide additional material that you or your readers think is needed.
3. Look back at the readings in this chapter to see how other writers have solved similar problems.

The following suggestions, which are organized according to the basic features of evaluation essays, will help you solve some common problems in this genre.

A Well-Presented Subject

- **Is the subject unclear or hard to identify?** Try to give it a name or to identify the general category to which it belongs. If you need more information about the subject, review your invention writing to see if you have left out any details you could now add. You may also need to revisit your subject or do further invention writing to answer questions that your classmates and instructor have raised or your intended readers might have.

- **Is the subject presented in too much detail?** Cut extraneous and repetitive details. If your subject is a film or book, consider whether you are giving away too much of the plot.

- **Is any of the information inaccurate or only partly true?** Reconsider the accuracy and completeness of the information you present. If any of the information will be surprising to readers, consider how you might reassure them that the information is accurate.

A Clear Overall Judgment

- **Is your overall judgment hard to find?** Announce your thesis more explicitly. If your judgment is mixed—pointing out what you like and do not like about the subject—let readers know this from the beginning. Use sentences that balance praise and criticism.

- **Does your overall judgment seem indecisive or too extreme?** If your readers do not know what your overall judgment is or if they think you are either too positive or too negative, you may need to clarify your thesis statement or qualify it more carefully.

Appropriate Reasons and Convincing Support

- **Do any of the reasons seem inappropriate to readers?** Explain why you think the reason is appropriate, or show that your argument employs a standard commonly used for evaluating subjects of this kind.

- **Is any of the support thin or unconvincing?** To find additional support, review your invention writing, or reexamine the subject. Look closely again at your subject for more details that would support your reasons. Consider comparing or contrasting aspects of your subject with those of other subjects like yours.

- **Are any of your reasons and support unclear?** To clarify them, you may need to explain your reasoning in more detail or use examples and comparisons to make your ideas understandable. You may need to do some additional exploratory writing or research to figure out how to explain your reasoning. Consider also whether any of the reasons should be combined, separated, or cut.

> **Checking Sentence Strategies Electronically**
> To check your draft for a sentence strategy especially useful in evaluation essays, use your word processor's highlighting function to mark sentences where you praise or criticize various aspects of the subject. Then think about whether you could make your evaluation more convincing to readers by making any of the sentences more balanced. For more on sentences that balance criticism and praise, see pp. 280–81.

Anticipation of Objections or Alternative Judgments

- **Are any important objections or questions overlooked?** Revisit your subject or invention notes to think more deeply about why and where readers might resist your argument. Try to imagine how a reader who strongly disagrees with your judgment (praising a movie or college program or restaurant, for example) might respond to your evaluation.

The Organization

- **Does the essay seem disorganized or confusing?** You may need to add a forecasting statement, transitions, summaries, or topic sentences. You may also need to do some major restructuring, such as moving your presentation of the subject or re-ordering your reasons.

- **Is the beginning weak?** Review your notes to find an interesting quotation, comparison, image, or example to use in your first paragraph.

- **Is the ending weak?** See if you can restate your judgment, summarize your reasoning, or frame the essay by echoing a point made earlier.

- **Can you add any visuals or design features to make the essay more interesting to read and to strengthen your argument?** Consider taking features from your subject or creating visual or audio elements of your own.

For a revision checklist, go to **bedfordstmartins.com/conciseguide**.

■ Editing and Proofreading

Now is the time to check your revised draft for errors in grammar, punctuation, and mechanics and to consider matters of style. Our research has identified several errors that are especially likely to occur in evaluative writing. The following guidelines will help you proofread and edit your revised draft for these common errors.

Checking Comparisons. Whenever you evaluate something, you are likely to engage in comparison. You might want to show that a new recording is inferior to an earlier one, that one film is stronger than another, that this café is better than that one. Make a point of checking to see that all comparisons in your writing are complete, logical, and clear.

> **A Note on Grammar and Spelling Checkers**
> These tools are good at catching certain types of errors, but currently there is no replacement for a good human proofreader. Grammar checkers in particular are extremely limited in what they can find. They also tend to give faulty advice for fixing problems and to flag correct items as wrong. Spelling checkers cause fewer problems but cannot catch misspellings that are themselves words, such as *to* for *too*.

Editing to Make Comparisons Complete

▶ *Jazz* is as good, ^as^ if not better than, Morrison's other novels.

▶ I liked the Lispector story because it's so different ^from anything else I've ever read.^

Editing to Make Comparisons Logical

▶ Will Smith's Muhammad Ali is more serious than any ^other^ role he's played.

▶ Ohio State's offense played much better than ~~Michigan.~~ ^Michigan's did.^

Check also to see that you say *different from* instead of *different than*.

▶ Carrying herself with a confident and brisk stride, Katherine Parker seems

different ^from^ ~~than~~ the other women in the office.

▶ Films like *Pulp Fiction* that glorify violence for its own sake are different ^from^ ~~than~~ films like *Apocalypse Now* that use violence to make a moral point.

For practice, go to bedfordstmartins.com/conciseguide/exercisecentral and click on Comparisons.

Combining Sentences.   When you evaluate something, you generally present your subject in some detail—defining it, describing it, placing it in some context. Inexperienced writers often give such details almost one by one, in separate sentences. Combining closely related sentences can make your writing more readable, helping readers to see how ideas relate.

▶ In paragraph 5, the details provide a different impression₍ˌ₎ ~~It is~~ a comic or

perhaps even pathetic impression₍ˌ₎ ~~The impression comes from~~ ^based on^ the boy's

attempts to dress up like a real westerner.

From three separate sentences, this writer combines details about the "different impression" into one sentence, using two common strategies for sentence combining:

- Changing a sentence into an appositive phrase (a noun phrase that renames the noun or pronoun that immediately precedes it: "a comic or perhaps even pathetic impression")
- Changing a sentence into a verbal phrase (phrases with verbals that function as adjectives, adverbs, or nouns: "based on the boy's attempts to dress up like a real westerner")

Using Appositive Phrases to Combine Sentences

▶ "Something Pacific" was created by Nam June Paik₍ˌ₎ ~~He is~~ a Korean artist who is considered a founder of video art.

▶ One of Dylan's songs ridiculed the John Birch Society. ~~This song was called "Talkin' John Birch Paranoid Blues."~~ ^, "Talkin' John Birch Paranoid Blues," ^

Using Verbal Phrases to Combine Sentences

▶ Spider-Man's lifesaving webbing ~~sprung~~ ^sprang^ from his wristbands₍ˌ₎ ~~They carried~~ ^carrying^ Mary Jane Watson and him out of peril.

▶ The coffee bar flanks the bookshelves₍ˌ₎ ~~It entices~~ ^enticing^ readers to relax with a book.

For practice, go to **bedfordstmartins.com/conciseguide/exercisecentral** and click on Combining Sentences.

Thinking About Document Design

Using Images to Support an Argument

In his comparison of the films *Emma* and *Clueless*, the student author described on p. 245 of this chapter selected movie stills to accompany his written text. He collected a number of stills from each film and chose two contrasting images that would best illustrate his argument that *Emma*, the film, looks more like Austen's England, but that *Clueless*, with its emphasis on today's social and cultural norms and its setting in contemporary suburban California, better captures the satirical spirit of the novel.

The writer used the still from *Emma* of Emma and Knightley dancing to emphasize the film's attention to aesthetics and romance. Details such as the hanging garlands, the ornate woodwork, the women's similar pale-toned dresses, the style of dancing, and the musicians in the background create an image of aristocratic wealth and elegance that, the student argues, satisfies audience expectations for a romantic period piece but obscures an important part of the novel's message.

Emma is, above all, a novel about class consciousness. Marriage is here, as in all of Austen's novels, a vehicle for exploring the rigidity of social class in nineteenth-century England. However, Emma the film (1996) is better at capturing the feel of the period than the intricacies of social dynamics. (See Fig. 1.) Though the characters come from a range of social classes, their homes and clothing look more similar than not. When Gwyneth Paltrow plays the occasionally lovable, occasionally irritating Emma, the focus on the heroine's failure at matchmaking overshadows the fact that she is obsessed not only with manners but also with wealth. For example, she has something that even her beloved Knightley does not, an estate that she will inherit from her father as long as she does not leave him. In the novel when Knightley agrees to live in the Woodhouse home after the two marry, he goes against traditional gender roles in order to make the most of the two characters' fortunes: his wealth and her property. As it does so many times, the film misses this cue, and instead focuses on Emma's emotional inability to leave her father. In the 1996 Emma, social distinctions get paved over for the audience's aesthetic expectations of a romance and of a period piece.

Fig. 1. Emma, dir. Douglas McGrath, perf. Gwyneth Paltrow, Toni Colette, Alan Cumming, and Jeremy Northam, Miramax, 1996.

To illustrate the flavor of *Clueless*, the student chose the picture of Cher descending the stairs wearing a minidress and an outrageous hat, with shopping bags, water bottle in its holder, and cell phone. This over-the-top satiric image in *Clueless*, the student argued, was designed to emphasize the social and economic distinctions in the novel. The image captures the ridiculousness of Cher in her obvious displays of wealth and posturing. While admired and well liked by her peers, she is also naive and too well-off for her own good.

The student builds to a concluding point that Cher's interest in reforming Tai is a result of her confidence that she could help someone to become as stylish and savvy as herself. Just as the novel makes fun of Emma for her lack of critical self-awareness, the student argued, so does *Clueless* make fun of Cher.

Clueless (1995), though it could not look less like Austen's England, better captures the spirit of the novel. Cher, who never leaves her cell phone at home and shops on Rodeo Drive, is both the consummate brat and the consummate charmer. (See Fig. 2.) Cher does more than just try to find a suitable match for the obviously not as well-off or stylish Tai; she actually works on transforming her, much as Emma does with Harriet Smith in the novel. Cher encourages Tai to cut her hair, buy new clothes, exercise, and read more nonacademic books, and she takes pride in the new person that she has tried to create. In this way, the film parallels the novel's attention not only to Emma's preoccupation with social status but also to the way she tries to use Harriet to further elevate her own reputation.

Fig. 2. Clueless, dir. Amy Heckerling, perf. Alicia Silverstone, Stacey Dash, Brittany Murphy, and Paul Rudd, Paramount, 1995.

Reflecting on Your Writing

Now that you have read and discussed several evaluation essays and written one of your own, take some time to think critically about what you have learned. What problems did you encounter as you were writing your essay, and how did you solve them?

Write a one-page explanation, telling your instructor about a problem you encountered in writing your essay and how you solved it. Before you begin, gather all of your writing—invention and planning notes, drafts, readers' comments, revision plan, and final revisions. Review these materials as you complete this writing task.

1. ***Identify one writing problem you needed to solve as you worked on the essay.*** Do not be concerned with grammar and punctuation problems; concentrate instead on problems unique to developing an evaluation essay. For example: Did you puzzle over how to present your subject? Did you have trouble acknowledging what you liked as well as what you disliked? Was it difficult to refute an important objection or answer a question you knew readers would raise?

2. ***Determine how you came to recognize the problem.*** When did you first discover it? What called it to your attention? If you did not become aware of the problem until someone else pointed it out to you, can you now see hints of it in your invention writings? If so, where specifically? When you first recognized the problem, how did you respond?

3. ***Reflect on how you went about solving the problem.*** Did you work on the wording of a passage, cut or add reasons or refutations, conduct further research, or move paragraphs or sentences around? Did you reread one of the essays in this chapter to see how another writer handled a similar problem, or did you look back at your invention writing? If you talked about the problem with another student, a tutor, or your instructor, did talking about it help? How useful was the advice you received?

4. ***Write a brief explanation of the problem and your solution.*** Be as specific as possible in reconstructing your efforts. Quote from your invention notes or draft essay, others' critical comments, your revision plan, or your revised essay to show the various changes that your writing—and thinking—underwent as you tried to solve the problem. If you are still uncertain about your solution, say so. Taking time to explain how you identified a particular problem, how you went about trying to solve it, and what you learned from this experience can help you solve future writing problems more easily.

Part Two

Strategies for Critical Thinking, Writing, and Research

8   A Catalog of Invention Strategies

Writers are like scientists: They ask questions, systematically inquiring about how things work, what they are, where they occur, and how more information can be learned about them. Writers are also like artists in that they use what they know and learn to create something new and imaginative.

The invention and inquiry strategies—also known as **heuristics**—described in this chapter are not mysterious or magical. They are available to all writers, and one or more of them may appeal to your common sense and experience. These techniques represent ways creative writers, engineers, scientists, composers—in fact, all of us—solve problems. Once you have mastered these strategies, you can use them to tackle many of the writing situations you will encounter in college, on the job, and in the community.

The strategies for invention and inquiry in this chapter are grouped into two categories:

Mapping: A brief visual representation of your thinking or planning

Writing: The composition of phrases or sentences to discover information and ideas and to make connections among them

These invention and inquiry strategies will help you explore and research a topic fully before you begin drafting and then help you creatively solve problems as you draft and revise. In this chapter, strategies are arranged alphabetically within each of the two categories.

▨ Mapping

Mapping strategies involve making a visual record of invention and inquiry. In making maps, writers usually use key words and phrases to record material they want to remember, questions they need to answer, and new sources of information they want to check. The maps show the ideas, details, and facts, as well as possible ways to connect and focus them. Mapping can be especially useful for working in collaborative writing situations, for preparing oral presentations, and for creating visual aids for written or oral reports. Mapping strategies include clustering, listing, and outlining.

Clustering

Clustering is a strategy for revealing possible relationships among facts and ideas. Unlike listing (the next mapping strategy), clustering requires a brief period of initial preparation when you divide your topic into parts or main ideas. Clustering works as follows:

1. In a word or phrase, write your topic in the center of a piece of paper. Circle it.

2. Also in words or phrases, write down the main parts or ideas of your topic. Circle these, and connect them with lines to the topic in the center.

3. Next, write down facts, details, examples, or ideas related to these main parts. Connect them with lines to the relevant main parts or ideas.

> **Software-based Diagramming Tools**
> Software vendors have created a variety of electronic tools to help people better visualize complex projects. These flowcharts, webs, and outlines can make it easier for you (or your instructor) to see how to proceed at any stage of your project.

Clustering can be useful in the early stages of planning an essay to find subtopics and organize information. You may try out and discard several clusters before finding one that is promising. Many writers also use clustering to plan brief sections of an essay as they are drafting or revising. (A model of clustering is shown in Figure 8.1 below.)

Figure 8.1 A model of clustering

Listing

Listing is a familiar activity. You make shopping lists and lists of errands to do or people to call. Listing can also be a great help in planning an essay. It enables you to recall what you already know about a topic and suggests what else you may need to find out.

A basic activity for all writers, listing is especially useful to those who have little time for planning—for example, reporters facing deadlines and college students taking essay exams. Listing lets you order your ideas quickly. It can also serve as a first step in discovering possible writing topics. Here is how listing works best for invention work:

1. Give your list a title that indicates your main idea or topic.
2. Write as fast as you can, relying on short phrases.
3. Include anything that seems at all useful. Try not to be judgmental at this point.
4. After you have finished or even as you write, reflect on the list, and organize it in the following way:

- Put an asterisk next to the most promising items.
- Number key items in order of importance.
- Put items in related groups.
- Cross out items that do not seem promising.
- Add new items.

Outlining

Like listing and clustering, **outlining** is both a means of inventing what you want to say in an essay and a way of organizing your ideas and information. As you outline, you nearly always see new possibilities in your subject, discovering new ways of dividing or grouping information and seeing where you need additional information to develop your ideas. Because outlining lets you see at a glance where your essay's strengths and weaknesses lie, outlining can also help you read and revise your essay with a critical eye.

There are two main forms of outlining: informal outlining and formal topic or sentence outlining. Among the several types of informal outlining, scratch outlines are perhaps the most adaptable to a variety of situations. Chunking is another useful method. (Clustering also may be considered a type of informal outlining.)

A *scratch outline* is little more than a list of the essay's main points. You have no doubt made scratch outlines many times—to plan essays or essay exams, to revise your own writing, and to analyze a difficult reading passage. Here are sample scratch outlines for two different kinds of essays. The first is an outline of the paragraphs in Rick Bragg's essay in Chapter 2 (pp. 24–27), and the second shows one way to organize a position paper (Chapter 5):

Scratch Outline: Essay about a Remembered Event

1. Gives background on his quest since boyhood for "a car built for speed"
2. Recalls the 1969 muscle car he bought the summer before his senior year of high school, how he paid for it, and his uncle's warning
3. Recalls how the car gave him status among his peers
4. Recalls winning his first parking-lot race in the car and his subsequent thrill over speeding the car down country roads
5. Turns to specific incident two weeks after he got the car when, during a high-speed race, he braked suddenly and flipped the car into a ditch
6. Describes how, miraculously, he was relatively unhurt, hanging upside down and pinned in by the low adjustment of the steering wheel
7. Reflects on the inappropriateness of his initial mental response: to turn down the radio
8. Describes being pulled from the car by a state trooper and the trooper's comment that he should have been killed in the accident ("The Lord was riding with you, son")
9. Describes his mother's stunned reaction
10. Tells about the authorities' decision not to charge him
11. Remembers the sight of the crushed car once it had been flipped back over
12. Recalls the wrecker operator's echo of the trooper's comment
13. Ends with a reflection about an imagined newspaper headline that humorously summarizes his experience

Scratch Outline: Essay Arguing a Position

Presentation of the issue

Concession of some aspect of an opposing position

Thesis statement

First reason with support

Second reason with support

(etc.)

Conclusion

Remember that the items in a scratch outline do not necessarily coincide with paragraphs. Sometimes two or more items may be developed in the same paragraph or one item may be covered in two or more paragraphs.

Chunking, a type of scratch outline commonly used by professional writers in business and industry and especially well suited to writing in the electronic age, consists of a set of headings describing the major points to be covered in the final document. What makes chunking distinctive is that the blocks of text — or "chunks" — under each heading are intended to be roughly the same length and scope. These headings can be discussed and passed around among several writers and editors before writing begins, and different chunks may be written by different authors, simply by typing notes or text on a word processor into the space under each heading. The list of headings is subject to change during the writing, and new headings may be added or old ones subdivided or discarded as part of the drafting and editing process.

The advantage of chunking in your own writing is that it breaks the large task of drafting into smaller tasks in a simple, evenly balanced way; once the headings are determined, the writing becomes just a matter of filling in the specifics that go in each chunk. Organization tends to improve as you get a sense of the weight of different parts of the document while filling in the blanks. Places where the essay needs more information or there is a problem with pacing tend to stand out because of the chunking structure, and the headings can either be taken out of the finished essay or left in as devices to help guide readers. If they are left in, they should be edited into parallel grammatical form like the items in a formal topic or sentence outline, as discussed below.

Topic and *sentence outlines* are considered more formal than scratch outlines because they follow a conventional format of numbered and lettered headings and subheadings:

I. (Main topic)
   A. (Subtopic of I)
   B.
      1. (Subtopic of I.B)
      2.
         a. (Subtopic of I.B.2)
         b.
            (1) (Subtopic of I.B.2.b)
            (2)
   C.
      1. (Subtopic of I.C)
      2.

The difference between a topic and sentence outline is obvious: Topic outlines simply name the topics and subtopics, whereas sentence outlines use complete or abbreviated sentences. To illustrate, here are two partial formal outlines of an essay arguing a position, Jessica Statsky's "Children Need to Play, Not Compete," from Chapter 5 (pp. 149–54).

Formal Topic Outline

I. Organized sports harmful to children
   A. Harmful physically
      1. Curve ball (Koppett)
      2. Tackle football (Tutko)

B. Harmful psychologically

   1. Fear of being hurt

      a. Little League Online

      b. Mother

      c. Reporter

   2. Competition

      a. Rablovsky

      b. Studies

Formal Sentence Outline

I. Highly organized competitive sports such as Peewee Football and Little League Baseball can be physically and psychologically harmful to children, as well as counterproductive for developing future players.

  A. Physically harmful because sports entice children into physical actions that are bad for growing bodies.

    1. Koppett claims throwing a curve ball may put abnormal strain on developing arm and shoulder muscles.

    2. Tutko argues that tackle football is too traumatic for young kids.

  B. Psychologically harmful to children for a number of reasons.

    1. Fear of being hurt detracts from their enjoyment of the sport.

      a. Little League Online ranks fear of injury seventh among the seven top reasons children quit.

      b. One mother says, "kids get so scared. . . . They'll sit on the bench and pretend their leg hurts."

      c. A reporter tells about a child who made himself vomit to get out of playing Peewee Football.

    2. Too much competition poses psychological dangers for children.

      a. Rablovsky reports: "The spirit of play suddenly disappears, and sport becomes joblike."

      b. Studies show that children prefer playing on a losing team to "warming the bench on a winning team."

In contrast to an informal outline in which anything goes, a formal outline must follow many conventions. The roman numerals and capital letters are followed by periods. In both topic and sentence outlines, the first word of each item is capitalized, but items in topic outlines do not end with a period as items in sentence outlines do. Every level of a formal outline except the top level (identified by the roman numeral *I*) must include at least two items. Items at the same level of indentation in a topic outline should be grammatically parallel — all beginning with the same part of speech. For example, *I.A.* and *I.B.* are parallel when they both begin with an adverb (*Physically harmful* and *Psychologically harmful*) or with an adjective

(*Harmful physically* and *Harmful psychologically*); they would not be parallel if one began with an adverb (*Physically harmful*) and the other with an adjective (*Harmful psychologically*).

Writing

Unlike most mapping strategies, **writing strategies** invite you to produce complete sentences. Sentences provide considerable generative power. Because they are complete statements, they take you further than listing or clustering. They enable you to explore ideas and define relationships, bring ideas together or show how they differ, and identify causes and effects. Sentences can also help you develop a logical chain of thought.

Some of these invention and inquiry strategies are systematic, while others are more flexible. Even though they call for complete sentences that are related to one another, they do not require preparation or revision. You can use them to develop oral as well as written presentations.

These writing strategies include cubing, dialoguing, dramatizing, keeping a journal, looping, questioning, and quick drafting.

Cubing

Cubing is useful for quickly exploring a writing topic, probing it from six different perspectives. It is known as *cubing* because a cube has six sides. These are the six perspectives in cubing:

Describing: What does your subject look like? What size is it? What is its color? Its shape? Its texture? Name its parts.

Comparing: What is your subject similar to? Different from?

Associating: What does your subject make you think of? What connections does it have to anything else in your experience?

Analyzing: What are the origins of your subject? What are the functions or significance of its parts? How are its parts related?

Applying: What can you do with your subject? What uses does it have?

Arguing: What arguments can you make for your subject? Against it?

Here are some guidelines to help you use cubing productively.

1. Select a topic, subject, or part of a subject. This can be a person, a scene, an event, an object, a problem, an idea, or an issue. Hold it in focus.

2. Limit your writing to three to five minutes for each perspective. The whole activity should take no more than half an hour.

3. Keep going until you have written about your subject from all six perspectives. Remember that cubing offers the special advantage of enabling you to generate multiple perspectives quickly.

4. As you write from each perspective, begin with what you know about your subject. However, do not limit yourself to your present knowledge. Indicate what else you would like to know about your subject, and suggest where you might find that information.

5. Reread what you have written. Look for bright spots, surprises. Recall the part that was easiest for you to write. Recall the part where you felt a special momentum and pleasure in writing. Look for an angle or an unexpected insight. These special parts may suggest a focus or topic within a larger subject, or they may provide specific details to include in a draft.

Dialoguing

A dialogue is a conversation between two or more people. You can use **dialoguing** to search for topics, find a focus, explore ideas, or consider opposing viewpoints. When you write a dialogue as an invention strategy, you need to make up all parts of the conversation (unless, of course, you are writing collaboratively). To construct a dialogue independently or collaboratively, follow these steps:

1. Write a conversation between two speakers. Label the participants *Speaker A* and *Speaker B*, or make up names for them.

2. If you get stuck, you might have one of the speakers ask the other a question.

3. Write brief responses to keep the conversation moving fast. Do not spend much time planning or rehearsing responses. Write what first occurs to you, just as in a real conversation, where people take quick turns to prevent any awkward silences.

Dialogues can be especially useful with personal experience and persuasive essays because they help you remember conversations and anticipate objections.

Dramatizing

Dramatizing is an invention activity developed by the philosopher Kenneth Burke as a way of thinking about how people interact and as a way of analyzing stories and films.

Thinking about human behavior in dramatic terms can be very productive for writers. Drama has action, actors, setting, motives, and methods. Since stars and acting go together, you can use a five-pointed star to remember these five points of dramatizing: Each point on the star provides a different perspective on human behavior (see Figure 8.2).

Action.   An action is anything that happens, has happened, will happen, or could happen. Action includes events that are physical (running a marathon), mental (thinking about a book you have read), and emotional (falling in love).

Actor.   The actor is involved in the action—either responsible for it or simply affected by it. (The actor does not have to be a person. It can be a force, something that causes

Figure 8.2 Dramatizing

an action. For example, if the action is a rise in the price of gasoline, the actor could be increased demand or short supply.) Dramatizing may also include a number of coactors working together or at odds.

Setting.   The setting is the situation or background of the action. We usually think of setting as the place and time of an event, but it may also be the historical background of an event or the childhood of a person.

Motive.   The motive is the purpose or reason for an action — the actor's intention. Actions may have multiple, even conflicting, motives.

Method.   The method explains how an action occurs, including the techniques an actor uses. It refers to whatever makes things happen.

Each of these points suggests a simple invention question:

Action: What?

Actor: Who?

Setting: When and where?

Motive: Why?

Method: How?

This list looks like the questions reporters typically ask. But dramatizing goes further: It enables us to consider relations between and among these five elements. We can think about actors' motives, the effect of the setting on the actors, the relations between actors, and so on.

You can use this invention strategy to learn more about yourself or about other significant people in your life. You can use it, as well, to explore, interpret, or evaluate characters in stories or movies. Moreover, dramatizing is especially useful in understanding the readers you want to inform or convince.

To use dramatizing, imagine the person you want to understand better in a particular situation. Holding this image in mind, write answers to any questions in the following list that apply. You may draw a blank on some questions, have little to say to some, and find a lot to say to others. Be exploratory and playful with the questions. Write responses quickly, relying on words and phrases, even drawings.

- What is the actor doing?
- How did the actor come to be involved in this situation?
- Why does the actor do what he or she does?
- What else might the actor do?
- What is the actor trying to accomplish?
- How do other actors influence—help or hinder—the main actor?
- What do the actor's actions reveal about him or her?
- What does the actor's language reveal about him or her?
- How does the event's setting influence the actor's actions?
- How does the time of the event influence what the actor does?
- Where does this actor come from?
- How is this actor different now from what he or she used to be?
- What might this actor become?
- How is this actor like or unlike the other actors?

Keeping a Journal

Professional writers often use **journals** to keep notes. Starting one is easy. Buy a special notebook, or open a new file on your computer, and start writing. Here are some possibilities:

- Keep a list of new words and concepts you learn in your courses. You could also write about the progress and direction of your learning in particular courses—the experience of being in the course, your feelings about what is happening, and what you are learning.
- Respond to your reading, both assigned and personal. As you read, write about your personal associations, reflections, reactions, and evaluations. Summarize or copy memorable or especially important passages, and comment on them. (Copying and commenting have been practiced by students and writers for centuries in special journals called *commonplace books*.)
- Write to prepare for particular class meetings. Write about the main ideas you have learned from assigned readings and about the relationship of these new ideas to other ideas in the course. After class, write to summarize what you have learned. List questions you have about the ideas or information discussed in class. Journal writing of this kind involves reflecting, evaluating, interpreting, synthesizing, summarizing, and questioning.

- Record observations and overheard conversations.
- Write for ten or fifteen minutes every day about whatever is on your mind. Focus these meditations on your new experiences as you try to understand, interpret, and reflect on them.
- Write sketches of people who catch your attention.
- Organize your time. Write about your goals and priorities, or list specific things to accomplish and what you plan to do.
- Keep a log over several days or weeks about a particular event unfolding in the news—a sensational trial, an environmental disaster, a political campaign, a campus controversy, the fortunes of a sports team.

You can use a journal in many ways. All of the writing in your journal has value for learning. You may also be able to use parts of your journal for writing in your other courses.

Looping

Looping is especially useful for the first stages of exploring a topic. As its name suggests, **looping** involves writing quickly to explore some aspect of a topic and then looping back to your original starting point or to a new starting point to explore another aspect. Beginning with almost any starting point, looping enables you to find a center of interest and eventually a thesis for your essay. The steps are simple:

1. Write down your area of interest. You may know only that you have to write about another person or a movie or a cultural trend that has caught your attention. Or you may want to search for a topic in a broad historical period or for one related to a major political event. Although you may wander from this topic as you write, you will want to keep coming back to it. Your purpose is to find a focus for writing.

2. Write nonstop for ten minutes. Start with the first thing that comes to mind. Write rapidly, without looking back to reread or to correct anything. *Do not stop writing. Keep your pencil moving or keystrokes clacking.* Continuous writing is the key to looping. If you get stuck for a moment, rewrite the last sentence. Follow diversions and digressions, but keep returning to your topic.

3. After ten minutes, pause to reread what you have written. Decide what is most important—a single insight, a pattern of ideas, an emerging theme, a visual detail, anything at all that stands out. Some writers call this a "center of gravity" or a "hot spot." To complete the first loop, restate this center in a single sentence.

4. Beginning with this sentence, write nonstop for another ten minutes.

5. Summarize in one sentence again to complete the second loop.

6. Keep looping until one of your summary sentences produces a focus or thesis. You may need only two or three loops; you may need more.

Questioning

Asking **questions** about a subject is a way to learn about it and decide what to write. When you first encounter a subject, however, your questions may be scattered. Also, you are not likely to think right away of all the important questions you ought to ask. The advantage of having a basic list of questions for invention, like the ones for cubing and for dramatizing discussed earlier in this chapter, is that it provides a systematic approach to exploring a subject.

The questions that follow come from classical rhetoric (what the Greek philosopher Aristotle called *topics*) and a modern approach to invention called *tagmemics*. Based on the work of linguist Kenneth Pike, tagmemics provides questions about different ways we make sense of the world, the ways we sort and classify experience in order to understand it.

Here are the steps in using questions for invention:

1. In a sentence or two, identify your subject. A subject could be any event, person, problem, project, idea, or issue—in other words, anything you might write about.

2. Start by writing a response to the first question in the following list, and move right through the list. Try to answer each question at least briefly with a word or a phrase. Some questions may invite several sentences or even a page or more of writing. You may draw a blank on a few questions. Skip them. Later, when you have more experience with questions for invention, you can start anywhere in the list.

3. Write your responses quickly, without much planning. Follow digressions or associations. Do not screen anything out. Be playful.

What Is Your Subject?

- What is your subject's name? What other names does it have? What names did it have in the past?
- What aspects of the subject do these different names emphasize?
- Imagine a still photograph or a moving picture of your subject. What would it look like?
- What would you put into a time capsule to stand for your subject?
- What are its causes and effects?
- How would it look from different vantage points or perspectives?
- What particular experiences have you had with the subject? What have you learned?

What Parts or Features Does Your Subject Have, and How Are They Related?

- Name the parts or features of your subject.
- Describe each one, using the questions in the preceding subject list.
- How is each part or feature related to the others?

How Is Your Subject Similar to and Different from Other Subjects?

- What is your subject similar to? In what ways?
- What is your subject different from? In what ways?
- What seems to you most unlike your subject? In what ways? Now, just for fun, note how they are alike.

How Much Can Your Subject Change and Still Remain the Same?

- How has your subject changed from what it once was?
- How is it changing now—moment to moment, day to day, year to year?
- How does each change alter your way of thinking about your subject?
- What are some different forms your subject takes?
- What does it become when it is no longer itself?

Where Does Your Subject Fit in the World?

- When and where did your subject originate?
- What would happen if at some future time your subject ceased to exist?
- When and where do you usually experience the subject?
- What is this subject a part of, and what are the other parts?
- What do other people think of your subject?

Quick Drafting

Sometimes you know what you want to say or have little time for invention. In these situations, **quick drafting** may be a good strategy. There are no special rules for quick drafting, but you should rely on it only if you know your subject well, have had experience with the kind of writing you are doing, and will have a chance to revise your draft. Quick drafting can help you discover what you already know about the subject and what you need to find out. It can also help you develop and organize your thoughts.

A Catalog of Reading Strategies   9

This chapter presents strategies to help you become a thoughtful reader. A thoughtful reader is above all a patient *re*reader, concerned not only with comprehending and remembering but also with interpreting and evaluating — on the one hand, striving to understand the text on its own terms; on the other hand, taking care to question its ideas.

The reading strategies in this chapter can help you enrich your thinking as a reader and participate in conversations as a writer. These strategies include the following:

- *Annotating:* Recording your reactions to, interpretations of, and questions about a text as you read it
- *Taking inventory:* Listing and grouping your annotations and other notes to find meaningful patterns
- *Outlining:* Listing the text's main ideas to reveal how it is organized
- *Paraphrasing:* Restating what you have read to clarify or refer to it
- *Summarizing:* Distilling the main ideas or gist of a text
- *Synthesizing:* Integrating into your own writing ideas and information gleaned from different sources
- *Contextualizing:* Placing a text in its historical and cultural contexts
- *Exploring the significance of figurative language:* Examining how metaphors, similes, and symbols are used in a text to convey meaning and evoke feelings
- *Looking for patterns of opposition:* Inferring the values and assumptions embodied in the language of a text
- *Reflecting on challenges to your beliefs and values:* Examining the bases of your personal responses to a text
- *Evaluating the logic of an argument:* Determining whether an argument is well reasoned and adequately supported
- *Recognizing emotional manipulation:* Identifying texts that unfairly and inappropriately use emotional appeals based on false or exaggerated claims
- *Judging the writer's credibility:* Considering whether writers represent different points of view fairly and know what they are writing about

Although mastering these strategies will not make critical reading easy, it can make your reading much more satisfying and productive and thus help you handle even difficult material with confidence. These reading strategies will, in addition, often be useful in your reading outside of school—for instance, these strategies can help you understand, evaluate, and comment on what political figures, advertisers, and other writers are saying.

◾ Annotating

Annotations are the marks—underlines, highlights, and comments—you make directly on the page as you read. **Annotating** can be used to record immediate reactions and questions, outline and summarize main points, and evaluate and relate the reading to other ideas and points of view. Your annotations can take many forms, such as the following:

> **Annotating Onscreen**
> Although this discussion of annotating assumes you are reading printed pages, you can also annotate many kinds of text on the computer screen by using your word processor's highlighting and commenting functions or simply by typing annotations into the text using a different color or font. If electronic annotation is impossible, print out the text, and annotate by hand.

Writing comments, questions, or definitions in the margins

Underlining or circling words, phrases, or sentences

Connecting ideas with lines or arrows

Numbering related points

Bracketing sections of the text

Noting anything that strikes you as interesting, important, or questionable

Most readers annotate in layers, adding further annotations on second and third readings. Annotations can be light or heavy, depending on the reader's purpose and the difficulty of the material. Your purpose for reading also determines how you use your annotations.

The following selection, excerpted from Martin Luther King Jr.'s "Letter from Birmingham Jail," illustrates some of the ways you can annotate as you read. Add your own annotations, if you like.

MARTIN LUTHER KING JR. (1929–1968) first came to national notice in 1955, when he led a successful boycott against the policy of restricting African American passengers to rear seats on city buses in Montgomery, Alabama, where he was minister of a Baptist church. He subsequently formed the Southern Christian Leadership Conference, which brought people of all races from all over the country to the South to fight nonviolently for racial integration. In 1963, King led demonstrations in Birmingham, Alabama, that were met with violence; a bomb was detonated in a black church, killing four young girls. King was arrested for his role in organizing the protests, and while in prison, he wrote his "Letter from Birmingham Jail" to justify his strategy of civil disobedience, which he called "nonviolent direct action."

King begins his letter by discussing his disappointment with the lack of support he has received from white moderates, such as the group of clergy who published criticism of his organization in the local newspaper. As you read the following excerpt, try to infer what the clergy's specific criticisms might have been. Also, notice the tone King uses. Would you characterize the writing as apologetic, conciliatory, accusatory, or something else?

An Annotated Excerpt from "Letter from Birmingham Jail"
Martin Luther King Jr.

¶1. *White moderates block progress.*

I must confess that over the past few years I have been gravely 1 disappointed with the white moderate. I have almost reached the regrettable conclusion that the Negro's [great stumbling block in his stride toward freedom] is not the White Citizen's Counciler or the Ku Klux Klanner, but the white moderate, who is more devoted

Contrasts: order vs. justice, negative vs. positive peace, ends vs. means

to "order" than to justice; who prefers a negative peace which is the absence of tension to a positive peace which is the presence of justice; who constantly says: "I agree with you in the goal you seek, but I cannot agree with your methods of direct action"; who

(treating others like children)

paternalistically believes he can set the timetable for another man's freedom; who lives by a mythical concept of time and who constantly advises the Negro to wait for a "more convenient season."

more contrasts

Shallow understanding from people of good will is more frustrating than absolute misunderstanding from people of ill will. Lukewarm acceptance is much more bewildering than outright rejection.

¶2. *Tension necessary for progress.*

I had hoped that the white moderate would understand that 2 law and order exist for the purpose of establishing justice and that when they fail in this purpose they become the [dangerously structured dams that block the flow of social progress.] I had

metaphor: law and order = dams (faulty?)

hoped that the white moderate would understand that the present tension in the South is a necessary phase of the transition

from an [obnoxious <u>negative peace</u>,] in which the Negro passively   *repeats*
contrast
accepted his unjust plight, to a [substantive and <u>positive peace</u>,]

in which all men will respect the dignity and worth of human per-

sonality. Actually, we <u>who engage in nonviolent direct action are</u>   *Tension already*
exists anyway.
<u>not the creators of tension</u>. We merely bring to the surface the hid-   *(True?)*

<u>den tension</u> that is already alive. We bring it out in the open, where

it can be seen and dealt with. [Like a boil that can never be cured   *simile: hidden*
tension is "like a
so long as it is covered up but must be opened with all its ugliness   *boil"*

to the natural medicines of air and light, injustice must be exposed,

with all the tension its exposure creates, to the <u>light of human con-</u>

<u>science and the air of national opinion</u> before it can be cured.]

In your statement you assert that <u>our actions</u>, even though 3   *¶3. Questions*
clergymen's logic:
peaceful, must be <u>condemned</u> because they precipitate violence.   *condemning his*
actions =
But is this a logical assertion? <u>Isn't this like condemning</u> (a robbed   *condemning*
victims, Socrates,
<u>man</u>) because his possession of money precipitated the evil act   *Jesus.*

of robbery? <u>Isn't this like condemning</u> (Socrates) because his

unswerving commitment to truth and his philosophical inquiries

precipitated the act by the misguided populace in which they

made him drink hemlock? <u>Isn't this like condemning</u> (Jesus)   *repetition ("Isn't*
this like . . .")
because his unique God-consciousness and never-ceasing devo-

tion to God's will precipitated the evil act of crucifixion? We must

come to see that, as the federal courts have consistently affirmed,

it is wrong to urge an individual to cease his efforts to gain his

<u>basic constitutional rights</u> because the question may precipitate

violence. [Society must <u>protect the robbed and punish the robber</u>.]   *(Yes!)*

I had also hoped that the white moderate would reject the 4

<u>myth concerning time</u> in relation to the struggle for freedom. I have

just received a letter from a white brother in Texas. He writes: "All   *example of a white*
moderate's view
Christians know that the colored people will receive equal rights

eventually, but it is possible that you are in <u>too great a religious</u>

hurry. It has taken Christianity almost two thousand years to accomplish what it has. The teachings of Christ take time to come to earth." Such an attitude stems from a tragic misconception of time, from the strangely irrational notion that there is something in the very flow of time that will inevitably cure all ills. Actually, time itself is neutral; it can be used either destructively or constructively. More and more I feel that the people of ill will have used time much more effectively than have the people of good will. We will have to repent in this generation not merely for the /hateful words and actions of the bad people/ but for the /appalling silence of the good people./ Human progress never rolls in on /wheels of inevitability;/ it comes through the tireless efforts of men willing to be co-workers with God, and without this hard work, time itself becomes an ally of the forces of social stagnation. /We must use time creatively, in the knowledge that the time is always ripe to do right./ Now is the time to make real the promise of democracy and transform our pending /national elegy/ into a creative /psalm of brotherhood./ Now is the time to lift our national policy from the /quicksand of racial injustice/ to the /solid rock of human dignity./

You speak of our activity in Birmingham as extreme. At first 5 I was rather disappointed that fellow clergymen would see my nonviolent efforts as those of an extremist. I began thinking about the fact that I stand in the middle of two opposing forces in the Negro community. One is a /force of complacency,/ made up in part of Negroes who, as a result of long years of oppression, are so drained of self-respect and a sense of "somebodiness" that they have adjusted to segregation; and in part of a few middle-class Negroes, who because of a degree of academic and economic security and because in some ways they profit by seg-regation, have become insensitive to the problems of the masses.

¶4. Time must be used to do right.

Silence is as bad as hateful words and actions.

metaphor (mechanical?)

(decay)

metaphors (song, natural world)

King accused of being an extremist.

¶5. Puts self in middle of two extremes: complacency and bitterness.

The other *[*force is one of bitterness and hatred,*]* and it comes perilously close to advocating violence. It is expressed in the various black nationalist *[*groups that are springing up*]* across the nation, the largest and best-known being Elijah Muhammad's Muslim movement. Nourished by the Negro's frustration over the continued existence of racial discrimination, this movement is made up of people who have lost faith in America, who have absolutely repudiated Christianity, and who have concluded that the white man is an incorrigible "devil."

Malcolm X?

I have tried to stand between these two forces, saying that 6 we need emulate neither the "do-nothingism" of the complacent nor the hatred and despair of the black nationalist. For there is the more excellent way of love and nonviolent protest. I am grateful to God that, through the influence of the Negro church, the way of nonviolence became an integral part of our struggle.

¶6. Offers better choice: nonviolent protest.

(How did nonviolence become part of King's movement?)

If this philosophy had not emerged, by now many streets of the 7 South would, I am convinced, be flowing with blood. And I am further convinced that if our white brothers dismiss as "rabble-rousers" and "outside agitators" those of us who employ nonviolent direct action, and if they refuse to support our nonviolent efforts, millions of Negroes will, out of frustration and despair, seek (solace) and security in black-nationalist ideologies—a development that would inevitably lead to a frightening racial nightmare.

¶7. Says movement prevented racial violence. (Threat?)

(Comfort)

(Oppressed people cannot remain oppressed forever.) The 8 yearning for freedom eventually manifests itself, and that is what has happened to the American Negro. Something within has reminded him of his birthright of freedom, and something without has reminded him that it can be gained. Consciously or unconsciously, he has been caught up by the (Zeitgeist,) and with his black brothers of Africa and his brown and yellow brothers of

(spirit of the times)

Asia, South America and the Caribbean, the United States Negro is moving with a sense of great urgency toward the *[promised land of racial justice.]* If one recognizes this *[vital urge that has engulfed the Negro community,]* one should readily understand why public demonstrations are taking place. The Negro has many *[pent-up resentments]* and latent frustrations, and he must release them. So let him march; let him make prayer pilgrimages to the city hall; let him go on freedom rides—and try to understand why he must do so. If his repressed emotions are not released in nonviolent ways, they will seek expression through violence; this is not a threat but a fact of history. So I have not said to my people: "Get rid of your discontent." Rather, I have tried to say that this normal and healthy discontent can be *[channeled into the creative outlet of nonviolent direct action.]* And now this approach is being termed extremist.

Not a threat, but a fact—?

¶18. Discontent is normal and healthy but must be channeled.

But though I was initially disappointed at being catego-   9
rized as an extremist, as I continued to think about the matter I gradually gained a measure of satisfaction from the label. Was not Jesus an extremist for love: "Love your enemies, bless them that curse you, do good to them that hate you, and pray for them which despitefully use you, and persecute you." Was not (Amos) an extremist for justice: "Let justice roll down like waters and righteousness like an ever-flowing stream." Was not (Paul) an extremist for the Christian gospel: "I bear in my body the marks of the Lord Jesus." Was not (Martin Luther) an extremist: "Here I stand; I cannot do otherwise, so help me God." And (John Bunyan:) "I will stay in jail to the end of my days before I make a butchery of my conscience." And (Abraham Lincoln:) "This nation cannot survive half slave and half free." And (Thomas Jefferson:) "We hold these truths to be self-evident, that all men are created equal. . . ." (So the question is not whether

¶19. Embraces "extremist" label. (!)

(Hebrew prophet)

(Christian apostle)

(Founded Protestantism)

(English preacher)

we will be extremists, but what kind of extremists we will be. Will we be extremists for hate or for love? Will we be extremists for the preservation of injustice or for the extension of justice? In that dramatic scene on Calvary's hill three men were crucified. We must never forget that all three were crucified for the same crime—the crime of extremism. Two were extremists for immorality, and thus fell below their environment. The other, Jesus Christ, was an extremist for love, truth and goodness, and thereby rose above his environment. Perhaps the South, the nation and the world are in dire need of creative extremists.

Compares self to great "extremists"— including Jesus

I had hoped that the white moderate would see this need. 10 Perhaps I was too optimistic; perhaps I expected too much. I suppose I should have realized that few members of the oppressor race can understand the deep groans and passionate yearnings of the oppressed race, and still fewer have the vision to see that [injustice must be rooted out] by strong, persistent and determined action. I am thankful, however, that some of our white brothers in the South have grasped the meaning of this social revolution and committed themselves to it. They are still all too few in quantity, but they are big in quality. Some—such as Ralph McGill, Lillian Smith, Harry Golden, James McBride Dabbs, Ann Braden and Sarah Patton Boyle—have written about our struggle in eloquent and prophetic terms. Others have marched with us down nameless streets of the South. They have languished in filthy, roach-infested jails, suffering the abuse and brutality of policemen who view them as "dirty nigger-lovers." Unlike so many of their moderate brothers and sisters, they have recognized the urgency of the moment and sensed the need for [powerful "action" antidotes] to combat the [disease of segregation.]

Disappointed in the white moderate

¶10. Praises whites who have supported King.

(Who are they?)

(been left unaided)

Metaphor: segregation is a disease.

1. Mark the text using notations like these:
   - Circle words to be defined in the margin.
   - Underline key words and phrases.
   - Bracket important sentences and passages.
   - Use lines or arrows to connect ideas or words.
2. Write marginal comments like these:
   - Number and summarize each paragraph.
   - Define unfamiliar words.
   - Note responses and questions.
   - Identify interesting writing strategies.
   - Point out patterns.
3. Layer additional markings on the text and comments in the margins as you reread for different purposes.

Taking Inventory

Taking inventory helps you analyze your annotations for different purposes. When you take inventory, you make various kinds of lists to explore patterns of meaning you find in the text. For instance, in reading the annotated passage by Martin Luther King Jr., you might have noticed that certain similes and metaphors are used or that many famous people are named. By listing the names (Socrates, Jesus, Luther, Lincoln, and so on) and then grouping them into categories (people who died for their beliefs, leaders, teachers, and religious figures), you could better understand why the writer refers to these particular people. Taking inventory of your annotations can be helpful if you plan to write about a text you are reading.

1. Examine your annotations for patterns or repetitions such as recurring images, stylistic features, repeated words and phrases, repeated examples or illustrations, and reliance on particular writing strategies.
2. List the items in a pattern.
3. Decide what the pattern might reveal about the reading.

Outlining

Outlining is an especially helpful reading strategy for understanding the content and structure of a reading. **Outlining,** which identifies the text's main ideas, may be part of the annotating process, or it may be done separately. Writing an outline in the margins of the text as you read and annotate makes it easier to find information later. Writing an outline on a separate piece of paper gives you more space to work with, and therefore such an outline usually includes more detail.

The key to outlining is distinguishing between the main ideas and the supporting material such as examples, quotations, comparisons, and reasons. The main ideas form the backbone, which holds the various parts of the text together. Outlining the main ideas helps you uncover this structure.

Making an outline, however, is not simple. The reader must exercise judgment in deciding which are the most important ideas. The words used in an outline reflect the reader's interpretation and emphasis. Readers also must decide when to use the writer's words, their own words, or a combination of the two.

You may make either a formal, multileveled outline or an informal scratch outline. A *formal outline* is harder to make and much more time-consuming than a scratch outline. You might choose to make a formal outline of a reading about which you are writing an in-depth interpretation or evaluation. For example, here is a formal outline a student wrote for an essay evaluating the logic of the King excerpt. Notice that the student uses roman numerals for the main ideas or claims, capital letters for the reasons, and arabic numerals for supporting evidence.

Formal Outline of "Letter from Birmingham Jail"

I.   "[T]he Negro's great stumbling block in his stride toward freedom is . . . the white moderate. . . ."
    A.   Because the white moderate is more devoted to "order" than to justice (paragraph 2)
        1.   Law and order exist to establish justice.
        2.   Law and order compare to "dangerously structured dams that block the flow of social progress."
    B.   Because the white moderate prefers a "negative peace" (absence of tension) to a "positive peace" (justice) (paragraph 2)
        1.   The tension already exists.
        2.   It is not created by nonviolent direct action.
        3.   Society that does not eliminate injustice compares to a boil that hides its infections. Both can be cured only by exposure (boil simile).
    C.   Because even though the white moderate agrees with the goals, he does not support the means to achieve them (paragraph 3)
        1.   The argument that the means — nonviolent direct action — are wrong because they precipitate violence is flawed.
        2.   An analogy compares black people to the robbed man who is condemned because he had money.
        3.   Analogies compare black people to Socrates and Jesus.
    D.   Because the white moderate paternalistically believes he can set a timetable for another man's freedom (paragraph 4)
        1.   King rebuts the white moderate's argument that Christianity will cure man's ills and man must wait patiently for that to happen.

      2.   He argues that "time itself is neutral" and that people "must use time creatively" for constructive rather than destructive ends.

  II. Creative extremism is preferable to moderation.

     A. Classifies himself as a moderate (paragraphs 5–8)

       1.   "I . . . stand between . . . two forces": the white moderate's complacency and the Black Muslim's rage.

       2.   If nonviolent direct action were stopped, more violence, not less, would result.

       3.   "[M]illions of Negroes will, out of frustration and despair, seek solace and security in black-nationalist ideologies . . ." (paragraph 7).

       4.   Repressed emotions will be expressed — if not in nonviolent ways, then through violence (paragraph 8).

     B. Redefines himself as a "creative extremist" (paragraph 9)

       1.   Extremism for love, truth, and goodness is creative extremism.

       2.   He identifies himself with other extremists — Jesus, Amos, Paul, Martin Luther, John Bunyan, Abraham Lincoln, and Thomas Jefferson.

     C. Not all white people are moderates; some are committed to "this social revolution" (paragraph 10).

       1.   He lists the names of white writers.

       2.   He refers to other white activists.

A *scratch outline* will not record as much information as a formal outline, but it is sufficient for most reading purposes. To make a scratch outline, you first need to locate the topic of each paragraph in the reading. The topic is usually stated in a word or phrase, and it may be repeated or referred to throughout the paragraph. For example, the opening paragraph of the King excerpt (p. 309) makes clear that its topic is the white moderate.

After you have found the topic of the paragraph, figure out what is being said about it. To return to our example: King immediately establishes the white moderate as the topic of the opening paragraph and at the beginning of the second sentence announces the conclusion he has come to — namely, that the white moderate is "the Negro's great stumbling block in his stride toward freedom." The rest of the paragraph specifies the ways the white moderate blocks progress.

The annotations include a summary of each paragraph's topic. Here is a scratch outline that lists the topics:

Scratch Outline of "Letter from Birmingham Jail"

¶1. White moderates block progress in the struggle for racial justice

¶2. Tension necessary for progress

¶3. Questions clergymen's logic

¶4. Time must be used to do right

¶5. Puts self in the middle of two extremes: complacency and bitterness

¶6. Offers better choice: nonviolent protest

¶7. Says movement prevented racial violence

¶8. Discontent normal and healthy but must be channeled

¶9. Embraces "extremist" label

¶10. Praises whites who have supported King

CHECKLIST: OUTLINING

1. Reread each paragraph, identifying the topic and the comments made about the topic. Do not include examples, specific details, quotations, or other explanatory and supporting material.

2. List the author's main ideas in the margin of the text or on a separate piece of paper.

Paraphrasing

Paraphrasing is restating a text you have read by using mostly your own words. It can help you clarify the meaning of an obscure or ambiguous passage. It is one of the three ways of integrating other people's ideas and information into your own writing, along with *quoting* (reproducing exactly the language of the source text) and *summarizing* (distilling the main ideas or gist of the source text) (p. 319). You might choose to paraphrase rather than quote when the source's language is not especially arresting or memorable. You might paraphrase short passages but summarize longer ones.

Following are two passages. The first is from paragraph 2 of the excerpt from King's "Letter." The second passage is a paraphrase of the first:

Original

I had hoped that the white moderate would understand that law and order exist for the purpose of establishing justice and that when they fail in this purpose they become the dangerously structured dams that block the flow of social progress. I had hoped that the white moderate would understand that the present tension in the South is a necessary phase of the transition from an obnoxious negative peace, in which the Negro passively accepted his unjust plight, to a substantive and positive peace, in which all men will respect the dignity and worth of human personality.

Paraphrase

King writes that he had hoped for more understanding from white moderates — specifically that they would recognize that law and order are not ends in themselves but means to the greater end of establishing justice. When law and order do not serve this greater end, they stand in the way of progress. King expected the white moderate to recognize that the current tense situation in the South is part of a transition process that is necessary for progress. The current situation is bad because although there is peace, it is an "obnoxious" and "negative" kind of peace based on blacks passively accepting the injustice of the status quo. A better kind of peace — one that is "substantive," real and not imaginary, as well as "positive" — requires that all people, regardless of race, be valued.

When you compare the paraphrase to the original, you can see that the paraphrase contains all the important information and ideas of the original. Notice also that the paraphrase is somewhat longer than the original, refers to the writer by name, and encloses King's original words in quotation marks. The paraphrase tries to be *neutral*, to avoid inserting the reader's opinions or distorting the original writer's ideas.

CHECKLIST: PARAPHRASING

1. Reread the passage to be paraphrased, looking up unfamiliar words in a college dictionary.
2. Translate the passage into your own words, putting quotation marks around any words or phrases you quote from the original.
3. Revise to ensure coherence.

◼ Summarizing

Summarizing is important because it helps you understand and remember what is most significant in a reading. Another advantage of summarizing is that it creates a condensed version of the reading's ideas and information, which you can refer to later or insert into your own writing. Along with quoting and paraphrasing, summarizing enables you to integrate other writers' ideas into your own writing.

A summary is a relatively brief restatement, primarily in the reader's own words, of the reading's main ideas. Summaries vary in length, depending on the reader's purpose. Some summaries are very brief — a sentence or even a subordinate clause. For example, if you were referring to the excerpt from "Letter from Birmingham Jail" and simply needed to indicate how it relates to your other sources, your summary might look something like this: "There have always been advocates of extremism in politics. Martin Luther King Jr., in 'Letter from Birmingham Jail,' for instance, defends nonviolent civil disobedience as an extreme but necessary means of bringing about racial justice." If, however, you were surveying the important texts of the civil rights movement, you might write a longer, more detailed summary that not only identifies the reading's main ideas but also shows how the ideas relate to one another.

Many writers find it useful to outline the reading as a preliminary to writing a summary. A paragraph-by-paragraph scratch outline (like the one on pp. 317–18) lists the reading's main ideas in the sequence in which they appear in the original. But summarizing requires more than merely stringing together the entries in an outline. It fills in the logical connections between the author's ideas. Notice also in the following example that the reader repeats selected words and phrases and refers to the author by name, indicating, with verbs like *expresses, acknowledges,* and *explains,* the writer's purpose and strategy at each point in the argument.

Summary

King expresses his disappointment with white moderates who, by opposing his program of nonviolent direct action, have become a barrier to progress toward racial justice. He acknowledges that his program has raised tension in the South, but he explains that tension is necessary to bring about change. Furthermore, he argues that tension already exists, but because it has been unexpressed, it is unhealthy and potentially dangerous.

He defends his actions against the clergy's criticisms, particularly their argument that he is in too much of a hurry. Responding to charges of extremism, King claims that he has actually prevented racial violence by channeling the natural frustrations of oppressed blacks into nonviolent protest. He asserts that extremism is precisely what is needed now—but it must be creative, rather than destructive, extremism. He concludes by again expressing disappointment with white moderates for not joining his effort as some other whites have.

A summary presents only ideas. While it may use certain key terms from the source, it does not otherwise attempt to reflect the source's language, imagery, or tone; and it avoids even a hint of agreement or disagreement with the ideas it summarizes. Of course, however, a writer might summarize ideas in a source like "Letter from Birmingham Jail" to show readers that he or she has read it carefully and then proceed to use the summary to praise, question, or challenge King's argument. In doing so, the writer might quote specific language that reveals word choice, imagery, or tone.

CHECKLIST: SUMMARIZING

1. Make a scratch outline of the reading.
2. Write a paragraph or more that presents the author's main ideas largely in your own words. Use the outline as a guide, but reread parts of the original text as necessary.
3. To make the summary coherent, fill in connections between the ideas you present.

■ Synthesizing

Synthesizing involves presenting ideas and information gleaned from different sources. It can help you see how different sources relate to one another. For example, one reading may provide information that fills out the information in another reading, or a reading could present arguments that challenge arguments in another reading.

When you synthesize material from different sources, you construct a conversation among your sources, a conversation in which you also participate. Synthesizing contributes most when writers use sources not only to support their ideas, but to challenge and extend them as well.

In the following example, the reader uses a variety of sources related to the King passage (pp. 309–14) and brings them together around a central idea. Notice how quotation, paraphrase, and summary are all used.

Synthesis

When King defends his campaign of nonviolent direct action against the clergymen's criticism that "our actions, even though peaceful, must be condemned because they precipitate violence" (King excerpt, paragraph 3), he is using what Vinit Haksar calls Mohandas Gandhi's "safety-valve argument" ("Civil Disobedience and Non-Cooperation" 117). According to Haksar, Gandhi gave a "non-threatening warning of worse things to come" if his demands were not met. King similarly makes clear that advocates of actions more extreme than those he advocates are waiting in the wings: "The other force is one of bitterness and hatred, and it comes perilously close to advocating violence" (King excerpt, paragraph 5). King identifies this force with Elijah Muhammad, and although he does not name him, King's contemporary readers would have known that he was referring also to his disciple Malcolm X, who, according to Herbert J. Storing, "urged that Negroes take seriously the idea of revolution" ("The Case against Civil Disobedience" 90). In fact, Malcolm X accused King of being a modern-day Uncle Tom, trying "to keep us under control, to keep us passive and peaceful and nonviolent" (Malcolm X Speaks 12).

CHECKLIST: SYNTHESIZING

1. Find and read a variety of sources on your topic, annotating the passages that give you ideas about the topic.
2. Look for patterns among your sources, possibly supporting or challenging your ideas or those of other sources.
3. Write a paragraph or more synthesizing your sources, using quotation, paraphrase, and summary to present what they say on the topic.

■ Contextualizing

All texts reflect historical and cultural assumptions, values, and attitudes that may differ from your own. To read thoughtfully, you need to become aware of these differences. **Contextualizing** is a critical reading strategy that enables you to make inferences about a reading's historical and cultural context and to examine the differences between its context and your own.

The excerpt from King's "Letter from Birmingham Jail" is a good example of a text that benefits from being read contextually. If you knew little about the history of slavery and segregation in the United States, it would be difficult to understand the passion expressed in this passage. To understand the historical and cultural context in which King wrote his "letter from Birmingham Jail," you could do some library or Internet research. Comparing the situation at the time King wrote the "Letter" to situations with which you are familiar would help you understand some of your own attitudes toward King and the civil rights movement.

Here is what one reader wrote to contextualize King's writing:

Notes from a Contextualized Reading

1. I am not old enough to know what it was like in the early 1960s when Dr. King was leading marches and sit-ins, but I have seen television documentaries showing de monstrators being attacked by dogs, doused by fire hoses, beaten and dragged by helmeted police. Such images give me a sense of the violence, fear, and hatred that King was responding to.

    The tension King writes about comes across in his writing. He uses his anger and frustration creatively to inspire his critics. He also threatens them, although he denies it. I saw a film on Malcolm X, so I could see that King was giving white people a choice between his own nonviolent way and Malcolm's more confrontational way.

2. Things have certainly changed since the sixties. Legal segregation has ended, but there are still racists like the detective in the O. J. Simpson trial. African Americans like Condoleezza Rice and Barack Obama are highly respected and powerful. The civil rights movement is over. So when I'm reading King today, I feel like I'm reading history. But then again, every once in a while there are reports of police brutality because of race (think of Amadou Diallo) and of what we now call hate crimes.

CHECKLIST: CONTEXTUALIZING

1. Describe the historical and cultural situation as it is represented in the reading and in other sources with which you are familiar. Your knowledge may come from other reading, television or film, school, or elsewhere. (If you know nothing about the historical and cultural context, you could do some library or Internet research.)

2. Compare the historical and cultural situation in which the text was written with your own historical and cultural situation. Consider how your understanding and judgment of the reading are affected by your own context.

Exploring the Significance of Figurative Language

Figurative language — metaphor, simile, and symbolism — enhances literal meaning by implying abstract ideas through vivid images and by evoking feelings and associations.

Metaphor implicitly compares two different things by identifying them with each other. For instance, when King calls the white moderate "the Negro's great stumbling block in his stride toward freedom" (par. 1), he does not mean that the white moderate literally trips the Negro who is attempting to walk toward freedom. The sentence makes sense only if understood figuratively: The white moderate trips up the Negro by frustrating every effort to achieve justice.

Simile, a more explicit form of comparison, uses the word *like* or *as* to signal the relationship of two seemingly unrelated things. King uses simile when he says that injustice is "like a boil that can never be cured so long as it is covered up" (par. 2). This simile makes several points of comparison between injustice and a boil. It suggests that injustice is a disease of society as a boil is a disease of the skin and that injustice, like a boil, must be exposed or it will fester and infect the entire body.

Symbolism compares two things by making one stand for the other. King uses the white moderate as a symbol for supposed liberals and would-be supporters of civil rights who are actually frustrating the cause.

How these figures of speech are used in a text reveals something of the writer's feelings about the subject. Exploring possible meanings in a text's figurative language involves (1) annotating and then listing the metaphors, similes, and symbols you find in a reading; (2) grouping and labeling the figures of speech that appear to express related feelings or attitudes; and (3) writing to explore the meaning of the patterns you have found.

The following example shows the process of exploring figures of speech in the King excerpt.

Listing Figures of Speech

"stumbling block in his stride toward freedom" (paragraph 1)

"law and order . . . become the dangerously structured dams" (2)

"the flow of social progress" (2)

"Like a boil that can never be cured" (2)

"the light of human conscience and the air of national opinion" (2)

"the quicksand of racial injustice" (4)

Grouping and Labeling Figures of Speech

Sickness: "like a boil" (2); "the disease of segregation" (10)

Underground: "hidden tension" (2); "injustice must be exposed" (2); "injustice must be rooted out" (10)

Blockage: "dams," "block the flow" (2); "Human progress never rolls in on wheels of inevitability" (4); "pent-up resentments" (8); "repressed emotions" (8)

Writing to Explore Meaning

The patterns labeled underground and blockage suggest a feeling of frustration. Inertia is a problem; movement forward toward progress or upward toward the promised land is stalled. The strong need to break through the resistance may represent King's feelings about both his attempt to lead purposeful, effective demonstrations and his effort to write a convincing argument.

The simile of injustice being "like a boil" links the two patterns of underground and sickness, suggesting that something bad, a disease, is inside the people or the society. The cure is to expose or to root out the blocked hatred and injustice as well as to release the tension or emotion that has long been repressed. This implies that repression itself is the evil, not simply what is repressed. Therefore, writing and speaking out through political action may have curative power for individuals and society alike.

CHECKLIST: EXPLORING THE SIGNIFICANCE OF FIGURATIVE LANGUAGE

1. Annotate all the figures of speech you find in the reading—metaphors, similes, and symbols—and then list them.

2. Group the figures of speech that appear to express related feelings and attitudes, and label each group.

3. Write one or two paragraphs exploring the meaning of these patterns. What do they tell you about the text?

■ Looking for Patterns of Opposition

All texts carry within themselves voices of opposition. These **patterns of opposition** may echo the views and values of readers the writer anticipates or predecessors to whom the writer is responding in some way; they may even reflect the writer's own conflicting values. Careful readers look closely for such a dialogue of opposing voices within the text.

When we think of oppositions, we ordinarily think of polarities: *yes* and *no, up* and *down, black* and *white, new* and *old*. Some oppositions, however, may be more subtle. The excerpt from King's "Letter from Birmingham Jail" is rich in such oppositions: *moderate* versus *extremist, order* versus *justice, direct action* versus *passive acceptance, expression* versus *repression*. These oppositions are not accidental; they form a significant pattern that gives a reader important information about the essay.

A careful reading will show that King always values one of the two terms in an opposition over the other. In the passage, for example, *extremist* is valued over *moderate* (par. 9). This preference for extremism is surprising. The reader should ask why, when white extremists like members of the Ku Klux Klan have committed so many outrages against African Americans, King would prefer extremism. If King is trying to convince his readers to accept his point of view, why would he represent himself as an extremist? Moreover, why would a clergyman advocate extremism instead of moderation?

Studying the patterns of opposition enables you to answer these questions. You will see that King sets up this opposition to force his readers to examine their own values and realize that they are in fact misplaced. Instead of working toward justice, he says, those who support law and order maintain the unjust status quo. By getting his readers to think of white moderates as blocking rather than facilitating peaceful change, King brings readers to align themselves with him and perhaps even embrace his strategy of nonviolent resistance.

Looking for patterns of opposition involves annotating words or phrases in the reading that indicate oppositions, listing the opposing terms in pairs, deciding which term in each pair is preferred by the writer, and reflecting on the meaning of the patterns. Here is a partial list of oppositions from the King excerpt, with the preferred terms marked by an asterisk:

Listing Patterns of Opposition

moderate	*extremist
order	*justice
negative peace	*positive peace
absence of justice	*presence of justice
goals	*methods
*direct action	passive acceptance
*exposed tension	hidden tension

CHECKLIST: LOOKING FOR PATTERNS OF OPPOSITION

1. Annotate the selection for words or phrases indicating oppositions.

2. List the pairs of oppositions. (You may have to paraphrase or even supply the opposite word or phrase if it is not stated directly in the text.)

3. For each pair of oppositions, put an asterisk next to the term that the writer seems to value or prefer over the other.

4. Study the patterns of opposition. How do they contribute to your understanding of the essay? What do they tell you about what the author wants you to believe?

■ Reflecting on Challenges to Your Beliefs and Values

To read thoughtfully, you need to scrutinize your own assumptions and attitudes as well as those expressed in the text you are reading. If you are like most readers, however, you will find that your assumptions and attitudes are so ingrained that you are not always fully aware of them. A good strategy for getting at these underlying beliefs and values is to identify and reflect on the ways the text challenges you, how it makes you feel — disturbed, threatened, ashamed, combative, pleased, exuberant, or some other way.

For example, here is what one student wrote about the King passage:

Reflections

In paragraph 1, Dr. King criticizes people who are "more devoted to 'order' than to justice." This criticism upsets me because today I think I would choose order over justice.
When I reflect on my feelings and try to figure out where they come from, I realize that
what I feel most is fear. I am terrified by the violence in society today. I'm afraid of
sociopaths who don't respect the rule of law, much less the value of human life.

I know Dr. King was writing in a time when the law itself was unjust, when order
was apparently used to keep people from protesting and changing the law. But things
are different now. Today, justice seems to serve criminals more than it serves law-
abiding citizens. That's why I'm for order over justice.

CHECKLIST: REFLECTING ON CHALLENGES TO YOUR BELIEFS AND VALUES

1. Identify challenges by marking the text where you feel your beliefs and values are being
   opposed, criticized, or unfairly characterized.
2. Write a few paragraphs reflecting on why you feel challenged. Do not defend your feelings; instead, search your memory to discover where they come from.

Evaluating the Logic of an Argument

An argument includes a thesis backed by reasons and support. The *thesis* asserts a position on a controversial issue or a solution to a problem that the writer wants readers to
accept. The *reasons* tell readers why they should accept the thesis, and the *support* (such
as examples, statistics, authorities, and textual evidence) gives readers grounds for
accepting it. For an argument to be considered logically acceptable, it must meet the
three conditions of what we call the ABC test:

The ABC Test

A. The reasons and support must be *appropriate* to the thesis.

B. The reasons and support must be *believable*.

C. The reasons and support must be *consistent* with one another as well as *complete*.

For more on argument, see Chapter 11. For an example of the ABC test, see Christine
Romano's essay in Chapter 7, pp. 259–63.

Testing for Appropriateness

To evaluate the logic of an argument, you first decide whether the argument's reasons
and support are appropriate. To test for appropriateness, ask these questions: How does

each reason or piece of support relate to the thesis? Is the connection between reasons and support and the thesis clear and compelling?

Readers most often question the appropriateness of reasons and support when the writer argues by analogy or by invoking authority. For example, in paragraph 2, King argues that when law and order fail to establish justice, "they become the dangerously structured dams that block the flow of social progress." The analogy asserts the following logical relationship: Law and order are to progress toward justice what a dam is to water. If you do not accept this analogy, the argument fails the test of appropriateness.

King uses both analogy and authority in paragraph 3: "Isn't this like condemning Socrates because his unswerving commitment to truth and his philosophical inquiries precipitated the act by the misguided populace in which they made him drink hemlock?" Not only must you judge the appropriateness of the analogy comparing the Greeks' condemnation of Socrates to the white moderates' condemnation of King, but you must also judge whether it is appropriate to accept Socrates as an authority. Since Socrates is generally respected for his teaching on justice, his words and actions are likely to be considered appropriate to King's situation in Birmingham.

For invoking authorities, see Chapter 11, pp. 350–51.

Testing for Believability

Believability is a measure of your willingness to accept as true the reasons and support the writer gives in defense of a thesis.

To test for believability, ask: On what basis am I being asked to believe this reason or support is true? If it cannot be proved true or false, how much weight does it carry?

In judging facts, examples, statistics, and authorities, consider the following points.

Facts are statements that can be proved objectively to be true. The believability of facts depends on their *accuracy* (they should not distort or misrepresent reality), their *completeness* (they should not omit important details), and the *trustworthiness* of their sources (sources should be qualified and unbiased). King, for instance, asserts as fact that the African American will not wait much longer for racial justice (par. 8). His critics might question the factuality of this assertion by asking, is it true of all African Americans? How does King know what African Americans will and will not do?

Examples and *anecdotes* are particular instances that may or may not make you believe a general statement. The believability of examples depends on their *representativeness* (whether they are truly typical and thus generalizable) and their *specificity* (whether particular details make them seem true to life). Even if a vivid example or gripping anecdote does not convince readers, it usually strengthens argumentative writing by clarifying the meaning and dramatizing the point. In paragraph 5 of the King excerpt, for example, King supports his generalization that some African American extremists are motivated by bitterness and hatred by citing the specific example of Elijah Muhammad's Black Muslim movement. Conversely, in paragraph 9, he refers to Jesus, Paul, Luther, and others as examples of extremists motivated by love and

Christianity. These examples support his assertion that extremism is not in itself wrong and that any judgment of extremism must be based on its motivation and cause.

Statistics are numerical data. The believability of statistics depends on the *comparability* of the data (the price of apples in 1985 cannot be compared with the price of apples in 2006 unless the figures are adjusted to account for inflation), the *precision* of the methods employed to gather and analyze data (representative samples should be used and variables accounted for), and the *trustworthiness* of the sources.

Authorities are people to whom the writer attributes expertise on a given subject. Not only must such authorities be appropriate, as mentioned earlier, but they must be credible as well—that is, the reader must accept them as experts on the topic at hand. King cites authorities repeatedly throughout his essay. He refers to religious leaders (Jesus and Luther) as well as to American political leaders (Lincoln and Jefferson). These figures are likely to have a high degree of credibility among King's readers.

Testing for Consistency and Completeness

In looking for consistency, you should be concerned that all the parts of the argument work together and that they are sufficient to convince readers to accept the thesis or at least take it seriously. To test for consistency and completeness, ask: Are any of the reasons and support contradictory? Do they provide sufficient grounds for accepting the thesis? Does the writer fail to counterargue (to acknowledge, accommodate, or refute any opposing arguments or important objections)?

A thoughtful reader might regard as contradictory King's characterizing himself first as a moderate and later as an extremist opposed to the forces of violence. (King attempts to reconcile this apparent contradiction by explicitly redefining extremism in paragraph 9.) Similarly, the fact that King fails to examine and refute every legal recourse available to his cause might allow a critical reader to question the sufficiency of his argument.

CHECKLIST: EVALUATING THE LOGIC OF AN ARGUMENT

Use the ABC test:

A. *Test for appropriateness* by checking that the reasons and support are clearly and directly related to the thesis.

B. *Test for believability* by deciding whether you can accept the reasons and support as likely to be true.

C. *Test for consistency and completeness* by deciding whether the argument has any contradictions and whether any important objections or opposing arguments have been ignored.

■ Recognizing Emotional Manipulation

Writers often try to arouse emotions in readers to excite their interest, make them care, or move them to take action. There is nothing wrong with appealing to readers' emotions. What is wrong is manipulating readers with false or exaggerated appeals.

Therefore, you should be suspicious of writing that is overly sentimental, that cites alarming statistics and frightening anecdotes, that demonizes others and identifies itself with revered authorities, or that uses potent symbols (for example, the American flag) or emotionally loaded words (such as *racist*).

King, for example, uses the emotionally loaded word *paternalistically* to refer to the white moderate's belief that "he can set the timetable for another man's freedom" (par. 1). In the same paragraph, King uses symbolism to get an emotional reaction from readers when he compares the white moderate to the "Ku Klux Klanner." To get readers to accept his ideas, he also relies on authorities whose names evoke the greatest respect, such as Jesus and Lincoln. But some readers might object that comparing his own crusade to that of Jesus is pretentious and manipulative. A critical reader might also consider King's discussion of African American extremists in paragraph 7 to be a veiled threat designed to frighten readers into agreement.

CHECKLIST: RECOGNIZING EMOTIONAL MANIPULATION

1. Annotate places in the text where you sense emotional appeals are being used.
2. Assess whether any of the emotional appeals are unfairly manipulative.

■ Judging the Writer's Credibility

Writers try to persuade readers by presenting an image of themselves in their writing that will gain their readers' confidence. This image must be created indirectly, through the arguments, language, and system of values and beliefs expressed or implied in the writing. Writers establish credibility in their writing in three ways:

By showing their knowledge of the subject

By building common ground with readers

By responding fairly to objections and opposing arguments

Testing for Knowledge

Writers demonstrate their knowledge through the facts and statistics they marshal, the sources they rely on for information, and the scope and depth of their understanding. You may not be sufficiently expert on the subject yourself to know whether the facts are accurate, the sources are reliable, and the understanding is sufficient. You may need to do some research to see what others say about the subject. You can also check credentials — the writer's educational and professional qualifications, the respectability of the publication in which the selection first appeared, and reviews of the writer's work — to determine whether the writer is a respected authority in the field. For example, King brings with him the authority that comes from being a member of the clergy and a respected leader of the Southern Christian Leadership Conference.

Testing for Common Ground

One way writers can establish common ground with their readers is by basing their reasoning on shared values, beliefs, and attitudes. They use language that includes their readers (*we*) and qualify their assertions to keep them from being too extreme. Above all, they acknowledge differences of opinion. You want to notice such appeals.

King creates common ground with readers by using the inclusive pronoun *we*, suggesting shared concerns between himself and his audience. Notice, however, his use of masculine pronouns and other references ("the Negro . . . he," "our brothers"). Although King addressed his letter to male clergy, he intended it to be published in the local newspaper, where it would be read by an audience of both men and women. By using language that excludes women, a common practice at the time the selection was written, King may have missed the opportunity to build common ground with more than half of his readers.

Testing for Fairness

Writers reveal their character by how they handle opposing arguments and objections to their argument. As a critical reader, pay particular attention to how writers treat possible differences of opinion. Be suspicious of those who ignore differences and pretend that everyone agrees with their viewpoints. When objections or opposing views are represented, consider whether they have been distorted in any way; if they are refuted, be sure they are challenged fairly — with sound reasoning and solid support.

One way to gauge the author's credibility is to identify the tone of the argument, for it conveys the writer's attitude toward the subject and toward the reader. Is the text angry? Sarcastic? Evenhanded? Shrill? Condescending? Bullying? Do you feel as if the writer is treating the subject — and you, as a reader — with fairness? King's tone might be characterized in different passages as patient (he doesn't lose his temper), respectful (he refers to white moderates as "people of good will"), or pompous (comparing himself to Jesus and Socrates).

CHECKLIST: JUDGING THE WRITER'S CREDIBILITY

1. Annotate for the writer's knowledge of the subject, how well common ground is established, and whether the writer deals fairly with objections and opposing arguments.

2. Decide what in the essay you find credible and what you question.

Cueing the Reader 10

Readers need guidance. To guide readers through a piece of writing, a writer can provide five basic kinds of **cues**, or signals:

1. Thesis and forecasting statements, to orient readers to ideas and organization
2. Paragraphing, to group related ideas and details
3. Cohesive devices, to connect ideas to one another and bring about clarity
4. Connectives, to signal relationships or shifts in meaning
5. Headings and subheadings, to group related paragraphs and help readers locate specific information quickly

This chapter illustrates how each of these cueing strategies works.

Orienting Statements

To help readers find their way, especially in difficult and lengthy texts, you can provide two kinds of **orienting statements**: a thesis statement, which declares the main point, and a forecasting statement, which previews subordinate points, showing the order in which they will be discussed in the essay.

Thesis Statements

To help readers understand what is being said about a subject, writers often provide a thesis statement early in the essay. The **thesis statement** operates as a cue by letting readers know which is the most important general idea among the writer's many ideas and observations. In "Love: The Right Chemistry" in Chapter 4, Anastasia Toufexis expresses her thesis at the end of the second paragraph:

> O.K., let's cut out all this nonsense about romantic love. Let's bring some scientific precision to the party. Let's put love under a microscope.

When rigorous people with Ph.D.s after their names do that, what they see is not some silly, senseless thing. No, their probe reveals that love rests firmly on the foundations of evolution, biology and chemistry.

Readers naturally look for something that will tell them the point of an essay, a focus for the many diverse details and ideas they encounter as they read. They expect to find some information early on that will give them a context for reading the essay, particularly if they are reading about a new and difficult subject. Therefore, a thesis statement, like Toufexis's, placed at the beginning of an essay enables readers to anticipate the content of the essay and helps them understand the relationships among its various ideas and details.

Occasionally, however, particularly in fairly short, informal essays, a writer may save a direct statement of the thesis until the conclusion. Writers also often reinstate the thesis at the end to bring together the various strands of information or supporting details introduced over the course of the essay.

EXERCISE 10.1

In the essay by Jessica Statsky in Chapter 5, underline the thesis statement, the last sentence in paragraph 1. Notice the key terms: "overzealous parents and coaches," "impose adult standards," "children's sports," "activities . . . neither satisfying nor beneficial." Then skim the essay, stopping to read the sentence at the beginning of each paragraph. Also read the last paragraph.

Consider whether the idea in every paragraph's first sentence is anticipated by the thesis's key terms. Consider also the connection between the ideas in the last paragraph and the thesis's key terms. What can you conclude about how a thesis might assert the point of an essay, anticipate the ideas that follow, and help readers relate the ideas to each other?

Forecasting Statements

Some thesis statements include **a forecast**, which overviews the way a thesis will be developed, as in the following example.

> In the three years from 1348 through 1350 the pandemic of plague known as the Black Death, or, as the Germans called it, the Great Dying, killed at least a fourth of the population of Europe. It was undoubtedly the worst disaster that has ever befallen mankind. Today we can have no real conception of the terror under which people lived in the shadow of the plague. For more than two centuries plague has not been a serious threat to mankind in the large, although it is still a grisly presence in parts of the Far East and Africa. Scholars continue to study the Great Dying, however, as a historical example of human behavior under the stress of universal catastrophe. In these days when the threat of plague has been replaced by the threat of mass human extermination by even more rapid means, there has been a sharp renewal of interest in the history of the fourteenth-century calamity. With new perspective, students are investigating its manifold effects: demographic, economic, psychological, moral and religious.
>
> —WILLIAM LANGER, "The Black Death"

This introductory paragraph informs us that Langer's article is about the effects of the Black Death. His thesis (highlighted) states that there is renewed interest in studying the social effects of the bubonic plague and forecasts the five main categories of effects of the Black Death that his essay will examine. As a reader would expect, Langer divides his essay into explanations of the research into these five effects, addressing them in the order in which they appear in the forecasting statement.

EXERCISE 10.2

Turn to Linh Kieu Ngo's essay in Chapter 4, and underline the forecasting statement in paragraph 6. Then skim the essay. Notice whether Ngo takes up every point he mentions in the forecasting statement and whether he sticks to the order he promises readers. How well does his forecasting statement help you follow his essay? What suggestions for improvement, if any, would you offer him?

Paragraphing

Paragraph cues as obvious as indentation keep readers on track. You can also arrange material in a paragraph to help readers see what is important or significant. For example, you can begin with a topic sentence, help readers see the relationship between the previous paragraph and the present one with an explicit transition, and place the most important information toward the end.

Paragraph Cues

One **paragraph cue**—the indentation that signals the beginning of a new paragraph—is a relatively modern printing convention. Old manuscripts show that paragraph divisions were not always marked. To make reading easier, scribes and printers began to use the symbol ¶ to mark paragraph breaks, and later, indenting became common practice. Even that relatively modern custom, however, has been abandoned by most business writers, who now distinguish one paragraph from another by leaving a line of space above and below each paragraph. Writing on the Internet is also usually paragraphed in this way.

Paragraphing helps readers by signaling when a sequence of related ideas begins and ends. Paragraphing also helps readers judge what is most important in what they are reading. Writers typically emphasize important information by placing it at the two points in the paragraph where readers are most attentive—the beginning and the end.

You can give special emphasis to information by placing it in its own paragraph.

EXERCISE 10.3

Turn to Patrick O'Malley's essay in Chapter 6, and read paragraphs 4–6 with the following questions in mind: Does all the material in each paragraph seem to be related? Do you feel a sense of closure at the end of each paragraph? Does the last sentence offer the most important or significant or weighty information in the paragraph?

Topic Sentence Strategies

A **topic sentence** lets readers know the focus of a paragraph in simple and direct terms. It is a cueing strategy for the paragraph, much as a thesis or forecasting statement is for the whole essay. Because paragraphing usually signals a shift in focus, readers expect some kind of reorientation in the opening sentence. They need to know whether the new paragraph will introduce another aspect of the topic or develop one already introduced.

Announcing the Topic.   Some topic sentences simply announce the topic. Here are some examples taken from Barry Lopez's book *Arctic Dreams*:

> A polar bear walks in a way all its own.

> What is so consistently striking about the way Eskimos used parts of an animal is the breadth of their understanding about what would work.

> The Mediterranean view of the Arctic, down to the time of the Elizabethan mariners, was shaped by two somewhat contradictory thoughts.

Lopez's topic sentences identify topics and also indicate how they will be developed in subsequent sentences. The following paragraph shows how one of his topic sentences (highlighted) is developed:

> What is so consistently striking about the way Eskimos used parts of an animal is the breadth of their understanding about what would work. Knowing that muskox horn is more flexible than caribou antler, they preferred it for making the side prongs of a fish spear. For a waterproof bag in which to carry sinews for clothing repair, they chose salmon skin. They selected the strong, translucent intestine of a bearded seal to make a window for a snowhouse — it would fold up for easy traveling and it would not frost over in cold weather. To make small snares for sea ducks, they needed a springy material that would not rot in salt water — baleen fibers. The down feather of a common eider, tethered at the end of a stick in the snow at an angle, would reveal the exhalation of a quietly surfacing seal. Polar bear bone was used anywhere a stout, sharp point was required, because it is the hardest bone.   — BARRY LOPEZ, *Arctic Dreams*

EXERCISE 10.4

Turn to Jessica Statsky's essay in Chapter 5. Underline the topic sentence (the first sentence) in paragraphs 3 and 5. Consider how these sentences help you anticipate the paragraph's topic and method of development.

Making a Transition.   Not all topic sentences simply point to what will follow. Some also refer to earlier sentences. Such sentences work both as topic sentences, stating the main point of the paragraph, and as transitions, linking that paragraph to the previous one. Here are a few topic sentences from "Quilts and Women's Culture," by Elaine Hedges, with transitions highlighted:

> Within its broad traditionalism and anonymity, however, variations and distinctions developed.

> Regionally, too, distinctions were introduced into quilt making through the interesting process of renaming.

Finally, out of such regional and other variations come individual, signed achievements.

Quilts, then, were an outlet for creative energy, a source and emblem of sisterhood and solidarity, and a graphic response to historical and political change.

Sometimes the first sentence of a paragraph serves as a transition, and a subsequent sentence states the topic, as in the following example:

> . . . What a convenience, what a relief it will be, they say, never to worry about how to dress for a job interview, a romantic tryst, or a funeral!
>
> Convenient, perhaps, but not exactly a relief. Such a utopia would give most of us the same kind of chill we feel when a stadium full of Communist-bloc athletes in identical sports outfits, shouting slogans in unison, appears on TV. Most people do not want to be told what to wear any more than they want to be told what to say. In Belfast recently four hundred Irish Republican prisoners "refused to wear any clothes at all, draping themselves day and night in blankets," rather than put on prison uniforms. Even the offer of civilian-style dress did not satisfy them; they insisted on wearing their own clothes brought from home, or nothing. Fashion is free speech, and one of the privileges, if not always one of the pleasures, of a free world.
>
> — ALISON LURIE, *The Language of Clothes*

Occasionally, whole paragraphs serve as transitions, linking one sequence of paragraphs with those that follow, as below:

> Yet it was not all contrast, after all. Different as they were — in background, in personality, in underlying aspiration — these two great soldiers had much in common. Under everything else, they were marvelous fighters. Furthermore, their fighting qualities were really very much alike.
>
> — BRUCE CATTON, "Grant and Lee: A Study in Contrasts"

This transition paragraph summarizes the contrasts between Grant and Lee and sets up an analysis of the similarities of the two men.

EXERCISE 10.5

Turn to the Karen Stabiner essay in Chapter 5 and read paragraphs 3–7. As you read, underline the part of the first sentence in paragraphs 4–7 that refers to the previous paragraph, creating a transition from one to the next. Notice the different ways Stabiner creates these transitions. Consider whether they are all equally effective.

Positioning the Topic Sentence.   Although topic sentences may occur anywhere in a paragraph, stating the topic in the first sentence has the advantage of giving readers a sense of how the paragraph is likely to be developed. The beginning of the paragraph is therefore the most common position.

A topic sentence that does not open a paragraph is most likely to appear at the end. When a topic sentence concludes a paragraph, it usually summarizes or generalizes preceding information:

> Even black Americans sometimes need to be reminded about the deceptiveness of television. Blacks retain their fascination with black characters on TV: Many of us buy *Jet* magazine primarily to read its weekly television feature, which lists every black

character (major or minor) to be seen on the screen that week. Yet our fixation with the presence of black characters on TV has blinded us to an important fact that *Cosby*, which began in 1984, and its offshoots over the years demonstrate convincingly: There is very little connection between the social status of black Americans and the fabricated images of black people that Americans consume each day. The representation of blacks on TV is a very poor index to our social advancement or political progress.

— Henry Louis Gates Jr., "TV's Black World Turns—but Stays Unreal"

When a topic sentence is used in a narrative, it often appears as the last sentence as a way to evaluate or reflect on events:

A cold sun was sliding down a gray fall sky. Some older boys had been playing tackle football in the field we took charge of every weekend. In a few years, they'd be called to Southeast Asia, some of them. Their locations would be tracked with pushpins in red, white, and blue on maps on nearly every kitchen wall. But that afternoon, they were quick as young deer. They leapt and dodged, dove from each other and collided in midair. Bulletlike passes flew to connect them. Or the ball spiraled in a high arc across the frosty sky one to another. In short, they were mindlessly agile in a way that captured as audience every little kid within running distance of the yellow goalposts.

— Mary Karr, *Cherry*

It is possible for a single topic sentence to introduce two or more paragraphs. Subsequent paragraphs in such a sequence have no separate topic sentences of their own:

Anthropologists Daniel Maltz and Ruth Borker point out that boys and girls socialize differently. Little girls tend to play in small groups or, even more common, in pairs. Their social life usually centers around a best friend, and friendships are made, maintained, and broken by talk—especially "secrets." If a little girl tells her friend's secret to another little girl, she may find herself with a new best friend. The secrets themselves may or may not be important, but the fact of telling them is all-important. It's hard for newcomers to get into these tight groups, but anyone who is admitted is treated as an equal. Girls like to play cooperatively; if they can't cooperate, the group breaks up.

Little boys tend to play in larger groups, often outdoors, and they spend more time doing things than talking. It's easy for boys to get into the group, but not everyone is accepted as an equal. Once in the group, boys must jockey for their status in it. One of the most important ways they do this is through talk: verbal display such as telling stories and jokes, challenging and sidetracking the verbal displays of other boys, and withstanding other boys' challenges in order to maintain their own story—and status. Their talk is often competitive talk about who is best at what.

— Deborah Tannen, *That's Not What I Meant!*

EXERCISE 10.6

Consider the variety and effectiveness of the topic sentences in your most recent essay. Begin by underlining the topic sentence in each paragraph after the first one. The topic sentence may not be the first sentence in a paragraph, though often it will be.

Then double-underline the part of the topic sentence that provides an explicit transition from one paragraph to the next. You may find a transition that is separate from the topic sentence. You may not always find a topic sentence.

Reflect on your topic sentences, and evaluate how well they serve to orient your readers to the sequence of topics or ideas in your essay.

Cohesive Devices

Cohesive devices guide readers, helping them follow your train of thought by connecting key words and phrases throughout a passage. Among such devices are pronoun reference, word repetition, synonyms, repetition of sentence structure, and collocation.

Pronoun Reference

One common cohesive device is **pronoun reference**. As noun substitutes, pronouns refer to nouns that either precede or follow them and thus serve to connect phrases or sentences. The nouns that come before the pronouns are called *antecedents*.

> In New York from dawn to dusk to dawn, day after day, you can hear the steady rumble of tires against the concrete span of the George Washington Bridge. The bridge is never completely still. It trembles with traffic. It moves in the wind. Its great veins of steel swell when hot and contract when cold; its span often is ten feet closer to the Hudson River in summer than in winter.   — GAY TALESE, "New York"

This example has only one pronoun-antecedent chain, and the antecedent comes first, so all the pronouns refer back to it. When there are multiple pronoun-antecedent chains with references forward as well as back, writers have to make sure that readers will not mistake one pronoun's antecedent for another's.

Word Repetition

To avoid confusion, writers often use **word repetition.** The device of repeating words and phrases is especially helpful if a pronoun might confuse readers:

> Some odd optical property of our highly polarized and unequal society makes the poor almost invisible to their economic superiors. The poor can see the affluent easily enough—on television, for example, or on the covers of magazines. But the affluent rarely see the poor or, if they do catch sight of them in some public space, rarely know what they're seeing, since—thanks to consignment stores and, yes, Wal-Mart—the poor are usually able to disguise themselves as members of the more comfortable classes.   — BARBARA EHRENREICH, *Nickel and Dimed*

In the next example, several overlapping chains of word repetition prevent confusion and help the reader follow the ideas:

> Natural selection is the central concept of Darwinian theory—the fittest survive and spread their favored traits through populations. Natural selection is defined by Spencer's phrase "survival of the fittest," but what does this famous bit of jargon really

mean? Who are the fittest? And how is "fitness" defined? We often read that fitness involves no more than "differential reproductive success"—the production of more surviving offspring than other competing members of the population. Whoa! cries Bethell, as many others have before him. This formulation defines fitness in terms of survival only. The crucial phrase of natural selection means no more than "the survival of those who survive"—a vacuous tautology. (A tautology is a phrase—like "my father is a man"—containing no information in the predicate ["a man"] not inherent in the subject ["my father"]. Tautologies are fine as definitions, but not as testable scientific statements—there can be nothing to test in a statement true by definition.)

— STEPHEN JAY GOULD, *Ever Since Darwin*

Synonyms

In addition to word repetition, you can use **synonyms**, words with identical or very similar meanings, to connect important ideas. In the following example, the author develops a careful chain of synonyms and word repetitions:

> Over time, small bits of knowledge about a region accumulate among local residents in the form of stories. These are remembered in the community; even what is unusual does not become lost and therefore irrelevant. These narratives comprise for a native an intricate, long-term view of a particular landscape. . . . Outside the region this complex but easily shared "reality" is hard to get across without reducing it to generalities, to misleading or imprecise abstraction. — BARRY LOPEZ, *Arctic Dreams*

Note the variety of synonym sequences:

"region," "particular landscape"

"local residents," "native"

"stories," "narratives"

"accumulate," "are remembered," "does not become lost"

"intricate, long-term view," "complex . . . reality"

The result is a coherent paragraph that constantly reinforces the author's point.

Sentence Structure Repetition

Writers occasionally use **sentence structure repetition** to emphasize the connections among their ideas, as in this example, in which Asimov repeats the same if/[then] sentence structure to show the relationship between his ideas.

> But the life forms are as much part of the structure of the Earth as any inanimate portion is. It is all an inseparable part of a whole. If any animal is isolated totally from other forms of life, then death by starvation will surely follow. If isolated from water, death by dehydration will follow even faster. If isolated from air, whether free or dissolved in water, death by asphyxiation will follow still faster. If isolated from the Sun, animals will survive for a time, but plants would die, and if all plants died, all animals would starve.
>
> — ISAAC ASIMOV, "The Case against Man"

Collocation

Collocation—the positioning of words together in expected ways around a particular topic—occurs quite naturally to writers and usually forms recognizable networks of meaning for readers. For example, in a paragraph on a high school graduation, a reader might expect to encounter such words as *valedictorian, diploma, commencement, honors, cap* and *gown,* and *senior class.* The paragraph that follows uses five collocation chains:

housewife, cooking, neighbor, home

clocks, calculated, progression, precise

obstinacy, vagaries, problem

sun, clear days, cloudy ones, sundial, cast its light, angle, seasons, sun, weather

cooking, fire, matches, hot coals, smoldering, ashes, go out, bed-warming pan

The seventeenth-century housewife not only had to make do without thermometers, she also had to make do without clocks, which were scarce and dear throughout the sixteen hundreds. She calculated cooking times by the progression of the sun; her cooking must have been more precise on clear days than on cloudy ones. Marks were sometimes painted on the floor, providing her with a rough sundial, but she still had to make allowance for the obstinacy of the sun in refusing to cast its light at the same angle as the seasons changed; but she was used to allowing for the vagaries of sun and weather. She also had a problem starting her fire in the morning; there were no matches. If she had allowed the hot coals smoldering under the ashes to go out, she had to borrow some from a neighbor, carrying them home with care, perhaps in a bed-warming pan.
— WAVERLY ROOT AND RICHARD DE ROUCHEMENT, *Eating in America*

EXERCISE 10.7

Now that you know more about pronoun reference, word repetition, synonyms, sentence structure repetition, and collocation, turn to Brian Cable's essay in Chapter 3 and identify the cohesive devices you find in paragraphs 1–4. Underline each cohesive device you can find; there will be many. You might also want to connect with lines the various pronoun, related-word, and synonym chains you find. You could also try listing the separate collocation chains. Consider how these cohesive devices help you read and make sense of the passage.

EXERCISE 10.8

Choose one of your recent essays, and select any three contiguous paragraphs. Underline every cohesive device you can find; there will be many. Try to connect with lines the various pronoun, related-word, and synonym chains you find. Also try listing the separate collocation chains.

You will be surprised and pleased at how extensively you rely on cohesive ties. Indeed, you could not produce readable text without cohesive ties. Consider these questions relevant to your development as a writer: Are all of your pronoun references clear? Are you straining for synonyms when repeated words would do? Do you ever repeat sentence structures to emphasize connections? Do you trust yourself to put collocation to work?

■ Connectives

A **connective** serves as a bridge to connect one paragraph, sentence, clause, or word with another. It also identifies the kind of connection by indicating to readers how the item preceding the connective relates to the one that follows it. Connectives help readers anticipate how the next paragraph or sentence will affect the meaning of what they have just read. There are three basic groups of connectives, based on the relationships they indicate: logical, temporal, and spatial.

Logical Relationships

Connectives help readers follow the **logical relationships** within an argument. How such connectives work is illustrated in this tightly and passionately reasoned paragraph by James Baldwin:

> The black man insists, by whatever means he finds at his disposal, that the white man cease to regard him as an exotic rarity and recognize him as a human being. This is a very charged and difficult moment, for there is a great deal of will power involved in the white man's naïveté. Most people are not naturally malicious, and the white man prefers to keep the black man at a certain human remove because it is easier for him thus to preserve his simplicity and to avoid being called to account for crimes committed by his forefathers, or his neighbors. He is inescapably aware, nevertheless, that he is in a better position in the world than black men are, nor can he quite put to death the suspicion that he is hated by black men therefore. He does not wish to be hated, neither does he wish to change places, and at this point in his uneasiness he can scarcely avoid having recourse to those legends which white men have created about black men, the most unusual effect of which is that the white man finds himself enmeshed, so to speak, in his own language which describes hell, as well as the attributes which lead one to hell, as being black as night.   — JAMES BALDWIN, "Stranger in the Village"

Connectives Showing Logical Relationships

- *To introduce another item in a series:* first, second; in the second place; for one thing . . . , for another; next; then; furthermore; moreover; in addition; finally; last; also; similarly; besides; and; as well as
- *To introduce an illustration or other specification:* in particular; specifically; for instance; for example; that is; namely
- *To introduce a result or a cause:* consequently; as a result; hence; accordingly; thus; so; therefore; then; because; since; for
- *To introduce a restatement:* that is; in other words; in simpler terms; to put it differently
- *To introduce a conclusion or summary:* in conclusion; finally; all in all; evidently; clearly; actually; to sum up; altogether; of course
- *To introduce an opposing point:* but; however; yet; nevertheless; on the contrary; on the other hand; in contrast; still; neither; nor

- *To introduce a concession to an opposing view:* certainly; naturally; of course; it is true; to be sure; granted
- *To resume the original line of reasoning after a concession:* nonetheless; all the same; even though; still; nevertheless

Temporal Relationships

In addition to showing logical connections, connectives may indicate **temporal relationships**—a sequence or progression in time—as this example illustrates:

> That night, we drank tea and then vodka with lemon peel steeped in it. The four of us talked in Russian and English about mutual friends and American railroads and the Rolling Stones. Seryozha loves the Stones, and his face grew wistful as we spoke about their recent album, *Some Girls*. He played a tape of "Let It Bleed" over and over, until we could translate some difficult phrases for him; after that, he came out with the phrases at intervals during the evening, in a pretty decent imitation of Jagger's Cockney snarl. He was an adroit and oddly formal host, inconspicuously filling our teacups and politely urging us to eat bread and cheese and chocolate. While he talked to us, he teased Anya, calling her "Piglet," and she shook back her bangs and glowered at him. It was clear that theirs was a fiery relationship. After a while, we talked about ourselves. Anya told us about painting and printmaking and about how hard it was to buy supplies in Moscow. There had been something angry in her dark face since the beginning of the evening; I thought at first that it meant she didn't like Americans; but now I realized that it was a constant, barely suppressed rage at her own situation.
>
> — ANDREA LEE, *Russian Journal*

Connectives Showing Temporal Relationships

- *To indicate frequency:* frequently; hourly; often; occasionally; now and then; day after day; every so often; again and again
- *To indicate duration:* during; briefly; for a long time; minute by minute; while
- *To indicate a particular time:* now; then; at that time; in those days; last Sunday; next Christmas; in 2003; at the beginning of August; at six o'clock; first thing in the morning; two months ago; when
- *To indicate the beginning:* at first; in the beginning; since; before then
- *To indicate the middle:* in the meantime; meanwhile; as it was happening; at that moment; at the same time; simultaneously; next; then
- *To indicate the end and beyond:* eventually; finally; at last; in the end; subsequently; later; afterward

Spatial Relationships

Connectives showing **spatial relationships** orient readers to the objects in a scene, as illustrated in these paragraphs:

On Georgia 155, I crossed Troublesome Creek, then went through groves of pecan trees aligned one with the next like fenceposts. The pastures grew a green almost blue, and syrupy water the color of a dusty sunset filled the ponds. Around the farmhouses, from wires strung high above the ground, swayed gourds hollowed out for purple martins.

The land rose again on the other side of the Chattahoochee River, and Highway 34 went to the ridgetops where long views over the hills opened in all directions. Here was the tail of the Appalachian backbone, its gradual descent to the Gulf. Near the Alabama stateline stood a couple of LAST CHANCE! bars. . . .

— WILLIAM LEAST HEAT MOON, *Blue Highways*

Connectives Showing Spatial Relationships

- *To indicate closeness:* close to; near; next to; alongside; adjacent to; facing
- *To indicate distance:* in the distance; far; beyond; away; there
- *To indicate direction:* up/down; sideways; along; across; to the right/left; in front of/behind; above/below; inside/outside; toward/away from

EXERCISE 10.9

Turn to Rick Bragg's essay in Chapter 2. Relying on the lists of connectives just given, underline the *logical* and *temporal* connectives in paragraphs 1–6. Consider how the connectives relate the ideas and events from sentence to sentence. Suggest any further connectives that could be added to make the relationships even clearer.

EXERCISE 10.10

Select a recent essay of your own. Choose at least three paragraphs, and underline the logical, temporal, and spatial connectives. Depending on the kind of writing you were doing, you may find few, if any, connectives in one category or another. For example, an essay speculating about causes may not include any spatial connectives; writing about a remembered event might not contain connectives showing logical relationships.

Consider how your connectives relate the ideas from sentence to sentence. Compare your connectives with those in the lists in this text. Do you find that you are making full use of the repertoire? Do you find gaps between any of your sentences that a well-chosen connective would close?

Headings and Subheadings

Headings and subheadings — brief phrases set off from the text in various ways — can provide visible cues to readers about the content and organization of a text. Headings can be distinguished from text in numerous ways, including the selective use of capital letters, bold or italic type, or different sizes of type. To be most helpful to readers, headings should be phrased similarly and follow a predictable system.

Heading Systems and Levels

In this chapter, the headings in the section Paragraphing, beginning on p. 333, provide a good example of a system of headings that can readily be outlined:

◼ Paragraphing

Paragraph Cues

Topic Sentence Strategies

Announcing the Topic.

Making a Transition.

Positioning the Topic Sentence.

Notice that in this example, the heading system has three levels. The first-level heading sits on its own line, includes a design element (a yellow square), and is set in a large, colored (blue) font; this heading stands out most visibly among the others. (It is one of five such headings in this chapter.) The second-level heading also sits on its own line, but it includes no design element and is set in a smaller font (also blue). The first of these second-level headings has no subheadings beneath it, while the second has three. These third-level headings, in black, do not sit on their own lines — they run into the paragraph they introduce, as you can see if you turn back to pp. 333–35

All of these headings follow a parallel grammatical structure: nouns at the first level; nouns at the second level ("cues" and "strategies"); and "-ing" nouns at the third level.

Headings and Genres

Headings may not be necessary in short essays: thesis statements, forecasting statements, well-positioned topic sentences, and transition sentences may be all the cues the reader needs. Headings are rare in some genres, such as essays about remembered events (Chapter 2) and essays profiling people and places (Chapter 3). Headings appear more frequently in genres such as concept explanations, position papers, public policy proposals, and evaluations (Chapters 4–7).

Frequency and Placement of Headings

Before dividing their essays into sections with headings and subheadings, writers need to make sure their discussion is detailed enough to support at least one heading at each level. The frequency and placement of headings depend entirely on the content and how it is divided and organized. Keep in mind that headings do not reduce the need for other cues to keep readers on track.

EXERCISE 10.11

Turn to Gian-Claudia Sciara's essay in Chapter 6 and survey that essay's system of headings. If you have not read the essay, read or skim it now. Consider how Sciara's headings help readers anticipate what is coming and how the argument is organized. Decide whether the headings substitute for or complement other cues for keeping readers on track. Consider whether the headings are grammatically parallel.

EXERCISE 10.12

Select one of your essays that might benefit from headings. Develop a system of headings, and insert them where appropriate. Be prepared to justify your headings in light of the discussion about headings in this section.

Arguing

11

This chapter presents the basic strategies for making arguments in writing. In it, we focus on asserting a thesis, backing it up with reasons and support, and anticipating readers' questions and objections.

Asserting a Thesis

Central to any argument is the **thesis**. In a sentence or two, a thesis asserts or states the main point of any argument you want to make. It can be assertive only if you make it clear and direct. The thesis statement usually appears at the beginning of an argument essay.

There are three kinds of argument essays in Part One of this book. Each of these essays requires a special kind of assertion and reasoning:

- *Assertion of opinion:* What is your position on a controversial issue? (Chapter 5, "Arguing a Position")

  When overzealous parents and coaches impose adult standards on children's sports, the result can be activities that are neither satisfying nor beneficial to children.
  — JESSICA STATSKY, "Children Need to Play, Not Compete"

- *Assertion of policy:* What is your understanding of a problem, and what do you think should be done to solve it? (Chapter 6, "Proposing a Solution")

  Although this last-minute anxiety about midterm and final exams is only too familiar to most college students, many professors may not realize how such major, infrequent, high-stakes exams work against the best interests of students both psychologically and intellectually. . . . If professors gave additional brief exams at frequent intervals, students would be spurred to study more regularly, learn more, worry less, and perform better.
  — PATRICK O'MALLEY, "More Testing, More Learning"

- *Assertion of evaluation:* What is your judgment of a subject? (Chapter 7, "Justifying an Evaluation")

  Overall, the Web site is well designed, amusing, and extremely helpful.
  — WENDY KIM, "Grading Professors"

As these different thesis statements indicate, the kind of thesis you assert depends on the occasion for which you are writing and the question you are trying to answer for your readers. Whatever the writing situation, to be effective, every thesis must satisfy the same three standards: It must be *arguable, clear,* and *appropriately qualified.*

Arguable Assertions

Reasoned argument is called for when informed people disagree over an issue or remain divided over how best to solve a problem, as is so often the case in social and political life. Hence the thesis statements in reasoned arguments make **arguable assertions**—possibilities or probabilities, not certainties.

Therefore, a statement of fact could not be an arguable thesis statement because facts are easy to verify—whether by checking an authoritative reference book, asking an authority, or observing the fact with your own eyes. For example, these statements assert facts:

Jem has a Ph.D. in history.

I am less than five feet tall.

Eucalyptus trees were originally imported into California from Australia.

Each of these assertions can be easily verified. To find out Jem's academic degree, you can ask him, among other things. To determine a person's height, you can use a tape measure. To discover where California got its eucalyptus trees, you can refer to a source in the library. There is no point in arguing such statements (though you might question the authority of a particular source or the accuracy of someone's measurement). If a writer asserts something as fact and attempts to support the assertion with authorities or statistics, the resulting essay is not an argument but a report.

Like facts, expressions of personal feelings are not arguable assertions. Whereas facts are unarguable because they can be definitively proved true or false, feelings are unarguable because they are purely subjective.

You can declare, for example, that you detest eight o'clock classes, but you cannot offer an argument to support this assertion. All you can do is explain why you feel as you do. If, however, you were to restate the assertion as "Eight o'clock classes are counterproductive," you could then construct an argument that does not depend solely on your subjective feelings, memories, or preferences. Your argument could be based on reasons and support that apply to others as well as to yourself. For example, you might argue that students' ability to learn is at an especially low ebb immediately after breakfast and provide scientific support for this assertion—in addition, perhaps, to personal experience and reports of interviews with your friends.

Clear and Precise Wording

The way a thesis is worded is as important as its arguability. The wording of a thesis, especially its key terms, must be clear and precise.

Consider the following assertion: "Democracy is a way of life." The meaning of this claim is uncertain, partly because the word *democracy* is abstract and partly because the phrase *way of life* is inexact. Abstract ideas like democracy, freedom, and patriotism are by their very nature hard to grasp, and they become even less clear with overuse. Too often, such words take on connotations that may obscure the meaning you want to emphasize. *Way of life* is fuzzy: What does it mean? Does it refer to daily life, to a general philosophy or attitude toward life, or to something else?

Thus a thesis is vague if its meaning is unclear; it is ambiguous if it has more than one possible meaning. For example, the statement "My English instructor is mad" can be understood in two ways: The teacher is either angry or insane. Obviously, these are two very different assertions. You would not want readers to think you mean one when you actually mean the other.

Whenever you write argument, you should pay special attention to the way you phrase your thesis and take care to avoid vague and ambiguous language.

Appropriate Qualification

In addition to being arguable and clear, an argument thesis must make **appropriate qualifications** that suit your writing situation. If you are confident that your case is so strong that readers will accept your argument without question, state your thesis emphatically and unconditionally. If, however, you expect readers to challenge your assumptions or conclusions, you must qualify your statement. Qualifying a thesis makes it more likely that readers will take it seriously. Expressions like *probably, very likely, apparently,* and *it seems* all serve to qualify a thesis.

EXERCISE 11.1

Write an assertion of opinion that states your position on one of the following controversial issues:

Should English be the official language of the United States and the only language used in local, state, and federal governments' oral and written communications?

Should teenagers be required to get their parents' permission to obtain birth control information and contraceptives?

Should high schools or colleges require students to perform community service as a condition for graduation?

Should girls and boys be treated differently by their families or schools?

Should businesses remain loyal to their communities, or should they move wherever labor costs, taxes, or other conditions are more favorable?

These issues are complicated and have been debated for a long time. Constructing a persuasive argument would obviously require careful deliberation and research. For this exercise, however, all you need to do is construct an arguable, clear, and appropriately qualified thesis.

EXERCISE 11.2

Find the thesis in one of the argument essays in Chapters 5–7. Then decide whether the thesis meets the three requirements: that it be arguable, clear, and appropriately qualified.

EXERCISE 11.3

If you have written or are currently working on one of the argument assignments in Chapters 5–7, consider whether your essay thesis is assertive, arguable, and appropriately qualified. If you believe it does not meet these requirements, revise it appropriately.

■ Giving Reasons and Support

Whether you are arguing a position, proposing a solution, justifying an evaluation, or speculating about causes, you need to give **reasons and support** for your thesis.

Think of reasons as the main points supporting your thesis. Often they answer the question "Why do you think so?" For example, if you assert among friends that you value a certain movie highly, one of your friends might ask, "Why do you like it so much?" And you might answer, "*Because* it has challenging ideas, unusual camera work, and memorable acting." Similarly, you might oppose restrictions on students' use of offensive language at your college *because* such restrictions would make students reluctant to enter into frank debates, *because* offensive speech is hard to define, and *because* restrictions violate the free-speech clause of the First Amendment. These *because* phrases are your reasons. You may have one or many reasons, depending on your subject and your writing situation.

For your argument to succeed with your readers, you must not only give reasons but also support your reasons. The main kinds of support writers use are examples, statistics, authorities, anecdotes, and textual evidence. Following is a discussion and illustration of each kind of support, along with standards for judging their reliability.

Examples

Examples may be used as support in all types of arguments. For examples to be believable and convincing, they must be representative (typical of all the relevant examples you might have chosen), consistent with the experience of your readers (familiar to them and not extreme), and adequate in number (numerous enough to be convincing and yet not likely to overwhelm readers).

The following illustration comes from a book on illiteracy in America by Jonathan Kozol, a prominent educator and writer.

> Illiterates cannot read the menu in a restaurant.
> They cannot read the cost of items on the menu in the window of the restaurant before they enter.

Illiterates cannot read the letters that their children bring home from their teachers. They cannot study school department circulars that tell them of the courses that their children must be taking if they hope to pass the SAT exams. They cannot help with homework. They cannot write a letter to the teacher. They are afraid to visit in the classroom. They do not want to humiliate their child or themselves.

Illiterates cannot read instructions on a bottle of prescription medicine. They cannot find out when a medicine is past the year of safe consumption; nor can they read of allergenic risks, warnings to diabetics, or the potential sedative effect of certain kinds of nonprescription pills. They cannot observe preventive health care admonitions. They cannot read about "the seven warning signs of cancer" or the indications of blood-sugar fluctuations or the risks of eating certain foods that aggravate the likelihood of cardiac arrest.   — JONATHAN KOZOL, *Illiterate America*

Kozol collected these examples in his many interviews with people who could neither read nor write. Though all of his readers are literate and have never experienced the frustrations of adult illiterates, Kozol assumes they will accept that the experiences are a familiar part of illiterates' lives. Most readers will believe the experiences to be neither atypical nor extreme.

EXERCISE 11.4

Identify the examples in paragraphs 9 and 11 in Jessica Statsky's essay "Children Need to Play, Not Compete" and paragraphs 16–18 in Amitai Etzioni's essay "Working at McDonald's" (both in Chapter 5). If you have not read the essays, pause to skim them so that you can evaluate these examples within the context of the entire essay. How well do the examples meet the standards of representativeness, consistency with experience of readers, and adequacy in number? You will not have all the information you need to evaluate the examples—you rarely do unless you are an expert on the subject—but make a judgment based on the information available to you in the headnotes and the essays.

Statistics

In many kinds of arguments about economic, educational, or social issues, **statistics** may be essential. When you use statistics in your own arguments, you will want to ensure that they are up-to-date, relevant, and accurate. In addition, take care to select statistics from reliable sources and to cite them from the sources in which they originally appeared if at all possible. For example, you would want to get medical statistics directly from a reputable and authoritative professional periodical like the *New England Journal of Medicine* rather than secondhand from a supermarket tabloid or an unaffiliated Web site, neither of which can be relied on for accuracy. If you are uncertain about the most authoritative sources, ask a reference librarian or a professor who knows your topic.

The following selection, written by a Harvard University professor, comes from an argument speculating about the decline of civic life in the United States. Civic life includes all of the clubs, organizations, and communal activities people choose to participate in.

The culprit is television.

First, the timing fits. The long civic generation was the last cohort of Americans to grow up without television, for television flashed into American society like lightning in the 1950s. In 1950 barely 10 percent of American homes had television sets, but by 1959, 90 percent did, probably the fastest diffusion of a major technological innovation ever recorded. The reverberations from this lightning bolt continued for decades, as viewing hours grew by 17–20 percent during the 1960s and by an additional 7–8 percent during the 1970s. In the early years, TV watching was concentrated among the less educated sectors of the population, but during the 1970s the viewing time of the more educated sectors of the population began to converge upward. Television viewing increases with age, particularly upon retirement, but each generation since the introduction of television has begun its life cycle at a higher starting point. By 1995 viewing per TV household was more than 50 percent higher than it had been in the 1950s.

Most studies estimate that the average American now watches roughly four hours per day (excluding periods in which television is merely playing in the background). Even a more conservative estimate of three hours means that television absorbs 40 percent of the average American's free time, an increase of about one-third since 1965. Moreover, multiple sets have proliferated: By the late 1980s three-quarters of all U.S. homes had more than one set, and these numbers too are rising steadily, allowing ever more private viewing . . . . This massive change in the way Americans spend their days and nights occurred precisely during the years of generational civic disengagement.

— Robert D. Putnam, "The Strange Disappearance of Civic America"

These statistics come primarily from the U.S. Bureau of the Census, a nationwide count of the number of Americans and a survey, in part, of their buying habits, levels of education, and leisure activities. The Census reports are widely considered to be accurate and trustworthy. They qualify as original sources of statistics.

Chapter 13 provides help finding statistical data in the library.

EXERCISE 11.5

In Chapter 5, underline the statistics in paragraphs 5 and 6 of Jessica Statsky's essay. If you have not read the essay, pause to skim it so that you can evaluate the writer's use of statistics within the context of the whole essay. How well do the statistics meet the standard of up-to-dateness, relevance, accuracy, and reliance on the original source? Does the writer indicate where the statistics come from? What do the statistics contribute to the argument?

Authorities

To support an argument, writers often cite experts on the subject. Quoting, paraphrasing, or even just referring to a respected **authority** can add to a writer's credibility. Authorities must be selected as carefully as facts and statistics, however. One qualification for authorities is suggested by the way we refer to them: They must be authoritative—that is, trustworthy and reputable. They must also be specially qualified to contribute to the subject you are writing about. For example, a well-known expert on the American presidency might be a perfect choice to support an argument about the achievements of a past president but a poor choice to support an argument on whether adolescents who commit serious crimes should be tried as adults. Finally, qualified authorities must have training at respected institutions or have unique real-world experiences, and they must have a record of research and publications recognized by other authorities.

The following example comes from a *New York Times* article about some parents' and experts' heightened concern over boys' behavior. The author believes that the concern is exaggerated and potentially dangerous. In the full argument, she is particularly concerned about the number of boys who are being given Ritalin, a popular drug for treating attention-deficit hyperactivity disorder (ADHD).

> Today, the world is no longer safe for boys. A boy being a shade too boyish risks finding himself under the scrutiny of parents, teachers, guidance counselors, child therapists — all of them on watch for the early glimmerings of a medical syndrome, a bona fide behavioral disorder. Does the boy disregard authority, make snide comments in class, push other kids around and play hooky? Maybe he has a conduct disorder. Is he fidgety, impulsive, disruptive, easily bored? Perhaps he is suffering from attention-deficit hyperactivity disorder, or ADHD, the disease of the hour and the most frequently diagnosed behavioral disorder of childhood. Does he prefer computer games and goofing off to homework? He might have dyslexia or another learning disorder.
>
> "There is now an attempt to pathologize what was once considered the normal range of behavior of boys," said Melvin Konner of the departments of anthropology and psychiatry at Emory University in Atlanta. "Today, Tom Sawyer and Huckleberry Finn surely would have been diagnosed with both conduct disorder and ADHD." And both, perhaps, would have been put on Ritalin, the drug of choice for treating attention-deficit disorder.
>
> — Natalie Angier, "Intolerance of Boyish Behavior"

In this example, Angier relies on *informal* citation within her essay to introduce Melvin Konner, the authority she quotes, along with a reference to his professional qualifications. Such informal citation is common in newspapers, magazines, and some books intended for general audiences. In other books and in academic contexts, writers use *formal* citation, providing a list of works cited at the end of the essay.

For examples of two formal citation styles often used in college essays, see Chapter 14.

EXERCISE 11.6

Analyze how authorities are used in paragraphs 4 and 5 of Patrick O'Malley's essay "More Testing, More Learning" in Chapter 6. Begin by underlining the authorities' contributions to these paragraphs, whether through quotation, summary, or paraphrase. On the basis of the evidence you have available, decide to what extent each source is authoritative on the subject: qualified to contribute to the subject, trained appropriately, and recognized widely. How does O'Malley establish each authority's credentials? Then decide what each authority contributes to the argument as a whole. (If you have not read the essay, take time to read or skim it.)

Anecdotes

Anecdotes are brief stories about events or experiences. If they are relevant to the argument, well told, and true to life, they can provide convincing support. To be relevant, an anecdote must strike readers as more than an entertaining diversion; it must seem to make an irreplaceable contribution to an argument. A well-told story is easy to follow, and the people and scenes are described memorably, even vividly. A true-to-life anecdote seems believable, even if the experience is foreign to readers' experiences.

The following anecdote appeared in an argument taking a position on gun control. The writer, an essayist, poet, and environmental writer who is also a rancher in South Dakota, always carries a pistol and believes that other people should have the right to do so.

> I was driving the half-mile to the highway mailbox one day when I saw a vehicle parked about midway down the road. Several men were standing in the ditch, relieving themselves. I have no objection to emergency urination, but I noticed they'd dumped several dozen beer cans in the road. Besides being ugly, cans can slash a cow's feet or stomach.
>
> The men noticed me before they finished and made quite a performance out of zipping their trousers while walking toward me. All four of them gathered around my small foreign car, and one of them demanded what the hell I wanted.
>
> "This is private land. I'd appreciate it if you'd pick up the beer cans."
>
> "What beer cans?" said the belligerent one, putting both hands on the car door and leaning in my window. His face was inches from mine, and the beer fumes were strong. The others laughed. One tried the passenger door, locked; another put his foot on the hood and rocked the car. They circled, lightly thumping the roof, discussing my good fortune in meeting them and the benefits they were likely to bestow upon me. I felt very small and very trapped and they knew it.
>
> "The ones you just threw out," I said politely.
>
> "I don't see no beer cans. Why don't you get out here and show them to me, honey?" said the belligerent one, reaching for the handle inside my door.
>
> "Right over there," I said, still being polite, " — there, and over there." I pointed with the pistol, which I'd slipped under my thigh. Within one minute the cans and the men were back in the car and headed down the road.
>
> I believe this incident illustrates several important principles. The men were trespassing and knew it; their judgment may have been impaired by alcohol. Their response to the polite request of a woman alone was to use their size, numbers, and sex to inspire fear. The pistol was a response in the same language. Politeness didn't work; I couldn't match them in size or number. Out of the car, I'd have been more vulnerable. The pistol just changed the balance of power.
>
> — LINDA M. HASSELSTROM, "Why One Peaceful Woman Carries a Pistol"

Most readers would readily agree that this anecdote is well told: it has many concrete, memorable details; there is action, suspense, climax, resolution, and even dialogue. It is about a believable, possible experience. Finally, the anecdote is clearly relevant to the author's argument about gun control.

See Chapter 2, Remembering an Event, for more information about narrating anecdotes.

EXERCISE 11.7

Evaluate the way an anecdote is used in paragraph 16 of Amitai Etzioni's essay "Working at McDonald's" in Chapter 5. Consider whether the story is well told and true to life. Decide whether it seems to be relevant to the whole argument. Does the writer make the relevance clear? Does the anecdote support Etzioni's argument?

Textual Evidence

When you argue claims of value (Chapter 7) and interpretation, **textual evidence** will be very important. In your college courses, if you are asked to evaluate a controversial book, you must quote, paraphrase, or summarize passages so that readers can understand why you think the author's argument is or is not credible. If you are interpreting a novel, you must include numerous excerpts to show just how you arrived at your conclusion.

For textual evidence to be considered effective support for an argument, it must be carefully selected to be relevant. You must help readers see the connection between each piece of evidence and the reason it supports. Textual evidence must also be highly selective—that is, chosen from among all the available evidence to provide the support needed without overwhelming the reader or weakening the argument with marginally relevant evidence. Textual evidence usually has more impact if it is balanced between quotation and paraphrase, and it must be smoothly integrated into the sentences of the argument.

The following example comes from a student essay in which the writer argues that the main character (referred to as "the boy") in the short story "Araby" by James Joyce is so self-absorbed that he learns nothing about himself or other people.

> The story opens and closes with images of blindness. The street is "blind" with an "uninhabited house . . . at the blind end." As he spies on Mangan's sister, from his own house, the boy intentionally limits what he is able to see by lowering the "blind" until it is only an inch from the window sash. At the bazaar in the closing scene, the "light was out," and the upper part of the hall was "completely dark." The boy is left "gazing up into the darkness," seeing nothing but an inner torment that burns his eyes.
>
> This pattern of imagery includes images of reading, and reading stands for the boy's inability to understand what is before his eyes. When he tries to read at night, for example, the girl's "image [comes] between [him] and the page," in effect blinding him. In fact, he seems blind to everything except this "image" of the "brown-clad figure cast by [his] imagination." The girl's "brown-clad figure" is also associated with the houses on "blind" North Richmond Street, with their "brown imperturbable faces." The houses stare back at the boy, unaffected by his presence and gaze.
>
> — SALLY CRANE, "Gazing into the Darkness"

Notice how the writer quotes selected words and phrases about blindness to support her reasoning that the boy learns nothing because he is blinded. There are twelve smoothly integrated quotations in these two paragraphs, along with a number of paraphrases, all of them relevant. The writer does not assume that the evidence speaks for itself; she comments and interprets throughout.

For information on paraphrasing, see pp. 318–19 in Chapter 9.

Analyze the use of evidence in paragraphs 3 and 4 of Christine Romano's evaluation in Chapter 7 of Jessica Statsky's essay. If you have not read this essay, read it now. Identify the quotes and paraphrases Romano uses, and then try to identify the phrases or sentences that comment on or explain this evidence. Consider whether Romano's evidence in these two paragraphs seems relevant to her thesis and reasons, appropriately selective, well balanced between quotes and paraphrases, integrated smoothly into the sentences she creates, and explained helpfully.

■ Counterarguing

Asserting a thesis and backing it with reasons and support are essential to a successful argument. Thoughtful writers go further, however, by **counterarguing**—anticipating and responding to their readers' objections, challenges, and questions.

To counterargue, writers rely on three basic strategies: acknowledging, accommodating or conceding, and refuting. Writers show they are aware of readers' objections and questions (acknowledge), modify their position to accept readers' concerns they think are legitimate (accommodate), or explicitly argue that readers' objections may be invalid or that their concerns may be irrelevant (refute). Writers may use one or more of these three strategies in the same essay. Readers find arguments more convincing when writers have anticipated their concerns in these ways.

Acknowledging Readers' Concerns

When you **acknowledge** readers' questions or objections, you show that you are aware of their point of view and you take it seriously even if you do not agree with it, as in the following example.

> The homeless, it seems, can be roughly divided into two groups: those who have had marginality and homelessness forced upon them and want nothing more than to escape them, and a smaller number who have at least in part chosen marginality, and now accept, or, in a few cases, embrace it.
>
> I understand how dangerous it can be to introduce the idea of choice into a discussion of homelessness. It can all too easily be used for all the wrong reasons by all the wrong people to justify indifference or brutality toward the homeless, or to argue that they are getting only what they deserve.
>
> And I understand, too, how complicated the notion can become: Many of the veterans on the street, or battered women, or abused and runaway children, have chosen this life only as the lesser of evils, and because, in this society, there is often no place else to go.
>
> And finally, I understand how much that happens on the street can combine to create an apparent acceptance of homelessness that is nothing more than the absolute absence of hope.
>
> Nonetheless we must learn to accept that there may indeed be people on the street who have seen so much of our world, or have seen it so clearly, that to live in it becomes impossible.
>
> — PETER MARIN, "Go Ask Alice"

You might think that acknowledging readers' objections in this way—addressing readers directly, listing their possible objections, and discussing each one—would weaken your argument. It might even seem reckless to suggest objections that not all readers would think of. On the contrary, however, most readers respond positively to this strategy because it makes you seem thoughtful and reasonable. By researching your subject and your readers, you will be able to use this strategy confidently in your own argumentative essays. And you will learn to look for it in arguments you read and use it to make judgments about the writer's credibility.

EXERCISE 11.9

Jessica Statsky acknowledges readers' concerns in paragraph 10 of her essay in Chapter 5. How, specifically, does Statsky attempt to acknowledge her readers' concerns? What do you find most and least successful in her acknowledgment? How does the acknowledgment affect your judgment of the writer's credibility?

Accommodating Readers' Concerns

To argue effectively, you must often take special care to **accommodate readers' concerns** by acknowledging their objections, questions, and alternative positions, causes, or solutions. Occasionally, however, you may have to go even further. Instead of merely acknowledging your readers' concerns, you may decide to accept some of them and incorporate them into your own argument. This strategy can be very disarming to readers. It is sometimes referred to as **concession**, for it seems to concede that opposing views have merit. The following example comes from an essay enthusiastically endorsing e-mail.

> To be sure, egalitarianism has its limits. The ease and economy of sending email, especially to multiple recipients, makes us all vulnerable to any bore, loony, or commercial or political salesman who can get our email address. It's still a lot less intrusive than the telephone, since you can read and answer or ignore email at your own convenience. But as normal people's email starts mounting into the hundreds daily, which is bound to happen, filtering mechanisms and conventions of etiquette that are still in their primitive stage will be desperately needed.
>
> Another supposed disadvantage of email is that it discourages face-to-face communication. At Microsoft, where people routinely send email back and forth all day to the person in the next office, this is certainly true. Some people believe this tendency has more to do with the underdeveloped social skills of computer geeks than with Microsoft's role in developing the technology email relies on. I wouldn't presume to comment on that. Whether you think email replacing live conversation is a good or bad thing depends, I guess, on how much of a misanthrope you are. I like it.
>
> — MICHAEL KINSLEY, "Email Culture"

Notice that Kinsley's accommodation or concession is not grudging. He readily concedes that e-mail brings users a lot of unwanted messages and may discourage conversation in the workplace.

How does Patrick O'Malley attempt to accommodate readers in paragraphs 8 and 9 of his Chapter 6 essay arguing for more frequent exams? What seems successful or unsuccessful in his argument? How do his efforts at accommodation make his argument seem more convincing?

Refuting Readers' Objections

Your readers' possible objections and views cannot always be accommodated. Sometimes they must be refuted. When you **refute readers' objections**, you assert that they are wrong and argue against them. Refutation does not have to be delivered arrogantly or dismissively, however. Because differences are inevitable, reasoned argument provides a peaceful and constructive way for informed, well-intentioned people who disagree strongly to air their differences.

In the following example, a social sciences professor refutes one argument for giving college students the opportunity to purchase lecture notes prepared by someone else.

> Now, it may well be argued that universities are already shortchanging their students by stuffing them into huge lecture halls where, unlike at rock concerts or basketball games, the lecturer can't even be seen on a giant screen in real time. If they're already short-changed with impersonal instruction, what's the harm in offering canned lecture notes?
>
> The amphitheater lecture is indeed, for all but the most engaging professors, a lesser form of instruction, and scarcely to be idealized. Still, Education by Download misses one of the keys to learning. Education is a meeting of minds, a process through which the student educes, draws from within, a response to what the teacher teaches.
>
> The very act of taking notes—not reading someone else's notes, no matter how stellar—is a way of engaging the material, wrestling with it, struggling to comprehend or take issue, but in any case entering into the work. The point is to decide, while you are listening, what matters in the presentation. And while I don't believe that most of life consists of showing up, education does begin with that—with immersing yourself in the activity at hand, listening, thinking, judging, offering active responses. A download is a poor substitute.
>
> — Todd Gitlin, "Disappearing Ink"

As this selection illustrates, writers cannot simply dismiss readers' possible concerns with a wave of their hand. Gitlin states a potential objection fully and fairly but then goes on to refute it by claiming that students need to take their own lecture notes to engage and comprehend the material that is being presented to them.

Effective refutation requires a restrained tone and careful argument. Although you may not accept this particular refutation, you can agree that it is well reasoned and supported. You need not feel attacked personally because the writer disagrees with you.

Evaluate Karen Stabiner's use of refutation in her essay "Boys Here, Girls There: Sure, If Equality's the Goal" (paragraphs 10–11) in Chapter 5. How does Stabiner signal or announce the refutation? How does she support the refutation? What is the tone of the refutation, and how effective do you think the tone would be in convincing readers to take the writer's argument seriously?

Logical Fallacies

Fallacies are errors or flaws in reasoning. Although essentially unsound, fallacious arguments seem superficially plausible and often have great persuasive power. Fallacies are not necessarily deliberate efforts to deceive readers. Writers may introduce a fallacy accidentally by not examining their own reasons or underlying assumptions, by failing to establish solid support, or by using unclear or ambiguous words. Here is a summary of the most common logical fallacies (listed alphabetically):

- *Begging the question:* Arguing that a claim is true by repeating the claim in different words (sometimes called *circular reasoning*)
- *Confusing chronology with causality:* Assuming that because one thing preceded another, the former caused the latter (also called *post hoc, ergo propter hoc*—Latin for "after this, therefore because of this")
- *Either-or reasoning:* Assuming that there are only two sides to a question and representing yours as the only correct one
- *Equivocating:* Misleading or hedging with ambiguous word choices
- *Failing to accept the burden of proof:* Asserting a claim without presenting a reasoned argument to support it
- *False analogy:* Assuming that because one thing resembles another, conclusions drawn from one also apply to the other
- *Hasty generalization:* Offering only weak or limited evidence to support a conclusion
- *Overreliance on authority:* Assuming that something is true simply because an expert says so and ignoring evidence to the contrary
- *Oversimplifying:* Giving easy answers to complicated questions, often by appealing to emotions rather than logic
- *Personal attack:* Demeaning the proponents of a claim instead of refuting their argument (also called *ad hominem*—Latin for "against the man"—*attack*)
- *Red herring:* Attempting to misdirect the discussion by raising an essentially unrelated point
- *Slanting:* Selecting or emphasizing the evidence that supports your claim and suppressing or playing down other evidence
- *Slippery slope:* Pretending that one thing inevitably leads to another
- *Sob story:* Manipulating readers' emotions to lead them to draw unjustified conclusions
- *Straw man:* Directing the argument against a claim that nobody actually makes or that everyone agrees is very weak

12 Field Research

In universities, government agencies, and the business world, field research can be as important as library research or experimental research. If you major in education, communication, or one of the social sciences, you will probably be asked to do writing based on your own observations, interviews, and questionnaire results. You will also read large amounts of information based on these methods of learning.

Observations and interviews are essential for writing profiles (Chapter 3). In proposing a solution to a problem (Chapter 6), you might want to interview people involved; or if many people are affected, you might find it useful to prepare a questionnaire. In writing to explain an academic concept (Chapter 4), you might want to interview a faculty member who is a specialist on the subject. As you consider how you might use such research most appropriately, ask your instructor whether your institution requires you to obtain approval for your field research.

■ Observations

This section offers guidelines for planning an observational visit, taking notes on your observations, writing them up, and preparing for follow-up visits. Some kinds of writing are based on observations from single visits—travel writing, social workers' case reports, insurance investigators' accident reports—but most observational writing is based on several visits. An anthropologist or a sociologist studying an unfamiliar group or activity might observe it for months, filling several notebooks with notes. If you are profiling a place (Chapter 3), you almost certainly will want to make more than one observational visit, some of them perhaps combined with interviews.

Planning the Visit

To ensure that your observational visits are productive, you must plan them carefully.

Getting Access. If the place you propose to visit is public, you will probably have easy access to it. If everything you need to see is within view of anyone passing by or using the place, you can make your observations without any special arrangements. However, most observational visits require special access. Hence, you will need to call ahead or stop by to introduce yourself and to make an appointment, if necessary.

Announcing Your Intentions.   State your intentions directly and fully. Say who you are, where you are from, and what you hope to do. You may be surprised at how receptive people can be to a college student on assignment. Not every place you wish to visit will welcome you, however. In addition, private businesses as well as public institutions place a variety of constraints on visitors.

Taking Your Tools.   Take a pen and a notebook with a firm back so that you will have a steady writing surface. Some writers dictate their observations, but because transcribing takes a lot of time, we recommend simply writing your notes.

Observing and Taking Notes

Here are some basic guidelines for observing and taking notes.

Observing.   Your purposes in observing are twofold: to describe what you observe and to analyze the activity or place, discovering a perspective that enables you to reveal insights into its meaning and significance.

Some activities invite the observer to watch from multiple vantage points, whereas others may limit the observer to a single perspective. Take advantage of every perspective available to you. Study the scene from a stationary position, and then try to move around it. The more varied your perspectives, the more details you are likely to observe.

Try initially to be an innocent observer: Pretend that you have never seen anything like this activity or place before. Then consider your own and your readers' likely preconceptions. Ask yourself which details are surprising and which confirm expectations.

Taking Notes.   Perhaps the most important advice about notetaking during an observational visit is to record as many details as possible about the place or activity and to write down your insights (ideas, interpretations, judgments) as they come to mind. You will undoubtedly find your own style of notetaking, but here are a few pointers.

- Take notes in words or phrases.
- Draw diagrams or sketches if they will help you recall details later on. Take photos if you are given permission to do so, but be aware that some people do not want their pictures taken.
- Use abbreviations as much as you like, but use them consistently and clearly.
- Note any impressions, ideas, questions, or personal insights that occur to you.
- If you are expecting to see a certain behavior, try not to let this expectation influence what you actually do see. But note how your expectations are overturned.
- Use quotation marks around any overheard remarks or conversations you record.

Do not worry about covering every aspect of the activity or place. At the same time, however, you want to be sure to include details about the setting, the people, and your reactions.

■ **The Setting.** Describe the setting: Name or list objects you see there, and record details about them—their color, shape, size, texture, function, relation to similar or dissimilar objects. Although your notes will probably contain mainly visual details, you might also want to record sounds and smells. Be sure to include some notes about the shape, dimensions, and layout of the place as a whole. How big is it? How is it organized?

■ **The People.** Note the number of people you observe, their activities, their movements and behavior, and their appearance or dress. Record parts of overheard conversations. Indicate whether you see more men than women, more members of one nationality or ethnic group than another, more older than younger people. Most important, note anything surprising, interesting, or unusual about the people and how they interact with each other.

Reflecting on Your Observations

Immediately after your visit (within a few minutes, if possible), find a quiet place to reflect on what you saw, review your notes, and fill in any gaps. Give yourself at least a half-hour to add to your notes and to write a few sentences about your perspective on the place or activity. Ask yourself the following questions:

- What did I learn?
- How did what I observed fit my own or my readers' likely preconceptions of the place or activity? Did it upset any of my preconceptions?
- What interests me the most about the activity or place? What are my readers likely to find interesting about it?
- What, if anything, seemed contradictory or out of place?

Writing Up Your Notes

Your instructor may ask you to write up your notes, as Brian Cable did after visiting the Goodbody Mortuaries for his profile essay (Chapter 3). If so, review your notes, looking for a meaningful pattern. You might find clustering or taking inventory useful for discovering patterns in your notes.

Assume that your readers have never been to the place, and decide on the perspective of the place you want to convey. Choose details that will convey this, and then draft a brief description of the place.

Clustering is described in Chapter 8, p. 295. Inventory-taking is described in Chapter 9, p. 315.

Arrange to meet with a small group (three or four students) for an observational visit somewhere on campus, such as the student center, campus gym, cafeteria, or restaurant. Assign each person in your group a specific task; one person can take notes on the appearance of the people, for example; another can take notes on their activities; another on their conversations; and another on what the place looks and smells like. After twenty to thirty minutes, report to each other on your observations. Discuss any difficulties that arise.

Preparing for Follow-Up Visits

It is important to develop a plan for your follow-up visits: questions to be answered, insights to be tested, types of information you would like to discover. If possible, do some interviewing and reading before a repeat visit so that you will have a greater understanding of the subject. For additional ideas on what to aim for in a follow-up visit, you might want to present your notes from your first visit to your instructor or to your class.

Interviews

Like making observations, interviewing tends to involve four basic steps: (1) planning and setting up the interview, (2) taking notes during the interview, (3) reflecting on the interview, and (4) writing up your notes.

Planning and Setting Up the Interview

The initial steps in interviewing involve choosing an interview subject and then arranging and planning for the interview.

Choosing an Interview Subject.   For a profile of an individual, most or all of your interviews would be with that person. If you are writing about some activity in which several people are involved, however, choose subjects representing a variety of perspectives. For instance, you might interview several members of an organization to gain a more complete picture of its mission or activities. You should be flexible because you may be unable to speak with the person you initially targeted and may wind up interviewing someone else — the person's assistant, perhaps. Do not assume that this interview subject will be of little use to you. With the right questions, you might even learn more from the assistant than you would from the person you had originally expected to see.

Arranging an Interview.   You may be nervous about calling up a busy person and asking for some of his or her time. Indeed, you may get turned down. But if so, it is possible that you will be referred to someone who will see you, perhaps someone whose job it is to talk to the public.

Do not feel that just because you are a student, you do not have the right to ask for people's time. Most people are delighted to be asked about themselves, particularly if you reach them when they are not feeling harried. Since you are a student on assignment, some people may even feel that they are performing a public service by talking with you.

When introducing yourself to arrange the interview, give a brief description of your project. If you talk too much, you could prejudice or limit the interviewee's response. At the same time, it is a good idea to exhibit some sincere enthusiasm for your project. If you lack enthusiasm, the person may see little reason to talk with you.

Keep in mind that the person you want to interview will be donating valuable time to you. Be certain that you call ahead to arrange a specific time for the interview. Arrive on time. Dress appropriately. Bring all the materials you need. Express your thanks when the interview is over. Finally, try to represent your institution well, whether your interview is for a single course assignment or part of a larger service-learning project.

Planning for the Interview.   The best interview is generally the well-planned interview. Making an observational visit and doing some background reading beforehand can be helpful. In preparation for the interview, you should consider your objectives:

- Do you want details, or a general orientation (the "big picture") from this interview?
- Do you want this interview to lead you to interviews with other key people?
- Do you want mainly facts or opinions?
- Do you need to clarify something you have observed or read? If so, what?

The key to good interviewing is flexibility. You may be looking for facts, but your interview subject may not have any to offer. In that case, you should be able to shift gears and go after whatever your subject is in a position to discuss. Be aware that the person you are interviewing represents only one point of view. You may need to speak with several people to get a more complete picture.

Composing Questions.   In addition to determining your objectives, you should prepare your questions in advance. Good questions can be the key to a successful interview.

Good questions come in two basic types: open and closed. **Open questions** give the respondent range and flexibility. They also generate anecdotes, personal revelations, and expressions of attitudes. **Closed questions** usually request specific information.

Suppose you are interviewing a small-business owner. You might begin with a specific (closed) question about when the business was established and then follow up with an open-ended question such as, "Could you take a few minutes to tell me something about your early days in the business? I'd be interested to hear how it got started, what your hopes were, and what problems you had to face." Consider asking directly for an anecdote ("What happened when your employees threatened to strike?"), encouraging reflection ("What do you think has helped you most? What has hampered you?"), or soliciting advice ("What advice would you give to someone trying to start a new business today?"). Here are some examples of open and closed questions:

Open Questions

- What do you think about (*name a person or an event*)?
- Describe your reaction when (*name an event*) happened.
- Tell me about a time you were (*name an emotion*).

Closed Questions

- How do you (*name a process*)?
- What does (*name a word or phrase*) mean?
- What does (*name a person, object, or place*) look like?
- How was (*name a product, process, etc.*) developed?

The best questions encourage the subject to talk freely but to the point. If an answer strays too far from the point, you may need to ask a follow-up question to refocus the talk. Another tack you might want to try is to rephrase the subject's answer, to say something like "Let me see if I have this right" or "Am I correct in saying that you feel . . . ?" Often, a person will take the opportunity to amplify the original response by adding just the anecdote or quotable comment you have been looking for.

Avoid questions that place unfair limits on respondents. These include forced-choice questions and leading questions.

Forced-choice questions impose your terms on respondents. If you are interviewing a counselor at a campus rape crisis center and want to know what he or she thinks is the motivation for rape, you could ask this question: "Do you think rape is about control or about rage?" But the counselor might not think that either control or rage satisfactorily explains the motivation for rape. A better way to phrase the question would be as follows: "People often fall into two camps on the issue of rape. Some think it is an expression of control, while others argue that it is an expression of rage. Do you think it is either of these? If not, what is your opinion?" Phrasing the question in this way allows interviewees to react to what others have said but also gives them freedom to set the terms for their response.

Leading questions assume too much. An example of this kind of question is this: "Do you think the number of rapes has increased because women are perceived as competitors in a highly competitive economy?" This question assumes that there is an increase in the occurrence of rape, that women are perceived (apparently by rapists) as economic competitors, and that the state of the economy is somehow related to acts of rape. A better way of asking the question might be to make the assumptions more explicit by dividing the question into its parts: "Has the occurrence of rape increased in recent years? If so, what could have caused this increase? I've heard some people argue that the state of the economy has something to do with rape. Some have suggested that rapists perceive women as competitors for jobs, and that this perception is linked to rape. Do you think there might be any truth to this?"

Bringing Your Tools. As for an observational visit, when you interview someone, you will need a pen and a notebook with a firm back so you can write in it easily without the benefit of a table or desk. You might find it useful to divide several pages into two columns by drawing a line about one-third of the width of the page from the left margin. Use the left-hand column to note details about the scene, the person, the mood of the interview, and other impressions. Head this column *Details and Impressions.* At the top of the right-hand column, write several questions. You may not use them, but they will jog your memory. This column should be titled *Information.* In it, you will record what you learn from answers to your questions.

Taking Notes during the Interview

In taking notes, your goals are to gather information and to record a few quotations, key words and phrases, and details of the scene, the person, and the mood of the interview. Remember that how something is said is as important as what is said. Look for material that will give texture to your writing — gesture, verbal inflection, facial expression, body language, physical appearance, dress, hair, or anything that makes the person an individual. In general, it is probably a good idea to do more listening than notetaking. You may not have much confidence in your memory, but if you pay close attention, you are likely to recall a good deal of the conversation afterward.

Reflecting on the Interview

As soon as you finish the interview, find a quiet place to reflect on it and review your notes. This reflection is essential because so much happens in an interview that you cannot record at the time. Spend at least a half-hour adding to your notes and thinking about what you learned.

At the end of this time, write a few sentences about your main impressions from the interview. Ask yourself these questions:

- What did I learn?
- What seemed contradictory or surprising about the interview?
- How did what was said fit my own or my readers' likely expectations about the person, activity, or place?
- How can I summarize my impressions?

Writing Up Your Notes

Your instructor may ask you to write up your interview notes. If so, review them for useful details and ideas. Decide what perspective you want to take on this person. Choose details that will contribute to this perspective. Select quotations and paraphrases of information you learned from the person.

You might also review notes from any related observations or from other interviews, especially if you plan to combine these materials in a profile, ethnographic study, or other project.

■ Questionnaires

Questionnaires let you survey the opinions and knowledge of large numbers of people. Compared to one-on-one interviews, they have the advantages of economy, efficiency, and anonymity. Some questionnaires, such as the ones you filled out when entering college, just collect demographic information: your name, age, sex, hometown, religious preference, intended major. Others, such as the Gallup and Harris polls, collect opinions on a wide range of issues. Before elections, we are bombarded with the results of such polls. Still other kinds of questionnaires, such as those used in academic research, are designed to help answer important questions about personal and societal problems.

This section briefly outlines procedures you can follow to carry out an informal questionnaire survey of people's opinions or knowledge.

Focusing Your Study

A questionnaire survey usually has a limited focus. You might need to interview a few people to find this focus, or you may already have a limited focus in mind. If you are developing a questionnaire as part of a service-learning project, discuss your focus with your supervisor or other staff members.

As an example, let us assume that you go to your campus student health clinic and have to wait over an hour to see a doctor. Sitting in the waiting room with many other students, you decide that this long wait is a problem that would be an ideal topic for an assignment you have been asked to do for your writing class, an essay proposing a solution to a problem (Chapter 6).

You do not have to explore the entire operation of the clinic to study this problem. You are not interested in how nurses and doctors are hired or in how efficient the clinic's system of ordering supplies is, for example. Your primary interests are how long students usually wait for appointments, what times are most convenient for students to schedule appointments, how the clinic accommodates students when demand is high, and whether the long wait discourages many students from getting the treatment they need. With this limited focus, you can collect valuable information using a fairly brief questionnaire. To be certain about your focus, however, you should talk informally with several students to find out whether they also think there is a problem with appointment scheduling at the clinic. You might want to talk with staff members, too, explaining your plans and asking for their views on the problem.

Whatever your interest, be sure to limit the scope of your survey. Try to focus on one or two important questions. With a limited focus, your questionnaire can be brief, and people will be more willing to fill it out. In addition, a survey based on a limited amount of information will be easier to organize and report on.

Writing Questions

The same two basic types of questions used for interviews, closed and open, are also useful in questionnaires. Figure 12.1 illustrates how these types of questions may be employed in the context of a questionnaire about the student health clinic problem. Notice that the questionnaire uses several forms of *closed questions* (in items 1–6): two-way questions, multiple-choice questions, ranking scales, and checklists. You will probably use more than one form of closed question in a questionnaire to collect different kinds of information. The sample questionnaire also uses several *open questions* (items 7–10) that ask for brief written answers. You may want to combine closed and open questions in your questionnaire because both offer advantages: Closed questions will give you definite answers, while open questions can elicit information you may not have anticipated as well as provide lively quotations for your essay explaining what you have learned.

Whatever types of questions you develop, try to phrase them in a fair and unbiased manner so that your results will be reliable and credible. As soon as you have a collection of possible questions, try them out on a few typical respondents. You need to know which questions are unclear, which seem to duplicate others, and which provide the most interesting responses. These tryouts will enable you to assess which questions will give you the information you need. Readers can also help you come up with additional questions.

Designing the Questionnaire

Begin your questionnaire with a brief, clear introduction stating the purpose of your survey and explaining how you intend to use the results. Give advice on answering the questions, and estimate the amount of time needed to complete the questionnaire (see Figure 12.1 for an example). You may opt to give this information orally if you plan to hand the questionnaire to groups of people and have them fill it out immediately. However, even in this case, your respondents will appreciate a written introduction that clarifies what you expect.

Select your most promising questions, and decide how to order them. Any logical order is appropriate. You might want to arrange the questions from least to most complicated or from general to specific. You may find it appropriate to group the questions by subject matter or format. Certain questions may lead to others. You might want to place open questions at the end (see Figure 12.1 for an example).

Design your questionnaire so that it looks attractive and readable. Make it look easy to complete. Do not crowd questions together to save paper. Provide plenty of space for readers to answer questions, especially open questions, and encourage them to use the back of the page if they need more space.

Testing the Questionnaire

Make a few copies of your first-draft questionnaire, and ask at least three readers to complete it. Time them as they respond, or ask them to keep track of how long they take to complete it. Discuss with them any confusion or problems they experience. Review their responses with them to be certain that each question is eliciting the information

Two-way question —————

This is a survey about the scheduling of appointments at the campus Student Health Clinic. Your participation will help determine how long students have to wait to use clinic services and how these services might be more conveniently scheduled. The survey should take only 3 to 4 minutes to complete. All responses are confidential. Thank you for your participation.

1. Have you ever made an appointment at the clinic?   (Circle one.)

   Yes   No

Multiple-choice questions —

2. How frequently have you had to wait more than 10 minutes at the clinic for a scheduled appointment?   (Circle one.)

   Always   Usually   Occasionally   Never

3. Have you ever had to wait more than 30 minutes at the clinic for a scheduled appointment?   (Circle one.)

   Yes   No   Uncertain

4. From your experience so far with the clinic, how would you rank its system for scheduling appointments?   (Circle one.)

Ranking scale —————

0	1	2	3	4	5
no experience	inadequate	poor	adequate	good	outstanding

5. Given your present work and class schedule, when are you able to visit the clinic?   (Check all applicable responses.)

Checklist —————

   _____ 8–10 AM   _____ 1–3 PM
   _____ 10 AM–Noon   _____ 3–5 PM
   _____ 12–1 PM

6. Given your present work and class schedule, which times during the day (Monday through Friday) would be the most and least convenient for you to schedule appointments at the clinic?   (Rank the four choices from 1 for most convenient time to 4 for least convenient time.)

Ranking scale —————

   _____ Morning (7 AM – Noon)   _____ Dinnertime (5–7 PM)
   _____ Afternoon (12–5 PM)   _____ Evening (7–10 PM)

7. How would you evaluate your most recent appointment at the clinic?

8. Based on your experiences with scheduling at the clinic, what advice would you give to other students about making appointments?

Open questions —————

9. What do you believe would most improve the scheduling of appointments at the clinic?

10. If you have additional comments about scheduling at the clinic, please write them on the back of this page.

Figure 12.1
Sample questionnaire: Scheduling at the Student Health Clinic

you want it to elicit. From what you learn, reconsider your questionnaire, and make any necessary revisions to your questions and design or format.

Administering the Questionnaire

Decide whom you want to fill out your questionnaire and how you can arrange for them to do so. The more respondents you have, the better, but constraints of time and expense will almost certainly limit the number. You can mail or e-mail questionnaires, distribute them to dormitories, or send them to campus or workplace mailboxes, but the return will likely be low. Half the people receiving questionnaires in the mail usually fail to return them. If you do mail the questionnaire, be sure to mention the deadline for returning it. Give directions for its return, and include a stamped, self-addressed envelope, if necessary. Instead of mailing the questionnaire, you might want to arrange to distribute it yourself to groups of people in class or around campus, at dormitory meetings, or at work. Some colleges and universities have restrictions about the use of questionnaires, so you should check your institution's policy before sending one out.

Note that if you want to do a formal questionnaire study, you will need a scientifically representative group of readers (a random or stratified random sample). Even for an informal study, you should try to get a reasonably representative group. For example, to study satisfaction with appointment scheduling at the clinic, you would want to include students who have been to the clinic as well as those who have avoided it. You might even want to include a concentration of seniors rather than first-year students because, after four years, seniors would have made more visits to the clinic. If many students commute, you would want to be sure to have commuters among your respondents. Your essay will be more convincing if you demonstrate that your respondents represent the group whose opinions or knowledge you claim to be studying. As few as twenty-five respondents could be adequate for an informal study.

Writing Up the Results

Once you have the completed questionnaires, how do you write up the results?

Summarizing the Results. Begin by tallying the results from the closed questions. Take an unused questionnaire, and tally the responses next to each choice. Suppose that you had administered the student health clinic questionnaire to twenty-five students. Here is how the tally might look for the checklist in question 5 of Figure 12.1.

5. Given your present work and class schedule, when are you able to visit the clinic? (Check all applicable responses.)

    _____ 8–10 AM ⅢⅣ ⅢⅣ ⅢⅣ III (*18*)   _____ 1–3 PM III (*3*)

    _____ 10 AM–Noon ⅢⅣ II (*7*)   _____ 3–5 PM ⅢⅣ IIII (*9*)

    _____ 12–1 PM ⅢⅣ ⅢⅣ III (*13*)

Each tally mark represents one response to that item. The totals add up to more than twenty-five because respondents were asked to check all the times when they could make appointments.

You can give the results from the closed questions as percentages, either within the text of your paper or in one or more tables or graphs. Conventional table formats for the social sciences are illustrated in the *Publication Manual of the American Psychological Association,* 5th edition (Washington, DC: American Psychological Association, 2001). For larger surveys, you can use computer spreadsheet programs to tabulate the results and even generate the tables and graphs.

Next, consider the open questions. Read all respondents' answers to each question separately to see the kinds and variety of responses they gave. Then decide whether you want to code any of the open questions so that you can summarize results from them quantitatively, as you would with closed questions. For example, you might want to classify the types of advice given as responses to question 8 in the clinic questionnaire: "Based on your experiences with scheduling at the clinic, what advice would you give to other students about making appointments?" You could then report the numbers of respondents (of your twenty-five) who gave each type of advice. For an opinion question (for example, "How would you evaluate your most recent appointment at the clinic?"), you might simply code the answers as positive, neutral, or negative and then tally the results accordingly for each kind of response. However, you'll probably want to use the responses to most open questions as a source of quotations for your report or essay.

Because readers' interests can be engaged more easily with quotations than with percentages, plan to use open responses in your essay, perhaps weaving them into your discussion like quoted material from published sources.

For strategies for integrating quoted material, see Chapter 14, pp. 409–10.

Organizing the Write-up.   In organizing your results, you might want to consider a plan that is commonly followed in the social sciences.

Reporting Your Survey

Statement of the problem

> Context for your study
> Question or questions you wanted to answer
> Need for your survey
> Brief preview of your survey and plan for your report

Review of other related surveys (if you know of any)

Procedures

> Questionnaire design
> Selection of participants
> Administration of the questionnaire
> Summary of the results

Results: Presentation of what you learned, with limited commentary or interpretation

Summary and discussion

> Brief summary of your results
> Brief discussion of their significance (commenting, interpreting, exploring implications, and possibly comparing with other related surveys)

13 Library and Internet Research

Research requires patience, careful planning, hard work, and even luck. The rewards are many, however. Each new research project leads you to unexplored regions of the library or of cyberspace. You may find yourself in a rare-book room reading a manuscript written hundreds of years ago or involved in a lively discussion on the Internet with people hundreds of miles away. One moment you may be surfing the Web, and the next you may be threading a microfilm reader, watching a DVD, or squinting at the fine print in a periodical index.

This chapter is designed to help you learn how to use all of the resources available to you. It gives advice on how to use the library and the Internet, develop efficient search strategies, keep track of your research, locate appropriate sources, and read them productively. Chapter 14 provides guidelines for using and acknowledging these sources in an essay and presents a sample research paper on home schooling.

■ Orienting Yourself to the Library

To conduct research in most college libraries, you will need to become familiar with a wide variety of resources. Library catalogs, almost all of them now electronic, provide information on books, journals, and other materials (such as DVDs) held by the library. Periodical indexes, used to locate magazine and journal articles, are available either in print or electronic form. The material you find may be in print, or microfilm or microfiche, or in downloadable electronic format.

Taking a Tour

Because nearly all college libraries are more complex than typical high school or public libraries, you should make a point of getting acquainted with your school's library. Your instructor may arrange a library orientation tour for your composition class. If not, you can join one of the orientation tours scheduled by the librarians or design your own tour (for suggestions, see Table 13.1).

Table 13.1 Designing Your Self-Guided Library Tour

Here is a list of important locations or departments to look for in your college library.

Library Location	What You Can Do at These Locations
Loan desk	Obtain library cards, check out materials, place holds and recalls, pay fees or fines.
Reference desk	Obtain help from reference librarians to locate and use library resources.
Information desk	Ask general and directional questions.
Reserves desk	Gain access to books and journal articles that are on reserve for specific classes.
Interlibrary loan department	Request materials not available on site; you can do this electronically through the catalog at many libraries.
Open-access computers	Gain access to the library catalog, electronic periodical indexes, the campus network, and the Internet.
Current periodicals	Locate unbound current issues of newspapers, journals, and magazines.
Reference collection	Find reference materials such as encyclopedias, dictionaries, handbooks, atlases, bibliographies, statistics, and periodical indexes and abstracts.
Government publications department	Locate publications from federal, state, and local government agencies.
Multimedia resources	Locate nonprint materials such as videos, CD-ROMs, and audiotapes.
Microforms	Locate materials on microfilm (reels) and microfiche (cards).
Special collections/Rare books room	Find rare or highly specialized materials not readily available in most library collections (in larger libraries only).
Archives	Find collections of papers from important individuals and organizations that provide source material for original research (in larger libraries only).
Maps and atlases	Locate maps and atlases (housed in a special location because of their size and format).
Copy service/Copiers	Have copies made or use self-service and special-function copiers.
Reading rooms	Read in quiet, comfortable areas.
Study rooms	Study in rooms reserved for individuals or small groups.
Computer labs	Use networked computers for word processing, research, and other functions.

Nearly every college library offers a Web site and handouts describing its resources and services. Pick up copies of any available pamphlets and guidelines, including a floor map of materials and facilities. See whether your library offers any research guidelines, special workshops, or presentations on strategies for locating resources. Many library Web sites offer tutorials for using the library's electronic resources.

Consulting a Librarian

Think of college librarians as instructors whose job is to help you understand the library and get your hands on sources you need to complete your research projects. Most librarians at the information or reference desk have years of experience answering the very questions you are likely to ask. You should not hesitate to approach them with any questions you have about locating sources. Remember, however, that they can be most helpful when you can explain your research assignment clearly and ask questions that are as specific as possible. You need not do so face-to-face: Many library Web sites now offer "virtual reference" chat rooms that connect library users to a reference librarian.

Knowing Your Research Task

Before you go to the library to start a research project, learn as much as you can about the assignment. Asking a question or two in advance can prevent hours—or even days—of misdirected work. Ask your instructor to clarify any confusing terms and to define the purpose and scope of the project. Find out how you can focus the project once you begin the research.

A Library Search Strategy

You should try to get to the library as soon as you understand the assignment. If many of your classmates will be working on similar projects, you may be competing with them for a limited number of books and other resources. More important, for your library research to be manageable and productive, you will want to work carefully and systematically, and this takes time. Although specific search strategies may vary to fit the needs of individual research tasks, the general process presented in Figure 13.1 should help you organize your time. Remember that you will be constantly refining and revising your research strategy as you find out more about your topic.

▮ Keeping Track of Your Research

As you research your topic, you will want to keep a careful record of all the sources you locate by setting up a working bibliography. You will also want to take notes on your sources in some systematic way.

Keeping a Working Bibliography

A **working bibliography** is a preliminary, ongoing record of books, articles, Web sites—all the sources of information you discover as you research your subject. In

Know your research task.

- Keep a research journal.
- Keep a working bibliography.
- Take notes.

Get an overview of your topic.

- Look in encyclopedias and subject guides.
- Review textbooks.
- Explore newspapers, magazines, and Internet sites.
- Construct a list of keywords and subject headings.
- Develop a preliminary topic statement.

Use subject guides to identify possible sources of information on specific topics.

Conduct a preliminary search for sources, using keywords and subject headings.

- Check the online catalog for books.
- Check periodical indexes for articles.
- Check Internet sites.

Evaluate and refine your search by asking yourself:

- Is this what I expected to find?
- Am I finding enough?
- Am I finding too much?
- Do I need to modify my keywords?
- Do I need to recheck background sources?
- Do I need to modify my topic statement?

Refine your search based on the answers.

Locate sources.

- Books
- Magazine and journal articles
- Newspaper articles
- Internet sites
- Government and statistical sources
- Other sources appropriate to your topic

Evaluate your sources.

- For information
- For relevance
- For accuracy
- For comprehensiveness
- For bias
- For currency

Continue to evaluate and refine your search strategy based on the research results.

Figure 13.1 Overview of an information search strategy

addition, you can use your working bibliography to keep track of any encyclopedias, bibliographies, and indexes you consult, even though these general sources are usually not identified in an essay.

Each entry in a working bibliography is called a **bibliographic citation**. The information you record in each bibliographic citation will help you to locate the source in the library and then, if you end up using it in your paper, to *cite* or *document* it in the list of references or works cited you provide at the end of an essay. Recording this information for each possible source as you identify it, rather than reconstructing it later, will save you hours of work. In addition to the bibliographic information, note the library location where the source is kept and any index or other reference work where you learned about it, just in case you have to track it down again. (See Figures 13.2 and 13.3 for guidelines on what to record for a book or a print periodical article. For guidelines for Internet sources, see Figure 13.6 on page 398.)

Author	
Title	
Place of publication	
Publisher	
Date of publication	
Location*	
Notes	

Figure 13.2 Information for working bibliography—books
*If found in hard copy, note name of library, special location (such as reference room, rare books room, or government publications department) if any, and call number. If found online, note URL, host site, and date of access.

Author of article	
Title of article	
Title of journal	
Volume / issue number	
Date of issue	
Page numbers	
Location*	
Notes	

Figure 13.3 Information for working bibliography—periodical articles
*If found in hard copy, note library location and format (bound journal, microfilm, etc.). If found online, note URL, date of access, and name of host site or periodicals database.

Chapter 14 presents two common documentation styles—one adopted by the Modern Language Association (MLA) and widely used in the humanities, and the other advocated by the American Psychological Association (APA) and used in the social sciences. Other disciplines have their own preferred styles of documentation. Confirm with your instructor which documentation style is required for your assignment so that you can follow that style for all the sources you put in your working bibliography.

Practiced researchers keep their working bibliography on index cards, in a notebook, or in a computer file. Many researchers find index cards convenient because they are portable and easy to arrange in the alphabetical order required for the list of works cited or references. Others find cards too easy to lose and prefer instead to keep everything—working bibliography, notes, and drafts—in one notebook. Still others prefer to record the information in a computer file, using either standard software (such as Word or Excel) or specialized software (such as Nota Bene or the Bedford Bibliographer*) designed for creating bibliographies.

Whether you use index cards, a notebook, or your computer for your working bibliography, your entries need to be accurate and complete. If the call number you record for a book is incomplete or inaccurate, for example, you may not be able to find the book easily in the stacks. If the author's name is misspelled, you may have trouble finding the book in the catalog. If the volume number for a periodical is incorrect, you may not be able to locate the article. If you initially get some bibliographic information from a catalog or index, check it for accuracy when you examine the source directly.

Taking Notes

After you have found some possible sources, you will want to begin taking notes. If you can make a photocopy of the relevant items or download them onto your computer, you may want to annotate on the page or on the screen. Otherwise, you should paraphrase, summarize, and outline useful information as separate notes. In addition, you will want to record quotations you might use in your essay.

You may already have a method of notetaking you prefer. Some researchers like to use index cards for notes as well as for their working bibliography. Other people prefer to keep their notes in a notebook, and still others enter their notes into a computer file. Whatever method you use, be sure to keep accurate notes.

Careful notetaking is the most important way to minimize the risks of misquoting and of copying facts incorrectly. Another common error in notetaking is copying an author's phrases and sentences without enclosing them in quotation marks. This error leads easily to **plagiarism**, the unacknowledged and therefore improper use of another's phrases and sentences or ideas. Double-check all your notes, and be as accurate as you can. Be sure to include the page numbers where you find information so that you can go back and reread if necessary; you will also need to give page numbers when you cite sources within your essay and in your list of works cited.

You might consider photocopying materials from print sources that look especially promising. All libraries house copy machines or offer a copying service. Photocopying can facilitate your work, allowing you to reread and analyze important sources as well as to highlight material you may wish to quote, summarize, or paraphrase. Because photocopying can be costly, you will want to be selective. Be sure to photocopy title pages or other publication information for each source you copy, or write this information on the photocopied text, especially if you are copying excerpts from several sources. Bring paper clips or a stapler with you to the library to organize your photocopies.

For electronic sources you find in the library, download the material to a disk, if possible. Even if you can download the complete text, it is a good idea to print it out, too. The printout serves as a backup in case your download disappears. Be sure your

---

*This free Web-based application, part of Bedford/St. Martin's *Re:Writing* collection of resources, can be accessed at http://bcs.bedfordstmartins.com/rewriting/rcBB.html.

downloaded version and the printout both include all the information required by the documentation system you are using.

Outlining, paraphrasing, and summarizing are discussed in Chapter 9, and quoting is discussed in Chapter 14. For tips on avoiding plagiarism, see Chapter 14, p. 406.

◼ Getting Started

"But where do I start?" That common question is easily answered. You first need an overview of your topic. If you are researching a concept or an issue in a course you are taking, a bibliography in your textbook or your course materials provides the obvious starting point. Your instructor can advise you about other sources that provide overviews of your topic. If your topic is currently in the news, you will want to consult newspapers, magazines, or Internet sites. For all other topics, encyclopedias and disciplinary (subject) guides are often the place to start.

Consulting Encyclopedias

General encyclopedias, such as the *Encyclopaedia Britannica* and the *Encyclopedia Americana*, give basic information about many topics; however, general encyclopedias alone are not adequate resources for college research. Specialized encyclopedias cover topics in the depth appropriate for college writing. In addition to providing an overview of a topic, a specialized encyclopedia often includes an explanation of issues related to the topic, definitions of specialized terminology, and selective bibliographies of additional sources.

As starting points, specialized encyclopedias have two distinct advantages: (1) They provide a comprehensive introduction to key terms related to your topic, terms that will help you find related material in catalogs and indexes, and (2) they provide a comprehensive presentation of a subject, enabling you to see many possibilities for focusing your research.

The following list identifies some specialized encyclopedias in the major academic disciplines:

ART	*Dictionary of Art.* 34 vols. 1996.
BIOLOGY	*Concise Encyclopedia Biology.* 1995.
CHEMISTRY	*Concise Encyclopedia Chemistry.* 1993.
COMPUTERS	*Encyclopedia of Computer Science and Technology.* 45 vols. 1975 – .
ECONOMICS	*Fortune Encyclopedia of Economics.* 1993.
EDUCATION	*Encyclopedia of Educational Research.* 1992.
ENVIRONMENT	*Encyclopedia of the Environment.* 1994.

FOREIGN RELATIONS	*Encyclopedia of U.S. Foreign Relations.* 1997.
	Encyclopedia of the Third World. 1992.
HISTORY	*Encyclopedia USA.* 29 vols. 1983–.
	New Cambridge Modern History. 14 vols. 1957–1980, 1990–.
LAW	*Corpus Juris Secundum.* 1936.
	American Jurisprudence, 2d series. 1962.
LITERATURE	*Encyclopedia of World Literature in the Twentieth Century.* 5 vols. 1981–1993.
	Encyclopedia of Literature and Criticism. 1990.
MEDICINE	*American Medical Association's Complete Medical Encyclopedia.* 2003.
MUSIC	*New Grove Dictionary of Music and Musicians,* 2nd ed. 29 vols. 2001.
NURSING	*Miller-Keane Encyclopedia and Dictionary of Medicine, Nursing, and Allied Health.* 1997
PHILOSOPHY	*Routledge Encyclopedia of Philosophy.* 10 vols. 1998.
PSYCHOLOGY	*Encyclopedia of Psychology.* 8 vols. 2000.
RELIGION	*Encyclopedia of Religion.* 15 vols. 2005.
SCIENCE	*McGraw-Hill Encyclopedia of Science and Technology.* 20 vols. 2002.
SOCIAL SCIENCES	*International Encyclopedia of the Social Sciences.* 19 vols. 1968–.
SOCIOLOGY	*Encyclopedia of Sociology.* 5 vols. 2000.
WOMEN'S STUDIES	*Women's Studies Encyclopedia,* Rev. ed. 3 vols. 1999.

You can locate any of these in the library by entering its title into the online catalog. Find other specialized encyclopedias by looking in the catalog under the subject heading for the discipline, such as "psychology," and adding the subheading "encyclopedia" or "dictionary."

Three reference sources can help you identify other specialized encyclopedias covering your topic:

- ***ARBA Guide to Subject Encyclopedias and Dictionaries,*** 2nd ed. (1997): Lists specialized encyclopedias by broad subject categories, with descriptions of coverage, focus, and any special features. Also available online.

- ***Subject Encyclopedias: User Guide, Review Citations, and Keyword Index*** (1999): Lists specialized encyclopedias by broad subject categories and provides information about articles within them. By looking under the key terms that describe a topic, you can search for related articles in any of over four hundred specialized encyclopedias.

- *Kister's Best Encyclopedias: A Comparative Guide to General and Specialized Encyclopedias,* 2nd ed. (1994): Surveys and evaluates more than a thousand encyclopedias, both print and electronic. Includes a title index and a topic index that you can use to find references to encyclopedias on special topics.

Consulting Disciplinary Guides

Once you have a general overview of your topic, you can consult one of the research guides within the college academic discipline where your topic resides. The following guides can help you identify the major handbooks, encyclopedias, bibliographies, journals, periodical indexes, and computer databases in the various disciplines. The *Guide to Reference Books,* 11th ed. (1996), edited by Robert Balay, will help you find disciplinary guides for subjects not listed here.

ANTHROPOLOGY	*Introduction to Library Research in Anthropology,* 2nd ed. 1998. By John M. Weeks.
ART	*Fine Arts: A Bibliographic Guide to Basic Reference Works, Histories, and Handbooks,* 3rd ed. 1990. By Donald L. Ehresmann.
	Visual Arts Research: A Handbook. 1986. By Elizabeth B. Pollard.
BUSINESS	*Encyclopedia of Business Information Sources,* 1970–(annual). Also available online.
	Strauss's Handbook of Business Information: A Guide for Librarians, Students, and Researchers, 2nd ed. 2004. By Rita W. Moss.
EDUCATION	*Education: A Guide to Reference and Information Sources,* 2nd ed. 2000. By Lois Buttlar and Nancy O'Brien.
FILM	*On the Screen: A Film, Television, and Video Research Guide.* 1986. By Kim N. Fisher.
GENERAL HISTORY	*Guide to Reference Books,* 11th ed. 1996. Edited by Robert Balay.
	A Student's Guide to History, 9th ed. 2004. By Jules R. Benjamin.
HUMANITIES	*The Humanities: A Selective Guide to Information Sources,* 5th ed. 2000. By Ron Blazek and Elizabeth S. Aversa. Also available online.
LITERATURE	*Reference Works in British and American Literature,* 2nd ed. 1998. By James K. Bracken. Also available online.
	Literary Research Guide: An Annotated Listing of Reference Sources in English Literary Studies, 4th ed. 2002. By James L. Harner.

MUSIC	*Music: A Guide to the Reference Literature.* 1987. By William S. Brockman.
PHILOSOPHY	*Philosophy: A Guide to the Reference Literature,* 2nd ed. 1997. By Hans E. Bynagle. Also available online.
POLITICAL SCIENCE	*Political Science: A Guide to Reference and Information Sources.* 1990. By Henry York.
PSYCHOLOGY	*Library Use: A Handbook for Psychology,* 3rd ed. 2003.
SCIENCE AND TECHNOLOGY	*Information Sources in Science and Technology.* 1998. By Charlie Hurt.
SOCIAL SCIENCES	*The Social Sciences: A Cross-Disciplinary Guide to Selected Sources,* 3rd ed. 2002. By Nancy L. Herron. Also available online.
SOCIOLOGY	*Sociology: A Guide to Reference and Information Sources,* 3rd ed. 2005. By Stephen H. Aby.
WOMEN'S STUDIES	*Women's Studies: A Guide to Information Sources.* 1990. By Sarah Carter and Maureen Ritchie.

Consulting Bibliographies

A **bibliography** is simply a list of publications on a given subject. All researched articles and books include bibliographies to document their sources of information. In addition, separately published, book-length bibliographies exist for many subjects that have attracted significant amounts of writing. Some of these bibliographies are exhaustive, including every title that can be found on a subject, but most are selective. To discover how selections were made, check the bibliography's preface or introduction. Occasionally, bibliographies are annotated with brief summaries and evaluations of the entries.

Even if you attend a large research university, your library is unlikely to hold every book or journal article that a bibliography might direct you to. If a source looks likely to be useful but your library does not have a copy, ask a reference librarian about the possibility of acquiring it through interlibrary loan.

■ Identifying Subject Headings and Keywords

To extend your research beyond encyclopedias, you need to find appropriate subject headings and keywords. **Subject headings** are specific words and phrases used in library catalogs, periodical indexes, and other databases to categorize the contents of books and articles so that people can look for materials about a particular topic. One way to begin your search for subject headings is to consult the *Library of Congress Subject*

Headings (LCSH), which your library probably makes available both in print and online. This work lists the standard subject headings used in library catalogs. Here is an example from the LCSH:

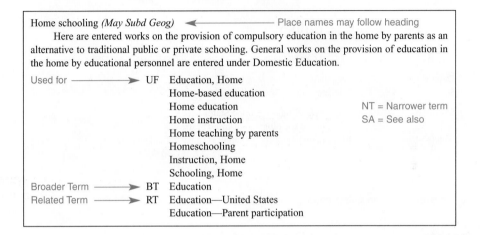

Home schooling *(May Subd Geog)* ◄─────────── Place names may follow heading
    Here are entered works on the provision of compulsory education in the home by parents as an alternative to traditional public or private schooling. General works on the provision of education in the home by educational personnel are entered under Domestic Education.

Used for ─────────► UF   Education, Home
                         Home-based education
                         Home education   NT = Narrower term
                         Home instruction   SA = See also
                         Home teaching by parents
                         Homeschooling
                         Instruction, Home
                         Schooling, Home
Broader Term ────► BT   Education
Related Term ─────► RT   Education—United States
                         Education—Parent participation

A student researching this topic but unable to find anything listed in the library catalog under "Home schooling," could use the other headings to find materials available in her library. Note that this LCSH entry explains the types of books that would be found under these headings and those that would be found elsewhere.

The LCSH can therefore be extremely helpful; however, you can often locate useful subject headings faster by searching the catalog or other database using **keywords**, words or phrases that you think describe your topic. As you read about your subject in an encyclopedia or other reference book, you should keep a list of keywords that may be useful. (Make sure you spell your keywords correctly. Databases are often unforgiving of spelling errors.) As you review the results of a keyword search, look for the titles that seem to match most closely the topics that you are looking for. When you call up the detailed information for these titles, look for the section labeled "Subject" or "Subject Heading," which will show the headings under which the book or article is classified. (In the example that follows, this section is abbreviated as "Subj-lcsh.") In many computerized catalogs and databases, these subject headings are links that you can click on to get a list of other materials on the same subject. Keep a list in your working bibliography of all the subject headings you find that relate to your topic, so that you can refer to them each time you look for more information. Here is an example of an online catalog listing for a book on home schooling:

Title:	Kingdom of children: culture and controversy in the homeschooling movement/ Mitchell L. Stevens
Imprint:	Princeton, NJ: Princeton University Press, c2001.

LOCATION	CALL NO	STATUS
Coe	LC40.S74 2001	NOT CHCKD OUT

Description:	xiii, 228 p.; 24 cm
Series:	Princeton studies in cultural sociology
Subj-lcsh	**Home Schooling – – United States** ⟶ Subject headings
	Educational sociology – – United States
Note(s):	Includes bibliographical references (p. 199 – 224) and index

For an example of an online catalog reference to a periodical, see p. 394.

Determining the Most Promising Sources

As you follow a subject heading into the library catalog and periodical indexes, you will discover many seemingly relevant books and articles. How do you decide which ones to track down and examine? You may have little to go on but author, title, date, and publisher or periodical name, but these details actually provide useful clues. Look again, for example, at the online catalog listing for *Kingdom of Children*. The title is the first clue to the subject coverage of the book. Note that the publication date, 2001, is fairly recent. From the subject headings, you can see that the geographic focus of the book is the United States. Finally, from the notes, you can see that the book includes an extensive bibliography that could lead you to other sources.

Now look at Figure 13.4, search results from *ERIC*, an electronic periodical database, searched through EBSCOhost.

This screen lists articles that address different aspects of home schooling, briefly describing some of the articles. You can see that the first article deals with the issue from a British point of view, which might provide an interesting cross-cultural perspective for your essay. The second and third articles, both from a journal devoted to the topic of college admissions, might give you a sense of how well home schooling prepares students for college. Be careful, though, to stay focused on your specific research topic or thesis, especially if you are pressed for time and cannot afford to become distracted exploring sources that sound interesting but are unlikely to be useful.

In addition, each entry contains the information that you will need to locate it in a library, and some databases provide links to the full text of articles from selected periodicals. Here is what each piece of information means:

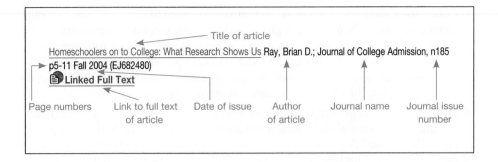

When you look in catalogs and indexes, consider the following points when deciding whether you should track down a particular source:

- **Relevance to your topic:** Examine the title, subtitle, subject headings, and abstract and try to determine how directly the particular source addresses your topic.

Figure 13.4 EBSCOhost: "Homeschooling," results of ERIC search

- *Publication date:* How recent is the source? For current controversies, emerging trends, and scientific or technological developments, you must consult recent material. For historical or biographical topics, you will want to start with present-day perspectives but eventually explore older sources that offer authoritative perspectives. You may also want or need to consult sources written at the time of the events or during the life of the person you are researching.

- *Description:* Does the length indicate a brief treatment of the topic or an extended treatment? Does the work include illustrations that may elaborate on concepts discussed in the text? Does it include a bibliography that could lead you to other works or an index that could give you an overview of what is discussed in the text?

From among the sources that look promising, select publications that seem by their titles to address different aspects of your topic or to approach it from different perspectives. Try to avoid selecting sources that are mostly by the same author, from the same publisher, or in the same journal.

For a discussion of periodical indexes, see p. 389.

Searching Online Library Catalogs and Databases

Computerized library catalogs and other databases consist of thousands or even millions of records, each representing an individual item such as a book, an article, or a government publication. The record is made up of different fields describing the item and allowing users to search for it and retrieve it from the database.

Using Different Search Techniques

Basic search strategies include author, title, and subject searches. When you perform an **author search**, the computer looks for a match between the name you type and the names listed in the author field of all the records in the online catalog or other database. When you perform a **title search** or a **subject search**, the computer looks for a match in the title field or the subject field, respectively. Computers are very literal. They try to match only the exact terms you enter, and most do not recognize incorrect spellings. That is an incentive to become a good speller and a good typist. However, because most library catalogs and databases also offer the option of searching for titles and subjects by keywords, you need not enter the full exact title or subject heading. Table 13.2 describes some search capabilities commonly offered by library catalogs and databases.

Doing Advanced Searches and Using Boolean Operators

The real power of using an online catalog or other database is demonstrated when you need to look up books or articles using more than one keyword. For example, suppose

Table 13.2 Common Search Capabilities Offered by Library Catalogs and Databases

Type of Search	How the Computer Conducts the Search	Things to Know
Author search (exact) • Individual *(Guterson, David)* • Organization *(U.S. Department of Education)*	Looks in the author field for the words entered	• Author searches generally are exact-match searches, so authors' names are entered *last name, first name* (for example, "Shakespeare, William"). • Organizations can be considered authors. Enter the name of the organization in natural word order. • An exact-match author search is useful for finding books and articles by a particular author.
Title search (exact) • Book title • Magazine or journal title • Article title	Looks in the title field for words in the exact order you enter them	An exact-match title search is useful for identifying the location of known items, such as when you are looking for a particular journal or book.
Subject search (exact)	Looks in the subject heading or descriptor field for words in the exact order you enter them	An exact-match subject search is useful when you are sure about the subject heading.
Keyword search	Looks in the title, note, subject, abstract, and text fields for the words entered	A keyword search is the broadest kind you can use. It is useful during early exploration of a subject.

you want information about home schooling in California. Rather than looking through an index listing all the articles on home schooling and picking out those that mention California, you can ask the computer to do the work for you by linking your two keywords. Most online catalogs and databases offer the option of an **advanced search**, sometimes on a separate page from the main search page, that allows you to search for more than one keyword at a time, search for certain keywords while excluding others, or search for an exact phrase. Or you may be able to create this kind of advanced search yourself by using the **Boolean operators** AND, OR, and NOT along with quotation marks and parentheses.

To understand the operation of **Boolean logic** (developed by and named after George Boole, a nineteenth-century mathematician), picture one set of articles about home schooling and another set of articles about California. A third set is formed by articles that are about both home schooling and California. The figures below provide an illustration of how each Boolean operator works.

Using Truncation

Another useful search strategy employs **truncation**. With this technique, you drop the ending of a word or term and replace it with a symbol, which indicates you want to retrieve records containing any term that begins the same way as your term. For example, by entering the term "home school#" you would retrieve all the records that have terms such as "home school," "home schooling," "home schools," "home schooled," or "home schoolers." Truncation is useful when you want to retrieve both the plural and the singular forms of a word or any word for which you are not sure of the ending. Truncation symbols vary with the catalog or database. The question mark (?), asterisk (*), and pound sign (#) are frequently used.

AND

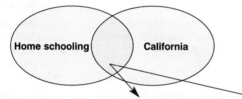

Returns references that contain both the term **home schooling** AND the term **California**
- Narrows the search
- Combines unrelated terms
- Is the default used by most online catalogs and databases

OR

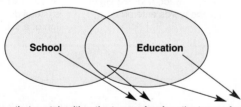

Returns all references that contain either the term **school** OR the term **education** OR both terms
- Broadens the search **("OR is more")**
- Is useful with synonyms and alternate spellings: ("home schooling" and "homeschooling")

NOT

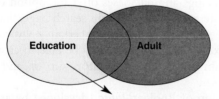

Returns references that include the term **education** but NOT the term **adult**
- Narrows the search

Caution: By narrowing your search, you may eliminate relevant material.

Table 13.3 Electronic Search Tips

If You Find Too Many Sources on Your Topic:	*If You Find Insufficient Information on Your Topic:*
• Use a subject search instead of a keyword search. • Add additional words to your search. • Use a more precise vocabulary to describe your topic. • Use an advanced search to restrict your findings by date, format, language, or other options.	• Use a keyword instead of a subject. • Eliminate words from your search terms. • Try truncated forms of your keyword. • Use different words to describe your topic. • Check the spelling of each term you type.

Table 13.3 offers some suggestions for expanding or narrowing your electronic search.

Locating Sources

The following are guidelines for finding books, various kinds of periodical articles, government documents and statistical information, and other types of sources.

Finding Books

The primary source for books is the library's computerized catalog. Besides allowing you to flexibly search keywords and subject headings, the catalog will tell you whether a book is currently available or checked out. It also allows you to print out source information rather than having to copy the material by hand. Look again at the sample catalog listing for a book on home schooling:

Title:	Kingdom of children: culture and controversy in the homeschooling movement/ Mitchell L. Stevens
Imprint:	Princeton, NJ: Princeton University Press, c2001.

LOCATION	CALL NO	STATUS
Coe	LC40.S74 2001	NOT CHCKD OUT

Description:	xiii, 228 p.; 24 cm
Series:	Princeton studies in cultural sociology
Subj-lcsh	**Home Schooling – – United States** **Educational sociology – – United States**
Note(s):	Includes bibliographical references (p. 199 – 224) and index

Whether you search a library catalog by author, title, subject, or keyword, each record you find will provide the following standard information.

1. *Call number:* This number is your key to finding the book in the library. Most college libraries use the Library of Congress system, and most public libraries and some small college libraries use the Dewey decimal system. Call numbers serve two purposes: They provide an exact location for every book in the library, and because they are assigned according to subject classifications, they group together books on the same topic. When you go to the stacks to locate the book, therefore, always browse for other useful material on the shelves around it.

2. *Author:* The author's name usually appears last name first, followed by birth and (if applicable) death dates. For books with multiple authors, the record includes an author entry under each author's name.

3. *Title:* The title appears exactly as it does on the title page of the book, except that only the first word and proper nouns and adjectives are capitalized.

4. *Publication information:* The place of publication (usually just the city), the publisher, and the year of publication are listed. If the book was published simultaneously in the United States and abroad, both places of publication and both publishers are indicated.

5. *Physical description:* This section provides information about the book's page length and size. A roman numeral indicates the number of pages devoted to front matter (such as a preface, table of contents, and acknowledgments).

6. *Notes:* Any special features such as a bibliography or an index are listed here.

7. *Subject headings:* Assigned by the Library of Congress, these headings indicate how the book is listed in the subject catalog. Often, these subject headings are active links; clicking on them will bring up a list of other books on the same subject.

For more on the Library of Congress Subject Headings (LCSH), see pp. 380–82. Examples of records in online catalogs are shown on p. 382.

Finding Periodical Articles

The most up-to-date information on a subject is usually found not in books but in articles published in periodicals. A **periodical** is a publication such as a magazine, newspaper, or scholarly journal that is published on an ongoing basis, at regular intervals (for instance, daily, weekly, monthly, or annually), and with different content in each issue. Examples of periodicals include *Sports Illustrated* (magazine), the *New York Times* (newspaper), *Tulsa Studies in Women's Literature* (scholarly journal), *Kairos* (online journal), and *Slate* (online magazine). Many print periodicals now publish online versions as well, although the contents may be somewhat different. In addition, some magazines and journals are published exclusively on the Web.

Articles in periodicals are usually not listed in the library catalog; to find them, you must use library reference works called **periodical indexes**. Some periodical indexes include **abstracts**, or short summaries of articles. In the library, indexes may be available in print, in microform, on CD-ROM, or as online databases. Many are available in both print and electronic formats, and some electronic indexes give you access to the full text of articles.

Distinguishing Scholarly Journals and Popular Magazines

Although they are both called periodicals, journals and magazines have important differences. **Journals** publish articles written by experts in a particular field of study, frequently professors or researchers in academic institutions. Journals are usually specialized in their subject focus, research oriented, and extensively reviewed by specialists prior to publication. They are intended to be read by experts and students conducting research. **Magazines**, in contrast, usually publish general-interest articles written by journalists. The articles are written to entertain and educate the general public, and they tend to appeal to a much broader audience than journal articles.

Journals contain a great deal of what is called **primary literature**, reporting the results of original research. For example, a scientist might publish an article in a medical journal about the results of a new treatment protocol for breast cancer. **Secondary literature**, published in magazines, is intended to inform the general public about new and interesting developments in scientific and other areas of research. If a reporter from *Newsweek* writes an article about this scientist's cancer research, this article is classified as secondary literature. Table 13.4 on p. 390 summarizes some of the important differences between scholarly journals and popular magazines.

Selecting an Appropriate Periodical Index or Abstract

Periodical indexes and abstracts are of two types: general and specialized. Both provide you with information that will help you locate articles on a topic. In addition to the lists on pp. 389–91, a reference librarian can help you identify other indexes and abstracts that may be useful for your topic.

General Indexes. These indexes are a good place to start your research because they cover a broad range of subjects. Most have separate author and subject listings. General indexes usually list only articles from popular magazines and newspapers, although some of them include listings from basic scholarly journals. Here is a list of the most common general indexes:

> *The Readers' Guide to Periodical Literature* (1900–; online, 1983–; updated quarterly): Covers about two hundred popular periodicals. Even for general topics, however, you should not rely on it exclusively, because it does not cover the research

Table 13.4 How to Distinguish a Scholarly Journal from a Popular Magazine

Scholarly Journal	Popular Magazine
• The front or back cover lists the contents of the issue.	• The cover features a color picture.
• The title of the publication contains the word *Journal*.	• The title may be catchy as well as descriptive.
• You see the journal only at the library.	• You see the magazine for sale at the grocery store, in an airport, or at a bookstore.
• It either does not include advertisements or advertises products such as textbooks, professional books, and scholarly conferences.	• It has lots of colorful advertisements in it.
• The authors of articles have *Ph.D.* or academic affiliations after their names.	• The authors of articles are journalists or reporters.
• Many articles have more than one author.	• Most articles have a single author but may quote experts.
• A short summary (abstract) of an article may appear on the first page.	• A headline or engaging description may precede the article.
• Most articles are fairly long, 5 to 20 pages.	• Most of the articles are fairly short, 1 to 5 pages.
• The articles may include charts, tables, figures, and quotations from other scholarly sources.	• The articles have color pictures and sidebar boxes.
• The articles have a bibliography (list of references to other books and articles) at the end.	• The articles do not include a bibliography.
• You probably would not read it at the beach.	• You might bring it to the beach to read.

journals that play such an important role in college writing. Here is an example of an entry for home education:

> **HOME SCHOOLING**
> Geography in the genes. il *National Geographic*
> v204 no5 p insert32 N 2003
> Keeping it in the family. S. Hunt. por *Black Issues Book Review* v5
> no5 p20–1 S/O 2003
> My home is my classroom. S. Payne. por *New York Times*
> *Upfront* v136 no2 p30 S 22 2003

Magazine Index (on microfilm, 1988–; online as part of InfoTrac, 1973–; see below): Indexes over four hundred magazines.

InfoTrac (online): Time coverage varies by subscription. Includes three indexes: (1) the *General Periodicals Index,* which covers over twelve hundred general-interest publications, incorporating the *Magazine Index* and including the *New York Times* and the *Wall Street Journal;* (2) the *Academic Index,* which covers four hundred scholarly and general-interest publications, including the *New York Times;* and (3) the *National Newspaper Index,* which covers the *Christian Science*

Monitor, Los Angeles Times, New York Times, Wall Street Journal, and *Washington Post.* Some entries include abstracts or the full text of articles.

Alternative Press Index (1970–; online through Biblioline): Indexes alternative and radical publications.

Humanities Index (1974–; online, 1984–): Covers more than five hundred periodicals in archaeology, history, classics, literature, performing arts, philosophy, and religion.

Social Sciences Index (1974–; online, 1983–): Covers more than five hundred periodicals in economics, geography, law, political science, psychology, public administration, and sociology.

Public Affairs Information Service Bulletin (1915–; online, 1972–): Covers articles and other publications by public and private agencies on economic and social conditions, international relations, and public administration. Subject listings only.

Specialized Indexes and Abstracts.   These publications list or summarize articles devoted to technical or scholarly research. As you learn more about your topic, you will turn to specialized indexes and abstracts to find references to scholarly articles. The

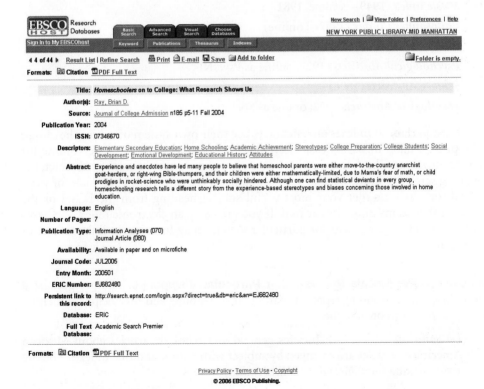

Figure 13.5 Entry from ERIC

example in Figure 13.5 from ERIC, which indexes and summarizes articles from a wide range of periodicals that publish educational research, is typical of entries found in specialized indexes.

Here is a list of specialized periodical indexes that cover various disciplines:

Accounting and Tax Index (1964–; online)

America: History and Life (1954–; online, 1964–)

American Statistics Index (1973–)

Applied Science and Technology Index (1958–; online, 1983–)

Art Index (1929–; online as *Art Abstracts,* 1984–)

Biological and Agricultural Index (1964–; online as *Bio Abstracts,* 1985–)

Education Index (1929–; online as *Education Abstracts,* 1983–)

Engineering Index (1920–; online)

Historical Abstracts (1955–; online, 1982–)

Index Medicus (1961–; online as MEDLINE)

MLA International Bibliography of Books and Articles in the Modern Languages and Literature (1921–; online)

Music Index (1949–; online, 1981–)

Philosopher's Index (1957–; online)

Physics Abstracts (1898; online as INSPEC)

Psychological Abstracts (1927; online as PsycINFO)

Science Abstracts (1898)

Sociological Abstracts 1952; online as Sociofile)

Most periodical indexes and abstracts use their own system of subject headings. The print version of *Sociological Abstracts,* for example, has a separate volume for subject headings. Check the opening pages or, for an electronic index or abstract, the opening screen or home page to see how subjects are classified. Then look for periodicals or articles under your most useful subject heading from the LCSH or the heading that seems most similar to it. If you are using an electronic index, the items in the subject heading field for particular articles may function as links to lists of related materials.

Indexes to Periodicals Representing Particular Viewpoints.   Some specialized periodical indexes tend to represent particular viewpoints and may help you identify different positions on an issue.

Chicano Index (1967–): Indexes general and scholarly articles about Mexican Americans. Articles are arranged by subject with author and title indexes. (Before 1989, the title was *Chicano Periodical Index.*)

G. K. Hall Index to Black Periodicals (1999–); previously published as *Index to Black Periodicals* (1984–1998): Provides an author and subject index to general and scholarly articles about African Americans.

Left Index (1982–; online only, 2000–): Indexes by author and subject over eighty periodicals with a Marxist, radical, or left perspective. Listings cover primarily topics in the social sciences and humanities.

Another useful source for identifying positions is *Editorials on File*, described on p. 395.

Full-Text Electronic Services.   In addition to the electronic indexes and abstracts listed earlier, many libraries subscribe to other electronic database services that provide the full text of periodical articles. Some of these services include the following:

ERIC (*Educational Resources Information Center*) (online, 1966–): Indexes, abstracts, and provides some full texts of articles from 750 education journals.

ABI/INFORM (1988–): Provides full-text articles from business periodicals.

PsycBOOKS (online, 2004–): Indexes books and book chapters in psychology.

IngentaConnect (1998–; http://www.ingentaconnect.com): An online document delivery service, Ingenta lists articles from more than 5,400 online journals and 26,000 other publications.

LEXIS-NEXIS Academic Universe (time coverage varies by source; http://www.lexis-nexis.com/lncc/academic): Provides the full text of articles from academic journals and other sources containing legal, news, and government information and statistics.

JSTOR (http://www.jstor.org): Provides the full text of articles from older issues of more than three hundred journals in the humanities and social sciences.

Project Muse (1996–; http://muse.jhu.edu): Provides the full text of articles from more than three hundred journals in the humanities, social sciences, and mathematics published by Johns Hopkins University Press and selected not-for-profit publishers.

Hein Online (2000–; http://www.11.georgetown.edu/lib/gulconly/hein/hein.html): Provides a collection of legal periodical titles with full-text access.

Science Direct (1997–; http://www.sciencedirect.com): Provides the full text of articles from more than a thousand journals in science, technology, medicine, and the social sciences published by Elsevier Press.

Interlibrary networks: Known by different names in different regions, these networks allow you to search in the catalogs of colleges and universities in your area and across the country. In many cases, you can request a book by interlibrary loan, although it may take several weeks to be delivered to your library. You can also request a copy of an article from a journal to which your own library does not subscribe. Most libraries do not lend their journals but will copy and forward articles for a fee.

Searching Electronic Periodical Databases

Although you can search an electronic periodical database by author or title, you will probably more often want to do searches using keywords. As with searches for books in the library catalog, make your keywords as precise as possible so that your search results in a manageable list of sources relevant to your topic. Most databases include an advanced-search mechanism or set of guidelines for using Boolean operators or other keyword-combining procedures. In addition, if you enter a very general keyword, many databases will provide a list of subtopics that you can use to narrow your search. Once you have entered your keywords, the computer searches the database and lists every reference to them that it finds. You can usually print or download the results.

Because online databases contain so much information, you may want to consult with a librarian to develop an efficient search strategy. Also keep in mind that some electronic indexes cover only the last fifteen to twenty years; you may need to consult older printed versions of indexes as well.

Locating Periodicals in the Library

When you identify a promising magazine or journal article in a periodical index, you must go to the library's catalog to learn whether the library subscribes to the periodical, whether the issue is available, and, if so, where you can find it. No library can subscribe to every periodical, so as you go through indexes and abstracts, be sure to identify more articles than you actually need. This will save you from having to repeat your search later.

Although every library arranges its print periodicals differently, recent issues are usually arranged alphabetically by title on open shelves. Older issues may be bound like books (shelved by call numbers or alphabetically by title) or filmed and available in microform.

Suppose you want to look up the article from *Journal of College Admission* that you found indexed in *ERIC*. Here is the record for the journal from one library's online catalog.

You searched TITLE   **Journal of College Admission**

Title of the journal

Where the journal is published

Title: Journal of college admission
Imprint: Skokie, Ill., National Association of College Admission Counselors [etc.]

Library where the journal is located and location of
current (unbound) issues

LOCATION: MAIN-Latest in Curr Per   LB 2301.A77x ◄——— Call number
LIB. HAS: B100-183(1984-2004) ◄—— Bound volumes and years the library owns
Latest Received: Fall 2005 No. 189 ◄——— Most recent issue received

From this record, you would learn that the library does subscribe to *Journal of College Admission* and that you could locate no. 185 (which has not yet been bound) in the library's current periodicals collection.

Finding Newspaper Articles and Other News Sources

Newspapers provide useful information for many research topics in such areas as foreign affairs, economics, public opinion, and social trends. Libraries usually photograph newspapers and store them in miniature form on microfilm (reels) or microfiche (cards) that must be placed in viewing machines to be read. Newspaper indexes such as the *Los Angeles Times Index, New York Times Index*, and *London Times Index*, which are available online as well as in print, can help you locate specific articles on your topic.

Your library may also subscribe to newspaper article and digest services, such as the following:

National Newspaper Index (microfilm, 1989–; online as part of InfoTrac, 1979–) (see p. 390): Indexes the *Christian Science Monitor, Los Angeles Times, New York Times, Wall Street Journal*, and *Washington Post*.

NewsBank (microfiche and CD-ROM, 1970–; online): Provides full-text articles from five hundred U.S. newspapers; a good source of information on local and regional issues and trends.

Newspaper Abstracts (1988–; online, 1989–): Indexes and gives brief abstracts of articles from nineteen major regional, national, and international newspapers; available through Proquest.

Facts on File (weekly; CD-ROM, 1980): Provides a digest of U.S. and international news events arranged by subject, such as foreign affairs, arts, education, religion, and sports.

Editorials on File (twice monthly): Provides a digest of editorials from 150 U.S. and Canadian newspapers with brief descriptions of editorial subjects followed by fifteen to twenty editorials on the subject, reprinted from different newspapers.

CQ Researcher (online, 1991–; previously published since 1924 as Editorial Research Reports): Reports on current and controversial topics, including brief histories, statistics, editorials, journal articles, endnotes, and supplementary reading lists.

Foreign Broadcast Information Service (FBIS) (1980–; online, 1990 –): Provides a digest of foreign broadcast scripts, newspaper articles, and government statements from Asia, Europe, Latin America, Africa, Russia, and the Middle East.

Keesing's Record of World Events (1931 – ; also online): Provides a monthly digest of events in all countries, compiled from British and other reporting services; includes speeches and statistics and chronological, geographic, and topical indexes.

Finding Government and Statistical Information

Federal, state, and local governments now make many of their publications and reference services available directly through the World Wide Web, though most college libraries still maintain print collections of government publications. Ask a reference librarian for assistance in locating governmental sources and other sources of statistical information in the library or on the Web. In particular, consider consulting the following sources for information on political subjects and national trends.

> ***Congressional Quarterly Almanac*** (annual): A summary of legislation; provides an overview of government policies and trends, including analysis as well as election results, records of roll-call votes, and the text of significant speeches and debates.

> ***CQ Weekly*** (online, 1998 –; formerly published as *Congressional Quarterly Weekly Report*): A news service; includes up-to-date summaries of congressional committee actions, congressional votes, and executive branch activities as well as overviews of current policy discussions and other activities of the federal government.

> ***Statistical Abstract of the United States*** (annual; some content online, http://www.census.gov/compendia/statab/): A publication of the Bureau of the Census; provides a variety of social, economic, and political statistics, often covering several years, including tables, graphs, charts, and references to additional sources of information.

> ***American Statistics Index*** (1974 –; annual with monthly supplements): Attempts to cover all federal government publications containing statistical information of research significance and includes brief descriptions of references.

> ***Statistical Reference Index*** (1980 –): Provides a selective guide to American statistical publications from sources other than the U.S. government, including economic, social, and political statistical sources.

> ***World Almanac and Book of Facts*** (annual): Presents information on a variety of subjects drawn from many sources, including a chronology of the year, climatological data, and lists of inventions and awards.

> ***The Gallup Poll: Public Opinion*** (1935 –): Provides a chronological listing of the results of public opinion polls, including information on social, economic, and political trends.

Finding Other Library Sources

Libraries hold vast amounts of useful materials other than books, periodicals, and government documents. Some of the following may be appropriate for your research.

- ***Vertical files:*** Pamphlets and brochures from government and private agencies
- ***Special collections:*** Manuscripts, rare books, and materials of local interest
- ***Audio collections:*** Records, audiotapes, music CDs, readings, and speeches

- *Video collections:* Slides, filmstrips, videotapes, and DVDs
- *Art collections:* Drawings, paintings, and engravings
- *Interlibrary loans:* As noted above, many libraries can arrange to borrow books from other libraries or have copies of journal articles sent from other libraries as part of an interlibrary network program. Ask your librarian how long it will take to get the material you need (usually several weeks) and how to use the loan service (some libraries allow you to send an electronic request to the local interlibrary loan office).
- *Computer resources:* Interactive computer programs that combine text, video, and audio resources in history, literature, business, and other disciplines

▓ Using the Internet for Research

By now, most of you are familiar with searching the Internet. This section introduces you to some tools and strategies that will help you use the Net more efficiently.

Keep the following guidelines in mind:

- *Many significant electronic sources require a paid subscription or other fees.* Electronic periodical indexes, full-text article databases, and other valuable electronic resources are often available only by subscription. If your college subscribes to these resources, your tuition grants you access to them. For these reasons (as well as the one discussed below), you should plan to use the library or campus computer system for much of your electronic research.

- *Open-access Internet sources are generally less reliable than print sources or electronic sources to which your library or campus subscribes.* Because it is relatively easy for anyone to publish on the Internet, judging the reliability of online information is a special concern. Depending on your topic, purpose, and audience, the sources you find on the Internet may not be as credible or authoritative as print sources or subscription electronic sources, which have usually been screened by publishers, editors, librarians, and authorities on the topic. For some topics, most of what you find on the Internet may be written by highly biased or amateur authors, so you will need to balance or supplement these sources with information from your library or campus and print sources. When in doubt about the reliability of an online source for a particular assignment, check with your instructor. (See Evaluating Sources on pp. 401–04 for more specific suggestions.)

- *Internet sources are not as stable as print sources or the electronic sources to which your library or campus subscribes.* A Web site that existed last week may no longer be available today, or its content may have changed.

- *Internet sources must be documented.* You will need to follow appropriate conventions for quoting, paraphrasing, summarizing, and documenting the online sources you use, just as you do for print sources. Because an Internet source can change or disappear quickly, be sure to record the information for the working-bibliography entry when you first find the source. Whenever possible, download and print out the source to preserve it. Make sure your download or printout includes all the items of information required for the entry or at least all those you can find. (See Figure 13.6 for guidelines on what to record for an Internet source.)

Citing Internet sources using MLA style is discussed in Chapter 14, pp. 416–29; APA style is discussed on pp. 429–36.

Author(s) of work	
Title of work	
Title of site	
Sponsor of site	
URL (address)	
Date of electronic publication or of latest update	
Date you accessed source	
Publication information for print version of work (if any)	
Notes	

Figure 13.6 Information for working bibliography—Internet sources

■ Finding the Best Information Online

Search tools like Google and Yahoo! are important resources for searching the Web for information on your topic. To use these tools effectively, you should understand their features, strengths, and limitations.

Most search tools now allow you to look for sources using both search engines and subject directories. **Search engines** are based on keywords. They are simply computer programs that scan the Web—or that part of the Web that is in the particular search engine's database—looking for the keyword(s) you have entered. **Subject directories** are based on categories, like the subject headings in a library catalog or periodical index. Beginning with a menu of general subjects, you click on increasingly narrow subjects (for example, going from Science to Biology to Genetics to DNA Mapping), until you reach either a list of specific Web sites or a point where you have to do a keyword search within the narrowest subject you have chosen. Search engines are useful whenever you have a good idea of the appropriate keywords for your topic or if you are not sure under what category the topic falls. But subject directories can help quickly narrow your search to those parts of the Web that are likely to be most productive and thus avoid keyword searches that produce hundreds or thousands of results.

Always click on the link called Help, Hints, or Tips on a search tool's home page to find out more about the recognized commands and advanced-search techniques for that specific search tool. Most search engines allow searches using the Boolean operators discussed on pp. 384–86. Many also let you limit a search to specific dates, languages, or other criteria.

As with searches of library catalogs and databases, the success of a Web search depends to a great extent on the keywords you choose. Remember that many different words often describe the same topic. If your topic is ecology, for example, you may find information under the keywords *ecosystem, environment, pollution,* and *endangered species,* as well as a number of other related keywords, depending on the focus of your research. When you find a source that seems promising, be sure to create a bookmark for the Web page so that you can return to it easily later on.

No matter how precise your keywords are, search engines can be unreliable, and you may not find the best available resources. You might instead begin your search at the Web site of a relevant and respected organization. If you want photos of constellations, go to the NASA Web page. If you want public laws, go to a government Web page like GPO Access. In addition, be sure to supplement your Internet research with other sources from your library, including books, reference works, and articles from appropriate periodicals.

Two other, more recent sources of online information are **blogs** and **RSS**. A blog, or Web log, is a Web site, often based on a particular topic, that is maintained by an individual or organization and updated on a regular basis, often many times a day. Blogs may contain postings written by the sponsor(s) of the site; information such as news articles, press releases, and commentary from other sites; and comments posted by readers. Blogs are usually organized chronologically, with the newest post at the top.

Because they are not subjected to the same editorial scrutiny as published books or periodical articles and may reflect just one person's opinions and biases, it's a good idea to find several blogs from multiple perspectives about your subject. Some Web sites, such as Blogwise (www.blogwise.com) and Blogger (www.blogger.com), provide directories and search functions to help you find blogs on a particular topic.

If you are researching a very current topic and need to follow constantly updated news sites and blogs, you can use a program called an **aggregator**, which obtains news automatically from many sources and assembles it through a process called RSS (Really Simple Syndication). Using an aggregator, you can scan the information from a variety of sources by referring to just one Web page and then click on links to the news stories to read further. Many aggregators, such as NetNewsWire, NewsGator, and SharpReader, are available as software that you can download to your computer; others are Web sites you can customize to your own preferences, such as Bloglines (www.bloglines.com) and NewsIsFree (www.newsisfree.com).

■ Using E-mail and Online Communities for Research

You may find it possible to use your computer to do research in ways other than those already discussed in this chapter. In particular, if you can find out the e-mail address of an expert on your topic, you may want to contact the person and ask whether he or she would agree to a brief online (or telephone) interview. In addition, several kinds of electronic communities available on the Internet may possibly be helpful. Many Web sites consist of or incorporate tools known as **bulletin boards** or **message boards**, in which anyone who registers may post messages to and receive them from other members. Older Internet servers known as news servers also provide access to bulletin boards or variants called **newsgroups**. Another kind of community, **mailing lists**, are groups of people who subscribe to and receive e-mail messages shared among all the members simultaneously. Finally, **chat rooms** allow users to meet together at the same time in a shared message space.

These different kinds of online communities often focus on a specific field of shared interest, and the people who frequent them are sometimes working professionals or academics with expertise in topics that are obscure or difficult to research otherwise. Such experts are often willing to answer both basic and advanced questions and will sometimes consent to an e-mail or telephone interview. Even if they are not authorities in the field, online community members may stimulate your thinking about the topic in new directions or save you a large amount of research time by pointing you to resources that might otherwise have taken you quite a while to uncover. Many communities provide some kind of indexing or search mechanism so that you can look for "threads" (conversations) related to your topic.

As with other sources, however, evaluate the credibility and reliability of online communities. Also be aware that while most communities welcome guests and newcomers, others may perceive your questions as intrusive or unwanted. What may seem new and exciting to you may be old news for veterans. Finally, remember that some online communities are more active than others; survey the dates of posts and frequency of activity to determine whether a given group is still lively or has gone defunct.

For most topics, you will be able to find a variety of related newsgroups; www.groups.google.com catalogs many of them (and allows you to start your own). For mailing lists, you have to register for a subscription to the list. Remember that unless a digest option is available, each subscription means you will be receiving a large amount of e-mail, so think about the implications before you sign up.

■ Evaluating Sources

From the beginning of your library and Internet search, you should evaluate potential sources to determine which ones you should take the time to examine more closely and then which of these you should use in your essay. Obviously, you must decide which sources provide information relevant to the topic. But you must also decide how credible or trustworthy the sources are. Just because a book or an essay appears in print or online does not necessarily mean that an author's information or opinions are reliable.

Selecting Relevant Sources

Begin your evaluation of sources by narrowing your working bibliography to the most relevant items. Consider them in terms of scope, date of publication, and viewpoint.

Scope and Approach.   To decide how relevant a particular source is to your topic, you need to examine the source in depth. Do not depend on title alone, for it may be misleading. If the source is a book, check its table of contents and index to see how many pages are devoted to the precise subject you are exploring. In most cases, you will want an in-depth, not a superficial, treatment of the subject. Read the preface or introduction to a book or the abstract or opening paragraphs of an article and any biographical information given about the author to determine the author's basic approach to the subject or special way of looking at it. As you attend to these elements, consider the following questions:

- Does the source provide a general or specialized view? General sources are helpful early in your research, but you will also need the authority or up-to-date coverage of specialized sources. Extremely specialized works, however, may be too technical.
- Is the source long enough to provide adequate detail?
- Is the source written for general readers? Specialists? Advocates? Critics?

- Is the author an expert on the topic? Does the author's way of looking at the topic support or challenge your own views? (The fact that an author's viewpoint challenges your own does not mean that you should reject the author as a source, as you will see from the discussion on viewpoints.)
- Is the information in the source substantiated elsewhere? Does its approach seem to be comparable to, or a significant challenge to, the approaches of other credible sources?

Date of Publication. Although you should always consult the most up-to-date sources available on your subject, older sources often establish the principles, theories, and data on which later work is based and may provide a useful perspective for evaluating it. If older works are considered authoritative, you may want to become familiar with them. To determine which sources are authoritative, note the ones that are cited most often in encyclopedia articles, bibliographies, and recent works on the subject. If your source is on the Web, consider whether it has been regularly updated.

Viewpoint. Your sources should represent multiple viewpoints on the subject. Just as you would not depend on a single author for all of your information, so you do not want to use only authors who belong to the same school of thought. (For suggestions on determining authors' viewpoints, see the following section on Identifying Bias.)

Using sources that represent a variety of different viewpoints is especially important when developing an argument for one of the essay assignments in Chapters 5–7. During the invention work in those chapters, you may want to research what others have said about your subject to see what positions have been staked out and what arguments have been made. You will then be able to define the issue more carefully, collect arguments supporting your position, and anticipate arguments opposing it.

Identifying Bias

One of the most important aspects of evaluating a source is identifying any bias in its treatment of the subject. Although the word *bias* may sound accusatory, most writing is not neutral or objective and does not try or claim to be. Authors come to their subjects with particular viewpoints. In using sources, you must consider carefully how these viewpoints are reflected in the writing and how they affect the way authors present their arguments.

Although the text of the source will give you the most precise indication of the author's viewpoint, you can often get a good idea of it by looking at the preface or introduction or at the sources the author cites. When you examine a reference, you can often determine the general point of view it represents by considering the following elements.

Title. Does the title or subtitle indicate the text's bias? Watch for loaded words or confrontational phrasing.

Author.   What is the author's professional title or affiliation? What is the author's perspective? Is the author in favor of something or at odds with it? What has persuaded the author to take this stance? How might the author's professional affiliation affect his or her perspective? What is the author's tone? Information on the author may be available in the book, article, or Web site itself or in biographical sources available in the library. You could also try entering the author's name into a search engine and see what you learn from sites that discuss him or her.

Presentation of Argument.   Almost every written work asserts a point of view or makes an argument for something the author considers important. To determine this position and the reason behind it, look for the main point. What evidence does the author provide as support for this point? Is the evidence from authoritative sources? Is the evidence persuasive? Does the author make concessions to or refute opposing arguments?

For more detail on these argumentative strategies, see Chapter 11.

Publication Information.   Is the book published by a commercial publisher, a corporation, a government agency, or an interest group? Is the Web site sponsored by a business, a professional group, a private organization, an educational institution, a government agency, or an individual? What is the publisher's or sponsor's position on the topic? Is the author funded by or affiliated with the publisher or sponsor?

Editorial Slant.   What kind of periodical published the article—popular, academic, alternative? If you found the article on a Web site, is the site maintained by a commercial or academic sponsor? Does the article provide links to other Web resources? For periodicals, knowing some background about the publisher can help to determine bias because all periodicals have their own editorial slants. Where the periodical's name does not indicate its bias, reference sources may help you determine this information. Two of the most common are the following:

> *Gale Directory of Publications and Broadcast Media* (1990–, updated yearly): A useful source providing descriptive information on newspapers and magazines. Entries often include an indication of intended audience and political or other bias.

> *Magazines for Libraries* (1997): A listing of over 6,500 periodicals arranged by academic discipline. For each discipline, this book lists basic indexes, abstracts, and periodicals. Each individual listing for a periodical includes its publisher, the date it was founded, the places it is indexed, its intended audience, and an evaluation of its content and editorial focus. Here is an example of one such listing:

>> 2605. *Growing Without Schooling.* [ISSN: 0745-5305]
>> 1977. bi-m. $25. Susannah Sheffer. Holt Assocs., 2269
>> Massachusetts Ave., Cambridge, MA 02140. Illus.,
>> index, adv. Sample. Circ: 5,000.
>> *Bk. rev:* 0–4, 400–600 words, signed. *Aud:* Ga, Sa.

GWS is a journal by and for home schoolers. Parents and students share their views as to why they chose home schooling and what they like about it. While lesson plans or activities are not included, home schoolers could get ideas for interesting activities from articles chronicling their experiences ("Helping Flood Victims," "Legislative Intern"). "News and Reports" offers home schoolers information on legal issues while the "Declassified Ads" suggest resources geared toward home schoolers. This is an important title for public libraries and should be available to students and faculty in teacher preparation programs.

Using Sources $\large 14$

In your college writing, you will be expected to use and acknowledge secondary sources—books, articles, interviews, Web sites, computer bulletin boards, lectures, and other print and nonprint materials—in addition to your own ideas and insights.

When you do use material from another source, you need to acknowledge the source, usually by citing the author and page or date in your text and including a list of works cited or references at the end of your essay. Failure to acknowledge sources constitutes *plagiarism*, a serious transgression. By citing sources correctly, you give appropriate credit to the originator of the words and ideas you are using, offer your readers the information they need to consult those sources directly, and build your own credibility.

This chapter provides guidelines for using sources effectively and acknowledging them accurately. It includes model citations for both the Modern Language Association (MLA) and the American Psychological Association (APA) documentation styles and presents a sample researched essay that follows the MLA format.

■ Acknowledging Sources

The only types of information that do not require acknowledgment are common knowledge (John F. Kennedy was assassinated in Dallas), facts widely available in many sources (U.S. presidents used to be inaugurated on March 4 rather than January 20), well-known quotations ("To be or not to be. That is the question"), or material you created or gathered yourself, such as photographs that you took or data from surveys that you conducted. Remember that you need to acknowledge the source of any visual (photograph, table, chart, graph, diagram, drawing, map, screen shot) that you did not create yourself or of any information that you used to create your own visual. (You should also request permission from the source of a visual you want to borrow if your essay is going to be posted on the Web.) When in doubt about whether you need to acknowledge a source, it is safer to do so.

The documentation guidelines later in this chapter present two styles for citing sources, MLA and APA. Whichever style you use, the most important thing is that your readers be able to tell where words or ideas that are not your own begin and end. You can accomplish this most readily by taking and transcribing notes carefully, by placing parenthetical source citations correctly, and by separating your words from those of the source with **signal phrases** such as "According to Smith," "Peters claims," and "As Olmos asserts." (When you cite a source for the first time in a signal phrase, you may use the author's full name; after that, use just the last name.)

Avoiding Plagiarism

Writers—students and professionals alike—occasionally fail to acknowledge sources properly. The word **plagiarism**, which derives from the Latin word for "kidnapping," refers to the unacknowledged use of another's words, ideas, or information. Students sometimes mistakenly assume that plagiarizing occurs only when another writer's exact words are used without acknowledgment. In fact, plagiarism also applies to such diverse forms of expression as musical compositions and visual images as well as ideas and statistics. Therefore, keep in mind that you must indicate the source of any borrowed information or ideas you use in your essay, whether you have paraphrased, summarized, or quoted directly from the source or have reproduced it or referred to it in some other way.

Remember especially the need to document electronic sources fully and accurately. Perhaps because it is so easy to access and distribute text and visuals online and to copy material from one electronic document and paste it into another, some students do not realize, or may forget, that information, ideas, and images from electronic sources require acknowledgment in even more detail than those from print sources (and are often easier to detect as plagiarism if they are not acknowledged).

Some people plagiarize simply because they do not know the conventions for using and acknowledging sources. If you are unfamiliar with these conventions, this chapter makes clear how to incorporate sources into your writing and how to acknowledge your use of those sources. Others plagiarize because they keep sloppy notes and thus fail to distinguish between their own and their sources' ideas. If you keep a working bibliography and careful notes, you will not make this serious mistake.

Another reason some people plagiarize is that they feel intimidated by the writing task or the deadline. If you experience this anxiety about your work, speak to your instructor. Do not run the risk of failing a course or being expelled from your college because of plagiarism.

If you are confused about what is and what is not plagiarism, be sure to ask your instructor.

For more on keeping a working bibliography, see Chapter 13, pp. 370–404.

Quoting, Paraphrasing, and Summarizing

Writers use sources by quoting directly, by paraphrasing, and by summarizing. This section provides guidelines for deciding when to use each of these three methods and for doing so effectively. Note that all examples in this section follow MLA style for in-text citations, which is explained in detail on pages 416–29.

Deciding Whether to Quote, Paraphrase, or Summarize

As a general rule, quote only in these situations: (1) when the wording of the source is particularly memorable or vivid or expresses a point so well that you cannot improve it, (2) when the words of reliable and respected authorities would lend support to your position, (3) when you wish to cite an author whose opinions challenge or vary greatly from those of other experts, or (4) when you are going to discuss the source's choice of words. Paraphrase passages whose details you wish to use but whose language is not particularly striking. Summarize any long passages whose main points you wish to record as support for a point you are making.

Quoting

Quotations should duplicate the source exactly. If the source has an error, copy it and add the notation *sic* (Latin for "thus") in brackets immediately after the error to indicate that it is not your error but your source's:

> According to a recent newspaper article, "Plagirism [sic] is a problem among journalists and scholars as well as students" (Berensen 62).

However, you can change quotations for the following purposes, as long as you signal your changes appropriately: (1) to emphasize particular words, (2) to omit irrelevant information, and (3) to insert information necessary for clarity, or (4) to make the quotation conform grammatically to your sentence. Note that *(Berensen 62)* represents a proper MLA-style in-text citation. For explanation of the rules for in-text citation, see pp. 416–19.

Using Italics for Emphasis.   You may italicize any words in the quotation that you want to emphasize; add a semicolon and the words *emphasis added* (in regular type, not italicized) to the parenthetical citation.

> In her 2001 exposé of the struggles of the working class, Ehrenreich writes, "The wages Winn-Dixie is offering--*$6 and a couple of dimes to start with*--are not enough, I decide, to compensate for this indignity" (14; emphasis added).

Using Ellipsis Marks for Omissions.   A writer may decide to omit words from a quotation because they are not relevant to the point being made. When you omit words from within a quotation, you must use ellipsis marks—three spaced periods (...)—in place of the missing words. When the omission occurs within a sentence, include a space before the first ellipsis mark and after the closing mark.

> Hermione Roddice is described in Lawrence's *Women in Love* as a "woman of the new school, full of intellectuality and . . . nerve-worn with consciousness" (17).

When the omission falls at the end of a sentence, place a sentence period *directly after* the final word of the sentence, followed by a space and three spaced ellipsis marks.

> But Grimaldi's commentary contends that for Aristotle rhetoric, like dialectic, had "no limited and unique subject matter upon which it must be exercised. . . . Instead,

rhetoric as an art transcends all specific disciplines and may be brought into play in them" (6).

A period plus ellipsis marks can indicate the omission of the rest of the sentence as well as whole sentences, paragraphs, or even pages.

When a parenthetical reference follows the ellipsis marks at the end of a sentence, place the three spaced periods after the quotation, and place the sentence period after the final parenthesis:

> But Grimaldi's commentary contends that for Aristotle rhetoric, like dialectic, had "no limited and unique subject matter upon which it must be exercised. . . . Instead, rhetoric as an art transcends all specific disciplines . . ." (6).

When you quote only single words or phrases, you do not need to use ellipsis marks because it will be obvious that you have left out some of the original.

> More specifically, Wharton's imagery of suffusing brightness transforms Undine before her glass into "some fabled creature whose home was in a beam of light" (21).

For the same reason, you need not use ellipsis marks if you omit the beginning of a quoted sentence unless the rest of the sentence begins with a capitalized word and still appears to be a complete sentence.

Using Brackets for Insertions or Changes.   Use brackets around an insertion or a change needed to make a quotation conform grammatically to your sentence, such as a change in the form of a verb or pronoun or in the capitalization of the first word of the quotation. In this example from an essay on James Joyce's short story "Araby," the writer adapts Joyce's phrases "we played till our bodies glowed" and "shook music from the buckled harness" to fit the grammar of her sentences:

> In the dark, cold streets during the "short days of winter," the boys must generate their own heat by "play[ing] till [their] bodies glowed." Music is "[shaken] from the buckled harness" as if it were unnatural, and the singers in the market chant nasally of "the troubles in our native land" (30).

You may also use brackets to add or substitute explanatory material in a quotation:

> Guterson notes that among Native Americans in Florida, "education was in the home; learning by doing was reinforced by the myths and legends which repeated the basic value system of their [the Seminoles'] way of life" (159).

Some changes that make a quotation conform grammatically to another sentence may be made without any signal to readers: (1) A period at the end of a quotation may be changed to a comma if you are using the quotation within your own sentence, and (2) double quotation marks enclosing a quotation may be changed to single quotation marks when the quotation is enclosed within a longer quotation.

Integrating Quotations

Depending on its length, a quotation may be incorporated into your text by being enclosed in quotation marks or set off from your text in a block without quotation marks. In either case, be sure to integrate the quotation into the language of your essay.

In-Text Quotations.   Incorporate brief quotations (no more than four typed lines of prose or three lines of poetry) into your text. You may place the quotation virtually anywhere in your sentence:

At the Beginning

"To live a life is not to cross a field," Sutherland, quoting Pasternak, writes at the beginning of her narrative (11).

In the Middle

Woolf begins and ends by speaking of the need of the woman writer to have "money and a room of her own" (4)--an idea that certainly spoke to Plath's condition.

At the End

In *The Second Sex*, Simone de Beauvoir describes such an experience as one in which the girl "becomes an object, and she sees herself as object" (378).

Divided by Your Own Words

"Science usually prefers the literal to the nonliteral term," Kinneavy writes, "--that is, figures of speech are often out of place in science" (177).

When you quote poetry within your text, use a slash (/) with spaces before and after to signal the end of each line of verse:

Alluding to St. Augustine's distinction between the City of God and the Earthly City, Lowell writes that "much against my will / I left the City of God where it belongs" (4-5).

Block Quotations.   In the MLA style, use the block form for prose quotations of five or more typed lines and for poetry quotations of four or more lines. Indent the quotation an inch (ten character spaces) from the left margin, as shown in the following example.

In "A Literary Legacy from Dunbar to Baraka," Margaret Walker says of Paul Lawrence Dunbar's dialect poems:

> He realized that the white world in the United States tolerated his literary genius only because of his "jingles in a broken tongue," and they found the old "darky" tales and speech amusing and within the vein of

> folklore into which they wished to classify all Negro life. This troubled
> Dunbar because he realized that white America was denigrating him as a
> writer and as a man. (70)

In the APA style, use block form for quotations of forty words or more. Indent the block quotation one-half inch (five to seven spaces), keeping your indents consistent throughout your paper.

In a block quotation, double-space between lines just as you do in your text. *Do not* enclose the passage within quotation marks. Use a colon to introduce a block quotation, unless the context calls for another punctuation mark or none at all. When quoting a single paragraph or part of one in the MLA style, do not indent the first line of the quotation more than the rest. In quoting two or more paragraphs, indent the first line of each paragraph an extra quarter inch (three spaces). If you are using the APA style, the first line of subsequent paragraphs in the block quotation indents an additional half inch or five to seven spaces from the block quotation indent. Note that, in MLA-style, the parenthetical page reference follows the period in block quotations.

Introducing Quotations

Statements that introduce in-text quotations take a range of punctuation marks and lead-in words. Here are some examples of ways writers typically introduce quotations.

Introducing a Quotation Using a Colon

A colon usually follows an independent clause placed before the quotation.

> As George Williams notes, protection of white privilege is critical to patterns of discrimi-
> nation: "Whenever a number of persons within a society have enjoyed for a considerable
> period of time certain opportunities for getting wealth, for exercising power and authority,
> and for successfully claiming prestige and social deference, there is a strong tendency for
> these people to feel that these benefits are theirs 'by right'" (727).

Introducing a Quotation Using a Comma

A comma usually follows an introduction that incorporates the quotation in its sentence structure.

> Similarly, Duncan Turner asserts, "As matters now stand, it is unwise to talk about com-
> munication without some understanding of Burke" (259).

Introducing a Quotation Using that

No punctuation is generally needed with *that,* and no capital letter is used to begin the quotation.

> Noting this failure, Alice Miller asserts **that** "the reason for her despair was not her suf-
> fering but the impossibility of communicating her suffering to another person" (255).

Punctuating within Quotations

Although punctuation within a quotation should reproduce the original, some adaptations may be necessary. Use single quotation marks for quotations within the quotation:

Original from David Guterson's Family Matters *(pages 16–17)*

E. D. Hirsch also recognizes the connection between family and learning, suggesting in his discussion of family background and academic achievement "that the significant part of our children's education has been going on outside rather than inside the schools."

Quoted Version

Guterson claims that E. D. Hirsch "also recognizes the connection between family and learning, suggesting in his discussion of family background and academic achievement 'that the significant part of our children's education has been going on outside rather than inside the schools'" (16-17).

If the quotation ends with a question mark or an exclamation point, retain the original punctuation:

"Did you think I loved you?" Edith later asks Dombey (566).

If a quotation ending with a question mark or an exclamation point concludes your sentence, retain the question mark or exclamation point, and put the parenthetical reference and sentence period outside the quotation marks:

Edith later asks Dombey, "Did you think I loved you?" (566).

Avoiding Grammatical Tangles

When you incorporate quotations into your writing, and especially when you omit words from quotations, you run the risk of creating ungrammatical sentences. Three common errors you should try to avoid are verb incompatibility, ungrammatical omissions, and sentence fragments.

Verb Incompatibility. When this error occurs, the verb form in the introductory statement is grammatically incompatible with the verb form in the quotation. When your quotation has a verb form that does not fit in with your text, it is usually possible to use just part of the quotation, thus avoiding verb incompatibility.

> ▶ The narrator suggests his bitter disappointment when ~~"I saw myself~~ *he describes seeing himself*
>
> "as a creature driven and derided by vanity" (35).

As this sentence illustrates, use the present tense when you refer to events in a literary work.

Ungrammatical Omission. Sometimes omitting text from a quotation leaves you with an ungrammatical sentence. Two ways of correcting the grammar are (1) adapting the quotation (with brackets) so that its parts fit together grammatically and (2) using only one part of the quotation.

▶ **From the moment of the boy's arrival in Araby, the bazaar is presented as a**

    commercial enterprise: "I could not find any sixpenny entrance and . . .
    hand[ed]
    ~~handing~~ **a shilling to a weary-looking man" (34).**
    ^

▶ **From the moment of the boy's arrival in Araby, the bazaar is presented as a**

                 He
    commercial enterprise: "~~I~~ "could not find any sixpenny entrance" and ▃▃
    so had to pay a shilling to get in (34).
    ~~handing a shilling to a weary-looking man" (34).~~
    ^

Sentence Fragment. Sometimes when a quotation is a complete sentence, writers neglect the sentence that introduces the quote—for example, by forgetting to include a verb. Make sure that the quotation is introduced by a complete sentence.

                                  leads
▶ **The girl's interest in the bazaar ~~leading~~ the narrator to make what amounts to a**
                               ^
    sacred oath: "If I go . . . I will bring you something" (32).

Paraphrasing and Summarizing

In addition to quoting sources, writers have the option of paraphrasing or summarizing what others have written.

Paraphrasing. In a **paraphrase**, the writer restates all the relevant information from a passage, without any additional comments or any suggestion of agreement or disagreement with the source's ideas. A paraphrase is useful for recording details of the passage when the order of the details is important but the source's wording is not. Because all the details of the passage are included, a paraphrase is often about the same length as the original passage. Paraphrasing allows you to avoid quoting too much. Anyway, it is better to paraphrase than to quote ordinary material, where the author's way of expressing things is not worth special attention.

    Here is a passage from a book on home schooling and an example of an acceptable paraphrase of it:

Original Source

Bruner and the discovery theorists have also illuminated conditions that apparently pave the way for learning. It is significant that these conditions are unique to each learner, so unique, in fact, that in many cases classrooms can't provide them. Bruner also contends that the more one discovers information in a great variety of circumstances, the more likely one is to develop the inner categories required to organize that information. Yet life at school, which is for the most part generic and predictable, daily keeps many children from the great variety of circumstances they need to learn well.

—David Guterson, *Family Matters: Why Homeschooling Makes Sense*, p. 172

Acceptable Paraphrase

According to Guterson, the "discovery theorists," particularly Bruner, have found that there seem to be certain conditions that help learning to take place. Because each individual requires different conditions, many children are not able to learn in the classroom. According to Bruner, when people can explore information in many different situations, they learn to classify and order what they discover. The general routine of the school day, however, does not provide children with the diverse activities and situations that would allow them to learn these skills (172).

Readers assume that some words in a paraphrase are taken from the source. Indeed, it would be nearly impossible for paraphrasers to avoid using any key terms from the source, and it would be counterproductive to try to do so, because the original and the paraphrase necessarily share the same information and concepts. Notice, though, that of the total of 86 words in the paraphrase, the paraphraser uses only a name (*Bruner*) and a few other key nouns and verbs (*discovery theorists, conditions, children, learn[ing], information, situations*) for which it would be awkward to substitute other words or phrases. If the paraphraser had wanted to use other, more distinctive language from the source—for example, the description of life at school as "generic and predictable"—these adjectives should have been enclosed in quotation marks. In fact, the paraphraser puts quotation marks around only one of the terms from the source: "discovery theorists," a technical term likely to be unfamiliar to readers.

Paraphrasers must, however, avoid borrowing too many words from a source and repeating the sentence structures of a source. Here is an unacceptable paraphrase of the first sentence in the Guterson passage:

Unacceptable Paraphrase: Too Many Borrowed Words and Phrases

Apparently, some conditions, which have been illuminated by Bruner and other discovery theorists, pave the way for people to learn.

If you compare the source's first sentence and the paraphrase of it, you will see that the paraphrase borrows almost all of its key language from the source sentence, including the entire phrase *pave the way for.* Even if you cite the source, this heavy borrowing would be considered plagiarism.

Here is another unacceptable paraphrase of the same sentence:

Unacceptable Paraphrase: Sentence Structure Repeated Too Closely

Bruner and other researchers have also identified circumstances that seem to ease the path to learning.

If you compare the source's first sentence and this paraphrase of it, you will see that the paraphraser has borrowed the phrases and clauses of the source and arranged them in an identical sequence, simply substituting synonyms for most of the key terms: *researchers* for *theorists, identified* for *illuminated, circumstances* for *conditions, seem to* for *apparently,* and *ease the path to* for *pave the way for.* This paraphrase would also be considered plagiarism.

Summarizing.   Unlike a paraphrase, a **summary** presents only the main ideas of a source, leaving out examples and details.

Here is one student's summary of five pages from *Family Matters.* You can see at a glance how drastically summaries can condense information, in this case from five pages to five sentences. Depending on the summarizer's purpose, the five pages could be summarized in one sentence, the five sentences here, or two or three dozen sentences.

In looking at different theories of learning that discuss individual-based programs (such as home schooling) versus the public school system, Guterson describes the disagreements among "cognitivist" theorists. One group, the "discovery theorists," believes that individual children learn by creating their own ways of sorting the information they take in from their experiences. Schools should help students develop better ways of organizing new material, not just present them with material that is already categorized, as traditional schools do. "Assimilationist theorists," by contrast, believe that children learn by linking what they don't know to information they already know. These theorists claim that traditional schools help students learn when they present information in ways that allow children to fit the new material into categories they have already developed (171-75).

Summaries like this one are more than a dry list of main ideas from a source. They are instead a coherent, readable new text composed of the source's main ideas. Summaries provide balanced coverage of a source, following the same sequence of ideas and avoiding any hint of agreement or disagreement with them.

Documenting Sources

Although there is no universally accepted system for acknowledging sources, most documentation styles use parenthetical in-text citations keyed to a separate list of works cited or references. The information required in the in-text citations and the order and content of the works-cited entries vary across academic disciplines. This section presents the basic features of two styles: the author-page system that is advocated by the Modern Language Association (MLA) and widely used in the humanities (for example, literature and history) and the author-year system that is advocated by the American

Psychological Association (APA) and widely used in the social sciences (for example, psychology and economics).

In Part One of this book, you can find examples of student essays that follow the MLA style (Linh Kieu Ngo, Chapter 4; Jessica Statsky, Chapter 5) and the APA style (Patrick O'Malley, Chapter 6). For more information about these documentation styles, consult the *MLA Handbook for Writers of Research Papers*, Seventh Edition (2009), or the *Publication Manual of the American Psychological Association*, Sixth Edition (2010).

Check with your instructor about which of these styles you should use or whether you should use some other style. A list of common documentation style manuals is provided in Table 14.1.

Table 14.1 Some Commonly Used Documentation Style Manuals

Subject	Style Manual	Online Source
General	*The Chicago Manual of Style.* 15th ed. 2003.	http://www.chicagomanualofstyle.org
	A Manual for Writers of Term Papers, Theses, and Dissertations. 6th ed. 1996.	—
Online sources	*Columbia Guide to Online Style.* 1998	http://www.columbia.edu/cu/cup/cgos/idx_basic.html
Biological sciences	*Scientific Style and Format: The CSE Manual for Authors, Editors, and Publishers.* 7th ed. 2006.	http://www.councilscienceeditors.org/publications/style.cfm
Chemistry	*The ACS Style Guide.* 2nd ed. 1997.	http://www.pubs.acs.org/books/references.shtml
Government documents	*The Complete Guide to Citing Government Documents.* Rev. ed. 1993.	http://exlibris.memphis.edu/resource/unclesam/citeweb.html
Humanities	*MLA Handbook for Writers of Research Papers.* 7th ed. 2009. *MLA Style Manual and Guide to Scholarly Publishing.* 3rd ed. 2008.	http://www.mla.org
Psychology/ Social sciences	*Publication Manual of the American Psychological Association.* 6th ed. 2010.	http://www.apastyle.apa.org

The MLA System of Documentation

Citations in Text

The MLA author-page system generally requires that in-text citations include the author's last name and the page number of the passage being cited. There is no punctuation between author and page. The parenthetical citation should follow the quoted, paraphrased, or summarized material as closely as possible without disrupting the flow of the sentence.

> Dr. James is described as a "not-too-skeletal Ichabod Crane" (Simon 68).

Note that the parenthetical citation comes before the final period. With block quotations, however, the citation comes after the final period, preceded by a space (see p. 410 for an example).

If you mention the author's name in your text, supply just the page reference in parentheses.

> Simon describes Dr. James as a "not-too-skeletal Ichabod Crane" (68).

A WORK WITH MORE THAN ONE AUTHOR

To cite a source by two or three authors, include all the authors' last names; for works with more than three authors, use all the authors' names or just the first author's name followed by *et al.*, meaning "and others," in regular type (not italicized or underlined).

> Dyal, Corning, and Willows identify several types of students, including the "Authority-Rebel" (4).

> The Authority-Rebel "tends to see himself as superior to other students in the class" (Dyal, Corning, and Willows 4).

> The drug AZT has been shown to reduce the risk of transmission from HIV-positive mothers to their infants by as much as two-thirds (Van de Perre et al. 4-5).

TWO OR MORE WORKS BY THE SAME AUTHOR

To cite one of two or more works by the same author, include the author's last name, a comma, a shortened version of the title you are citing, and the page number(s).

> When old paint becomes transparent, it sometimes shows the artist's original plans: "a tree will show through a woman's dress" (Hellman, *Pentimento* 1).

A WORK WITH AN UNKNOWN AUTHOR

Use a shortened version of the title, beginning with the word by which the title is alphabetized in the works-cited list. ("Awash in Garbage" was the title in the following example.)

An international pollution treaty still to be ratified would prohibit all plastic garbage from being dumped at sea ("Awash" 26).

TWO OR MORE AUTHORS WITH THE SAME LAST NAME CITED IN YOUR ESSAY

In addition to the last name, include each author's first initial in the citation. If the first initials are also the same, spell out the authors' first names.

Chaplin's *Modern Times* provides a good example of montage used to make an editorial statement (E. Roberts 246).

A CORPORATE OR GOVERNMENT AUTHOR

In a parenthetical citation, give the full name of the author if it is brief or a shortened version if it is long. If you name the author in your text, give the full name even if it is long.

A tuition increase has been proposed for community and technical colleges to offset budget deficits from Initiative 601 (Washington State Board 4).

According to the Washington State Board for Community and Technical Colleges, a tuition increase . . . from Initiative 601 (4).

A MULTIVOLUME WORK

When you use two or more volumes of a multivolume work in your paper, include the volume number and the page number(s), separated by a colon and one space, in each citation.

According to Forster, modernist writers valued experimentation and gradually sought to blur the line between poetry and prose (3: 150).

If you cite only one volume, give the volume number in the works cited (see p. 421) and include only the page number(s) in the parenthetical citation.

A LITERARY WORK

For a novel or other prose work available in various editions, provide the page numbers from the edition used as well as other information that will help readers locate the quotation in a different edition, such as the part or chapter number.

In *Hard Times*, Tom reveals his utter narcissism by blaming Louisa for his own failure: "'You have regularly given me up. You never cared for me'"(Dickens 262; bk. 3, ch. 9).

For a play in verse, such as a Shakespearean play, indicate the act, scene, and line numbers instead of the page numbers.

At the beginning, Regan's fawning rhetoric hides her true attitude toward Lear: "I profess / myself an enemy to all other joys . . . / And find that I am alone felicitate / In your dear highness' love" (*King Lear* 1.1.74-75, 77-78).

For a poem, indicate the line numbers and stanzas or sections (if they are numbered), instead of the page numbers. If the source gives only line numbers, use the term *lines* in the first citation and give only the numbers in subsequent citations.

> In "Song of Myself," Whitman finds poetic details in busy urban settings, as when he describes "the blab of the pave, tires of carts . . . the driver with his interrogating thumb" (8.153-54).

A RELIGIOUS WORK

For the Bible, indicate the book, chapter, and verse instead of the page numbers. Abbreviate books with names of five or more letters in your parenthetical citation, but spell out full names of books in your text.

> She ignored the admonition "Pride goes before destruction, and a haughty spirit before a fall" (*New Oxford Annotated Bible*, Prov. 16.18).

A WORK IN AN ANTHOLOGY

Use the name of the author of the work, not the editor of the anthology, but use the page number(s) from the anthology.

> In "Six Days: Some Rememberings," Grace Paley recalls that when she was in jail for protesting the Vietnam War, her pen and paper were taken away and she felt "a terrible pain in the area of my heart--a nausea" (191).

A QUOTATION FROM A SECONDARY SOURCE

Include the secondary source in your list of works cited. In your parenthetical citation, use the abbreviation *qtd. in* (in regular type, not italicized or underlined) to acknowledge that the original was quoted in a secondary source.

> E. M. Forster says "the collapse of all civilization, so realistic for us, sounded in Matthew Arnold's ears like a distant and harmonious cataract" (qtd. in Trilling 11).

AN ENTIRE WORK

Include the reference in the text without any page numbers or parentheses.

> In *The Structure of Scientific Revolutions*, Thomas Kuhn discusses how scientists change their thinking.

A WORK WITHOUT PAGE NUMBERS

If a work has no page numbers or is only one page long, you may omit the page number. If a work uses paragraph numbers instead, use the abbreviation *par.* (or *pars.,* plural) in regular type, not italicized or underlined, and use a comma after the author's name.

The average speed on Montana's interstate highways, for example, has risen by only 2 miles per hour since the repeal of the federal speed limit, with most drivers topping out at 75 (Schmid).

Whitman considered African American speech "a source of a native grand opera" (Ellison, par. 13).

TWO OR MORE WORKS CITED IN THE SAME PARENTHESES

When two or more different sources are used in the same passage of your essay, it may be necessary to cite them in the same parentheses. Separate the citations with a semicolon. Include any specific pages, or omit pages to refer to the whole work.

A few studies have considered differences between oral and written discourse production (Scardamalia, Bereiter, and Goelman; Gould).

MATERIAL FROM THE INTERNET

Give enough information in the citation to enable readers to locate the Internet source in the list of works cited. If the author is not named, give the document title. Include page, section, paragraph, or screen numbers, if available.

In handling livestock, "many people attempt to restrain animals with sheer force instead of using behavioral principles" (Grandin).

List of Works Cited

The list of works cited provides full information for all the sources the writer uses. Entries are alphabetized according to the first author's last name or by the title if the author is unknown. Every source cited in the text must refer to an entry in the list of works cited. Conversely, every entry in the list of works cited must correspond to at least one in-text citation.

In the MLA style, multiple works by the same author (or same group of authors) are alphabetized by title. The author's name is given for the first entry only; in subsequent entries, three hyphens and a period are used.

Kingsolver, Barbara. *High Tide in Tucson: Essays from Now or Never*. New York: HarperCollins, 1995. Print.

---. *Small Wonder*. New York: HarperCollins, 2002. Print.

The information presented in a works-cited entry for a book follows this order: author, title, publication source, year of publication, and medium of publication. The MLA style requires a "hanging indent," which means that the first line of a works-cited entry is not indented but subsequent lines of the entry are. The MLA specifies an indent of half an inch or five character spaces.

Note that, in the list of Works Cited, publishers' names are given in shortened form. Compound or hyphenated names are usually limited to the first name only (with *Bedford*, for example, used for *Bedford/St. Martin's*). The words *University* and *Press* are shortened to *U* and *P*, respectively.

Books

Here is an example of a basic MLA-style entry for a book:

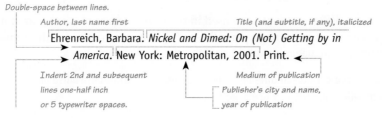

Double-space between lines.

Author, last name first | Title (and subtitle, if any), italicized

Ehrenreich, Barbara. *Nickel and Dimed: On (Not) Getting by in*
America. New York: Metropolitan, 2001. Print.

Indent 2nd and subsequent lines one-half inch or 5 typewriter spaces. | Medium of publication | Publisher's city and name, year of publication

A BOOK BY A SINGLE AUTHOR

Lamb, Sharon. *The Secret Lives of Girls*. New York: Free, 2002. Print.

A BOOK BY AN AGENCY OR A CORPORATION

American Medical Association. *Family Medical Guide*. 4th ed. Hoboken: Wiley, 2004. Print.

A BOOK BY MORE THAN ONE AUTHOR

Saba, Laura, and Julie Gattis. *The McGraw-Hill Homeschooling Companion*. New York: McGraw, 2002. Print.

Wilmut, Ian, Keith Campbell, and Colin Tudge. *The Second Creation: Dolly and the Age of Biological Control*. New York: Farrar, 2000. Print.

A WORK BY MORE THAN THREE AUTHORS

The MLA lists all the authors' names *or* the name of the first author followed by *et al.* (in regular type, not italicized).

Hunt, Lynn, et al. *The Making of the West: Peoples and Cultures*. Boston: Bedford, 2001. Print.

A BOOK BY AN UNKNOWN AUTHOR

Use the title in place of the author.

Rand McNally Commercial Atlas and Marketing Guide. Skokie: Rand, 2003. Print.

A BOOK WITH AN AUTHOR AND AN EDITOR

If you refer to the author's text, begin the entry with the author's name.

> Arnold, Matthew. *Culture and Anarchy*. Ed. Samuel Lipman. New Haven: Yale UP, 1994. Print.

If you cite the editor in your paper, begin the entry with the editor's name.

> Lipman, Samuel, ed. *Culture and Anarchy*. By Matthew Arnold. 1869. New Haven: Yale UP, 1994. Print.

AN EDITED COLLECTION

> Waldman, Diane, and Janet Walker, eds. *Feminism and Documentary*. Minneapolis: U of Minnesota P, 1999. Print.

A WORK IN AN ANTHOLOGY OR A COLLECTION

> Lahiri, Jhumpa. "Nobody's Business." *The Best American Short Stories 2002*. Ed. Sue Miller. Boston: Houghton, 2002. 136-72. Print.

TWO OR MORE WORKS FROM THE SAME ANTHOLOGY

To avoid repetition, you may create an entry for the collection and cite the collection's editor to cross-reference individual works to the entry.

> Boyd, Herb, ed. *The Harlem Reader*. New York: Three Rivers, 2003. Print.

> Wallace, Michelle. "Memories of a Sixties Girlhood: The Harlem I Love." Boyd 243-50.

ONE VOLUME OF A MULTIVOLUME WORK

If only one volume from a multivolume set is used, indicate the volume number after the title.

> Freud, Sigmund. *The Standard Edition of the Complete Psychological Works of Sigmund Freud*. Vol. 8. Trans. and ed. James Strachey. New York: Norton, 2000. Print.

TWO OR MORE VOLUMES OF A MULTIVOLUME WORK

> Sandburg, Carl. *Abraham Lincoln*. 6 vols. New York: Scribner's, 1939. Print.

A BOOK THAT IS PART OF A SERIES

After the medium of publication, include the series title in regular type (not italicized or in quotation marks), followed by the series number and a period. If the word *Series* is part of the name, include *Ser.* before the number. Common abbreviations may be used for selected words in the series title.

Zigova, Tanya, et al. *Neural Stem Cells: Methods and Protocols*. Totowa: Humana, 2002. Print. Methods in Molecular Biology 198.

A REPUBLISHED BOOK

Provide the original year of publication after the title of the book, followed by publication information for the edition you are using.

Alcott, Louisa May. *An Old-Fashioned Girl*. 1870. New York: Puffin, 1995. Print.

A LATER EDITION OF A BOOK

Rottenberg, Annette T., and Donna Haisty Winchell. *The Structure of Argument*. 6th ed. Boston: Bedford, 2009. Print.

A BOOK WITH A TITLE IN ITS TITLE

Do not italicize a title normally italicized when it appears within the title of a book.

Hertenstein, Mike. *The Double Vision of* Star Trek: *Half-Humans, Evil Twins, and Science Fiction*. Chicago: Cornerstone, 1998. Print.

O'Neill, Terry, ed. *Readings on* To Kill a Mockingbird. San Diego: Greenhaven, 2000. Print.

Use quotation marks around a work normally enclosed in quotation marks when it appears within the title of a book.

Miller, Edwin Haviland. *Walt Whitman's "Song of Myself": A Mosaic of Interpretation*. Iowa City: U of Iowa P, 1989. Print.

A TRANSLATION

If you refer to the work itself, begin the entry with the author's name.

Tolstoy, Leo. *War and Peace*. Trans. Constance Garnett. New York: Modern, 2002. Print.

If you cite the translator in your text, begin the entry with the translator's name.

Garnett, Constance, trans. *War and Peace*. By Leo Tolstoy. 1869. New York: Modern, 2002. Print.

A DICTIONARY ENTRY OR AN ARTICLE IN A REFERENCE BOOK

"Homeopathy." *Webster's New World College Dictionary*. 4th ed. 1999. Print.

Rowland, Lewis P. "Myasthenia Gravis." *The Encyclopedia Americana*. 2001 ed. Print.

AN INTRODUCTION, PREFACE, FOREWORD, OR AFTERWORD

Graff, Gerald, and James Phelan. Preface. *Adventures of Huckleberry Finn*. By Mark Twain. 2nd ed. New York: Bedford, 2004. iii-vii. Print.

Articles

Here is an example of a basic MLA-style entry for an article in a periodical:

> *Author, last name first*   *Article title, in quotation marks*
>
> Simon, Robin W. "Revisiting the Relationship among Gender, Marital Status, and Mental
>
> ➤ Health." *American Journal of Sociology*   107.4   (2002):   1065-96.   Print.
>
> *Double-space between*   *Periodical title, italicized*   *Volume*   *Date, in*   *Page numbers* *Medium*
> *lines; indent second*   *and*   *parentheses,*
> *and subsequent*   *issue*   *followed by*
> *lines one-half inch.*   *number*   *colon*

Scholarly journals are typically identified using their volume and issue numbers, separated by a period. If a journal does not use volume numbers, provide the issue number only, following the title of the journal.

> Fee, Margery. "Predators and Gardens." *Canadian Literature* 197 (2008): 6-9. Print.

If the article is not on a continuous sequence of pages, give the first page number followed by a plus sign, as in the following example.

AN ARTICLE FROM A DAILY NEWSPAPER

> Stoll, John D., et al. "U.S. Squeezes Auto Creditors." *Wall Street Journal* 10 Apr. 2009: A1+.
>   Print.

Note that magazines and newspapers are identified not by volume and issue number but by date with the names of most months abbreviated.

AN ARTICLE FROM A WEEKLY OR BIWEEKLY MAGAZINE

> Doig, Will. "America's Real First Family." *Advocate* 17 July 2007: 46-50. Print.

AN ARTICLE FROM A MONTHLY OR BIMONTHLY MAGAZINE

> Shelby, Ashley. "Good Going: Alaska's Glacier Crossroads." *Sierra* Sept.-Oct. 2005: 23. Print.

AN EDITORIAL

> "Addiction Behind Bars." Editorial. *New York Times* 12 Apr. 2009: A20. Print.

A LETTER TO THE EDITOR

> Orent, Wendy, and Alan Zelicoff. Letter. *New Republic* 18 Nov. 2002: 4-5. Print.

A REVIEW

> Cassidy, John. "Master of Disaster." Rev. of *Globalization and Its Discontents*, by Joseph
>   Stiglitz. *New Yorker* 12 July 2002: 82-86. Print.

If the review does not include an author's name, start the entry with the title of the review and alphabetize by that title. If the review is untitled, begin with the words *Rev. of* and alphabetize under the title of the work being reviewed.

AN UNSIGNED ARTICLE

Begin with the article title, alphabetizing the entry according to the first word after any initial *A, An,* or *The.*

"A Shot of Reality." *U.S. News & World Report* 1 July 2003: 13. Print.

Electronic Sources

Much of the information required in citations of electronic sources takes the same form as in corresponding kinds of print sources. For example, if you are citing an article from an online periodical, put the article title in quotation marks and italicize the name of the periodical. If the source has been previously or simultaneously published in print, include the print publication information if it is available. You also should include information specific to electronic sources, where it is appropriate and available, including the following:

- The version or edition used
- The publisher or sponsor of the site, if not available, use *N.p.*
- Date of publication, if not available, use *n.d.*
- Medium of publication (*Web*)
- The date you accessed the source

Electronic content frequently changes or disappears without notice, and because it is not organized in the kinds of standard ways that print book and periodicals are, finding the information needed for documentation is often difficult. If you cannot find some of this information, include what you do find. Always keep your goal in mind: to provide enough information so that your reader could track the source down later.

Here is an example of a basic MLA-style entry for the most commonly cited kind of electronic source, a specific document from a Web site:

Author, last name first	Title of document, in quotation marks		Title of site, italicized

Cuddy-Keane, Melba. "History of IVWS." *The International Virginia Woolf Society Web Page.*

International Virginia Woolf Society, 23 June 2003. Web. 7 Oct. 2008.

Sponsor of site	Date of publication or most recent update	Medium of publication	Date of access

AN ENTIRE WEB SITE

Gardner, James Alan. *A Seminar on Writing Prose*. N. p., 2001. Web. 4 June 2008.

If the author's name is not known, begin the citation with the title.

The International Virginia Woolf Society Web Page. International Virginia Woolf Society,
 31 Aug. 2002. Web. 21 Feb. 2008.

For an untitled personal site, put a description such as *Home page* (in regular type,
not italicized), followed by a period, in the position a title would normally be
cited.

Chesson, Frederick W. Home page. N. p., 1 Apr. 2003. Web. 26 Apr. 2008.

AN ONLINE SCHOLARLY PROJECT

For a complete project, provide the title, italicized, and the name of the editor, if given.
Then give the electronic publication information—the version number (if any), the
name of the sponsoring organization, and the date of electronic publication or latest
update—followed by the medium and date of access.

The Darwin Correspondence Project. Ed. Duncan Porter. Cambridge U Library, 2 June 2003.
 Web. 28 Nov. 2008.

A BOOK OR SHORT WORK WITHIN A SCHOLARLY PROJECT

Begin with the author's name and the title (italicized for a book or in quotation marks
for an article, essay, poem, or other short work). Follow with the print publication
information, if any, and the information about the project.

Corelli, Marie. *The Treasure of Heaven*. London: Constable, 1906. *Victorian Women Writer's
 Project*. Ed. Percy Willett. Indiana U, 10 July 1999. Web. 10 Sept. 2008.

Heims, Marjorie. "The Strange Case of Sarah Jones." *The Free Expression Policy Project*. FEPP,
 24 Jan. 2003. Web. 13 Mar. 2006.

MATERIAL FROM AN ONLINE DATABASE

If you accessed material through an online database, give the database name (in italics),
the medium, and the date of access after the print publication information.

Braus, Patricia. "Sex and the Single Spender." *American Demographics* 15.11 (1993): 28-34.
 Academic Search Premier. Web. 13 Aug. 2008.

A NONPERIODICAL PUBLICATION ON A CD-ROM

Picasso: The Man, His Works, the Legend. Danbury: Grolier Interactive, 1996. CD-ROM.

AN ARTICLE FROM AN ONLINE SCHOLARLY JOURNAL

Include the volume number and issue number, if given, after the title of the journal. Also include the number of pages, paragraphs, or other sections, if given, after the date of publication; if none are given, use *n. pag.*

Cesarini, Paul. "Computers, Technology, and Literacies." *The Journal of Literacy and Technology* 4.1 (2004/2005): n. pag. Web. 12 Oct. 2008.

A POSTING TO A DISCUSSION GROUP OR NEWSGROUP

Include the author's name (if you know it), the title or subject line of the posting (in quotation marks), the group name, the sponsor, the posting date, the medium, and the access date.

Willie, Otis. "In the Heat of the Battle." *soc.history.war.us-revolution.* Google, 27 Sept. 2005. Web. 7 Oct. 2008.

Martin, Francesca Alys. "Wait—Did Somebody Say 'Buffy'?" *Cultstud-L.* U of S Florida, 8 Mar. 2000. Web. 8 Mar. 2008.

AN E-MAIL MESSAGE

The subject line of the message is enclosed in quotation marks. Identify the persons who sent and received it and the date it was sent. End with the medium (*E-mail*).

Olson, Kate. "Update on State Legislative Grants." Message to the author. 5 Nov. 2008. E-mail.

Note that MLA style hyphenates *E-mail.*

COMPUTER SOFTWARE

Home Computers Work. Indianapolis: Que, 1998. CD-ROM.

Other Sources

A LECTURE OR PUBLIC ADDRESS

Birnbaum, Jack. "The Domestication of Computers." Conf. of the Usability Professionals Association. Hyatt Grand Cypress Resort, Orlando. 10 July 2002. Lecture.

A GOVERNMENT DOCUMENT

If the author is known, the author's name may either come first or be placed after the title, introduced with the word *By*.

> United States. Dept. of Health and Human Services. *Trends in Underage Drinking in the United States, 1991-2007*. By Gabriella Newes-Adeyi, et al. Washington: GPO, 2009. Print.

A PAMPHLET

> BoatU.S. Foundation for Boating Safety and Clean Water. *Hypothermia and Cold Water Survival*. Alexandria, VA: BoatU.S. Foundation, 2001. Print.

PUBLISHED PROCEEDINGS OF A CONFERENCE

If the name of the conference is part of the title of the publication, it need not be repeated. Use the format for a work in an anthology (see p. 421) to cite an individual presentation.

> Duffett, John, ed. *Against the Crime of Silence: Proceedings of the International War Crimes Tribunal*. Nov. 1967, Stockholm. New York: Clarion-Simon, 1970. Print.

A PUBLISHED DOCTORAL DISSERTATION

Cite as you would a book, but add pertinent dissertation information before publication data.

> Botts, Roderic C. *Influences in the Teaching of English, 1917-1935: An Illusion of Progress*. Diss. Northeastern U, 1970. Ann Arbor: UMI, 1971. Print.

> Jones, Anna Maria. *Problem Novels/Perverse Readers: Late-Victorian Fiction and the Perilous Pleasures of Identification*. Diss. U of Notre Dame, 2001. Ann Arbor: UMI, 2001. Print.

AN UNPUBLISHED DOCTORAL DISSERTATION

Enclose the title of an unpublished dissertation in quotation marks.

> Bullock, Barbara. "Basic Needs Fulfillment among Less Developed Countries: Social Progress over Two Decades of Growth." Diss. Vanderbilt U, 1986. Print.

A LETTER

Use *MS* ("manuscript") if written by hand, and *TS* ("typescript") if produced using technology.

> Duhamel, Grace. Letter to the author. 22 Mar. 2008. TS.

A MAP OR CHART

Map of Afghanistan and Surrounding Territory. Map. Burlington: GiziMap, 2001. Print.

A CARTOON OR COMIC STRIP

Provide the title (if given) in quotation marks directly following the artist's name.

Cheney, Tom. Cartoon. *New Yorker*. 10 Oct. 2005: 55. Print.

AN ADVERTISEMENT

Hospital for Special Surgery. Advertisement. *New York Times* 13 Apr. 2009: A7. Print.

A WORK OF ART OR MUSICAL COMPOSITION

De Goya, Francisco. *The Sleep of Reason Produces Monsters*. 1799. Etching with watercolor. Norton Simon Museum, Pasadena.

Beethoven, Ludwig van. *Violin Concerto in D Major, Op. 61*. 1809. New York: Adwin F. Kalmus, n.d. Print.

Gershwin, George. *Porgy and Bess*. 1935. New York: Alfred, 1999. Print.

If a photograph is not part of a collection, identify the subject, the name of the person who photographed it, and when it was photographed.

Washington Square Park, New York. Personal photograph by author. 24 June 2006.

A PERFORMANCE

Proof. By David Auburn. Dir. Daniel Sullivan. Perf. Mary-Louise Parker. Walter Kerr Theatre, New York. 9 Sept. 2001. Performance.

A TELEVISION PROGRAM

"Murder of the Century." *American Experience*. Narr. David Ogden Stiers. Writ. and prod. Carl Charlson. PBS. WEDU, Tampa, 14 July 2003. Television.

A FILM OR VIDEO RECORDING

Space Station. Prod. and dir. Toni Myers. Narr. Tom Cruise. IMAX, 2002. Film.

Casablanca. Dir. Michael Curtiz. Perf. Humphrey Bogart, Ingrid Bergman, and Paul Henreid. 1942. Warner Home Video, 2003. DVD.

A MUSIC RECORDING

Begin the entry with the name of the musician, composer, or group. Follow with the title at the recording (in italics unless your citation is for an instrumental piece designated only by form, key, or number); and the performers or conductor (if applicable). End with publication information and the medium (such as *LP*, *CD*, or *Audiocassette*).

> Beethoven, Ludwig van. *Violin Concerto in D Major*, Op. 61. U.S.S.R. State Orchestra. Cond. Alexander Gauk. Perf. David Oistrakh. Allegro, 1980. Audiocassette.

> Springsteen, Bruce. "Dancing in the Dark." *Born in the USA*. Columbia, 1984. CD.

AN INTERVIEW

> Ashrawi, Hanan. "Tanks vs. Olive Branches." Interview with Rose Marie Berger. *Sojourners Magazine* Feb. 2005: 22-26. Print.

> Ellis, Trey. Personal interview. 3 Sept. 2008.

The APA System of Documentation

Citations in Text

AUTHOR INDICATED IN PARENTHESES

The APA author-year system calls for the last name of the author and the year of publication of the original work in the citation. If the cited material is a quotation, you also need to include the page number(s) of the original. If the cited material is not a quotation, the page reference is optional. Use commas to separate author, year, and page in a parenthetical citation. The page number is preceded by *p.* for a single page or *pp.* for a range. Use an ampersand (&) to join the names of multiple authors.

> The conditions in the stockyards were so dangerous that workers "fell into the vats; and when they were fished out, there was never enough of them left to be worth exhibiting" (Sinclair, 2005, p. 134).

> Racial bias does not necessarily diminish through exposure to individuals of other races (Jamison & Tyree, 2001).

If you are citing an electronic source without page numbers, give the paragraph number if it is provided, preceded by the abbreviation *para*. If no paragraph number is given, give the heading of the section and the number of the paragraph within it where the material appears, if possible.

The subjects were tested for their responses to various stimuli, both positive and negative (Simpson, 2002, para. 4).

AUTHOR INDICATED IN SIGNAL PHRASE

If the author's name is mentioned in your text, cite the year in parentheses directly following the author's name, and place the page reference in parentheses before the final sentence period. Use *and* to join the names of multiple authors.

Sinclair (2005) wrote that workers sometimes "fell into the vats; and when they were fished out, there was never enough of them left to be worth exhibiting" (p. 134).

As Jamison and Tyree (2001) have found, racial bias does not diminish merely through exposure to individuals of other races (Conclusion section, para. 2).

SOURCE WITH MORE THAN TWO AUTHORS

To cite works with three to five authors, use all the authors' last names the first time the reference occurs and the last name of the first author followed by *et al.* (in regular type, not italicized or underlined) subsequently. If a source has six or more authors, use only the last name of the first author and *et al.* at first and subsequent references.

First Citation in Text

Rosenzweig, Breedlove, and Watson (2005) wrote that biological psychology is an interdisciplinary field that includes scientists from "quite different backgrounds" (p. 3).

Subsequent Citations

Biological psychology is "the field that relates behavior to bodily processes, especially the workings of the brain" (Rosenzweig et al., 2005, p. 3).

TWO OR MORE WORKS BY THE SAME AUTHOR

To cite one of two or more works by the same author or group of authors, use the author's last name plus the year (and the page, if you are citing a quotation). When more than one work being cited was published by an author in the same year, the works are alphabetized by title and then assigned lowercase letters after the date (2005a, 2005b).

Middle-class unemployed workers are better off than their lower-class counterparts, because "the white collar unemployed are likely to have some assets to invest in their job search" (Ehrenreich, 2005b, p. 16).

UNKNOWN AUTHOR

To cite a work listed only by its title, the APA uses a shortened version of the title.

An international pollution treaty still to be ratified would prohibit all plastic garbage from being dumped at sea ("Awash," 1987).

SECONDARY SOURCE

To quote material taken not from the original source but from a secondary source that quotes the original, give the secondary source in the reference list, and in your essay acknowledge that the original was quoted in a secondary source.

E. M. Forster said "the collapse of all civilization, so realistic for us, sounded in Matthew Arnold's ears like a distant and harmonious cataract" (as cited in Trilling, 1955, p. 11).

List of References

The APA follows this order in the presentation of information for each source listed: author, publication year, title, and publication source; for an article, the page range is given as well. Titles of books, periodicals, and the like should be italicized. For books and articles, capitalize only the first word of the title, proper nouns, and the first word following a colon (if any). Capitalize the titles of magazines and journals as you would normally capitalize them.

When the list of references includes several works by the same author, the APA provides the following rules for arranging these entries in the list:

- Same-name single-author entries precede multiple-author entries:

  Zettelmeyer, F. (2000).

  Zettelmeyer, F., Morton, F. S., & Silva-Risso, J. (2006).

- Entries with the same first author and a different second author are alphabetized under the first author according to the second author's last name:

  Dhar, R., & Nowlis, S. M. (2004).

  Dhar, R., & Simonson, I. (2003).

- Entries by the same authors are arranged by year of publication, in chronological order:

  Golder, P. N., & Tellis, G. J. (2003).

  Golder, P. N., & Tellis, G. J. (2004).

- Entries by the same authors with the same publication year should be arranged alphabetically by title (according to the first word after *A*, *An*, or *The*), and lower-case letters (*a*, *b*, *c*, and so on) are appended to the year in parentheses:

  Aaron, P. (1990a). *Basic . . .*

  Aaron, P. (1990b). *Elements . . .*

The APA recommends that the first line of each entry be indented one-half inch (or five spaces) in papers intended for publication but notes that student writers may use a hanging indent of five spaces. Ask your instructor which format is preferred. The following examples demonstrate a hanging indent of one-half inch.

Books

A BOOK BY A SINGLE AUTHOR

Ehrenreich, B. (2001). *Nickel and dimed: On (not) getting by in America*. New York, NY: Metropolitan.

A BOOK BY AN AGENCY OR A CORPORATION

American Medical Association. (2004). *Family medical guide*. Hoboken, NJ: Wiley.

A BOOK BY MORE THAN ONE AUTHOR

Saba, L., & Gattis, J. (2002). *The McGraw-Hill homeschooling companion*. New York, NY: McGraw-Hill.

Hunt, L., Po-Chia Hsia, R., Martin, T. R., Rosenwein, B. H., Rosenwein, H., & Smith, B. G. (2001). *The making of the West: Peoples and cultures*. Boston, MA: Bedford/St. Martin's.

If there are more than seven authors, list only the first six, then insert three ellipses, and add the last author's name.

A BOOK BY AN UNKNOWN AUTHOR

Use the title in place of the author.

Rand McNally commercial atlas and marketing guide. (2003). Skokie, IL: Rand McNally.

When an author is designated as "Anonymous," identify the work as "Anonymous" in the text, and alphabetize it as "Anonymous" in the reference list.

A BOOK WITH AN AUTHOR AND AN EDITOR

Arnold, M. (1994). *Culture and anarchy* (S. Lipman, Ed.). New Haven, CT: Yale University Press. (Original work published 1869)

AN EDITED COLLECTION

Waldman, D., & Walker, J. (Eds.). (1999). *Feminism and documentary*. Minneapolis, MN: University of Minnesota Press.

A WORK IN AN ANTHOLOGY OR A COLLECTION

Fairbairn-Dunlop, P. (1993). Women and agriculture in western Samoa. In J. H. Momsen & V. Kinnaird (Eds.), *Different places, different voices* (pp. 211-226). London, England: Routledge.

A TRANSLATION

Tolstoy, L. (2002). *War and peace* (C. Garnett, Trans.). New York, NY: Modern Library. (Original work published 1869)

AN ARTICLE IN A REFERENCE BOOK

Rowland, R. P. (2001). Myasthenia gravis. In *Encyclopedia Americana* (Vol. 19, p. 683). Danbury, CT: Grolier.

AN INTRODUCTION, PREFACE, FOREWORD, OR AFTERWORD

Graff, G., & Phelan, J. Preface (2004). In M. Twain, *Adventures of Huckleberry Finn* (pp. iii-vii). New York, NY: Bedford/St. Martin's.

Articles

AN ARTICLE FROM A DAILY NEWSPAPER

Peterson, A. (2003, May 20). Finding a cure for old age. *The Wall Street Journal*, pp. D1, D5.

AN ARTICLE FROM A WEEKLY OR BIWEEKLY MAGAZINE

Gross, M. J. (2003, April 29). Family life during war time. *The Advocate*, 42-48.

AN ARTICLE FROM A MONTHLY OR BIMONTHLY MAGAZINE

Shelby, A. (2005, September/October). Good going: Alaska's glacier crossroads. *Sierra, 90*, 23.

AN ARTICLE IN A SCHOLARLY JOURNAL WITH CONTINUOUS ANNUAL PAGINATION

The volume number follows the title of the journal.

Shan, J. Z., Morris, A. G., & Sun, F. (2001). Financial development and economic growth: A chicken and egg problem? *Review of Economics, 9*, 443-454.

AN ARTICLE IN A SCHOLARLY JOURNAL THAT PAGINATES EACH ISSUE SEPARATELY

The issue number appears in parentheses after the volume number.

Tran, D. (2002). Personal income by state, second quarter 2002. *Current Business, 82*(11), 55-73.

AN ANONYMOUS ARTICLE

Communities blowing whistle on street basketball. (2003). *USA Today*, p. 20A.

A REVIEW

Cassidy, J. (2002, July 12). Master of disaster [Review of the book *Globalization and its discontents*]. *The New Yorker*, 82-86.

If the review is untitled, use the bracketed information as the title, retaining the brackets.

Electronic Sources

While the APA guidelines for citing online resources are still something of a work in progress, a rule of thumb is that citation information must allow readers to access and retrieve the information cited. The following guidelines are derived from the *Publication Manual of the American Psychological Association*, Sixth Edition (2010). Regular updates are posted on the APA's Web site (www.apastyle.apa.org).

For most sources accessed on the Internet, you should provide the following information:

- Name of author (if available)
- Date of publication or most recent update (in parentheses; if unavailable, use the abbreviation *n.d.*)
- Title of document
- Publication information, including volume and issue numbers for periodicals
- Retrieval information necessary to locate the document. Note that the APA now requires the date of access *only* for content that is likely to be changed or updated.

For more information on using the Internet for research, see Chapter 13, pp. 397–98.

DOCUMENT FROM A WEB SITE

When you cite an entire Web site, the APA does not require an entry in the list of references. You may instead give the name of the site in your text and its Web address in parentheses. To cite a document that you have accessed through a Web site, follow these formats:

American Cancer Society. (2003). How to fight teen smoking. Retrieved from http://www
.cancer.org/docroot/ped/content/ped_10_14_how_to_fight_teen_smoking.asp

Heins, M. (2003, January 24). The strange case of Sarah Jones. *The Free Expression Policy Project*. Retrieved from http://www.fepproject.org/commentaries/sarahjones
.html

ARTICLE FROM A DATABASE

Follow the guidelines for a comparable print source, but conclude with the article's DOI (Digital Object Identifier), if one is assigned. If there is no DOI, conclude with the URL of the journal's home page.

Houston, R. G., & Toma, F. (2003). Home schooling: An alternative school choice. *Southern Economic Journal, 69*(4), 920-936. Retrieved from http://www. southerneconomic.org

Tharp, R. G. (1989). Psychocultural variables and constants: Effects on teaching and learning in schools. *American Psychologist, 44*(2), 249–359. doi:10.1037/0003-066X.44.2.349

AN ARTICLE FROM AN ONLINE PERIODICAL

Include the same information you would for a print article. If the article has a DOI, include it; if not, include the URL for the article or the periodical's home page.

Jauhar, S. (2003, July 15). A malady that mimics depression. *The New York Times.* Retrieved from http://www.nytimes.com

Retrieval information is always required for periodicals that are published only online.

Cesarini, P. (2004/2005). Computers, technology, and literacies. *The Journal of Literacy and Technology, 4*(1). Retrieved from http://www.literacyandtechnology.org/v4/cesarini.htm

ONLINE POSTINGS

Include online postings in your list of references only if you can provide data that would allow retrieval of the source. Provide the author's name, the date of the posting, the subject line, and any other identifier in brackets after the title. Include the words *Retrieved from* followed by the URL where the message can be found. Include the name of the list, newsgroup, or blog, if this information is not part of the URL.

Paikeday, T. (2005, October 10). "Esquivalience" is out [Electronic mailing list message]. Retrieved from http://listserv.linguistlist.org/cgi-bin/wa?A1=ind0510b&L=ads-1#1

Ditmire, S. (2005, February 10). NJ tea party [Newsgroup message]. Retrieved from http:// groups.google.com/group/TeaParty

AN E-MAIL MESSAGE

In the APA style, it is not necessary to list personal correspondence, including e-mail, in your reference list. Simply cite the person's name in your text, and in parentheses give the notation *personal communication* (in regular type, not underlined or italicized) and the date.

COMPUTER SOFTWARE

If an individual has proprietary rights to the software, cite that person's name as you would for a print text. Otherwise, cite as you would an anonymous print text.

> How Computers Work [Software]. (1998). Available from Que: http://www. howcomputerswork.net

Other Sources

A GOVERNMENT DOCUMENT

> U.S. Department of Health and Human Services. (1999). *Building communities together: Federal programs guide 1999-2000.* Washington, DC: GPO.

Note: when the author and publisher are the same, as in the example above, use the word *Author* (not italicized) as the name of the publisher.

AN UNPUBLISHED DOCTORAL DISSERTATION

> Bullock, B. (1986). *Basic needs fulfillment among less developed countries: Social progress over two decades of growth* (Unpublished doctoral dissertation). Vanderbilt University, Nashville, TN.

A TELEVISION PROGRAM

> Charlsen, C. (Writer and producer). (2003, July 14). Murder of the century [Television series episode]. In M. Samels (Executive producer), *American Experience.* Boston, MA: WGBH.

A FILM OR VIDEO RECORDING

> Myers, T. (Writer and producer). (2002). *Space station* [Film]. New York, NY: IMAX.

A MUSIC RECORDING

If the recording date differs from the copyright date, the APA requires that it appear in parentheses after the name of the label. If it is necessary to include a number for the recording, use parentheses for the medium; otherwise, use brackets.

> Beethoven, L. van. (1806). Violin concerto in D major, op. 61 [Recorded by USSR State Orchestra]. (Cassette Recording No. ACS 8044). New York, NY: Allegro. (1980).

> Springsteen, B. (1984). Dancing in the dark. On *Born in the U.S.A.* [CD]. New York, NY: Columbia.

AN INTERVIEW

When using the APA style, do not list personal interviews in your references list. Simply cite the person's name (last name and initials) in your text, and in parentheses give the notation *personal communication* (in regular type, not italicized or underlined) followed by a comma and the date of the interview. For published interviews, use the appropriate format for an article.

■ Some Sample Research Papers

As a writer, you will want or need to use sources on many occasions. You may be assigned to write a research paper, complete with formal documentation of outside sources. Several of the writing assignments in this book present opportunities to do library or field research — in other words, to turn to outside sources. Among the readings in Part One, the essays listed here cite and document sources. (The documentation style each follows is given in parentheses.)

"Cannibalism: It Still Exists," by Linh Kieu Ngo, Chapter 4, pp. 101–05 (MLA)

"Children Need to Play, Not Compete," by Jessica Statsky, Chapter 5, pp. 149–54 (MLA)

"More Testing, More Learning," by Patrick O'Malley, Chapter 6, pp. 195–99 (APA)

"Win-Win Flexibility," by Karen Kornbluh, Chapter 6, pp. 200–204 (MLA)

"Grading Professors," by Wendy Kim, Chapter 7, pp. 247–53 (MLA)

■ An Annotated Research Paper

On the following pages is a student research paper speculating about the causes of a trend — the increase in homeschooling. The author cites statistics, quotes authorities, and paraphrases and summarizes background information and support for her argument. She uses the MLA documentation style.

1/2"
Dinh 1

1"

Cristina Dinh

Double-spaced

Professor Cooper

1"

English 100

15 May 2009

Double-spaced

Title centered;
no underlining,
quotes, or italics

Educating Kids at Home

Every morning, Mary Jane, who is nine, doesn't have to worry about
gulping down her cereal so she can be on time for school. School for Mary
Jane is literally right at her doorstep.

Paragraphs
indented
one-half inch

In this era of serious concern about the quality of public education, increasing numbers of parents across the United States are choosing to edu-

1"

cate their children at home. These parents believe they can do a better job
teaching their children than their local schools can. *Homeschooling*, as
this practice is known, has become a national trend over the past thirty

Author named in
text; no paren-
thetical page ref-
erence, because
source not pagi-
nated

years, and, according to education specialist Brian D. Ray, the homeschooled population is growing at a rate between 5 percent and 12 percent
per year. A 2008 report by the U.S. Department of Education's Institute of
Education Sciences estimated that, nationwide, the number of homeschooled children rose from 850,000 in 1999 to approximately 1.5 million

in 2007 (*1.5 Million* 2). Some homeschooling advocates believe that even

Abbreviated title
used in parentheti-
cal citation, be-
cause Works Cited
lists two sources
by government
author (named in
text); no punctua-
tion between title
and page number

these numbers may be low because not all states require formal notification when parents decide to teach their children at home.

What is homeschooling, and who are the parents choosing to be homeschoolers? David Guterson, a pioneer in the homeschooling movement, defines homeschooling as "the attempt to gain an education outside of
institutions" (5). Homeschooled children spend the majority of the conventional school day learning in or near their homes rather than in traditional

Author named
in text; paren-
thetical page
reference falls at
end of sentence

schools; parents or guardians are the prime educators. Former teacher and
homeschooler Rebecca Rupp notes that homeschooling parents vary consid-
erably in what they teach and how they teach, ranging from those
who follow a highly traditional curriculum within a structure that parallels
the typical classroom to those who essentially allow their children to pursue

1"

Dinh 2

whatever interests them at their own pace (3). Homeschoolers commonly
combine formal instruction with life skills instruction, learning fractions, for
example, in terms of monetary units or cooking measurements (Saba and   *Work by two*
Gattis 89). According to the U.S. Department of Education's 2008 report,   *authors cited*
while homeschoolers are also a diverse group politically and philosophi-
cally--libertarians, conservatives, Christian fundamentalists--most say they
homeschool for one of three reasons: they are concerned about the quality
of academic instruction, the general school environment, or the lack of religious or moral instruction (*1.5 Million* 2).

    The first group generally believes that children need individual
attention and the opportunity to learn at their own pace to learn well.
This group says that one teacher in a classroom of twenty to thirty
children (the size of typical public-school classes) cannot give this kind
of attention. These parents believe they can give their children greater
enrichment and more specialized instruction than public schools can
provide. At home, parents can work one-on-one with each child and be
flexible about time, allowing their children to pursue their interests at
earlier ages. Many of these parents, like homeschooler Peter Bergson,
believe that

> home schooling provides more of an opportunity to continue   *Quotation of*
> the natural learning process that's in evidence in all children.   *more than four*
> [In school,] you change the learning process from self-directed   *lines typed as*
> to other-directed, from the child asking questions to the   *a block and*
> teacher asking questions. You shut down areas of potential in-   *indented ten*
> terest. (qtd. in Kohn 22)   *spaces*

*Brackets indi-
cate addition to
quotation*

*Parenthetical
citation of
secondary
source falls after
period*

    This trend can be traced back to the 1960s, when many people began
criticizing traditional schools. Various types of "alternative schools" were
created, and some parents began teaching their children at home
(Friedlander 20). Parents like this mention several reasons for their disappointment with public schools and for their decision to homeschool. A
lack of funding, for example, leaves children without new textbooks. In a

Dinh 3

2002 survey, 31 percent of teachers said that their students are using text-books that are more than ten years old, and 29 percent said that they do *Corporate au-* not have enough textbooks for all of their students (National Education *thor's name* *cited* — Association). Many schools also cannot afford to buy laboratory equipment and other teaching materials. At my own high school, the chemistry teacher told me that most of the lab equipment we used came from a re-search firm he worked for. In a 2006 Gallup poll, lack of proper financial support ranked first on the list of the problems in public schools (Rose and Gallup).

Parents also cite overcrowding as a reason for taking their kids out of school. The more students in a classroom, the less learning that goes on, as Cafi Cohen discovered before choosing to homeschool; after spending several days observing what went on in her child's classroom, she found that administrative duties, including disciplining, took up to 80 percent of a teacher's time with only 20 percent of the day devoted to learning (6). Moreover, faced with a large group of children, a teacher ends up gearing lessons to the students in the middle level, so children at both ends miss out. Gifted children and those with learning disabilities partic-ularly suffer in this situation. At home, parents of these children say they can tailor the material and the pace for each child. Studies show that homeschooling methods seem to work well in preparing children academically. Lawrence Rudner, director of the ERIC Clearinghouse on Assessment and Evaluation at the University of Maryland and a researcher on homeschooling, found that testing of homeschooled students showed them to be between one and three years ahead of public school students their age (xi). Homeschooled children have also made particularly strong showings in academic competitions; since the late 1990s, 10 percent of National Spelling Bee participants have been Homeschooled, as have two National Spelling Bee and two National Geographic Bee winners (Lyman). More and more selective colleges are admitting, and even recruiting, homeschooled applicants (Basham, Merrifield, and Hepburn 15).

Dinh 4

Parents in the second group--those concerned with the general school environment--claim that their children are more well-rounded than those in school. Because they don't have to sit in classrooms all day, homeschooled kids can pursue their own projects, often combining crafts or technical skills with academic subjects. Homeschoolers participate in outside activities such as 4-H competitions, field trips with peers in homeschool support groups, science fairs, musical and dramatic productions, church activities, and Boy Scouts or Girl Scouts (Saba and Gattis 59-62). In fact, they may even be able to participate to some extent in actual school activities. A 1999 survey conducted by the U.S. Department of Education's Institute of Education Sciences found that 28 percent of public schools allowed homeschooled students to participate in extracurricular activities alongside enrolled students, and 20 percent allowed homeschooled students to attend some classes (Blumenfeld 12).

Many homeschooling parents believe that these activities provide the social opportunities kids need without exposing their children to the peer pressure they would have to deal with as regular school students. For example, many kids think that drinking and using drugs are cool. When I was in high school, my friends would tell me a few drinks wouldn't hurt or affect driving. If I had listened to them, I wouldn't be alive today. Four of my friends were killed under the influence of alcohol. Between 1992 and 2008, the number of high school seniors surveyed who had used any illicit drug in the last year climbed from 27.1 percent to 36.6 percent (Johnston, et al. 59).

——Work by more than three authors cited

Another reason many parents decide to homeschool their kids is that they are concerned for their children's safety. Samuel L. Blumenfeld notes that "physical risk" is an important reason many parents remove their children from public schools as "[m]ore and more children are assaulted, robbed, and murdered in school" and a "culture of violence, abetted by rap music, drug trafficking, . . . and racial tension, has engulfed teenagers" (4). Beginning in the mid-1990s, a string of school shootings--including the 1999 massacres in Littleton, Colorado, and Conyers, Georgia, and the 2001 massacre in Santee, California--has led to increasing fears that young people are simply not safe at school.

   While all of the reasons mentioned so far are important, perhaps the single most significant cause of the growing homeschooling trend is Christian fundamentalist dissatisfaction with "godless" public schools. Sociologist Mitchell L. Stevens, author of one of the first comprehensive studies of homeschooling, cites a mailing sent out by Basic Christian Education, a company that markets homeschooling materials, titled "What Really Happens in Public Schools." This publication sums up the fears of fundamentalist homeschoolers about public schools: that they encourage high levels of teenage sexual activity and pregnancies "out of wedlock"; expose children to "violence, crime, lack of discipline, and, of course, drugs of every kind"; present positive portrayals of communism and socialism and negative portrayals of capitalism; and undermine children's Christian beliefs by promoting "New Age philosophies, Yoga, Transcendental Meditation, witchcraft demonstrations, and Eastern religions" (51).

   As early as 1988, Luanne Shackelford and Susan White, two Christian homeschooling mothers, were claiming that because schools expose children to "[p]eer pressure, perverts, secular textbooks, values clarification, TV, pornography, rock music, bad movies . . . [h]ome schooling seems to be the best plan to achieve our goal [to raise good Christians]" (160). As another mother more recently put it:

Brackets used to indicate changes in capitalization and addition to quotation for clarification

Ellipsis marks used to indicate words left out of quotations

> I don't like the way schools are going. . . . What's wrong with Christianity all of a sudden? You know? This country was founded on Christian, on religious principles. [People] came over here for religious freedom, and now all of a sudden all religious references

Dinh 6

seem to be stricken out of the public school, and I don't like that

at all. (qtd. in Stevens 67)   —————— *Quotation cited in a secondary source*

Although many nonfundamentalist homeschoolers make some of these

same criticisms, those who cite the lack of "Christian values" in public

schools have particular concerns of their own. For example, homeschooling

leader Raymond Moore talks of parents who are "'sick and tired of the   — *Single quotation marks indicate a quotation within a quotation*

teaching of evolution in the schools as a cut-and-dried fact,' along with

other evidence of so-called secular humanism" (Kohn 21), such as text-

books that contain material contradicting Christian beliefs. Moreover, par-

ents worry that schools undermine their children's moral values. In   *Citation placed close to quotation, before comma but after quotation marks*

particular, some Christian fundamentalist parents object to sex education

in schools, saying that it encourages children to become sexually active

early, challenging values taught at home. They see the family as the core

and believe that the best place to instill family values is within the fam-

ily. These Christian homeschooling parents want to provide their children

not only with academic knowledge but also with a moral grounding con-

sistent with their religious beliefs.

Still other homeschooling parents object to a perceived government-

mandated value system that they believe attempts to override the values,

not necessarily religious in nature, of individual families. For these par-

ents, homeschooling is a way of resisting what they see as unwarranted

intrusion by the federal government into personal concerns (*Alliance*). —— *Internet source cited by shortened form of title; author's name and page numbers unavailable*

Armed with their convictions, parents such as those who belong to

the Christian Home School Legal Defense Association have fought in court

and lobbied for legislation that allows them the option of homeschooling.

In the 1970s, most states had compulsory attendance laws that made it

difficult, if not illegal, to keep school-age children home from school.

Today, homeschooling is permitted in every state, with strict regulation

required by only a few (Home School). As a result, Mary Jane is one of—— *Shortened form of corporate author's name cited*

hundreds of thousands of American children who can start their school

day without leaving the house.

1"

Works Cited

Dinh 7

Alliance for the Separation of School and State. Home page. Alliance for the
   Separation of School and State, 26 Feb. 2009. Web. 10 Apr. 2009.

Basham, Patrick, John Merrifield, and Claudia R. Hepburn. *Home
   Schooling: From the Extreme to the Mainstream*. 2nd ed. Vancouver:
   The Fraser Institute, 2007. Studies in Education Policy. *Fraser
   Institute*. Web. 13 Apr. 2009.

Blumenfeld, Samuel L. *Homeschooling: A Parent's Guide to Teaching Children*.
   Bridgewater: Replica, 1999. Print.

Cohen, Cafi. *And What about College?: How Homeschooling Leads to
   Admissions to the Best Colleges and Universities*. Cambridge: Holt,
   1997. Print.

Friedlander, Tom. "A Decade of Home Schooling." *The Homeschool Reader*.
   Ed. Mark Hegener and Helen Hegener. Tonasket: Home Education, 1988.
   Print.

Guterson, David. *Family Matters: Why Homeschooling Makes Sense*. San
   Diego: Harcourt, 1992. Print.

Home School Legal Defense Association. "State Action Map." *HSLDA:
   Advocates for Homeschooling*. HSLDA, 2009. Web. 5 Apr. 2009.

Johnston, Lloyd D., et al. *Monitoring the Future: National Results on
   Adolescent Drug Use, Overview of Key Findings, 2008*. Bethesda: National
   Institute on Drug Abuse, 2009. Web. 20 Apr. 2009.

Kohn, Alfie. "Home Schooling." *Atlantic Monthly* Apr. 1988: 20-25. Print.

Lyman, Isabel. "Generation Two." *American Enterprise* Oct./Nov. 2002:
   48-49. *InfoTrac OneFile*. Web. 10 May 2009.

National Education Association. *2002 Instructional Materials Survey*. Sept.
   2002. Association of American Publishers, 2002. Web. 21 Apr. 2009.

Ray, Brian D. "Research Facts on Homeschooling." *National Home Education
   Research Institute*. NHERI, 2008. Web. 10 Apr. 2009.

Rose, Lowell C., and Alec M. Gallup. "The 38th Annual PDK/Gallup Poll of
   the Public's Attitudes Toward the Public Schools." *Phi Delta Kappan*
   88.1 (2006): n. pag. *Phi Delta Kappa International*. Web. 1 May 2009.

Dinh 8

Rudner, Lawrence. Foreword. *The McGraw-Hill Homeschooling Companion*. By
    Laura Saba and Julie Gattis. New York: McGraw, 2002. Print.

Rupp, Rebecca. *The Complete Home Learning Source Book*. New York: Three
    Rivers, 1998. Print.

Saba, Laura, and Julie Gattis. *The McGraw-Hill Homeschooling Companion*.
    New York: McGraw, 2002. Print.

Shackelford, Luanne, and Susan White. *A Survivor's Guide to Home Schooling*.
    Westchester: Crossway, 1988. Print.

Stevens, Mitchell L. *Kingdom of Children: Culture and Controversy in the
    Homeschooling Movement*. Princeton: Princeton UP, 2001. Print.

United States. Dept. of Education. Institute of Education Sciences.
    Homeschooling in the United States: 1999. Washington: GPO, 2001.
    National Center for Education Statistics. Web. 23 Apr. 2009.

---. ---. ---. *1.5 Million Homeschooled Students in the United States in 2007*.
    Washington: GPO, 2008. *National Center for Education Statistics*. Web.
    23 Apr. 2009.

15 Designing Documents

The arrangement of text, visuals, and white space on a page—called **page layout**—has a major impact on the readability of a document and may influence the reader's attitude toward it. This chapter introduces basic components of page layout, discusses some common formats for paper and electronic documents you may be asked to create in your college courses or in the workplace, and offers guidelines for designing effective documents.

Considering Context

When considering page layout and other aspects of document design, you will want to understand the context in which your document will be read. For instance, if you are writing an essay for a college course, your instructor will read it carefully. Your design decisions should make sustained reading as easy as possible; therefore, you will want to present a neat, clearly printed paper. Fonts that are too small to read easily or print that is too light to see clearly will make the reader's job unnecessarily difficult. Use double-spaced text and one-inch margins to leave your instructor room to write comments on the page.

When you write for other audiences, however, you cannot expect all readers to read your writing closely. Some readers may skim through your blog entries looking for interesting points; others might scan a report or memo for information important specifically to them. Design elements such as headings, bullets, and chunking will help these readers find the information of most interest to them.

Frequently, too, your page-layout and document design decisions will be predetermined by the kind of document you are preparing. Business letters and memos, for example, traditionally follow specific formats. Because your readers will bring certain expectations to these kinds of documents, altering an established format can cause confusion.

It is important to note that MLA, APA, and other style systems have specific rules regarding such things as spacing, margins, and heading formats. Be sure to ask your instructor whether you will be expected to adhere closely to these rules; if so, your choices regarding document design will be limited.

To analyze the context in which a document is read or used, ask yourself the following questions:

- *Where will my document be read?* Will the document be read on paper in a well-lighted, quiet room? Or will it be read on a laptop in a noisy, dimly lit coffee shop?
- *Do my readers have specific expectations for this kind of document?* Am I writing a memo, letter, or report that requires certain design conventions? Does my instructor expect me to follow MLA style, APA style, or another system?
- *How will the information be used?* Are my readers reading to learn, or to be entertained? Do I expect them to skim the document or to read it carefully?

Elements of Document Design

Readable fonts, informative headings, bulleted or numbered lists, and appropriate use of color, white space, and visuals like photographs, charts, and diagrams all help readers learn from your document.

Font Style and Size

Typography is a design term for the letters and symbols that make up the print on a page or a screen. You are already using important aspects of typography when you use capital letters, italics, boldface, or different sizes of type to signal a new sentence, identify the title of a book, or distinguish a heading from body text.

Word processing programs enable you to use dozens of different fonts, or typefaces; bold and italic versions of these fonts; and a range of font sizes. Fortunately, you can rely on some simple design principles to make good typographic choices for your documents.

Perhaps the most important advice for working with typography is to choose fonts that are easy to read. Some fonts are meant for decorative or otherwise very minimal use, and are hard to read in extended passages. Font style, font size, and combinations of style and size are features that can add to or distract from readability.

Considering Font Style.   For most academic and business writing, you will probably want to choose a traditional font that is easy to read, such as Arial or Times New Roman. This book is set in Minion. Sentences and paragraphs printed in fonts that imitate *calligraphy* (typically called script fonts) or those that mimic Handwriting are not only difficult to read but also too informal in appearance for most academic and business purposes.

Some Fonts Appropriate for Academic and Business Writing

Arial
Georgia
Tahoma

Times New Roman
Verdana

Considering Font Size.   To ensure that your documents can be read easily, you also need to choose an appropriate font size (traditionally measured in units called **points**). For most types of academic writing, a 12-point font is standard for the main (body) text. For Web pages, however, you should consider using a slightly larger font to compensate for the difficulty of reading from a computer monitor. For overhead transparencies and computer-projected displays, you should use an even larger font size (such as 32-point, and typically no smaller than 18-point) to ensure that the text can be read from a distance.

Combining Font Styles and Sizes.   Although computers now make hundreds of font styles and sizes available to writers, you should avoid confusing readers with too many different fonts in one document. Limit the fonts in a document to one or two that complement each other well. A common practice, for instance, is to choose one font for all titles and headings (such as Arial, 14-pt, boldface) and another for the body text (such as Times New Roman, 12-pt), as shown in the example here.

> ## This is an Example Heading
>
> This is body text. This is body text.
> This is body text. This is body text.
> This is body text. This is body text.
>
> ## This is an Example Heading
>
> This is body text. This is body text.
> This is body text. This is body text.
> This is body text. This is body text.

Headings and Body Text

Titles and headings are often distinguished from body text by boldface, italics, or font size. Headings are helpful in calling attention to certain parts or sections of a piece of writing and in offering readers visual cues to its overall organization. Always check with your instructor about the conventions for using (or not using) these elements in the particular discipline you are studying.

Distinguishing between Headings and Subheadings.   Typically, headings for major sections (level-one headings) must have more visual impact than those subdividing these sections (level-two headings), which should be more prominent than headings within the subdivisions (level-three headings). The typography should reflect this hierarchy of headings. Here is one possible system for distinguishing among three levels of headings:

LEVEL-ONE HEADING
Level-Two Heading
Level-Three Heading

Notice that the level-one and level-two headings are given the greatest prominence by the use of boldface and that they are distinguished from one another by the use of all capital letters for the major heading versus capital and lowercase letters for the sub-heading. The third-level heading, italicized but not boldfaced, is less prominent than the other two headings but can still be readily distinguished from body text. Whatever system you use to distinguish headings and subheadings, be sure to apply it consistently throughout your document.

Positioning Headings Consistently.   In addition to keeping track of the font size and style of headings, you need to position headings in the same way throughout a piece of writing. You will want to consider the spacing above and below headings and determine whether the headings should be aligned with the left margin, indented a fixed amount of space, or centered. In this book, headings like the one that begins this paragraph — **Positioning Headings Consistently** — are aligned with the left margin and followed by a period and a fixed amount of space.

Using Type Size to Differentiate Headings from Text.   In documents that do not need to observe the MLA or APA style, which have specific rules about format-ting, you may wish to use font size to help make headings visually distinct from the body of the text. If you do so, avoid making the headings too large. To accompany 12-point body text, for instance, a 14-point heading will do. The default settings for heading and body text styles on most word processing and desktop publishing pro-grams are effective, and you may want to use them to autoformat your heading and text styles.

For more on selecting appropriate headings and subheadings, see Chapter 10, pp. 342–44.

Numbered and Bulleted Lists

Lists are often an effective way to present information in a logical and visually coherent way. Use a **numbered list** (1, 2, 3) to present the steps in a process or to list items that readers will need to refer back to easily (for instance, see the sample e-mail message on p. 465). Use a **bulleted list** (marking each new item with a "bullet" — a dash, circle, or box) to highlight key points when the order of the items is not significant (for instance, see the sample memo on p. 462). Written instructions, such as recipes, are typically formatted using numbered lists, whereas a list of supplies, for example, is more often presented in the form of a bulleted list.

Colors

Color printers, photocopiers, and online technology facilitate the use of color, but color does not necessarily make text easier to read. In most academic print documents, the only color you should use is black. While color is typically used more freely in academic writing produced in other media (for example, Web pages or slideshow presentations), it should still be used in moderation and always with the aim of increasing your readers' understanding of what you have to say. Always consider, too, whether your readers might be color-blind and whether they will have access to a full-color version of the document.

Although the slideshow design in Figure 15.1 is visually interesting and the heading is readable, the bulleted text is very hard to read because there is too little contrast between the text color and the background color.

In Figure 15.2, it is clear that the person who created the pie chart carefully chose the colors to represent the different data. What the person did not consider, however, is how the colors would look when printed out on a black-and-white printer. It is nearly impossible to associate the labels with the slices of the pie and thus to read the chart.

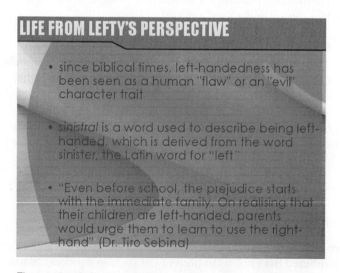

Figure 15.1 A document with too little color contrast

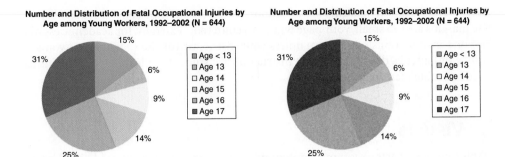

Figure 15.2 A pie chart that requires a color printer to be understandable
Source: National Institute for Occupational Safety and Health, "Data on Young Worker Injuries and Illnesses in Worker Health" (2004).

Also consider the meanings associated with different colors. For example, in the United States and other Western cultures, white typically is associated with goodness and purity; in China, however, white represents grief and mourning. Although your use of color in an essay, a Web page, or a slideshow presentation might not carry such deep meaning, bear in mind that most people have emotional or psychological responses to colors and color combinations.

White Space

Another basic element of document design, white space, is the open, or blank, space surrounding the text. White space is usually used between a heading, for instance, and the paragraph that follows the heading. You also use white space when you set the margins on the page, and even when you double-space between lines of text. In all of these cases, the space makes your document easier to read. When used generously, white space facilitates reading by keeping the pages of a document uncluttered and by helping the eye find and follow the text.

Chunking.   **Chunking**, the breaking up of text into smaller units, also facilitates reading. Paragraphing is a form of chunking that divides text into units of closely related information. In most academic essays and reports, text is double-spaced, and paragraphs are distinguished by indenting the first line one-half inch.

In single-spaced text, you may want to make reading easier by adding extra space between paragraphs, rather than indenting the first lines of paragraphs. This format, referred to as **block style**, is often used in memos, letters, and electronic documents. When creating electronic documents, especially Web pages, you might consider chunking your material into separate "pages" or screens, with links connecting the chunks.

Margins.   Adequate margins are an important component of general readability. If the margins are too small, your page will seem cluttered. Generally, for academic essays, use one-inch margins on all sides unless your instructor (or the style manual you are following) advises differently. Some instructors ask students to leave large margins to accommodate marginal comments.

■ Visuals

Tables, graphs, charts, diagrams, photographs, maps, and screen shots add visual interest and are often more effective in conveying information than prose alone. Be certain, however, that each visual has a valid role to play in your work; if the visual is merely a decoration, leave it out or replace it with a visual that is more appropriate.

You can create visuals on a computer, using the drawing tools of a word processing program, the charting tools of a spreadsheet program, or software specifically designed for creating visuals. You can also download visuals from the World Wide Web or photocopy or scan visuals from print materials. If your essay is going to be posted on the Web on a site that is not password-protected and a visual you want to use is from a source that is copyrighted, you should request written permission from the copyright holder (such as the photographer, publisher, or site sponsor). For any visual that you borrow from or create based on data from a source, be sure to cite the source in the caption, your bibliography, or both, according to the guidelines of the documentation system you are using.

Choose Appropriate Visuals and Design the Visuals with Their Final Use in Mind

Select the types of visuals that will best suit your purpose. The following list identifies various types, explains what they are best used for, and provides examples. If you plan to incorporate a visual into an overhead transparency or a computer-projected display, try to envision the original version as it would appear enlarged on a screen. Similarly, if you intend the visual for use on a Web page, consider how it will appear when displayed on a computer screen.

- *Tables.* A table is used to display numerical or textual data that is organized into columns and rows to make it easy to understand. A table usually includes several items as well as variables for each item. For example, the first column of Table 15.1 includes cities and states; the next two columns show the city population in 1990 and in 2000; and the final two columns show the change in population from 1990 to 2000 in number and percentage.
- *Bar graphs.* A bar graph typically compares numerical differences, often over time, for one or more items. For example, Figure 15.3 shows the rise in Internet access across five years (1997–2001) for U.S. households of varying incomes.
- *Line graphs.* A line graph charts change over time, typically with only one variable represented (unlike in Figure 15.3, where the bar chart data are organized into six

Table 15.1 Population Change for the Ten Largest U.S. Cities, 1990 to 2000

	Population		Change, 1990 to 2000	
City and State	*April 1, 2000*	*April 1, 1990*	*Number*	*Percentage*
New York, NY	8,008,278	7,322,564	685,714	9.4
Los Angeles, CA	3,694,820	3,485,398	209,422	6.0
Chicago, IL	2,896,016	2,783,726	112,290	4.0
Houston, TX	1,953,631	1,630,553	323,078	19.8
Philadelphia, PA	1,517,550	1,585,577	−68,027	−4.3
Phoenix, AZ	1,321,045	983,403	337,642	34.3
San Diego, CA	1,223,400	1,110,549	112,851	10.2
Dallas, TX	1,188,580	1,006,877	181,703	18.0
San Antonio, TX	1,144,646	935,933	208,713	22.3
Detroit, MI	951,270	1,027,974	−76,704	−7.5

Source: U.S. Census Bureau, Census 2000; 1990 Census, Population and Housing Unit Counts, United States (1990 CPH-2-1).

variables). For example, Figure 15.4 shows the amount of government spending for low-income children between 1966 and 2002.

- *Pie charts.* A pie chart shows the sizes of parts making up a whole. For instance, the whole (100 percent) in the chart shown in Figure 15.5 is the average annual

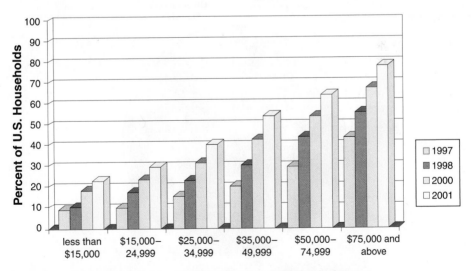

Figure 15.3 Percent of U.S. households with Internet access by income
Source: http://www.bc-net.org/Broadband/FixedWirelessBroadbandProject.nsf/
c39905004594509b85256c020048da39/fd5c34c8ce893c7185256c06004b05b5/
$FILE/bringing_a_nation.pdf

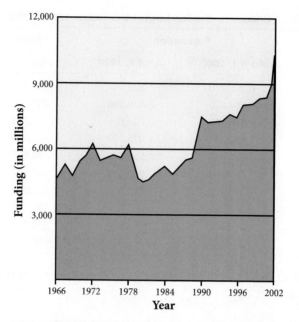

Figure 15.4 Title I spending for low-income children (in constant dollars)
Source: U.S. Department of Education.

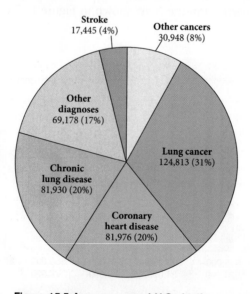

Figure 15.5 Average annual U.S. deaths attributable to cigarette smoking, 1995–1999
Source: Data from U.S. Centers for Disease Control.
Note: Total annual average is 406,290 deaths.

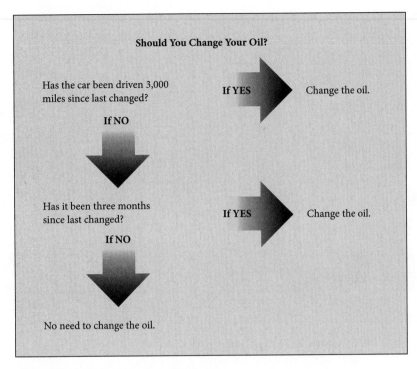

Figure 15.6 Oil-changing decision process

number of deaths in the United States attributable to cigarette smoking; the parts are the specific causes of death, such as lung cancer (31 percent) and coronary heart disease (20 percent).

- *Flowcharts.* A flowchart shows a process broken down into parts or stages. Flowcharts are particularly helpful for explaining a process or facilitating a decision based on a set of circumstances, as shown, for instance, in Figure 15.6.

- *Organization charts.* An organization chart does what its name suggests—it creates a map of lines of authority within an organization, such as a company. Typically, the most important person—the person to whom most employees report—appears at the top of the chart, as seen in Figure 15.7, where the managing editor, who oversees the entire daily newspaper, appears at the top.

- *Diagrams.* A diagram depicts an item or its properties, often using symbols. It is typically used to show relationships or how things function. (See Figure 15.8.)

- *Drawings and cartoons.* A drawing shows a simplified version or an artist's interpretation of an object or situation. Cartoons, like the one in Figure 15.9, are drawings typically used to make an argumentative point, usually in a humorous way.

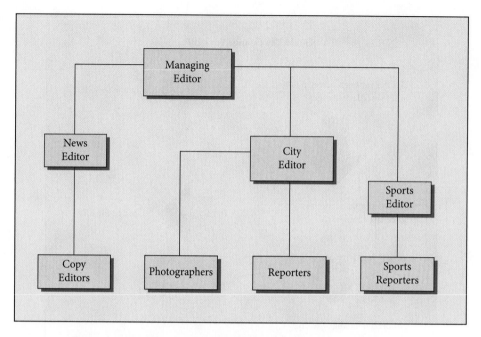

Figure 15.7 The newsroom of a typical small daily newspaper

- *Photographs.* Photographs are used when an author wants to represent a real and specific object, place, or person, often for its emotional impact. For instance, a student selected Figure 15.10, a photo of a burrowing owl, to be included in a report about the ways in which local development was affecting endangered species. Although photographic images are generally assumed to duplicate what the eye sees, a photograph may, in fact, be manipulated in a variety of ways for special effects. Photographs that have been altered should be so identified.

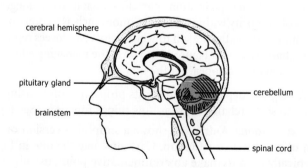

Figure 15.8 A cross-section of the human brain

Figure 15.9 A cartoon that makes an argument about using Native American Names for sports teams

- *Maps.* Maps are used to show geographical areas, lay out the spatial relationships of objects, or make a historical or political point. Figure 15.11 identifies Western Relocation Authority Centers and states that had a high Japanese American population. The map reveals that people were often relocated a great distance from their homes. (See Figure 15.11).

Figure 15.10 The burrowing owl

Figure 15.11 Western relocation authority centers
During World War II, ethnic prejudice was strong, and although they posed no threat to national security, Japanese Americans were forced to go to "Western Relocation Authority" camps. As the map indicates, people were often taken a great distance from their homes.

- *Screen shots.* A screen shot duplicates the appearance of a specific computer screen or of a window or other section within it. Screen shots can be used to capture a Web page to include in a print document or to describe steps or instructions for using a piece of software (see Figure 15.12).

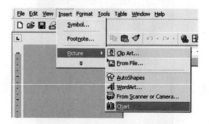

Figure 15.12 Screen capture to accompany written instructions, "How to insert a chart into a word processing document"

Number and Title Your Visuals

Number your visuals in sequential order and give each one a title. Refer to tables as *Table 1, Table 2,* and so on, and to other types of visuals as *Figure 1, Figure 2,* and so on. (In a long work with chapters or sections, you may also need to include the chapter or section number [*Figure 15.1*], as is done in this chapter of this book.)

Make sure each visual has a title that reflects the subject of the visual (for example, income levels) and its purpose (to compare and illustrate changes in those income levels): *Figure 1. Percentage of U.S. Households in Three Income Ranges, 1990–2000.* Notice that MLA style requires that the title for a table be placed above the table and the title for a figure be placed below the figure.

Label the Parts of Your Visuals and Include Descriptive Captions

To help readers understand a visual, clearly label all of its parts. In a table, for instance, give each column a heading; likewise, label each section of a pie chart with the percentage and the item it represents. You may place the label on the chart itself if it is readable and clear; if that is not practical, place a legend next to the chart.

Some visuals may require a caption that provides a fuller description than the title alone does. Your caption might also include an explanation helpful to understand the visual, as in Figure 15.11.

Cite Your Visual Sources

Finally, if you borrow a visual from another source or create a visual from borrowed information, you must cite the source, following the guidelines for the documentation style you are using (see Figure 15.2 and Table 15.1 for examples). In addition, be sure to document the source in your list of works cited or references at the end of your document.

Integrate the Visual into the Text

Visuals should facilitate, not disrupt, the reading of the body text. To achieve this goal, you need to first introduce and discuss the visual in your text and then insert the visual in an appropriate location.

Introducing the Visual. Ideally, you should introduce each visual by referring to it in your text immediately *before* the visual appears. An effective textual reference answers the following questions:

- What is the number of the visual?
- Where is it located?
- What kind of information does it contain?
- What important point does it make or support?

Here is an example of an effective introduction for the line graph shown earlier (Figure 15.4):

> Note the sharp increase between 1990 and 2002 in federal spending for disadvantaged children (see Figure 15.4), which rose steadily over this period despite fluctuations in partisan control of Congress and the White House.

Placing the Visual in an Appropriate Location. MLA style requires and APA style recommends that you place a visual in the body of your text as soon after the discussion as possible, particularly when the reader will need to consult the visual. In APA style, visuals can also be grouped at the end of an essay if they contain supplemental information that may not be of interest to the reader or if the visuals take up multiple pages. (See Figure 15.13 for a page from a sample student paper with a figure included. Note that the figure is mentioned in the text and placed directly after this introduction, and that it includes a descriptive title with source information.)

Use Common Sense When Creating Visuals on a Computer

If you use a computer program to create visuals, keep this advice in mind:

- *Make the decisions that your computer cannot make for you.* A computer can automatically turn spreadsheet data into a pie chart or bar graph, but only you can decide which visual — or what use of color, if any — is most appropriate for your purpose.
- *Avoid "chart junk."* Many computer programs provide an array of special effects that can be used to alter visuals, including three-dimensional renderings, textured backgrounds, and shadowed text. Such special effects often detract from the intended message of the visual by calling attention to themselves instead. Use them sparingly, and only when they emphasize key information.
- *Use clip art sparingly, if at all.* Clip art consists of icons, symbols, and other simple, typically abstract, copyright-free drawings. Because clip art simplifies ideas, it is of limited use in conveying the complex information contained in most academic writing.

■ Sample Documents

Earlier in this chapter you saw examples of various types of visuals; in this section you will take a look at various types of documents that you may be asked to prepare. Each sample document is accompanied by a discussion of appropriate design conventions.

As you examine the documents, try also to analyze the way that typography, color, white space, and visuals are used to guide the reader's eye across the page. What design features make the documents easy to read? What features make finding specific information within the documents easy? What features make the document easy to use?

In addition to examining the sample documents with these questions in mind, look at the sample research paper in Chapter 14, pp. 438–45.

Stanford University anchors the reputation and identity of their law school via their Web site (see Figure 1). The page features strongly contrasting colors—red, black, and light grey—and includes graphics that change each time the page is reloaded: photos of students and professors, in class and on campus, as well as questions whose answers are likely to be of interest to prospective students and other visitors to the site. These rotating graphics are meant to represent the various facets of Stanford Law School.

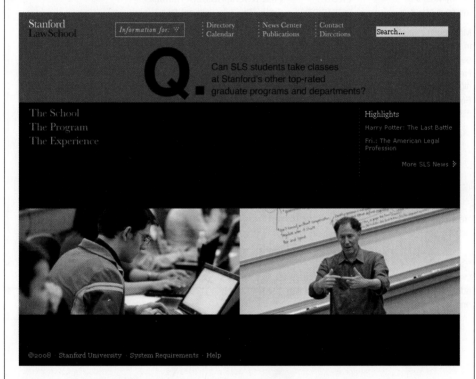

FIGURE 1: Home Page of Stanford Law School (image captured on March 14, 2008 from http://www.law.stanford.edu).

The question and photos are the most prominent features of the page, but the basic information about the law school (linked from "The School," "The Program," and "The Experience" at left) is easy to locate.

Figure 15.13 Excerpt from sample student paper with figure

Memos

Memos, such as the one shown in Figure 15.14, are documents sent between employees of the same organization (in contrast to business letters, which are sent to people

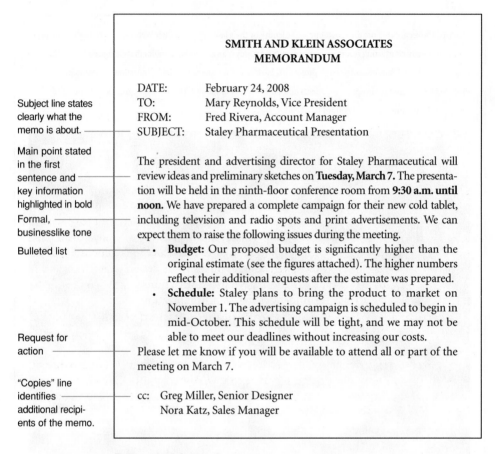

SMITH AND KLEIN ASSOCIATES
MEMORANDUM

DATE: February 24, 2008
TO: Mary Reynolds, Vice President
FROM: Fred Rivera, Account Manager
SUBJECT: Staley Pharmaceutical Presentation

The president and advertising director for Staley Pharmaceutical will review ideas and preliminary sketches on **Tuesday, March 7.** The presentation will be held in the ninth-floor conference room from **9:30 a.m. until noon.** We have prepared a complete campaign for their new cold tablet, including television and radio spots and print advertisements. We can expect them to raise the following issues during the meeting.

• **Budget:** Our proposed budget is significantly higher than the original estimate (see the figures attached). The higher numbers reflect their additional requests after the estimate was prepared.

• **Schedule:** Staley plans to bring the product to market on November 1. The advertising campaign is scheduled to begin in mid-October. This schedule will be tight, and we may not be able to meet our deadlines without increasing our costs.

Please let me know if you will be available to attend all or part of the meeting on March 7.

cc: Greg Miller, Senior Designer
      Nora Katz, Sales Manager

Labels (left column):
Subject line states clearly what the memo is about.

Main point stated in the first sentence and key information highlighted in bold

Formal, businesslike tone

Bulleted list

Request for action

"Copies" line identifies additional recipients of the memo.

Figure 15.14 A sample memo

outside the organization). The following conventions for writing a memo are well established and should rarely be altered. In addition, some organizations have specific guidelines for memos (such as the use of letterhead).

• *Heading.* A memo should carry the major heading *Memorandum* or *Memo.* If you are using letterhead stationery, position the heading just below the letterhead. The heading may be centered on the page or positioned at the left margin (depending on your organization's guidelines). In either case, the heading should be distinguished in some way from the rest of the body text, such as by a large font size, boldface type, or capital letters.

• *Content headings.* Just below the heading and separated by at least one line of space are the content headings: *Date, To, From,* and *Subject.* Place the content headings at the left margin and in the same size font as the body text.

- *Body text.* The main text of a memo is usually presented in block style: single-spaced with an extra line of space between paragraphs. (Do not indent the first line of paragraphs in block style.) If you need to call attention to specific information, consider presenting it in a numbered or bulleted list, or highlight the information visually by using boldface or extra white space above and below it. In a memo announcing a meeting, for example, you might boldface the date, time, and place of the meeting so the reader can quickly find the information, or you might set off the date, time, and place on separate lines.

Letters

The **business letter** (such as the one shown in Figure 15.15) is the document most often used for correspondence between representatives of one organization and representatives of another, though e-mail messages are increasingly being used in place of business letters. Business letters are written to obtain information about a company's products, to register a complaint, to respond to a complaint, or to introduce other documents (such as a proposal) that accompany the letter. As with memos, the design conventions for letters are long-established, although letters have more variations. Check to see whether there are specific business letter guidelines for your organization.

The heading of a business letter consists of the contact information for both the sender and the recipient of the letter. Block style is the most commonly used format for business letters.

Be sure to state the purpose of your letter in the first few lines and to provide supporting information in the paragraphs that follow. Always maintain a courteous and professional tone throughout a business letter. Include enough information to identify clearly any documents you refer to in the letter.

E-mail

Increasingly, students and instructors rely on electronic mail to exchange information about assignments and schedules as well as to follow up on class discussions (see Figure 15.16 on p. 465). **E-mail** messages are usually concise, direct, relatively informal, and limited to a single subject. Effective e-mails include a clear subject line.

In many organizations, e-mail messages are replacing handwritten or typed memos. When you send a memo electronically, make sure the headings automatically provided by the e-mail program convey the same essential information as the content headings in a traditional memo. If you are part of a large or complex organization, you may want to repeat your name and add such information as your job title, division, and telephone extension in a "signature" at the end of the document.

E-mail is a broader medium of communication than the business memo. Nevertheless, in anything other than quick e-mails to friends, you should maintain a professional tone. Avoid sarcasm and humor, which may not come across as you intend, and be sure to proofread and spell-check your message before sending it. Also, because e-mail messages are accessible to many people other than the person to whom you are writing, always be careful about what you write in an e-mail message.

Letterhead providing information the recipient will need to communicate with the sender

MetroType
409 South 8th Street
Pawkett, KY 45397
Phone: 502.555.1234   Fax: 502.555.4321   Email: type@micran.net

January 26, 2008

Full-block format: Each new line starts at the left margin:

Mr. Carl Boyer
Boyer Advertising Co.
1714 North 20th Street, Suite 16
Pawkett, KY 45397

Letter is single-spaced, with double-spacing between paragraphs and other major parts.

Dear Mr. Boyer:

The author refers to earlier correspondence to state purpose of the letter.

Thank you for your letter of January 16, 2008. You asked whether MetroType could provide one of your clients with mail-merged letters after first converting your client's files from Corel WordPerfect to Microsoft Word. We certainly can. As I mentioned on the phone earlier today, creating mail-merge documents is one of our key services, and we frequently convert word-processing files for customers who are moving from one program to another.

Elaboration, support, and detail

Much of the file conversion is done automatically; however, we have noticed that some parts of a file (such as accented characters and graphics) aren't always converted accurately. For this reason, we will compare a printout of your client's original files to a printout of the converted files and then make whatever corrections are necessary. For an additional fee, we can also proofread the final documents. If your client is interested in having us proofread the documents, I would be happy to furnish you with a quote.

If you have any other questions, please call me at (502) 555-1234. In the meantime, I'll look forward to hearing from you again.

Sincerely yours,

Signature

Trudy L. Philips

Trudy L. Philips
Owner/Director

Author's initials, followed by typist's (if typist is not author)

TLP/dmp

Figure 15.15 A sample business letter

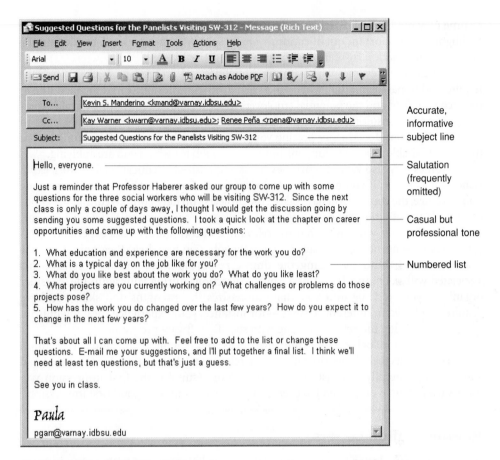

Figure 15.16 A sample e-mail message

While e-mail messages are among the simplest forms of electronic documents, new software programs allow you to attach files, insert hypertext links, and even insert pictures and graphics into your e-mail documents. As a matter of courtesy, check to be sure that the recipient of your e-mail message has the software to read these electronic files before you include them with the message.

Résumés

A **résumé** is used to acquaint a prospective employer with your work experience, education, and accomplishments. All résumés contain such basic information as your name, address, phone number, and e-mail address.

The résumé is a good example of why the context in which a document is read is so important. An employer may receive dozens of résumés for one position. Your résumé may not be read closely in a first screening. Consequently, your résumé should highlight your important qualifications visually so that the reader can quickly find the pertinent information by scanning the page.

The format of résumés varies among disciplines and professions. Some professions require traditional formatting, while others allow for some flexibility in design. Be sure to research your field and the potential employers to see if a particular résumé format is preferred; consider consulting recently published reference books that show examples of good résumés. Also consider whether posting your résumé on a Web site such as Monster.com might be advisable. Always tailor your résumé to the job for which you are applying.

Résumés may also vary in terms of what is emphasized—educational or work experience, for example. If you have little work experience, focus your résumé on your grade point average, the courses you have taken, the projects you have completed, and the applicable skills and abilities you have acquired in college. (For an example of such a résumé, see Figure 15.17.) If you have extensive, relevant, and continuous work experience, consider a reverse-chronological résumé, listing the jobs you have held (beginning with the most recent job) and describing the duties, responsibilities, and accomplishments associated with each one. If you have shifted directions during your adult life, consider organizing your résumé in a way that emphasizes the strengths and skills you have acquired and used in different settings—for instance, your experience speaking in front of groups, handling money, or working with specific software programs.

Do not include such personal information as your height, weight, and age. Mention personal interests or hobbies only if they are relevant to the position. Finally, proofread your résumé carefully; it must be error-free. Your résumé is the first impression you make on a potential employer. Do everything you can to make a good first impression.

Job-Application Letters

A **job-application letter** (sometimes called a **cover letter**) is sent with a résumé when you apply for a job. The primary purpose of the job-application letter is to persuade your reader that you are a qualified candidate for employment and to introduce your résumé. For college students and recent graduates, most job-application letters (such as the one shown in Figure 15.18) consist of four paragraphs:

1. The *first paragraph* identifies the position you are applying for and how you became aware of its availability. If you are not applying for a particular position, the first paragraph expresses your desire to work for the particular organization.

2. The *second paragraph* briefly describes your education, focusing on specific achievements, projects, and relevant course work.

3. The *third paragraph* briefly describes your work experience, focusing on relevant responsibilities and accomplishments.

Note that the second and third paragraphs should not merely restate what is in your résumé; rather, they should help persuade your reader that you are qualified for the job.

Kim Hua
Current Address: MS 1789, Union College, Union, PA 55342 ———— Contact
Permanent Address: 702 Good Street, Borah, ID 83702   information
Phone: (412) 555-1234 E-mail: khua@mailer.union.edu

Ample margins

EDUCATION

| Union College | Bachelor of Arts, | Anticipated May 2009 |
| Union, PA | Child Development | GPA: 3.7 |

Relevant Courses: Lifespan Human Development, Infancy and
Early Childhood, Parent-Child Relations, Fundamentals of
Nutrition, Education of the Preschool Child

Relevant Projects: Coordinator, collaborative research project analyzing educational goals for local Head Start program. Lead writer, report
on parent-child relations, delivered to the Borah, Idaho, School Board.

CHILD DEVELOPMENT WORK EXPERIENCE

- *Summer 2007, Union College Child-Care Center, Union College,* ———— Work experience
  Union, PA   begins with
                                                                          most current
  Child Care Provider: Provided educational experiences and daily   employment
  care for three 2-year-olds and four 3-year-olds. Prepared daily
  activity agendas.

- *Summer 2006, St. Alphonsus Day Care Center, St. Alphonsus*
  Hospital, Union, PA

  Child Care Provider: Provided educational experiences and daily
  care for a group of nine children ages six through ten.

- *Fall 2005, Governor's Commission for the Prevention of Child*
  Abuse, Union, PA

  Intern: Located online resources relevant to the prevention of ———— Relevant
  child abuse. Recommended which resources to include in the   volunteer work
  Web site of the Governor's Commission.

OTHER WORK EXPERIENCE

2005 to present, Union Falls Bed & Breakfast, Union, PA
Payroll Manager: Maintain daily payroll records for all employ- ———— Other experience
ees, compile daily and weekly reports of payroll costs for the   showing
manager, and ensure compliance with all applicable state and   dependability and
federal laws governing payroll matters.   responsibility

PROFESSIONAL AFFILIATIONS

Past President, Union College Child and Family Studies Club;
Student Member, American Society of Child Care Professionals;
Member, National Child Care Providers

Figure 15.17 A sample résumé

Modified block format: Your address, the date, and the signature block begin five spaces to the right of center.

308 Fairmont Street
Warren, CA 07812
June 9, 2006

Ms. Ronda Green
Software Engineer
Santa Clara Technology
P.O. Box 679
Santa Clara, CA 09145

Dear Ms. Green:

Purpose of the letter

I am responding to your February 10 posting on Monster.com (reference #91921) announcing that Santa Clara Technology is accepting résumés for an entry-level engineer position in the Quality Assurance Department. I think that my experience as an intern in quality assurance and my educational background qualify me for this position.

Education paragraph

As my résumé states, I graduated this past May from the University of Southern California (USC) with a Bachelor of Science degree in Interdisciplinary Studies. The Interdisciplinary Studies program at USC allows students to develop a degree plan spanning at least two disciplines. My degree plan included courses in computer science, marketing, and technical communication. In addition to university courses, I have completed courses in team dynamics, project management, and C and C++ programming offered by the training department at PrintCom, a manufacturer of high-end laser printers.

Work-experience paragraph

Throughout last summer, I worked as an intern in the quality-assurance department of PrintCom. I assisted quality-assurance engineers in testing printer drivers, installers, and utilities. In addition, I maintained a database containing the results of these tests and summarized the results in weekly reports. This experience gave me valuable knowledge of the principles of quality assurance and of the techniques used in testing software.

Concluding paragraph

I would appreciate the opportunity to discuss further the education, skills, and abilities I could bring to Santa Clara Technology. You can reach me any workday after 3 p.m. (PDT) at (907) 555-1234 or by e-mail at sstur17@axl.com.

Sincerely yours,

Shelley Sturman

Shelley Sturman

Enclosure: résumé

Figure 15.18 A sample job-application letter

4. The *fourth paragraph* expresses your willingness to provide additional information and to be interviewed at the employer's convenience.

Lab Reports

A **lab report** is written to summarize the results of an experiment or test, and generally consists of the following five sections:

1. The *Introduction* provides background information: the hypothesis of the experiment, the question to be answered, how the question arose.

2. The *Methods* section describes how the research was conducted or how the experiment was performed.

3. The *Results* section describes what happened as a result of your research or experiment.

4. The *Discussion* section consists of your explanation of and reasoning about your results.

5. The *References* section cites the sources used in conducting the research, performing the experiment, or writing the report.

The content and format of a lab report may vary from discipline to discipline or from course to course. Before writing a lab report, be certain that you understand your instructor's requirements. The sample in Figure 15.19 shows excerpts from a lab report written by two students in a soils science course. It uses the documentation format advocated by the Council of Science Editors (CSE).

Web Pages

While Web pages offer the potential for expanded use of color and visuals (including animation and video), the general principles of design used for paper documents can be applied to them. Again, you will want to evaluate the context in which the document will be read. Will your reader be reading from a computer screen or printing the document on paper for reading? If the reading takes place on a computer screen, how big is the screen and how good is its resolution? Reading from a computer screen can be more difficult than reading on paper, so you will want to avoid small fonts and confusing backgrounds that distract from the core content.

Web pages and other electronic texts differ from print texts in large part because of the links they can include to additional text or graphics, to other Web pages, or to short clips of video, animation, or sound. As an author, you must consider that, because of these links, readers may navigate your text in a nonlinear fashion, starting almost anywhere they like and branching off whenever a link piques their curiosity. To help readers find their way around, Web authors often provide a navigation scheme, usually in the form of site maps or "index" pages.

HTML (hypertext markup language) is the standard language used for creating Web pages. Software programs called **HTML editors** provide novices with an easy way

Bulk Density and Total Pore Space

Joe Aquino and Sheila Norris

Soils 101

Lab Section 1

February 20, 2008

Introduction

Background
information that
the reader will
need to
understand the
experiment

Soil is an arrangement of solids and voids. The voids, called pore spaces, are important for root growth, water movement, water storage, and gas exchange between the soil and atmosphere. A medium-textured soil good for plant growth will have a pore-space content of about 0.50 (half solids, half pore space). The total pore space is the space between sand, silt, and clay particles (micropore space) plus the space between soil aggregates (macropore space).[1]

[The Introduction continues with a discussion of the formulas used to calculate bulk density, particle density, and porosity.]

Methods

Detailed
explanation of
the methods
used

To determine the bulk density[2] and total pore space of two soil samples, we hammered cans into the wall of a soil pit (Hagerstown silt loam). We collected samples from the Ap horizon and a Bt horizon. We then placed a block of wood over the cans so that the hammer did not smash them. After hammering the cans into the soil, we dug the cans, now full of soil, out of the horizons; we trimmed off any excess soil. The samples were dried in an oven at 105°C for two days and weighed. We then determined the volume of the cans by measuring the height and radius, as follows:

volume $= 1/4 \ r^2 h$

We used the formulas noted in the Introduction to determine bulk density and porosity of the samples. Particle density was assumed to be 2.65 g/cm^3. The textural class of each horizon was determined by feel; that is, we squeezed and kneaded each sample and assigned it to a particular textural class.

Figure 15.19 A sample lab report

Results

We found both soils to have relatively light bulk densities and large porosities, but the Bt horizon had greater porosity than the Ap. Furthermore, we determined that the Ap horizon was a silt loam, whereas the Bt was a clay (see Table 1).

Table 1 Textural class, bulk density, and porosity of two Hagerstown soil horizons

Textural Class	Ap Silt Loam	Bt Clay
Bulk density (g/cm³)	1.20	1.08
Porosity	0.55	0.59

Presents the results of the experiment, with a table showing quantitative data

[The Results section continues with sample calculations.]

Discussion

Both soils had bulk densities and porosities in the range we would have expected from the discussions in the lab manual and textbook. The Ap horizon is a medium-textured soil and is considered a good topsoil for plant growth, so a porosity around 0.5 is consistent with those facts. The Bt horizon is a fine-textured horizon (containing a large amount of clay), and the bulk density is in the predicted range.

Explains what was significant about the results of the research

[The Discussion section continues with further discussion of the results.]

[The References section begins on a new page.]

References

1. Brady NC, Weil RR. The nature and properties of soils. 11th ed. New York: Prentice-Hall; 1996. 291 p.

2. Blake GR, Hartge KH. Bulk density. In: Klute A, editor. Methods of soil analysis. Part 1. 2nd ed. Agronomy 1986;9:363-376.

The references are in the format recommended by the Council of Science Editors (CSE)

to create Web pages, and most new word processing programs allow a document to be converted into HTML and saved as a Web page.

As you design a Web page, beware of letting unnecessary graphics and multimedia elements distract from your message. Yes, you *can* add a textured background to the screen that will make it look like marble or cloth, but will that background make reading the text easier? Will a sound file improve communication of your main points, or are you adding sound simply because you can? Consider the following guidelines when designing a Web page:

- *Make sure your text is easy to read.* Many Web pages are difficult to read because of textured and brightly colored backgrounds. Keep the background of a Web page light in tone so that your text can be read with ease. Because color type can also be difficult to read, avoid vibrant colors for long blocks of text. Bear in mind that most readers are used to reading dark (typically black) text on a light (typically white) background.

- *Chunk information carefully and keep your Web pages short.* Because many people have difficulty reading long documents on a computer screen, be sure to chunk your information into concise paragraphs. Also, readers often find it difficult to read a Web page that requires extensive scrolling down the screen. Break up long text blocks into separate Web pages that require no more than one or two screens of scrolling. Use hypertext links to connect the text blocks and to help readers navigate across the pages.

- *Limit the file size of your Web pages.* A Web page that is filled with visuals and sound files can be slow and clunky to load, especially for users with old computers or dial-up connections to the Internet. Limiting your use of visuals and sound files so that your pages load quickly will help ensure that your documents are read.

- *Use hypertext links effectively.* Make sure that all of your links work correctly and that all the pages of your Web site include a link back to your home page so that readers can access it easily. You can make your text easier to read by judiciously limiting the number of links you embed in it. In addition to embedded text links, consider including a list of important links on a separate page for readers' convenience.

- *Use the elements of document design.* Remember what you have learned in this chapter about typography, white space, color, and visuals when you create Web pages. Most principles of good print document design apply to Web page design as well.

Acknowledgments

Text Credits

Rick Bragg. "100 Miles per Hour, Upside Down and Sideways." From *All Over but the Shoutin'.* Copyright © 1997 by Rick Bragg. Reprinted with the permission of Pantheon Books, a division of Random House, Inc.

Annie Dillard. Pp. 45–49 from *An American Childhood,* by Annie Dillard. Copyright © 1987 by Annie Dillard. Reprinted by permission of HarperCollins Publishers and Russell and Volkening, Inc.

John T. Edge. "I'm Not Leaving Until I Eat This Thing." From *The Oxford American* (September/October 1999). Copyright © 1999 by John T. Edge. Reprinted with the permission of the author. Photo by Sharon Brinkman. www.sharonbrinkman.com. Reproduced with permission.

Amitai Etzioni. "Working at McDonald's." Copyright © 1986 by Amitai Etzioni, author of *The Spirit of Community.* Director, George Washington University Center for Communitarian Policy Studies. Reprinted with the permission of the author.

Bob Holmes. "In the Blink of an Eye." From *New Scientist Magazine,* July 2005. Copyright © 2005 by New Scientist. Reprinted with the permission of New Scientist. www.newscientist.com.

Martin Luther King, Jr. An annotated sample from "Letter from Birmingham Jail." Copyright © 1963 Martin Luther King, Jr., copyright renewed 1991 by the Heirs to the Estate of Martin Luther King, Jr. Reprinted by arrangement with the Heirs to the Estate of Martin Luther King, Jr., c/o Writer's House as agent for the proprietor.

Karen Kornbluh. "Win-Win Flexibility." A policy brief written for the New America Foundation, 2005. Copyright © 2005 Karen Kornbluh. Reprinted with permission of the author.

John McPhee. "The New York Pickpocket Academy." From *Giving Good Weight* by John McPhee. Copyright © 1979 by John McPhee. Reprinted by permission of Farrar, Straus & Giroux, and LLC.

Gian-Claudia Sciara. "Making Communities Safe for Bicycles." From *Access 22* (Spring 2003): 28–33 (with visuals by Melanie Curry), the official journal of the University of California Transportation Center. Copyright © 2003 by the Regents of the University of California. Reprinted with permission of the author.

A. O. Scott. "News in Black, White and Shades of Gray." From *The New York Times,* Movies Section, September 23, 2005 issue, page E1. Copyright © 2005 by The New York Times. All rights reserved. Used with permission and protected by the Copyright Laws of the United States. The printing, copying, redistribution, or retransmission of the Material without express written permission is prohibited. www.nytimes.com.

Karen Stabiner. "Boys Here, Girls There" (originally titled, "Boys Here, Girls There: Sure, If Equality's the Goal"). From *The Washington Post,* May 12, 2002. Copyright © 2002. Reprinted with the permission of the author, and By the Word, Inc.

Anastasia Toufexis. "Love: The Right Chemistry." From *Time,* February 15, 1993. Originally titled "The Right Chemistry." (Includes "imprinting" figure.) Copyright © 1993 Time, Inc. Reprinted with permission. All rights reserved.

Photo Credits

12 (top) © Zave Smith/zefa/Corbis; (middle) David Epperson/Getty Images; (bottom) Image 100/Alamy; **52** (top) © Bill Aron/PhotoEdit, Inc.; (middle) © David Young-Wolff/PhotoEdit, Inc.; (bottom) © Jon Feingersh/Corbis; **98** (top) © David Young-Wolff/PhotoEdit, Inc.; (middle) DigitalGlobe/Getty Images; (bottom) Comstock Images/Alamy; **146** (top) David DeLossy/GettyImages; (middle) © Michael Newman/PhotoEdit; (bottom) © Roger Ressmeyer/Corbis; **189** (top) "Wall Street's Glass Ceiling" from *Business Week,* July 26, 2004. © 2004 Business Week, Inc. Reprinted with permission; (bottom) "Still an All Boy's Club" from *Business Week,* November 22, 1999. © 1999 Business Week, Inc. Reprinted with permission; **192** (top) Children's Television Workshop/GettyImages; (middle) © David Young-Wolff/PhotoEdit, Inc.; (bottom) Blend Images/Alamy; **242** (bottom) © Gabe Palmer/Palmer Kane Studio; **244** (top) PhotoFest; (middle) © Nancy Richmond/The Image Works; (bottom) © Norbert Schaefer/Corbis; **248** © mtvU. Reprinted with permission; **255** "Good Night and Good Luck" still image. Photographer: Melinda Sue Gordon. Reproduced with permission of Warner Bros. Entertainment, Inc.; Warner Bros. and 2929 Productions; **290** © PhotoFest; **291** © PhotoFest; **383** © 2006 EBSCO Publishing, Inc. All rights reserved; **458** JH Pete Carmichael/ Getty Images; **461** Courtesy of Stanford Law School. Reprinted with permission.

Subject Index

About the Authors

RISE B. AXELROD is director of English composition and McSweeney Professor of Rhetoric and Teaching Excellence at the University of California, Riverside. She has previously been professor of English at California State University, San Bernardino; director of the College Expository Program at the University of Colorado, Boulder; and assistant director of the Third College Composition Program at the University of California, San Bernardino.

CHARLES R. COOPER is an emeritus professor in the department of literature at the University of California, San Diego, where he served as coordinator of the Third College Composition Program, Dimensions of Culture Program, and Campus Writing Programs. He has also been codirector of the San Diego Writing Project, one of the National Writing Project Centers. He is coeditor, with Lee Odell, of *Evaluating Writing* and *Research on Composing: Points of Departure,* and coauthor, with Susan Peck MacDonald, of *Writing the World* (Bedford/St. Martin's, 2000).

Together, Axelrod and Cooper have coauthored *The St. Martin's Guide to Writing* and, with Alison M. Warriner, *Reading Critically, Writing Well.*

Submitting Your Essays for Publication

We hope that we'll be able to include many new essays by students in the next editions of *Axelrod & Cooper's Concise Guide* to *Writing* and its companion collections. Please let us see the best essays you've written using the *Concise Guide*. Send them with this submission form and copies of the agreement form on the back of this page (one for each essay you submit) to English Editor—Student Essays, Bedford/St. Martin's, 33 Irving Place, 10th Floor, New York, NY 10003.

PAPER SUBMISSION FORM

Student's Name_____

Instructor's Name _____

School _____

Department _____

Writing Assignment (circle one)

Remembering an Event   Arguing a Position

Writing Profiles   Proposing a Solution

Explaining a Concept   Justifying an Evaluation

Agreement Form

I hereby assign to Bedford/St. Martin's ("Bedford") all of my right, title and interest throughout the world, including without limitation, all copyrights, in and to my essay, _____, and any notes and drafts pertaining to it (the sample essay and such materials being referred to as the "Essay").

I understand that Bedford in its discretion has the right but not the obligation to publish the Essay in any form(s) or format(s) that it may desire; that Bedford may edit, revise, condense, or otherwise alter the Essay as it deems appropriate in order to prepare the same for publication. I understand that Bedford has the right to use and to authorize the use of my name as author of the Essay in connection with any work that contains the Essay (or a portion of it).

I represent that the Essay is wholly original and was completely written by me, that publication of it will not infringe upon the rights of any third party, and that I have not granted any rights in it to any third party.

In the event Bedford determines to publish any part of the Essay in one of its print books, I will receive one free copy of the work in which it appears.

Student's signature _____

Name_____Date_____

Permanent address _____

_____

Phone number(s) _____

E-mail address(es)_____

A Note to the Student:

When a writer creates something—a story, an essay, a poem—he or she automatically possesses all of the rights to that piece of writing, no trip to the U.S. Copyright Office needed. When a writer—an historian, a novelist, a sportswriter—publishes his or her work, he or she normally transfers some or all of those rights to the publisher, by formal agreement. The form above is one such formal agreement. By entering into this agreement, you are engaging in a modern publishing ritual—the transfer of rights from writer to publisher. If this is your first experience submitting something for publication, you should know that you are in good company: every student who has published an essay in one of our books entered into this agreement, and just about every published writer has entered into a similar one.

Thank you for submitting your essay.